ITALY 1980

THE CONTRIBUTORS

Project coordinator for this book is **Charles E. Cabell III,** an American who lives in Rome. Charles has been managing editor for Rome's English-language daily the *International Courier,* and Rome correspondent for *Taxi* magazine.

The Milan and Lombardy chapters are by **Cathy Crane.** Cathy has collaborated on a number of television projects, including *Cosmos,* with Charles Sagan and *Age of Uncertainty,* with John Kenneth Galbraith.

The art essays throughout this volume, the Michelangelo tours of Rome and Florence, and the Cultural Timeline are the work of **Michael Hinden,** professor of English and Integrated Liberal Studies at the University of Wisconsin–Madison.

Architecture essays are by **Mary Beth Betts** and **Charles Ayes.** Mary Beth is an architectural historian teaching at the Cooper Union; Charles, a New York-based architect.

Information for the "Travel Arrangements" section was compiled by **Taryn Schneider,** a writer whose credits include *Natural History* magazine, *Travel Agent* magazine, and *ASTA Travel News.* The vocabulary section was put together by **Giuseppe Manca,** who teaches Italian in New York City. The "Business Brief" is by **Sondra Snowdon,** author of *The Global Edge: How Your Company Can Win in the International Marketplace.*

Research on hotels and restaurants in the Veneto section was compiled by Italian architect **Adriano Sorrentino.** Other collaborators in the field include: Graziella Giovannini, Danila Niboli, Rodolfo and Alberto Collodi, Fleride Piacenza, Giovanni Gatti, Ugo Falcone, Carlo Menditto, and Constantino Scalabrone.

The New York editor for this book is Debra Bernardi; assistant editor is Charlotte Savidge. Maps are by R.V. Reise und Verkehrsverlag, and Swanston Graphics.

A BANTAM TRAVEL GUIDE

ITALY

1989

BANTAM
NEW YORK ● TORONTO ● LONDON ● SYDNEY ● AUCKLAND

ITALY 1989

A Bantam Book / April 1989

Grateful acknowledgment is made for permission to reprint the following excerpts: From Italian Journey *by Johann Wolfgang Goethe, translated by W. H. Auden and Elizabeth Mayer. Published 1962 by Pantheon Books, a division of Random House, Inc. From* D. H. Lawrence and Italy *by D. H. Lawrence. Copyright 1921 by Thomas Seltzer, Inc. Copyright renewed 1949 by Frieda Lawrence. Reprinted by permission of Viking Penguin Inc. All rights reserved. From* Venice Observed *by Mary McCarthy, reprinted by permission of Harcourt Brace Jovanovich, Inc. From* Italian Hours *by Henry James, first published in 1987 by Ecco Press. Reprinted by permission. From* Italy: The Fatal Gift *by William Murray, first published in 1958 by Dodd, Mead & Company, Inc. Reprinted by permission. From* Venice, Frail Barrier *by Richard De Combray, first published 1975 by Doubleday. Reprinted by the author's permission.*

ISBN 0-553-34637-7

Published simultaneously in the United States and Canada

Bantam Books are published by Bantam Books, a division of Bantam Double-day Dell Publishing Group, Inc. Its trademark, consisting of the words "Bantam Books" and the portrayal of a rooster, is Registered in U.S. Patent and Trademark Office and in other countries, Marca Registrada, Bantam Books, 666 Fifth Avenue, New York, New York 10103

PRINTED IN THE UNITED STATES OF AMERICA

0 9 8 7 6 5 4 3 2 1

CONTENTS

FOREWORD

Anyone who's ever used a travel guidebook knows how addictive they become when they're good, but how annoying they are when they're bad. We at Bantam launched this new guidebook series because we honestly believed we could improve on the best of what's already out there.

The Bantam team had one major goal—that of producing the only travel guides that both the experienced and the inexperienced traveler would ever need for a given destination. You're holding an example of how well we succeeded. Can we document this success? Let's take a look.

- One of the first things you'll notice is that **Bantam Travel Guides** include a full-color travel atlas with maps detailed enough for the most demanding travel needs.
- Upon closer scrutiny you'll find that the guide is organized geographically rather than alphabetically. Descriptions of what's available in a contiguous geographical area make it easier to get the most out of a city neighborhood or a country region.
- A real convenience is the way that restaurants and hotels in major cities are keyed into the maps so that you can locate these places easily.
- At the end of key chapters you'll find a feature called "City Listings," where museums, churches, major sights, and shops are listed with their addresses, phone numbers, and map-location code.
- Bantam guides will be revised every year. Travel conditions change and so do our guides.
- Finally, we think you'll enjoy reading our guidebooks. We've tried hard to find not only well-informed writers, but good writers. The writing is literate and lively.

Still, no guidebook can cover everything that's worth seeing or doing. We ask you to bear in mind, too, that prices can change at any time, and that today's well-managed restaurant or hotel can change owners or managers tomorrow. We've recommended places as they are now and as we expect them to be in the future, but there are no guarantees. We welcome your comments and suggestions. Our address is Bantam Travel Guides, 666 Fifth Avenue, New York, N.Y. 10103.

Richard T. Scott
Publisher

Tips on Getting the Most Out of This Guide

1. You'll find a special **"Travel Arrangements"** section, easily identified by the black-bordered pages, toward the back of the book. This section can be invaluable in planning your trip.

2. The **"Priorities"** chapter and the corresponding sections in the city chapters will insure that you see and do the most important things when you visit your destination. Whether you're spending two days or two weeks, you'll want to make the most of your time.

3. Note that in addition to our main selection of important restaurants you'll also find described in the text informal places to stop for lunch, a snack, or a drink.

4. To help you instantly identify restaurant and hotel writeups, whether they're in a list or mentioned in the text, we've designed the following two little versions of our friendly Bantam rooster. Miniatures of these roosters will appear at the beginning of restaurant and hotel lists and in the margin of the text whenever a restaurant or hotel is described there.

RESTAURANTS

HOTELS

1

THE EXPERIENCE: ITALY, 1989

The eccentricities and idiosyncrasies are legendary; Italy is a different dimension. This is a land of contrasting extremes where excessive expectations can result in frustration. Many of the amenities that travelers from service-oriented countries take for granted may be missing, but when does the visiting team determine the ground rules?

The world's fifth most industrialized nation, Italy today is enjoying unparalleled prosperity, and the traveler expecting a deal in goods and services could be disappointed. Bargain-basement days have been relegated to the past. And with the final folding of barriers between European Economic Community nations in 1992, the purchasing power of American visitors is not likely to be rising. (If, in fact, the opposite is true—which it may well be—it's never again going to be cheaper to visit Italy than now.) Still, the true value of an Italian holiday is the artistic, historical, and cultural experience: the superb food and wine, captivating provincial charm, and the awesome array of scenic beauty.

Yet Italy is not the magic kingdom. Ingenuity and creativity have evolved to majestic proportions in a land where the natural resources for a modern industrialized nation are mostly lacking. The country compensates with the uncanny ability of *arrangiarsi,* truly the foremost indigenous trait. Nothing could be more alien to the understanding of a foreign visitor. The term defies a literal translation, but basically means an ability to play it by ear, to incorporate a creative sense of adventure into even the most banal aspects of daily routines, while being as inventive as possible. A collateral effect is that strong sense of independence so cherished by the Italians.

More than being seen, Italy should be absorbed. And nowhere is more conducive to the possibility than the hinterland, the peninsula's provinces, as much the spine of the nation as the Apennines. Although Rome, Naples, Venice, Milan, and

Florence are truly the highlights of an Italian holiday, urban chaos, impatience and cultural unfamiliarity can cloud their traditional appeal.

Too often ignored in the haste to consume highway mileage, the heartbeat of the hinterland sounds along the major connecting arteries. Many cultural events staged in smaller cities and towns have achieved international acclaim. Verona's Arena—better preserved than Rome's Colosseum—annually hosts open-air opera that attracts leading international performers and conductors. Spoleto's Festival of Two Worlds has spread to the United States and Australia. The classical theater calendar in Syracuse (Siracusa), Sicily, provides due attention to the most extensive and important archaeological reminders of the rule of Magna Graecia.

The canals of Treviso and La Reggia at Caserta are just a few of the hundreds of architectural offerings in and around provincial centers. Smaller towns such as Aosta, Merano, Gubbio, and Erice, almost unchanged by time, are literally living museums illustrating the tremendous cultural variations of a nation that stretches from the Alps to the middle of the Mediterranean.

Italy's gastronomic diversities only add to The Experience. Superb food and wines are available practically everywhere. Renaissance recipes have become Italy's response to France's nouvelle cuisine. Italian ingenuity and creativity in peasant kitchens created *piatti dei poveri* (food for the poor) to make the most inexpensive produce as appetizing as possible. *Pasta e fagioli* alone has scores of variations from north to south.

Italian chefs today are competing in the revival of these and other recipes forgotten in time. The result, along with traditional fare such as *polenta, risotti,* and an incalculable number of *minestrone* and pasta combinations, is a true diner's delight.

With a heterogeneous population as diverse as the Swiss and the Tunisian, Italy is a fledgling 42-year-old democratic republic. Its roots stretch through history to the days when Rome was the ruler of the Mediterranean world, as well as through invasions by hordes of Saracens, Byzantines, Bourbons, Napoleonic troops, and the Austro-Hungarian Empire.

Contemporary Italy was not united into a single nation until 1870, when the Risorgimento—the movement for Italian unification—culminated in the establishment of Rome as the capital of a monarchy under the House of Savoy. Following World War II a national referendum condemned new King Umberto II to exile, along with successors to the throne. His son, Victor Emmanuel, now resides in Switzerland. Highly controversial, he is allegedly responsible for the gunshot death of a German tourist aboard a yacht moored off Corsica a decade ago.

Two unfortunate aspects of traveling in Italy today are terrorism and petty crime. Political violence in recent years has dissuaded many from visiting, and petty crime has convinced many never to return. Yet in spite of revolving-door, musical-chair governments, Italy has dealt a crushing defeat to left and right-wing plotters alike in what must be considered a textbook case of democratic survival, and an involvement with a terrorist act today appears as remote as Oliver North stopping by for lunch.

Not so remote, however, is the threat of pickpockets, purse snatchers, and automobile break-ins, as well as the harassment of insistent gypsy beggars. Millions of careless and forgetful travelers, national and foreign alike, have created lucrative opportunities for the unscrupulous. But crime exists in every urban metropolis, and the mature traveler does not abandon elementary precautions in a land where he may not even speak the language. Common sense should prevail. Valuables should be kept in hotel safety-deposit facilities. Shoulder bags should be carried away from the curb—between oneself and one's companion, if possible—and with the strap bandolier-style across the chest. Under no circumstances should a baggage-packed vehicle ever be left unattended. Out-of-town license plates are like neon signs announcing goodies up for grabs.

Language can be a problem, even for travelers of Italian origin who have mastered an obscure and perhaps obsolete dialect. Phrase books are very useful for asking a question, but can leave you on a limb with the answer. Don't judge Italian hospitality by an awkward experience with language on a chaotic urban street corner. Imagine the predicament of an Italian in Times Square.

In the provinces, people are more generous with their time. A quest for information often may be resolved with a series of exotic gestures. And don't be surprised if there is an accompanying increase in volume; Italians are inclined to believe that your chances of understanding improve if the reply is loud.

Fortunately, tourism plays a key role in the Italian economy. There are information booths at all major air and rail terminals, with people speaking varying degrees of English. But beware: the same terminals are filled with hawkers peddling taxis, hotels, and so forth; say "No!"

Don't be sidetracked. Don't feel abandoned. Don't be upset if you feel foreign, barely tolerated. This is just the perimeter of a new cultural dimension. The Experience is only a few more steps away.

A Note About Restaurants

The specifics of each region's cuisine are discussed in the individual chapters. However, there are a few general things to be aware of if you're a first-time traveler to Italy—and a few things that may have changed or that return visitors may need to be reminded of since their last trip.

First off, return American visitors especially will be amazed at how expensive everything is. The days of four-course meals with a good wine for $10 are gone—probably forever. Prices in the major Italian cities are comparable to those in New York. And though, of course, you'll find more reasonably priced meals in the hinterland—even here, things are not cheap.

But remember what you're getting for your money. This isn't a simple meal of pasta and a salad that may pass for an Italian dinner back home. What we consider a full meal throughout this book consists of four courses. The antipasto is a teaser before your first course of pasta or soup, then your second course—meat, fish, or fowl; followed by fruit, cheese, or a sweet.

If a restaurant isn't too busy, you'll be able to eat one course before deciding on the next. Unlike the usual U.S. practice, there's no need to order everything at once. This, of course, takes longer—but dinner is an all-evening activity in Italy.

For meat or fish, you may see an *etto* price on the menu—this means that the menu price refers to each 100 grams (about 4 ounces)—and so the price on the menu is not the price of your dinner.

DOC wines are those wines certified by the state not to be diluted with low-quality grapes. Specifics are given in each chapter.

Throughout Italy you'll see numerous establishments labeled bars. These are not akin to the American establishments of the same name, but instead are places to get coffee and possibly a sweet and/or a sandwich. Yes, you can get alcoholic beverages here, but most people are really there for a quick shot of espresso.

Credit cards are accepted widely. Throughout this book the following abbreviations are used: AE—American Express, DC—Diner's Club, MC—MasterCard, V—Visa.

2

ORIENTING YOURSELF

The boot-shaped peninsula, Italy extends from northern Alpine borders with France, Switzerland, Austria, and Yugoslavia to the middle of the Mediterranean. See the color orientation map of Italy at the back of the book.

Its 116,304-square-mile territory is smaller than the state of California, but its population is nearly 20 percent that of all the United States and fairly evenly divided between urban and rural areas.

The Italian coastline extends for 2,685 miles, not including Sardinia and Sicily. Maximum north–south and east–west distances are 708 and 130 miles, respectively.

Though the geopolitical division of the country is limited to north and central-south, there are six distinct topographical divisions of "The Continent" (as islanders refer to mainland Italy).

The southern slopes of the Alps run to the perimeter of the Po Valley. Through this fertile plain flows Italy's largest river, the Po, collecting most of the country's other principal waterways originating in the Alps or the valley's southern Apennine perimeter.

The lagoon lowlands extend northeast of Venice confining the Adriatic Sea. These marshes and beaches open onto fertile land extending to the southern slopes of the Dolomite Alps.

From the French border near Nice the Apennines run the entire length of the country to Reggio Calabria on the toe of the boot. This rugged spine divides the country's eastern Adriatic and western Tyrrhenian sea provinces.

Two distinctive areas are the Apulia (Puglia) lowlands that are the heel of the boot and the western highlands-plains on the boot's shin. Of the latter lowlands, Tuscany's Maremma and Lazio's Agro Pontina are rich farmlands.

Italy is served by an excellent but costly turnpike network throughout the north and along most of both coasts. Most state highways (indicated by SS and a number) are well surfaced two- or three-lane scenic routes often shaded by characteristic cyprus and Mediterranean pine trees.

State highways generally link major urban areas, while good two-lane provincial roads criss-cross more remote areas. See "Travel Arrangements" at the back of the book for more detailed information.

Italy's 95 provinces are distributed over twenty administrative regions. Following a general north to south pattern:

Valle d'Aosta. This smallest region is a delightful series of valleys snaking between Alpine peaks that attract summer as well as winter holiday travelers. The Monte Bianco (Mont Blanc) tunnel is the gateway to France. In fact, the local patois is more French than it is Italian. The combination of French and Mediterranean characteristics means an area that combines graceful, warm sophistication with a sober outdoorsiness. One of Italy's four casinò's is at St. Vincent near the town of Aosta. See the chapter "Northwestern Italy."

The Piedmont (Piemonte). The largest mainland region in Italy, the Piedmont extends south, east, and west of the Valle d'Aosta. Sixty-two miles from Aosta is the seat of the Piedmont, Turin, one of the country's main industrial centers. Before Rome was wrenched from the papacy, Turin was the capital of the monarchy under the House of Savoy; the royal palace is open to visitors today. Only about an hour's drive away are trout streams, ski resorts, and beautiful Lake Maggiore. Again, see "Northwestern Italy."

Lombardy (Lombardia). **Milan** is pacesetter of the region of Lombardy, east of the Piedmont, bordering Switzerland. The financial capital of the nation, it has sights as famous as Leonardo da Vinci's *Last Supper* and the opera house La Scala. Industrial areas in the rest of the region are balanced by the scenic lake district, which includes the western shores of Lake Garda and Lake Como. The region is rich in history, with towns like Pavia (within which is the Certosa di Pavia, the Carthusian monastery) and Cremona, home of violin makers, including Stradivarius. A train from Milan to Turin takes around 1½ hours, Milan–Rome, 6 hours.

Trentino-Alto Adige. With the primarily German-speaking province of Bolzano (Bozen), once Austria's South Tyrol (Südtirol), and the Italian area of Trento (also called Trent or Trentino), the region, east of Lombardy, offers two international experiences. Visitors can explore colorful Austro-Germanic towns like Bolzano by day and sleep in castles by night. See "Northeastern Italy."

Veneto. South of Trentino-Alto Adige, this is a region of lakes, mountains, beaches, as well as the famed canals of **Venice** and Treviso, Palladian villas, Verona's Arena, and the setting for many of Shakespeare's plays. Few regions offer so much for so many. This once predominantly pre-Alp agricultural area has been vitalized with the development of a highly successful manufacturing industry. Venice is about three hours from Milan by train, about six hours from Rome.

Friuli-Venezia Giulia. Primarily a rugged, mountainous area, this region is east of the Veneto, bordering Austria and Yugoslavia. Also here is Trieste, the country's leading Adriatic port, whose union with Italy in 1954 symbolized Italy's emergence from the debacle of World War II. In the Lignano beach complex, wide, sandy beaches line the Adriatic. Consider a houseboat as your accommodation here, traveling perhaps between Trieste and Venice, or simply anchoring offshore to avoid beach crowds. See "Northeastern Italy."

Liguria. This slim, coastal sliver sloping to the Tyrrhenian, is south of the Piedmont, stretching from Tuscany to France. The region has a rich seafaring tradition. Ponente and Levante rivieras flank the massive ship-building and port facilities in Savona and Genoa—birthplace of Christopher Columbus, once home to some of the world's wealthiest merchants. Visitors to Genoa today can explore fine palaces, several of which house distinguished art collections. The riviera town Portofino and the coastal towns known as the Cinque Terre are two prime attractions near the growing port of La Spezia. It will take about two hours to travel from Milan to Genoa by train; Genoa is about a seven-hour train ride from Rome.

Emilia-Romagna. Emilia-Romagna, south of Lombardy and the Veneto, is the heart of Italy's "Red Belt," with an antipapal past that still dominates the region's political profile. A highly developed agricultural system nourishes one of the country's strongest gastronomical traditions, epitomized in the restaurants of Bologna. The Adriatic beaches are some of Europe's most popular summer resorts. Prices are in stark contrast to the more selective Ligurian rivieras. Also in the region is Ravenna, famous for its mosaics; Ferrara, Modena, and Reggio nell' Emilia, whose prominence was once determined by the rise and fall of the fortunes of the Este family; and Parma and Piacenza, prominent cultural centers in the 16th century. Bologna is almost 2 hours from Milan by train, 2½ hours from Venice, 3½ hours from Rome.

Tuscany (Toscana). This region, south of Emilia-Romagna, is much more than **Florence**—undoubtedly one of the cultural capitals of the West. An entire holiday could be spent exploring the art in the city alone. Renaissance beauty is complemented by the rolling Chianti vineyards, the island of

Elba, the Carrara marble country, the ancient port of Pisa, and Siena, where words like "charming" and "picturesque" take on new meaning. The train between Milan and Florence will take about three hours; between Genoa and Florence, four hours; Venice–Florence, three hours; Rome–Florence, three hours.

The Marches (Marche). Here, east of Tuscany, rugged Apennine terrain interrupts sandy beaches along the Adriatic. The principal city of Ancona is the base of one of Italy's largest fishing fleets as well as a major sea link with Yugoslavia and Greece. Urbino is only one of a number of picturesque towns dominating hillsides in the hinterland. Ancona is four hours from Milan by train, three hours from Rome.

Umbria. The only landlocked region south of the Alpine border regions, Umbria, southeast of Tuscany and west of the Marches, is one of the greenest and most picturesque areas of the country. The regional seat of Perugia is obliged to share the limelight with smaller cities and towns that truly reflect the country's medieval past and provincial charm: Orvieto, Assisi, Spoleto, Gubbio, Todi, to name a few. Perugia is about 2 ½ hours from Florence by train, almost 3 hours from Rome.

Lazio. It's no surprise that **Rome,** with its mini-state Vatican City neighbor, dominates the region southwest of Umbria with its artistic, historical, and political importance. Though nearby beaches, once beautiful black-sand stretches, now leave much to be desired, there are many other attractions surrounding "The Eternal City." Follow the trail of the Etruscans in Palestrina; visit little-known, but still suggestive, medieval towns such as Sermoneta and Viterbo; and spend time at Emperor Hadrian's Villa, just outside Tivoli.

Abruzzi (Abruzzo). East of Lazio and south of the Marches, Abruzzi is rugged and mountainous. The region's national park has been ringed with ski-resort developments for middle-class Romans and Neapolitans. Tradition has bagpipe-playing shepherds descending the mountains toward cities at Christmastime to add a touch of folklore to the holiday season. Sea resorts vie with the mountains as tourist attractions.

Molise. The territory south of the Sangro River—and south of Abruzzi—was once part of the Abruzzi region; now it has a separate administrative status centered in Campobasso. The least-populated region, primarily agricultural, Molise has remote, historic towns, Adriatic beaches, and can boast of artisans such as the Marinelli brothers, whose foundry at Agonone has forged bells for churches from Sri Lanka to New York.

Campania. Farther south is Campania. The sense of decadence that now shrouds the principal city of **Naples** is a textbook case of almost nonexistent administration. But the extroverted nature of the people always makes a visit enjoyable. The surrounding sights are many: the 18th-century palace La Reggia, near Caserta; the islands Ischia and Capri; the beautiful coastline along the Sorrentine peninsula and Amalfi Drive; historic sights like Vesuvius, Pompeii, and Paestum.

Basilicata. This region borders Campania on the south. The hinterland could qualify as a forgotten territory. Three types of terrain predominate: sandy beaches on the Gulf of Taranto in the south, craggy coastline on the eastern Gulf of Policastro, and rugged interior. See "The Deep South" chapter.

Apulia (Puglia). Too often ignored by travelers hustling to Brindisi for the ferry to Greece, the area, east of Campania and Basilicata, the heel of the boot, boasts the natural wonders of the Gargano coast (woods, beaches, and rocky coastline) and the Castellana Grotte (caverns). Contrasting with the North African appearance of many coastal dwellings are the characteristic white-washed, cone-shaped homes, called *trulli*, in the Valle d'Itria. Again, see "The Deep South."

Calabria. This mountainous region, the toe of the boot, with an extensive coastline, still reflects Byzantine, Greek, and Roman dominations. The bronze Greek statues discovered off the coast of Riace are in the National Museum at Reggio di Calabria, almost at the toe's point. Whereas the Silla mountains are an ecological eden, most of the Tyrrhenian coast has been marred by indiscriminate development. It's about 300 miles from Naples to Reggio. See "The Deep South."

Sicily (Sicilia). Etna aptly symbolizes island character: apparently dormant, brooding, then explosive. The rich history of the region, Italy's largest, is easily discovered in the towns of Taormina, with a Greek theater dating from the third-century B.C., the once-walled town Erice, and Agrigento's Valley of Temples, one of the most important reminders of Magna Graecia. Ferries connect Sicily with the continent (you can fly as well). The ferry from Reggio to the closest Sicilian port, Messina, takes less than one hour.

Sardinia (Sardegna). Italy's other island region has little in common with Sicily. Historically a sheep-raising and agricultural area, the island was revolutionized by the Aga Khan's development of the Costa Smeralda. The transparent waters have elevated the island to one of the major summer holiday attractions in Europe. Sardinia's is the only Italian dialect officially recognized as a language in itself. As with Sicily, Sardinia is connected to the mainland via planes and ferries. These ferries take considerably longer than those to Sicily, ranging from eight to 17 hours—depending on your ports.

3

SETTING PRIORITIES

Flexibility tops the list of essentials for anyone planning a visit to Italy. Individual tastes, habits, and customs can be accommodated by a guidebook, advice from a friend, and attractive brochures and promotional literature. But will these satisfy every whim of an entire two- to three-week vacation? Or even a business trip for less than a week?

The business traveler will have a full itinerary dictated by necessity. Generally, even spare time will be appropriated for informal get-togethers that could well be the real key for a successful junket. Europeans can conclude more at a caffè or over a dinner table than in a boardroom.

On the other hand, the holiday traveler must loosely organize an itinerary that will permit the best possible use of time. For the inexperienced traveler, group excursions eliminate organizational headaches. Everything is highly organized—even down to the collection of baggage—too often at 5 A.M.

First-timers with more of a taste for adventure can also do it alone or with friends by either rail or automobile. Rail is the best option for first-timers wanting to take in just the Big Four: Venice, Florence, Rome, and the Gulf of Naples.

The main advantage of traveling by auto is the possibility it allows for travelers to take sidetrips between major destinations. The disadvantage of traveling in Italy by automobile is that the vehicle is practically useless in any major city. In addition to traffic problems, many urban areas have designated pedestrian-only sections. You'll need to decide whether you want to stay in the center of cities like Florence or Rome, or if a more suburban location might be sufficient. Staying out of town usually offers a savings on accommodations, and parking will not be a problem so you'll eliminate the need for a garage, which can be costly.

To take in the Big Four you'll need at least two days for Venice, two for Florence, and at least three days each for

Rome and the Gulf of Naples. That's already ten days without considering travel time. If you're on a two-week junket, cover the main sights and lay the groundwork for a more comprehensive return trip, which can include one or two specific stops as well as rewarding hinterland touring.

Venice requires at least a day simply for visitors to get acclimated. This is best done on the Grand Canal and in and around the Piazza San Marco (St. Mark's Square). The next day can be spent in museums and art galleries, or simply wandering the back canals.

The biggest problem with **Florence** is where to start. Sightseeing or shopping? Besides the major sights (outlined in the Florence chapter), there will always be a special exhibit of some sort that will certainly merit a visit.

Rome is in a league by itself. No other Italian city has so many major monuments and archaeological sites or anything to compete with St. Peter's and the Vatican museums. Unfortunately quite often more time is spent standing in line than actually seeing the sights. Rome is also more spread out than Florence or Venice. The Rome chapter in this book is divided into three basic sectors: religious (the Vatican), monumental, and archaeological. On the run, with one day for each, the visitor can look around and at least say, "I was there."

The attraction of the **Gulf of Naples** is not so much the city of Parthenope, but the entire gulf area from Bàcoli around the coast to Sorrento; the isles of Capri, Ischia, and Procida; and the Amalfi Drive on the coast from Sorrento toward Salerno (a stop at Positano is a must). In this sweep around the gulf are the famous archaeological sights of Pompeii, Herculaneum, and Vesuvius.

This is one of the most scenic parts of the country. But, Naples itself can be mind-boggling. In-city accommodations have been listed in our "Naples and Campania" chapter, but the best suggestion is to use one of the smaller surrounding towns as a base of operations. Here an auto is a definite asset. Two of the most beautiful views on the old continent are those offered by Capri toward Vesuvius and from the point of the Sorrentine peninsula above Nerano, which provides a sweeping panorama over both the gulfs of Naples and Salerno as well as the length of the Sorrentine peninsula.

These are the highlights for any trip to Italy, but other sights and experiences can be just as rewarding. After your tour of Venice, consider stops at some of the surrounding islands. Or explore the **Veneto region:** the palatial villas—called the Ville Venete—including those in Vicenza, the town that is the center of Andrea Palladio's architecture. Or walk in the legendary steps of Shakespeare's star-crossed lovers in picturesque Verona. These can be explored on a trip between Venice and Milan—a trip that is in itself a full holiday. And **Milan,** "the Manhattan of Italy" has its own unique charms in a northern sophistication rooted in Italian provincialism. Among its attractions are museums, the famous Duomo, and some great shopping. (Bargain hunters should be advised that better prices can be found in Florence and Rome.) Excursions from Milan can take travelers into the **Italian lake country**—for dramatic scenery. (If it's water sports you're interested in, choose Lake Garda.)

Trips from Florence will take you into **Tuscany,** the garden of Florence. From here you can explore Pisa and its Piazza del Duomo complex (part of this is the famous Leaning Tower), and atmospheric Siena, where the light is said to be like nowhere else in the world.

Travel between Rome and Florence into **Umbria**'s medieval splendors, towns like Gubbio, Assisi, and Spoleto where the past seems very much alive.

Skiers should investigate the northeast and northwest corners of the country. **Northwestern ski resorts** are set up on the slopes of Monte Bianco (Mont Blanc), Cervinia (the Matterhorn), and Monte Rosa. In the northeast you can obtain a pass to ski 11 **Dolomite resorts.** Some Dolomite skiing is actually in the Veneto region (and covered in that chapter), including the skiing at Cortina d'Ampezzo, site of the 1956 winter Olympics. Farther south, **Emilia-Romagna** has highly organized resorts (with the ubiquitous Emilia-Romagna discotheques).

Beach goers may especially want to sample the shores of **Sardinia,** which are supposed to line Italy's cleanest waters; the **rivieras in Liguria**—especially the five towns that comprise the area of coast known as the Cinque Terre; the long stretch of **Tyrrhenian coast of Calabria,** from Lamezia Terme to Reggio di Calabria. A beach holiday in **Sicily** can combine with tours to major archaeological sights such as the Valley of the Temples outside Agrigento.

Wherever you're coming from or going to, along any given route in Italy, there is an abundance of sights, both natural and man-made, that can make your trip much longer than you may expect. We've organized much of this book around driving excursions, for those of you who are exploring outside the major sights on this trip to Italy. And this is why we've put so much emphasis on that Italian trait of *arrangiarsi:* So much in Italy is well worth a detour; you'll need to be spontaneous to make the most of your trip. Set your priorities, but don't let them rule. The best type of Italian holiday may well be one in which the traveler has come up with no list of things to see and do; remember, as we've said elsewhere, more than being seen, Italy should be absorbed.

4

ROME

Rome has to be eternal. What other city so severely and consistently tested has always managed to survive?

Motor vehicles are the scourge of the twentieth century. Over the past thirty years they have provoked more damage than nearly two thousand years of quakes, fires, plagues, looting, complacency, and pure quests for power. Modern Neroes fiddle through brief reigns as daily traffic throughout the metropolitan area increasingly paralyzes routine life, and creates the pollution that is crumbling ancient Rome's monuments. Municipal inadequacy and national inefficiency in dealing with the problem have created a quagmire to rival the marshland bogs where legend says that Romulus founded Rome on April 21, 753 B.C.

Archaeologists today are reassessing Rome's historical role in the development of the city-state. Until now, ancient Rome has been considered a military power that usurped the technical and cultural advancements of the Etruscans and Greeks; based on recent digs at the Palatine site that reputedly have uncovered ruins of the original village, scholars now believe Rome originated more than the civilization has been given credit for, and are reevaluating the cultural impact of ancient Rome.

Ancient Romans were convinced they were deified, preordained to rule the world. Their constant quest for conquest circled the Mediterranean in their effort to dominate the known world. Then came the invasions of Gaul and Britain, and all roads truly led to Rome, *caput mundi,* "capital of the world." The immense grandeur of the achievement has captivated the imagination of the centuries.

Charismatic politician-generals such as Julius Caesar and his great-nephew Octavius (who assumed the name Augustus as emperor) provided early leadership that is unknown in the petty politicking that disrupts Italy today. But in ensuing years, political feuds and plots corrupted the Empire, and it was divided into East and West. The papacy's political emer-

gence forced hotly contested rivalry between imperialists, re-
publicans, and papists. This continued throughout the Middle
Ages, in the city-states of the warring Guelphs and Ghibellines.

In 1308 the papacy was forced to seek refuge in Avignon,
France. It did not return to Rome until 1377, but even then
there were rivals to Peter's throne. With the reign of Pope
Alexander VI (Rodrigo Borgia), who freely wielded the sword
of excommunication against any and all opponents who escaped the ire of his infamous offspring Cesare and Lucretia,
Rome began to accumulate a powerful artistic patrimony
through Alexander's patronage of such artists as Michelangelo, Raphael, and Bramante. Rome went on to become the baroque capital of the world with Urban VIII's commissioning
of the architectural genius of Gianlorenzo Bernini and Borromini to revitalize Rome. Their artistic legacy is truly one
of the beauties of the city.

The Risorgimento's unification of Italy under the House of
Savoy in 1861 formally terminated the political power of the
papacy. When Rome became capital of the Savoy kingdom in
1870, more subtle means of influence were applied to internal
Italian affairs.

Boundaries were drawn with the 1922 Lateran Pact that established the Holy See as an independent state and achieved
church recognition for the Fascist regime of Benito Mussolini.

The Vatican has undergone sharp criticism for its conduct
during the Nazi occupation of Rome, especially for failure to
intervene before the Fosse Ardeatine reprisal killings of some
three hundred Italians. But individual acts of heroism were
not rare. A brave Irish priest spirited a number of Allied avia-
tors to freedom as well as the wife and son of the SS major
who supervised the Fosse Ardeatine massacre.

During the occupation, Allied bombing of the San Lorenzo
rail freight depot caused death and destruction among the civilian population, and forced a rare exit of then-Pope Pius XII
from Vatican City.

Recently the streets of Rome have appeared more war-
ravaged than following the city's liberation by the Allies in
1944, as the capital prepares for two major events. In 1990
Italy will host the World Cup soccer tournament, and in 1992
the final erasing of national barriers between European Economic Community nations is scheduled (the first steps toward
European integration were signed in Rome on March 23,
1957). Hardly a street in Rome has escaped excavation to ren-
ovate and expand phone, gas, electric, water, and sewer lines
to handle the expected crowds. With time-tested lack of coordination seemingly inherent in Italian bureaucracy, repeated
street closings have added to the already desperate traffic
snarl in Rome, complicated by the constant and abrupt rever-
sal of the direction of one-way streets. And contractors live

in constant fear of uncovering artifacts of archaeological significance: the Fine Arts Commission will then block all work—sometimes for months—pending a decision on the fate of the new find.

The same bureaucratic neglect has dogged the effort to save Rome's crumbling architectural heritage. The first-century Arch of Constantine has remained under scaffolding erected for renovation seven years ago. Work on the Palace of Justice took so long that grass grew on the scaffolding. And yet much of Rome's charm lies in its cavalier attitude toward its own greatness.

This cavalier attitude unfortunately can show up as a lack of courtesy and civic pride. Service in downtown shops can be appalling. One Rome daily newspaper was prompted to run a clerk of the week contest; the effect was totally undetectable. Sales personnel snarl today as beautifully as they did yesterday.

The dream of every neighborhood is that a local resident will be elected mayor. This will assure that their streets are properly lit, that garbage will be collected daily and the streets swept at least once a week. Impersonality has taken its toll as condominium lifestyles trade simplicity for modern convenience.

The southernization of Rome has taken its toll, manning the lethargic bureaucracy less common in the industrious, Austro-Hungarian-influenced north. (Southern Italy was controlled by the Bourbons who reigned at a maximum level of exploitation, giving nothing in return. After the Bourbons, the popular attitude saw the state as the goose that laid the golden egg, with everyone entitled to as many as they could wrangle.)

Leftist labor laws have greatly restricted private employers and state supervisors. The former maintain an institutional independence; the latter are tied to political nepotism with overtones of Third World mentality. Under such circumstances, providing adequate and accurate tourist assistance is a real catch-22, and without tourism Rome and its entrepreneurs would be in dire straits.

Don't be scared off; forewarned is forearmed, and the objective—the Eternal City—is worth your patience. Not all Rome's inhabitants are gruff, indifferent, or hustling—after all, they are Italians. The city can be amazingly hospitable; much can depend on the visitor. Therein lies the secret to a successful Roman holiday: proper perspective, and a share in the admiration of the ages for this decadent queen of cities. At times it may resemble Looney Tunes, but it's not Disney World.

ORIENTING YOURSELF

Where to start is the real Roman dilemma. Unlike other great cities in Italy, Rome's major attractions are so many and so widely dispersed that it is impossible to see them all by foot in a limited amount of time. To simplify the task, think of Rome as three general areas: the Vatican, monumental Rome, and archaeological Rome.

The Vatican includes the Basilica of St. Peter's, the Vatican Museums (including the Sistine Chapel and the Raphael Rooms), and the papal fortress of Castel Sant'Angelo. For purposes of simplification, we're also considering the residential Prati area nearby as part of the Vatican area. The Vatican area is across the Tiber, directly west of the center of modern downtown Rome. It is easily accessible by the subway A line (Ottaviano, the last stop); the number 30 tram (Piazza Risorgimento, the last stop), which makes one long sweep around most of central Rome; and the number 64 bus, which terminates its run in the shadow of the colonnades embracing St. Peter's Square. (The number 64 line runs from the central Termini train station through the heart of Rome—Via Nazionale, Piazza Venezia, and Corso Vittorio Emanuele II.)

Monumental Rome is the area of palaces and monuments on both sides of the central Via del Corso from Piazza del Popolo to Piazza Venezia. It is bounded on the west by the Tiber, and on the east by the Pincio area, down Trinita dei Monti to the Spanish Steps, and along Via Sistina to Piazza Barberini. This area is well-serviced by the A line, with stops at Piazza Barberini, Piazza di Spagna, and Piazzale Flaminio (just outside Piazza del Popolo).

Most of this area is a pedestrian island; only public vehicles and those with special permits are allowed. Sundays and holidays are the best for daytime visits, since traffic will be reduced to a bare minimum. Most of the area is especially attractive in the evening, when the illuminated sights seem even more impressive.

This area is also the main shopping area, offering pleasant distractions and no lack of places for a snack or refreshment. Distances shrink amazingly when traveling by foot, since major monuments, churches, and fountains are never more than five minutes apart.

The concentration of sights becomes more intensive heading down the Corso toward the archaeological area, the excavations of what was once ancient Rome. The monumental area ends in Piazza del Campidoglio, the square designed by Michelangelo atop the Capitoline Hill, offering a balcony view over the major ancient ruins, with the Colosseum as a backdrop.

To reach **archaeological Rome,** take the street downhill east, from the Campidoglio to Via dei Fori Imperiali, which leads directly to the Colosseum, across from the entrance to the Roman Forum and Palatine Hill. This is the heart of ancient Rome, once ruler of the Mediterranean world. Interesting mosaic maps on the embankment walls along the right side of Via dei Fori Imperiali illustrate the expansion of the Roman Empire.

To the left, across the street from the Colosseum, is the B line metro stop, the most convenient means for reaching the archaeological area. Up the hill behind the Colosseum are numerous bus and tram stops, including the number 118 bus to the Via Appia Antica and the Catacombs. The most interesting are San Calisto and San Sebastiano; since the catacombs alternate closing days, one of these is always open.

Between the two catacombs, on Via delle Sette Chiese, is the Fosse Ardeatine site where more than three hundred Italians were executed in tufo caves on direct orders from Hitler after a German police patrol was bombed in the center of Rome. An impressive monument marks the site.

As part of a visit to archaeological Rome, you can make a sidetrip to San Giovanni in Laterano (the cathedral of Rome) and the Holy Stairs, just off the A line stop at the beginning of the modern Via Appia.

Beyond this basic breakdown of the major sights in Rome are the following:

- The complex in front of Stazione **Termini** includes the church of Santa Maria degli Angeli and Diocletian's Baths, housing the National Museum of Rome. The basilica of Santa Maria Maggiore is also near the rail terminal, just off the B line.
- **Trastevere,** meaning "across the Tiber," is basically the area between the Tiber and Gianicolo hill. Once considered the last bastion of "true" Romans, the area was discovered by expatriates who considered it quaint. Prices soared, places were renovated, and it is no longer quite so quaint— with residents that include royalty and some of the world's wealthiest individuals. It is still known as a good dining area, with a number of trattorias and restaurants for all tastes and price ranges, even though fast food and foreign fare have encroached on the previously purely Roman domain. The area of the Sunday flea market, Trastevere is also the site of the church of Santa Maria in Trastevere, only a five-minute walk from Piazza Sonnino on Viale di Trastevere. The area is accessible by the number 280 bus from Prati and the Vatican, and the number 710, 718, and 719 buses which have terminals in the Piazza Venezia area.

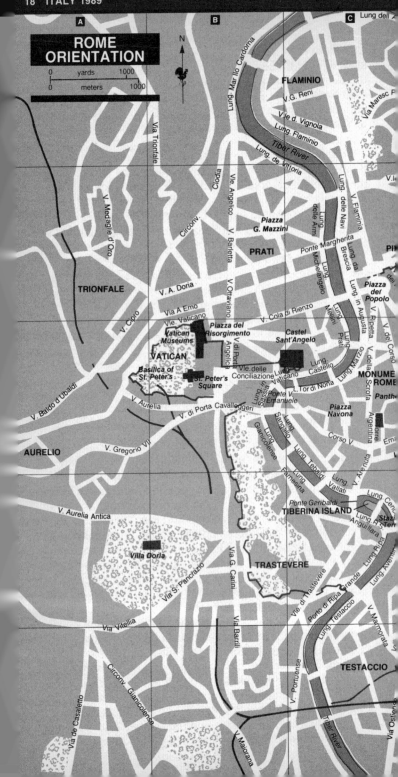

ROME ORIENTATION

D **E** **F**

SALARIO

Villa Ada

Via Tripoli

V. Nomentana

1

Viale dei Parioli

PARIOLI

V. Rossini

V.le Liegi

Via Salana

V.R. Lanciani

V. Paisiello

Via Po Tagliamento

Nomentana

Circonv. Nomentana

V.le Reg. Margherita

Villa Borghese

Via Pinciane

Villa Torlonia

2

RGHESE

Corso d'Italia

V. Piave

V. G. Morgagni

V. Bari V. Catania

V. della Lega Lombarda

di na

V.le del Policlinico

V.le Reg. Elena

V. Veneto

Piazza Barberini

V. Tiburtina

stina

V. delle Quattro Fontane

V. XX Settembre

V.le Castro Pret.

TERMINI

V. le Università

ain

V. Quirinale

V. Nazionale

Piazza Repubblica

Piazza V. Emanuele

V. Agostino Depretis

Stazione Termini

Via Marsala

Via Ramni

Via Scalo S. Lorenzo

3

Teatro dell'Opera

Santa Maria Maggiore

V. Giolitti

V. Cavour

Piazza Magnanapoli

n

San Pietro in Vincoli

Terme di Traiano

Piazza V. Emanuele

V. Principe Eugenio

V. Porta Maggiore

Imperiali

del doglio

ARCHAEOLOGICAL ROME

V. Merulana

V.le Manzoni

Via Prenestina

Piazza del Colosseo

Colosseum

V. Labicana

V. Emanuele Filiberto

Piazza di Porta Maggiore

V. Casilina

latine Hill

V. di S. Gregorio

V. Claudia Navicella

Piazza S. Giovanni in Laterano

V. Casilina Vecchia

4

Piazza di Porta Capena

irco

ventino

V. della

V. A. Aradam

San Giovanni in Laterano

Via La Spezia

Vie delle Terme di Caracalla

V. Gallia

V. Etruria

Baths of Caracalla

V. di Porta S. Sebastiano

V. di Porta S. Sebastiano

V. Acaia

V. Appia Nuova

TUSCOLANO

5

Marco Polo

Via Latina

onv. Ostiense

Immediately north of Piazza Sonnino are **Tiberina Island** and the main synagogue on Lungotevere de'Cenci in the old **ghetto.**

• The **Borghese area** lies north of the city center. Consider a brief tour of the Galleria Borghese, Modern Art Gallery, and Villa Giulia Etruscan museum, which edge the north and east of the largest park in Rome, Villa Borghese, which also contains the Rome zoo. **Pincio** is another park area; the "balcony of Rome," it overlooks Piazza del Popolo and extends into Villa Borghese. The **Parioli** area borders Villa Borghese on the north. There are a number of embassies here, as well as the official residence of the U.S. ambassador.

• The **Via Veneto,** running south from Villa Borghese, is no longer the street of *La Dolce Vita.* Today, hookers must compete with tourists for space on the streets, and the major attractions are some good restaurants and shopping.

PRIORITIES

It's difficult to imagine needing less than three days to see just the basics of Rome. One day is required to visit the Vatican, its museums, and Castel Sant'Angelo. Another day can be exhausted touring the fountains, monuments, and churches in monumental old Rome. Archaeological Rome can be just as demanding, with the Colosseum, the Roman Forum, and many other important ruins.

Fortunately, you can sightsee at night, taking pleasant evening strolls around the Trevi Fountain, the Pantheon, and Piazza Navona, where there is pleasant caffè life and a number of good restaurants.

Since the Colosseum and Forum can easily be seen on the same day, tour this area any day other than Tuesday, when the Forum is closed, and include the church of San Clemente on your tour, just a ten-minute stroll behind the Colosseum on Piazza San Clemente, between Via Labicana and Via San Giovanni in Laterano.

The following sights should be on any list of things to see and do in Rome. The order is alphabetical; decide for yourself what to do first. Sights are keyed in to areas of Rome, as well as to the color map of the city at the back of the book. In the neighborhood key, reference is made to the page number of the color insert and the appropriate map coordinates.

Baths of Caracalla
(Terme di Caracalla)   ARCHAEOLOGICAL ROME, P. 25, D5

These second-century baths were among the largest and most important in ancient Rome. Open-air opera is staged here in summer. Open Tuesday through Saturday 9 A.M. to 6 P.M., to 1 P.M. Sunday and Monday. Take the number 118 bus from behind the Colosseum; you can stop here on your way to the Catacombs.

Capitol (Campidoglio)
MONUMENTAL ROME, P. 24, D3.

The Piazza del Campidoglio, designed by Michelangelo, sits at the top of Capitoline Hill. To the left of the square is the Church of Santa Maria d'Aracoeli, with frescoes by Pinturicchio. Facing each other are the Palazzo Nuovo and Palazzo dei Conservatori, now the Capitoline Museums. The Nuovo houses mainly classical statues; the Conservatori features a picture gallery, with famous works such as Caravaggio's *John the Baptist.* The museums are open 9 A.M. to 2 P.M. Tuesday through Friday; to 11:30 P.M. on Saturday; to 1 P.M. on Sundays and holidays; also from 5 to 8 P.M. on Tuesdays and Thursdays. Telephone 6782862 to confirm days and hours. Behind the Campidoglio, there's a wonderful view of the Colosseum and Roman Forum.

Castel Sant'Angelo
VATICAN, P. 24, B2

First completed in A.D. 139 as the emperor Hadrian's tomb, the Castel was converted into a citadel because of its strategic position on the Tiber; it later became a fortified residence for a number of popes. Within you can visit papal apartments and galleries. The Castel is on Lungotevere Castello, across the Tiber from downtown Rome. Take the A line metro, the number 30 tram, or the number 64 bus.

Nearby: St. Peter's Square and Basilica; the Vatican Museums.

Catacombs
ARCHAEOLOGICAL ROME

These underground Christian cemeteries line the ancient Appian Way, Via Appia Antica. You can see tombs of various sizes, chapels that have been carved out of the rock, and early examples of Christian carvings and paintings on the walls. Two of the best known are San Calisto, at number 110, and San Sebastiano, at number 136. Tours are available in English. Open 8:30 A.M. to noon and 2:30 to 5:30 P.M., to 5 P.M. in winter. Take the number 118 bus from behind the Colosseum.

Colosseum
ARCHAEOLOGICAL ROME, P. 24, D4

Probably the best-known symbol of ancient Rome, this imposing arena dates from A.D. 80. It accommodated up to 50,000 for spectacles ranging from gladiator combats to mock sea battles. Located at the end of Via dei Fori Imperiali, the Colosseum is open from 9 A.M. to 3:30 P.M. in winter, to 7 P.M. in summer; to 1 P.M. only on Sunday and holidays. The B line metro stops across the street.

Nearby: The Roman Forum; the Palatine Hill; and the bus to the Catacombs (the Baths of Caracalla are along the way).

Palatine Hill
ARCHAEOLOGICAL ROME, P. 24, D4

Romulus and Remus were said to have been found on this hill, once covered with public buildings and homes of prominent Romans. Highlights include the House of Livia, the Palace of the Flavians, and the baths of Septimus Severus. Open 9 A.M. to 7 P.M., to 5 P.M. in winter. Take the B line metro to the Colosseum.

Nearby: The Colosseum; and the Roman Forum.

Pantheon
MONUMENTAL ROME, P. 24, C3

Standing on Piazza della Rotonda, this is the most complete building remaining from Imperial Rome. Originally constructed in about 27 B.C., it was rebuilt by the Emperor Hadrian around 118–125. A temple to the gods as well as a symbol of Hadrian's power, the structure is especially impressive because of its dome, wider than that of St. Peter's. There is active nightlife in the area, so an evening visit is a good idea. You can take the A line metro and walk from Piazza di Spagna; the number 119 tram passes through Piazza Rotonda; you can also take bus number 90 or 70.

Nearby: The Trevi Fountain and Piazza Navona.

Piazza del Popolo
MONUMENTAL ROME, P. 24, C1

The entrance to the city is the third-century Porta del Popolo, adorned by Bernini. The church of Santa Maria del Popolo contains frescoes by Pinturicchio and two masterpieces by Caravaggio, *The Conversion of St. Paul* and the *Crucifixion of St. Peter.* The obelisk in the center of the piazza was taken from an Egyptian sun temple and brought to Rome for the Circus Maximus. Take the A line metro to Flaminio.

Nearby: There is good shopping along Via del Babuino to Piazza di Spagna.

Piazza di Spagna
MONUMENTAL ROME, P. 24, D2

Named after the residence of the Spanish ambassador to the Vatican, the square and the famous Spanish Steps are favorite gathering spots, especially for young people. Pietro Bernini's Barcaccia fountain stands at the foot of the stairway. Next to the stairs is the Keats-Shelley memorial, the house where Keats died (open Monday through Friday 9 A.M. to 12:30 P.M. and 3:30 to 6 P.M., 2:30 to 5 P.M. in winter). The A line metro stops just off the square.

Nearby: Piazza del Popolo; the Trevi Fountain; and some great shopping.

Piazza Navona
MONUMENTAL ROME, P. 24, C3

One of the world's most beautiful squares, the Piazza Navona is dominated by Bernini's Fountain of the Four Rivers. Facing the fountain is Borromini's Church of Sant'Agnese in Agone. The Square has an active nightlife, with a number of caffès and great people-watching.

Nearby: The Pantheon.

Roman Forum
ARCHAEOLOGICAL ROME, P. 24, D3/D4

The center of life in ancient Rome, the Forum contains ruins of numerous temples; the Curia, where the Senate met; the house of the Vestal Virgins; and triumphal arches that commemorated the victories of individual emperors. Open from 9 A.M. to one hour before sunset, Sun. from 10 A.M.; closed Tuesday. Take the B line metro to the Colosseo stop.

Nearby: The Colosseum and the Palatine Hill.

St. Peter's Square
VATICAN, P. 24, A2

The world's largest church, St. Peter's Basilica is framed by a magnificent piazza begun in 1656 by Bernini. The church itself, said to stand where St. Peter was buried, is the product of the architectural efforts of Bramante, Michelangelo, Maderno, and Bernini. Within the church is Michelangelo's famous *Pietà*. Take the A line metro to Ottaviano; the number 30 tram to Piazza Risorgimento; or the number 64 bus to the end of the line.

Nearby: The Vatican Museums and Castel Sant'Angelo.

San Giovanni in Laterano (St. John Lateran) and the Holy Stairs
ARCHAEOLOGICAL ROME, P. 25, F4

The cathedral of Rome, the cathedral of the Pope, stands in the piazza of the same name. The baptistery (open 8 A.M. to noon and 4 to 6 P.M.) is worth a visit for its eight mosaics of the life of John the Baptist. The Holy Stairs (8 A.M. to 12:30 P.M. and 3 to 7 P.M., from 3:30 P.M. May to September) are reputedly the original 28 marble stairs that Christ climbed in Pilate's palace in Jerusalem. The cathedral is just off the A line metro, at the beginning of the Via Appia Nuova.

San Pietro in Vincoli (St. Peter in Chains)
ARCHAEOLOGICAL ROME, P. 24, D3/E3

This fifth-century church houses the alleged chains of St. Peter, but the major point of interest is Michelangelo's great sculpture of *Moses*. Take the B line metro to Cavour.

Nearby: The Colosseum and Santa Maria Maggiore.

Santa Maria Maggiore
TERMINI, P. 24, E3

One of Rome's four major basilicas, this church was begun in the fifth century. Of special interest are the baroque Chapel of Sixtus V and Pauline Chapel. The campanile is the highest in Rome. The church stands in the Piazza Santa Maria Maggiore, just off the B metro line, near the Termini stop.

Nearby: The church of Santa Maria degli Angeli; the Diocletian Baths; and the National Museum of Rome.

Trevi Fountain
MONUMENTAL ROME, P. 24, D2

Rome's most famous fountain was built in the 18th century. The fountain is turned off in the evenings these days (continued renovation may mean more extensive closing), but that doesn't keep tourists from tossing their coins in to ensure their return to Rome. Nightlife is active here. Take the A line metro; the Barberini or Spagna stops are the closest.
Nearby: The Piazza di Spagna and the Pantheon.

Vatican Museums
VATICAN, P. 24, A2

The most famous section of these museums, which house an enormous collection of works, is the Sistine Chapel. Right before you enter the chapel are the Raphael Rooms, painted by Raphael for Pope Julius II while Michelangelo was working on the Sistine ceiling. (Michelangelo's *Last Judgment* on the Sistine wall was painted more than twenty years after he completed work on the ceiling.) The Vatican Museums are open 9 A.M. to 2 P.M. Monday through Saturday, and the last Sunday of the month (when they're free). During July, August, September and at Easter, hours extend to 5 P.M. Take the A line metro, the number 30 tram, or the number 64 bus, all to the end of the line.
Nearby: St. Peter's Square and Basilica; Castel Sant'Angelo.

Excursions into rural Lazio, including Tivoli, are discussed later in this chapter.

Museum Hours

Unless otherwise specified, museums usually are open from 9 A.M. to 2 P.M. Tuesday through Saturday, to 1 P.M. on Sunday and holidays. You cannot enter during the last hour; some more abrupt ticket takers close even earlier.

Though afternoon and evening hours are sometimes given, sites often are not actually open. Check before making special trips: Telephone the gallery or museum directly to confirm the hours.

TRAVEL

Rome has three airports, seven state-run rail terminals and three private rail depots. Provincial bus service is based at depots throughout the city; there are two subway lines and an extensive city bus system. Despite all this, transportation is clogged and traffic heavy.

Rome is rapidly being strangled by automobile traffic that city authorities seem unequipped to regulate. And despite the numerous services and depots available, ninety percent of rail and air traffic is concentrated on Stazione Termini and Leonardo da Vinci (Fiumicino) Airport.

Arriving at the Airport

Leonardo da Vinci is the official name of Rome's international airport near the small port town of Fiumicino. This can create confusion for the traveler, since abroad the airport is referred to as da Vinci, while in Rome it is always **Fiumicino**. (It also explains why some identification tags on luggage destined for Rome read FCO.)

The international and domestic terminals at Fiumicino are side by side. The airport information number is (06) 60121; information is available in English, and the switchboard can transfer calls to all airlines. Most airline offices in Rome are in the area between Via Veneto, Via Barberini, and Via Bissolati. All are closed noon Sat.–9 A.M. Mon.

Only Alitalia has a 24-hour, seven-day-a-week all-service number: (06) 5456. You can't reach other airlines (for reservations, confirmation, etc.) during the weekend.

Bus service from the airport to Termini Station is Lit. 5,000 per person. The 22-mile ride takes 45 min., traffic permitting; buses leave from Termini's Via Giolitti Air Terminal, and from both the international and domestic terminals at Fiumicino, every 15 min. 7 A.M.–9 P.M. and every 30 min. 9 P.M.–7 A.M. There are train, bus, and subway connections at Termini.

Once the Rome airport, **Ciampino** is now basically a military facility that handles charters and acts as a backup for Fiumicino in bad weather. (Being close to the coast, Fiumicino is more likely to be subject to rare fogs.) The Ciampino information number is (06) 724241; information is available in Italian only.

Besides taxi, the best means of reaching Rome from Ciampino is to take the ACOTRAL bus from the airport to the Anagnina subway (metro) stop, then take the A line (in the direction of Ottaviano) into Rome.

Having lire with you on arrival is a must at Ciampino; there are no banking facilities. Designed more to accommodate bank employees than international travelers, limited banking is available at Fiumicino.

When leaving from Fiumicino, if you want to exchange lire for the currency of your next destination, you must present a foreign-exchange slip from a Rome bank as proof that an official lire transaction was originally made.

Airport taxis are assigned to Fiumicino and Ciampino for two-week stints. Cabs assigned to the airport cannot work in the city, and vice versa. This obliges cabs to return to the airport empty, at the original passenger's expense. A run to Fiumicino thus has Lit. 14,000 added to the meter fare; from Fiumicino to the city, the added fee is Lit. 10,000. The taxi ride will total around Lit. 50,000, not including extra cost for luggage. To and from Ciampino the added fee is Lit. 7,000 (with total cost around Lit. 40,000).

Train Connections

Trains from the main Rome station of Termini connect Italy's capital with the rest of the country as well as Western and Eastern European destinations. Information can be obtained from the English-language information counter in the station at Piazza dei Cinquecento, or by telephoning (06) 4775 (in Italian only).

Other Rome train stations are:

Ostiense, Piazzale Partigiani, tel. (06) 5750732 (connections to Ostia, Viterbo, Naples via Formia, and Nettuno)

Prenestina, Piazzale della Stazione Prenestina, tel. (06) 272072 (to Avezzano and Pescara)

San Pietro, Via Stazione San Pietro, tel. (06) 631391 (to Viterbo via la Storta)

Tiburtina, Circonvallazione Nomentana, tel. (06) 4956626 (to Ancona via Foligno, Florence, Bologna, Naples via Formia, Pescara via Avezzano, Nettuno, Velletri, and Viterbo)

Trastevere, Piazzale Biondo, tel. (06) 5816076 (to Genoa via Pisa, Nettuno, and Viterbo)

Tuscolana, Via Mestre, tel. (06) 7576359 (to Naples via Formia, and Nettuno).

There also are three local train services under ACOTRAL, with departure points at Piazzale Flaminio (connections to Civita Castellana and Viterbo, plus an urban link to Parioli's Piazza Euclide); Roma Laziali, on Via Giolitti behind Termini; and Porta San Paolo, across the street from the Pyramid metro stop (connections to Ostia Lido and Ostia Antica, every 30 min. 5:30 A.M.–midnight). An hourly bus service to Ostia substitutes for the trains after midnight. For ACOTRAL information call (06) 57531.

Bus Connections

ACOTRAL's extraurban blue buses serve the province of Rome and other key points in Lazio. Depots are along the metro lines, thereby offering fast and easy connections between provincial bus lines and inner-city destinations.

ACOTRAL information can be obtained from the main office, Via Ostiense 131; tel. (06) 57531. Buses depart from Via Castro Pretorio, Viale Giulio Cesare (Lepanto metro stop), the EUR-Fermi metro station, Piazza dei Cinquecento (in front of the Termini FS station), Piazzale Flaminio (just outside Piazza del Popolo), Via Gaeta (near Termini), Via Giolitti (the Termini departure point for da Vinci-Fiumicino airport), Piazza M. Fanti, Piazza di Cinecittà, and the Pyramid (Piramide) metro stop.

Public Transportation within the City

The Roman's near-masochistic sense of individualism manifests itself in the insistence on driving in inner Rome, most of which is banned to private autos except for those of residents, merchants, and such friends of city hall who have acquired permanent windshield permits. Traffic often paralyzes what could otherwise be an efficient transit system. This makes the Metropolitana (subway) much more efficient than surface transportation. The metro is also the spine of the urban transportation system; a number of city bus lines terminate at or near metro stops.

State tourist board (EPT) information offices at the turnpike stations Roma Nord and Roma Sud, the international airport (da Vinci-Fiumicino), and Termini (a kiosk at track number 3) provide free city maps of principal bus, tram, and metro routes.

The metro is run by ACOTRAL, which also operates provincial bus service; city buses are run by ATAC.

TAKING THE SUBWAY

The two metro lines are simply designated A and B. Direction is indicated by the terminals at the end of each line. The A and B lines intersect under Termini train station. You can change lines without paying another fare. The fare is Lit. 700 per ride regardless of distance. Booklets of ten tickets may be purchased at the reduced rate of Lit. 6,000. These may be purchased at most underground stops; those not equipped with vendor booths have coin-operated vending machines. For information call (06) 57531.

TAKING THE BUS OR TRAM

ACOTRAL ticket vendors sell a daily BIG ticket (Lit. 2,400) valid for 24 hours on both metro and all city bus and tram (ATAC) lines. This is the only bus-tram-metro ticket combination.

The city transit company (ATAC) issues regular monthly one-line and multi-line passes for residents. For tourists, a weekly multi-line pass (Lit. 10,000) is available at the ATAC kiosk in front of Termini, in Piazza dei Cinquecento. As are all urban buses in Italy, ATAC buses and trams are yellow.

Individual tickets for trams and buses are purchased at newsstands and tobacco counters near ATAC stops for Lit. 700 each, or Lit. 6,000 for a booklet of ten. Ticket holders board at the back of the bus or tram, and must cancel tickets in the machine to the left of the aisle. Pass holders board at the front of the bus or tram. Everyone exits through the center door.

Company inspectors regularly patrol city routes. Anyone found without a properly cancelled ticket will be fined Lit. 10,000 on the spot. Keep this in mind if you feel like doing as the Romans do and don't buy a ticket.

Taxis

Taxis are an interesting undertaking in Rome—which is our polite way of saying you should watch what you're doing. All legitimate taxis are yellow. No licensed cab driver will approach anyone at train stations and airports offering his services. Legitimate cabs are in line in front of terminals, often under the watchful eye of a city policeman. At the air terminal less scrupulous drivers sometimes will exploit jet lag and travelers' unfamiliarity with Rome and Italian currency. If the driver refuses to turn on his meter, ask him to stop; call a policeman; or sit back, enjoy the ride, and refuse to pay upon reaching your destination—but be prepared for a screaming match, and call the local police precinct.

When a meter is turned on, a starting fee is registered. If a cab has been called from an outdoor stand or radio taxi co-op, the driver turns on his meter for the drive to the pickup point, and the meter will be running on arrival. There is a flat Lit. 3,000 night fee in effect 10 P.M.–7 A.M., added onto the meter fee. The same is done on Sundays and holidays. There is no such thing as a per passenger charge, but there is a charge for each piece of baggage. All taxi regulations should be available on a printed fare sheet under the seal of the city of Rome in each and every yellow cab.

When tipping, round off to the next highest thousand, or empty your pockets of change. But use your own discretion when deciding how deserving your driver is.

Driving

Regardless of what has been written and said about Rome traffic, nothing can match the initial impact. The only relief is in August, when fools rush in where angels fear to tread. Most of a broiling city has been deserted for the annual holiday, which means very little traffic and an abundance of usually nonexistent parking. But try to find a restaurant, dry cleaner, or laundry, and then you'll know who went on vacation.

Rome is surrounded by a beltway indicated by green turnpike signs reading "GRA" (Grande Raccordo Anulare). All turnpikes and major roads to Rome are linked to this ring road, which can help drivers avoid much grief if they arrive in Rome on the opposite side of the city from their final destination.

Clockwise around the beltway arrival routes are:

SS3 Via Flaminia (due north)
SS4 Via Salaria
The A1 Rome–Milan turnpike approach road to Roma Nord
SS5 Via Tiburtina (to Tivoli)
the A24 Rome–L'Aquila
SS6 Via Casilina (to Palestrina)
the A2 Rome-Naples approach road for Roma Sud
SS215 Via Tuscolana (for Frascati and the Albani Hills)
SS7 Via Appia (passing Ciampino and the lakes of Castel Gandolfo and Nemi en route to Naples)
SS148, practically due south of the city, which is an extension of Via Cristoforo Colombo, which pierces EUR (this is the road for the industrial zone at Pomezia en route to Latina, San Felice Circeo, and the Terracina ferry port for the island of Ponza)
SS201, the main route to Fiumicino, southwest of Rome, with a turnoff that becomes the A12 to Civitavecchia
SS1 Via Aurelia, due west, entering Rome behind the Vatican (connecting with the Circonvallazione Cornelia, crossing the Via Olimpica inner loop, and arriving at the Tiber on Via Gregorio VII: then chaos reigns)
SS2 Via Cassia (to Siena), running northwest and completing the GRA loop

The Cassia and Casilina are the worst roads to use to enter Rome. The best are the Colombo, Salaria, and Flaminia, in that order. Try to arrive between 2 and 4 P.M. Mon.–Sat. and

between 10 A.M. and 6 P.M. Sun. Otherwise rush-hour and end-of-the weekend traffic is impossible.

CAR RENTALS

Auto rental facilities are available in Rome, but tourists beginning their travels in Rome should forget the convenience factor of picking up an automobile at the airport and weigh it against the inconvenience of major traffic snarls en route to a hotel in Rome. For touring Rome, cars are an invitation to frustration. Main one-way streets change directions seemingly at whim, adding to the chaos.

These are the best international organizations, plus two reliable national agencies:

Leonardo da Vinci–Fiumicino: (International terminal) Avis, tel. (06) 601579; Europcar, tel. (06) 601879, telex 614564; Hertz, tel. (06) 601241, telex 610201; Maggiore, tel. (06) 601678. (National terminal) Avis, tel. (06) 601531; Europcar, tel. (06) 601977; Hertz, tel. (06) 601553; Maggiore, tel. (06) 601508.

Ciampino Airport: Avis, tel. (06) 6001955; Europcar, tel. (06) 7240387; Hertz, tel. (06) 600095; Maggiore, tel. (06) 7240368.

Rome: Avis, Via Sardegna 38A; tel. (06) 4701229. Europcar, Via Lombardia 7; tel. (06) 465802; telex 612358. Hertz, Via Salustiana 28; tel. (06) 463334; telex 621068. Maggiore, Via Po 8A; tel. (06) 858696. Prestige, Via Marco Aurelio 47B; tel. (06) 732542; telex 620889.

To avoid Saturday afternoon and Sunday pickup and return problems, clear your plans in advance; the car rental firms normally close their offices at these times. Alternative arrangements are possible.

Bike Rentals

It is possible to tour Rome by bicycle. Rentals are available at the exit of the Piazza di Spagna A line metro stop. Fees are Lit. 3,000 an hour or Lit. 10,000 for an entire day (9 A.M.–midnight). To obtain a bike you must leave an identity card or passport on deposit to assure the bike's return. If you value your life you'll limit bike riding to the city's pedestrian island, between Piazza di Spagna and Via del Corso, and Piazza del Popolo and Via del Tritone.

TOURS

Since a normal lifetime does not offer the opportunity to properly visit all that both Rome and the Vatican have to offer, organized tours merit special consideration here. As always, tours mean running with the herd, but they provide a reasonable means of visiting the most in the least amount of time.

There are a number of reputable tour operators in Rome. Each has its share of arrangements with hotels ranging from luxury to economy class. Some will make pickup arrangements, others require that clients reach a central meeting point.

Practically all hotels have arrangements with a tour company; the desk will provide brochures upon request, collect payment, and provide tickets for excursions.

The city is basically divided into four half-day excursions by all companies.

Half-day excursions out of the city take in Tivoli, the ancient Roman seaport of Ostia, and the Albani Hills, which include the summer papal residence at Castel Gandolfo.

Most tour companies will arrange for a papal audience either in Rome or Castel Gandolfo. There are a number of combination tours to Capri, Pompeii, Sorrento, and Amalfi. One-day tours go to Florence, Assisi, Anzio, and Nettuno (to visit the U.S. war cemetery), as well as an Etruscan tour that is one of the best of the lot.

Leading agencies are:

American Express, Piazza di Spagna 35; tel. (06) 6796108. Appian Line, Via Barberini 109; tel. (06) 464151. CIT, Piazza della Repubblica 68; tel. (06) 47941. Carrani, Via V.E. Orlando 95; tel. (06) 4742501. Green Line, Via Farini 5a; tel. (06) 4744857. Vastours, Via Piemonte 34; tel. (06) 4814309.

✤ ACCOMMODATIONS

Foreign visitors are generally surprised by the high cost of hotels in Rome. Travelers who have not made reservations should consult with the EPT kiosks at Termini or the airport, or turnpike offices near the Roma Nord and Roma Sud exits on the A1 and A2 toll roads. EPT will make phone reservations free of charge; they have information on types of accommodation and price ranges, and will call specific hotels upon request.

Large concentrations of hotels are found around Termini, the Via Veneto, the monumental area of the old town—monumental Rome—on both sides of central Via del Corso (west to the Tiber and east towards Piazza di Spagna), and in the immediate Vatican area and adjacent neighborhood of Prati.

The Termini area is convenient for rail and air travelers. It is also the prime gathering area for illegal aliens, drug traffic, and male, female, and transsexual prostitutes. Various assorted creatures will appear along with the first shadows of evening.

Both houses of Parliament are situated in the monumental area, along with the prime minister's office, many banks, and the best shopping area.

The staid neighborhood around the Vatican is populated by a large number of religious institutes. Adjacent Prati is evolving more and more into a service area, with offices replacing apartment residences due to the law courts on Viale Giulio Cesare and Piazzale Clodio, and many RAI (state radio-TV) offices, stages, and broadcast studios.

The Via Veneto of Fellini's *La Dolce Vita* has long turned to dust. Hookers and hustlers abound amid the tourists and traffic fumes. However, the area still has some fine restaurants and good shopping.

Rates given below indicate the range between single and double rooms.

Credit cards are listed as accepted. "All cards" means that all of the following are accepted: AE—American Express; DC—Diner's Club; MC—MasterCard; V—Visa.

As with priorities, we've keyed hotels into the color map at the back of the book, referring to the page number of the insert as well as to the map coordinates at which the hotel is located.

AMERICAN CHAINS

Three names familiar to North American travelers are Hilton, Holiday Inn, and Sheraton. They have four hotels that are convenient by car off the proper access road from the GRA. None of the four is centrally located, but each will provide bus service to the city as well as the airport.

Cavalieri Hilton
OUTSKIRTS, P. 24, A1

Via Cadlolo 101, 00136; tel. (06) 31511; telex 625337 HI-ROME-I. On Monte Mario, this 387-room, 5-star luxury hotel is a weak financial link in the chain, but is maintained for prestige. (Then came 1988's call-girl scandal.) The pool and La Pergola, a roof-garden discotheque, are popular with Rome's status seekers. The summer salad buffet is actually one of Rome's best noontime bargains (in Trattoria del Cavaliere). All the amenities and a polite, professional staff still make the Hilton one of the best safehouses in Rome for North Americans. Rooms are Lit. 300,000–430,000 with air-conditioning. All cards.

Holiday Inns
OUTSKIRTS

The two Holiday Inns are located at Via Aurelia Antica 415, 00165; tel. (06) 5872; telex 625434; and Via Castello della Magliana 65, 00148; tel. (06) 68581; telex 613302. The first is somewhat near the Vatican; the second is on the approach route to Fiumicino. Both have more than 300 rooms, a restaurant, bar, swimming pool, and tennis court. Both are air-conditioned 4-star hotels with ample parking facilities. Rates in both average Lit. 180,000–230,000. All cards.

Sheraton Roma
OUTSKIRTS

Viale del Pattinaggio, 00144; tel. (06) 5453; telex 614223. This 587-room, 4-star colossus is in the EUR section, east of Rome. Totally air-conditioned, the hotel has large conference and banquet facilities requiring substantial advance booking. There is a pool, tennis court, restaurant, bar, and private garage. Rooms run Lit. 235,000–305,000. All cards.

LUXURY HOTELS

Luxury hotels usually won't accept group excursions, while first-class hotels often aim for that fourth star in order to attract tour operators obliged to book "first-class accommodations" for coach tours. Here are two 5-star, luxury-class suggestions:

Excelsior
VIA VENETO, P. 24, D2

Via Vittorio Veneto 125, 00187; tel. (06) 4708; telex 610232. The CIGA mark is always an assurance. This 383-room hotel across the street from the U.S. Embassy also embraces the famed Doney caffè and piano bar on the Veneto stretch where Marcello Triumphed. One of the first acts of both German and Allied generals when commanding Rome was to require that the Excelsior provide first-class comfort during the rigors of war. Reception and banquet facilities are among the best in Rome. Rooms range Lit. 380,000–542,000. All cards.

Le Grand Hotel et de Rome
TERMINI, P. 25, E2

Via V.E. Orlando 3, 00185; tel. (06) 4709; telex 610210. The 175 rooms of this CIGA hotel are popular with visiting VIPs who don't suffer from hay fever. The ornate trimmings can be havens for dust. Near Piazza della Repubblica (previously called Esedra), the hotel's majestic salons are a desired setting for fashion presentations by leading Rome designers such as Valentino. Rooms are Lit. 350,000–500,000. All cards.

EXPENSIVE

De la Ville
MONUMENTAL ROME, P. 24, D2

Via Sistina 69, 00187; tel. (06) 6733; telex 620836. This 4-star, 189-room, air-conditioned hotel is next to the luxurious Hassler. A restaurant, bar, parking, and courtyard garden make it attractive to its own fashion and entertainment clientele. Rome's leading theater (the Sistina) is 100 yards down the street towards nearby Piazza Barberini. Rooms are Lit. 220,000–300,000. All cards.

D'Inghilterra
MONUMENTAL ROME, P. 24, C2

Via Bocca di Leone 14, 00187; tel. (06) 672161; telex 614552 Hoting I. This 4-star, 102-room, air-conditioned hotel has been extensively renovated and has regained the splendor that once made this former Torlonia Palace guest house the most fashionable hotel in Rome. Guests have included Mark Twain, Henry James, Hans Christian Andersen, Felix Mendelssohn, and Ernest Hemingway. Valentino is next door and Fendi and Ferre are just around the corner. Rooms are Lit. 233,000–302,000. All cards.

Forum
ARCHAEOLOGICAL ROME, P. 24, D3

Via Tor de'Conti 25, 00184; tel. (06) 6792446; telex 622549. This 4-star, 79-room air-conditioned hotel is a fine example of how the Roman ruins were once exploited as a quarry. Wood paneling and marble columns create an on-the-spot and relaxing ambience overlooking the Imperial Forums. The rooms are small, but the roof garden offers the best outdoor dining spectacle in Rome. Rooms run Lit. 210,000–300,000. All cards.

Hassler Villa Medici
MONUMENTAL ROME, P. 24, D2

Piazza Trinità dei Monti 6, 00187; tel. (06) 6782651; telex 610208. Next to the picturesque Trinità dei Monti church at the top of the monumental Spanish Steps descending to Bernini's Barcaccia fountain, this 101-room luxury jewel's suites have always been a Kennedy family favorite. The roof-garden restaurant offers one of the best inner-city views of Rome. Thoroughly air-conditioned, the hotel is automatically associated with luxury. Rooms run Lit. 365,000–520,000. AE.

Raphael
MONUMENTAL ROME, P. 24, C3

Largo Febo 2, 00180; tel. (06) 650881; telex 622396. This 4-star, air-conditioned 83-room hotel is just around the corner from Piazza Navona on a picturesque side street that is usually well guarded, since the hotel is the Rome residence of Socialist leader Bettino Craxi. The machine guns and bulletproof vests detract from an otherwise charming ambience. There is a bar and restaurant. Rooms are Lit. 160,000–236,000. All cards.

Visconti Palace
VATICAN, P. 24, C2

Via Federico Cesi 37, 00193; tel. (06) 3684; telex 622489 VPOL-TEL. Completely air-conditioned and soundproofed, this 4-star, 250-room hotel is one block from the Tiber and a 10-min. walk across the river from Piazza del Popolo at the top of Via del Corso. There is a restaurant, cocktail lounge, piano bar, private garage, and conference and reception facilities for up to 200. There's also a roof garden, and some rooms have private balconies. Room rates, with continental breakfast, are Lit. 178,000–256,000. All cards.

MODERATELY PRICED

Colosseum
ARCHAEOLOGICAL ROME, P. 24, E3

Via Sforza 10, 00184; tel. (06) 4827228; telex 611151. In a charming area between Santa Maria Maggiore and San Pietro in Vincoli (St. Peter in Chains), housing the famous sculpture of *Moses* by Michelangelo, this 3-star hotel is a 10-min. walk from the Colosseum. All 45 comfortable rooms have baths, but there is no restaurant and no air conditioning. The hotel has a strong entertainment clientele due to special arrangements with a number of Rome agents. Rooms average Lit. 64,000–110,000. All cards.

Columbus
VATICAN, P. 24, B2

Via della Conciliazione 33, 00193; (06) tel. 6865435; telex 620096. This 3-star, 107-room hotel in a renovated 15th-century building is on the main road from the Tiber to the Vatican. The public rooms are well decorated; some are even frescoed. The Columbus has always had a popular following, and reservations should be made well in advance during major religious festivals. There's a restaurant and bar, but no air-conditioning. Not all of the rooms have private baths; but rates for rooms with private bath are Lit. 108,000–168,000, including continental breakfast. All cards.

Fontana
MONUMENTAL ROME, P. 24, D2

Piazza di Trevi 96, 00187; tel. (06) 6786113. Part of a converted medieval monastery facing Rome's most famous fountain, this 3-star, 28-room hotel has undergone extensive renovation since 1960, when it charged just Lit. 750 for a single with bath. With restaurant and bar (but no elevator), the Fontana's locale is unique, and much quieter now that the fountain's waters are turned off in the late evening and automobile traffic is banned in front of the hotel. Air-conditioning is Lit. 16,000 extra. Room rates are Lit. 66,000–102,000. All cards.

Forti's Guest House
VATICAN, P. 24, B1

Via Fornovo 7, 00192; tel. (06) 6799390. This clean, efficient, 22-room hotel, conveniently located near the Lepanto metro and bus and tram lines, is one block from the Tiber. The evolution of Prati, the neighborhood next to the Vatican, is clearly evident in the Forti's clientele, which includes magistrates, actors, musicians, and Italian sales reps. There is an attractive breakfast buffet, but it's not mandatory. Rooms with bath are Lit. 42,000–59,900. All cards.

Gerber
VATICAN, P. 24, B1

Via degli Scipioni 241, 00192; tel. (06) 3221001. This 3-star, 27-room hotel is on a side street a 5-min. walk from the Lepanto metro stop. The hotel offers a small pergola-covered court and a sun terrace. There is a bar and a restaurant, but no air-conditioning. Rooms run Lit. 68,000–105,000 with continental breakfast. All cards.

Porta Maggiore
TERMINI, P. 24, F3

Piazza di Porta Maggiore 25, 00185; tel. (06) 7598751; telex 612612. This 3-star, 200-room hotel has undergone a thorough renovation. The modern amenities, clean linens, and efficiency may allow you to overlook the kitschy effort to create an ancient Roman atmosphere in the entrance. Pleasant terrace dining and a solarium are available on the roof. Behind Termini facing the Porta Maggiore, the hotel is minutes from the archaeological zone, the Casilina exit for Palestrina, and the A24 for L'Aquila. Rooms are Lit. 93,000–140,000. AE.

Sant'Anna
VATICAN, P. 24, B2

Borgo Pio 134, 00193; tel. (06) 6541602. This small, 3-star, 18-room hotel is in one of the most picturesque areas around the Vatican, having survived Mussolini-era rebuilding. Just 50 yards from St. Peter's, the air-conditioned hotel has a charming little breakfast room. Rooms with breakfast run Lit. 95,000–142,000. All cards.

Scalinata di Spagna
MONUMENTAL ROME, P. 24, D2

Piazza Trinità dei Monti 17, 00187; tel. (06) 6793006. Just 2 stars and only 14 rooms, all with private bath or shower. This pensione has probably the best spot in Rome, at the top of the Spanish Steps. The courteous, efficient management is an added bonus. The mandatory continental breakfast is served on a roof terrace. Rates for rooms with breakfast run Lit. 85,000–140,000. AE.

Sole al Pantheon,
MONUMENTAL ROME, P. 24, C3

Via del Pantheon 63, 00186; tel. (06) 6780441; telex 630054. This 15th-century inn has just undergone extensive renovation inside and out and should have a 4th star by 1989. The 28-room hotel is on Piazza del Rotonda, 30 seconds from the Pantheon. A 1513 guest was Ariosto (the author of *Orlando Furioso*), and Mascagni (*Cavalleria Rusticana*) wrote several of his operatic compositions here in the 1800s. There is a bar only, but the surrounding area has an abundance of trattorias and restaurants within a 5-min. walk. Air-conditioned. Rooms run Lit. 125,000–190,000 with continental breakfast. All cards.

Villa Mangili
PARIOLI

Via G. Mangili 31, 00197; tel. (06) 3609594. Roberto Anconetani is a young Roman architect who renovated a seedy *pensione* in a turn-of-the-century villa in one of the greenest areas of Parioli. The results are outstanding, and so was the cost. Anconetani and his wife, Luciana, who works with French television, are now majority shareholders of this charming, air-conditioned, 11-room hotel with garden and bar. With continental breakfast, rooms are Lit. 70,000–90,000. All cards.

The Vatican

Combining all the sights at the Vatican into one day of sightseeing can be a mammoth task, one that is simplified in the summer and during Holy Week, when the Vatican Museums are open for an additional three hours in the afternoon.

Castel Sant'Angelo

Start your tour at the Castel Sant'Angelo, Lungotevere Castello, where art exhibits or shows are sometimes staged. Originally Hadrian's tomb, the mausoleum was completed in A.D. 139, a year after the emperor's death. Amazingly well preserved, the cylindrical mausoleum was later converted into a citadel due to its strategic position on the Tiber. The Ponte Sant'Angelo crossing the river in front of the Castel once led to a drawbridge at the entrance of the fort. The moat around Castel Sant'Angelo was fed by the Tiber's waters, but the road running parallel to the river makes this difficult to imagine now.

The **bronze statue of the angel** atop the castle has just returned by helicopter from extensive restoration. It represents a vision received by St. Gregory at the end of a 6th-century plague. When the statue was first erected the fortress was renamed Sant'Angelo. In the 9th century Pope Leo IV walled in the Vatican and surrounding area up to the castle, which became a fortified residence. There is a passageway (the Passetto) atop the walls that connects the castle with Vatican City.

The citadel has been modified by several popes. A number of interesting **papal apartments and galleries** may be visited; **medieval arms** are also on display. The top of the castle affords a fine view. It was from this point that Puccini had his *Tosca* leap to her death.

The Vatican Museums

The Vatican Museums, Viale Vaticano, are closed Sunday, except for the last Sunday of the month, when admission is free. During most of the year they're open 9 A.M. to 2 P.M.; to 5 P.M. during July, August, September, and two weeks at Easter. There will never be enough time to properly visit all the wonders proposed in this museum. So much is on display that it can be overwhelming, and majestic works of art can seem to lose their significance.

Michelangelo, *The Sistine Chapel Ceiling* (1508–1512)

"I'm no painter," Michelangelo protested, trying to fob off the job on Raphael. But Pope Julius II prevailed, and in 1508, the renowned sculptor mounted scaffolding to begin the most ambitious artistic undertaking of the Renaissance. Always impatient, Michelangelo fired his assistants early on. Four years later, after back-wrenching toil in contorted positions, he was finished. Michelangelo's frescoes cover nearly 6,000 square feet of a difficult vaulted surface and include hundreds of figures: Old Testament prophets, sibyls, and various supporting characters for the great biblical epic from *Genesis* that spans the central vault.

The ceiling is crowded with drama. Picture the nine central panels as a tragedy in three acts, each divided into three scenes. Act I, shrouded in mystery, hints at the Creation: In the beginning, God separates light from darkness, creates the heavens, and separates the waters from the land. Act II begins in hope and ends in despair: the Creation of Adam and Eve, and the Temptation and Expulsion from the Garden. Act III depicts the Flood: Noah's Sacrifice, the Deluge, and Noah's Drunkenness. The scenes were painted in reverse narrative order; Michelangelo began with Noah's sin, and then inched his way across the ceiling toward that moment of visionary creation when the universe first sprang into being at God's command.

In all of Western art, there is no more famous image than the central panel, where an all-powerful Creator, with flowing robe and beard, extends his hand to Adam, linking the human and the Divine. Pictured before the Fall, Adam, godlike himself, truly is formed in his maker's image. Waiting to receive the spark of life, he is separated from perfection by a fingertip only.

—Michael Hinden

The prime attraction is the **Sistine Chapel,** considered the masterpiece of Michelangelo. This is a particularly interesting time to visit, as the controversial restoration of the frescoes is still underway (and will take at least another three years to complete). The restoration has revealed bright colors that some art historians blame on the restoration process, an alarming theory that is gaining sway; but the vibrant new look to the murals has attracted much attention.

During high tourist season the Sistine is the one point that everyone heads for. Since access is limited already by the narrow Vatican passageways, leave early and head directly for the chapel, before the herd hits. When the chapel is packed, viewing the *Last Judgment* can be more trying than exhilarating. Just before the Sistine, stop to see the Raphael Rooms.

The four frescoed **Raphael Rooms** were the private apartments of Pope Julius II, decorated by Raphael and his

Michelangelo, *The Last Judgment* (1535–1541)

The far wall of the Sistine Chapel boasts a masterpiece every bit as impressive as the ceiling frescoes, but this awe-inspiring *Last Judgment* was painted more than twenty years later and represents a different phase in Michelangelo's career. In style and conception, the *Last Judgment* reflects the anxieties of a waning Renaissance. The design is cramped, the figures agitated, grotesque, writhing in defeat. Anger and confusion reign. The Rome that Michelangelo knew had changed drastically in the intervening years. Christendom now was split in two; in 1527 Charles V's invading army had stabled its horses in the Sistine Chapel. In response, the Counter-Reformation was underway, battering the Renaissance ideal of humanism.

In executing the *Last Judgment,* Michelangelo gave vent to his dismay, adding a terrifying final act to the drama of human destiny depicted on the ceiling. Angels summon the dead with trumpet blasts; corpses and skeletons rise from the grave; the righteous (on the left) ascend, while the wicked (on the right) are cast down. At the center, a beardless, powerful Christ threatens evildoers with an upraised arm, while Charon waits below to ferry the damned. Christ's gesture of condemnation in the *Last Judgment* is dramatic contrast to the *Creation of Adam* on the ceiling. There, the Father reaches out to man, while here the Son angrily sweeps him away.

Michelangelo spent four years laboring on the Sistine ceiling. The *Last Judgment* cost him six more. Toward the end, the artist drew his own self-portrait on the flayed skin dangling from the hand of martyred St. Bartholomew, who sits at Christ's left knee. By painting his facial signature on this grisly trophy, Michelangelo may have been expressing his anguish at the world's injustice— and his own spiritual exhaustion.

—Michael Hinden

students while Michelangelo was painting the Sistine Chapel ceiling. In the second room, Stanza della Signatura, is Raphael's masterpiece, *The School at Athens.*

Other sections of the museums include: the new wing collection of second-century mosaics and Greek statues; modern religious art; tapestry and candelabra galleries; medal collections, the Chiaromonti collection of ancient sculptures; the Gregorian Etruscan Museum; the Egyptian museum; the ethnological museum; the Pio-Clementino Museum of Greek and Roman sculptures; the Pio Christian museum of objects from the catacombs; the Apostolic Library containing both Etruscan and Roman material; a gallery containing tapestries designed by Raphael; Italian paintings of Byzantine inspiration; Greek and Etruscan vases; and a hall dedicated to Greek originals.

Raphael, *The School at Athens* (1508–1511)

Balance, harmony, and grace are the characteristics of Raphael's style, but the tensions that are brought under control in this sweeping narrative of ancient philosophy must have tested his unifying powers. In *The School at Athens,* formal balance mirrors the reconciliation of philosophical opposites.

At the center of the painting, Plato and Aristotle resume their age-old quarrel. Plato gestures upward, asserting the realm of Pure Ideas; Aristotle extends a downward palm, claiming the domain of Nature. Between them, they divide ancient philosophy into two camps. On Plato's side are the metaphysicians such as Pythagoras (in the foreground), shown working on his harmonic tablets, while Aristotle gathers on his side the scientists and mathematicians, such as Euclid, drawing with his compass.

It has been suggested, considering the fresco's placement in the heart of the papal court, that the painting may have been intended to convey a timely message to Raphael's contemporaries: If science and metaphysics are reconciliable, then might not the entire tradition of pagan philosophy be reconciled with the Church? Such was the hope of the Renaissance humanists, and Raphael had enlisted in their cause.

As his model for Plato, Raphael chose Leonardo da Vinci. The young artist himself (wearing a black cap) peers out of the painting at the far right. Michelangelo inspired the dejected figure in the foreground, hunched on the steps, head in hand. Only Michelangelo appears unmollified, unable to resolve his lifelong struggle to synthesize pagan and Christian teachings.

Symbolically, the majestic vault encompasses them all, repeating its design in a series of distant arches and hemispheres of sky, suggesting an endless progression of visual and philosophical horizons.

—Michael Hinden

St. Peter's Square and Basilica

St. Peter's Basilica and its Bernini-framed piazza are the only parts of the independent Vatican state that are readily accessible free of charge to visitors. The independence of the Vatican was established by the first Lateran Pact, between Fascist Italy and the Holy See. The pact was altered recently, confirming many of the church's rights in the Italian state, but it was established by the government of then-Premier Bettino Craxi, a Socialist, that Catholicism was no longer to be considered the state religion.

The basilica that replaced the original one built by Emperor Constantine over St. Peter's tomb in A.D. 324 is the combination of efforts by Bramante, Michelangelo, Maderna, and Bernini. Of the five entrances into the world's largest church, (610 feet by 443 feet and 144 feet high), on the far right is the Holy Door, opened only during Holy Years. To the immediate right inside the basilica is Michelangelo's triumph in marble, the *Pietà.* It is now under protective glass and fully restored, after being damaged by a hammer-wielding Australian twenty years ago. Farther toward the front, on the right, is the entrance to the dome; you can walk all the way up or travel part way by elevator, part way by stairs. It's a tiring trip, but the view makes the effort worthwhile.

The center altar is dominated by Bernini's half-styled, half-sculptured *baldacchino.* Only the pope celebrates mass from the high altar, which sits above the remains of St. Peter.

The left side of the Latin-cross church is the richest in sculpture, and features the **tombs of Innocent VIII, Leo XI de'Medici,** and **Alexander VII.** Entrance to the **Treasury** is to the left of the high altar, near the monument to Pius VIII.

In the apse in the front of the basilica is the **Throne of St. Peter** by Bernini, a great bronze work encasing a wooden chair said to have been St. Peter's; the throne floats on clouds toward the Holy Spirit in the stained-glass window above.

On the left of the basilica is the **Vatican information office,** tel. (06) 6982, where arrangements may be made for the two-hour tours (Lit. 9,000) of the **Vatican gardens** every morning except Wednesday and Sunday (when papal audiences and the papal benediction to the faithful gathered in the square are held if the Pope is in Rome). The tours are limited to 33 persons; no reservations are taken by telephone.

Arrangements to visit the **catacombs** under St. Peter's may be made at the Ufficio Scavi, tel. (06) 6985318. You probably will have to wait, due to the great number of people who want to make this tour. Underground paths lead as far as the obelisk in the center of St. Peter's Square.

The **twin fountains** in the piazza were originally one; it was moved to make room for the obelisk and a replica of the fountain was constructed to balance the other side of the square.

Papal Audiences

Tickets for papal audiences, held on Wednesdays, should be sought through local dioceses before leaving home. There is often a last-minute possibility at the Vatican Prefecture (at the top of the stairs that begin under the colonnade on the right side of the basilica), where all uncollected tickets are returned and made available Tuesday on a first-come, first-served basis. Commercial tour companies also have tickets available to members of their coach tours. No tickets are needed for the Sunday blessing, held at noon, when the Pope appears at his apartment window in Rome or at the balcony of his summer house at Castel Gandolfo.

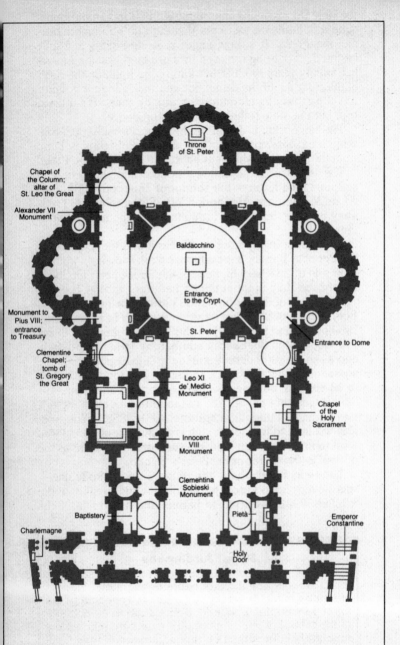

Throne of St. Peter

Chapel of the Column; altar of St. Leo the Great

Alexander VII Monument

Baldacchino

Entrance to the Crypt

St. Peter

Entrance to Dome

Monument to Pius VIII; entrance to Treasury

Clementine Chapel; tomb of St. Gregory the Great

Leo XI de' Medici Monument

Chapel of the Holy Sacrament

Innocent VIII Monument

Clementina Sobieski Monument

Baptistery

Pietà

Emperor Constantine

Charlemagne

Holy Door

ST. PETER'S

N

A Tour of Michelangelo's Rome

In 1505, Michelangelo was summoned from Florence to Rome by Pope Julius II. With his departure, the center of gravity of the Italian Renaissance shifted south. Michelangelo's Roman commissions transformed some of the city's most important landmarks.

Begin in the morning with a visit to Vatican City, starting in **St. Peter's Square (Piazza San Pietro).** Michelangelo adapted plans by Bramante in designing the present **basilica** soon after his arrival. Later architects significantly altered his cohesive design, but the colossal dome, surely the most beautiful in Europe, retains his lofty vision. It was not built until after Michelangelo's death.

Entering the huge basilica, locate the *Pietà* in the first chapel to the right. Carved in 1499 when the sculptor was only 24 years old, this was Michelangelo's first masterpiece, and it gained him immediate fame. Its poignancy and beauty of expression are unrivaled. Visitors praise the anatomical accuracy of the figures, but in fact Mary is larger than Christ and paradoxically younger. Through these subtle reversals, Michelangelo stresses the Virgin's eternal youth and at the same time her motherly embrace of her martyred son.

Devote the remainder of the morning and early afternoon to the **Vatican Museums,** which include the Sistine Chapel. The various rooms are open from 9 A.M. to 2 P.M., to 5 P.M. in July, August, and September; closed Sunday. Choose one of the self-guided tours depending on the amount of time at your disposal, and follow the colored arrows. Highlights of a Michelangelo tour might include the *Laocoön Group* in the Octagonal Court and the *Apollo Belvedere* in an adjacent room, two masterpieces of sculpture from antiquity that Michelangelo admired. The **Sistine Chapel** itself is overpowering and simply cannot be absorbed by just walking through. Bring opera glasses or binoculars and plan to linger.

After a late lunch, visit Michelangelo's modification of Roman civic architecture on the **Capitoline Hill** (the **Campidoglio**). Both the **Piazza del Campidoglio** and the **Palazzo Nuovo** were built to Michelangelo's specifications.

Conclude the tour with a visit to the Church of **San Pietro in Vincoli (St. Peter in Chains),** in the vicinity of the Colosseum. Michelangelo's majestic *Moses* (1515) is here, although it was originally designed for Pope Julius's unfinished tomb. This wrathful, muscular giant appears about to rise from his seat, transported with fury at those who have rejected God's laws. Along with *David* and the *Pietà,* the *Moses* is one of Michelangelo's supreme achievements in sculpture.

In this connection I wish to say one word about Michelangelo Buonarroti. I used to worship the mighty genius of Michelangelo—that man who was great in poetry, painting, sculpture, architecture—great in everything he undertook. But I do not want Michelangelo for breakfast—for luncheon—for dinner—for tea—for supper—for between meals. I like a change occasionally. In Genoa he designed everything; in Milan he or his pupils designed everything; he designed the Lake of Como; in Padua, Verona, Venice, Bologna, who did we ever hear of from guides but Michelangelo? In Florence he painted everything, designed everything nearly, and what he did not design he used to sit on a favorite stone and look at, and they showed us the stone. In Pisa he designed everything but the old shot tower, and they would have attributed that to him if it had not been so awfully out of the perpendicular. He designed the piers of Leghorn and the custom-house regulations of Civitavecchia. But here—here it is frightful. He designed St. Peter's; he designed the Pope; he designed the Pantheon, the uniform of the Pope's soldiers, the Tiber, the Vatican, the Coliseum, the Capitol, the Tarpeian Rock, the Barberini Palace, St. John Lateran, the Campagna, the Appian Way, the Seven Hills, the Baths of Caracalla, the Claudian Aqueduct, the Cloaca Maxima—the eternal bore designed the Eternal City, and unless all men and books do lie, he painted everything in it! Dan said the other day to the guide, "Enough, enough, enough! Say no more! Lump the whole thing! Say that the Creator made Italy from designs by Michelangelo!"

I never felt so fervently thankful, so soothed, so tranquil, so filled with a blessed peace as I did yesterday when I learned that Michelangelo was dead.

—Mark Twain
The Innocents Abroad, 1869

Monumental Rome

Piazza del Popolo

Bernini's 17th-century facade decorating the ancient **Porta del Popolo** is the entrance to monumental Rome at Giuseppe Valadier's Piazza del Popolo. Inside the church to the immediate right, **Santa Maria del Popolo,** are works by Caravaggio and Pinturicchio. The piazza's central **obelisk** was removed from the Egyptian sun temple and brought to Rome for the Circus Maximus. Moved here on orders from Sixtus V in 1589, it was ornamented with four basins and marble lions by Valadier in 1823. Up the terrace on the left is the **Pincio** park entrance to Villa Borghese, often called the **Balcony of Rome.** Opposite Porta del Popolo are the twin churches of **Santa Maria di Monte Santi** and **Santa Maria dei Miracoli,** which frame the central Via del Corso. Via di Ripetta, towards the Tiber, leads to the Mausoleum of

Caravaggio, *Conversion of St. Paul* (1601–1602), Cerasi Chapel, Church of Santa Maria del Popolo

Unlike the patrons of the Renaissance, who valued stateliness and order above all, the public of the baroque period in the early 17th century thrilled to the drama of unruly passions. A fascination with religious mysticism swept Italy, as well as a taste for violent and theatrical subject matter in art. Caravaggio was well equipped by temperament to satisfy the craving. A notorious ruffian, he was forced to flee Rome in 1606 after murdering a rival at a tennis match.

His undisciplined genius is evident in the *Conversion of St. Paul.* This painting, hidden in a dark alcove of the church, is meant to bewilder. (A coin-activated lamp dimly illuminates the work.) St. Paul is shown at the moment of his conversion, overpowered by a religious vision that sweeps him from his horse as he travels the road to Damascus. Like the fallen rider, the viewer at first may feel somewhat disoriented. The low angle of vision draws the eye close to the ground, where St. Paul seems in danger of being trampled. The foreground is enlarged by the curtain of darkness behind it, and the combined effects of radical foreshortening, eerie light, crowding, and overlapping limbs contribute to an impression of claustrophobia; the transition in the saint's life is a violent one.

The painting's realism is unrelenting. Notice the furrowed brow and the varicose veins on the leg of the servant who is trying to control the horse. In an age of highly stylized baroque, Caravaggio insisted on the literal. His grubby exuberance shocked his contemporaries, but by the time he died at 38 (appropriately, of a fever), he was acknowledged as a master throughout Italy.

—Michael Hinden

Augustus, while Via del Babuino on the left is a direct route to Piazza di Spagna.

 At opposite sides of the square are the well-known **Rosati** (just completely renovated, amid cries of scandal when it was rumored that the new tenant would be McDonald's) and **Canova** caffès, gathering spots to see and at which to be seen.

Along the Tiber

At Piazza Augustus Imperatore is the imposing circular brick ruin of the **Mausoleum of Augustus.** Now closed to the public, it was used as a fortress, circus, and concert hall before extensive archaeological excavations that ended in 1936.

Glassed in atop the embankment along the Tiber is the reconstructed **Ara Pacis Augustae.** (The embankments replaced the former port at Ripetta to prevent flooding by the Tiber.) This monumental altar was built by order of the Roman Senate to honor Augustus and the peace that followed his victories in Spain and Gaul. In addition to the usual hours, the monument is open Tuesday, Thursday, and Saturday from 4:30 to 8 P.M., April to October.

Piazza di Spagna

Follow Via di Ripetta south to Via del Clementino, turn left, and head towards the well-framed view of Piazza di Spagna. Twenty yards to the left is **Piazza Borghese** and an **open-air market** that features prints of all dimensions as well as old books. Continuing straight and crossing Via del Corso, you'll be on **Via Condotti,** which is lined with fine shops and leads to the center of Piazza di Spagna and the **Barcaccia Fountain** by Pietro Bernini, the father of the more famous Gianlorenzo.

Just before the square is the famous **Caffè Greco,** on the left, which has always attracted artists and intellectuals. A brief closing by health authorities has not tainted its reputation, though some cynics say the coffee is no longer the same. Here one pays for the atmosphere and indifferent waiters in tails.

In the Piazza di Spagna (Spanish Square), named after **Palazzo di Spagna,** the residence of the Spanish ambassador to the Vatican, are two reminders of Old England: **Babington's Tea Rooms,** where prices assure a selective clientele, and the **Keats–Shelley memorial,** the house where Keats died, on the immediate right of the square (open 9 A.M. to 12:30 P.M. and 3:30 to 6 P.M., 2:30 to 5 P.M. in winter; closed weekends). A favorite gathering place for youngsters, the **Spanish Steps** have served as a beautiful backdrop for international fashion shows and open-air concerts.

Atop the stairs is Carlo Maderna's **Trinità dei Monti.** The most notable work besides the 16th-century facade of the church is Daniele da Volterra's *Assumption.* The second-century **obelisk** at the top of the Spanish Steps was put here by Pius VI in 1788.

The Trevi Fountain

From Piazza di Spagna down Via della Propaganda—the Vatican Office of Propagation of the Faith is on the left—you pass a Rome outlet of the designer Nazareno Gabrielli on the way to the Trevi Fountain. Cross Via del Tritone and just follow the tourist signs.

Nicolò Salvi's 18th-century fountain of Neptune's seahorse-drawn chariot is the most famous in Rome. The central figure of Neptune appears to call for calm. The City shows up promptly every evening to remove the coins tossed in by tourists, which had caused rivalry between juvenile gangs after the money. Turned off in the evening, the fountain invites contemplation in spite of the masses of tourists. On the square are a number of shoe stores catering to the bargain-conscious.

For daytime or evening refreshment at number 90 is **Claudio Patassini's** bar, with a wide assortment of ice cream and fruit drinks to beat the summer heat, and an excellent hot chocolate to accompany an equally large number of pastries in cooler weather.

The Quirinale Area

Overlooking the fountain from the Quirinale hill is the **Palazzo del Quirinale,** former royal palace that is now the official residence of the president of Italy. Visits can be arranged, depending on state functions; tel. (06) 46991. The **obelisk** in the Piazza del Quirinale is identical to the one in Piazza dell'Esquilino. The two originally stood at the entrance to the Mausoleum of Augustus. They were moved to their present locations by Pope Sixtus V in 1587. The gardens inside the palace are a beautiful oasis of green and silence in the center of a cacophonous city.

Across the street from the palazzo, at the corner of Via del Quirinale and Via delle Quattro Fontane, is the church of **San Carlo alle Quattro Fontane** (familiarly known as **San Carlino**). The church was designed by Francesco Borromini in the 17th century.

Back toward Via del Corso, at Via della Pilotta 17, is **Galleria Colonna,** in the Palazzo Colonna, facing Piazza Santi Apostoli. This 17th-century gallery of a Roman family of princes contains works by Van Dyck, Tintoretto, Veronese, and Annibale Caracci, among others. Open Saturdays only; closed August; tel. (06) 6794362.

The Pantheon

Heading toward the river, wind your way into Piazza della Rotonda, in front of the **Pantheon.** Originally built around 27 B.C. and rebuilt by Emperor Hadrian around A.D. 118 to 125, this is the most well-preserved building remaining from the Imperial period of Rome. Circular, with a Greek-style porch, the building has been stripped of all its original ornamentation. The bronze from the beams of the portico was ordered removed by Urban VIII for use in construction of the *baldacchino* at St. Peter's. The superb dome, wider than St. Peter's, has a central oculus that provides natural lighting for the tombs of Raphael and several Italian monarchs.

At one point the square in front of the Pantheon was surfaced with wood that was a gift from the Argentine. According to old-timers the wood diminished the noise of passing carriages, which disturbed the nobility, wealthy merchants, and clergy who resided in the area.

Francesco Borromini, San Carlo alle Quattro Fontane (1633–1683)

Some have called the passion and drama of this church wanton and immoral. Before receiving the commission for San Carlo, Borromini apprenticed with his uncle, the architect Maderna, on the completion of St. Peter's. For San Carlo, Borromini rejected Maderna's use of clear, geometric forms, favoring ovals and polygons, which resulted in a new dynamism. The design is a case of a master in control of his powers, working with a modest commission and a restricted urban site to produce a brilliant tour de force.

San Carlino (as it is familiarly known) is imbedded in baroque Rome. The church incorporates one of the four fountains built by Pope Sixtus V as part of his plan to mark significant places and call attention to important views.

Movement is the major issue in Borromini's church. The facade displays compressed and distorted forms combined with sinuous, undulating lines. The campanile and cupola bulge out at the corner, making the front shrug its "shoulders."

The interior of the church arouses both awe and anxiety. As with the facade, tension is created by classical forms thrusting here and pulling there, stretching and compressing the idea of the centrally aligned church. The dome is articulated with coffers in the shapes of crosses, hexagons, and octagons, exaggerating its depth. The columns seem to offer tenuous support in the face of all this activity.

—Mary Beth Betts and Charles Ayes

An Italian fast-food eatery is behind the **obelisk,** placed here in 1711 by Pope Clement XI. Redecorated with dolphins and the pope's coat of arms, the original obelisk dates to the sixth century B.C. and bears hieroglyphic inscriptions that mention Ramses II. A similar **obelisk** stands in nearby Piazza della Minerva (to the left of the Pantheon), on a marble elephant base by a pupil of Bernini. It stands in front of **Santa Maria sopra Minerva** church, which was founded in the eighth century on the remains of a temple to Minerva and rebuilt in Gothic style in the 12th. The facade was rebuilt and the interior redone during the Renaissance.

Just up Via della Maddalena is the **Caffè delle Palme,** offering one of the widest selections of homemade *gelati* in Rome. In the back is a video bar for youngsters. Around the corner to the right is **Giolitti,** at Via Uffici del Vicario 40, which serves its giant sundaes until 2 A.M.

South of the Pantheon, towards the Torre Argentina on Via del Torre Argentina, in little more than a hole in the wall at number 20 is **Pascucci,** the home of the best fruit shakes in the city. Though not strictly a warm-weather drink, these can be especially refreshing during torrid summer months.

West of the Pantheon, in Piazza Sant'Eustachio at number 82 is the **Sant'Eustachio** caffè, noted for its creamy espresso

The Pantheon
(around 27 B.C.; A.D. 118–125)

No one knows exactly how the Pantheon was constructed. Legends tell of a mountain of earth supporting the dome as the liquid concrete hardened and set. The Emperor Hadrian, according to these tales, had this mound sprinkled with gold to ensure its removal. Even standard wood scaffolding seems unlikely. Nevertheless, the Pantheon pairs innovative construction with spectacular form.

Surprisingly, the unusual interior of this Roman monument has a rather traditional temple exterior in front. A rectangular vestibule masks the circular shape of the building on the exterior. Within, the building is a domed cylinder 143 feet high awash with color and light. On sunny days the open round window (oculus) of the roof projects a moving beam of sunlight into the interior. On rainy days a column of water and light streams into the center of the space. Alternating recessed niches and projecting shrines sculpturally define the ground level. Above this, a portion of the original paneled band of richly colored marbles can still be seen, over the niche to the right of the central apse. The space culminates in the coffered dome with its open oculus.

Rebuilt by the Emperor Hadrian over a 27 B.C. structure by Agrippa, the Pantheon was both a temple to all the gods and a sign of Hadrian's political power. The building's harmony of form produced a potent symbol of the spiritual unity of the cosmos and the worldly order of the Roman Empire.

—Mary Beth Betts and Charles Ayes

coffee. If you're a cappuccino buff you won't find any place in Italy that can top this. If you don't want it sweetened say so when ordering, as sugar is automatically added to both espresso and cappuccino here. Don't be bashful, or you'll never make it through the crowds to the bar.

Piazza Navona

Cross Corso del Rinascimento, which runs in front of the Senate quarters housed in the 16th-century Medici Palazzo Madama, and take any of the small alleyways to enter Piazza Navona.

This rectangular piazza is a baroque masterpiece, one of the finest in Europe, dominated by Bernini's **Fountain of the Four Rivers.** His **Moor** and **Neptune fountains** at opposite extremes of the piazza complete the spectacle. Facing the central Bernini fountain is the **Church of Sant'Agnese in Agone,** with a baroque facade by Borromini. Bernini and Borromini were intense rivals, and local legend says Bernini purposefully fashioned the fountain's figures to recoil from the church. Borromini responded with an indignant Sant' Agnese atop the facade, whose turned head totally ignores the fountain below.

Up Corso Vittorio Emanuele towards the Tiber is one of the finer Renaissance buildings in Rome, **Palazzo della Cancelleria,** attributed to Bramante, and the church of **Santa Maria in Vallicella,** more commonly known as the **Chiesa Nuova** (New Church). The 16th-century church contains a fine high altarpiece flanked by paintings by Rubens.

Campo dei Fiori Area

Returning down Corso Vittorio Emanuele, turn right (south) after Palazzo della Cancelleria and walk straight into **Piazza Campo dei Fiori,** in the heart of one of the most picturesque sections of old Rome. The **open-air market** appears unweathered by time. On the sidelines are some of the most notable usurers in Rome, ready to conclude loans at ultraorbital rates of interest.

Part of the area is an overflow from the Jewish ghetto, and was one of the last bastions of Roman craftsmen. For early-morning shoppers there is a wide variety of **shops** between the square and Via Arenula, to the east. Tradition has it that shopkeepers consider it lucky to make a sale to the first client of the day. So if you're number one, bargain—good discounts may be in the wind.

The real treasure in the neighborhood is the **Palazzo Farnese,** between Campo dei Fiore and the Tiber. Now the French Embassy, this finest of Renaissance buildings in Rome has a number of frescoes by Raphael; Sangallo the Younger and Michelangelo contributed to the palazzo's design. The building is closed to tourists.

Heading east to Piazza Venezia, Corso Vittorio Emanuele ends at the Imperial ruins (**Area Sacra**) of **Largo di Torre Argentina.** Continue into Piazza Venezia with its exaggerated white marble **monument to King Victor Emmanuel II.** On the right of the monument is **Palazzo Venezia,** which was the seat of Fascism; the central first-floor balcony was where Mussolini announced Italy's ill-fated venture in World War II.

Capitoline Hill

Off to the right on Via del Teatro di Marcello, a five-minute uphill walk takes you to stairs that lead to the Capitoline Hill. The beautiful **Piazza del Campidoglio** was designed by Michelangelo. The equestrian statue of Marcus Aurelius was once in the center of the square, but has been removed and is undergoing renovation.

The traditional symbol of the Eternal City is the She-Wolf who raised the abandoned twins Romulus and Remus, the legendary founders of Rome. Until the 1960s a live wolf was kept in a cage to the right of the stairs rising to the Campidoglio. Since all efforts to have her reproduce in captivity failed, the cage has remained empty since she died.

The stairs to the left lead to the church of **Santa Maria d'Aracoeli,** also accessible from behind Palazzo Nuovo in the main square. Frescoes by Pinturicchio decorate a chapel in the church, which was built on the site of an ancient fortress and the Temple of Juno.

Opposite the stairs is the **Campidoglio,** Rome's city hall, mayoral offices, and city council chamber. On the left and right of the square, facing one another, are the **Palazzo Nuovo** and **Palazzo dei Conservatori,** housing the **Capitoline Museums.** In addition to normal hours, the museums are open 5 to 8 P.M. Tuesday and Thursday and 9 to 11:30 P.M. Saturday; telephone (06) 6782862. The Palazzo Nuovo is primarily dedicated to classical statues, while the Conservatori has antique art including the 6th-century B.C. Etruscan bronze of the She-Wolf, to which Romulus and Remus were added in the 15th century. The Conservatori art gallery contains Caravaggio's *John the Baptist* in the Cini Gallery and Pietro da Cortona's *Rape of the Sabines* in the Hall of Hercules.

(Civil weddings are conducted in the ground-floor chambers of the Conservatori, explaining all the young brides in the square.)

Walk behind the Campidoglio and take in the panorama of the Roman Forum, with the Colosseum in the background. For the foot-weary, taxi stands are in Piazza Venezia.

Archaeological Rome

The Imperial Forums

To the left of Piazza Venezia is one of the more remarkable surviving monuments of ancient Roman, **Trajan's Column.** Spiraling bas-reliefs illustrate scenes from the war against the Dacians. The column is in the **Trajan Forum** (A.D. 111–114, the most recent of the Imperial Forums) next to the three-story **Trajan Markets,** which contained shops. Access to the area is near the Via Magnanapoli off Via IV Novembre (hours are 9 A.M. to 1 P.M. and 3 to 6 P.M.; mornings only on Sunday; Oct. 1 to May 31, 10 A.M. to 4 P.M.; closed Sunday and holidays). The **Torre delle Milizie,** one of the best-preserved medieval buildings in Rome, is also here. Known as Nero's tower, this is the legendary site from which the mad emperor watched the burning of Rome. It is now closed for restoration.

Mussolini ordered construction of **Via dei Fori Imperiali** in a 1930s urban renewal program. It covers portions of the

Trajan, Caesar, Augustus, Nerva, and Vespasian forums (in that order, as you head toward the Colosseum). The archaeological digs now in progress in the Roman Forum were part of a former Communist junta's project to remove the Fascist military parade route and restore the splendor of Imperial Rome. The project was derided as being motivated by politics rather than history. The route is still used for military parades that celebrate the Italian republic on the first of June. The parades were suspended for several years during the height of the last decade's terrorism.

The Arch of Constantine and the Roman Forum

The Roman Forum lies in what was once a marshy valley between the sloping hills of Quirinale, Viminale, Palatine, and Capitoline. ("Forum" is derived from the Latin for "beyond inhabited areas.") The adjacent forums were constructed when this center became too small for meetings, judicial hearings, and sessions on public and commercial affairs. A detailed map of the ruins is essential to fully appreciate this heartland of Imperial Rome (open 9 A.M. to one hour before sunset, from 10 A.M. Sunday; closed Tuesday).

Among the more important ruins are the 179 B.C. **Basilica Emilia;** the **Curia** meeting place for senators; the **Tomb of Romulus** with the oldest known Latin inscription, "lapis niger"; the **Triumphal Arch of Septimus Severus** (A.D. 203); the A.D. 608 **Column of Phocas** (ruler of the Eastern Empire); and the **Via Sacra,** which led to a number of sanctuaries.

On the Via Sacra is the **Basilica Giulia** law courts next to the **Temple of Saturn.** Opposite the basilica are the remains of the **Temple of Caesar,** which was dedicated in 29 B.C. by Octavius on the spot where Caesar had been cremated.

The **Church of Santa Maria Antiqua** is the oldest Christian building in the forum (but closed at press time). Early frescoes are in the former imperial building. Back on the Via Sacra is the **House of the Vestal Virgins,** where the Vestals lived, completely cut off from the outside world. If the sacred flame in their circular **temple** ever went out it was interpreted as an omen of impending misfortune.

Near the **Temple of Antoninus and Faustina** (A.D. 141) is the **cemetery** of the first Palatine inhabitants (ninth to sixth century B.C.). After the **Temple of the Diefied Romulus** (Tomb of Romulus), built by Maxentius after his son Romulus died in A.D. 309, is the fourth-century **Basilica of Maxentius,** where summer concerts are held.

These concerts are now the only evening activity in the Roman Forum. A "Sound and Light" show was evicted after

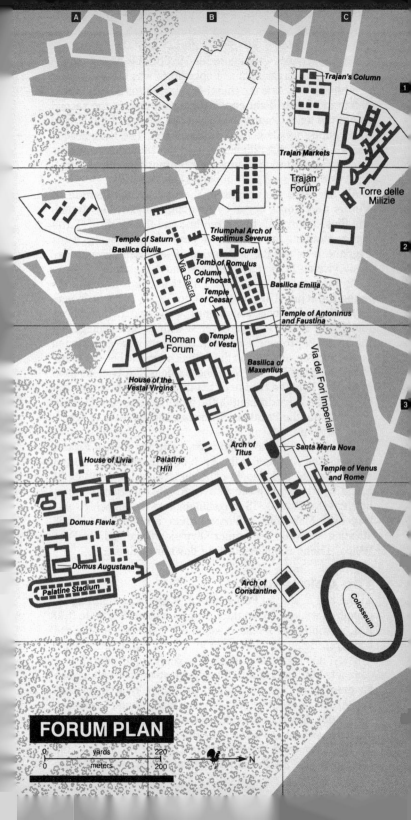

FORUM PLAN

Trajan's Column

Trajan Markets

Trajan Forum

Torre delle Milizie

Temple of Saturn

Basilica Giulia

Triumphal Arch of Septimus Severus

Curia

Tomb of Romulus

Column of Phocas

Via Sacra

Temple of Ceasar

Basilica Emilia

Temple of Antoninus and Faustina

Roman Forum

Temple of Vesta

House of the Vestal Virgins

Basilica of Maxentius

Via dei Fori Imperiali

Arch of Titus

Santa Maria Nova

House of Livia

Palatine Hill

Temple of Venus and Rome

Domus Flavia

Domus Augustana

Palatine Stadium

Arch of Constantine

Colosseum

A   B   C

1

2

3

0   yards   220
0   meters   200

N

several spectators were injured and irreparable damage to the ruins by both organizers and spectators was alleged.

Near the basilica is the church known both as **Santa Maria Nova** and **Santa Francesca Romana,** built in the second half of the tenth century to replace Santa Maria Antiqua. The 17th-century facade is by Carlo Lombardi. The Romanesque bell tower is of the 12th century. In the adjoining convent is the **Antiquarium Forense,** the Forum museum (open 9 A.M. to 6 P.M., to 3 P.M. in winter).

As you leave the church, to the right is the **Temple of Venus and Rome** begun by Hadrian, completed by Antoninus Pius, and rebuilt by Maxentius; and the **Arch of Titus** commemorating the victories of Vespasian and his son Titus over the Jews and the destruction of Jerusalem. Even today many visiting Jews refuse to pass under the arch.

To the right is the **Clivus Palatinus,** a path that leads to the **Palatine Hill** (open 9 A.M. to 7 P.M., to 5 P.M. in winter), where Romulus and Remus were said to have been found. The area was once covered with public buildings and the homes of prominent Romans. Convents were constructed on the ancient ruins, and in the 16th century the hill was transformed into the Farnese Villa and Gardens. Excavations have brought to light the **House of Livia, Domus Flavia** (probably official state apartments), the imperial residence **Domus Augustana,** the **Palatine Stadium,** and the baths of **Septimus Severus.**

In front of the Colosseum entrance to the Roman Forum, at the end of Via Sacra, is the **Arch of Constantine,** erected by the Senate and People of Rome (that's the meaning of *S.P.Q.R.,* which you'll see all over Rome, especially on manhole covers) in A.D. 315 to commemorate the emperor's victory over Maxentius at Ponte Milvio, a bridge that is still standing, between the former Olympic village and the Foro Italico athletic complex north of downtown Rome.

The Colosseum

At the end of Via dei Fori Imperiali is the most imposing reminder of ancient Rome, the Colosseum (open 9 A.M. to 3:30 P.M. in winter, to 7 P.M. in summer, to 1 P.M. Sunday and holidays). Begun by Vespasian in A.D. 72 during the Flavian dynasty, it is also known as the Flavian Amphitheater. It was completed by Titus in A.D. 80, when festivities lasted for one hundred days. The four-tiered arena could accommodate 50,000 spectators at its gladiator combats, "hunts," and mock sea battles. Much of the Colosseum's deterioration was due to its use as a quarry in the mid-15th century. Stone and marble were removed for the construction of St. Peter's, the Palazzo di Venezia, Palazzo della Cancelleria, and the Ripetta river port (once on the Tiber near Piazza del Popolo), among other structures.

In modern times, pollution has caused more damage in thirty years than stone-looting, quakes, fire, and foreign invasion had in nearly two thousand years. During extensive restoration at the outset of the 1980s, interesting areas were uncovered in a lower level beneath the arena that give further insight into the operation of the Colosseum (they're open 9 A.M. to noon, Tuesday through Saturday.)

SIDETRIP

San Pietro in Vincoli (St. Peter in Chains) is in the piazza of the same name off Via Cavour, near the B line metro Cavour stop. Stop here as a detour from Piazza Venezia to the Colosseum or en route to the Colosseum from Santa Maria Maggiore in the Termini area. In this 5th-century church are the alleged chains of St. Peter and the beginning of the tomb the megalomaniacal Pope Julius II commissioned Michelangelo to build. The skyscraper proportions of the tomb, which was to be placed in St. Peter's, were never realized, but Michelangelo's overpowering Carrara marble statue of *Moses* is considered by many to be his greatest sculpture. Folklore has the master rapping his hammer against the work when completed and ordering, "Speak!"

San Giovanni Area

San Clemente church is down Via di San Giovanni in Laterano, behind the Colosseum. Various levels of ancient Rome are exposed as you descend into the 4th-century lower church. (Open Monday through Saturday 9 to 11:30 A.M. and 3:30 to 6:30 P.M.; Sunday from 10 A.M.) A splendid mosaic is in the apse of the upper church; there are frescoes by Masolino da Panicale. Irish Dominicans have cared for the complex since 1677.

Farther down the street, **San Giovanni in Laterano** (St. John Lateran) and the **Holy Stairs (Scala Sancta)** are in Piazza di San Giovanni in Laterano, near the beginning of the Via Appia Nuova and the metro A line stop San Giovanni. This is the cathedral of the pope, who is bishop of Rome. The **Lateran Palace,** nearby, was once the official residence of the pope. Also in the square are the **Baptistery** (open 8 A.M. to noon and 4 to 6 P.M.) and the **Holy Stairs.** The fifth-century baptistery replaced an earlier one sacked by the Goths. The eight scenes from the life of John the Baptist are by Andrea Sacchi. The heavy bronze doors reportedly came from the Baths of Caracalla. The Holy Stairs are said to be the original 28 marble steps to Pilate's palace in Jerusalem, brought to Rome by St. Helena, mother of Constantine. They lead to the former papal oratory, the only part of the original Lateran Palace to have survived a fire in 1308. Many devout

Catholics ascend the stairs on their knees. (Open 6 A.M. to 12:30 P.M. and 3 to 7 P.M., from 3:30 P.M. May to September.)

The Baths of Caracalla

The Baths of Caracalla (Terme di Caracalla) are off the Viale delle Terme di Caracalla, along the number 118 bus route from the Colosseum to Via Appia, and down the Via Amba Aradam and Via Druso from San Giovanni. (Open 9 A.M. to 6 P.M., to 1 P.M. Sunday and Monday.) The second-century baths were one of the largest and most important of ancient Rome. Summer open-air opera is staged here; acoustics are poor, so vie for central seats, but bring a sweater—even the warmest summer can have cool nights. For information on the opera call the Teatro dell'Opera, telephone (06) 461755, or Caracalla, telephone (06) 5758300.

Northwest of the baths, at the foot of the Palatine Hill, is a rectangular field that was once the **Circus Maximus,** used for chariot races. Now stripped of all artifacts, the area at times is used for summer film shows and cultural events.

A five-minute walk away is the medieval **Santa Maria in Cosmedin** church and the **Bocca della Verita** (Mouth of Truth). The sixth-century church and its seven-story bell tower are among the most beautiful in Rome, in a pretty piazza near the Tiber. Legend says anyone putting a hand in the Bocca (an ancient Roman drain cover sculpted as a mask-face) will lose it if telling a lie.

The Appian Way

Opened in 312 B.C., the "queen of roads" originally went from Rome only as far as Capua, but it was later extended to Brindisi, on the Adriatic coast. In the Roman fashion, the Via Appia Antica (Old Appian Way) was lined with tombs; number 110 are the **San Calisto Catacombs,** and the **San Sebastiano Catacombs** are at number 136. (They both are open 8:30 A.M. to noon and 2:30 to 5:30 P.M. in summer; to 5 P.M. in winter. San Calisto is closed Wednesday; San Sebastiano, Thursday.) To reach the Via Appia Antica, catch the number 118 bus behind the Colosseum. The **Fosse Ardeatine Memorial,** to the memory of 335 Italians ordered killed by Hitler, is between the two on Vicolo delle Sette Chiese.

Other Areas of Interest

Termini Area

The **Diocletian Baths** are in Piazza della Repubblica, on the metro A line and near the Termini station. Housed amid its ruins are the **National Museum of Rome** and the church of **Santa Maria degli Angeli.** Michelangelo transformed part of the fourth-century baths into a church on a commission from Pius IV. The museum has one of the largest collections of relics from ancient Rome. (Museum open 9 A.M. to 1:45 P.M., to noon Sunday, closed Monday.)

Near the baths, on Via XX Settembre, is the **Church of Santa Maria della Vittoria,** notable for Bernini's *St. Teresa in Ecstasy,* in the Cornaro Chapel.

Gianlorenzo Bernini, *St. Teresa in Ecstasy* (1645–52)

In the 17th century, while Protestant churches were being stripped of decoration, the spirit of the Counter-Reformation came alive in Rome, fighting to win back the soul of Europe through prodigious works of art. In Bernini, the movement found a sculptor whose talent was said to rival Michelangelo's.

More than an exquisite statue—although it certainly is that—*St. Teresa* orchestrates a multimedia environment, combining sculpture (the central figures carved in gleaming marble), architecture (the opulent canopy above), metallurgy (the heavenly rays of gilded bronze), painting (the chapel's ornate ceiling), and theatrical design (the ensemble as a whole). The work might be thought of as a grandiloquent opera without sound.

The story of St. Teresa of Avila was known to everyone. A Spanish mystic of the 16th century, she recorded in her *Autobiography* a series of strange visitations by an angel who repeatedly plunged a dart into her bosom, causing her to swoon in delicious pain. To Teresa, this was the arrow of Divine love. Of course, there have been Freudian explanations of Teresa's fainting spells. Bernini himself seems well aware of the erotic parallels in his treatment of the subject. The saint's parted lips, curled toes, and posture of abandon suggest that the sculptor based his interpretation of mystical transport on his knowledge of sexual response. Baroque artists often thought of physical and spiritual rapture as mutually enlightening. Bernini was devout, and the religiosity of the ensemble is indisputable, as is his astonishing skill in three-dimensional representation.

Bernini's stamp as an architect is visible all over Rome, in the city's fountains, buildings, and piazzas, and most noticeably St. Peter's Square.

—Michael Hinden

Santa Maria Maggiore (St. Mary Major) is between Piazza dell'Esquilino and Piazza Santa Maria Maggiore, on the top of the Esquiline Hill, not far from Termini. The original church that stood here was built by Pope Liberius on the site of his vision of a mid-August snow storm, reenacted every year with artificial snow. The interior of the Sistine Chapel is by Domenico Fontana and the Pauline Chapel is by Flaminio Ponzio. The 14th-century bell tower is the highest in Rome.

The obelisk in Piazza dell'Esquilino was removed from the Mausoleum of Augustus by Pope Sixtus V in 1587.

San Prassede, Via San Martino ai Monti, just behind Santa Maria Maggiore, is the most important Byzantine monument in Rome. The **Flagellation Column** in the church was brought to Rome in 1223, and is believed to be the column to which Christ was tied and whipped in Jerusalem.

The Jewish Ghetto and Trastevere

Rome's **ghetto** is second in size only to that in Venice, from which it derived. The old Jewish quarter centers around the main **synagogue** on Lungotevere de'Cenci between Via Arenula, Via del Teatro di Marcello, and the **Teatro di Marcello,** built by Julius Caesar and Augustus.

In the Tiber, near the Teatro di Marcello, is the **Isola Tiberina,** an island supposedly shaped like the boat of the god of medicine, Aesculapius. A hospital and the **San Bartolomeo church** have been built atop the ruins of the Temple of Aesculapius. Across the river is the area known as Trastevere, literally "across the Tiber," a popular area known for its good restaurants.

Santa Maria in Trastevere is west of Piazza Sidney Sonnino down Via della Lungaretta. The origin of the church (third or fourth century) is uncertain, but the present basilica was built in the 12th century and renovated several times. Of particular interest are the 12th- to 13th-century mosaics on the facade, and the ornate wood ceiling. Once a month, in front of the church, a group of Sicilian doctors distributes, free of charge, a cancer drug that Italian authorities refuse to legalize. (Under the Lateran Pacts the Vatican has extraterritorial rights over the church property, and the doctors are protected.)

The Borghese Area

The **Villa Borghese** was created by Cardinal Scipione Borghese in the 17th century; the three-and-a-half-mile-square park surrounding it was later purchased by King Umberto I and presented to the city of Rome. The trees, lawns, fountains, and lakes are a delightful respite from the traffic chaos of the city.

The **Borghese Museum and Gallery** is in the Borghese Palace at Piazza Scipione Borghese 3; telephone (06) 858577. The museum, which features sculpture by Bernini and paintings by 16th- and 17th-century Italian masters, has been undergoing extensive renovation and may have limited access. Some of its major works consequently are being displayed elsewhere in the city, so telephone the museum directly to obtain specific information. (Usually open 9 A.M. to 2 P.M., to 1 p.m. Sunday; closed Monday.)

Rome's **Modern Art Gallery,** Viale delle Belle Arti 131, telephone (06) 802751, is on the outer rim of Villa Borghese. The gallery stages worthy exhibits throughout the year to accompany permanent exhibits of Italian Impressionists, as well as futurist Umberto Boccioni and the metaphysical Giorgio De Chirico. (Open 9 A.M. to 2 P.M., to 1 p.m. Sunday and holidays; closed Monday.)

Villa Giulia, at Piazzale di Villa Giulia 9, is off the Viale delle Belle Arti; take tram 30. This 16th-century Renaissance villa was built for Pope Julius III. Now it houses the **National Etruscan Museum** featuring artifacts from digs at Cerveteri (off the Via Aurelia) and Vei-o (near Isola Farnese off the Via Cassia). Both areas are just outside Rome, and provide good picnic grounds on afternoon tours out of the city proper. (The museum is open Tuesday through Saturday 9 A.M. to 2 P.M.; Wednesday to 6:30 P.M. in winter, and from 3 to 7:30 P.M. in summer; Sunday to 1 P.M. Closed Monday. But it's a good idea to confirm: 06-3601951.)

The Roman Walls

The city **walls of ancient Rome** extend around a good portion of the city. They begin at Porta del Popolo and run parallel to Viale del Muro Torto up to Porta Pinciana (at the top of the Via Veneto), then along Corso d'Italia to Porta Salaria, and around the Pretorian Camp as far as Porta Tiburtina and Porta San Lorenzo; then comes the stretch that is most evocative of their original defensive purpose—from Porta Latina to **Porta San Sebastiano,** which opens onto the Appian Way. The walls here are open to visitors, at Via di Porta San Sebastiano 18. (Open 9 A.M. to 1:50 P.M., to 1 P.M. Sunday and holidays; from 4 to 7 P.M. Tuesday and Thursday in summer; closed Monday.)

The walls continue west from San Sebastiano; at Porta San Paolo is the beginning of the Via Ostiense, the road to Ostia. South on Via Ostiense is **San Paolo Fuori le Mura** (St. Paul's Beyond the Walls). The basilica is just beyond the main Rome wholesale produce market on the way to the area called EUR, the so-called "new Rome," which Mussolini started to symbolize his empire. A shrine to the martyred St. Paul (he was beheaded almost two miles further south, where the Tre Fontane Abbey stands on the Via Laurentina), the basilica is a required stop for Holy Year pilgrims, along with San Giovanni in Laterano, Santa Maria Maggiore, and St. Peter's. The original fourth-century church was destroyed by a July 15, 1823 fire; this new custodian of the remains of St. Paul was rebuilt in the early Christian style after the disaster, and contains masterpieces salvaged from the blaze. You can take the B line Metro.

Etruscans

The Etruscans were the most important inhabitants of Italy prior to the Romans. From the eighth century B.C. to the third century B.C., when they were finally conquered, their military and cultural superiority over the Italian tribes allowed them to dominate almost a third of Italy, including present day Tuscany, Umbria, and parts of Campania.

The Etruscan states were never a unified nation; rather, there were three main concentrations—Etruria, Campania, and the Po Valley—each with twelve capital cities. Among the cities ruled by the Etruscans were Perugia and Bologna in the north, Tarquinia and Caere (Cerveteri) in the environs of Rome, and Pompeii in the south. Historical evidence indicates that these cities felt no alliance with one another and were often engaged in civil wars. This, in addition to a series of invasions by the Gauls in the north and the Romans in the south, led to their decline. Today, for a number of reasons, little is known about the Etruscans; the only historical records of them come from their Roman conquerers who absorbed their civilization. Most information about Etruscan society comes from the burial tombs.

Throughout Etruria the typical burial rite was cremation. The Etruscans believed that death was a journey rather than an end and treated their tombs as shrines for the dead. Many tombs were decorated with frescoes of daily life, jewelry, vases, and terracottas. While many of the tombs were looted or destroyed during excavations, you can still visit a few and the artifacts from many others have been preserved in Italy's museums. Among the Etruscan places worth visiting are Tarquinia, for the Museo Nazionale Etrusco and the Necropolis of Tarquinia where frescoes date from the sixth century B.C. to the second century B.C., representing all phases of tomb painting; Perugia, for the Museo Archeologico Nazionale dell' Umbria and the Ipogeo dei Volumni, one of the finest Etruscan tombs dating from the second century B.C., and Cerveteri, the Etruscan city of Caere, for the Necropolis of the Banditaccia. Italy's largest and best collection of Etruscan artifacts is in the Villa Giulia in Rome.

—Charlotte Savidge

SHOPPING

Complaining about prices in Rome shops is as much a national as an international pastime. For the foreign traveler, the scales can tip noticeably according to the whims of the international exchange rate. For Italians, prices can roller-coaster from inventory time to the legitimate *saldi* (sales), at the end of the winter and summer seasons in particular. The between-season offerings in late spring and late fall often don't amount to much.

Sales generally begin after January 6, when the long Christmas break is over, and at the end of July and early August, before most stores close shop to take their August holidays.

August is not the month to shop in Rome, it can be difficult enough to find an open restaurant, much less a shoe store. Stores that do remain open are usually geared exclusively to the tourist market, since locals are on holiday.

A new gimmick in Rome is the *vendita promozionale* (promotional sale), which can be presented in a variety of forms. Many are honest clearance sales; some are testing grounds for coming sales; others are smoke screens, with sales on a few current products but mostly on outdated items that have been gathering dust.

The secret to wise shopping in Rome is basically knowing what is stylish and what is passé. Decide what you want, and don't be in a hurry to purchase it the very first time you see it.

Unfortunately, time is against the traveler, who may not have the time to make a reconnaissance tour of prime shopping areas at sales times to compare prices.

Your best bet is to keep a keen eye on shop windows while you're touring or taking an evening stroll—so that when you're ready to shop you'll have some context for the prices you see.

STORE HOURS

Rome stores generally are open 9 A.M. to 1 P.M. and 3:30 to 7:30 P.M. winter, 4–8 P.M. summer, Tuesday through Saturday. Stores close on Sundays and for one half-day during the week. Clothing and apparel stores, jewelers, gift shops, and so forth close Monday morning; department stores generally remain open. Food stores close Thursday afternoon; hardware, paint stores, and the like close Saturday afternoon. During the summer months this half-day closing schedule is abandoned, and all stores close Saturday afternoon. Some stores have opted for the *orario unico,* and are open from 9 A.M. until 6 P.M. without the *siesta* break. All stores are obliged to post the hours they are open where they can easily be seen by the public.

Efforts have been made to extend late-evening shopping hours until 10 P.M. This met with mixed results last year; no clear policy is certain for 1989.

Shopping Areas

The prime shopping area in Rome is along **Via dei Condotti** and **Via Frattina** from **Via del Corso** to **Piazza di Spagna.** This is the area where most of the prime names in Italian fashion are quartered. This is also the high-rent district (with corresponding prices), so check out the shops on the area's perimeter, where the range of products may not be as vast, but prices are often lower than a block or two away.

The upper area of **Via del Corso** towards Piazza del Popolo has an abundance of shops catering to youthful whims and kitsch crazes. This same is true for most of **Via Nazionale,** especially the lower portion after the Quirino Theater. Occasional exceptions can be found around the intersection of Via Nazionale and Via delle Quattro Fontane.

The upper half of **Via Veneto** is noted for high prices, but often offers surprises. Since Arab oil money emanates from the first-class hotels around the Veneto, Middle Eastern, European, and North American concepts of chic can clash, but at least display windows here are well lit into the late evening, offering an opportunity to compare prices during a stroll.

In the vicinity is the high-rent but high-quality **Via Barberini,** extending from Piazza Barberini to Via Bissolati. This is also the major airline offices area.

Across the Tiber from Piazza del Popolo is **Via Cola di Rienzo,** which records one of the highest volumes of business in the capital. Most of the shops are found west of Piazza Cola di Rienzo to Piazza del Risorgimento, halfway between St. Peter's and the Vatican Museums. These privately owned shops usually have concession arrangements with leading stylists; the shop owner is generally on the premises, and amenable to "rounding off" prices on larger purchases, which can amount to a small savings.

In the monumental area around the **Pantheon** small shops alternate with restaurants, caffès, and sweets shops; keep an eye peeled for bargains. Around the **Trevi Fountain** avid competition flourishes between economy-class shoe stores for those who have been scared off by exorbitant prices in the Veneto and Piazza di Spagna areas (these prices are often up to twenty percent less than prices in Florence, the backyard for Tuscan shoe factories, since the abundance of stores in Rome has created a more competitive market).

An area not to be ignored by the serious shopper is the beginning of the **Via Appia Nuova** at Porta San Giovanni. This is where the Coin department store is located, and the number of shops on both sides of Via Appia Nuova down to Piazza Re di Roma is impressive. The area is making a serious effort to rival more centrally located competition, and can offer especially attractive sales.

Open-Air Markets

There are a number of open-air markets throughout Rome. Every section of Rome offers a similiar market on a smaller scale. All attract *ambulanti*—roving vendors who rotate around five or six market areas across the city. Their goods can vary from factory rejects (a rare commodity in Italy) to a store's entire leftover inventory after *saldi* season. These sales are usually conducted by weight, and the sidewalk vendor can then offer vastly reduced prices.

Appearances can often be deceiving. Some of the stubble-chinned vendors who appear on the verge of starvation are often well-traveled entrepreneurs who import directly from India or China, and who simply prefer a more independent lifestyle to the confines of a store. **Piazza Vittorio** offers the largest fruit and vegetable market, with a scattering of stalls offering meats, *insaccati,* fish, and fowl.

The granddaddy of Rome's open-air markets is found every Sunday morning along the stretch of Via Portuense from **Porta Portese** to the underpass that leads into Piazza della Radio. Including the stalls on the side streets there are nearly two miles of stands, selling everything from used cars to newly born pups.

Of the estimated 2,200 vendors, only nine hundred have regular city licenses. The ever-increasing size of the Porta Portese Sunday-only market has sparked protests from area residents who want the city to move the market elsewhere. The city has expressed a willingness to consider the move if another suitable site can be found for this Roman tradition, as much a folk fair as a simple market.

The Porta Portese market is a haven for pickpockets, purse snatchers, and shell games—take precautions. Though the area is patrolled by city police, they are outnumbered.

In addition to the traditional fare of alleged antiques, spare parts for out-of-stock old motors and electric appliances, cheap clothes and leather goods, stamps, coins, and prints, there is now an international element in the market. African and Arab peddlers offer native handicrafts, carpets, and similar items that can also be found for sale throughout the city on sidewalks in a number of well-trafficked areas. Russian and Iranian refugees and other emigrants offer goods for sale when their funds are low. This is where serious bartering enters the scene, since such items often have personal value to the vendor.

The umbrella-covered **Via Sannio** market, behind the Coin department store at the San Giovanni metro A line stop, can offer tremendous bargains in leather goods and accessories. Here the asking price is never paid, and a sharp-eyed comparison shopper who is prepared to wrangle can get a good deal.

Department Stores

Rome's department stores range from the Coin and Rinascente to UPIM and Standa. Of these, Rinascente makes serious attempts to attract the foreign shopper, with such incentives as flat 10 percent discounts upon presentation of a passport (even with charge purchases) and money-changing services if purchases are made with traveler's checks. Some prices occasionally are also posted in U.S. dollars, at a very advantageous exchange rate.

Coin is in Piazzale Appio at Porta San Giovanni.

Rinascente is in Piazza Colonna and Piazza Fiume.

The **UPIM** locations at Via Nazionale 211, Piazza Santa Maria Maggiore, and Via del Tritone 172 are the most centrally located of their 17 outlets in Rome.

Standa's locations at Via Cola di Rienzo 173/181, Viale di Trastevere 60/64, and Via Appia Nuova 181/183 are among the most accessible of Standa's 36 Rome outlets.

International Designers

Giorgio Armani, Via del Babuino 102, tel. (06) 6793777, and **Emporio Armani,** Via del Babuino 140, tel. (06) 6788454, sell clothing for men and women, with Emporio Armani offering a more affordable end of the collection.

Benetton, Via dei Condotti 59, tel. (06) 6797982, and Via Cola di Rienzo 225, are just a few of the hundreds of outlets throughout the city for men's and women's clothing.

Brioni, Via Barberini 75/83, tel. (06) 484517.

Bulgari, Via dei Condotti 70, tel. (06) 6793876, is home base for the most internationally acclaimed jeweler in Rome.

Fendi, Via Borgognona 39, tel. (06) 6797641, sells leather and fur that needs no introduction.

Salvatore Ferragamo, Via dei Condotti 66 and 73/74, tel. (06) 6781130, is the Rome base for the famous Florentine cobbler. Ladies' apparel and accessories are also sold.

Gianfranco Ferre is at Via Borgognona 8, tel. (06) 6797445, and on the same street at 42B, tel. (06) 6790050; the Milanese fashion school keeps expanding its Rome base.

Richard Ginori, with stores at Via Cola di Rienzo 223, tel. (06) 352138, Via dei Condotti 87/90, tel. (06) 6784151, and Via del Tritone 177, tel. (06) 6793836, sells quality porcelain, ceramics, and crystal.

Gucci, Via dei Condotti 8, tel. (06) 6789340, is, of course, one of the most popular international names in leather goods.

Krizia is at Piazza di Spagna 77/8, tel. (06) 6793419; her castle outside Rome testifies to the popularity of this women's designer.

Bruno Magli sells men's and ladies' shoes at Via del Gambero 1, tel. (06) 6793802, Via Barberini 94, tel. (06) 486850, Via Veneto 70A, tel. (06) 464355, Via Cola di Rienzo 237, tel. (06) 351972.

Missoni offers colorful knits at Via Borgognona 38B, tel. (06) 6797971; for men only at Piazza di Spagna 78, tel. (06) 6792555; and for women only at Via del Babuino, tel. (06) 679791.

Luisa Spagnoli locations at Via Veneto 130, tel. (06) 465881, Via Frattina 116, tel. (06) 6795517, Via del Corso 385, tel. (06) 6793983, and Via Barberini 84, tel. (06) 460757, are main outlets in central Rome for the Perugia women's stylist.

Stefanel has a dozen Rome outlets; the most central are Via Frattina 31/32, tel. (06) 6792667; Via Cola di Rienzo 191/193, tel. (06) 352954; and Via Nazionale 227, tel. (06) 485914.

Valentino's high-fashion center is at Via Gregoriana 24; tel. (06) 67391. Women's wear is at Via Bocca di Leone 15/18, tel. (06) 6795862, and men's clothing at Via Mario dei Fiori 22 (corner of Via dei Condotti), tel. (06) 6783656.

Mario Valentino at Via Frattina 58, tel. (06) 6791242, and Via Frattina 84, tel. (06) 6791246, represent the Neapolitan leather stylist.

Gianni Versace sells Milanese styling in Rome at Via Bocca di Leone 27, tel. (06) 6780521, and Via Borgognona 29, tel. (06) 6795292.

Fabrics

Cesari, is at Via del Babuino 16, tel. (06) 3611441; linen and lingerie can also be found in the shop at Via Barberini 1; tel. (06) 463035.

Fallani, Via Vitelleschi 20/24 and 28/32, tel. (06) 6542652, also sells linen, men's and women's wear, and lingerie at wholesale prices, near the Vatican.

Polidori is at Via dei Condotti 21; tel. (06) 6784842.

Jewelry and Silverware

Bezzi, Via Colonna 43, tel. (06) 3604800, is run by the Bezzi brothers—they compete with the women in the family, who have set up a shop called **Giannotti 1880** at Lungotevere Mellini 44, Scala Valadier; tel. (06) 3213996. Both are conveniently located in Prati, near the Vatican.

Fornari, Via dei Condotti 80, tel. (06) 6794285, is a Rome byword for quality silverware. Fornari also sells jewelry.

Giansanti, Via Sicilia 40, tel. (06) 493594—Carlo is gracious and accommodating in this reliable shop just off the Via Veneto. Custom orders are filled by experienced goldsmiths.

Leather Goods

Pier Caranti, Piazza di Spagna 43, tel. (06) 6791621, sells bags, belts, and briefcases.

Di Cori, Piazza di Spagna 53, tel. (06) 6784439, sells gloves.

Volterra, Via Barberini 102/104, tel. (06) 4819315, has quality luggage and men's and ladies' apparel.

Valigeria Romana, Via Silla 51; tel. (06) 318437. Besides making trunks and luggage, this is the Samsonite concessionaire in Rome, and repairs are made on luggage that has succumbed to the ordeals of international travel.

Shoes
FOR MEN AND WOMEN
Raphael Salato, Piazza di Spagna 34, tel. (06) 6795646; Via Veneto 149, tel. (06) 493507; or Via Veneto 104, tel. (06) 484677.

Trancanelli, Piazza Cola di Rienzo 84, tel. (06) 6878753; the store at Via Sabotino 52, tel. (06) 319156, sells the same shoes at reduced prices.

Clothes
FOR MEN
For Man, Via Cola di Rienzo 184; tel. (06) 6874661.

Gaj, Piazza Cola di Rienzo 120/122; Aldo's wife has **Vedette** for the ladies next door at number 116/118.

Red and Blue, Via Due Macelli 57/58, just off Piazza di Spagna; tel. (06) 6791933.

Testa, Via Frattina 104, tel. (06) 6791298; and Via Borgognona 13, tel. (06) 6796174.

Uomo In, Via A. Regolo 15; tel. (06) 3598363.

Volpi, Via Barberini 76.

FOR WOMEN
DiPorto, Via Cola di Rienzo 186.

Max Mara, Via Frattina 28, tel. (06) 6793683; Via dei Condotti 46, tel. (06) 6787946; and a new location at Via Cola di Rienzo 275.

FOR YOUNG MEN
Antinco Caffè Moda, Via Genova 12; tel. (06) 4743323; also sells unisex clothing just off Via Nazionale.

FOR YOUNG WOMEN
Cipria, Via Ottaviano 58/64, is just down from the metro A line terminal on the way to the Vatican.

FOR CHILDREN
Chicco, Via della Penna 13/19 (just off Piazza del Popolo).

Cicogna, Via Frattina 138, tel. (06) 6791912; Via Cola di Rienzo, tel. (06) 6530557.

Raphael Junior, Via Veneto 98; tel. (06) 465692.

Gifts
Cose così, Via Candia 75A, tel. (06) 352184, offers a wide assortment of gifts at reasonable prices; it's near the Ottavi-

ano metro stop on the A line. (Via Candia is the extension of Viale Giulio Cesare.)

Factory Outlets

Serious shoppers who are traveling elsewhere in Italy should stop at the I.C.E., the Italian Institute for Foreign Trade (Istituto Nazionale per il Commercio con l'Estero), Via Listz 21; tel. (06) 59921. Near the EUR Marconi metro stop on the B line, this is a government agency promoting Italian products, and can provide merchandise lists of factory outlets that include names, addresses, and telephone numbers of factories throughout the country. This may be a bit ambitious for the average tourist, but since it's along the walk to the Roman Civilization Museum, a stop may be worth the effort a week or so later when touring Tuscany, Veneto, the Marches, and other areas.

☙ RESTAURANTS

If you think Rome hotels are expensive, wait until you try the restaurants. But first impressions can be misleading, because what constitutes a full meal for one in Rome would feed two anywhere else. *Antipasto* is followed by pasta or soup; then comes the *secondo* (second) course of meat, fowl, or fish followed by fruit, cheese, or a sweet. You are not obligated (or expected) to order everything (even though some waiters may give it a try).

Have a good breakfast and a light lunch as a break from sightseeing. It is all but impossible to eat before 7:30 P.M., so return to your hotel for a shower, and then stop at a sidewalk caffè for an *aperitivo.* By then it's restaurant time, and you'll be ready to enjoy a full Roman meal.

An old saying in Rome is that the rich are never hungry. But although servings may seem meager in the more expensive restaurants, a plate of pasta in a picturesque Trastevere trattoria can be overwhelmingly ample. Roman cuisine is not for weight watchers. It is hardy and tasty, and requires a chilled Frascati or another Albani Hills wine to stave off after-dinner thirst. The famous pasta dish *spaghetti alla carbonara* is actually Roman soul food modified. After World War II a black GI added an egg yoke or two to the heavily peppered spaghetti with bacon bits. His idea caught on, and *presto,* the foreign encroachment was complete.

Roman cooking makes heavy use of legumes, oxtails, entrails, spices, and pasta. Meat specialties are *abbacchio* (lamb) and *porchetta* (roast pig). Many restaurants feature fish despite rising costs; remember the menu's *etto* price refers to each 100 grams of weight (about four ounces) and not the price of the dinner.

Service is not a strong point in even the fancier Roman restaurants, so don't expect miracles in the more economical spots.

If you have difficulty in getting your check, just stand up and head for the door—this usually gets results.

Foreign fare is abundant in Rome. The invasion of Chinese restaurants has seemingly emptied Peking. But we're emphasizing Italian restaurants here; of course, Rome has many restaurants featuring every other region in Italy. These pages include a good cross section of all.

The monumental area has many offerings. Trastevere has an impressive concentration of large, small, expensive, and economical restaurants and trattorias. Good neighborhood spots usually run about Lit. 30,000 for a full meal with house wine. In Rome you can eat just as well or just as poorly as anywhere else. As fame increases, so does the tab; this should be remembered in selecting a restaurant. Listings include a neighborhood code for easy reference.

Prices given below are for a complete meal for one person, from antipasto to dessert. Credit cards are listed as accepted. "All cards" means that all of the following are accepted: AE—American Express; DC—Diner's Club; MC—MasterCard; V—Visa.

Neighborhood keys refer to page number of color map insert and the map coordinates at which restaurant is located.

EXPENSIVE

Ai Tre Scalini   ARCHAEOLOGICAL ROME, P. 25, E4
Via SS. Quattro 30; tel. (06) 732695. Rossana and Matteo add a gastronomical touch to the best daily market produce, making a trip to the Colosseum even more enjoyable. A 5-min. walk behind the amphitheater, the restaurant is in a picturesque part of old Rome. Try the ravioli with goat cheese. Meals run Lit. 65,000. Closed Sat. noon, Sun. evening, Mon., July, Aug. All cards.

Alberto Ciarla   TRASTEVERE, P. 24, C4
Piazza San Cosimato 40; tel. (06) 5818668. On the rim of the largest open-air produce market in the heart of popular Trastevere, the menu has a solid accent on fish, with aquariums displaying the menu offerings—fresh, fresh, fresh. Besides a good Italian and French wine list, Alberto offers a Bianco di Velletri Vigna Ciarla from the family vineyards. The *pasta e fagioli* soup with shellfish is first-class and a fine first course. No air conditioning, but outdoor tables in the summer. The waiters seem to be always undergoing on-the-job training. Meals run Lit. 80,000–100,000. Closed Sun., Aug. 5–25, Dec. 23–Jan. 10. All cards.

Fabrizio   TRASTEVERE, P. 24, B3
Via Santa Dorotea 15; tel. (06) 5806244. Raised in the best of old Trastevere tradition, Fabrizio has chosen a more ambitious cooking path. Neptune reigns here, under Fabrizio's watchful eye; he personally selects each day's offerings from the fish stalls at Fiumicino. Traditional Roman dishes are also served, but the best are imaginative creations like *pasta e fagioli* with cuttlefish. Meals run Lit. 65,000. Closed Sun., Aug. 8–31. AE, MC.

Hostaria dell'Orso

Via dei Soldati 25; tel. (06) 6864250. Open only in the evening, this 15th-century former inn often has an elite gathering at its ground-floor watering hole, where the subdued lighting makes it hard to see anyone. The elegant, refined restaurant on the first floor is perfect for romantic occasions, with background piano music to set the mood. The gracious service is a forgotten commodity in most of Rome, and it's air-conditioned, too. The food caps an evening to be remembered; try oysters au gratin with spinach sauce. Reservations recommended. (If the rafters creak under an occasional after-10 P.M. stomp, it's the second-floor disco coming to life.) Meals run Lit. 90,000. Closed Sun. All cards.

Mimi

Via G. Belli 59; tel. (06) 3210962. The best restaurant on the isle of Ponza (off the southern coast of Lazio) is well represented in Rome by this elegant, intimate little restaurant, offering seafood specialties just around the corner from Piazza Cavour and the Palace of Justice. Table telephones ensure privacy. Meals are Lit. 65,000. Closed Mon. AE, DC. In Ponza, Mimi is on Via dietro la Chiesa; tel. (0771) 80338, and remains open seven days a week for the entire summer season. Seafood is less expensive here; meals run Lit. 50,000. Closed Mon. AE, DC.

Papà Giovanni

Via dei Sediari 4; tel. (06) 6565308. Just off Piazza Navona. Renato Sentuti has an avid local following for his creative use of what produce each season provides. Fully realizing the maxim that "the eye deserves its share," the choreography of a tried and talented hand is most apparent in his salads. Renato's sherbets are true and tasty. Dinners run Lit. 70,000–80,000. Closed Sun., Aug. All cards.

If the tab is a bit exorbitant, Renato's wife, Marisa, has her own little place, **G.B. Il Cardinale,** Via delle Carceri 6; tel. (06) 6569336. Kosher and Roman specialties are featured, in addition to an abbreviated selection of Giovanni's fare. A dinner here costs Lit. 40,000–45,000. Closed Sun., Aug., AE.

Patrizia e Roberto del Pianeta Terra

Via Arco del Monte 94/95; tel. (06) 6869893. This little oasis of culinary creativity is tucked into a side street between Campo dei Fiori and Via Arenula, behind the Justice Ministry. Open only in the evening and with only 30 settings (so reservations are a must), it is one of the leading new-wave restaurants, which are becoming increasingly popular. Let Patrizia call the signals for ex-rugby-player husband Roberto in the kitchen. Meals run Lit. 75,000. Closed Sun., Aug. 8–28. AE, DC, MC.

Pino e Dino

Piazza di Montevecchio 22; tel. (06) 6861319. Off the Piazza Navona, this spot has had the same name for years, but not the same principals. Now it's Peppino and Tonino who are equally devoted to serving a panorama of Italy's cuisines. Here is positive proof that there is no one all-embracing style of Italian cooking. An elegant and intimate atmosphere in the evening relaxes to become suitable for a working lunch. At noon expect to pay around Lit. 35,000; for dinner, about Lit. 60,000. Closed Mon., 1 week in Aug., 3 in Jan. AE, DC.

Ranieri
MONUMENTAL ROME, P. 24, C2

Via Mario dei Fiori 26; tel. (06) 6791592. Mario and Giovanni Forti are regaining the fame that once made this one of the best restaurants in the center of Rome (near the Piazza di Spagna). Founded by Neapolitan Giuseppe Ranieri, who was chef to England's Queen Victoria, the restaurant offers old world atmosphere to an army of foreign shoppers and tourers, but now the Italians are beginning to return. Specialties include spinach and ricotta cannellone, melanzana parmigiano, and a wide assortment of meat and fowl. Meals run Lit. 60,000 Closed Sun., 2 weeks in Aug. All cards.

Rooftop Dining

Charles, Hotel Eden, Via Ludovisi 49; tel. (06) 4742401. When the name of a hotel's restaurant derives from its maître d', the service has to be good. Soft music accompanies beautiful views from atop this hotel between the Via Veneto and Piazza di Spagna. The tab runs Lit. 80,000–100,000, but you can stop in for just a drink until midnight, for an unforgettable nightcap. Closed Sun., Aug. All cards.

Les Etoiles, Atlante Star Hotel, Via Vitelleschi 34; tel. (06) 6879558. It's difficult to imagine that this 5-star hotel was once a *pensione* with a fleet of roadside hustlers soliciting foreigners entering Rome on the old consular roads. Over 25 years the pensione took over the entire building and became a hotel that was associated with the Best Western chain, before renovating its way to luxury class. The roof garden offers a fine view of St. Peter's and Rome from the other side of the Tiber. Meals run Lit. 80,000. All cards.

Forum Roof-Garden, Hotel Forum, Via Tor de' Conti 25; tel. (06) 6792446. Most exciting is the overview of the main archaeological section of ancient Rome. Food, wine, and service are pleasant, but come here for the atmosphere; you'll have no doubt as to what city you're in. Meals run Lit. 70,000. All cards.

Hassler Roof-Garden, Hassler Villa Medici Hotel, Piazza Trinità dei Monti 6; tel. (06) 6782651. Atop the Spanish Steps, this elegant, refined, air-conditioned restaurant has a beautiful view of monumental Rome. Service is impeccable and helps create a luxurious dining atmosphere. Meals average Lit. 120,000–135,000. All cards.

La Pergola, Cavalieri Hilton, Via Cadlolo 101; tel. (06) 3151. Open for dinner only, this is probably the best restaurant on the list. Rome will be at your feet from this Monte Mario perch. From the *degustazione* to *alla carta* alternatives, the tab can run Lit. 70,000–110,000. Closed Sun.; first 3 weeks of Jan. All cards.

Sans Souci

Via Sicilia 20; tel. (06) 4456194. Serving dinner only, this ultr-aelegant restaurant half a block off the Via Veneto is also ultrasmall. Reservations are necessary to assure a table. Have an *aperitivo* in the small lounge after descending into the restaurant, and take the opportunity to contemplate the mixed menu of nouvelle cuisine and inviting Italian fare. Fine crystal, porcelain, and linen and soft music complete a delightful atmosphere. Air-conditioned. Meals run Lit. 80,000–100,000. Closed Mon., Aug. All cards.

MODERATELY PRICED
Ambasciata d'Abruzzo

Via Pietro Tacchini 26; tel. (06) 878256. This air-conditioned restaurant is a favorite with foreign tourists for its unique service. *Antipasto* is a basket of Abruzzo *insaccati,* ham, and cheese. A full meat meal runs Lit. 35,000, but can climb to Lit. 40,000 with fish. Closed Sun., 3 weeks in Aug. When the "embassy" is closed in summer, son Roberto's **Vicariato d'Abruzzo,** Via delle Fornaci 8/10, tel. (06) 633438, fills the gap with a similar dining experience and identical prices. Closed Mon. All cards at both.

Andrea

Via Sardegna 28; tel. (06) 493707. With wife Francesca running the kitchen, Aldo De Cesare has guided this comfortable, air-conditioned restaurant into the limelight with some of the area's most tempting *antipasti,* fish, sweets, and wines. The crispy, plain pizza bread is rushed hot from the wood oven of the pizzeria across the street. The high demand at dinner and for business lunches means reservations are essential. Meals run Lit. 60,000. Closed Sun., Aug. 10–30. All cards.

Antico Romagnolo

Via Panisperna 231; tel. (06) 4740620. In the 1930s this was a favorite meeting place for Italy's famed "boys of Via Panisperna," the group of physicists who included Enrico Fermi, Pontecorvo, Majorana, Amaldi, and Segré. Renovated by ex-Alitalia stewards Giacomo Ramenghi and Lino Menegon, but maintaining a comfortable old osteria air, the restaurant provides a vast assortment of regional dishes to satisfy practically any desire. There's an especially good antipasto spread; for your *secondo,* try *faraona* (guinea hen) breast with peppers. Meals run Lit. 30,000–35,000. Closed Sat. noon, Sun. AE, DC, V.

Il Caminetto

Viale Parioli 89; tel. (06) 803946. Air-conditioned inside for lunch, dinner is served outside during the summer. A comfortable, neighborhood restaurant with a fine panorama of regional cuisine. You'll find a good antipasto spread and a wide assortment of pastas, always al dente. Meals run Lit. 35,000–40,000. Closed Thurs., 1 week in mid-Aug. AE, DC, MC.

Dante
VATICAN, P. 24, B2

Taberna dei Gracchi, Via dei Gracchi 266/268; tel. (06) 383757. Dante Mililli's success story since abandoning an old Trastevere eatery 26 years ago is reflected in every corner of this modern, air-conditioned restaurant. But Dante has remained faithful to his old Trastevere roots, and serves as a Roman gastronomical ambassador abroad, in London, Berlin, and New York (at Girafe, 208 E. 58th St.). In Rome, customers include printers who have remained faithful over the years, the Lazio professional soccer team, attorneys, judges, and tourists from neighboring first-class hotels. Meals run Lit. 45,000–50,000. Closed Sun., Mon., noon, Aug. 5–25. AE, DC, V.

On the Tiber

The old *Roman Holiday* barge of Audrey Hepburn and Gregory Peck today is no more than a burned-out hull on the banks of the Tiber. The river is so polluted that swimming is prohibited; a sip of its waters would be lethal. But riverside dining can still be attractive. Two possibilities both have sun decks for tanning buffs.

Il Canto del Riso, under Ponte Cavour (enter by the stairs across from Lungotevere Mellini 7); tel. (06) 3610430. Alvaro Silvestri is an authentic boat person, but a pragmatic one. The riverside Canto features rice first courses and seafood seconds. Meals average Lit. 30,000–40,000. Closed Sun. evening, Mon., Nov. 1–March 31. No cards.

Isola del Sole, Lungotevere Arnaldo da Brescia; tel. (06) 3601400. Giulio Bendandi's barge restaurant is open year-round, though it closes at high tide. Reservations are a must for the 1–3 P.M. lunch and 8:30–11:30 P.M. dinner. Meals run Lit. 35,000–40,000. Closed Mon. AE.

Sister Clelia manages **Isola del Sole No. 2** (also known as al Khadir) at Porto Ercole, Via dei Cannoni 4, Banchina Santa Barbara; tel. (0546) 831248. Prices run Lit. 40,000–50,000. No cards.

Fortunato
MONUMENTAL ROME, P. 24, C3

Via del Pantheon 55; tel. (06) 6792788. Near the Pantheon, between the Senate and Chamber of Deputies, this restaurant attracts Parliamentarians. Fresh fish is guaranteed every day, as well as vegetables that are a house specialty, spaghetti with clams, and *gnocchi.* Ricotta cheese is featured in crepes and a rustic Roman pie. Expect to pay Lit. 40,000–50,000 for dinner. Closed Sun., Aug. 10–31. AE.

Girone VI
MONUMENTAL ROME, P. 24, C3

Vicolo Sinibaldi 2; tel. (06) 6542831. In a picturesque alley off Via del Torre Argentina, 5 min. from the Pantheon, is Gabriele and Antonietta Oreggia's elegant little restaurant in a 15th-century crypt. The seven tables inside are bolstered by another four or five in the alley during the summer. Open evenings only, 8 P.M.–midnight, year-round. A former Alitalia flight steward, Gabriele is aided by son Marco, an aspiring sommelier, in adding an appealing personal touch to old Italian recipes. When you leave you're almost one of the family. Dinner runs Lit. 55,000. Closed Sun., 10 days over Christmas. AE, MC, V.

Grottino
VATICAN

Via Oslavia 54; tel. (06) 3612703. A little beyond the Vatican's perimeter, but the husband-wife team of Alfredo and Alberta Fiorio hosts an elegant, air-conditioned, totally renovated basement restaurant featuring the renaissance of traditional recipes with an inventive flare. The menu changes nightly; but try the linguine with crab meat if available. Going into its second year, the restaurant already draws heavily from the nearby radio and television studios. Meals run Lit. 35,000. Closed Sun., Aug. 10–20. AE, V.

Piazza Navona

Two restaurants that take advantage of incredible locations on one of the most beautiful piazzas in Europe are **Mastrostefano,** Piazza Navona 94/100; tel. (06) 6542855 (closed Mon., Jan 10–27, Aug. 18–31), and **Tre Scalini,** Piazza Navona 30; tel. (06) 6861234 (closed Wed.). Tabs at both can orbit up to Lit. 50,000–60,000, including wine. Both take all cards. Make reservations for an outdoor table and feast your eyes on Bernini's Fountain of Four Rivers. But be aware that it's the atmosphere, not the food you're paying for.

Il Matriciano
VATICAN, P. 24, B2

Via dei Gracchi 55; tel. (06) 3212327. Next to the area's largest city market, Giuseppe Colasanti's traditional fare can be appreciated until midnight. Tables can flow onto the sidewalks in warmer weather, and it is better to reserve a table in advance. Obliging waiters are ready to advise on a vast assortment of selections that include regional and classic specialties, including the pasta dish *buccattini* alla matriciana and grilled meats. Meals run Lit. 35,000–40,000. Closed Sat., Aug. 5–29. All cards.

Al Moro
MONUMENTAL ROME, P. 24, D2

Vicolo delle Bollette 13; tel. (06) 6783495. In its 60th year this restaurant near the Trevi Fountain is a little labyrinth of small rooms from various past expansions. Franco Romagnoli maintains a good dining tradition in the second generation. (His late father submitted to Federico Fellini's powers of persuasion to play a prime supporting role in *Satyricon,* between turns of directing waiters and the kitchen staff.) Here the *carbonara* is prepared with red peppers instead of black pepper. A steady clientele makes reservations a must. Air-conditioned. Meals run Lit. 45,000–50,000. Closed Sun., Aug. No cards.

Da Pancrazio
MONUMENTAL ROME, P. 24, C3

Piazza del Biscione 92; tel. (06) 6861246. There is outdoor dining on the small square just off Campo dei Fiori, but for atmosphere, romantics prefer the lower level inside, amid the ruins of the first-century B.C. Pompeo Theater, where Caesar was believed to have been assassinated. In such an atmosphere

Roman specialties are a must, but the fish is also tempting. Dinners run Lit. 35,000–40,000. Closed Wed., Aug. 12–18. All cards.

Piperno
GHETTO, P. 24, C3

Monte dei Cenci 9; tel. (06) 6540629. In the heart of the old Jewish quarter, the air-conditioned restaurant's kosher cooking has an appeal that surpasses religious belief. Artichokes abound in the Roman countryside, and "Jewish style" *(alla giudiea)* is the way to order them in Rome. It is a house specialty here, along with a wide assortment of vegetable *antipasti* and baccala. Meals run Lit. 40,000–65,000. Closed Sun. evening, Mon., Aug. No cards.

Regno Sardo
VATICAN, P. 24, B1/2

Via Fabio Massimo 101; tel. (06) 3212501. It's been a long way from Ortueri, in Sardinia, for Giovanni Bonu, but since he set up shop in an old osteria, that seemed to have seen the wrath of God, things have never been the same. Nowhere in Rome can a seafood spread—from antipasto to spaghetti with clams to a mixed, grilled seafood platter—be found at Giovanni's prices. He cuts corners elsewhere—and accommodates clients with a smile. The hurried, demanding, and pretentious should go elsewhere. For Giovanni, dinner in his restaurant is an evening to be enjoyed—relax and loosen your belt. Meals are Lit. 35,000–40,000 depending on wine. Closed Mon., Aug. 10–25. AE, DC, V.

Romolo a Porta Settimiana
TRASTEVERE, P. 24, B3

Via Porta Settimiana 8; tel. (06) 5818284. Legend has it that this was the osteria Raphael frequented while adorning the walls of the Farnese Palace. The exuberant master was attracted by a local barmaid. In succeeding generations the likes of Trilussa (Rome's favorite poet) and Guttuso (an acclaimed contemporary artist, who favored friend Romolo with a sketch for the menu) joined the rank and file of the famous who have passed these portals. The Casali clan has reigned since Romolo set up shop in 1923 in one of the most picturesque corners of old Rome. Daughter Marisa continues the tradition with the best of Roman cuisine and other regions' specialties. Ox-tail is a winter favorite. A large courtyard can accommodate 180 diners, but reservations are suggested. Meals are Lit. 45,000–55,000. Closed Mon., Aug. 5–29. AE, DC, V.

Sabatini in Trastevere
TRASTEVERE, P. 24, C4

Back-to-back are two restaurants in one: at Vicolo Santa Maria in Trastevere 18; tel. (06) 5818307 (closed Tues.), and at Piazza Santa Maria in Trastevere 13; tel. (06) 582026 (closed Wed.). Salvatore, Silvestro, and Francesco Sabatini continue one of the best traditions in Trastevere. The sober, intimate, labyrinthed interior is offset by outdoor summer dining on the square, opposite one of the more beautiful churches in Rome. Seafood occupies a prime role, but the principal fare is still traditional Roman, which couldn't have a more appropriate setting. For dinner on the square reservations are a must. Meals run Lit. 40,000–55,000. Both closed Aug. 14–17. All cards.

Trastevere

No one eats and runs in Trastevere; the experience is a leisurely evening in old Rome. The Trastevere food tradition could fill volumes, and high prices are not necessary. There still exist purely family-style *osterie* with paper-covered wooden tables; foreign food; fast food; gay bars; and cabarets. A stroll through the area between Santa Maria in Trastevere and Piazza San Cosimato, on the right of Viale di Trastevere, or from Piazza Sidney Sonnino to Piazza dei Mercanti on the left, will always turn up a pot luck alternative and a pleasant evening.

Osteria Santa Ana   MONUMENTAL ROME, P. 24, C1

Via della Penna 68/69; tel. (06) 3610291. Around the corner from Piazza del Popolo is a fine, elegant restaurant that offers good food in a pleasant atmosphere. Two steps down (watch your head) and you're almost in Osteria St. Ana (there's outside dining in warmer months). Here the best of Roman specialties, seafood, veal, and imaginative pasta courses follow an attractive antipasto cart. Meals run Lit. 45,000. Closed Sun., 2nd half Aug. All cards.

BASIC BARGAINS
Bella Napoli   VATICAN, P. 24, A1

Via S. De Saint Bon 59; tel. (06) 314712. Roman and Molise cuisine, seafood recipes, and good pizza from two young men who have renovated this old neighborhood eatery and smashed doubts that quality would suffer. The expansion and outdoor tables in summer can make service less than immediate, but the wait is worth the effort. The sauté di frutti di mare is exceptional. Weekend evenings are impossible without reservations. Meals are Lit. 25,000–30,000. Closed Mon., Aug. No cards.

Hosteria del 104   ARCHAEOLOGICAL ROME, P. 24, E3

Via Urbana 104; tel. (06) 484556. This delightful little restaurant is a Sicilian-American effort featuring specialties from the native lands of both partners, plus some. Baked ham with pineapple, spaghetti with eggplant, Mexican chili, and lemon pie are a few. The daily menu is limited to several house specialties. You can expect a satisfying meal in this comfortable, clean, but small restaurant; reservations may be smart. A perfect lunch stop between Santa Maria Maggiore and the Colosseum, for Lit. 15,000. Dinners run Lit. 19,000, beverages extra. Closed Wed., Aug. AE.

Otello alla Concordia   MONUMENTAL ROME, P. 24, C2

Via della Croce 81; tel. (06) 6791178. A pleasant stop while shopping; take the last left off Piazza di Spagna before entering Via del Babuino. The narrow street of Via della Croce opens onto a pleasant courtyard where Otello successfully caters to foot-weary tourists and a clientele from the nearby art galleries and antique shops. A bowl of pasta and a salad make a satisfying lunch. Several set tourist menus with house wine are available. Dinners run Lit. 20,000–30,000. Closed Sun., 2 weeks at Christmas. AE.

Palmerie   ARCHAEOLOGICAL ROME, P. 24, D3
Via Cimarra 4/5; tel. (06) 4744110. Reservations are a must in this little osteria with a steady clientele. A quick coat of paint, and Nicola and Beatrice Cerazoli joined the ranks of young couples in Rome who offer economical dining alternatives. A quick, light lunch featuring exotic salads (Tues.–Fri.) runs Lit. 20,000–25,000; dinner runs about Lit. 30,000. Closed Mon., Aug. 10–20. No cards.

ENTERTAINMENT

Rome is far from being the entertainment capital of the Western world. And in August, there is more happening in the middle of the Dead Sea than in the stiflingly hot Eternal City.

In the Summer

The local tourist board (EPT) makes an admirable effort on the Isola Tiberina every evening, with games, music, snacks, and pizza stands to help you unwind after hours of walking in the sun or stuffy museums. (Air-conditioning is still considered a luxury by state and city officials.)

Discos, piano bars, jazz retreats, cabarets, theaters, and cinemas all close for a month or more. The more ambitious enterprises follow the beautiful people to the beach or the more fashionable mountain resorts and set up shop for the holiday. Those who do not close out of desperation—Rome's heat can be brutal in August.

The main musical attraction is the **summer open-air opera** season at the Baths of Caracalla. (See Baths of Caracalla in the sightseeing section for ticket information.) Most public bus service has terminated for the evening by the time the performance is over, but the city's ATAC provides a special fleet of buses to cover general routes into all main sections of the city to assure transportation for most of the way back to hotels. The EPT is working to secure the same service for its Isola Tiberina street fair when it ends at 1 A.M.

Another option for a summer evening is the only **English-language movie house,** Pasquino, at Vicolo dei Piedi 19; telephone (06) 5803622.

But if neither of the above appeals to you, it's best to join that untarnished Roman pastime, people watching.

When the city begins to repopulate in September, theater season manifests are posted, and the piano bars, discos, and cabarets return to the usual grind for another season.

People Watching

Gawking finds its maximum expression in Rome. The Via Veneto is most attractive during the day, when the shops are open. Here **Doney** and **Café de Paris** are old favorites, but there are less crowded perches such as at **Carpano,** up a block towards the Porta Pinciana. During July or August, it's tourist watching tourist—almost like being back at JFK waiting for your flight to Europe.

Things are a bit brighter in Piazza Navona, or even the Pantheon. The street artists, fire-eaters, and other exhibitionists provide pleasant diversion while you're admiring Bernini's fountains. The popularity of caffès can change from year to year, but two favorites with tourists on Piazza Navona are **Tre Scalini,** which features a chocolate ice cream *tartufo* with bits of chocolate, and **Mastrostefano,** which offers a special *coppa gigante* that is a meal of ice cream and fruit cocktail. A comfortable little caffè that recently replaced an art gallery is the **Barberini,** in the end zone near the Fountain of Neptune.

A pleasant *passeggiata* (stroll) from Piazza Navona will take you across Corso Rinascimento into Piazza Sant'Eustachio, for a creamy espresso at the **Caffè Sant'Eustachio,** then on to Piazza della Rotonda (near the Pantheon), which attracts Roman youths. As a result, there are a never-ending number of caffès, bars, ice cream parlors, video bars, and so forth in the area. Stroll up around the Parliament's Chamber of Deputies in the evening, when traffic is quiet, to savor the real flavor of Rome.

The metro runs until 11:30 P.M. Although it's relatively safe, petty thievery is an ever-present possibility. Have a caffè call a cab for your return to your hotel, instead.

Clubs and Discos

Two discos that are especially popular with the young and young at heart are **Bella Blu,** Via Luciani 21; tel. (06) 3608840 (open 9 P.M. to 3:30 A.M.), and **Much More,** Via Luciani 52; tel. (06) 870504 (open 11 P.M. to 3 A.M., and also 4 to 8 P.M. Saturday and Sunday; closed Monday). These two spots have rejuvenated staid Parioli, to a point.

The **Jackie O',** Via Boncompagni 11; tel. (06) 461401 (open 11 P.M. to 3:30 A.M.; closed Monday), is just off the Via Veneto and convenient to area hotels. Phone for reservations, since the club is often used for private parties. Across the Via Veneto is the **Club 84,** Via Emilia 84; tel. (06) 4751538 (open 10 P.M. to 3:30 A.M.), another of the very few legitimate night spots in town.

Too many clubs have sidewalk hustlers who use every imaginable ploy to con singles into astronomical tabs, ruining the vacations of unsuspecting tourists.

The temple of Italian rock in the 1960s was the Piper Club. Now the **Piper '80,** Via Tagliamento 9, tel. (06) 854459, it still stages live shows to punctuate its more regular videos.

Piano Bars

Once upon a time (about twenty years ago) there was a young American following in the wake of two expatriates who had long been on the piano-bar scene in Paris, Bricktop and Charlie Beal. Bricktop had her own basement place on the Veneto, and Charlie entertained the nostalgic at the American-owned Luau, which used to be on the Via Sardegna, off Via Veneto.

The young man had his playing in order, but the Italians didn't give him much of a chance to prove his real worth. Finally he packed up, returned stateside, and achieved international success with the score for *Rocky.* The likes of Bill Conti, Bricktop, and Charlie Beal are now missing from the Rome piano-bar scene. But who knows when another genius may wander in?

Every now and then Romano Mussolini, youngest son of the Fascist dictator, shows up at a piano with his lifelong passion for jazz.

For a casual drink and a few sounds, try:

Little Bar, Via Gregoriana 54A; tel. (06) 6796386. **Manuia,** Vicolo del Cinque 54; tel. (06) 58170716, features Brazilian music; there's a restaurant with a courtyard garden next door, so you can make it a complete evening without traveling very far. **La Prugna,** Piazza dei Ponziani 3; tel. (06) 5890555. **Tartarughino,** Via della Scrofa 2; tel. (06) 6786037, draws a crowd from Roman personalities.

Concerts, Theater, and Special Events

Rome has an active **concert season** from the fall to the beginning of summer. In June and into July concerts are staged in parks around the city, and there is **Jazz on a Tiber Barge** at Foro Italico, Italy's largest athletic complex, 15 minutes from the Prati area.

Rome has finally cracked the major rock-concert tours. Pink Floyd and Michael Jackson are just a few of the international favorites who played the Flaminio Stadium last year. The traveler's chance of obtaining tickets to big-name concerts unfortunately is likely limited to buying from scalpers the night of the concert.

For concerts, special events, and what-have-you, the entertainment section of the Rome daily *Il Messaggero* is probably the best list of happenings in Rome. Too often there is not much advance publicity for events.

Rome always draws a **circus** or two at Christmas. Though the Italian troupes may lack the kitsch that is common in the U.S., they provide an entertaining afternoon or evening. And there are generally visiting East European and Asian troupes which, with glasnost, may now find U.S. bookings.

Theater is naturally all in Italian, but musicals may at times be worth a trip to non-speakers of Italian for just the music and dance. Theater troupes take off Sunday evening and Monday. This can mean that a concert will be sandwiched into the theater's idle moment. Often foreign performers are featured, especially at the **Sistina,** Via Sistine 29; telephone (06) 4756841.

Sports

The sporting scene is dominated by the **soccer** season from September to May. Italy is preparing to host the 1990 World Cup tournament, and local heroes are being closely scrutinized along with the foreign stars who toil in the ranks of leading Italian teams.

Rome's two professional teams are Roma and Lazio. Between them they have captured only three Italian titles. But in recent years Roma has usually been a contender. Lazio has just returned to the A League in an interesting rotation formula that relegates one year's cellar dwellers to the B League, and promotes the top three teams of the B League to the A League. This always assures a lively battle for the league championship, and an elimination of complacency in the bottom of the standings among teams battling to remain in the major league.

League games are limited to Sunday; with both Rome teams in the A League, the city is practically assured a major-league game every week at the Olympic Stadium, Foro Italico. Italian Cup matches and friendlies (exhibition games) may be played during the week.

The national team should have a rich schedule of friendlies until cup time, since as tournament host Italy will not play in a qualification round.

You can take the number 911 bus to Foro Italico; there are also special buses running to and from the stadium on Sundays—but these tend to be outrageously crowded. Bars around the city sometimes sell tickets the week before the game.

Basketball is the second most popular sport in the country, and Italy probably has the world's highest-paid amateur players. Under the guise of industrial ball (teams sponsored by corporations), the Italian league attracts a number of U.S. players who had full careers in the NBA. And there is always a player or two who survived all but the final NBA team cut, and remains active in Italy in hopes of getting a second shot the next time around. Rome's Banco Roma team has enthusiastic followers who almost rival the frenzy that engulfs the more powerful northern teams. Home games are generally played at the Sports Palace that was constructed in EUR for the 1960 Olympic games. Take the metro B line.

This is also the arena for major **boxing** matches, but Rome is no longer the center of this sport in Italy; the recent death of promoter Rodolfo Sabatini left a tremendous void in local boxing organizations. Do-it-yourself enthusiasts won't be denied, but public boxing facilities are severely lacking. The gym scene is dominated by private clubs that often have difficulty in accommodating their own members.

In and around Rome there are two **horse,** one **dog,** and one **auto racing** circuit. Regular horse racing is near the Ciampino airport at the Capannelle, Via Appia Nuova, km. 12; telephone (06) 7993144; the **trotters** are at Tor di Valle, Via del Mare, km. 9; telephone (06) 6564129. To get to Capannelle, take the A line metro to the Colli Albani Stop and the ATAC bus 664 to the track. The trotters go under the lights, as do the dogs at the Ponte Marconi track near EUR, Via della Vasca Navale 6; telephone (06) 5566258.

Auto racing is twenty miles out on the Via Cassia at Valle Lunga; telephone (06) 9041417.

Il Corriere dello Sport is a daily sports newspaper in Rome that has complete information on activity at all of these tracks. The local racing form is *Il Cavallo,* for those who want to get serious. There is off-track betting in Italy, and a visit to a local betting shop will find characters even Damon Runyon never imagined.

Participant Sports

The largest **outdoor pool** and an **indoor pool** are in the Olympic Committee complex at Foro Italico, across the Tiber in northern Rome. Opening hours can vary, depending on scheduled lessons and competitions; telphone (06) 3601498 for specific information.

For active **tennis** enthusiasts attempts may be made to make reservations with the courts at EUR, Viale dell'Artigianato 2, telephone (06) 5924693; Foro Italico, Lungotevere Maresciallo Diaz, telephone (06) 3619021; the Tennis Club Belle Arti, Via Flaminia 158, telephone (06) 3600602; or the Tre Fontane complex near EUR, Via delle Tre Fontane, telephone (06) 5926386. Courts are very hard to come by; early morning times are your best bet.

For a round of **golf,** you must apply well in advance for a temporary membership with either of the two local clubs that have 18-hole courses: Acqua Santa, Via Appia Nuova 716, telephone (06) 783407; or Olgiata, Largo Olgiata 15, telephone (06) 3789141.

Bowlers can always find a lane with Enrico Vietri at the Bowling Brunswick, Lungotevere Acqua Acetosa; telephone (06) 3966696. To keep youngsters occupied, there is a wide assortment of video games. Facilities are smaller at Bowling Roma, at the more central Viale Regina Margherita 181; telephone (06) 861184.

The most complete **health club** in Rome is the Roman Sport Center, Via del Galoppatoio 33; telephone (06) 3601667. Adjacent to the underground parking facility in Villa Borghese, it is open from 8:30 A.M. to 11 P.M.

SHORT TRIPS OUT OF ROME

The overpowering presence of Rome can outshine many of the attractions elsewhere in the region of Lazio. But the Eternal City's mind-boggling abundance of monuments, fountains, museums, and art and artifacts can create the need for relief and relaxation, for the quaint, the calm, the picturesque. The Lazio countryside's minor provinces offer not-so-minor attractions that would be more prominent farther from Rome.

Anzio is now a popular beach resort 36 miles south of Rome. You can take ACOTRAL buses near the San Giovanni A line metro stop. On January 22, 1944, Anzio was where Anglo-American troops landed against weak German resistance, then camped while the Germans regrouped. Reminders of this Allied indecision are the 8,000 U.S. graves in nearby Nettuno and the 1,000 British graves in a cemetery along the road to Albano.

Best Beaches. The coast around Rome and most of Lazio is only for the most desperate beach buff. The best beach areas are at **Santa Marinella** (41 miles north of Rome on the Via Aurelia; you can take ACOTRAL buses from Viale Giulio Cesare) and **San Felice Circeo** (60 miles south of Rome on the Via Pontina). But the best suggestion is **Ponza** in the Pontine Islands. Ferry service is available from Anzio, Circeo, Terracina, and Formia. (Circeo, Terracina, and Formia are also served by ACOTRAL.) But don't go in August; if you're wondering why Rome is so deserted, you'll rapidly discover where everyone went when you arrive in Ponza.

If you're having difficulty conversing, try English. The local dialect is more an offshoot of Neapolitan, and difficult to understand; but many of the fishing folk and their families split their time between Ponza and Brooklyn.

⚜ RESTAURANTS

South of Rome, along the way to the ferry port at Formia, a pleasant restaurant is **Italo,** Via Unita d'Italia, tel. (0771) 21529. A good, complete seafood meal with wine in this modern, seaside restaurant with summer dining terrace is Lit. 40,000. Closed Mon., Dec. 22–Jan. 5. AE, DC, V.

SIDETRIP TO GAETA

Below Formia on the coast is the town of Gaeta and its fortress-prison, where Nazi SS officers convicted for atrocities in Italy were incarcerated. One died after being taken out of a Rome military hospital in a suitcase; another was returned to Austria by then-Premier Bettino Craxi, in spite of public referendums explicitly against his release.

Cassino. Just south of Formia on the Via Appia is a good road (SS630) for the 35-mile drive to Cassino, a recommended stop on a drive through Lazio or to Naples. Cassino is on the SS6 Via Casilina, and just off the A2 Rome–Naples turnpike, at the base of the hilltop **Abbey of Montecassino,** the cradle of the Benedictine Order. Founded by St. Benedict in A.D. 529, the abbey was completely destroyed for the fourth time in 1944 by Allied bombing and artillery that sought to dislodge the German garrison that was controlling the roads to Rome. Fortunately for posterity, the abbey's rich historic archives had been transferred to the Vatican. Ironically, the abbey became more fortified by the destruction, as debris bolstered the massive walls. The view of Cassino is eerie, with its vacant lots marked only by the foundations of former houses, remaining as a reminder of the price of war paid by the civilian population. Free Polish forces led the attacks up the hill, and near an obelisk that commemorates the battle is a cemetery containing the remains of 1,100 Polish soldiers who helped to liberate the road to Rome.

The abbey is open to the public 7 A.M. to 12:30 P.M. and 3:15 P.M. to sunset. Under the high altar in the richly decorated basilica is an urn containing the remains of St. Benedict and his sister St. Scolastica. Both died here in A.D. 543.

Ostia Antica is 15 miles southwest of Rome on the Via del Mare to Ostia beach. The old Roman seaport can also be reached by train from Rome's Porta San Paolo station (to Ostiense). All of the **ruins** are open to a scorching summer sun, so wear a hat, or visit late in the afternoon. Open 9 A.M. to one hour before sunset. Closed Monday. Lit. 2000.

🐎 RESTAURANTS

Drive over to the fishing port of **Fiumicino** for dinner at **Bastianelli al Molo,** Via Torre Clementina 312; tel. (06) 6440118. One of the best seafood restaurants on the Roman coast. Dinner runs Lit. 40,000–60,000. Closed Mon. All cards.

Palestrina is 23 miles southeast of Rome off the Via Casilina (SS6). An important Etruscan seventh-century B.C. religious center, Palestrina also drew the Romans, who built the first-century B.C. terraced **Temple of Fortune,** which suffered bomb damage in World War II. The bombing uncovered previously unknown areas of the temple. Though most Etruscan artifacts from the area have been put on exhibit in the Villa

Giulia in Rome, there is an interesting museum in the town's Piazza della Cortina.

❦ RESTAURANTS

At **Labico,** a short drive south from Palestrina, is one of the best little restaurants in Rome's environs: **Antonello Colonna's Vecchia Osteria,** Via Casilina, km. 38.3; tel. (06) 9510032. The 23-mile drive from Rome isn't so very far for a comfortable, elegant evening of dining away from the masses. This old carriage stop has been converted into an elegant restaurant; reservations required. Antonello's *degustazione* special is a gastronomic delight and explains why he is often on call as an ambassador of Roman culinary prowess in presenting the renaissance of traditional recipes in the U.S. and West Germany. Try the ceci bean soup, wild boar. Meals run Lit. 80,000. Closed Sun. evening, Mon., Aug. All cards.

Rieti. Reiti's province is rich in **religious shrines,** most notably the four sanctuaries founded by St. Francis of Assisi along the perimeter of the Reatina Holy Valley. The **ski resort of Monte Terminillo** was proclaimed by Mussolini "the mountain of Rome." There is no direct rail link to Rome; bus service connects Rieti's Piazza Mazzini rail terminal with the Castro Pretorio and Corso d'Italia terminals in Rome. But since most points of interest are in the province, a car is practically a necessity. Rieti is 48 miles from Rome on Via Salaria.

The geographical center of Italy is in the provincial seat's Piazza S. Rufo, connected to central Corso Garibaldi by Via Cerroni. The point is marked by a plaque inscribed in twenty languages.

The four sanctuaries in the Holy Valley are:

Poggio Bustone, ten miles north of Rieti off SS79, where St. Francis prayed and meditated in two caves.
Santa Maria della Foresta, two and a half miles directly north of Rieti, a stop on the saint's travels in 1225.
Fonte Colombo, three miles southwest of Rieti. Here, in 1223, St. Francis reportedly dictated the rules of his order.
Greccio, ten and a half miles from Rieti at the western end of the valley. In the winter of 1223, St. Francis created the first nativity scene by saying mass at a manger; every year the occasion is commemorated locally with a "living" reproduction of the event on Christmas Eve.

❦ RESTAURANTS

The town of **Greccio** has the unique restaurant **Il Nido del Corvo,** tel. (0746) 753181. Ample signs from the town square lead to this hill-clinging restaurant adorned with religious artifacts of debatable origin. Outside dining overlooking the valley in summer. "The Crow" greets guests in a straw cowboy hat, Hawaiian shirt, short leather pants, and cowboy boots. His plates of the day are for serious eaters only, with *antipasto,* two pasta or rice courses, two meat or fowl dishes, dessert, wine, coffee, and more. Meals are Lit. 35,000. Open daily. AE, DC.

Sermoneta. The train from Rome's Termini Station to Latina Scalo takes less than half an hour. For under Lit. 10,000 a taxi will then take you, in less than 15 minutes, to the charming little medieval town of Sermoneta, around the 13th-century **Caetani castle.** Castle tours are conducted in Italian from March to October hourly from 10 A.M. to noon and 3 to 6 P.M.; closed Thursday (Lit. 3000). Plans indicate that English information sheets will soon be available. The castle, which briefly belonged to the Borgias, is amazingly well preserved. The town itself is so clean and well preserved it seems more Umbrian than Lazio.

☙ RESTAURANTS

A pleasant surprise in **Sermoneta** is Michele Sabba's **Black Rose,** Via G. Garibaldi 17; tel. (0773) 30021. After 20 years in Sydney, Australia, Michele and family returned home to open this pizzeria-trattoria that has everything from hot dogs and hamburgers to meat pies and pizzas from a wood oven, as well as homemade pasta. Going into his second year, Michele hopes negotiations for credit cards will soon be complete. Closed Tues., Jan.

If the sweet tooth is commanding, head for **Engelberto Carosi's** ice cream at Via del Castello 8, just before the entrance to the Caetani castle. There is a little garden with tables; the well—well don't talk about it. While renovating the building Carosi found hundreds of old books and manuscripts that he thought were worthless; he chucked them all into the well. He still has nightmares thinking about their value, estimated by his antique-dealer brother. Two skeletons were found in the building's walls; villagers believe they were victims of Lucretia Borgia, who was given the castle by Borgia Pope Alexander VI when the Caetanis were excommunicated and momentarily turned out into the cold.

Also in the area is the "medieval Pompeii" of **Ninfa,** annihilated by malaria in the 17th century. Nestled along a small lake fed by the Ninfa River, the beautiful little village has botanical gardens that can be visited on the first Saturday and following Sunday of each month, from April through October. Another local attraction is the 13th-century **Abbey of Valvisciolo,** open 8 A.M. to noon and 3 to 6 P.M. in winter, from 3:30 to 7 P.M. afternoons in summer. Visit the spirits shop next to the abbey, which sells liqueurs made by the monks. You'll want a car to visit Ninfa.

Tivoli was to the Roman emperors what Southampton is to New York's investment banking set: an escape from the city. The town is 15 miles from Rome on the Via Tiburtina (SS5).

You can take a bus from Via Gaeta near Termini and Piazza della Repubblica.

About half a mile before Tivoli, to the right as you travel from Rome, is **Hadrian's Villa** (Villa Adriana), entrance is Lit. 4,000 (open 9 A.M. to one and a half hours before sunset). The massive second-century complex built by the emperor as his country place consisted of thermal baths and the re-creation of his favorite monuments from sites throughout the empire. One of the most impressive: Canopus on the Nile; Hadrian re-created this Egyptian town with its canal lined with statues and gardens. A fine reproduction at the entrance to the ruins provides orientation, and there's a museum displaying finds from the excavations. The size of the complex is evocative of the grandiose sense of scale of the Roman Empire.

In Tivoli itself is the Renaissance **Villa d'Este,** built by Cardinal Ippolito d'Este in the middle of the 16th century as his retreat. (Open 9 A.M.; evening hours have been suspended, since night lighting is believed to have caused damage to fauna in the villa. Admission is Lit. 5,000.) The gardens surrounding the house present a formidable display of streams, fountains, cascades, and waterfalls against a lush background of greenery.

RESTAURANTS

Behind Tivoli overlooking the old town is the **Hotel Torre Sant' Angelo,** Via Quintilio Varo; tel. (0774) 23292, a restructured 10th-century castle with pool and private park for its 40 rooms with private baths. There's also a restaurant here. When not hosting political refugees at the expense of the Italian government the rates are Lit. 35,500–52,100. (No cards).

In Tivoli's old town is the **Sibilla Restaurant,** Via della Sibilla 50; tel. (0774) 20281. Sibilla is also the entrance to the Temple of Vesta. Dine on a terrace with a fine view; tables are actually placed among the ruins of the temple, dating from the Roman Republic. Meals run Lit. 30,000–40,000. Closed Mon. AE, DC, V.

Viterbo still has the air of a medieval city. Rail service from Rome leaves from Piazzale Flaminio. Viterbo is 50 miles away, on Via Cassia. A one-hour stroll can take in most of the sights within the walled city, including **Piazza San Lorenzo,** which covers the former Etruscan acropolis; the 12th-century **cathedral,** and the 13th-century Gothic **Papal Palace** where several popes were elected.

CITY LISTINGS

Neighborhood keys refer to page number of color map insert and map coordinates at which sight/establishment is located. Page numbers within the listings refer to the text page(s) on which sight/establishment is discussed.

Churches

Chiesa Nuova (New Church)   MONUMENTAL ROME, P. 24,
                                                                            B3
See Santa Maria in Vallicella

San Carlo alle Quattro Fontane
(San Carlino)   MONUMENTAL ROME, P. 24, D2
Via Quirinale and Via Quattro Fontane; p. 45, 46

San Clemente   ARCHAEOLOGICAL ROME, P. 24, E4
Via di San Giovanni in Laterano; Mon.–Sat. 9–11:30 A.M., 3:30–6:30 P.M.,
Sun. 10–11:30 A.M., 3:30–6:30 P.M.; p. 53

San Giovanni in Laterano   ARCHAEOLOGICAL ROME, P. 25,
                                                                            F4
Piazza di San Giovanni in Laterano, near beginning of Via Appia Nuova;
Baptistery: 8 A.M.–noon, 4–6 P.M.; Holy Stairs: 6 A.M.–12:30 P.M., 3–7 P.M.;
May–Sept. from 3:30 P.M. only; pp. 17, 23, 53

San Paolo Fuori le Mura
(St. Peter's Beyond the Walls)   OUTSKIRTS
Via Ostiense, pp. 57

San Pietro in Vincoli
(St. Peter in Chains)   ARCHAEOLOGICAL ROME, P. 24, D3/E3
Piazza San Pietro in Vincoli off Via Cavour, pp. 23, 41, 53

San Prassede   TERMINI, P. 24, E3
Via San Martino ai Monti, p. 56

Sant'Agnese in Agone   MONUMENTAL ROME, P. 24, C3
Piazza Navona, pp. 22, 47–48

Santa Maria d'Aracoeli   MONUMENTAL ROME, P. 24, D4
Piazza del Campidoglio, p. 49

Santa Maria degli Angeli   TERMINI, P. 24, E2
Piazza della Repubblica, pp. 17, 54

Santa Maria dei Miracoli   MONUMENTAL ROME, P. 24, C1
Via del Corso, Piazza del Popolo, p. 42

Santa Maria del Popolo   MONUMENTAL ROME, P. 24, C1
Piazza del Popolo, p. 42–43

Santa Maria della Vittoria   TERMINI, P. 24, E2
Via XX Settembre, p. 55

Santa Maria di Monte Santi   MONUMENTAL ROME, P. 24, C1
Via del Corso, Piazza del Popolo, p. 42

Santa Maria in Cosmedin   ARCHAEOLOGICAL ROME,
                                                                      P. 24, D4
Piazza Bocca della Verita, p. 54

Santa Maria in Trastevere   TRASTEVERE, P. 24, C4
Off Via della Lungaretta, in Piazza Santa Maria in Trastevere, pp. 17, 56

Santa Maria in Vallicella (Chiesa Nuova)   MONUMENTAL
                                                                  ROME, P. 24, B3
Via Chiesa Nuova, off Corso Vittorio Emanuele, p. 48

Santa Maria Maggiore   TERMINI, P. 24, E3
Between Piazza dell'Esquilino and Piazza Santa Maria Maggiore, pp. 23,
55–56

Santa Maria sopra Minerva   MONUMENTAL ROME, P. 24, C3
Piazza della Minerva (near the Pantheon), p. 46

Sistine Chapel   VATICAN, P. 24, A2
See Vatican Museums

St. Peter's Basilica   VATICAN, P. 24, A2
St. Peter's Square, pp. 23, 38–41

Historical Sights

Ara Pacis Augustae   MONUMENTAL ROME, P. 24, C2
Lungotevere in Augusta, p. 43

Arch of Constantine   ARCHAEOLOGICAL ROME, P. 24, D4
In front of Colosseum, at entrance to Via Sacra, p. 50

Area Sacra of Largo di Torre Argentino   MONUMENTAL
                                                    ROME, P. 24, D3
Corso Vittorio Emanuele, Piazza Venezia, p. 48

Barcaccia Fountain   MONUMENTAL ROME, P. 24, D2
Piazza di Spagna, pp. 22, 44

Baths of Caracalla   ARCHAEOLOGICAL ROME, P. 25, D5
Viale delle Terme di Caracalla; Tues.–Sat. 9 A.M.–6 P.M., Sun. and Mon.
to 1 P.M.; for opera information tel. (06) 5758300; pp. 20–21, 54

Bernini's Fountain of Four Rivers   MONUMENTAL ROME, P.
                                                    24, C3
Piazza Navona, pp. 22, 47

Capitol (Campidoglio)   MONUMENTAL ROME, P. 24, D3
Piazza del Campidoglio, pp. 16, 21, 41, 49

Castel Sant'Angelo   VATICAN, P. 24, B2
Lungotevere Castello, pp. 16, 21, 35

Catacombs   ARCHAEOLOGICAL ROME
San Callisto, Appian Way 110; San Sebastiano, Appian Way 136; 8:30
A.M.–noon, 2:30–5:30 P.M. in summer, in winter, to 5 P.M., pp. 17, 21, 54

Circus Maximus   ARCHAEOLOGICAL ROME, P. 25, D4
Foot of Palatine Hill, p. 54

Colosseum   ARCHAEOLOGICAL ROME, P. 24, D4
Via Dei Fori Imperiali; 9 A.M.–3:30 P.M. in winter, to 7 P.M. in summer,
Sun. to 1 P.M., pp. 16–17, 20, 21, 52–53

Diocletian Baths   TERMINI, P. 24, E2
Piazza della Repubblica, pp. 17, 54

Mausoleum of Augustus   MONUMENTAL ROME, P. 24, C2
Piazza Augustus Imperatore, p. 43

Moor Fountain   MONUMENTAL ROME, P. 24, C3
Piazza Navona, p. 47

Neptune Fountain   MONUMENTAL ROME, P. 24, C3
Piazza Navona, p. 47

Palatine Hill   ARCHAEOLOGICAL ROME, P. 24, D4
9 A.M.–7 P.M., winters to 5 P.M., pp. 17, 22, 52

Palazzo del Quirinale   MONUMENTAL ROME, P. 24, D3
Quirinale Hill; tel. (06) 46991; open by appt. only, p. 45

Palazzo della Cancelleria   MONUMENTAL ROME, P. 24, C3
Corso Vittorio Emanuele, p. 48

Palazzo Farnese   MONUMENTAL ROME, P. 24, C3
Piazza Farnese, p. 48

Palazzo Venezia   MONUMENTAL ROME, P. 24, D3
Piazza Venezia, p. 48

Pantheon   MONUMENTAL ROME, P. 24, C3
Piazza della Rotonda, pp. 22, 45, 47

Piazza del Campidoglio, pp. 41, 48   MONUMENTAL ROME, P.
                                                                   24, D3

Piazza Navona, pp. 22, 41, 47   MONUMENTAL ROME, P. 24,
                                                                      C3

Piazza del Popolo, pp. 22, 42   MONUMENTAL ROME, P. 24, C1

Piazza di Spagna, pp. 22, 44   MONUMENTAL ROME, P. 24, D2

Porto del Popolo   MONUMENTAL ROME, P. 24, C1
Piazza del Popolo, p. 22, 42

Roman Forum   ARCHAEOLOGICAL ROME, P. 24, D3/D4
9 A.M.–one hour before sunset, from 10 A.M. Sun., closed Tues., pp. 17,
23, 50–52

Trajan Forum   ARCHAEOLOGICAL ROME, P. 24, D3
Via Magnanapoli off Via IV Novembre; 9 A.M.–1 P.M., 3–6 P.M.; mornings
only on Sun.; Oct. 1–May 31, 10 A.M.–4 P.M., closed Sun. p. 49

Trevi Fountain   MONUMENTAL ROME, P. 24, D2
Off Via del Tritone, pp. 24, 44

Walls of Ancient Rome   OUTSKIRTS
Porta del Popolo to Porta Pinciana; Corso d'Italia to Porta Salaria, then
around Pretorian Camp to Porta Tiburtina and Porta San Lorenzo; Porta La-
tina to Porta San Sebastiano at Appian Way; open to visitors at Via di Porta
San Sebastiano 18, Tues.–Sat. 9 A.M.–1:50 P.M., Sun. and holidays 9 A.M.–1
P.M., Tues., Thurs. in summer, 4–7 P.M., closed Mon., p. 57

Museums

Borghese Museum and Gallery   BORGHESE, P. 24, D1
Piazza Scipione Borghese 3; tel. (06) 858577; Tues.–Sat. 9 A.M.–2 P.M.,
Sun. to 1 P.M., closed Mon., pp. 20, 56

Capitoline Museums (Palazzo Nuovo
and Palazzo dei Conservatori)   MONUMENTAL ROME, P. 24, D3
Piazza del Campidoglio; tel. (06) 6782862; Tues.–Fri. 9 A.M.–2 P.M., Tues.
and Thurs. also 5–8 P.M., Sat. to 11:30 P.M., Sun. to 1 P.M., closed Mon.,
pp. 21, 41, 49

Galleria Colonna   MONUMENTAL ROME, P. 24, D3
Via della Pilotta 17; tel. (06) 6794362; open Sat. only, closed in Aug., p.
45

Keats-Shelley Memorial   MONUMENTAL ROME, P. 24, D2
Piazza di Spagna; Mon.–Fri. 9 A.M.–12:30 P.M., 3:30–6 P.M., winter 2:30–5
P.M., closed Sat., Sun., pp. 22, 44

Modern Art Gallery   BORGHESE, P. 24, D1
Viale delle Belle Arti 131; tel. (06) 802751; Tues.–Sat. 9 A.M.–2 P.M., Sun.
to 1 P.M., closed Mon., pp. 20, 57

National Museum of Rome   TERMINI, P. 24, E2
Piazza della Repubblica; 9 A.M.–1:45 P.M., Sun. to noon, closed Mon., pp.
17, 54

Vatican Museums (including the **Sistine Chapel**) **VATICAN, P. 24, A2**

Viale Vaticano; Mon.–Sat. 9 A.M.–2 P.M., to 5 P.M. during July, Aug., Easter, closed Sun. except the last Sun. in the month, pp. 24, 35–38, 41

Villa Giulia (Etruscan Museum) **BORGHESE, P. 24, C1**

Piazzale di Villa Giulia 9; tel. (06) 3601951. 9 A.M.–2 P.M.; Wed. to 6:30 P.M. in winter, 3–7:30 in summer; Sun. to 1 P.M., closed Mon., p. 57

Parks and Gardens

Villa Borghese, pp. 20, 56 **BORGHESE, P. 24, D1**

Shops

Antinco Caffè Moda **TERMINI, P. 24, D3**

Via Genova 12; tel. 4743323, p. 64

Benetton **MONUMENTAL ROME, P. 24, C2; VATICAN, P. 24, B2**

Via dei Condotti 59, tel. 6797982; and Via Cola di Rienzo 225, p. 62

Bezzi **VATICAN, P. X, XX**

Via Colonna 43; tel. 3604800, p. 63

Brioni **NEAR MONUMENTAL, P. 24, D2**

Via Barberini 75–83; tel. 484517, p. 62

Bruno Magli **MONUMENTAL, P. 24, C3 and D2; VIA VENETO, P. 24, D2; VATICAN, P. 24, B2**

Via del Gambero 1, tel. 6793802; Via Barberini 94, tel. 486850; Via Veneto 70a, tel. 464355; and Via Cola di Rienzo 237, tel. 351972, p. 62

Bulgari **MONUMENTAL ROME, P. 24, D2**

Via dei Condotti 70; tel. 6793876, p. 62

Cesari **MONUMENTAL ROME, P. 24, C2 and D2**

Via del Babuino 16, tel. 3611441; Via Barberini 1, tel. 463035, p. 63

Chicco **NEAR MONUMENTAL ROME, P. 24, C1**

Via della Penna 13–19, p. 64

Cicogna **MONUMENTAL ROME, P. 24, C/D2, VATICAN, P. 24, B2**

Via Frattina 138, tel. 6791912; Via Cola di Rienzo, tel. 6530557, p. 64

Cipria **VATICAN, P. 24, B2**

Via Ottaviano 58–64, p. 64

Coin **ARCHAEOLOGICAL ROME, P. 25, F4**

Piazzale Appia, Porta San Giovanni, p. 62

Cose cosi **VATICAN, P. 24, A2**

Via Candia 75A; tel. 352184, p. 64

Di Cori **MONUMENTAL ROME, P. 24, D2**

Piazza di Spagna 53; tel. 6784439, p. 63

DiPorto **VATICAN, P. 24, B2**

Via Cola di Rienzo 186, p. 64

Emporio Armani **MONUMENTAL ROME, P. 24, C2**

Via del Babuino 140; tel. 6788454, p. 62

Fallani **VATICAN, P. 24, B2**

Via Vitelleschi 20–24 and 28–32; tel. 6542652, p. 63

Fendi **MONUMENTAL ROME, P. 24, C2**

Via Borgognona 39; tel. 6797641, p. 62

For Man   VATICAN, P. 24, B2
   Via Cola di Rienzo 184; tel. 6874661, p. 64

Fornari   MONUMENTAL ROME, P. 24, C2
   Via dei Condotti 80; tel. 6794285, p. 63

Gaj   VATICAN, P. 24, B2
   Piazza Cola di Rienzo 120–122, p. 64

Gianfranco Ferre   MONUMENTAL ROME, P. 24, C2
   Via Borgognona 8, tel. 6797445; Via Borgognona 42B; tel. 6790050, p. 62

Gianni Versace   MONUMENTAL ROME, P. 24, D2 and C2
   Via Bocca di Leone 27, tel. 6780521; Via Borgognona 29; tel. 6795492, p.
63

Giannotti 1880   VATICAN, P. 24, C2
   Longotevere Mellini 44, Scala Valadier; tel. 3213996, p. 63

Giansanti   VIA VENETO AREA, P. 24, D2
   Via Sicilia 40; tel. 493594, p. 63

Giorgio Armani   MONUMENTAL ROME, P. 24, C2
   Via del Babuino 102; tel. 6793777, p. 62

Gucci   MONUMENTAL ROME, P. 24, C2
   Via dei Condotti 8; tel. 6789340, p. 62

Krizia   MONUMENTAL ROME, P. 24, D2
   Piazza di Spagna 77–78; tel. 6793419, p. 62

Luisa Spagnoli   VIA VENETO, P. 24, D2; MONUMENTAL ROME,
                                            P. 24, C/D2; C2; D2
   Via Veneto 130, tel. 465881; Via Frattina 116, tel. 6795517; Via del Corso
385, tel. 6793983; and Via Barberini 84, 460757, p. 63

Mario Valentino   MONUMENTAL ROME, P. 24, D2
   Via Frattina 58, tel. 6791242; Frattina 84, tel. 6791246, p. 63

Max Mara   MONUMENTAL ROME, P. 24, D2 and C2; VATICAN,
                                                    P. 24, B2
   Via Frattina 28, tel. 6793683; Via dei Condotti 46, tel. 6787946; Via Cola
di Rienzo 275, p. 64

Missoni   MONUMENTAL ROME, P. 24, D2, D2, AND C2
   Via Borgognona 38B, tel. 6797971; for men: Piazza di Spagna 78, tel.
6792555; for women: Via del Babuino, tel. 679791, p. 62

Pier Caranti   MONUMENTAL ROME, P. 24, D2
   Piazza di Spagna 43; tel. 6791621, p. 63

Polidori   MONUMENTAL ROME, P. 24, C2
   Via dei Condotti 21; tel. 6784842, p. 63

Raphael Junior   VIA VENETO, P. 25, D2
   Via Veneto 98; tel. 465692, p. 64

Raphael Salato   MONUMENTAL ROME, P. 24, D2; VIA VENETO,
                                                    P. 24, D2
   Piazza di Spagna 34, tel. 6795646; Via Veneto 149, tel. 493507; Via Veneto
104, tel. 484677, p. 64

Red and Blue   MONUMENTAL ROME, P. 24, D2
   Via Due Macelli 57–58; tel. 6791933, p. 64

Richard Ginori   VATICAN, P. 24, B2 AND C2; MONUMENTAL
                                               ROME, P. 24, D2
   Via Cola di Rienzo 223, tel. 352138; Via dei Condotti 87–90, tel. 6784151;
and Via del Tritone 177, tel. 6793836, p. 62

Rinascente MONUMENTAL ROME, 24, C2; NEAR BORGHESE, P. 24, E1
Piazza Colonna; Piazza Fiume, p. 62

Salvatore Ferragamo MONUMENTAL ROME, P. 24, C2
Via dei Condotti 66 and 73–74; tel. 6781130, p. 62

Standa VATICAN, P. 24, B2; TRASTEVERE, P. 24, C4/ARCHAEOLOGICAL ROME, P. 25, F5
Via Cola di Rienzo 173–181; Viale Trastevere 60–64; Via Appia Nuova 181–183, p. 62

Stefanel MONUMENTAL ROME, P. 24, D2; VATICAN, P. 24, B2; TERMINI, P. 24, D3
Via Frattina 31–32, tel. 6792667; Via Cola di Rienzo 191–193, tel. 352954; and Via Nazionale 227, tel. 485914, p. 63

Testa MONUMENTAL ROME, P. 24, C2
Via Frattina 104, tel. 6791298; Via Borgognona 13, tel. 6796174, p. 64

Trancanelli VATICAN, P. 24, B2 AND B1
Piazza Cola di Rienzo 84, tel. 6878753; Via Sabotino 52, tel. 319156, p. 64

Uomo In VATICAN, P. 24, B2
Via A. Regolo 15; tel. 3598363, p. 64

UPIM TERMINI, P. 24, D3 AND E3; MONUMENTAL ROME, P. 24, D2
Via Nazionale 211; Piazza Santa Maria Maggiore; Via del Tritone 172, p. 62

Valentino MONUMENTAL ROME, P. 24, D2 AND C2 AND D2
Via Gregoriana 24, tel. 67391; for women: Via Bocca di Leone 15–18; 6795862; for men: Via Mario de Fiori 22, tel. 6783656, p. 63

Valigeria Romana VATICAN, P. 24, B2
Via Silla 51; tel. 318437, p. 64

Vedette VATICAN, P. 24, B2
Piazza Cola di Rienzo 116–118, p. 64

Volpi MONUMENTAL ROME, P. 24, D2
Via Barberini 76, p. 64

Volterra VATICAN, P. 24, D2
Via Barberini 102–104; tel. 4819315; Via Cola di Rienzo 188, p. 64

5

UMBRIA

A landlocked window on the Middle Ages, Umbria offers a welcome respite from more torrid tourist trails. In the same way that 14th- and 15th-century pontiffs sought refuge from insurrections and political feuds, the harried tourist—when all churches begin to look the same—can break from the thundering herds and take to pasture in the "green heart of Italy."

Umbria's rolling, terraced terrain boasts cool, clear air and room to breathe. It is the only Italian region south of the peninsula's Alpine borders void of coastline and thereby free of the summer beach frenzy. More sedate Italian vacationers flee to the freshness and the marked medieval atmosphere. Once a conglomerate of city-states, Umbria is now a village-region. Except for Umbria's two provincial capitals, Perugia and Terni, practically all urban settlements have diligently maintained their stone facades, closely paved streets, and other medieval characteristics. Todi, Gubbio, Spoleto, and Città di Castello are excellent examples.

The two predominant powers—church and state—are proudly poised on the main squares of ancient towns. The cathedral and the palace of the local lord or commune were the keystones in 13th- and 14th-century development, which assumed a homogeneous character in popular as well as aristocratic building.

This was the heyday of Umbrian city-states. Perugia, today the regional capital, was the predominant political force until 1540, when the city succumbed to forces of Pope Paul III in the so-called "salt wars" (the Perugians had refused to pay the pope's tax on the precious commodity salt).

Umbria—the denomination existed in the Augustan era of the Roman Empire (27 B.C. to A.D. 14)—remained a papal state until House of Savoy troops arrived in September 1860. These nationalist-minded Piedmontese forces ended the Perugian massacres by papal troops, and Umbria joined the Risorgimento's unification of Italy.

A strong religious sense is evident in this land that sired saints revered throughout the Catholic world: St. Francis of Assisi, St. Rita of Norcia, and Europe's patron St. Benedict of Nursia (Norcia). Dominican as well as Franciscan and Benedictine monasteries abound throughout the region. And the sepulcher of the saint who has touched everyone's heart is in Terni's Basilica of St. Valentine.

Lake Trasimeno, where Hannibal of Carthage routed Roman legions in 217 B.C., is one of Italy's largest freshwater bodies. Other attractions are the Roman-engineered Marmore falls near Terni, the Clitumnus (Clitunno) springs outside Spoleto, and the over 200-foot-deep well of St. Patrick in Orvieto.

WINING AND DINING

Umbrian DOC wines (wines certified not to be diluted with low-quality grapes) are Torgiano, Montefalco, Colli Perugino, Colli Alto Tiberini, Orvieto, and Colli del Trasimeno. The local liqueur is a Monte Ingino brew.

The region's cuisine is tasty and hearty, utilizing the excellent local olive oil and a wide variety of spices and herbs. When in season, truffels and mushrooms are prized additions to many local recipes. An antipasto is usually a wide variety of local *insaccati* (sausages) and ham.

Typical first courses are *tagliatelle* with a nut-cream sauce and a Castelluccio lentil soup. Second courses usually are pork or lamb, as well as local game including boar and hare. Often featured are roast stuffed pigeon and river shrimp, especially popular around Terni. Wild asparagus is a local treat, often used in a risotto first course. For a different sweet, try Terni's Christmas cake, *pampepato,* which includes dried fruit, chocolate, and pepper.

Dining out poses no serious problems in Umbria; clean, relatively inexpensive spots can always be found around the corner. When on a day tour, don't forget picnic possibilities. Just about any *salumeria* (a deli-like butcher) will make sandwiches on the spot. Or buy bread at a *panetteria* (bakery) and make your own sandwich with cold cuts from a nearby *norceria.*

Credit cards for our recommended restaurants are listed as accepted. "All cards" means that all of the following are accepted: AE—American Express; DC—Diner's Club; MC—MasterCard; V—Visa. Prices given are for a complete dinner (antipasto to dessert) for one person, unless specified otherwise.

TRAVEL

Flying

For those not traveling by automobile, Perugia is recommended as a base. Its St. Egidio airport—the only one in Umbria—provides a daily flight to Milan, as well as to Rome Mon.–Fri.

Flight times to Milan's Linate and Rome's Ciampino airports are 50 and 20 min. respectively. Bus service is available from Piazza Italia. For flight information, telephone (075) 66940. Considering the time involved in traveling between Ciampino and downtown Rome by bus, a Rome–Perugia flight isn't much more convenient than a drive.

Taking the Train

By rail, Perugia is 2¼ hours from Florence via Arezzo and 2¾ hours from Rome via Terni. The main station is in Piazza Vittorio Veneto.

Taking the Bus

For those who can cope with provincial bus service, the Perugia depot is in Piazza dei Partigiani, connected to the railroad station by bus routes 32 and 57. From Piazza dei Partigiani there is also an escalator going to Piazza Italia at one extreme of Corso Vannucci. This is one of the most convenient means of reaching the station from the center of the old town, since a bus from Piazza dei Partigiani to the main rail station is available about every 5 min.

When traveling out of town by provincial bus, always confirm return times after reaching your destination. Night service is rare indeed, so don't run the risk of needing another hotel.

Driving

The most practical way to visit Umbria is by automobile. The region lies halfway between Rome and Florence, and its capital, Perugia, is approximately 2 hours from each. The Milan–Rome Autostrada del Sole (A1) flanks the western perimeter of the region.

From Florence, the exit from A1 is at Val di Chiana, onto SS75bis, which skirts scenic Lake Trasimeno before arriving at Perugia. From Rome, take the Orte exit to Narni and Terni on the SS3. This road continues to Spoleto and Foligno, where the superstrada becomes SS75, and continues northwest to Assisi before reaching Perugia. An alternative route before Narni is the SS3bis, which passes Todi and Deruta before arriving at Perugia. Or you can take the Orvieto exit to visit the cathedral, then proceed up the Tiber valley to Todi on the SS79bis.

The Perugia–Todi–Terni–Foligno–Perugia oval is all excellent superstrada and can be driven in 2 hours.

Two interesting stops north of Perugia are Città di Castello and Gubbio. They can easily be visited in one day on a circular route from Perugia. The SS3bis north via Bagno di Romagna is a rewarding route to the Adriatic coast, and eliminates a Florence–Rome turnpike dash on any Venice–Rome itinerary.

CAR RENTALS
Auto rental facilities are available in Perugia through Europcar, Via Ruggero D'Andreotto 7; tel. (075) 61804. Neither Hertz nor Avis have outlets in Umbria.

ACCOMMODATIONS

Assisi (year-round) and Spoleto (during the Festival of Two Worlds, last week of June–first week of July), require confirmed bookings months in advance. But distances in Umbria are neither great nor time-consuming, and practically anywhere along the Perugia–Todi–Terni–Foligno–Perugia superstrada oval can provide a touring base. Credit cards are listed as accepted. "All cards" means that all of the following are accepted: AE—American Express; DC—Diner's Club; MC—MasterCard; V—Visa. Room rates given show the range between single and double rooms, unless otherwise specified.

Camping
Alternative accommodations are camping areas, which may provide furnished bungalows and/or minichalets that sleep four to six and are ideal for families. Several examples are:

Il Collaccio, 06047 Preci (PG); tel. (0743) 99430 or 99138. This is also a farm cooperative and asks Lit. 60,000 for minibungalows and Lit. 90,000 for three-room chalets. In addition to a pool and tennis courts, horseback riding is available. The restaurant serves produce from the farm co-op almost exclusively. This is the heart of Umbrian salami, sausage, and ham country; off-season courses are available on preparation and curing of meats. There are more than 20 acres of camper and camping space, and a number of interesting weekend packages are proposed for the spring and fall.

Centro Turistico Camping Pian di Boccio, Località Caglioli, 06031 Bevagna (PG); tel. (0742) 360391 or 360472. Over 200 acres in the heart of Umbria (21 miles from Perugia, 15 from Assisi, 12 from Spoleto, 15 from Todi, and 30 from Gubbio), just off the SS3 7 miles from Foligno. Primarily a campground in the strictest sense, but there are nine bungalows available that can accommodate as many as six. There are also flood-lit tennis courts and a pool, restaurant, bar, disco, pizzeria, and market.

For the less adventurous, here are suggested standard accommodations in cities and towns. Hotels are open year-round, unless indicated otherwise. Don't expect air-conditioning, unless noted.

Assisi
San Francesco, Via San Francesco 48, 06081 (PG); tel. (075) 812281; telex 660122 SF Azitur. With dining facilities, this 3-star,

45-room hotel, built in 1962, faces the Basilica of St. Francis (a 100-yard walk). Room rates are about Lit. 44,000–65,000, breakfast not required. All cards.

Subasio, Via Frate Elia 2, 06081 (PG); tel. (075) 812206; telex 662029 H Subi I. Year-round rates for the 66 rooms in this 4-star hotel that has hosted royalty and thespians alike are Lit. 90,000–150,000, which includes a required breakfast (called *colazione*). Scenic dining is possible on a vine-covered terrace overlooking the Basilica of St. Francis. The restaurant is closed Jan.–Feb. DC, MC, V.

Città di Castello
Garden, Via Aldo Bologni, 06012 (PG); tel. (075) 8550587. This 3-star, 61-room hotel was built in 1980. Rates, about Lit. 44,000–63,000. AE, DC, V. Dining facilities available, but under different management, which only accepts CartaSi (MC in Italy).

Gubbio
Bosone Palace, Via XX Settembre 22, 06024 (PG); tel. (075) 9272008 or 9271398. A beautiful location just 50 yards from Piazza della Signoria. Advance bookings a must. Also obtain detailed instructions on how to arrive by auto, as area traffic is restricted. This 3-star, 33-room hotel closes Feb. Dining arranged with the **Tana del Lupo,** Via Ansidei 21a; tel. 9274368 (closed Mon. and Jan.), once considered the best restaurant in Gubbio. Room rates are about Lit. 41,000–65,000. All cards.

Orvieto
Maitani, Via Maitani 5, 05018 (TR); tel. (0763) 42011. This 14th-century building near the cathedral was restructured in 1963 into a 4-star, 40-room hotel. Since the acclaimed Morino restaurant closed, it has had no dining facilities. Air-conditioning included in room rates: Lit. 77,000–120,000; mini-apartments, Lit. 141,000. All cards.

Virgilio, Piazza Duomo 5/6, 05018 (TR); tel. (0763) 41882. A 3-star, 13-room hotel, without restaurant, facing the cathedral. Rates are moderate—Lit. 44,000–63,000. No credit cards.

Perugia
Brufani, Piazza Italia 12, 06100; tel. (075) 62541–42–43; telex 662104 Gabb I. Five stars with all the amenities; conference facilities make it suitable for business trips. The 24 rooms with a view can go for Lit. 220,000–330,000. Air-conditioning is an additional Lit. 6,000. The Mr. Collins caffè-restaurant in the hotel is best at lunchtime. All cards.

Della Posta, Corso Vannucci 97, 06100; tel. (075) 61345. Perugia's oldest hotel dates from the early 1700s. It has an ornate facade and Gucci's next door for easy shopping. Mini-bars have been added to most of the 56 rooms. The 3-star hotel should have undergone its planned renovation by now. No restaurant.

Rates from Lit. 48,000–73,000 with optional breakfast (colazione). AE, DC, V.

La Rosetta, Piazza Italia 19, 06100; tel. (075) 20841. Across the street from the tourist information office, this 4-star hotel's 96 clean, comfortable rooms are governed by a polite, competent staff. Laundry actually returns in 24 hours. There's also a reasonably priced restaurant. Rates range Lit. 50,000–160,000. All cards.

Spoleto
Europa, Viale Trento e Trieste 201, 06043 (PG); tel. (0743) 46949. A 3-star hotel built in 1983 near the rail station and just half a mile from the central pedestrian island—public transportation readily available. Rates for the 24 rooms run Lit. 49,000–74,000 with optional breakfast. Air-conditioning is an additional Lit. 6,000 per day. AE, DC, MC.

Gattapone, Via del Ponte 6, 06043 (PG); tel. (0743) 36147. An elegant, 4-star hotel that has just doubled its capacity to 16 decorous rooms with wood-paneled baths. During festival time rooms are impossible to obtain; they're reserved for leading Italian and multinational corporations. A comfortable bar, lounge, and conference facilities are available (air-conditioning and restaurant projects are, alas, knotted in local bureaucratic red tape). Rates run Lit. 65,000–90,000. All cards.

Todi
Bramante, Via Orvietana, 06059 (PG); tel. (075) 8848381. A tastefully restored and expanded stone abbey half a mile from the center of Todi on the provincial road to Orvieto (24 miles away). Dining overlooks a scenic view of the Tiber valley. The 4-star hotel is open year-round. Rates for its 43 rooms are Lit. 80,000–110,000. AE, DC.

Cavour, Corso Cavour 12, 06059 (PG); tel. (075) 882417. This is a pure convenience pick. Ten of the 2-star hotel's 19 rooms have private baths. The one-hundred-year-old hotel does not have an elevator for its three stories, but it compensates by looking onto Piazza Garibaldi and is just half a minute from Piazza del Popolo. Closed Jan. 10–Feb. 15. Rates are Lit. 30,000–45,000. AE, MC, V.

San Valentino Country House, Contrada Fiori, 06059 (PG); tel. (075) 884103. This beautifully restored 12th-century convent and adjoining manor house in the same re-created styling is in an oasis of tranquility just half a mile from the center of Todi. The hotel has a pool and tennis courts. The 12 rooms are not numbered, but named in accordance with the authentic furnishings of each: Renaissance (from the 16th century), Paolina Borghese (from the 19th), etc. Advance reservations are a must June–Sept. Rates with breakfast: Lit. 179,000 single, 260,000 double. Average meal (antipasto to dessert without wine) Lit. 50,000 from *alla carta* menu. Open year-round. AE, DC.

The Umbria Oval

Perugia

A stark contrast to the modern structures and busy superstrada that first hit the eye on arrival is Perugia's walled old town, tracing its origin to the sixth century B.C., when it was the Etruscan town of Perusia. Compact and harmonious, its soothing atmosphere is a balm for the stress of contemporary urban life. A stroll down central **Corso Vannucci** (the promenade lined with stores, pastry shops, and caffès) leads into that urban *salotto* (literally, drawing room), **Piazza IV Novembre.** Here the past hosts the future as students from Italy's University for Foreigners gather around the 13th-century **Fontana Maggiore,** with sculptures by Nicola and Giovanni Pisano. (For a tour of piazzas in Perugia and elsewhere in northern Italy, see the Touring Section of Travel Arrangements, at the back of this book.) Joining the 13th-century **San Lorenzo Cathedral** (or Duomo) on the square are the Gothic **Priors' Palace** (1293–1443) and its **National Gallery of Umbria,** which houses works by Fra Angelico, Gentile da Fabriano, Piero della Francesca, Pietro (Il Perugino) Vannucci, and Pinturicchio, as well as a number of early Umbrian painters. Also on the square is the 15th-century **Collegio del Cambio** (a financial center built for moneylenders), with elegant 15th-century frescoes by Perugino. Perugia's most moody street, the medieval Via delle Volte della Pace, leads from the square, medieval **Maestà delle Volte church.** Also in the northern section of town is the 15th-century **San Severo church,** with a fresco by Raphael.

At the opposite end of the corso are the **Carducci Gardens,** built on the ruins of Rocca Paolina, the ancient underground fortress built by architect Antonio Sangallo for Pope Paul III in 1540; the gardens afford a fine view over the southern part of the city. Just a five-minute walk away is the second-century B.C. Etruscan gateway, **Porta Marzia,** which leads to the spooky, underground **Via Bagliona Sotterranea,** lined with 15th-century houses. (It's open regular museum hours.) Nearby is the **Umbrian National Archaeological Museum,** housing a collection of Roman and Etruscan relics.

One of the most popular local festivals is **Umbria Jazz,** usually held the first half of July.

Unless otherwise noted, museums and historic sites are open Tuesday to Sunday mornings.

❧ RESTAURANTS

Renato Sommella, Via Baldeschi 5, tel. (075) 65819. Renato and his English wife, Kate Jones, have just opened this small (thirty settings at the most), well-cured restaurant featuring seafood, all prepared in full view in a glassed-in kitchen. Fresh flowers, candles, and subdued lighting add to a refined, intimate atmosphere to accompany Renato's culinary prowess. Lit. 40,000–50,000 for dinner with wine, depending on main course selection. Closed Sun. and Mon., late July–early Sept., and over Christmas. No credit cards at press time.

La Taverna, Via delle Streghe 8; tel. (075) 61028. Down the stairs and just a block off central Corso Vannucci in the heart of Perugia, Gianfranco Marlucci offers good Umbrian fare in two clean, characteristic rooms seating a maximum of sixty. With a house wine the tab can still be under Lit. 30,000. Closed Mon. and July 15–31. V.

In Torgiano (9½ miles from Perugia) is **Le Tre Vaselle,** Via Garibaldi 48; tel. (075) 982447. This restaurant is part of a luxury hotel, often hosting conventions and conferences, in a restructured palace. There is a gourmet corner here for more serious gastronomical encounters. Following the chef's suggestions of the day can provide a delightful panorama of Umbrian cuisine. A meal costs approximately Lit. 60,000, including wine. AE, DC, V.

South of Perugia, off the superstrada, is one of Italy's most noted ceramic centers, Deruta. The SS3bis is lined with roadside vendors, but swing off onto the Via Tiburtina; at number 330 is Ivan Ranocchia's Maioliche Originali Deruta, which produces on the premises all merchandise displayed.

Todi

This immaculate little town best preserves the essence of medieval planning. Facing the splended **Piazza del Popolo** are the 14th-century **Priors' Palace,** the 12th-century **cathedral** with its pink and white marble facade punctuated by an ornate Gothic rose, and the **Popolo** and **Capitano palaces.** Although these palaces are not officially open to tourists, no one will refuse you if you ask to peek inside.

The **Gran Caffè Duomo** offers tables in the square for intensive contemplation. It also has a back room full of video games for restless children.

Fine views of the surrounding countryside are available from the adjacent **Piazza Garibaldi** and from the cloister of a former convent. Now the local administrative offices, the cloister offers a panorama that is worth the five-minute walk, down the narrow street to the left of the cathedral, which winds down to a small arch.

Another interesting church is **San Fortunato,** custodian of the crypt of Saint Jacopone da Todi, the Franciscan believed to be the author of *Stabat Mater.* This church is now undergoing extensive renovation. A number of **antique shops** are found both at the foot of the stairs leading to San Fortunato on Via Ciufelli, and just off Piazza del Popolo on Via del Duomo and Via del Seminario.

❦ RESTAURANTS

Umbria, Via San Bonaventura 13; tel. (075) 882737. Just off Piazza Garibaldi behind the Popolo and Capitano palaces, the summer terrace is a treat in itself. A full Umbrian meal from antipasto to espresso may hit Lit. 35,000. With just pasta and wine it's much less for a noontime break. Closed Tues. and Dec. 19–Jan. 8. AE, DC, MC.

Orvieto

Orvieto is west of Todi, and actually off the oval. The **cathedral** here is one of the most beautiful in Italy. Considered the apex of Italian Gothic architecture, the cathedral, from its splendid mosaic facade to its richly frescoed interior, reflects the artistic genius that thrived during the nearly three hundred years of construction, begun in 1295. The frescoes, begun in 1447 by Fra Angelico in the Cappella Nuova (New Chapel—also known as the Cappella della Madonna San Brizio), were completed by Luca Signorelli in 1504. Relics of the Miracle of Bolsena (the origin of the feast of Corpus Christi) are contained in goldsmith Ugolino di Vieri's Reliquiario Corporale (1338). Also to be admired are the wood sculptures (1331–40) by Giovanni Ammannati of Siena. The bronze doors by Emilio Greco were added in 1964.

Next to the cathedral are the 13th-century **Soliano** and **Papal palaces,** which preserve records on the history of the cathedral's three centuries of construction and planning. In front of the cathedral is an **Etruscan museum** in the **Faina Palace.** Off to the left (a five-minute walk) is the **Pozzo di San Patrizio** (St. Patrick's Well) that Antonio di Sangallo constructed in 1527 on orders from Pope Clement VII, who feared Orvieto would be without water if the forces of Charles V besieged the town after sacking Rome. The well is over two hundred feet into volcanic rock and is accessed by two 248-step spiral stairways, one for descent and one for ascent. The well derives its name from its alleged similarity to the cavern in Ireland, supposedly created by a miracle of St. Patrick's.

May in Orvieto is full of celebrations, especially the twenty days devoted to local wines (the dry white needs no introduction) and cuisine. For the Pentecostal Palombella (dating from the 15th century), a white dove slides down a cable to the front of the cathedral amid festive fireworks.

Try to avoid Orvieto on Sundays, when recruits from the air force basic training center have the day off and are met by family and friends; they overrun practically every square foot of local attractions and restaurants.

🐾 RESTAURANTS

Six miles from Orvieto on the Baschi-Todi road is tiny Civitella del Lago. Here father and son complement one another on the artificial Corbara Lake. Son Gian Carlo's quality menus at **Vissani** attract serious gourmets from near and far. Seven servings with different types of homemade bread to accompany each are just an indication of what's in store in this exclusive little Umbrian oasis that seats no more than twenty. A music menu is offered, so you can set your own mood for the evening. The tab can hit Lit. 100,000, but this is a prime example of the renaissance in Italian kitchens. Closed Wed. AE.

Il Padrino is Papa Vissani's two-hundred-seat restaurant next door, and if anyone has any doubts about who's boss in the family. . . . Traditional Umbrian fare is available here at more modest prices; a complete meal runs Lit. 30,000–40,000. And sometimes, when it's a slow night at Gian Carlo's. . . . Closed Wed. and July. AE, DC.

Both restaurants have the same telephone number: (0744) 950206.

Terni

Terni was severely damaged by Allied bombing during World War II because a steel plant and arms factory were aiding the Axis cause. Founded by the Romans in the seventh century B.C., Terni is gateway to the picturesque Val Nerina and only 25 miles from Rieti, capital of the northernmost province of Latium (Lazio). St. Valentine is patron of Terni; the saint's sepulcher is in the **Basilica of St. Valentine,** Via Papa Zaccaria, in the San Valentino district, which avidly celebrates the saint's feast day February 11–20. The basilica is located approximately half a mile from the first Terni exit on SS3 when coming from Rome.

Near Terni are the **Marmore falls** and the beautiful little village of **Labro,** which overlooks Piediluco Lake. Five miles from Terni, the man-made, three-tier Marmore falls were constructed by the Romans in 271 B.C. to keep the Velino river from flooding the Rieti valley. At the top of the 528-foot falls is an observation area reached by walking two hundred yards parallel to the canals from a small parking area. Below is the Nera River, which collects water from the falls when they are operating. Since the waters are utilized by local factories, the falls function at various hours depending on the season and day of the week.

Foligno

Situated on a plain (the only such Umbrian town except for Terni), Foligno has seen much of its medieval luster tarnished by expansion and industrialization. But the past is revived from the second Saturday to the third Sunday each September, when the annual **Quintana ring-lancing tournament**

features horsemen in 17th-century costumes representing
various quarters of town.

On display in the **city library (Biblioteca Comunale)**
is the press that, on April 11, 1472, printed Dante Alighieri's
Divine Comedy, the first printing in Italy of a book in Vernacu-
lar Italian.

Joining the Romanesque 12th-century **cathedral** and 13th-
century **town hall** on Foligno's central **Piazza della Repubblica** is the 15th-century **Trinci Palace** and its **art gallery,** adorned with 15th-century frescoes. Open mornings
daily, afternoons weekdays only, October through April.

Spoleto

Spoleto today is best known for Gian Carlo Menotti's **"Festival of Two Worlds"** (held the last week of June and first
week of July), a highlight of Italy's summer cultural calendar
with its fascinating combination of classical, contemporary,
and avant-garde drama, music, and dance. Of Etruscan-Roman
origin, in an elbow of the Tessino waterway, Spoleto was once
center of the Longobard duchy, which extended over most
of central Italy. Centered in town is the impressive **Piazza
del Duomo** and its 12th-century **cathedral** with frescoes
by Pinturicchio and Fra Filippo Lippi. Off the square is the
Via dell'Anfiteatro that leads to the second-century B.C.
Roman amphitheater. Nearby Via Cecili runs along an
Etruscan wall dating from the sixth to first century B.C.,
and leads to the town's modern **art gallery** in a former convent. In the opposite direction from the cathedral is the imposing **Ponte delle Torri,** reached from Via del Ponte
beyond the cathedral's parking lot.

RESTAURANTS
Il Tartufo, Piazza Garibaldi 24, tel. (0743) 40236. Emilio Di
Marco is an avid supporter of Spoleto's culinary traditions, but
also keeps an eye on the calorie count to accommodate weight
watchers. With his creative touch, flavor is not sacrificed. The
fare can vary in price from Lit. 35,000–45,000, depending on
wine and one's eye on the Valerina truffles. Closed Wed. and
July 15–Aug. 5. All cards.

SIDETRIP
Only eight miles north of Spoleto, off the SS3 headed for Perugia, are the romantic **Clitumnus (Clitunno) springs** (the
geese here have been known to go for the feet of curious children), the fourth- or fifth-century Roman **Clitumnus temple**—now a church—and, to the right, the conic cascade of
houses that is **Trevi.**

Assisi

One of Christianity's most revered shrines, the **Basilica of St. Francis** dominates Assisi. Actually the basilica is two churches in one. The lower church, custodian of St. Francis's crypt, is enriched with frescoes by Cimabue as well as leading exponents of the Umbrian school. The upper church is adorned with 28 frescoes, 24 by Giotto, that relate the life of the saint. Other Giotto frescoes can be seen in the church of **Santa Chiara** (St. Clare).

The town lives well in the shadow of its saint. Assisi is as immaculate as it is beautifully suggestive of its medieval roots. But its peaceful air is disrupted by the throngs of visitors in July and August during a yearly **music festival.** On Thursday, Friday, and Saturday of the first week of May, the **Calendimaggio folk festival** features archery competition in medieval costume.

❧ RESTAURANTS

Buca di San Francesco, Via Brizi 1; tel. (075) 812204. In the heart of Assisi under a medieval palace, this restaurant features typical Umbrian dishes as well as imaginative creations by the distaff of the husband-and-wife team of Giovanni and Graziella Betti. Giovanni is an accomplished sommelier capable of satisfying even the most capricious wine whim. A meal costs about Lit. 35,000, wine included. Closed Mon. and July 1–20. All cards.

St. Francis

St. Francis was born in 1182, the son of an Italian linen-draper. Taken a prisoner of war in Perugia in 1201, he came down with a fever and had a number of visions of Christ and the Virgin— during one of which he received the stigmata. Until this point in his life, Francis had been interested in a military career; his visions changed all that, and he was converted to Catholicism. A poet as well as a mystic, he preached a life of prayer and penitence, as well as love of nature and animals.

North of the Oval

Gubbio

Considered by many "the perfect medieval town," much of Gubbio, which is built against Monte Ingino, is a pedestrian island. Corso Garibaldi becomes the main promenade on holidays. Up the hill is spacious **Piazza della Signoria** overlooking the lower town. Facing the square are the **Consuls' Palace** and **Pretorio Palace** (both open daily, mornings and afternoons), and the **cathedral.** In the Consuls' Palace are the Eugubine Tablets—seven bronze plaques engraved with Umbrian and Latin script. These are among the oldest records of the Umbrians, one of the first ethnic groups known to have resided in Italy.

The square is the site of two May folk festivals. On May 15 is the annual **Race of the Ceri:** Three large, candle-shaped figures on huge platforms are sped by alternating 20-man teams in traditional garb over a three-mile course up the hill to St. Ubald Basilica. (A cable car is available for the less energetic tourist.) The three teams represent local farmers, merchants, and masons. The basilica is custodian of the "candles" *(ceri)* the rest of the year. The second festival, the **Crossbow Palio,** takes place on the last Sunday of May. The archers of Gubbio and San Sepolcro appear in costume for parades, flag tossing, and other events.

Also facing the main square are several **ceramic shops,** including Valentino Biagioli's La Mastro Giorgio. Gubbio has long been noted for its ceramics and artisans, of which Mastro Giorgio was one of the most prominent, having created certain colors, notably an iridescent red, that have defied imitation.

When walking through the streets around the main square, note one of Gubbio's most peculiar traits, the "doors of death." These squat little portals, often next to the main entrance of a home, served for the passage of coffins.

❦ RESTAURANTS

Alla Balestra, Via della Repubblica 41; tel. (075) 9273810. Umbrian specialties are served in renovated, characteristic 14th-century surroundings, or, during the summer, in an inner garden with a fine view over the lower city. The central location is at the beginning of Corso Garibaldi, which is closed to traffic on holidays when it serves as the promenade. Around Lit. 30,000 for dinner with wine. (Slightly less than proprietor Rodolfo Mencarelli's other local restaurant, **Taverna del Lupo,** via G. Ansidei 21; tel. (075) 9274368. Closed Mon. and Feb. All cards.) Alla Balestra is closed Tues. and Feb. All cards.

Fornace di Mastro Giorgio, Via Mastro Giorgio 2; tel. (075) 9275740. A refined restaurant has been restructured around the oven where the ceramics master purportedly prepared his masterpieces. Proprietor Ignazio Mongelli oversees the revitalized, almost forgotten local fare with imagination and creativity. The pecorino and pear antipasto and the pasta *maccheroni* with a bean and onion cream sauce are two delicious examples. Fresh flowers, soft lights, and courteous service make the complete dinner price of Lit. 30,000 hardly seem possible. There is even a tourist special for Lit. 22,000, but with some limitations. Closed Mon. and Feb. AE, DC, V.

Città di Castello

The famous medieval cultural and artistic center of Città di Castello is only a 45-minute drive north of Perugia on SS3. Medieval printing and ceramic traditions still flourish here.

The art gallery in the **Vitelli Palace** contains Luca Signorelli's *Martyrdom of St. Sebastian* and Ghirlandaio's *Coronation of the Madonna*.

Trasimeno

The 60-square-mile lake of Trasimeno is known as the "lido of Perugia." Hannibal wouldn't recognize the site where his Carthaginians routed Roman legions on June 24, 217 B.C. **Passignano** is divided into the old town, with characteristic towered walls, and the new area, with hotels, restaurants, and bathing facilities. Rooms are generally easy to get in Passignano except in August. Bungalows and trailers are available at **Villaggio Cerguestra** (see "Camping," this chapter). Motorboat service is available from Passignano to Maggiore Island, as well as to the town of Castiglione del Lago, across the lake, with its 14th-century medieval castle.

6

THE MARCHES, ABRUZZI, MOLISE

The Marches, Abruzzi, and Molise are three central, predominantly mountainous regions with over two hundred miles of Adriatic coastline forming the calf of the boot-shaped Italian peninsula. Isolation and rugged climate have bred a fierce spirit of independence here that dates from the ancient Samnite tribes who resisted advancing Roman legions longer than any other ethnic group.

For centuries the mountains and sea were the sole source of livelihood in these regions isolated by nature. The profane claim that the only escape from trawler or pasture was to the kitchen; regardless of the motive, the local cuisine is well represented in all major cities.

In an area deprived of a dominant artistic and cultural heritage, where survival was often the only question, Urbino is a fruitful exception. Yet the regions can claim numerous figures of prominence besides Urbino's raucous Renaissance master Raphael, such as Sulmona's Augustan-era Latin poet Ovid, Pesaro composer Gioacchino Rossini, Pescara's poet-adventurer Gabriele D'Annunzio, and Pescasseroli philosopher Benedetto Croce.

The natural beauty of the hinterland belies the hardships endured over the ages. Modern conveniences have alleviated the struggle but have detracted from the charm in recent times. No longer do shepherds gather flocks before winter snows to walk the hundred-mile-plus paths to Apulian plains. Now sheep are tiered in trucks for one-day turnpike trips.

And families are no longer divided for months on end. Just forty years ago in Pescasseroli, the main Abruzzi National Park town, men and women literally spoke different languages. The women, obliged to remain home to mind house and children, always conversed in the local dialect. The men, who journeyed south with their flocks for extended stays, tended to use the dialects of northern Apulia. (The annual migration of flocks is down to 200,000 sheep today, but 17th-century tax records show that migration once reached 5,500,000 head.)

The house-bound women of these regions developed wool-weaving skills that are still a major local handicraft. There are often roadside stands where these weavings can be found, especially on the drive between Teramo and Campotosto. Among the men, wood-carving flourished; examples can still be found throughout the regions.

Best Buys

If you're looking to buy local specialty items, try the following:

- Abruzzese bedspreads throughout the Abruzzi
- accordions in Castelfidardo (just southwest of Ancona)
- ceramics throughout the Marches
- furniture from factories near Francavilla al Mare
- handmade paper in Fabriano
- handmade pipes in Pesaro (at Mastro de Paja, Via A. Faggi 39)
- shoes from factories in Civitanova Marche

Hiking the old pastoral paths has become increasingly popular in the summer. Two highlights are the slopes of the Gran Sasso (the Apennine peaks of which Corno Grande is the highest) and the Abruzzi National Park. A number of towns and villages dot the sheep trails. Some have faded, others have prospered from the days when local markets filled with milk, lamb, and pecorino cheese.

An ever-increasing number of ski resorts have blossomed, geared mainly to middle-class Romans and Neapolitans (although there are resort hotels and rentals that cater to foreigners). Ski season generally is mid-December through the end of March. Definitely a local shortcoming, however, organization has not kept pace with development.

Environmental League red flags flutter along extensive areas of the Adriatic coast, indicating polluted waters (a problem clearly not limited to the northeastern United States). Development continues at a rapid pace, but too often safeguards for holiday beachgoers are lacking.

A "dead-end" sea, the Adriatic has insufficient currents north of Puglia's Gargano spur to rinse clean a basin subject to continued industrial and tourist development.

The best swimming is south of Vasto or in the small rocky inlet at Sirolo, 12 miles south of Ancona. Stretches of sandy beaches—the most extensive is the 12 miles from Francavilla al Mare to Pescara—are found all along the coast. Though hotels and concessionaires control most bathing areas, every town along the coast has designated public beaches. Concessionaires may attempt to extort swimming fees—often in no uncertain terms—but don't pay; the 15 feet inland from the high-tide line is public domain throughout Italy.

Most resorts in these three regions draw families with young children. The beaches are excellent for children, as the slope of the sea floor is so gradual that fifty to one hundred yards offshore the water is only waist-high on an adult.

But sun and fun are not prime motives for visiting these regions—better beaches are found elsewhere. Most of the area is virgin territory for foreign travelers; it is presented here as a north–south tour between more classical points of interest. On a Venice-to-Rome drive, the Marches, Abruzzi, and Molise will open a nostalgic eye on an Italian lifestyle that has not totally been sealed in the past.

WINING AND DINING

The sea and the mountains have molded gastronomic tradition in the three regions of the Marches, Abruzzi, and Molise. But most of the area's wines are produced in the Marches. State controls guarantee the following wines (labeled "DOC"): Bianco dei Colli, Bianchello del Metauro, Falerio dei Colli Ascolani, Lacrima di Morro, Montepulciano d'Abruzzo, Pentro, Rosso Conero, Rosso Piceno, Sangiovese dei Colli Pescaresi, Trebbiano d'Abruzzo, Verdicchio dei Castelli di Jesi, Verdicchio di Matelica, Vernaccia di Sferrapetronia.

Fish will be on the menu baked, broiled, boiled, fried, grilled, and in the widest variety of sauces. But be wary: Improper reading of the menu finds first-timers shocked when the bill arrives. The key word is *etto* (meaning hectogram, about four ounces)—diners are billed by the weight of the fish they order. To guarantee freshness, many restaurants present uncooked fish for the diner to choose from. The chosen fish is weighed in the kitchen; the number of *etti* are multiplied by the unit price listed on the menu to determine the total cost. (The same system is used for calculating the tab on a Florentine-style steak.)

Also keep an eye trained for an asterisk next to any entry. If so, check the bottom of the menu for reference to *congelato* or *surgelato*, meaning that particular entry is frozen. This indication is required by law; any restaurant serving frozen food without properly indicating that it is not fresh will have its license suspended, and revoked upon a repeat offense.

An exception to the rule is *baccalà* or *stoccafisso* (stockfish), usually cod, that has been dried and often salted.

Gnocchi, lasagna, and *pasta alla chitarra* (rectangular noodles) are favorite first courses after an antipasto of shellfish, local *insaccate,* or cooked greens. Most meat dishes will call for lamb or *porchetta* (roast pig). Sparerib buffs may be in for a surprise; *spuntature* in the tri-region area of Marches-

Abruzzi-Molise does not indicate spareribs, but lamb entrails, which can be interesting if one is seeking a spicy adventure.

When it's all over, if a good *digestivo* is needed, Abruzzi is noted for a liqueur that will disintegrate anything: Centerbe, about 150 proof and up.

Credit cards in the restaurant recommendations are listed as accepted. "All cards" means that all of the following are accepted: AE—American Express; DC—Diner's Club; MC—MasterCard; V—Visa. The prices given are for a full meal (antipasto to dessert) for one person, unless otherwise specified.

TRAVEL

The Marches and Abruzzi capitals of Ancona and Pescara, respectively, are well served by public transportation. Ancona is northeast of Rome; Pescara is due east.

Flying

Ancona's Falconara airport is 11½ miles from the central Piazza Roma airport bus pickup point. Daily, direct flights head for Milan (1 hour by air), Pescara, and Rome (1 hour by air). In Rome connecting flights are available to elsewhere in Italy.

Pescara's Pasquale Liberi airport is only 4½ miles from the old rail terminal on Via Guglielmo Marconi in the center of town, where the orange city line number 4 provides airport connections. Flights head for Ancona, Bari, Bologna, Milan (2 hours, 10 min.), Naples (55 min.), Rome (55 min.), and Turin.

Taking the Train

Ancona and Pescara are both on the Milan–Bologna–Lecce rail line, 1 hour, 25 min. apart by inter-city service. Milan is a 4-hour train ride from Ancona.

Direct rail links from Rome are via Orte, Terni, and Spoleto to Ancona (approximately 3 hours, Rome–Ancona); and via Avezzano, Sulmona, and Chieti to Pescara (about 3 hours, 40 min., Rome–Pescara).

Driving

Rail and bus traffic throughout these three regions can be annoyingly adventurous. Use of an automobile is recommended—especially if you want to move inland from the coast.

Small towns and villages along state and provincial roads that once made the journey to Rome a twisting, all-day affair are once again being passed by due to the two turnpikes linking the central Adriatic to Rome and to the Bologna–Taranto turnpike, which runs along the coast.

The 65-mile A24, the Rome–L'Aquila autostrada, connects with the 6-mile Gran Sasso tunnel. At this point, turnpike stretching from hilltop to hilltop narrows into two lanes before cloverleafing onto SS150 to cover the remaining 15 miles to Roseto degli Abruzzi on the Adriatic coast.

Roseto is on the A14, the Bologna–Taranto autostrada, which is the most viable route for Italy's central and southern Adriatic coast. Parallel to the coast is the SS16. From Roseto, Ancona is 78 miles north, Pescara is only 15 miles south, and Rome is 135 miles west; Ancona is about 130 miles from Bologna.

In addition to the A24, the A25 also crosses the Apennines. This completed 70-mile autostrada joins the A24 west of L'Aquila for a nonstop 135-mile Rome–Pescara drive that can easily be covered in less than 2½ hours. If time is important, connect with the A25; otherwise the Gran Sasso tunnel is the more interesting route.

CAR RENTALS

Rental facilities are:

Pescara: Avis, Corso V. Emanuele 161b; tel. (085) 4212442. Europcar, Viale Bove 46; tel. (085) 41017. Hertz, Via Tiburtina 289/1; tel. (085) 53900.

Ancona: Avis, Via Marconi; tel. (071) 50369. Europcar, Piazza Roselli 16; tel. (071) 203100. Hertz, Via Flaminia 32; tel. (071) 41314.

All three rental agencies can arrange airport pickups and drop-offs on prior notice. All offices are near the train stations.

❦ ACCOMMODATIONS

Lacking much of a hotel tradition, the Marches-Abruzzi-Molise must be appreciated for their simplicity and desire to please, though even the latter can be missing on the coast during the weighty July–Aug. demand. Inland the foreign traveler can evoke curiosity, and subsequently find pleasant surprises in reception.

An independent mountain streak in local character hampers local control. Coastal waters are too frequently dotted with Environmental League tags prohibiting bathing. But contrary to northern neighbors in Romagna, local administrators have responded slowly to improving conditions of the area's 200-mile coastline.

Dining service may often be considered rustic and nonchalant. But considering the basic simplicity of local recipes, yielding to nature's course may be appropriate.

If your priority is to avoid crowds, then try the peaceful isolation of Abruzzi National Park. Isernia and Campobasso are farther off the beaten path and can be good bases for hikers. Combine the Apennine foothills with the sea by swinging a half-hour inland to stay in Urbino, Macerata, or Ascoli Piceno, or try Chieti, just 8½ miles from the Adriatic.

Beach accommodations (in towns such as Civitanova Marche, Fano, Francavilla al Mare, Pesaro, and San Benedetto del Tronto) are a dime a dozen (regarding choice, not expense) and are often separated from stretches of sandy beach by shade-providing pine groves. In some areas rail tracks run parallel to the beach. For the best bathing either stay at Vasto or commute to Sirolo from Ancona (12 miles) and walk through a small wooded area to reach the coast.

The most developed beach area is in and around Pescara, which is Abruzzi's hub for air and train travel. Here there is ferry service to Yugoslavia.

The Marches air and rail hub is Ancona. Not nearly as modern as Pescara, Ancona is a leading Adriatic port with ferry services to Cyprus, Greece, Israel, Turkey, and Yugoslavia.

Air-conditioning is still considered a luxury here; don't expect it, unless noted. (Remember that it won't be necessary in most mountain towns.) Expect hotels and restaurants to be open year-round unless specified otherwise.

Credit cards are listed as accepted. "All cards" means that all of the following are accepted: AE—American Express; DC—Diner's Club; MC—MasterCard; V—Visa. Room rates given indicate the range between single and double rooms.

Ancona

Fortuna, Piazza Rosselli, 15, 60100; tel. (071) 42662 or 561286. In front of the rail terminal, this 58-room hotel is also near the port. Rates are moderate—Lit. 50,000–70,000; additional Lit. 5,000 for air-conditioning. All cards.

Grand Hotel Passetto, Via Theon de Revel 1, 60100; tel. (071) 31307. A fine view is available from this hotel, on the opposite coast from the port. Near the tourist information office and the best restaurant in town (see Ancona, below), the hotel provides elevator service to private beach facilities. Rates run Lit. 95,000–140,000 (air-conditioning included). AE, DC, V.

Ascoli Piceno

Pennile, Via Spalvieri (Pennile di Sopra), 63100; tel. (0736) 41645. Peace and quiet are assured in this 33-room hillside hotel just minutes from the center of the old city. No restaurant. Rates run Lit. 42,000–63,000. AE.

Campobasso

Skanderberg, Via Novelli, 86100; tel. (0874) 93341. Located near the railroad terminal, this modern, comfortable 68-room hotel is of neo-rustic design. Rates are Lit. 40,000–58,000. AE, MC, V.

Chieti

Hotel Dangiò, Via Solferino 20 (Tricalle), 66100; tel. (0871) 34356. This is a modern, hillside, 38-room hotel just off the road leading to Chieti proper. The commanding view of the countryside to and along the Adriatic makes it worth staying here, 5 min. outside the center of town. The restaurant (see La Regina in the Chieti section, below) is probably the town's best. Rates: Lit. 40,000–50,000. AE, DC.

Civitanova Marche

Miramare, Viale Matteotti 1, 62012 (MC); tel. (0733) 770888; telex 561431. The outstanding feature of this 4-star, beachfront

61-room hotel is its restaurant (Ciaccio, see below), the best in town. Room rates are Lit. 73,000–95,000. All cards.

Pamir, Via Santone di Santarosa 17/19, 62012 (MC); tel. (0733) 771777. This 26-room hotel with a typical summer-resort restaurant may require that meals be included when the season peaks in July–Aug. Rates are quite reasonable: Lit. 35,000–60,000; you won't be on a beach, however. All cards.

Fano
Continental, Viale Adriatico 148, 61032 (PS); tel. (0721) 84670. Located across the street from the beach, this 52-room hotel offers a fine view over the Adriatic. Both the hotel and restaurant are open from May 20 to Sept. 20 only. Rates are Lit. 39,000–57,000. No cards.

Corallo, Via Leonardo da Vinci 3, 61032 (PS); tel. (0721) 804200. This 3-star hotel with 22 rooms is just around the corner from the Viale Adriatico shoreline drive. Room rates are Lit. 36,000–56,000. If you're required to take meals it's a blessing in disguise (see restaurant listings below). No cards.

Francavilla al Mare
Punta de l'Est, Viale Adriatico 188, 66023 (CH); tel. (085) 4910474. A 48-room family resort hotel located on the beach. Rates will run about Lit. 37,000–53,000 a night with free parking. Open May 1–Sept. 25. DC, V.

Isernia
La Tequila, Via San Lazzaro, 86170; tel. (0865) 51346. Rates are Lit. 46,000–66,000 for this 60-room modern hotel offering a pool, a garden, and tranquility. Air-conditioning included in price. AE, DC, MC.

L'Aquila
Hotel Duca degli Abruzzi, Viale Giovanni XXIII 10, 67100; tel. (0862) 28341. The 35 new rooms and conference center under construction will probably net this 120-room hotel its fourth star. Parking available between the stilts supporting this hillside building. The best view is from the rooftop restaurant, Il Tetto (see below). Rates run Lit. 50,000–70,000. Traveler's checks accepted. AE.

Macerata
Hotel della Piaggia, Via Santa Maria della Porta 18, 62100; tel. (0733) 40387. This 25-room, 3-star hotel is centrally located in a renovated building. There is a bar but no restaurant. Reservations are a must during the July–Aug. opera season. Room rates, Lit. 35,000–58,000. Air-conditioning is Lit. 4,000 extra. All cards.

Pesaro

Most of the major hotels in Pesaro are along the seafront Viale Trieste. Cited because of its good restaurant (Da Teresa; see below) is the **Hotel Principe,** Viale Trieste 180, 61100; tel. (0721) 30096. This modern, 3-star hotel on the seaside strip has a bar and offers parking. Rates are Lit. 40,000–58,000. Closed Dec.–Jan. All cards.

Pescara

Hotel Esplanada, Piazza 1 Maggio 46, 65100; tel. (085) 292141. This is a 4-star, 145-room hotel facing a pleasant park along the beach. Parking and beach facilities available. Modern and comfortable. Rates run Lit. 75,000–90,000 per night; air-conditioning Lit. 6,000 more. All cards.

Hotel Holiday, Lungomare C. Colombo 104, 65100; tel. (085) 60913. This 51-room, 3-star hotel opposite the beach is handy for those traveling to or from Yugoslavia by ferry. Rates are relatively inexpensive—Lit. 25,000–46,000 per night, although meals may be mandatory in Aug. and rates will rise accordingly.

San Benedetto del Tronto

Roxy, Viale Bruno Buozzi 6, 63039 (AP); tel. (0735) 44414. This 4-star hotel with 74 air-conditioned rooms is the most expensive in town, but rightly so. Though the hotel is open year-round, restaurant service is limited to July and Aug. Off-season consolation can be found at the bar. Private pool and garden, hotel bus service to rail depot. Room rates, Lit. 84,000–132,000. All cards.

Urbino

Hotel Bonconte, Via della Mura 28, 61029 (PS); tel. (0722) 2463. There is ample parking across the street from this modern, 4-star, 20-room hotel a 4-min. walk from the center of old town. There is a bar, but no restaurant. Room rates, Lit. 55,000–73,000. AE, DC.

Raffaello, Vicolo S. Margherita 40, 61029 (PS); tel. (0722) 4896. Nadia Pecci bubbles over with enthusiasm when discussing her charming little 16-room, 3-star hotel just behind Raffaello's house. A three-story, 17th-century seminary has been totally restructured inside, with Carrara marble. In the historic old town, the Raffaello has a bar, but no restaurant. Closed Dec. 15–27, Jan. 10–20. Rooms are Lit. 59,000 (doubles only). (Nadia claims that her hotel chooses not to have air-conditioning, because it's a health hazard.) DC.

Vasto

Hotel Caravel, Viale Dalmazia 126, 66054 (CH); tel. (0873) 801477. These 18 rooms on the Marina di Vasto are convenient to the hydroplane for the Tremiti Islands. Rates run on the inexpensive side: Lit. 36,000–50,000. AE, DC, V.

The Northern Marches

Pesaro

Where the Apennines appear to step into the Adriatic, Pesaro, the seat of the northernmost Marches province, lies in a gentle cove at the mouth of the Foglia River, on A14 and SS16, 18 miles south of Rimini. There are many beaches in this coastal city, as well as a beautiful shoreline drive running between the sea and the hotels.

The **home of Gioacchino Rossini** (composer of *The Barber of Seville, William Tell*) is now a museum at Via Rossini 34. The house has been undergoing extensive renovations, but at press time was scheduled to open in 1989. Hours will be Tuesday to Saturday 9 A.M. to 12:30 P.M., and 4 to 6:30 P.M.; Sunday 9 A.M. to 12:30 P.M.; closed Monday.

Other points of interest are the 15th-century **Ducal Palace** that overlooks **Piazza del Popolo,** and the **Municipal Museum** (hours from April 1 through September 30 are Tuesday to Saturday 9:30 A.M. to 12:30 P.M. and 4 to 7 P.M.; from October 1 through March 31, Tuesday to Saturday 8:30 A.M. to 1:30 P.M.; closed Monday and holidays). Several prominent works by Giovanni Bellini are displayed in the art section of the museum, including the famous altarpiece Pala di Pesaro. The ceramics gallery not only testifies as to why 15th-century local artisans were among the most acclaimed in Europe, but also devotes space to masters from Deruta and Gubbio. Of particular interest is the center case of room 9, devoted to Mastro Giorgio of Gubbio.

RESTAURANTS

Il Castiglione, Viale Trento 148; tel. (0721) 64934. Luigi Antonioli's imaginative fish and vegetable recipes, the rustic ambience characteristic of the area, plus a well-shaded garden for summer dining combine for a pleasant experience. A dinner without wine will cost about Lit. 35,000. Closed Mon. and Nov. 1–15. All cards.

Da Teresa, Viale Trieste 180; tel. (0721) 30096. Teresa's seafood recipes seem to improve with time. Consider her son Otello's wine suggestions. Dinner with wine will run around Lit. 40,000. Open daily Apr. 15–Sept. 30. AE, DC, V.

Fano

Fano is just six and a half miles south of Pesaro on SS16. Situated in an inlet where the Metauro Valley opens onto the Adriatic, the town's fishing port is bordered by wide sandy beaches. Of historic interest are the **Arc of Augustus** (second century B.C.), the **cathedral** (12th century), and the **San Michele Loggia** (15th century). The SS3 arrives here from Rome; there is a superstrada through the Metauro Valley inland to Fossombrone. (Once an additional eight-mile stretch under construction is completed, Urbino will be even more accessible from Fano and the Adriatic coast.)

❦ RESTAURANTS

The Hotel Corallo's restaurant, Via Leonardo da Vinci 3; tel. (0721) 80400, offers good home-style cooking that makes any trip to Fano worth the effort. Specializing in seafood, the Panaroni family even has its own fishing boat, the *Corallo II,* to guarantee the freshest fare possible. Closed Sat. and Sun. evenings and Dec. 24–Jan. 10. A full meal without wine will run Lit. 30,000–35,000. (No cards.)

Long Beach, Via A. De Gasperi 9; tel. (0721) 82613, is a popular local favorite, with a mind-boggling number of choices. Dinner without wine will run about Lit. 25,000. Closed Wed. in off-season and Nov. AE, DC, V.

Urbino

Adjectives fail to do justice to the harmony, spaces, and artistic value of the once-isolated gem Urbino. There are other inland trips in Marches–Abruzzi–Molise, but this half-hour drive from the coast is the most worthwhile. The **Ducal Palace** here was commissioned by Federico da Montefeltro (whose family had dominated the area since the 12th century). Federico commissioned the building in 1444; the project was taken over by Dalmatian architect Luciano Laurana in 1465, and was completed 38 years later. No structure has so brilliantly unified old Gothic with new Renaissance design. Connecting the medieval castle and cathedral, the structure gives a palatial atmosphere to the entire town. The Ducal Palace is open Monday through Saturday from 9 A.M. to 2 P.M.; Sunday and holidays it closes at 1 P.M.

Urbino was where one of Italy's most gifted Renaissance masters was born. The childhood **home of Raphael Sanzio** (1483–1520)—with its noble courtyard—is now a museum containing some of his early sketches. Open November 1 to March 15, Tuesday to Saturday 9 A.M. to 2 P.M., Sunday 9 A.M. to 1 P.M., closed Monday; March 15 to November 1, Monday to Sunday, 9 A.M. to 1 P.M. and 3 to 6 P.M. As well as works by Raphael, the **Marches National Gallery** in the Ducal Palace also contains works by Paolo Uccello, Titian, Verrocchio, and Piero della Francesca.

The **Strada Panoramica,** a road starting from Piazza Roma, provides an exceptional view of the Ducal Palace as well as the lower part of Urbino.

Unless otherwise noted, expect museums and historic sights to be open 9 A.M. to noon, Tuesday to Sunday.

Luciano Laurana,
Palazzo Ducale (c. 1465–72)

The serenely elegant Ducal Palace at Urbino summarizes 15th-century cultural concerns. The building's patron, Duke Federico da Montefeltro, was a paragon of Renaissance noblemen. Trained as a soldier, the duke was a noted scholar and supporter of the arts.

The hilltop palace and city are entered through Francesco di Giorgio's enormous spiral ramp, a remarkably efficient form of transportation which parallels Leonardo da Vinci's concerns with engineering. Above this, the exterior facade of the palace combines fortifications with balconies providing bucolic views of the surrounding landscape. Entry to the complex is on the other side of the building, through the main city square. Fragments of stone cladding still in place indicate the intention to transform this square into a monumental public space.

The focus of the palace, however, is the interior courtyard. Four equal sides, composed of an open arcade on the ground floor and pilastered upper stories, gracefully encircle the space. A radiating pavement marks the center of the court, its sides, and corners. Beautifully crafted brick and stone emphasize the refined resolution of details. Given the harmony of this courtyard, it is not surprising to learn that Raphael's father was an artist at the Duke's court.

The interior of the palace, now a museum, continues the elegance of the courtyard. Of particular interest are the broad ceremonial stairs, the duke's throne room, the ornamental wood inlay of the *studiolo,* and the delicately carved balconies.

—Mary Beth Betts and Charles Ayes

🦅 RESTAURANTS

Enoteca da Bruno, Via V. Veneto 45; tel. (0722) 2598, can be hectic, with the tourist and student traffic, but the wide variety of food offerings and price make it worthwhile. Dinner with house wine will cost about Lit. 20,000. Closed Sun. and 15 days in Sept. DC.

Vecchia Urbino, Via dei Vasari 3/5; tel. (0722) 4447, is in a 17th-century structure once used to store grain, now elegantly renovated. Dinner will run about Lit. 25,000 without wine. Closed Tues. except Apr.–Sept. All cards.

SIDETRIPS

A scenic detour before returning to the Adriatic or heading into Umbria on the SS3 (only 8 miles from Gubbio at the SS298 intersection at Scheggia) is the trip to **Acqualagna,** where more than one-third of the truffles on the Italian market are found.

🦅 In Acqualagna, stop for a meal at **Al Cantinone,** Via Arco d'Augusto 62; tel. (0721) 803980. The wine cellar alone makes it worth the trip. Meals must be ordered in advance, so telephone Leonardo Gentili, who is at his best in the fall, when mushrooms and truffles are in season. Dinner without wine will cost about Lit. 30,000–35,000. Closed Tues. No cards.

Outside Acqualagna at the SS3 intersection, turn right for Umbria, but left to return to Fano on the Adriatic via Fossombrone. The 6 miles along the Candigliano River toward Fossombrone traverse the wild, deep **Furlo Pass** carved between Mts. Paganuccio and Pietralata. The artificial lake is a reservoir to satisfy coastal water needs.

Heading toward Umbria there is a pleasant detour to the **Fonte Avellana Monastery** on 2,240-foot Mount Catria overlooking the Cesano River. Nothing is more suggestive of medieval Italy than the sound of silence in front of this monastery, which once offered refuge to Dante. The bell tower dates from 1483. To reach the monastery, turn off the SS3 at Cagli and head toward Gramale and Frontone; in about 10 miles there is a second right turn to Caprile, then the monastery.

Near the Fonte Avellana Monastery is **Taverna della Rocca,** Via G. Leopardi; tel. (0721) 786109. A medieval ambience surrounds a rustic fireplace that provides a tempting variety of roasts. Dinner will run about Lit. 25,000. Closed Wed. and 10 days in Oct. No cards.

A halfway house between Urbino and Gubbio is **Da Secondo,** Via G. Leopardi 24; tel. (0733) 787404. The good local cooking is enhanced by the homemade *tagliatelle*. Dinner without wine will run around Lit. 20,000. Closed Sat. and Oct. No cards.

North of Ancona

North of the major Marches port of Ancona are two pleasant inland towns worth a visit: Corinaldo and Jesi.

Corinaldo is only ten minutes from the town of San Michele on SS424, which begins at the coastal town of Cesano, just north of Senigallia. To avoid the same road on return, just complete the twenty-mile loop to Senigallia. Corinaldo's 14th–15th-century medieval castle walls are the best preserved in the Marches. A nearly one-thousand-yard stretch practically encloses the entire town.

Jesi is less than seven miles west of the Ancona Nord A14 exit on SS76. The beautifully walled medieval old town traces its origin to 247 B.C. when it was a Roman colony. Piazza Federico II is named for the German emperor, allegedly born there under a tent on December 26, 1194.

The nearby **Bar Centrale** in the piazza is a good stop for coffee or the famous Verdicchio wine of the Jesi castles.

Ancona

The regional capital of Marches, Ancona was founded by the seafaring Syracusans in the fourth century B.C. With a population of over one hundred thousand, Ancona is one of Italy's busiest Adriatic ports and fishing centers. Ferry service is available to Cyprus, Greece, Israel, Turkey, and Yugoslavia, making the port very active in the summer with Italian and foreign vacationers.

Ancona centers around a natural harbor and was used by the Syracusans for commerce with Greece when Magna Graecia was the center of the Western world. With the Roman conquest the port was enlarged, and became prey for the Byzantines after the fall of the Roman Empire. One of the city's most important monuments is at the entrance to the town from the port, the **Trajan Arch,** remarkably well preserved.

Other major points of interest are the **San Ciriaco Cathedral,** near the Trajan Arch, a beacon above the port dating from the 11th–13th centuries; then, heading inland, the **archaeological museum** in a palazzo, featuring works by Titian, Lotto, Guercino, Andrea Lilli, and the most prominent Marches artists, Ferretti; the **Podesti Art Gallery;** the 13th-century church of **Santa Maria della Piazza;** and just down Via della Loggia, the **Loggia dei Mercanti** (Merchant's Loggia), from the 15th century; and Antonio Sangallo's 16th-century **fortress.**

For bathing enthusiasts, one of the three regions' better beaches is the sandy and rocky shore at **Sirolo,** 12 miles south.

❦ RESTAURANTS

La Moretta, Piazza Plebiscito 52; tel. (071) 58382. Near the port, Corrado Bilo makes the most of what the local fishing fleet provides daily. His trattoria is simple, characteristic of the region, and above all, friendly. Dinners without wine run Lit. 35,000–40,000. Closed Sun. and Aug. 10–20. All cards.

Passetto, Piazza IV Novembre; tel. (071) 33214. The best location has the best restaurant in town thanks to the never-ending efforts of Ideale Carini and Giancarlo Magnarelli. The terrace and view must also be in the tab, which is out of proportion with local standards: a dinner without wine can cost Lit. 40,000–60,000. Closed Wed. AE, DC, V.

The Southern Marches

Macerata

Macerata is easily accessible on a half-hour ride from the coast, either on SS571 just south of Porto Recanati or SS485 from Civitanova Marche. It is a typical Marches town with **Roman ruins, castle walls**—(with 32 towers), a **loggia** dating to 1500, and an 18th-century **cathedral.** Its **Piazza della Liberta** and **Corso della Repubblica** are promenades where local citizens meet and go to be seen.

Over the past decade the local summer **open-air opera** performances have acquired increased national importance and critical acclaim. Staged in the half-moon **Sferisterio amphitheater**—originally built for tournaments featuring a local variety of handball—the illuminated arches and columns provide an unusual setting over six hundred feet above sea level. Tickets go on sale in January.

You may purchase tickets at the box office (tel. 0733-45807; open Mon.–Fri., 10:30 A.M.–1 P.M. and 3–8 P.M. To purchase tickets prior to departure write: Biglietteria Arena Sferisterio, Casella Postale 92, 62100 Macerato.

❦ RESTAURANTS
Da Secondo, Via Pescheria Vecchia 28; tel. (0733) 49912. Mimma and Secondo Moretti's family-run restaurant is a local favorite, utilizing every square inch for its maximum sixty settings. Don't get carried away with the *antipasti,* there's more to come. A meal without wine will cost about Lit. 30,000. Closed Mon. and Aug. 18–31. V.

Civitanova Marche
Overlooking coastal villas, restaurants, and shoe factories, the attractive old town of Civitanova Marche, thirty miles south of Ancona, is perched four hundred feet above the Adriatic and some spectacular **beaches.** The old town's narrow, winding streets divide 13th- and 14th-century structures within the confines of fortress walls. The year-round Saturday **market** around Piazza XX Settembre is as much a local attraction as a tourist attraction.

❦ RESTAURANTS
Ciaccio, Viale Matteotti 1; tel. (0733) 770888. The tab can be expensive for an Adriatic resort, but "we have no rivals," declares director Luigi Sironi. An experienced sommelier, Sironi also boasts the availability of over five hundred French and Italian wines. Dinner without wine will run to Lit. 50,000. Closed Fri. All cards.

Da Peppe, Viale V. Veneto 241; tel. (0733) 74263. Peppe offers enough to satisfy most tastes, but he's mentioned here on the merits of his spaghetti with shrimp in a pizzaiolo sauce. Dinner with wine will cost about Lit. 40,000. Closed Tues. No cards.

San Benedetto del Tronto
Billed as "the pearl of the Adriatic," the popular resort of San Benedetto del Tronto is near the Marches–Abruzzi border. Extensive **beaches** are flanked by a long, seafront drive lined with palms and other exotic plants. Shopping appears to be as much a pastime as sunbathing. Ample space is given to products from local artisans and shoe factories, as well as top Italian and international designers. The town also is base for

a large fishing fleet; the local fish soup is the bonus on a brief stop.

❦ RESTAURANTS

Angelici, Via Piemonte 1; tel. (0735) 84674. When a fish restaurant is popular in a fisherman's town there has to be a substantial reason. Chef Ivo and sommelier Dino also draw heavily from the summer vacation crowd, so it's best to reserve as space is limited. Dinners run Lit. 30,000–35,000 with local wine. Closed Dec. 23–Jan. 20 and Mon. (except in July and Aug.). No cards.

Ascoli Piceno

In less than a half-hour one can cover the superstrada from the A14 Ascoli–San Benedetto exit inland to Ascoli Piceno. A Roman outpost over two thousand years ago, the seat of Ascoli Piceno province has spread beyond the original confines of the Tronto and Castellano rivers. The old triangle between the two rivers is typical of Roman urbanization, with characteristic walls and gates. The central **St. Francis' Church** faces one of the most beautiful squares in Italy, **Piazza del Popolo.** The flagstone piazza warrants a mid-morning or late afternoon visit for espresso or an *aperitivo.*

On the first Sunday of August the town hosts the **Quintana tournament,** where galloping horsemen in colorful period garb "joust" with a straw-stuffed Saracen warrior.

❦ RESTAURANTS

Kursaal, Corso Mazzini 221; tel. (0736) 53140. This restaurant, decorated in the popular European Liberty style of the late 19th century, is in the center of the old town near Piazza del Popolo. Regional meats and vegetables dominate the menu; a dinner without wine will run Lit. 25,000–30,000. Closed Sun. AE, DC, V.

Pennile, Via Spalvieri 13; tel. (0736) 42504. Heading a long list of local recipes are the *fritto misto* and *olive all'Ascolana.* Dinner will cost Lit. 18,000 with house wine. Closed Tues. and 15 days in Nov. DC.

Tornasacco, Via Tornasacco 29; tel. (0736) 54151. Probably the most popular local favorite, this relaxingly comfortable and courteous restaurant specializes in typical Marches cooking. Dinners without wine cost Lit. 25,000–30,000. Closed Fri. and July 1–15. AE, DC, V.

Northern Abruzzi

Teramo

The small town of **Teramo** is considered the cradle of Abruzzese gastronomical tradition. Superb is the *zuppa primavera* (spring soup) found at harvest time in May. This specialty can take at least a week of preparation to obtain maximum blending of ingredients.

The main point of artistic interest in Teramo is the **Romanesque-Gothic cathedral,** started in 1158. The upper facade and Ghibelline merlons were added in 1300; the ornate entrance is decorated with statues and mosaics. Inside is a superb 1433 gold sculpture by Nicola di Guardiagrele. Teramo is still not linked to the national turnpike network, though it is connected to neighboring L'Aquila by A24 via the Gran Sasso tunnel. The coast is only a ten-mile drive away on SS80.

RESTAURANTS

Il Carpaccio, Via De Gasperi 41; tel. (0861) 414723. Lit. 18,000 for menu of the day; Lit. 30,000 *alla carta* for local specialties with regional wine. Closed Mon. and Aug. 14–21. All cards.

Duomo, Via Stazio 9; tel. (0861) 321274. Carlo Rossi has few rivals in presenting the best of Abruzzese gastronomical tradition. Located in the center of the old city, this restaurant has a good assortment of local wines. Dinner will run Lit. 25,000–40,000 with house wine. Closed Mon. and Aug. All cards.

Campotosto and Amatrice

Welcome to the wilderness. One of the highest in the Apennines, the village of Campotosto, on the largest lake in Abruzzi, is known not only for good fishing but also for one of the best mortadellas (the pink pork *insaccato* dotted with lard) in Italy. The V-shaped **Lake Campotosto,** at 4,700 feet, is overshadowed by Gran Sasso. The lake resort is a good spot to hike, swim, or relax. The forty-mile drive from Teramo to Campotosto can take at least an hour, taking SS80 to the provincial road (on the right) some eight miles after Senarica.

Once part of the Abruzzi, but now in the Rieti province of Latium, **Amatrice** is 14 miles north of the lake. Known primarily for its food, Amatrice is home to one of the most satisfying pasta dishes, *bucatini all'amatriciana.* These fat, hollow noodles defy even the most able fork-winding, so a good bib may be needed; the spicy tomato sauce with thick, diced bacon is garnished with pecorino cheese.

Atri

The 13th-century **cathedral** in Atri was built in the transitional Romanseque-Gothic style, making it one of the most interesting churches in central Italy. Atri is twenty miles northwest of Pescara and just six miles from the coastal A14 Atri–Pineto exit.

🐾 RESTAURANTS

Facing the famous Atri cathedral, the air-conditioned oasis of **Alla Campana d'Oro,** Piazza d'Uomo 23; tel. (085) 870177, is perfect for a midday break from the rigors of touring. Be patient; many local recipes can take time. A complete meal here will run about Lit. 25,000 without wine. Closed Tues. AE, V.

Pescara

Pescara is the most modern city in the three regions of Marches, Abruzzi, and Molise. Here the past has not been allowed to prevail on the present. Manufacturing, seasonal hotels, and maritime services have attracted mountain folk seeking to abandon pastoral life. A nine-mile seafront drive parallels sandy **beaches** and an ever-expanding coastal development of condos and hotels attracting a national clientele. Under construction is a yacht basin south of the mouth of the Pescara River, which flows through the city into the Adriatic. Farther south is the commercial port, which provides ferry service to Yugoslavia. Poet-adventurer Gabriele D'Annunzio was born in Pescara in 1863. The two-story **D'Annunzio home** on Corso Manthone is now a museum. The museum is open Tues.–Sat. 9 A.M.–1 P.M. in winter; Tues.–Sat. 9 A.M.–1 P.M. and 6–8 P.M., Sun. 9 A.M.–1 P.M. in summer.

🐾 RESTAURANTS

La Cantina di Jozz, Via delle Caserme 61; tel. (085) 690383. Ideal for those with a large appetite and adventurous palate. Giovanni and Maria Teresa select and then impose on their guests three first courses, one second, a choice of roast, and a sweet. An enjoyable marathon: about Lit. 30,000 without wine. Closed Sun. evening, Mon., and Dec. 23–Jan. 8. All cards.

Taverna 58, Corso Manthoné 58; tel. (085) 690724. Giovanni Marrone's characteristic little restaurant is a local favorite, so telephone ahead of time. Dinner without wine will cost around Lit. 28,000. Near the D'Annunzio museum. Closed Sun., Aug., and holidays. AE, V.

SIDETRIP

About 30 miles west of Pescara on SS5 toward Popoli are a series of **churches and abbeys** representative of a once-predominant religious influence. The ninth-century **St. Clement at Casauria** near Torre de'Passeri is the best example of Romanesque-Cistercian architecture in the region. Popoli's **Church of St. Francis** in the central piazza preserves a fine majolica altar front and wood sculpture.

Sulmona

Ancient Sulmo, which fell to the Romans about 200 B.C., is today's Sulmona, just off A25 44 miles inland from Pescara and 92 miles from Rome. This medieval town is the country's *confetti* capital. Confetti are sugar-coated nuts that traditionally accompany Italian birth and wedding announcements. The town's main street, **Corso Ovidio,** is named after its most famous son—Publius Ovidius Naso, the Augustan-era Latin poet more commonly called Ovid. Navigating many of the narrow streets in an automobile can be more interesting than bumper cars at an amusement park. The main point of artistic interest in town is the Renaissance-baroque **Palazzo dell'Annunziata,** dating from the early 1400s. A market-town air is perpetuated every Wednesday and Saturday in nearby Piazza Garibaldi, which is bordered by a medieval aqueduct.

RESTAURANTS
Italia, Piazza XX Settembre 26; tel. (0864) 33070. Centrally located off the main Corso Ovidio, this simple, accommodating restaurant gained fame through the inventive prowess of Nicola Pavia. Siblings Luisa, Lucia, and Gino continue a family tradition in delightful dining. Dinner with a local wine runs about Lit. 29,000. A Lit. 16,000 tourist menu is also available. Closed Mon. and July. AE, DC, V.

Two nearby caffès offer a wide assortment of snacks, ice cream, and bakery goods: **Bar Grand Caffè** and **Caffè Gelateria Europa.**

Scanno
On SS479, 19 miles south of Sulmona, is Scanno, a summer retreat-winter ski station. Many local women excel in **embroidery, weaving,** and **filigree,** which can be purchased at many of the town's shops. The townsfolk can be seen in native dress on holidays and feast days. From its hillside perch Scanno offers a fine view over the Sagittario River valley and Lake Scanno. An even better view is from **Colle Rotondo** after a 15-minute **chair-lift ride** two thousand feet up from the village. During the ski season, which lasts until about the end of March, the chair operates sporadically.

L'Aquila
L'Aquila is a medieval market town in the mountain basin between the Gran Sasso and Monte Ocre, 65 miles from Rome on A24. Most of its low-lying stone buildings appear to roll over the city's hills. Once the most important southern town after Naples (with its own mint), L'Aquila, though the largest commercial center in western Abruzzi, has lost much of its glory; perhaps time has simply passed it by. But many reminders of a prestigious past are still evident. Of the legendary 99 castles and 99 squares that formed the ancient town, however, only the **Fountain of 99 Spouts** near Porta Rivera and San Vito church remains.

The most impressive church in L'Aquila is **Santa Maria di Collemaggio Basilica,** where the hermit founder of the

Celestine Order, Pietro da Morrone, became Pope Celestine V in 1294. In 1313 he was canonized St. Peter Celestine; his sepulcher is in the right chapel of the upper altar. A white-and-reddish marble facade with rose windows was added to the Romanesque church in the 14th century. The octagonal base outside the church was the foundation of an old bell tower that has been demolished. The town has an unforgettable history of earth tremors; a 1915 quake took a high toll.

To the left of the basilica is **Porta Bazzano,** one of seven gates through the ancient walls. Down Via Strinella is **Porta Castello,** which opens onto a park and the Spanish-style fort ordered by the viceroy of Naples, Pedro de Toledo, in 1530. This well-preserved fortress-castle is now custodian of the **National Museum of Abruzzi,** featuring Roman archaeological remains, medieval wood sculpture, and the prehistoric mammut *(Elephas meridionalis)* discovered at nearby Madonna della Strade in 1954. The museum is open Tuesday through Saturday from 9 A.M. to 2 P.M. and Sunday from 9 A.M. to 1 P.M. It is closed Monday and holidays.

Down Via Sara is the **Basilica of San Bernardino of Siena.** The sepulcher of the saint is in this late 15th-century church that is Abruzzi's best Renaissance expression. Note the carvings and frescoes adorning the wood ceiling. The bell in nearby **Torre Civica** (1300) tolls 99 times at sunset.

❧ RESTAURANTS

Il Tetto, Viale Giovanni XXIII 10; tel. (0862) 28341. This glass-enclosed, air-conditioned restaurant features Abruzzese specialties and splendid views across the city's rooftops to the Gran Sasso and other surrounding Apennine peaks. The restaurant serves all meals, seven days a week. Dinner will cost about Lit. 28,000 per person without wine. AE.

Tre Marie, Via Tre Marie 3; tel. (0862) 20191. Nestled in an alley just a block off the city's open-air market square, this national monument reflects Paolo Scipioni's devotion to his Abruzzese heritage. Local recipes and wine accentuate nearly a century of family tradition. Few Italian restaurants have such an abundance of regional character and charm. The hand-painted ceramic plates, tablecloths woven with regional patterns, and hand-painted, decorative wooden ceiling add to this testament to Abruzzese folk charm and tradition. A complete dinner without wine will cost in the neighborhood of Lit. 45,000. No cards.

Gran Sasso d'Italia

To reach the massif Gran Sasso d'Italia, travel 13 miles from L'Aquila on either A24 or SS17bis (Via della Funivia del Gran Sasso). By this reading, the **cable car** *(funivia)* to the highest peak in the Apennines may be open. It had been closed for three years due to lack of progress on restoration of the city-owned hotel at Campo Imperatore (where German paratroopers rescued Fascist dictator Benito Mussolini after his arrest in 1943). The cable car station can also be reached by city bus service from L'Aquila, 5 A.M. to 8 P.M. The 30- to 40-minute bus ride departs from Via Castello.

The town of **Campo Imperatore** (nearly six thousand feet up) is at the base of the **Corno Grande,** which, at nine thousand feet, is the highest Apennine peak. A number of **ski runs** are accessible from the *piazzale* further down the mountain, where there are also several hotels and restaurants. For more information contact Tourist Information, EPT, Piazza S. Maria di Paganica 5, 67100 L'Aquila.

Abruzzi National Park

First conceived in 1910, Abruzzi National Park was not formally recognized by the state until 1923. From A25, exit at Celano to reach Pescasseroli in the center of the park.

An elbow A24-A25 turnpike route can be used from L'Aquila, but the scenic Rocca di Cambio–Ovindoli–Celano route warrants navigating the winding SS5bis, especially for the view from the ski and summer resort of Ovindoli.

Visitors can camp in the park; no reservations are necessary. For those who want to arrange a hiking trip in advance, good maps can be obtained from IGM, Viale Strozzi 44, 50123 Firenze; tel. (055) 262341.

For more information on the park contact **Tourist Information,** Parco Nazionale D'Abruzzo, Via Piave, 67032 Pescasseroli (AQ); tel. (0863) 91461.

Southern Abruzzi

Chieti

Chieti is seat of the province of the same name, and is only eight and a half miles inland from Pescara. The town is nearly one thousand feet above sea level and offers an extended panorama of the Abruzzi coast. The main point of interest is the **Villa Comunale National Museum of Abruzzi and Molise Antiquity,** where most of the archaeological findings from the two regions are on display. Its prize piece is the Capestrano Warrior, dating from the sixth century B.C.

RESTAURANTS

Nino, Via Principessa di Piemonte 7; tel. (0871) 65396. New twists are provided to old local recipes here. In addition to a good house wine, there is a variety of local brands. Dinner with wine will run about Lit. 25,000. Closed Fri. and Aug. No cards.

La Regina, Via Solferino 20 (Tricalle); tel. (0871) 34358. Restaurant of the Hotel Dangiò, located just off the road leading to Chieti proper, this is probably Chieti's best restaurant, with a fine hillside view to the coast. Proprietor Nicola Ranieri's dedication to Italian cuisine in general and Abruzzese in particular is reflected by an inviting menu that can change substantially from season to season. Dinner with wine will run somewhere around Lit. 35,000–40,000. Closed Mon. AE, DC.

The Sea Resorts

Chieti's main sea resorts are **Ortona, Vasto,** and **Francavilla al Mare.** The quickest transportation to the **Tremiti Islands** (1 hour, 15 minutes by hydroplane) departs from Marina di Vasto (see The Deep South chapter). Another point of interest in the province is **Lanciano,** between the Maiella Apennines and the Adriatic. Its **Santa Maria Maggiore church** was built in 1227 on the ruins of the Temple of Apollo, and the town's cathedral was erected in 1389 on a triple-arched Roman bridge. The cathedral is custodian of a fine silver cross by Nicola di Guardiagrele.

🦐 RESTAURANTS

In **Francavilla al Mare** is **Casa Mia,** Via Alcione 115A; tel. (085) 87147. This local favorite can suffer from the crunch of the July–Aug. seasonal rush. Dinner with wine will cost Lit. 35,000–40,000. Closed Mon. and Jan. AE, DC.

In **Lanciano,** try **Taverna Ranieri,** Via Luigi De Crecchio 42; tel. (0872) 32102. Previous owner Nicola Ranieri was a local legend. Carlino Caroselli is trying to perfect his master's touch. Dinner with wine: around Lit. 35,000. Closed Mon. and Sept. 15–30. AE, DC, V.

In **Ortona,** the recommended restaurant is **Miramare,** Largo Farnese 15; tel. (086) 912593. Suggestively located in the walls of the Farnese Palace, this is a rare commodity—it maintains a steady pace even under the surge of summer holiday makers. Seafood, liver sausages, and roast *scamorza* cheese are recommended. Dinner with wine will run Lit. 25,000–40,000. Closed Sun. and Nov. 15–Dec. 15. AE, DC.

Vasto's best is **Il Corsaro,** Via Osca 32 (Punta Penne Porto, 4 miles north); tel. (0873) 50113. "Pirate" proprietor Claudio Cusci provides a seafood feast on the sea to accompany his guitar and multilingual repertoire. A meal will cost about Lit. 50,000–60,000 including wine. Closed Mon., except during the summer. AE, DC.

Molise

Mountainous Molise is the least populated Italian region. Created in 1963 from the southern extremity of the Abruzzi, Molise now consists of the provinces of Campobasso and Isernia, most of which once belonged to Lazio's (Latium) Frosinone. The state turnpike network has yet to penetrate the area, which must rely on SS87 from the Adriatic resort of Termoli (to reach Campobasso, fifty miles) and the SS17 south from the Rome–Pescara A25 (to Isernia). These two provincial seats (Campobasso is also the regional administrative center) are only thirty miles apart, via SS17 and SS87. Many mountain settlements are so remote it was once said they were only accessible in four days by mule and two hours by eagle.

Termoli

The old section of Termoli is atop a rocky coastal spur jutting into the Adriatic. Adjacent are some typical Adriatic yellow-sand beaches. The town's **12th-century Romanesque cathedral** has survived pirates, bandits, and various restoration attempts. In a crypt beneath the church is a mosaic of Eastern inspiration dating to the 6th and 7th centuries. The **fortress** ordered by Frederick II was the first in an extended chain of protective outposts along the Adriatic and over the mountains of Basilicata and Calabria.

Campobasso

Inland, the town of Campobasso climbs a hill dominated by the 16th-century **Monforte castle** dating from Lombard domination.

RESTAURANTS

Il Potestà, Vicolo Persichillo 3; tel. (0874) 311101. The Neapolitan influence is strong in this local favorite, but local fare is the true flare. Except to pay Lit. 45,000 for a complete dinner with wine. Closed Sun. and Aug. AE.

Pub, Via Palombo 38; tel. (0874) 94665. No name could be more deceiving in this certainly Molise trattoria. Dinner will run Lit. 25,000–30,000 with wine. Closed Sun.

Just two and a half miles away in Ferrazzano is a **15th-century castle** worth seeing. You can tour the castle any day from 8 A.M. to 1 P.M. Also in the area, seven miles north toward Termoli, is the 12th-century Romanesque **Santa Maria della Strada** with its tall bell tower, surprisingly intact. The church contains a 15th-century Gothic tomb.

Isernia

The town of Isernia has been ravaged repeatedly by war and natural calamities. Remains of this ancient Samnitic settlement are found in the **Civic Museum,** once a convent. One of the town's most curious traditions is the June **onion festival,** held every year June 27 to 29. (June 29 is the feast day of Sts. Peter and Paul.) It dates from the year 1250, when it was held in front of the **cathedral of San Pietro** (St. Peter), which was the center of the mountain village that is now the capital of the province of Isernia. The festival today is basically a county fair and has expanded to occupy most of the main street of the town, Corso Risorgimento. It features any and all local produce, from onions to livestock. The gypsy camp gets into the act with "luna park" rides, games, and amusements. However, the onion still reigns supreme throughout the festivities.

RESTAURANTS

Taverna Maresca, Corso Macelli 186; tel. (0865) 3976. Situated in a renovated 13th-century building, this tavern is nearly 200 years old. A nearby gypsy camp has influenced preparation of the best local fare in town. A dinner with local wine will cost about Lit. 18,000–22,000. Closed Sun. and Aug. No cards.

SIDETRIP

In remote **Agnone,** on secondary SS86 from Isernia to coastal Vasto, is a family foundry that since the 13th century has provided church bells for the four corners of the earth, from New York to Ceylon. Pope John XXIII personally contacted the owners, the Marinelli brothers, to order bells for St. Paul's Basilica in Rome.

7

FLORENCE AND TUSCANY

Tuscany is the garden of Florence (Firenze). The regional capital, considered by many to be the cultural capital of Europe, overshadows its province. But the city of the Medici as seen today is easily traced to November 4, 1966, when the dark, murky waters of the Arno roared over their embankments and poured destruction through the city and its priceless treasures.

Every malaise of Italian bureaucracy came to light as the list of masterpieces lost forever or seriously damaged grew. Cimabue's *Crucifixion* fresco was damaged beyond repair, as were many lesser known works.

Somewhat symbolic was the Italian state television news the evening of the disaster, which used as its lead story then-President Giuseppe Saragat at a long-since-forgotten ribbon-cutting ceremony. Then came coverage of the Florence flood.

But the intensive pride of the Florentine—a trait that in less trying times can seem provincial arrogance—emerged on all fronts. The city's leading cultural and intellectual figures took to the streets in hip boots to wallow through subsiding waters and mounds of mud, leading armies of volunteers in recovering, cataloging, cleaning, and storing works of art and volumes upon volumes of ancient books, records, and ledgers. The race against time centered on the books and manuscripts, since glue from bindings had seeped between pages and threatened to seal them forever. Relief caravans were stopped at the city limits and diverted to other disaster areas in the country; Florence had decided not to accept overtures of solidarity from the national government.

In the end, the city survived the flood. The cleanup operation even opened underground storage areas that had all but been forgotten, and sculptures and paintings were uncovered that negligent bureaucrats had condemned to oblivion. As Florentines began to rediscover the beauty of their city, years of complacency were swept aside, and a city that had been mired in time was restored to beauty.

The Renaissance capital was indeed reborn. For the future of Florence the flood was a blessing in disguise.

The city's documented history dates to 59 B.C., when a Roman colony was established on the remains of an ancient village in the marshland along the Arno river. Its geographical position was an asset to its rise as a major trade center, for which supremacy was often contested.

In medieval times Florence was a Guelph city allied with the papacy. By the mid-15th century when the Medici came to power, Florence dominated all of Tuscany except for Siena and Lucca with its explosion of the creative arts and sciences. Another century was needed to bring Siena into the fold, but Lucca resisted until 1847. Twelve years later, Florence and all of Tuscany joined the unification of Italy under the Savoys, Florence even serving as capital of the united kingdom for five years in the 1860s.

Florence's Roman past has created serious controversy in recent times. Ruins were discovered during the resurfacing of the Piazza della Signoria, and the dispute continues on whether to unearth the Roman remains and deface one of the world's most charming Renaissance squares, once the center of power among Tuscan city states in the never-ending Guelph and Ghibelline conflicts.

Today Florence maintains its Renaissance legacy of artistic beauty and grace together with an ever-sharpening sense of its commercial and trading traditions. Its able craftsmen are internationally noted for their prowess in working leather, textiles, glass, metals, and wood. Its museums are legendary and exhaustive.

Tuscany's other eight provinces pale next to Florence's abundances. Yet they contain breathtaking medieval towns like Siena, where the light and architecture are unforgettable, and Pisa, with its famous Leaning Tower. Tuscany, the most continuously civilized region of Italy, is its cultural crown, and Florence is its jewel.

WINING AND DINING

Chianti is usually the first wine that comes to mind when thinking of Tuscany. The hardy, dry red nectar has a distinguished heritage. A grand duchy of Tuscany decree established the territorial limits of Chianti country in 1716, in the provinces of Florence and Siena. Local producers have been producing high-quality wine for over 250 years.

Chianti is a blend of four regional grapes. The black Canaroto provides 70–80 percent of the blend; the others are Sangiovese and the white Trebbiano Toscano and Malvasia del Chianti grapes. Chianti Classico country centers around

Greve in Chianti, 16 miles from Florence. Superior Chianti has a *gallo nero* (black rooster) logo on the seal on the neck of the bottle. Next in quality is *putto,* indicated by a cherub on the label. Other Tuscan DOC wines are Vernaccia di San Gimignano, Brunello di Montalcino, Pitigliano white, Nobile di Montepulciano, red and white from Elba, Colline Lucchesi red, Montecarlo, Morellino di Scansano, Val di Chiana Vergine white, Montescudaio, Carmignano, Apuani hill white, Parrina, Val di Nievole white, Bianco Pisano di S. Torpè, Pomino, and Bolgheri.

Tuscan cuisine is usually associated with salty *insaccati* (sausages, salami, etc.) such as the *finocchiona,* made with fennel; bread without salt; and *bistecca alla fiorentina,* the only real Italian steak.

Tuscans generally prefer their steaks singed on the outside and practically raw inside. Anyone not liking rare meat should always specify *molto bene cotto.* Remember that the lire price is *per etto,* unless it is substituted by *S. Q.* (according to quantity). Per etto means you pay by the weight (an *etto* is about four ounces), including bone and fat.

Pasta is not as much of a local tradition as are soups served with bread and olive oil: *ribollita* (a vegetable soup) and *pappa al pomodoro* (a tomato soup). Both are savory means devised by frugal Tuscans for disposing of leftover bread. Local cannellini (white beans) served warm with regional olive oil are a treat.

Popular desserts are *crostate,* large pastry tarts glazed with fresh fruit jam. The local *focaccia* is a sweet bread best made in wood ovens. End your meal in the best Tuscan fashion with a *vin santo,* literally, "holy wine," a sweet dessert wine ideal with focaccia and hard Tuscan cookies.

This is the inland side of Tuscan tradition; the region's Tyrrhenian coast has nurtured a taste for seafood. *Cacciucco* is a delightful fish stew that varies from town to town.

Credit cards are listed as accepted in our restaurant recommendations. "All cards" means that all of the following are accepted: AE—American Express; DC—Diner's Club; MC—MasterCard; V—Visa. Prices given are for a complete meal (antipasto to dessert) for one person.

Unità Festivals

The Unità festivals make their annual appearance throughout Tuscany during the summer months. They are held everywhere, from the smallest villages to Florence and the other provincial seats. Despite their Communist party sponsorship, the festivals are gathering points for other political groups as well. Ignore the political propaganda and head for the chow line, where strictly regional fare undercuts local restaurant prices.

TRAVEL

The regional capital of Florence is best served by turnpike and rail traffic. The main Tuscan airport is at Pisa; the smaller Florence airport was reopened two years ago and has some international flights.

Flying

Florence's Peretola Airport is on Via del Termine near the A11, and is 3½ miles from the center of town. The most practical means of reaching the airport is by taxi (the fare runs Lit. 10,000). City bus service is available on ATAF line number 23C from the main Santa Maria Novella rail terminal.

Domestic air service is provided by Alitalia, ATI, and Aliblu, Lungarno degli Acciaiuoli 10/12, tel. (055) 27889; and Alisarda and Avianova, Via Alamanni 23, tel. (055) 213585. Domestic flights are available to Bari (1 hour, 40 min.), Milan (1 hour), Naples, (1 hour, 35 min.), Pisa (25 min.), Rome (65 min.), and Turin (65 min.)

Besides Alitalia, international carriers in Florence are Air France, Borgo Santi Apostoli 9, tel. (055) 218335; British Air, Via della Vigna Nuova 36R, tel. (055) 218655; and Lufthansa, Pelliceria 6, tel. (055) 262890. Florence flights are available to Munich and Paris. These offices also service international flights at Pisa.

Pisa's Galileo Galilei Airport is 1¼ miles from the center of town. It has a train depot, where ATUM number 5 buses leave for Pisa's Piazza della Stazione (a 10-min. ride). There is regular rail service from Florence to the Pisa airport depot. Cost of the 1-hour ride is Lit. 4,200.

Domestic service at Pisa is provided by Alitalia, ATI, and Aliblu, tel. (050) 501570; and Alisarda and Avianova, tel. (050) 20256.

Flights connect with Alghero (55 min.), Cagliari (65 min.), Catania (1 hour, 20 min.), Elba (30 min.), Florence (25 min.), Genoa (35 min.), Milan (45 min.), Olbia (50 min.), Palermo (1 hour, 20 min.), Rome (50 min.), and Siena (25 min.) Alitalia and British Air provide daily (2-hour) service to London's Heathrow Airport. Daily flights to Paris (1 hour, 40 min.) are made by Alitalia and Air France, tel. (050) 21842 (at the airport).

For information on seasonal shuttles between Elba and Florence, Lucca and Pisa, as well as Siena–Pisa flights, contact Alitalia at Pisa.

Taking the Train

Florence is the hub of north-south rail traffic on the principal line through the heart of the country. There is also a west coast route from Genoa to Rome via La Spezia, Massa, Viareggio, Pisa, Livorno, Grosseto, and Civitavecchia.

Lucca, Siena, and Pistoia are not on these two main rail lines and must rely on secondary connections.

Florence's Santa Maria Novella train station in Piazza della Stazione, tel. (055) 278785, is the main terminal. The substation of Rifredi on Via Vasco de Gama, tel. (055) 411138, has trains to Pisa, Pistoia, Lucca, and Viareggio. There is another station, between the stadium and the Arno, which services other secondary routes: the Campo di Marte Station, Via Mannelli, tel. (055) 243344.

Connections from Florence to Siena (to the south) are through Empoli (to the west). The ride takes 1 hour, 18 min. if no change is required at Empoli. From Florence to Grosseto and the Argentario island the ride is about 3 hours.

Travel times from Florence are: to Rome, 2 hours, 10 min.; Milan, 2 hours, 47 min.; Verona, 2 hours, 34 min.; Venice, 2 hours, 30 min.; and Bologna, 1 hour, 6 min. Local service from Florence to Arezzo takes 45 min.; to Lucca, 1 hour, 27 min.; Pistoia, 35 min.; and to Pisa, 1 hour, plus an additional 5 min. to the airport depot.

Taking the Bus

Except for Florence, provincial bus service is almost exclusively confined to routes within each of the eight other provinces.

Six companies are based in Florence: Brunellesca, Piazza Santa Maria Novella, tel. (055) 298411; CAP, Via Nazionale 13r, tel. (055) 214637; CAT, Via Fiume 2r, tel. (055) 283400; COPIT, Piazza Santa Maria Novella 22r, tel. (055) 215451; Lazzi, Piazza Adua at the corner of Piazza della Stazione, tel. (055) 215154; and SITA, Via di Santa Caterina da Siena 15r, tel. (055) 211487.

These companies provide service to Arezzo, La Spezia, Livorno, Lucca, Grosseto, Marina di Carrara, Prato, Pistoia, and Siena. Other routes include the ski areas of Cavalese in Trentino and Pievepelago in Emilia-Romagna; the beaches at Rimini, Forte dei Marmi, and Viareggio; as well as Montecatini, Empoli, Faenza, Greve in Chianti, and Sansepolcro.

Driving

Main highways in Tuscany are the A1 Milan–Rome and A11 Firenze–Mare turnpikes. The A11 passes through Lucca via Prato, Pistoia, and Montecatini, then splits south for Pisa and north for Viareggio and the A12 to Genoa by way of Livorno. Should the Lazio region resolve bureaucratic problems, the A12 eventually will connect the entire west coast from Genoa to Rome. Until then, the coastal road from Livorno to Civitavecchia is the old SS1 (named Aurelia) route. This 144-mile stretch also takes in Orbetello, where a man-made isthmus ties to the Argentario island and its resort towns of Porto Santo Stefano and Port'Ercole.

Siena is on the SS2 (also known as the Via Cassia), which heads southeast. From Florence there is a superstrada beginning at Galluzzo (3½ miles from the center) that covers the 33½ miles to Siena. From Siena SS273 heads southwest to Grosseto. There are no service areas on these express routes, which avoid the tortuous winding provincial routes through the Tuscan hill country.

CAR RENTALS

Once outside Florence, driving is probably the best means to visit Tuscany. Auto rental facilities in the region are:

Arezzo: Avis, Piazza della Repubblica 1; tel. (0575) 354232.

Florence: (Peretola Airport) Avis, tel. (055) 213629; Europcar, tel. (055) 318609.

(City) Avis, Via Borgo Ognissanti 128r; tel. (055) 213629. Europcar, Via Borgo Ognissanti 53/59r; tel. (055) 293444; telex 571337. Hertz, Via Maso Finiguerra 33; tel. (055) 298205; telex 570222. Maggiore, Via Maso Finiguerra 11r; tel. (055) 210238.

Grosseto: Avis, Via Telamonio 16/4; tel. (0564) 413704.

Livorno Avis, Via Garibaldi 49; tel. (0586) 888090. Hertz, Via Mastacchi 59/63; tel. (0586) 410515; telex 570222. Maggiore, Via Fiume 3/33; tel. (0586) 892240.

Marina di Carrara: Avis, Via Venezia 5; tel. (0585) 630112.

Montecatini: Avis, Viale Manin 8; tel. (0572) 72946.

Piombino: Hertz, Via U. Dini 13; tel. (0565) 32466; telex 500238.

Pisa: (Airport) Avis, tel. (050) 42028; Europcar, tel. (050) 41017; telex 501178; Hertz, tel. (050) 44426; telex 501305; Maggiore, tel. (050) 42574.

(City) Hertz, Via Vespucci 106/A; tel. (050) 44389; telex 590261. Maggiore, Via P. Mascagni; tel. (050) 502429.

Port'Ercole: Avis, Marina di Cala Galeca, tel. (0564) 833131.

Portoferraio: Maggiore (seasonal office), Calata Italia 8; tel. (0565) 915368.

Taking the Ferry

Livorno is Tuscany's principal seaport. Primarily a container-cargo facility, Livorno is also the base for ferry service to Sardinia, Sicily, Corsica, and Elba.

For information on service to Sardinia contact Sardinia Ferries, Via Calafati 4; tel. (0586) 896001. For Sicily, contact the Tirrenia Line, Scali D'Azeglio 6, tel. (0586) 890332; and for Corsica, either Sardinia Ferries or NAVARMA Lines, Via Veneto 24, tel. (0586) 895214.

NAVARMA services Elba, as does TOREMAR, Via Calafati 4; tel. (0586) 896113. From Porto Santo Stefano on the Argentario island there is service to Bastia, Corsica by Corsica Ferries, Banchina Toscana; tel. (0564) 813707.

❦ ACCOMMODATIONS

Florence, the city of arts and leather, should be a prime consideration on any visit to Italy. It is attractive to international business; the city has a highly organized conference and trade-show board and attracts national and international buyers and sales representatives. And a number of American universities have year-abroad study programs that fill the more economical pensioni year-round. Thus, it can be difficult at times to find preferred lodgings; planning ahead is seriously suggested.

Many economical Florence hotels and pensioni set a 4 or 3 P.M. check-in time that is rigorously applied unless a deposit has been made or a credit card number given to guarantee arrival.

Americans in particular have a bad track record on cancellations, and the frugal Florentines have no intention of paying the consequences.

Always try to book a room several days in advance, if not before leaving home. You can send a *vaglia telegrafica* (money order) from any post office in Italy for the first night's lodging; the *vaglia* will arrive within 24 hours, if not the same day. On the post office form there is space for *"comunicazioni";* write your name, dates of arrival and departure, and type of reservation. You will then have a receipt from the post office and the reservation will be 99.9 percent secure.

The Tuscan countryside has become increasingly popular for summer vacations. A home base here provides easy access not only to Florence but to the region. The *New York Times* and *London Times* classified sections list summer rentals of private villas and apartments. One local agency specializing in the rental of castles, old country homes, and modern villas with swimming pools as well as apartments is Solemar, Via Cavour 80, 50129 Florence; tel. (055) 218112. Illustrated catalogs and price lists are available upon request. (Specify that you want price lists in U.S. dollars or they will be furnished in Swiss francs.)

Beach resorts on the coast (Viareggio, Forte dei Marmi, etc.) have lost much of their past luster, but in August accommodations can still be impossible.

Credit cards are listed as accepted. "All cards" means that all of the following are accepted: AE—American Express; DC—Diner's Club; MC—MasterCard; V—Visa. Rates given below show the range between single and double rooms.

Florence

Aprile, Via della Scala 6, 50123; tel. (055) 216237. This efficient 3-star hotel is near the central rail terminal. Not all of its 29 rooms have private bath, but there is a small, pleasant garden in the courtyard of this Medici palace. There is a bar, but no restaurant. Rates for rooms with bath run Lit. 67,000–99,000. All cards.

Bologna, Via Orcagna 50, 50121; tel. (055) 678359. Near the inner-city viale loop with easy access to the Firenze Sud (South) A1 connection, this 2-star hotel is managed by two accommodating brothers. Most of the 20 rooms have private baths. A bar, but no restaurant. Street parking and easy access to the center of town make this a good choice for the more economy-minded traveling by car. Avoid the back rooms during the school year—they are next to a playground. Rates for rooms with private bath, including breakfast and air-conditioning, run Lit. 57,000–77,000. All cards.

Calzaiuoli, Via dei Calzaiuoli 6, 50122; tel. (055) 212456; telex 580589 CALZAI. A thorough, modern renovation of an old Florentine building on the city's pedestrian-only promenade between Piazza di San Giovanni and Piazza della Signoria, this 3-

star, 37-room hotel would be more centrally located only if it were on David's shoulders. There's a pleasant breakfast room but no bar. Rates are Lit. 70,000–106,000. All cards.

Continental, Lungarno degli Acciaiuoli 2, 50123; tel. (055) 282392; telex 580525 CONTAL. Elevated to 4-star status, this hotel near Ponte Vecchio has authentic antiques and period furnishings. There are 61 air-conditioned rooms. No restaurant, but snacks are available at the hotel bar. Rates run Lit. 105,000–151,000. All cards.

Excelsior, Piazza d'Ognissanti 3, 50123; tel. (055) 264201; telex 570022 EXCEFI. Frequented by fashion stylists, buyers, and entertainers, this 5-star CIGA luxury hotel with 205 lavish air-conditioned rooms (suites and apartments also available) is on the Arno. A summer roof garden with a good restaurant offers a fine view over the city. Room rates are Lit. 393,000–575,000. All cards.

Grand Hotel Baglioni, Piazza dell'Unità Italiana 6, 50123; tel. (055) 218441; telex 5270225 HOTBAG I. This 4-star hotel is in a 19th-century patrician villa furnished and decorated in Florentine style. There are 195 air-conditioned rooms and comfortable convention facilities. The roof-garden restaurant has a fine view of central Florence. Rates here run Lit. 170,000–225,000. All cards.

Losanna, Via Vittorio Alfieri 9, 50121; tel. (055) 245840. For the tight budget traveler, this 1-star hotel-*pensione* is a 15-min. walk from the center of Florence. Inside the viale loop, it has only nine rooms and is fairly well known, so reserve in advance. The hotel across the street may seem more attractive, but appearances are deceiving. Rates for rooms without bath are Lit. 28,500–44,500; for a double with private bath, Lit. 58,000. No cards.

Lungarno, Borgo San Jacopo 14, 50123; tel. (055) 264211; telex 570129 LUNGAR. This 4-star hotel with 71 air-conditioned rooms in the Oltrarno has a bar, but no restaurant. In the 13th-century Torre de'Marsili, the hotel has a fine collection of modern art, and is in the only stretch of downtown Florence where the buildings are directly over the Arno. Rooms in the back look down directly on the river. Only 10 min. from the Pitti Palace and two from the Ponte Vecchio. Lit. 143,000–209,000. All cards.

Martelli, Via dei Panzani 8, 50123; tel. (055) 217151; telex 573137 MARTEL. This 3-star hotel with 44 rooms is in a Medici palace near the cathedral. Air-conditioning is Lit. 3,000 extra. Rates for room with breakfast are Lit. 83,000–128,000. All cards.

Silla, Via dei Renai 5, 50125; tel. (055) 284810. Most of the 32 rooms in this 3-star hotel-*pensione* have private baths. The hotel is on the quieter left bank of the Arno, 15 min. from Ponte Vecchio on the way to Piazzale Michelangiolo. Meals or breakfast may be required in season. Rates for rooms with private baths are Lit. 60,000–92,000. All cards.

Villa Medici, Via il Prato 42, 50123; tel. (055) 261331; telex 570179 MEDICI. This 5-star luxury hotel with 107 air-conditioned rooms is in a quiet zone 10 min. from the center of Florence. Its patrician villa facade covers a modern, efficient hotel, with a pool in the inner courtyard. There's a bar and restaurant. Rooms range Lit. 330,000–550,000. All cards.

Villa sull'Arno, Lungarno Cristoforo Colombo 1, 50136; tel. (055) 670971; telex 573297 VILARN I. This 4-star hotel is in a restored villa and has a garden with a heated pool. The 47 rooms are air-conditioned. There's a bar and a garage, but no restaurant. The hotel is on the Arno, but beyond the viale loop around the inner city. Rooms are Lit. 115,000–196,000. All cards.

Altopascio

Astoria, Via Roma 86, 55011 (LU); tel. (0583) 24746. This modern, 3-star, 42-room hotel has a steady clientele of sales agents and buyers. But most of the nearby factories close in Aug., so rooms are available when Florence and nearby beach resorts are full. Nothing is worse than not being able to find a hotel in the middle of the night; even the roosters crowing at the crack of dawn can be contended with. The Astoria is ½ mile from the Firenze–Mare A11, 11 miles from Lucca and 35 miles from Florence. Lit. 38,000–55,000. No cards.

Elba

It's close to impossible to find rooms in July and Aug. on Napoleon's exile isle. But May, June, and Sept. are much less crowded, though minimum sojourns of one week are required in the **Camping Village Rosselba le Palme** on the northern coast near Portoferraio. There is daily ferry service to Bastia (on Corsica), Capraia Island, Livorno, and Piombino (see "Taking the Ferry"). Chalets for 4–5 run Lit. 55,000–85,000 daily in low season, and Lit. 35,000–50,000 daily for furnished trailers and bungalows that sleep 2–4. Contact Rosselba le Palme, Località Ottone 3, 57037 Portoferraio (LI); tel. (0565) 966101. In winter, contact Rosselba le Palme, Strada S. Fermo 11, 37121 Verona; tel. (045) 592488.

Fiesole

Just northeast of Florence in the immediate hill country is Fiesole, away from the confusion of a tourist-packed city. Here are two suggestions:

Villa Bonelli, Via Francesco Poeti 1, 50014; tel. (055) 59513. Tucked into a labyrinth of narrow streets, this 2-star *pensione* is clean and efficient; most of the 23 rooms have private bath. The restaurant/breakfast room on the top floor offers a view from under a wood-beam roof. The nearby number 7 bus makes the short ride to the center of Florence every 20 min. Meals are usually required in high season; air-conditioning is an extra Lit. 3,000. Rates for room only with private bath are Lit. 42,000–62,000. All cards.

Villa San Michele, Via di Doccia 4, 50014; tel. (055) 59451; telex 570643 SANMIC I. In a converted 16th-century monastery designed by Michelangelo is one of the best-known hotels in Italy. The 5-star luxury Cipriani hotel (of Venice fame) has just 29 rooms. Surrounded by a lush park with a pool, the hotel has a bar and excellent restaurant. Reservations are essential for the restaurant as well as the hotel; the experience is unforgettable. Rooms are Lit. 418,000–625,000. All cards.

Greve

To combine a visit to Florence with a country sojourn, consider staying in Greve, in the heart of Chianti Classico wine country, 17 miles from the center of Florence. Evenings are much cooler there than in Florence; advance bookings are suggested, since the area's Tuscan hiking trails attract groups.

Giovanni da Verrazzano, Piazza Matteotti 28, 50022; tel. (055) 853189. Most of the 11 rooms in this 3-star hotel have private bath. A good regional restaurant is on the veranda atop the porticoes that line the triangular piazza, which has a statue honoring the navigator Giovanni da Verrazzano. (Why did New York remove a "z" when giving his name to a bridge?) Avoid rooms in the front of the hotel on Friday nights: The weekly Saturday market begins at dawn—if not before—and sleep is impossible. Rates for rooms with private bath are Lit. 52,000–82,000. AE, DC.

Livorno

Gran Duca, Piazza Micheli 16, 57100; tel. (0586) 891024. This 3-star, 51-room hotel is a converted 1450 fort overlooking the port (with ferries to Sardinia and Corsica). The hotel has a bar, a good restaurant featuring local seafood, and parking facilities. Rooms are Lit. 48,000–74,000. No cards.

Lucca

Celide, Viale Giuseppe Giuisti 27, 55100; tel. (0583) 954106. This 3-star, 56-room hotel on the viale loop paralleling the old fortress walls of Lucca has easy access to the A11 and to the center of Lucca. No restaurant, but there is a bar. Limited parking. Rates are Lit. 54,000–80,000. AE, V.

Pisa

Ariston, Via Cardinale Maffi 42, 56100; tel. (050) 561834. Behind the cathedral just 100 yards from the Leaning Tower, this 3-star hotel has 33 rooms, most with bath or shower, but no restaurant. Rates for rooms with private bath are Lit. 45,000–68,000. AE, MC.

Siena

Certosa di Maggiano, Strada di Certosa 82, 53100; tel. (0577) 288180; telex 574421. This 4-star, 14-room hotel is a converted 14th-century monastery, with a restaurant, garden, a heated pool, and a tennis court. The hotel is ½ mile from the Porta Romana in Siena's old city wall. Rooms are Lit. 240,000–290,000. Closed Dec.–Jan. All cards.

Palazzo Ravizza, Piano dei Mantellini 34; tel. (0577) 280462; telex 575304. This 3-star *pensione* with 28 rooms is behind the cathedral and 10 min. from the central Piazza del Campo, where the Palio is held twice each summer. The 17th-century building has a pleasant inner courtyard garden. Meals may be required in season. Rooms are spacious. Rates are Lit. 50,000–79,000. All cards.

Beach Towns

The main Tuscan beach area includes Viareggio, Forte dei Marmi, and Camaiore. For information on the so-called Versilian Riviera and the rest of the region's Tyrrhenian coast, contact: Francesco Sesto Rubino, EPT di Lucca, Piazza Giudiccioni 2, 55100 Lucca, tel. (0583) 41205; or Leda Zeni Piccoli, EPT di Massa–Carrara, Piazza 2 Giugno 14, 54023 Carrara, tel. (0585) 70668.

Florence

Even under wraps, Florence inspires awe. The intense concentration of creative culture and majestic historical monuments is said to be the cause of a so-called Stendhal Syndrome that afflicts visitors from countries lacking everyday reminders of a historical past.

Florence is the easiest of the Italian cities to visit. Naples, Rome, and even tiny Venice are more difficult to navigate; in Florence, the next masterpiece or monument is just two steps away.

Don't try to see and do everything in this incredibly cultured city—you can't. Florence can mean claustrophobic culture shock for the unprepared. (Initial, but scarce, statistics say that the most affected are Americans, Australians, and Northern Europeans between twenty and forty years of age, not traveling in groups and intent on visiting all the city's cultural heritage in a maximum of two days.) Choose the few sights most important to you and discover what else is on the way.

Many of Florence's outdoor statues and monuments are undergoing restoration or are being replaced by copies to prevent further damage from acid rain and exhaust fumes. (Unleaded petrol has appeared on the horizon and may be mandatory by the year 2,000. Florence has experimented with limiting auto access to older areas to residents only, to protect its priceless buildings and artworks from pollution. But initial enthusiasm has eroded, though the plan is still in effect.)

Piazza Duomo

A good starting point for tackling Florence is **Piazza Duomo,** where three of the city's celebrated attractions await the visitor: the cathedral, the Baptistery, and the Campanile.

The Cathedral (Duomo) of Santa Maria del Fiore was originally designed by Arnolfo di Cambio in 1296; Brunelleschi's imposing dome was begun in 1420, and completed 16 years later, the major engineering feat of the Renaissance. If Florence can be thought of as a symbol of the Italian genius that was the Renaissance, then its Cathedral was a symbol of the wealth, power, and talent that was Florence—this was to be the greatest cathedral man had ever built.

The Cathedral's odd neo-Gothic facade by De Fabris was added in 1887, replacing one that was destroyed in the late 1500s. The space inside the cathedral, the world's fourth largest, seems bare, echoing. There are works by such masters as Ghiberti (the stained-glass windows at the rear), Paolo Uccello (the trompe l'oeil fresco of a mercenary general in the left aisle), and Andrea del Castagno (the second fresco of a local mercenary leader in the left aisle). Behind the bronze doors of the New Sacristy (look for the Luca della Robbia terra-cottas over the doors), Lorenzo *Il Magnifico* Medici fled to escape Pazzi assassins on April 26, 1478 (the Pazzi were Medici rivals); his brother Giuliano was slain.

Brunelleschi's tomb is under the vast cathedral, as are remains of the Romanesque church (Santa Reparata) that originally occupied this spot, itself formerly an early Christian church. (The cathedral is open 10 A.M. to 5:30 P.M.)

You can climb to an inner gallery in the dome (the fresco of the *Last Judgment* is by Vasari), then continue to the top for a view of Florence and surrounding Tuscany. (The dome can be visited 10 A.M. to 5:30 P.M.)

The **Cathedral Museum** (Museo dell'Opera del Duomo), directly behind, is one of the more important in Florence, originally created in 1891 to store sculptures for both the interior and exterior of the church, as well as equipment used in the dome's construction. The museum today displays most of the cathedral's original sculpture. At the top of the first stairs, the 1550 *Pietà* by Michelangelo was intended for the artist's own tomb, but, not pleased with the final product, he broke the statue and left it unfinished. (The museum is open 9 A.M. to 8 P.M., to 6 P.M. in winter; 10 A.M. to 1 P.M. Sundays and holidays. Admission is free Sunday.)

The **Campanile** is Giotto's famous bell tower, which he began in 1334; he died two years later, and his tower was completed by Pisano and Talenti. The most beautiful in Italy, the tower measures 280 feet high and nearly 48 feet wide, the walls are almost 12 feet thick. The climb is rewarded by a closer look at Brunelleschi's dome and a panorama of Florence. (Open 9 A.M. to 7:30 P.M., to 5:30 P.M. in winter.)

A Walking Tour of Michelangelo's Florence

For Michelangelo, all Florence was an open-air school. This walking tour takes in Michelangelo's contributions to the city as well as key works of earlier Florentine artists who inspired him. The tour should take one day and takes into account the early closing times at important sites. Get an early start and avoid Mondays, when nearly all the museums in Florence are closed.

Begin in the **Piazza della Signoria,** which was the center of political and cultural life under the Medicis. It was here that Savonarola was hanged and burned in 1498, when Michelangelo was 23. (A bronze plaque near the Fountain of Neptune marks the spot.) The event greatly disturbed Michelangelo; he had been moved, along with the rest of Florence, by the monk's fanatical sermons. Amid other outdoor statues in the square stands a copy of Michelangelo's *David,* his most famous nude (and a work that Savonarola would have despised).

From the Piazza della Signoria, walk northeast a short distance, crossing the Piazza di San Firenze to the **Bargello Museum** (Palazzo del Bargello). This fortified palace, begun in 1255, houses many important works, among them some of Michelangelo's earliest statues, including a drunken *Bacchus* (ground floor). Here you will find Donatello's bronze *David* (first floor) and Verrocchio's bronze *David* (second floor), both of which Michelangelo studied.

Continue north on the Via del Proconsolo a few blocks to the **Piazza del Duomo,** where the imposing Cathedral, Giotto's bell tower, and the Baptistery comprise the city's most recognizable landmarks. The great dome of the Cathedral was mounted by Brunelleschi between 1420 and 1436. Michelangelo was awed by it, and used the cupola as the inspiration for the even larger dome he later designed for St. Peter's Basilica in Rome. After circling the Cathedral, stroll to the octagonal **Baptistery,** where you can admire, as Michelangelo did, the magnificent bronze doors sculpted by Lorenzo Ghiberti for the east entrance. It took Ghiberti 27 years to complete them; Michelangelo scrutinized the doors and pronounced them fit to be the *"Gates of Paradise,"* the name by which they have been known ever since.

Return to the north side of the Duomo, find the Via Ricasoli, and continue to **the Academy** (Galleria dell'Accademia), entrance at number 60. This is the highlight for lovers of Michelangelo's work. Here, in addition to the toweringly graceful original *David,* are his *Palestrina Pietà* and the wonderfully expressive figures of *St. Matthew* and the unfinished *Four Prisoners,* who seem to be struggling to escape their enslaving blocks of stone, as souls battling against the flesh.

After lunch, retrace your steps on the Via Ricasoli to the Via dei Pucci, which crosses it. Turn right and walk a block to the **Medici Palace** (Palazzo Medici–Riccardi). Florence's first Medici ruler, Cosimo the Elder, built this palace for his descendants.

Here Lorenzo the Magnificent was born, and here Michelangelo lived as a young man while he studied sculpture with Bertoldo.

Continue a short distance to the **Church of San Lorenzo,** where the Medicis worshipped. Through the cloisters you may enter the **Laurentian Library** at Piazza di San Lorenzo 9, which Michelangelo designed to house the Medici manuscript collection. His massive yet whimsical staircase is one of the most original architectural designs of the period.

Behind the church, enter the dazzlingly oppulent **Medici Chapels** (on the Piazza di Madonna degli Aldobrandini). The stately architectural details of the **New Sacristy,** which Michelangelo designed and partly executed, lend this cool marble chapel a profound meditative atmosphere. Seven statues by the master sculptor decorate tombs, among them the allegorical figures *Day, Night, Dawn,* and *Dusk,* in the setting that Michelangelo envisioned for them.

To end the day, walk west from San Lorenzo to the bus station (Piazza della Stazione), where you can take a bus or cab to the **Piazzale Michelangiolo.** From this height above the Arno, another copy of Michelangelo's *David* looks out on a splendid panorama of the city. Follow its gaze; straight ahead, unmistakably, is the Duomo. To its left is the turret of the **Palazzo Vecchio,** and to its right, in the near distance, is the **Church of Santa Croce,** where Michelangelo is buried.

—Michael Hinden

The **Baptistery** is in front of the Cathedral, in Piazza San Giovanni. Its exact date of origin is uncertain, but it is believed to have been built between 1059 and 1150 to honor St. John the Baptist. Marble from Roman monuments was used in building the Romanesque edifice; its paved interior is majestic. The three sets of gilded bronze doors are by Andrea Pisano (on the left as you leave the cathedral) and Lorenzo Ghiberti (center and right). The most noted are the 1425 doors facing the cathedral, called the "Gates of Paradise" by Michelangelo. These doors are said to mark the beginning of the Renaissance, when realistic three-dimensional perspective replaced Gothic stylized formality. Two panels of Ghiberti's masterpiece have been restored and the originals are on display in the Duomo Museum. (The Baptistery is open 9:30 A.M. to 12:30 P.M. and 2:30 to 5:30 P.M.)

On the left of the Piazza del Duomo is the sculptured marble parapet of the 14th-century **Loggia del Bigallo.** To the left is Via dei Calzaiuoli, widened in the 19th century and now a pleasant promenade lined with shops. It leads to the **Piazza della Signoria.** Along the promenade is the 14th-century **Loggia Orsanmichele,** a grain market transformed into a church and decorated with a panorama of 14th- to 16th-century Florentine statues of the patron saints of the arts (open 7 A.M. to noon and 2 to 7 P.M.). The **Palazzo dell'Arte**

della Lana, nearby, once employed 30,000 workers. At one corner of the 14th-century tower is the tabernacle of Santa Maria della Tromba.

Piazza della Signoria

South on the Via dei Calzaiuoli is the **Piazza della Signoria,** the medieval center of the city's political life. The homes of Ghibelline families were destroyed between the 13th and 14th centuries to enlarge the square. Many of the sculptures on the square are in front of the Palazzo Vecchio (or della Signoria). Donatello's *Marzocco* lion and bronze statue of *Judith and Holofernes* join Michelangelo's *David* and *Hercules,* among others. These are copies; the original works are now housed in museums throughout the city.

Across the square, next to the equestrian statue of Cosimo de'Medici by Giambologna, is a marble disk marking the spot where Savonarola (the "heretic friar") was hanged and then burned. Nearby is the *Neptune Fountain* and statues of *Hercules and Cacus* by Bandinelli.

The **Palazzo Vecchio** was built at the turn of the 14th century and is the best example of Florentine civic architecture of its period. The ornate interior and its collection of art, including statues by Michelangelo and paintings by Bronzino and Vasari, along with the Quartieri Monumentali, Medici apartments, is open 9 A.M. to 7 P.M., 8 A.M. to 1 P.M. holidays; closed Sunday. Admission is Lit. 4,000.

The **Loggia dei Lanzi** (or dei Priori) was built in 1380, in front of the palace; its name comes from the *Lanzichenecchi* guards of Cosimo the Younger. The loggia houses Roman and Renaissance statues, including *Perseus and Medusa* by Cellini and Giambologna's *Rape of the Sabine Women.* Now covered by scaffolding, the loggia is undergoing extensive renovation that has returned to light Donatello's *Faith,* among the statues of the Virtues in the niches between the loggia's rounded arches.

Unless specified otherwise, attractions will be open Tuesday to Sunday mornings; closed Monday. However, if you're counting on a certain museum being open while you're in Florence, do double-check for any late-breaking changes.

Off the square is Piazzale degli Uffizi, which opens onto the Arno. Here is the famous **Uffizi Gallery** (open 9 A.M. to 7 P.M., to 1 P.M. holidays; closed Mon.), once the administrative center for the Medici (*uffizi* means offices). Now it is one of the world's leading museums, with a collection begun by Cosimo I and enriched by other Medici and the Lorraine dukes who also ruled from Florence. The 16th-century building is considered Vasari's architectural masterpiece. The gallery has paintings of the Florentine school, including works by Cimabue, Giotto, Masaccio, Fra Angelico, Paolo Uccello, Filippo Lippi, Botticelli, Leonardo da Vinci, and Michelangelo. Other Italian masters represented are Simone Martini, Piero della Francesca, Pollaiuolo, Mantegna, Raphael, Titian, and Caravaggio. Heading the list of foreign masters are Rubens, Rembrandt, and Goya.

Expect crowds; enter the museum determined to be patient, determined not to let tour groups distract; you may have to wait to get close to some paintings. Try to go as early in the day as possible; buy a guide to the Uffizi (on sale outside) the day before you go so you can plan what's most important to you to see. But leave yourself open: Painters you know almost nothing about may surprise you. You can't see this entire, amazing collection in one day; when you've seen enough, go for coffee. The Uffizi and Florence will wait for you.

The **Vasarian Corridor** once connected the Uffizi with

Sandro Botticelli, *Birth of Venus*
(c. 1480)

The sweetness of Botticelli's imagination delights the spirit. His ethereal figures seem partly of this world and partly of some other, where absolute beauty reigns. The sureness of his line is unsurpassed, but it is the purity of his artistic vision that has endeared Botticelli to hundreds of thousands of visitors to the Uffizi.

Like others of his generation, he embraced the Neoplatonic doctrine of union with spiritual reality through art, a belief in the possibility of a sensuous apprehension of truth. His goddess symbolizes religious as well as physical grace and no doubt was conceived as a fusion of pagan and Christian ideals.

The painting proclaims the mystery of eternal beauty by celebrating its earthly counterpart. Born of the sea, this Venus is as demure as a Madonna, yet naked for all that. Modestly (or coyly?) she covers herself, using available means, as zephyrs waft her ashore on a fanciful scallop shell. An attendant prepares to drape her with a sumptuous cloak that billows in the wind.

Stylistically, the painting emphasizes the dreamlike quality of Botticelli's vision. The two wind gods, erotically entwined, scatter flowers in their wake, while the floral pattern is repeated in the cloak and gown of Venus' servant. The ocean waves are artificially stylized, as is the shoreline and the horizon. A few odd details enhance the painting's charm: the cattails on the bank, the clunky toes of the zephyrs pedaling in the air, the pebbled beach, Venus' doughy left arm, and the unusual trees, whose foliage echoes the shape of the zephyrs' wings. If Botticelli seems less interested than his contemporaries in achieving complete verisimilitude, remember that he was painting more for the imagination than for the eye.

—Michael Hinden

Parmigianino, *Madonna of the Long Neck*
Uffizi (1534)

He was the Andy Warhol of his generation. For Warhol and his postmodernist allies, Picasso was a hard act to follow; after abstraction, how could art continue to be inventive unless it became outrageous? Parmigianino and his contemporaries faced a similar impasse. After the heroic era that produced Leonardo, Michelangelo, and Raphael, what, they wondered, was left to be accomplished in the arts? The High Renaissance lasted only 25 years or so (1500–1525); the post-Renaissance reaction is called Mannerism, a bizarre and fascinating episode in Western art that anticipates contemporary attitudes.

Whereas the High Renaissance masters strove for balance, harmony, and correct proportion, the Mannerists purposefully undid the rules. Their works are studied, self-conscious, and reflexive—in a word, "mannered"—driven by a compulsion for originality that is well understood in terms of today's tastes.

Thus, Parmigianino's *Madonna of the Long Neck* coolly subverts the Renaissance standards of anatomical accuracy. The sinuous figures are unnaturally elongated, almost grotesque. The composition seems to parody Michelangelo's *Pietà,* which it superficially resembles in subject matter and pyramidal organization. But nothing here seems stable or quite logical. The Madonna's head is too small for her neck, while her extended hand is overlong. The entire composition is off-center, crowded to the left by an arbitrary column in the background, supporting empty space. The five squashed figures on the left appear to hop on a communal leg that juts out of nowhere, and the tiny figure on the right violates perspective. This audacious painting emphasizes playfulness and wit—as does much of today's "experimental" art.

—Michael Hinden

the Pitti Palace across the Arno, and included a passage atop the picturesque Ponte Vecchio. The corridor enabled the Medici to move about Florence unobserved. Now filled with self-portraits by masters from Raphael to Rembrandt, the corridor is open by appointment only; telephone (055) 218341 to arrange a visit.

The famous bridge, **Ponte Vecchio,** is lined with shops, a number of which offer gold, silver, and other types of jewelry. A gaping hole was torn through one of the shops during the 1966 flood. A cry of scandal arose when it was learned that the shopkeepers had removed their precious products before the Arno flooded; the question was, why were the shopkeepers alone warned of the flood? It was revealed that the shopkeepers keep a regular eye on the level of the river, and automatically remove their wares whenever it becomes threatening. The Ponte Vecchio is one of several bridges crossing to the Oltrarno.

The Bargello Area

Returning to Piazza della Signoria and crossing the square to the right is Via del Proconsolo. At number 4 is the **Bargello National Museum.** Built in 1255 as the Governor's Palace, it became the residence of the chief of police (*Bargello*) in 1574. Since 1859 it has been a museum featuring important Tuscan sculptures from the 1300s to the 1600s, with works by Donatello and Michelangelo, in addition to Cellini, Bernini, Luca della Robbia, Laurana, Rossellino, Benedetto da Maiano, Pollaiuolo, and Giambologna's *Mercury.* The Carrand collection of gems and ivories occupies several rooms. (Open 9 A.M. to 2 P.M., to 1 P.M. Sunday and holidays; closed Monday and some holidays; you can telephone (055) 210801.

Across Via del Proconsolo, which follows the path of Florence's old Roman walls, is the **Badia Fiorentina.** This former Benedictine abbey was founded in 978 and rebuilt in 1285 and 1627. During the Middle Ages it was the richest monastery in Florence.

Santa Croce Area

Walking east from the south end of Piazza di Santa Firenze, ten minutes down Borgo dei Greci, is **Santa Croce.** This Franciscan church features frescoes by Giotto, Donatello's famous crucifix, and Michelangelo's tomb, resting among enough illustrious Italians to have earned Santa Croce the nickname "Pantheon of the Italians." Buried here are Alfieri, Machiavelli, Galileo, Bruni, Rossini, and Ghiberti. There is also an empty sarcophagus for Dante, but the poet was exiled from Florence and is buried in Ravenna. The **cloisters** and **Pazzi Chapel** by Brunelleschi are to the right of the main church. (These and the church **museum** are open 9 A.M. to 12:30 P.M. and 3 to 6:30 P.M. in summer, to 5 P.M. in winter, closed Wednesday.) Santa Croce was the church that suffered the most damage during the 1966 flood; water reached a height of 13 feet inside the church. The high-water mark is indicated on the walls.

North from Piazza di Santa Croce on Via da Verrazzano, a five-minute walk to Via Ghibellina 70, is the house of Michelangelo. **Casa Buonarroti** is open from 9 A.M. to 1 P.M. only, and is closed Tuesday, but it's worth the early start. Among the displays are some of the great artist's earliest works. When you get out, there are a number of good restaurants on Via Ghibellina (one of the better concentrations in Florence).

Across the Arno (the Oltrarno)

Across the Arno is the artisan area called, appropriately, the Oltrarno. Several bridges cross the Arno, but the Ponte Vec-

Filippo Brunelleschi, Pazzi Chapel, (1433–1473), Santa Croce

Miracles *can* happen. This lovely chapter house for the convent of Santa Croce represents the seldom-attained ideal of enlightened private patronage combined with innovative artistry. Brunelleschi was at the forefront of the Florentine artistic scene, and his chapel is the epitome of the Florentine Renaissance style in art and architecture, another exercise in applying new ways of thinking about art and building. His artistic vision was stimulated by the rebirth of science, perspective, and engineering, and the rediscovery of the classical past.

The Pazzi Chapel is a perfectly proportioned reproduction of Roman antiquity. Ancient Roman motifs appear on the columns and in the portico's barrel vaults and central dome. The simple proportions of the dome are echoed by the arches and classical pilasters on the walls. Blue and white terra-cotta medallions by della Robbia depict the saints at good works and imitate the form of the dome.

Because the decoration is spare and clearly related, the room has a harmony rarely found in spaces at this time. The space is clear and calm, proof that the world can be ordered and peaceful, a powerful statement especially in the anxious medieval times.

—Mary Beth Betts and
Charles Ayes

chio goes into the heart of the district. Straight down Via de'Guicciardini are the **Pitti Palace and Boboli Gardens,** in Piazza Pitti. The original palace by Brunelleschi, commissioned by Florentine merchant Luca Pitti, was bought by the Medici family in 1549. Progressively enlarged through the 18th century, the palace was the residence of the Medici and their successors, the Lorraine dukes. Pitti was seat of the Savoy court when Florence was capital of a united Italy, from 1865 to 1870, and is now the backdrop for special exhibits and Florence fashion shows. It houses five museums, including the **Palatine Gallery** collection of 15th- to 18th-century masters including Raphael, Giorgione, Titian, and Rubens. The others are the **Gallery of Modern Art** (featuring 19th-century Tuscan works), the **Silver Museum, Porcelain Museum,** and the **Contini-Bonacossi Painting collection.** The amazing **Boboli Gardens** with their acres of fountains and sculpture are behind the palace. (The palace is open 9 A.M. to 2 P.M., to 1 P.M. Sunday and holidays; closed Monday. Admission is free to the Boboli Gardens and the Contini-Bonacossi collection Tuesday, Thursday, and Saturday at 10 A.M., but arrangements must be made in advance through the Uffizi offices; telephone 055-218341.)

Wander towards the Arno through the shopping streets across Via de'Guicciardini from the Pitti Palace, and you will eventually reach Piazza di Santo Spirito and the church of **Santo Spirito.** This 15th-century church by Brunelleschi represents one of the purest architectural creations of the Renaissance. The 1490 bell tower is by Baccio d'Agnolo. Don't be fooled by the outward look of neglect; the interior is considered an authentic museum of 14th- to 17th-century Florentine art.

Masaccio, *The Tribute Money*
(1427)

This unimposing fresco in a corner of the gloomy Church of Santa Maria del Carmine bears examining. Although dimmed by time, the historical importance of *The Tribute Money* is great. Its grasp of perspective was revolutionary; to other artists of the time, its subtle modeling of figures seemed a revelation.

Medieval artists recognized, of course, that space had three dimensions, but for them, the interplay between Heaven and earth was all-important. Our eyes are directed upwards toward a golden sky by their paintings, and to modern viewers their works appear flat, organized vertically.

Masaccio for the first time drew the viewer *into* the painting with his invention of atmospheric perspective, modulating light, shapes, and shadows to suggest depth. Here the figures are distinguished by the actual light that falls upon them from a chapel window. Vasari wrote in the 16th century that Masaccio's painted human figures were the first to really stand on their own two feet.

Considering its technical boldness, the subject of the fresco is particularly appropriate: the conflict between worldly and otherworldly allegiances, a narrative told in three episodes. In the center, Christ instructs Peter to go to the river, where he will find a fish with a coin in its mouth that can be used to pay the tax collector, who stands disputing with the Disciples, his back to the viewer. At the far left, Peter catches the fish, and at the far right he delivers the coin. "Render therefore unto Caesar the things that are Caesar's; and unto God the things that are God's."

Masaccio died young, at the age of 27, leaving works that were studied by Michelangelo, Leonardo, and many others.

—Michael Hinden

Leave Piazza di Santo Spirito by Via Sant'Agostino and continue northwest (it will change names to Via Santa Monica at Via de'Serragli) to reach Piazza del Carmine and the **Church of Santa Maria del Carmine.** Its Brancacci Chapel has some excellent frescoes by Masaccio, plus some by Masolino and Flippino Lippi.

The San Lorenzo Area

The **Basilica of San Lorenzo,** with its **Laurentian Library** and **Medici Chapels,** continues Florence's incomprehensible parade of great art. Brunelleschi's church in Piazza San Lorenzo, funded by the Medici, has many pieces by Donatello, including two bronze pulpits; nearby is a marble tabernacle by Desiderio da Settignano. The **old sacristy,** decorated by Donatello, contains a sarcophagus by Verrocchio. Filippino Lippi's *Annunciation* altarpiece is across the Transept.

The Michelangelo-designed **Laurentian Library** (open 10 A.M. to 1 P.M., closed Sunday and holidays) can be reached through the church. The **cloisters** are by Brunelleschi, the staircase by Vasari from a design by Michelangelo. Over 10,000 manuscripts are cataloged.

The opulent **Medici Chapels,** in Piazza di Madonna degli Aldobrandini, are back-to-back with San Lorenzo (open 9 A.M. to 2 P.M., to 1 P.M. Sunday and holidays; closed Monday). Four Medici are entombed in the **New Sacristy,** which was designed by Michelangelo; his **tombs** for Lorenzo and Giuliano are compelling. The **Princes' Chapel** is a vast vault of precious stones and marble.

The **Medici-Riccardi Palace,** at Via Cavour 1 (open 9 A.M. to 12:30 P.M. and 3 to 5 P.M.; 9 A.M. to noon Sunday and holidays; closed Wednesday), was the residence of the Medici before they moved to the Palazzo Vecchio. It was built by Michelozzo for Cosimo the Elder; the Medici occupied it from 1460 to 1540. Now the Prefecture of Florence, it was once the court of Lorenzo Il Magnifico. Benozzo Gozzoli's *The Procession of the Magi* is in the first-floor chapel. On the same floor are Luca Giordano's brilliant frescoes in the vault of the gallery.

Santa Maria Novella

West of San Lorenzo, near the train station, is the church of **Santa Maria Novella,** facing Piazza di Santa Maria Novella. This 13th-century Dominican church has a curious Romanesque-Gothic marble facade; the upper green and white portion was an addition by Leon Battista Alberti. Featured in the Gothic interior are Brunelleschi's wooden crucifix and Masaccio's *Trinity* fresco. **Cloisters** frescoed by Paolo Uccello lead to the **Chapel of the Spaniards,** with 14th-century frescoes by Andrea di Buonaiuto. (Museum open 9 A.M. to 2 P.M.; 8 A.M. to 1 P.M. Sunday and holidays; closed Friday.)

San Marco and the Academy

A few blocks northeast of San Lorenzo is the Museum of San Marco and the Academy Gallery, with perhaps the most recognized Florentine masterpiece, Michelangelo's *David.*

The **Museum of San Marco,** in Piazza San Marco, is in

The Medici

Throughout Florence and Tuscany, a traveler senses the impact of the Medici family on the art and architecture in the region. Prominent landowners in the Mugello Valley, they rose to power in the 15th century, ruling Florence and Tuscany until the mid-1700s. The Medici family came from a questionable background consisting of criminals as well as merchants and artisans, and was therefore excluded from Florentine government in the early 14th century. However, Giovanni de Bicci, son of Averardo de Medici, established himself as a successful businessman throughout Europe, and in 1421 he was elected gonfalonier, allowing the Medici family to gain a foothold in city politics. Their position was solidified by Giovanni's oldest son, Cosimo, a prosperous businessman whose wealth helped him rise to political power in Florence, where politics and economics were closely linked. His influence extended to the city's architecture and he commissioned a number of buildings including the Palazzo Medici, the dormitory of Santa Croce, and the Basilica of San Lorenzo. Cosimo passed his power on to his son Piero, who passed it on to his oldest son, Lorenzo. Lorenzo was known as Il Magnifico as he was a patron of the arts and a poet as well as a prominent political leader—a true Renaissance man. His rule was followed by a brief interruption in power when the family was forced to leave Florence. Lorenzo's second son Cardinal Giovanni reestablished the family's position. Giovanni's two younger brothers, Lorenzo and Giuliano, who died early in life, were remembered in Michelangelo's Medici tombs of the New Sacristy, erected in 1524.

Cosimo I was the first Grand Duke of Tuscany and the last of the Medici to contribute significantly to the arts in Florence. Among the works produced under his rule are the Neptune Fountain and the equestrian statue of himself in the Piazza della Signoria. In the field of architecture he commissioned Vasari to design Fort Belvedere. The fort stands across the Arno from the Pitti Palace, which was acquired by the Medici in the 1500s and now houses the Medici treasure in the Silver Museum. Other works commissioned by the Medici include portraits by Botticelli and Rubens in the Uffizi Gallery and Giambologna's bronze animals in the National Museum.

—Charlotte Savidge

a Dominican monastery enlarged by Michelozzo in 1437. Fra Angelico lived here, and much of the museum is dedicated to his graceful paintings. (Museum open 9 to 2 P.M., Sunday and holidays 9 to 1 P.M.; closed Monday.)

The Academy (**Galleria dell'Accademia**), at Via Ricasoli 60, is an unassuming building with a treasury of Michelangelo masterpieces (open 9 A.M. to 2 P.M., to 1 P.M. Sunday and holidays; closed Monday). Topping the list is the original *David* and four unfinished statues intended for the tomb of

Pope Julius II. In an adjoining gallery is a wide collection of 13th- to 16th-century Italian artists.

Michelangelo, *David* (1501–1504)

Florentines loved to hear the story of how young David conquered Goliath through resourcefulness. In Florence, bravery was admirable, but cleverness was a cause for civic pride. Both Donatello and Verrocchio had carved earlier versions of the biblical hero, but in light of Michelangelo's noble giant (more than 14 feet tall without its pedestal), their smaller, delicate interpretations seem but preludes.

Michelangelo endowed his David with a moral presence that transcends physical beauty. Superbly proportioned, his David is sublime, a vision in stone of human perfection. Florence honored the statue by placing it in front of the Palazzo Vecchio, where it dominated the Piazza della Signoria until 1873, when it was moved to its present indoor site to protect it from the elements.

The *David* establishes the Renaissance ideal of power harmonized with grace. At the peak of physical development, David lolls confidently, resting his weight casually on one leg. The serenity of his pose is belied by the dynamic tension of his musculature, his brow knit in concentration. His sinewed right hand conceals a stone, the sling resting on his shoulder. David is poised at the ready, his triumph assured. With his *David,* Michelangelo dramatizes the supreme confidence of the High Renaissance in individual potential and achievement. Hamlet's words express a similar attitude and might fittingly be chiseled on the pedestal as an epigraph: "What a piece of work is man, how noble in reason, how infinite in faculties, in form and moving how express and admirable, in action how like an angel, in apprehension how like a god."

—Michael Hinden

East of the Academy is the **Piazza della Santissima Annuziata,** with an equestrian statue of Ferdinand I de'Medici by Giambologna and two 17th-century baroque fountains. On the square are the **Foundlings' Hospital (Spedale degli Innocenti)** and **Santissima Annunziata** church.

Children are the main theme in the gallery of the Foundlings' Hospital, at number 12. Children abandoned on the steps of the hospital received the surname Innocenti, which is now common in Tuscany. (Tours of the gallery given from 9:30 A.M. to 1 P.M. and 2 to 5:30 P.M., 4:30 P.M. in winter.)

The **Annunciation Church (Santissima Annunziata)** was founded in 1250 and rebuilt by Michelozzo in the mid-15th century. Cellini's tomb is in the Chapel of St. Luke, reached from the north transept (open 8 A.M. to noon and 3 to 7 P.M., to 5 P.M. in winter). In the cloister in front of the church are a number of frescoes, most by Andrea del Sarto. In the right-hand corner is the painting *Birth of the Virgin.* The focus in this painting actually seems to be neither the baby nor her mother but a woman standing in the middle: Supposedly this woman was Lucrezia, loved by Andrea del Sarto to distraction (to the detriment of his art, some thought, including Giorgio Vasari, author of *The Lives of the Painters*). On the wall perpendicular to this one is the *Procession of the Magi.* The figure in the orange robe is a self portrait of Andrea. If you look carefully, it certainly seems that Andrea and Lucrezia in the other painting are looking directly into each other's eyes.

SHOPPING

Fashion, leather, shoes, gloves, purses, luggage, gifts, embroidered linens—the list could go on and on. The offerings of Florence and environs are mind-boggling.

In Florence elegance is a byword, practically inherent in the city's soul. The most exclusive shopping is along **Via de'Tornabuoni,** often called Europe's most elegant shopping street. Here just the stroll is pure pleasure, past the Florence base of such illustrious international names as Gucci, Ferragamo, Armani, Fendi, and Gianni Versace. The overflow onto the intersecting Via della Vigna Nuova includes Valentino, Enrico Coveri, and others.

The parallel **Via dei Calzaiuoli** has Beltrami and Franco Rizzo and then some. Florence is the center of Italy's prominent **shoe industry.** The proximity of the factories does not always mean the prices are good—but the selection is wide. In Rome, where competition may be keener due to the larger number of stores, prices may be lower—so keep this in mind if Rome is your next stop.

Emilio Pucci is a name dear to Florentines and international shoppers. The noble name is based in **Pucci Palace,** at Via dei Pucci 6.

The **Ponte Vecchio** is lined with shops, and is a charming place to browse for **jewelry,** gold, silver, and cameos (but remember the lower prices in Torre del Greco if Naples is on your itinerary). When pricing, also keep in mind that most Italian gold is 18 carat, instead of the 14 carat that prevails in the North American market.

Florence offers exceptional gift items. The **crafts fairs** at **Fortezza da Basso,** behind the train station, in September and February are a panorama of the ingenuity and skill of local craftspeople. In the tangle of streets beyond the Pitti Palace, practically the entire length of **Via della Chiesa** (west of Piazza di San Felice), is lined all the way to Piazza Tasso with diligent craftspeople who supply material for prominent international names. Don't expect ultra-cheap prices, since wholesale prices are not given to walk-in trade. But the savings at **Biondi** (at number 49r), **Vannini** (number 18), and **Nannini** (number 84) can be considerable.

There are two main **open-air markets** in Florence: at **Piazza del Mercato Nuovo** (closed Sunday and Monday morning) and **Piazza San Lorenzo** (closed Sunday and Monday). The best open-air buys can be found at the Tuesday-only market along the Arno in the **Cascine Park.** There are fakes and the real thing too, here and elsewhere; browsing and wrangling can be fruitful.

Once **embroidery** was a flourishing cottage industry throughout Tuscany. Some handmade items can still be found, but in Florentine shops prices are often prohibitive, and there is a good chance the goods are Chinese, not Italian.

In nearby **Pistoia** the embroidery industry has been mechanized in grand style. In Quarrata, between Florence and Pistoia, there seem to be about as many embroidering establishments as residences. Most have outlets on the premises, and for serious shoppers the short drive is worth the effort. Elsewhere in Tuscany, **Greve** in Chianti, 17 miles south of Florence, still has a few places that produce hand-embroidered towels, bed sets, and spreads, another reason to visit the Chianti Classico countryside. One particularly good shop can be found on the right side of the road, by the town limits, as you come from Florence.

RESTAURANTS

Florence is a safe city: choose your restaurant and enjoy the walk there and back to your hotel. Part of the fun of an evening in Florence includes the stroll home through out-of-the-way streets—perhaps topped off with a coffee in the Piazza della Signoria.

Il Barone di Porta Romana, Via Romana 123; tel. (055) 220585. Full of local color, this typical Florentine restaurant has a large garden for summer dining. In the Oltrarno, Via Romana runs almost to the Pitti Palace from Porta Romana. House offerings range from spaghetti with crabmeat to tripe and chicken livers in white wine. Meals run Lit. 40,000 with house wine. Closed Sun. All cards.

Coco Lezzone, Via Parioncino 26r; tel. (055) 287178. "The rancid chef" in name only, this basic Tuscan trattoria features regional fare in its three small rooms just off Lungarno Corsini. Good elbows assure a seat to enjoy *pappa a pomodoro,* the soup *ribollita, pasta e fagioli* and thick *fiorentina* steaks. Meals run Lit. 35,000–40,000. Closed Sat., Sun., Tues. evening in winter, July 20–Aug. 20. No cards.

Dante al Lume di Candela, Via delle Terme 23r; tel. (055) 294566. Near the Ponte Vecchio, Dante Poggiali's air-conditioned, refined, exclusive restaurant (the name means "Dante by Candlelight") is an intimate experience, with four seasonal menus based on local tradition and produce. House specialties include *agnolotti* with salmon and crab sauce. Reservations usually required. Meals run Lit. 50,000–60,000. Closed Sun., Aug. 10–25. All cards.

Dino, Via Ghibellina 51r; tel. (055) 241452. The Carini family's menu of old Tuscan and experimental recipes is a solid local favorite. Try pasta with artichokes or a triple sauce of rabbit, duck, and herbs, or veal with myrtle. Dino is always trying something new. The average meal in this air-conditioned former wine shop, across the street from Michelangelo's house, costs Lit. 35,000 with house wine. Closed Sun. evening, Mon., Aug. All cards.

Don Chisciotti, Via Cosimo Ridolfi 4/6r; tel. (055) 475430. Walter Viligardi's menu passes from the inventive to pure Tuscan, but the latter reigns. A happy medium is ricotta and spinach ravioli and a fillet with mushrooms and a truffle sauce (when in season). Meals with house wine run Lit. 40,000. The restaurant is behind the train station, just off Piazza dell'Independenza. All cards.

Enoteca Pane e Vino, Via Poggio Bracciolini 48; tel. (055) 683746. Across the Verrazzano bridge, near Piazza Ravenna. Barbara, Marco, Antonella, Gilberto, and Ubaldo let the market dictate the daily menu. *Gnocchi* and *brasato* warrant consideration when available. Meals are Lit. 25,000 without wine. Closed Sun., Aug. No cards.

"Private" Clubs

A number of private clubs catering to the young and the young at heart have opened around inner Florence. Many have no more than a nameplate on a locked door. Knock or ring to enter and obtain instant membership (if you pass the rapid look-over). Some of the clubs charge a nominal membership fee of Lit. 1,000–2,000 for a card valid for one year. For others, a brief application form is a formality only. Two examples are:

Il Canapone (Clinica Gastronomica), Via Mazzetta, just beyond Pitti Palace, between Santo Spirito and Piazza di San Felice. Snacks and a limited menu provide refreshment with a tap wine for as little as Lit. 20,000. No cards.

Anziche, Via d'Ardiglione, on the left bank of the Arno not far from the Pitti Palace. The street is parallel to Via de'Serragli, 5 min. from Ponte alla Carraia. A quick lunch with wine is only Lit. 10,000. Dinner, including an antipasto, is Lit. 18,000. Anziche stays open until midnight sometimes, which is quite late for Florence. No cards.

Enoteca Pinchiorri, Via Ghibellina 87; tel. (055) 242777. Giorgio Pinchiorri and Annie Feolde's menu of French and Tuscan recipes has gained fame in one of the best restaurants in the country. The 15th-century palace setting is air-conditioned and centrally located, and there is a pleasant courtyard for summer dining. The Tuscan seafood dishes are special. Reservation only. With wine, lunch can run Lit. 50,000, dinner can climb past Lit. 80,000. Closed Sun., Mon. noon, Aug., Christmas. All cards.

Harry's Bar, Lungarno Vespucci 22; tel. (055) 296700. Reservations are suggested for this small, air-conditioned restaurant along the Arno near the Excelsior hotel. Its elegant caffè atmosphere is a favorite with visiting Americans. No relation to the Harry's in Venice, this establishment serves homemade pasta, pasta e fagioli, and Tuscan specialties. Meals run Lit. 45,000–60,000. Closed Sun., Dec. 15–Jan. 1. AE.

La Loggia, Piazza Michelangiolo 1; tel. (055) 2342832. From the most panoramic point overlooking Florence, this elegant, air-conditioned restaurant across the Arno offers refined dining to accompany its spectacular location. Specialties are the pasta dish *panzarotti dello chef* and green pepper beef fillet. Meals run Lit. 40,000–50,000. Closed Wed., Aug. 10–25. All cards.

San Zanobi, Via San Zanobi 33r; tel. (055) 475286. Sisters Delia and Mariangela Fiore offer a pleasant, low-key atmosphere and good home cooking near Piazza dell'Indipendenza. Check the list of the day for *sformati* (baked vegetable and cheese dishes), or *stufato al Chianti* (a stew). Meals run Lit. 35,000. Closed Sun., Aug. AE, V.

Sostanza (Il Troia), Via del Porcellana 25r; tel. (055) 212691. Don't get confused with the definite article in Italian: "*La Troia*" means "The whore." This old Florentine trattoria discourages the pretentious. The accent is on hardy regional fare, thick Florentine steaks with Tuscan *cannellini* (beans) are at their best. Meals run Lit. 30,000–35,000. Closed Sun., Aug. No cards.

SIDETRIP TO FIESOLE

Fiesole is a small town in the hills overlooking Florence; four and a half miles northeast, offering archaeological collections and an amphitheater that testify to the area's Etruscan and Roman past. The panorama of Florence makes the trip worthwhile. You can reach Fiesole by taking city bus number 7 from the cathedral to the end of the line.

❧ RESTAURANTS

Cave di Maiano, Località Maiano, Via delle Cave 16; tel. (055) 59133. Breezes are more likely in the summer garden, offering welcome relief from torrid Florentine heat. Aldo and Romolo cater to serious eating (such as roast ham with turnip greens *alla Toscana*). The *antipasti* are a true house specialty. Meals run Lit. 35,000–45,000. Closed Thurs., Sun. evening in Aug. AE, DC.

Northwestern Tuscany

Pistoia

Pistoia is too close to Florence to excite much appreciation for its **12th-century cathedral, 14th-century baptistery** by Giovanni Pisano, and other attractive monuments and galleries. The province surrounding the town has fared somewhat better with the internationally renowned spa at **Montecatini Terme** and Tuscany's **ski area** at more than 5,500-foot-high Abetone Pass. Pistoia is 23 miles from Florence and can be visited as a day-trip or a brief stop for travelers headed elsewhere.

The **Pescia flower market** is the largest one in Italy that is not on the Ligurian coast. In the pleasant little village of **Collodi,** home of the author of *Pinocchio,* there is an attractive garden in the 17th-century **Villa Garzoni,** an amusement park, and a statue dedicated to the little puppet known to generations of youngsters around the world.

Lucca

High embankments surround the provincial seat of Lucca, west of Pistoia, 46 miles from Florence. Once a Roman colony and dominated successively by the Goths, Longobards, Pisans, Napoleonic forces, Hapsburgs, and Bourbons, Lucca was not annexed by Florence until 1847, 13 years before the unification of Italy.

In the town are the marble-rich **Cathedral** of San Martino, **San Michele in Foro,** and 6th- and 12th-century **San Frediano.** The Cathedral and San Michele are elaborately embroidered Romanesque marble masterpieces. Founded in the sixth century and rebuilt in 1060, the Cathedral was dressed in its Romanesque facade in the 13th century. San Michele and its brick-and-marble bell tower are a fine example of Pisan-Lucchese architecture of the 12th century.

One of the more interesting areas of the old town is the circular **Piazza del Anfiteatro,** on the site of a Roman amphitheater, just off the shop-lined promenade of **Via Fillungo.**

An **antique fair** is held the third weekend of every month in the area around Piazza Antelminelli. The city also stages concerts, ballets, and folk shows every summer between July and September.

Visit Lucca as a day-trip from Florence, or combine an overnight visit here with a visit to Pisa, 13½ miles away.

In the province are hillside villages that have been discovered by Northern European tourists, and the **beaches** along the Tyrrhenian coast that have long been popular with Italians. Between Lucca and Viareggio is the **Torre del Lago home of composer Giacomo Puccini,** open to the public for guided tours everyday during the summer.

Massa–Carrara

Two of the world's most productive marble centers give this coastal province its name. The hills along the route between Massa and Carrara are covered with white dust from the marble quarries that have been exploited for over 2,000 years, providing the majestic white stone that Michelangelo and other masters transformed into the artistic triumphs of all time.

Pisa

No longer directly on the sea, this ancient Roman port on the northern Tuscan coast was once one of the major Italian maritime republics. In Pisa's **Piazza dei Miracoli (Piazza del Duomo),** there is much more than the leaning tower. An immense grass carpet, the square embraces an 11th-century cathedral and 12th-century baptistery; a 13th-century monumental cemetery borders one side. (Open 9 A.M. to 4:30 P.M., hours adjusted seasonally.)

The bronze doors of the **Cathedral** (from the Giambologna school) and the bronze transept doors by Bonanno Pisano (facing the tower) accent the marble patterns of the cathedral. The ceiling and Giovanni Pisano's **pulpit** were rebuilt after being damaged in a 1596 fire. Gables were added to the first two stories of the **Baptistery** in the 14th century. Under the impressive 115-foot-diameter interior dome is Nicolò Pisano's 13th-century pulpit.

Baptistery, Cathedral, Leaning Tower, Cemetery (1063–1464), Piazza del Duomo

The tilt of Pisa's famed *campanile* is an accident of faulty foundations. The richly ornamented appearance of the Piazza del Duomo complex, however, was a deliberate symbol of Pisa's wealth. Medieval Pisa was one of Italy's most powerful seafaring merchant cities, rivaled only by Genoa and Venice.

The square's gleaming white buildings are separated by an intense green lawn. The circular Baptistery, the cross-shaped Cathedral, and the Leaning Tower are backed by the rectangular Camposanto cemetery. The recurrent use of colored stones inset against the white marble and facades of stacked arcades unify the complex.

The predominant classically rounded arches revived an interest in Italy's Roman past, evident in the Baptistery pulpit by Nicolò Pisano and the duomo pulpit by his son Giovanni. The buildings were also shaped by their medieval context; Pisa was a major stopping point for the Crusaders on their way to the Near East, and the Camposanto is supposedly filled with earth from Jerusalem's Hill of Calvary. The dizzying ascent up the Leaning Tower provides the best view of the complex and the city of Pisa.

—Mary Beth Betts and
Charles Ayes

The Romanesque white marble **Leaning Tower** of Pisa by Bonanno Pisano is a bell tower with 294 steps.

Climbing the tilting tower can produce curious effects. Avoid the climb in damp weather; the marble steps become slick and not all of the open portals of the tower are blocked by railings.

The **Camposanto** (cemetery) is allegedly formed from soil that Crusaders brought from the Hill of Calvary. The Gothic galleries are faced by 600 tombstones.

If it's more than just a day-trip to the tower from Florence, head down Via Santa Maria (behind the cathedral) onto Via del Mille, which leads to the 16th- and 17th-century **Piazza dei Cavalieri** and Vasari's **Palazzo dei Cavalieri.** The church and bell tower of **Santo Stefano,** on the piazza, were built in 1569 from a design by Vasari. The square was the base for the Crusading Knights of St. Stephen (the *Cavalieri*).

On the banks of the Arno, on Lungarno Mediceo, is the **National Museum** (open 9 A.M. to 1 P.M. and 3 to 6 P.M. in summer; 9 A.M. to 2 P.M. in winter; 9 A.M. to 1 P.M. Sunday and holidays; closed Monday). In rooms around the 15th-century cloisters of the former San Matteo monastery, the museum features works by native sons Giovanni and Andrea Pisano. The first floor has sculptures and paintings from the Pisan school.

❦ RESTAURANTS

Pisa offers some fine choices, such as **Al Ristoro dei Vecchi Macelli,** Via Volturno 49; tel. (050) 20424, and **Sergio,** Lungarno Pacinotti 1; tel. (050) 48245. On a day trip from Florence, stop en route in Montopoli (20 miles from Pisa and 32 from Florence) at the **4 Gigli,** Piazza San Michele 2; tel. (0571) 466940. In the old Governor's Palace overlooking the Tuscan hills, this country restaurant has pure Tuscan fare with a strong local accent, from *antipasti* to game, to sweets and regional wines. Dinner runs Lit. 30,000–40,000. Closed Sun. evening, Mon., Aug. 10–25. AE, DC, V.

Livorno

South of Pisa, the origins of Tuscany's principal seaport of Livorno are traced to 904. Livorno was dominated by Genoa from 1046 to 1425, when it was sold to Florence and became part of the Grand Duchy of Tuscany. The 16th-century **Fortezza Vecchia** (Old Fort) on Viale Caprera was commissioned by Giulio de'Medici; Antonio da Sangallo built it. The 16th- and early **17th-century cathedral** in Piazza Grande was severely damaged, as was most of the city, in Allied bombing raids in 1943. The cathedral has been totally rebuilt.

You can take a ferry from Livorno to a number of islands, including Elba (see "Taking the Ferry," this chapter). Livorno is 72 miles from Florence.

❦ RESTAURANTS

Rossi Torre di Calafuria, Via del Litorale 248; tel. (0586) 580547. The Nardis are often called from their kitchen to represent Tuscany with their fish and meat dishes in foreign gastronomical festivals. Dinners run Lit. 30,000–45,000. Closed Tues., Nov. AE, V.

Central Tuscany

Arezzo

The city of Petrach, Vasari, and Guido d'Arezzo (who invented the musical scale in the 11th century), Arezzo is of Etruscan origin and commands a hillside overlooking four valleys. Fifty miles from Florence, the town makes a good break for travelers heading south—perhaps into Umbria. The major attraction is Piero della Francesca's **Legend of the Holy Cross frescoes** in the 14th-century **Basilica of San Francesco.** The **home of Giorgio Vasari,** at Via XX Settembre 55, is open to the public (8 A.M. to 2 P.M.; closed Monday). The versatile Vasari personally directed construction of his 16th-century house and its furnishings and frescoes.

Piero della Francesca,
Legend of the Holy Cross (1453–1464)

This pleasing cycle of frescoes by Piero della Francesca is based on a popularized account of scripture. The *Legend of the Holy Cross* recounts ten episodes of the miraculous history of the True Cross. For Piero the story seems mainly an occasion for a display of technical virtuosity. The variety of subject matter is impressive, ranging from the stillness of the *Announcement of Christ's Death to the Virgin* (notice the austere column dividing her private space from that of the angel) to the chaos of battle in *The Victory of Heraclius over Chosroes* (who had attempted to steal the cross). Piero's grasp of space, design, and volume is most notable in the pageantry of *The Queen of Sheba's Meeting with King Solomon,* as is his colorist's eye for subtle shadings.

The most interesting panel of all is the *Dream of Constantine* (lower right, central wall), which depicts a night scene of supreme originality. A swooping angel brings tidings of victory to Constantine, who lies sleeping in his tent. The campsite is aglow; over the shoulder of the standing guard shows the bored gaze of a servant keeping watch. A third soldier senses the intruder, but no one looks up: The angel plunging out of the night is invisible to them as he enters the sleeper's dream.

Piero's figures are round-faced and squat, as bound to the earth as were the Tuscan peasants who probably served as his models. Several stare boldly at the viewer with dark, frank eyes. Piero's colors are drawn from the earth, as well: soft greens, browns, ochers, and wine-purple, which he favored. At the same time, the frescoes radiate a mysterious, otherworldly quality, distilled in the pale blue skies.

—Michael Hinden

An interesting folk festival is the **Giostra del Saracino** (Saracen Joust) staged the first Sunday in September. Horsemen in 12th-century costume charge a Saracen dummy with lances, hoping to strike and escape unscathed from the ricocheting dummy. An **antique fair** is also held the first weekend of every month.

SIDETRIP

Nearby Cortona has harmoniously blended the Etruscan, medieval, and Renaissance behind its old walls atop Monte Sant'Egidio. The **Etruscan Museum** in **Palazzo Casali** has few but notable Etruscan objects (open 10 A.M.–1 P.M. and 4–7 P.M. April 1–September 30; 9 A.M.–1 P.M. and 3–5 P.M. October 1–March 31).

Siena

Florence is a must on any visit to Italy, and Siena is a must on any visit to Tuscany. According to legend, the children of Remus staked out the boundaries of Siena, but the Sienese prefer staking their own claim to an Etruscan heritage. The center of the old walled city is **Piazza del Campo,** site of the famous **Palio delle Contrade,** staged every July 2 and now August 16 as well. (The Palio began July 2, 1656; the August date was recently added to attract tourists.) The brick square is covered with dirt for this immensely popular medieval horse race between representatives of the city's *contrade* (parishes). The Sienese take these races to heart. Many a losing jockey has been obliged to head for the hills until the ire ebbed. And if contrada residents feel he fell into the race eve smoke-filled room trap and accepted a payoff to hold back . . .

On the square is the 13th-century **Palazzo Pubblico** (Town Hall), considered the best example of public Gothic architecture in Tuscany. Inside are famous frescoes by Lorenzetti. Prior to the Palio the horses enter the square from the building's courtyard. Next to the palace is the nearly 300-feet-high **Torre del Mangia.** This 14th-century bell tower offers a splendid view over the old city, bathed red with Sienese brick and roof tiles. Surprising are the cultivated orchards inside the old city walls.

Construction on the **Cathedral,** in Piazza Duomo, began in the mid-12th century. In 1339 it was decided to expand the Gothic church into Christianity's largest cathedral, but the plague of 1348 shelved further construction. Giovanni and Nicolò Pisano collaborated in the decoration of the interior: Admire the inlaid marble floor. Down the left nave is the **Libreria Piccolomini,** built by the future Pius III (open 9 A.M. to 7:30 P.M.), with a large rectangular hall frescoed by Pinturicchio. The **Chapel of the Madonna** has sculptures by Bernini.

To the right of the Duomo are stairs leading down to Piazza San Giovanni and the entrance to the **Baptistery** (open 9 A.M. to 1 P.M. and 3 to 5 P.M.). Among the 15th-century frescoes in the interior is Jacopo della Quercia's marble tabernacle.

Ambrogio Lorenzetti,
Allegory of Good Government (1337–1339)

Lorenzetti's vision of well-regulated town and country life is prominent in Siena's town hall, along with its *Bad Government* counterpart. Although the painting's political intent may have been important to its original viewers, what attracts today are the delightful glimpses afforded of everyday life in the 14th century. Ambrogio was also a mapmaker, and this 27-foot-long panorama combines a firm grasp of spatial relations, draftsmanship, and an eye for small detail.

His ideal city hums with commerce and daily pleasures. In the central marketplace, winsome young ladies sing and dance in a circle to a tambourine. Drawn by the music, another young woman looks down from her window. A class is in session in the building below, which also houses a shoemaker's shop and a wine bar. Tradesmen of every description go about their business. A wealthy entourage on horseback exits left, while a goatherd at right drives his flock toward the town gate. On high, roofers complete a new building, while below, donkeys laden with small logs or sacks of grain clop through the streets. A bird cage hangs in one window, and there are flowerpots and pitchers here and there on sills. The buildings themselves, with their crenellated parapets, balconies, and arcades, are a blend of reality and imagination, a notion of Siena as it should be, a delight to the eye in every nook and corner.

The city wall at right divides the country from the town. On the road, activity is brisk, as various social classes mingle peaceably. The sweeping bird's-eye view of the distance shows fields that are neatly tended; all is well here, too. On the opposite wall, the hellish alternative of bad government is also allegorized.

—Michael Hinden

Although the Palio is Siena's most popular attraction, it's impossible to get the real feel of Siena then. The spring and early fall are a real delight for wandering through the stone-paved streets or reclining at a caffè in Piazza del Campo. Here the words "charming" and "picturesque" find new dimensions.

RESTAURANTS
Antica Trattoria Bottega Nova, Strada Chiantigiana 29; tel. (0577) 284230. Ettore Silvestri has a good staff, good Chianti, and good beef, worth the drive beyond the old city walls to this rustic country-style Tuscan trattoria. Dinners range Lit. 28,000–33,000. Closed Sun., Jan. 1–10, Aug. 16–31. All cards.

SIDETRIP
Besides the spa at Chianciano Terme, the province of Siena offers the medieval gem of **San Gimignano,** a town of Etruscan origin. Three sets of city walls testify to the town's Guelph and

Ghibelline conflicts (Guelphs supported papal rule, Ghibellines the emperor); 14 towers that look like medieval skyscrapers line the ramparts. In medieval times a status symbol among local nobility, the towers, intended as strongholds, became prestigiously higher and higher in the effort to "keep up with the Rossis" (there were no Joneses in Tuscany at the time).

Southern Tuscany

Grosseto

The agricultural center of Grosseto is the seat of the southernmost province in Tuscany, which borders the region of Lazio. It is in the southern **Maremma,** the land of Tuscan cowboys. (The Wild West show of Buffalo Bill came out second-best to these Tuscan wranglers during a rodeo that was staged in Piazza del Popolo over one hundred years ago in Rome.) Southeast of Grosseto is the charming little village of Saturnia, with its **sulfur baths.**

The summer resorts of **Porto Santo Stefano** and **Port'Ercole** on the **Argentario** island are linked to the mainland by a man-made isthmus at Orbetello, on the SS1 (the Via Aurelia Etrusca).

Elba

Elba is the largest island in the Tuscan archipelago. It is only 6½ miles off the mainland point of Piombino near Livorno. Portoferraio is the main town on the island and prime ferry connection to the mainland (Piombino and Livorno).

The residence of Napoleon I after abdication, the island is now known as a summer vacationland. Natural harbors abound on most of the eastern, northern, and southern perimeters of the island providing excellent access for fishing and water sports enthusiasts.

8

EMILIA-ROMAGNA

Politically, Emilia-Romagna is the core of Italy's "Red Belt." The postwar "peaceful conflict" between Roman Catholic clergy and Communist politicians was immortalized in Giovanni Guareschi's *Tales of Don Camillo and Peppone,* which romanticized the political strife. The imagery is not farfetched— it is not unusual to find a sea of red flags following a torchlit religious procession, in a typically pragmatic blend of contrasts.

The region's "red" streak is most evident in its strong cooperative sense, typified by agricultural programs that are often praised as models for continental development by European Economic Community officials. This cooperative spirit has helped to make Emilia-Romagna one of Europe's most developed summer recreational and entertainment areas, with the most extensive stretch of seaside hotels along the coast of Romagna. This area is popular nationally and internationally, particularly with northern Europeans. Ironically, Germans sparked the postwar beach boom, as well as a riviera sexual revolution, such that in the mid-1960s a prominent Frankfurt daily felt compelled to editorialize an appeal to young frauleins heading for Rimini and environs to modify their behavior with local lifeguards and beach boys.

Such incidents have fanned the flames of legends in this land of coarse exaggeration. Emilian journalist Enzo Biagi in his book *Italia* chronicles the boast of another Emilian who claimed his sexual prowess was so exceptional that the completion of a performance under a scene depicting the Last Supper was rewarded with a standing ovation by all the disciples. In Romagna this is low key.

Geographically, Emilia-Romagna is the fertile buffer between Italy's industrial north and more isolated central and southern lands. The region extends for nearly 14,000 square miles, from the River Po to the Apennines, from Liguria to the Adriatic. The area has two subregions: northern and western Emilia, with its Apennines and broad fields, and eastern and southern Romagna, with its valleys and beaches.

Agriculture has flourished here for two thousand years, since Emilia-Romagna's rich plains were the breadbasket of the Roman Empire. The region takes its name from the ancient Via Aemilia (Emilia), which Roman Consul Marcus Aemilius Lepidus had built in 187 B.C. from Ariminum (Rimini), on the Adriatic, to northwestern Placentia (Piacenza).

Emilia-Romagna's strategic geography has long shaped the region's history. The Apennines, stretching along western Emilia, formed the infamous "Gothic Line" of World War II that stymied Allied advances for two months in 1944, exposing the Italian population behind German lines to incessant Allied bombing intended to disrupt German supply lines. Partisan resistance to the Germans resulted in the reprisal mass murder of 1,836 people at Marzabotto. Today's winter ski resorts—where Olympic champion Alberto Tomba began developing his slalom skills—belie the tremendous price paid in human lives for the liberation of the area just 45 years ago.

Geography has played other tricks on the region. The fertile River Po, Italy's largest, overflowed its banks in November 1951 in one of the country's worst modern calamities, and spread destruction and death across the river's Adriatic delta.

On July 14, 1948, an assassin's bullet seriously wounded Communist Party leader Palmiro Togliatti as he left Parliament in Rome. The news flash sparked tension-packed civil unrest throughout Emilia-Romagna's "red belt." Government riot squads squared off against demonstrators, many of whom had belonged to leftist partisan groups in the waning years of Nazi occupation. From his hospital bed Togliatti appealed for calm, but his words were not as effective as those from a radio sports commentator reporting the Herculean effort of a solitary cyclist furiously pedaling against time on the back roads of France.

Italian cyclist Gino Bartali had won the Tour de France in 1938, but World War II had canceled the prime of his career. A decade later, the 34-year-old Tuscan again emerged to capture that Superbowl of cycling. When he crossed the finish line in Paris, Bartali gave a wounded and divided nation reason to rejoice and reflect. Together, riot policemen and demonstrators toasted Bartali's incredible defiance of time, then went separate ways. It was not a day for letting blood.

The famous and infamous who have called this region home typify the contrasts inherent here. Native sons Guglielmo Marconi and Benito Mussolini made historic contributions to mankind—in completely opposite directions. Music-mad Emilia-Romagna was the birthplace of composer Giuseppe Verdi and conductor Arturo Toscanini, though the music that still reigns—despite booming disco beats—is the *liscio,* an agrarian tango. Ballrooms swell throughout the region and know no age limits. There is even a multi-million dollar liscio palace near Ravenna.

The list of native-born film directors reads like a who's who of Italian cinema: Bernardo Bertolucci, Federico Fellini, Michelangelo Antonioni, Liliana Cavani, and Pier Paolo Pasolini, to name a few. And outside Modena, at Maranello, is the hometown of the most famous name in international Formula One auto racing, Enzo Ferrari.

Family dynasties also have emerged: Rimini's ruthless Malatestas; the cultured but cruel Estes (of *New York Times* crossword puzzle fame) from Ferrara, Modena, and Reggio nell'Emilia; Bologna's Renaissance Bentivoglios; and the patronal Farneses of Parma and Piacenza.

WINING AND DINING

Dining well is practically a religion in Emilia-Romagna. Heretics can find fast food. For the rest, there are tortellini, tortelloni, lasagna, Bolognese cutlets, *zampone* (pig's feet), *bolliti* (boiled meats), even eels from the Comacchio Lagoon—Ferrara's bread alone is worth the trip. There is fine seafood on the Adriatic coast, and *piedina,* a Romagnola pizza stuffed with ham and cheese, or sausage and cooked greens. In Emilia-Romagna, weight-watchers must take a holiday.

Government-regulated DOC wines are not in abundance, but with the likes of Lambrusco and Sangiovese di Romagna there is little demand for a wider variety. Other inviting regional wines are Albana di Romagna, Bianco di Scaniano, Colli Bolognese, Colli di Parma, Monte San Pietro, Reggiano di Sorbana di Santa Croce, and Trebbiano di Romagna.

In Bologna the joys of dining late and caffè nightlife are being rediscovered. A number of places remain open to 3 and 4 A.M., rivaling the 5–6 A.M. closings found on the Romagna coast, where a tableful of revelers might be concluding the night out with a late *spaghettata* next to a party of early-risers facing a sizable breakfast.

Restaurant suggestions for Bologna cover an extensive price range to accommodate longer stays. Recommendations for the Romagna coast are limited since hotels there usually require meal plans, especially in high season. The small-town listings are restaurants considered the best in the region and worth a detour. All recommended restaurants (unless otherwise noted) feature typical Emilia-Romagna fare.

Credit cards are listed as accepted in our recommended restaurants described below. "All cards" means that all of the following are accepted: AE—American Express; DC—Diner's Club; MC—MasterCard; V—Visa. Prices given are for a complete dinner (antipasto to dessert) for one person, unless otherwise specified.

TRAVEL

Volume is the biggest obstacle to travel in Emilia-Romagna. All major north–south highways and rail lines converge on centrally located Bologna. Turnpike tie-ups in August bear a closer resemblance to downtown Rome than to extraurban eight-lane highways.

Turnpike workers' strikes are welcomed by motorists, since unmanned tollbooths mean free travel on one of the most expensive toll-road networks in Europe. Train strikes, however, are disastrous in Bologna and practically paralyze north–south movement. This strategic location is what prompted the terrorist bombing of the Bologna rail terminal by neo-fascist extremists on August 2, 1980. Happily, such terrorism seems to be a thing of the past in Italy today.

Flying

Bologna's international Guglielmo Marconi Airport is at Borgo Panigale, just 4 miles from the central rail terminal. The ride on the city number 91 bus from the train station to the airport is only half an hour. The 15-min. ride by cab should cost about Lit. 12,000.

Flight information can be obtained from Alitalia, ATI, tel. (051) 311952; Aliblu, tel. (051) 311850; Alisarda, tel. (051) 384856; Lufthansa, tel. (051) 52001; and British Airways, tel. (051) 247215.

Lufthansa flies directly to Frankfurt (1½ hours) and Munich (1 hour, 25 min.). Alitalia flies daily to London-Heathrow (2 hours) and Paris (1 hour, 35 min.). British Air has direct flights Monday, Wednesday, Friday, and Sunday to London-Gatwick (2 hours).

Two other regional airports are Forli's Luigi Ridolfi and Rimini's Miramare.

There is also a small airport 2 miles from downtown Parma. Taxis provide the only service to Parma. For flight information, call (0921) 994356.

Taxi is the most convenient means of reaching the Forli airport for Alisarda and Avianova flights to Milan, Olbia, and Rome, but fortunately the airport is just 2 miles from the center of town. For flight information, tel. (0543) 780678.

Alitalia, ATI, and Aliblu serve the Rimini airport, which is kept busy with charter flights from northern Europe during the summer beach season. Regularly scheduled flights are available to both Milan and Rome. Bus service is available for the 4-mile ride to central Piazza Tripoli. For flight information, tel. (0541) 373132.

Domestic Flights

	Bologna (Guglielmo Marconi)	Parma	Rimini (Miramare)	Forlì (Luigi Ridolfi)
Alghero	1 hr., 5 min.			
Bari	1 hr., 30 min.			
Cagliari	1 hr., 15 min.			
Catania	1 hr., 30 min.			
Milan	55 min.		1 hr., 5 min.	50 min.
Naples	1 hr., 40 min.			
Olbia	1 hr.			1 hr., 20 min.
Palermo	1 hr., 20 min.			
Pescara	1 hr., 10 min.			
Rome	55 min.	50 min.	1 hr., 5 min.	1 hr., 10 min.

Taking the Train

Bologna is the hub of the two principal rail routes in Italy. The Turin–Milan line extends south through all the Via Emilia provincial capitals to the Adriatic, and continues down the eastern coast through Ancona, Pescara, Foggia, and Bari to Lecce, in the extreme south of Puglia. Going north, it is a major route for international traffic via Chiasso, Domodossola, and Ventimiglia.

The principal west coast route goes from Reggio Calabria (with connections to Sicily) north through Naples, Rome, and Florence. Two other northern routes go to Verona, Trento, and Bolzano, to the Brenner Pass; and to Padua and Venice, with connections to Udine and into Austria, or to Trieste and into Yugoslavia.

Inter-city service (with respective times from Bologna) are: Milan (1 hour, 50 min.), Rome (3½ hours), Turin (Torino) (3½ hours), Brenner (4½ hours), Venice (2 hours, 20 min.), and Rimini (1¼ hours).

Driving

The turnpike system in Emilia-Romagna follows basically the same pattern as rail travel, with major turnpikes converging on the northern semi-circular Tangenziale bypass of Bologna proper.

Converging on the Tangenziale are the Rome–Milan A1, the A14 south to Taranto, and the A13 north to Padua via Ferrara (29 miles from Bologna). The latter joins with the Turin–Trieste A4 at Padua.

On the A1 at Modena (24 miles northwest of Bologna) is a junction with the A22 Modena-Brenner, which crosses the A4 at Verona.

At the Piacenza A1 exit (93 miles west of Bologna) there is a junction with the A21 Turin-Brescia which also ties into the A4, at Brescia. At the Parma A1 exit (60 miles west of Bologna) there is a connection with the A15 to La Spezia, on the Riviera di Levante.

Bologna is 235 turnpike miles from Rome, 65 from Florence, 130 from Milan, and 94 from Venice.

CAR RENTALS

The following auto rental facilities are available in Emilia-Romagna.

Bologna: City—Avis, Viale Pietramellara 35l; tel. (051) 550647. Europcar, Via Boldoni 3A; tel. (051) 247101; telex 216008. Hertz, Via Stalingrado 22B; tel. (051) 370631; telex 570222. Maggiore, Via Cairoli 4; tel. (051) 553553.

Airport (Borgo Panigale)—Avis, tel. (051) 380754; Europcar, tel. (051) 312175; Hertz, tel. (051) 311811; Maggiore, tel. (051) 311552.

Ferrara: City—Avis, Via Padova 207; tel. (0532) 461994.

Forlì: Airport (Ridolfi)—Avis, through Ravenna office, tel. (0544) 420581; Europcar, tel. (0543) 782105; Hertz, tel. (0543) 782288 or through Ravenna office, tel. (0544) 33674.

Modena: City—Avis, Via Malmusi 26; tel. (059) 2300966. Europcar, Via Ciro Menotti 4; tel. (059) 217657; telex 583262. Hertz, Via Canaletto 60; tel. (059) 315344; telex 570222. Maggiore, Via Trento e Trieste 43; tel. (059) 216920.

Parma: City—Avis, Via Fratti 24; tel. (0521) 722418. Hertz, Viale Mentana 124; tel. (0521) 32481; telex 570222. Maggiore, Via Brescia 7; tel. (0521) 76880.

Piacenza: City—Avis, Piazzale Marconi 5; tel. (0523) 29345.

Pomposa: Avis, Via Lovara 22, Codigoro; tel. (0533) 710125. Seasonal office Apr. 1–Oct. 31.

Ravenna: City—Avis, Via Trieste 25; tel. (0544) 420581. Europcar, Via di Roma 153; tel. (0544) 28376. Hertz, Garage Roma, Via Beatrice Alighieri 20; tel. (0544) 33674. Maggiore, Via Beatrice Alighieri 40; tel. (0544) 31078.

Reggio nell'Emilia: City—Europcar, Viale Isonzo 9C; tel. (0522) 40976.

Rimini: City—Avis, Viale Trieste 16; tel. (0541) 51256. Europcar, Via Giovanni XXII 126; tel. (0541) 54746; telex 550667. Hertz, Viale Trieste 16A; tel. (0541) 53110.

Airport (Miramare)—Europcar, tel. (0541) 374606. Advance reservations required.

✤ ACCOMMODATIONS

Supply strains to meet the demand on the coast of Romagna during July and Aug., and in and around Bologna during the city's heavy industrial fair schedule Sept.–early June. During Bologna's popular Dec. motor show, accommodations are all but impossible to get without reservations.

Coastal hotels (the best coastal towns are Cattolica, Rimini, and Riccione) offer special rates in May, June, and Sept. in an effort to extend summer business. (Use Riccione as a very convenient base for exploring the tiny Republic of San Marino.) University students have a stranglehold on economy lodgings, particularly in Bologna, and many budget lodgings close during Aug. Rates quoted here are for the high season.

However, since the region's turnpike system is so efficient, any base on the Via Emilia can suffice for the traveler by car. The towns of the House of Este can all be explored from Modena, Reggio nell'Emilia, Parma, or Piacenza. Ferrara, worth a visit in its own right, is a bit farther afield. Tourist information offices on the autostradas can provide information on the numerous small hotels popping up in smaller urban areas.

Credit cards are listed as accepted. "All cards" means that all of the following are accepted: AE—American Express; DC—Diner's Club; MC—MasterCard; V—Visa. Ranges given for room rates indicate the span between single and double rooms.

Bologna

City Hotel, Via Magenta 10, 40100; tel. (051) 372676. This modern, 3-star, 50-room hotel with air-conditioning is just off the Tangenziale at exit (*uscita*) 6 and only 800 yards from the industrial fair site. There is no restaurant, but parking is available. Room rates run Lit. 60,000–90,000. All cards.

Donatello, Via dell'Indipendenza 65, 40100; tel. (051) 248174. This air-conditioned, 38-room, comfortable 3-star hotel is on Bologna's main street halfway between the rail terminal and the heart of the city. Private TV and telephone. There are two garages in the vicinity. Room rates are Lit. 60,000–89,000. AE, DC, V.

Grand Hotel Baglioni, Via dell'Indipendenza 8, 40100; tel. (051) 225445; telex 510242. This 5-star, 16th-century palace is one of Italy's best extra-luxury hotels. It reopened in March 1987 after a decade of extensive renovation. An original stretch of the Roman Via Emilia was uncovered under the hotel, and is open to inspection by guests. Frescoes of the 16th and 17th centuries by Bartolomeo Ceci and the Caracci family adorn the bar and restaurant, the most fashionable in town. It's not unusual to find Bolognans weekending here for a luxurious touch during a wedding anniversary. The hotel has 125 air-conditioned rooms. Rates run Lit. 210,000–300,000 with breakfast. All cards.

Maggiore, Via Emilia Ponente 62, 40100; tel. (051) 381634; telex 226262. Beyond the viale loop around old town, this 3-star, 60-room hotel is halfway between the airport and the center of Bologna (about 1¼ mile each way). There is no restaurant, but ample parking. Air-conditioning should have been installed by this reading. Room rates with continental breakfast run Lit. 70,000–110,000. Closed the first three weeks of Aug. All cards.

Royal Hotel Carlton, Via Montebello 8, 40100; tel. (051) 249361; telex 510356. This spacious, elegant, well-cared-for, 5-star hotel was built in 1974 just off the main street of Bologna and only 150 yards from the main rail terminal. Rates for its 250 air-conditioned rooms, including a buffet breakfast, run Lit. 210,000–280,000. All cards.

Cattolica

Three quick suggestions are the seasonal 4-star **Caravelle,** Via Padova 6, 47033 (FO); tel. (0541) 962416, with rates of Lit. 132,000; **Negresco,** Via del Turismo 6, 47033 (FO); tel. (0541) 963281, with rooms for Lit. 78,000; and 3-star **Cormoran,** Via Francia 2, 47033 (FO); tel. (0541) 951002, rooms, Lit. 50,000. All have private pools. Prices include full board.

For more economical accommodations, contact: I.A.T.—
Cattolica, Piazza Nettuno, 47033 Cattolica (FO); tel. (0541)
963341.

Ferrara
Touring, Viale Cavour 11, 44100; tel. (0532) 26096. A 3-star,
39-room hotel just around the corner from the Largo Castello
tourist information office and Este Castle. Facilities for the handicapped. There is parking, but no restaurant. Room rates run Lit.
38,000–65,000. AE, DC, V.

Modena
Roma, Via Farini 44, 41100; tel. (059) 222218. This 3-star, 53-
room hotel is in a 17th-century palace considered a national
monument by the Italian Fine Arts Commission. It is centrally located, just off the Via Emilia and 200 yards from the tourist information office, and has garage facilities. Room rates (breakfast
included during summer months) run Lit. 52,000–74,000. All
cards.

Parma
Torino, Borgo Angelo Mazza 7, 43100; tel. (0521) 281046.
Centrally located between the cathedral and Pilotta Palace, this
3-star, 33-room hotel is near the theater in the old quarter, on
a pedestrian island. *"Vado al Hotel Torino"* will placate city police while you try to reach the hotel by auto. Garage and private
TV, but no air-conditioning. Just 10 min. from the rail station.
Room rates run Lit. 48,000–72,000. Closed one week at Christmas and the first three weeks of Aug. All cards.

Piacenza
Milano, Viale Risorgimento 47, 29100; tel. (0523) 36843. This
3-star, 43-room hotel is just behind the Farnese Palace, with
easy access from A21 (Piacenza Ovest exit), and just 5 min.
from the rail terminal. Parking, but no restaurant (there is one
next door). The rooms were recently renovated and each has
private TV. Room rates run Lit. 42,000–66,000. AE, MC, V.

Ravenna
Argentario, Via di Roma 45, 29100; tel. (0544) 22555. This
3-star, 34-room hotel is just beyond the old-town pedestrian island and only 50 yards from Sant'Apollinare Nuovo and the city
art gallery. No restaurant, but facilities for the handicapped.
Rooms are Lit. 43,000–67,500. No cards, but traveler's checks
accepted.

Reggio nell'Emilia
Albergo Posta, Piazza Cesare Battisti 4, 42100; tel. (0522)
32944; telex 530036. In the old-town pedestrian island, this recently renovated 4-star, 45-room hotel in the 13th-century
Palazzo del Capitano del Popolo combines an overnight stay
with a museum visit. The hotel has a bar and breakfast room,

but no restaurant. Air-conditioning in some rooms, at added fee. Room rates with continental breakfast run Lit. 95,000–135,000. All cards.

Riccione
Savioli Spiaggia, Viale d'Annunzio 2, 47036 (FO); tel. (0541) 43252; telex 551038. Located on the beach, this air-conditioned, 4-star, 70-room hotel also has a heated pool. Per-person room and full board costs Lit. 139,000. All cards.

For more economical accommodations, contact the Riccione Tourist Board, Piazzale Ceccarini 10, 47036 Riccione (FO); tel. (0541) 43361. For last-minute arrivals there also is a seasonal information booth at the rail terminal.

Rimini
Bellevue, Piazzale Kennedy 12, 47037 (FO); tel. (0541) 54116; telex 550546. This 4-star, 67-room, air-conditioned hotel just across the beachfront drive is open all year. The restaurant is open only for conventions. Room rates range from Lit. 110,000–160,000 to Lit. 150,000–210,000, continental breakfast included. All cards.

Grand Hotel, Via Ramusio 1, 47037 (FO); tel. (0541) 56000; telex 550022. This 5-star, 128-room hotel is Rimini's best. On Piazza Indipendenza, just across the shoreline drive, it's the only hotel with a private beach (the contract expires in 1999). Open all year, the air-conditioned hotel also has a tennis court, heated pool, and private parking. High season bed-and-breakfast rates are Lit. 145,000–225,000. All cards.

Rosabianca, Viale Tripoli 195, 47037 (FO); tel. (0541) 22577. This modern, 52-room hotel recently gained its fourth star. The small rooms are comfortable and efficient, and are just 5 min. from the airport bus connection at Piazza Tripoli and 10 min. from Rimini's industrial fairgrounds. Rooms run Lit. 60,000–100,000. Closed the last 10 days of Dec. AE, DC.

SKIING

Ski resorts in Emilia-Romagna are among the best organized in the Apennines. Ski season generally runs Dec.–Mar., but some areas have snow in Nov. and Apr.

Equipment rentals, ski schools, and chair lifts are available, as are hotels, restaurants, bars, medical aid, and mechanical assistance including the Italian Automobile Club. And since this is lively Emilia-Romagna, there is the ever-present discotheque, and sometimes movie theaters.

Snow-removal equipment keeps roads open, and an efficient provincial bus system connects skiing areas to rail depots, guaranteeing access by mass transit throughout the region.

The most frequented resorts are those in the provinces of Modena and Bologna, near the region's southern boundary with Tuscany:

Monte Cimone: This four-station complex (Fanano, Montecreto, Riolunato, and Sestola), 40–50 miles from Modena, is connected by over 28 miles of interwinding ski runs; a single pass is valid for the entire network. Cross-country courses and sled runs are also available. Hotels in the four stations can accommodate more than 1,800 persons. Also available are apartments and private rooms. Full information on the Monte Cimone complex and stations at Pievepelago, Fiumalbo, Mocogno, and Frassinoro can be obtained from the Modena Provincial Tourist Office, Corso Canalgrande 3, 41100 Modena; tel. (059) 230513.

Corno alle Scale: Including Budiara and Val Carlina, the station is about 50 miles from Bologna and 59 miles from Florence. Hotels in the area can accommodate more than 1,800 persons, and apartments and private rooms also are available. There are nearly 20 miles of ski runs as well as cross-country skiing. Complete information on this area and other ski resorts in the province of Bologna can be obtained from the Bologna Provincial Tourist Office, Via Marconi 45, 40100 Bologna; tel. (051) 237410.

Other regional ski information can be obtained from: Forli Provincial Tourist Office, Corso della Repubblica 23, 47100 Forli; tel. (0543) 25532. Parma Provincial Tourist Office, Piazza Duomo 5, 43100 Parma; tel. (0521) 33951. Piacenza Provincial Tourist Office, Via S. Siro 17, 29100 Piacenza; tel. (0523) 34347. Reggio nell'Emilia Provincial Tourist Office, Piazza C. Battisti 4, 42100 Reggio nell'Emilia; tel. (0522) 43370.

Bologna

"Fat," "learned," and "towered," Bologna is Emilia-Romagna's centrally located administrative capital.

"Fat" for its fertile terrain between the Reno and Savena rivers at the base of the Apennine foothills, an area that supplies one of Italy's most acclaimed gastronomical traditions.

"Learned" for a long-standing academic tradition fostered by Europe's oldest university, which has just celebrated its nine-hundredth anniversary. The University of Bologna's medical and nuclear physics schools are world-renowned.

"Towered" for its turrets and towers, which characterize a city also known for arcades and covered walks (constructed to shelter the poor) that rarely expose the stroller to the rigors of inclement weather.

Bologna basks in a fascinating provincialism that, unlike the aura of other major regional capitals, does not eclipse Emilia-Romagna's other provincial capitals—some of which were more prominent in the past. Bologna's low profile is not conducive to generating mass tourist appeal, but an appeal exists.

The center of Bologna is the "T" junction of Via dell'Indipendenza, Via Ugo Bassi, and Via Rizzoli at **Piazza del Nettuno,** with its 16th-century Giambologna **Neptune**

fountain (now caged and under restoration). The piazza is an antichamber for the more predominant Piazza Maggiore.

Facing Maggiore is the **Basilica of San Petronio** (patron of Bologna), which was under construction for 350 years, from 1309 to 1659. Here, in 1530, Charles V was crowned Holy Roman Emperor by Pope Clement VII. Across the square are the 13th-century **Palazzo del Podestà** (Governor's Palace), now the mayor's office and city council chamber, and the 13th- to 14th-century **Palazzo Comunale,** which frames a statue of Pope Gregory XIII, responsible for the Gregorian calendar. Also known as Palazzo d'Accursio, the Comunale contains the city's **art museum** in salons on its first and second floors (open 9 A.M. to 2 P.M., Sundays 9 A.M. to 12:30 P.M. Closed Tuesday and holidays).

Along the short walk to Via Rizzoli is **Piazza Re Enzo** and the **13th-century palace** where Enzo, king of Sardinia and son of King Frederick II, was incarcerated for 23 years. Visitors can see the inner courtyard.

Via Rizzoli is one of the most fashionable streets of Bologna with its elegant shops and caffès. It leads into **Piazza di Porta Ravegnana** and the two leaning towers that are the symbol of Bologna. The 325-foot **Asineli** has nearly a four-foot lean, and is open to the daring public 9 A.M. to 6 P.M. A fine view of the city center awaits the adventurous who can manage the 486 steps. The smaller, 162-foot **Garisenda** has a ten-foot lean. It originally rivaled the 12th-century Asineli in height, but the unstable upper portion was removed in 1351.

Other interesting sights are the 13th-century **Casa Isolani** (at 19 Strada Maggiore) and, at number 44, the **Palazzo Davia Bargellini** where, in seven large rooms, paintings, ceramics, and furniture from the 14th to 18th centuries are on display (9 A.M. to 2 P.M.; 9 A.M. to 12:30 P.M. Sunday; closed Tuesday). Across the street is the Gothic 14th-century **Santa Maria dei Servi,** one of the most beautiful churches in Bologna. At the end of Strada Maggiore and to the right, at Piazza Carducci, is the **house-museum of poet Giosuè Carducci,** the patriot-poet. The house is open Tuesday through Saturday, 9 A.M. to noon and 3 to 5 P.M., 9 A.M. to 1 P.M. Sunday and holidays; closed Monday.

The **city archaeological museum,** on Via Archiginnasio, houses prehistoric, Egyptian, Greek, Etruscan, and Roman artifacts; medieval and Renaissance sculptures; ceramics; arms, musical instruments; and more. It is open 9 A.M. to 2 P.M., 9 A.M. to 12:30 P.M. Sunday and holidays; closed Monday.

The **National Art Gallery** (with hours the same as the city museum), on Via delle Belle Arti, is divided into three sections: primitive, Bologna artists, and the Renaissance and baroque. Emilian artists of the 14th to 18th centuries prevail, but there are also interesting works by Raphael, Perugino, Giotto, and Parmigianino.

The **University of Bologna** is on Via Zamboni. At the corner of Via Belmeloro is **University Palace,** which contains naval, astronomy, and history museums, as well as the university library.

Across Via Zamboni at the corner of Via delle Moline is the **city theater,** which was constructed in 1756 on the ruins of the palace of the Bentivoglio family, once the *signori* of Bologna, who opened the city to the Renaissance.

The Bentivoglio family funeral chapel, with 15th-century frescoes, is in the **church of San Giacomo Maggiore.** Begun in 1267, the church has a Gothic facade, but the interior is adorned in mid-15th-century Renaissance style. Look for the Bentivoglio tomb by Jacopo della Quercia.

Worth a drive is the circular series of *viali* around the old city center, passing each of the 12 city gates. By public transportation, take either the number 32 bus (clockwise) or number 33 (counterclockwise) from the main rail terminal.

RESTAURANTS

I Carracci, Via Manzoni 2; tel. (051) 270815. This first-class restaurant of the Baglioni Hotel is named after the 16th–17th-century family of artists who adorned the restaurant with the "Four Seasons" frescoes. Choose your meat and fowl from serving carts, where portions are carved as requested. Other specialties include ricotta soufflé and sweet-and-sour breast of duck. The air-conditioned restaurant is the most fashionable in town. Dinners cost about Lit. 60,000–80,000. Closed Sun. and Aug. All cards.

Diana, Via dell'Indipendenza 24; tel. (051) 231302. One of the oldest restaurants in Bologna, and a local favorite. The decor is yesteryear, the cuisine Bologna today with a flare for fantasy. For antipasto try mortadella tarts, with *mortadella spuma*—whipped—served on thin slices of toasted bread. Dinner costs about Lit. 35,000. Closed Mon. and Aug. AE, DC, V.

Osteria Matusel, Bertolini 2; tel. (051) 231718. Eat, drink, and be merry. Near the university, on the first floor of a 13th-century building under the tutelage of the State Fine Arts Commission, this restaurant caters to a youthful (both in body and in spirit) clientele. Old, country cooking with regional wine for only Lit. 10,000–15,000. And if you're toting a guitar, a sing-along crowd is ready and willing. Closed Sun. and mid-July–Sept.

Fast Food

Places for midday snacks and fast food are in abundance across the region. On Via dell'Indipendenza in the heart of Bologna there is **Italy and Italy** (a local franchise); **McDonald's;** and **Il Centro,** a regular evening restaurant that has self-service at noon, where one can obtain a quick lunch for less than Lit. 10,000. At Piazza 8 Agosto is **Il Ragu,** also good for a quick lunch.

Notai, Via de' Pignattari 1; tel. (051) 228694. Sometimes consistency suffers, but mostly, innovation is successfully applied to traditional regional cuisine. Try, for instance, traditional tortelloni with grated mushrooms. During the summer, dine at one of the outdoor tables near the San Petronio Basilica. Dinners range Lit. 50,000–60,000. Closed Sun. and the last half of Aug. AE, DC, V.

Pappagallo, Piazza della Mercanzia 3c; tel. (051) 232807. Living off a glorious past, the elegant atmosphere provides a pleasant (if somewhat overpriced) evening of traditional Bolognese food. Air-conditioned. Reservations are recommended. Dinners cost Lit. 40,000–65,000. Closed Sun. evening, Mon., one week in Jan., and three weeks in Aug. All cards.

Osteria dei Poeti, Via dei Poeti 1b; tel. (051) 236166. This was a favorite with both contemporary poets Carducci and Pascoli. The food here is strictly Bolognese fare (tortelloni, lasagna, roasts, cutlets). Open until 4 A.M., the air-conditioned locale is divided into two sections: a restaurant with soft dining music, and a piano bar encouraging public participation. A full meal in the restaurant costs Lit. 40,000–50,000 with wine. Closed Mon. All cards.

Silverio, Via Nosadella 37a; tel. (051) 330604. This small, comfortable restaurant 400 yards from San Petronio specializes in the unusual, and Silverio Cineri's efforts have a local cult following. Try figs with prosciutto mousse or *pappardella* with sage and cedar leaves. Reservations suggested. Dinner runs about Lit. 35,000 without wine. Closed Mon. and Aug. AE, DC, V.

Al Solito Posto, Via Turati 112; tel. (051) 410415. A good alternative to strictly Bolognese fare, as only a Neapolitan with a Spanish wife could provide. Small and characteristic. The paella is abundant. Dinner with local wine runs Lit. 40,000–50,000. Closed Tues., Wed. lunch, Jan. 1–10, and Aug. All cards.

SIDETRIP

Just 3 miles from Bologna's Porta Saragozza, on SS64 toward Casalecchio, the **Madonna di San Luca Sanctuary** stands atop Monte della Guardia and offers a fine overview of Bologna. A covered 17th–18th-century, 2½-mile walk with 666 arches leads to the 18th-century sanctuary, which contains an icon of St. Mary with the infant Jesus, allegedly painted by the apostle Luke, though more likely from the 12th century. Founded in 1194, the present sanctuary was constructed between 1723 and 1757.

Ravenna

Now five and a half miles from the Adriatic, Ravenna was once a lagoon city on piles, like Venice. In A.D. 402 it succeeded Rome as capital of the Roman Empire; by the sixth century it had fallen to the Byzantines, and was capital of their western empire.

Ravenna's origins are buried in time. Some scholars claim they date to 1403 B.C. and an obscure people called the Tessaglians. The city's prominence under Roman rule made Ravenna one of the most contested cities on Italy's eastern coast. But it was Byzantine domination that left the city its most impressive legacy, the richest collection of mosaics in Europe—and the best reason for traveling to Ravenna today.

When the Longobards ousted the Byzantine presence, Ravenna swayed in and out of the papal sphere of influence. Venice had its turn at dominating the Adriatic for nearly a century, but by mid-16th century Ravenna, again in the Vatican fold, became capital of Romagna. The city's importance diminished with the arrival of the French, who divided Romagna into two sectors that remained intact when papal rule was restored after the collapse of the Napoleonic Empire. In 1859 Ravenna became part of the united Italian kingdom.

The city was severely damaged by Allied bombing raids during the German retreat in late 1944. Tragically destroyed was the 11th- and 12th-century Romanesque church of Santa Maria in Porta Fuori, with its Rimini-school frescoes and fifth-century sarcophagus.

The city's most beautiful church (**Sant'Apollinare in Classe**) is actually three miles from downtown Ravenna and is all that remains of the Roman port of Classe. This is the ideal starting point for visiting Ravenna's beautiful collection of sixth- and seventh-century **mosaics.** (Its *Transfiguration* and other mosaics no longer have the brilliancy of other churches' mosaics, so a visit here after seeing the others might be anticlimatic.)

The main **tourist information office** is at **Piazza San Francesco** in front of the **church** of the same name, next to the **tomb of Dante Alighieri.** The celebrated author of the *Divine Comedy* died in exile here in 1321 after fleeing first to Verona when he was banished from Florence. The mini-mausoleum was built in 1780.

This point is halfway between two mosaic musts: **Sant'Apollinare Nuovo** on Via di Roma and the **Battistero,** behind the **Archbishop's Palace museum** (also worthy of a visit) off Via De Gasperi. Five hundred yards north are the fifth-century **Mausoleum of Galla Placida** and sixth-century Byzantine **San Vitale church,** which is one of Italy's foremost expressions of early Christian art.

North of the canal, just off the Via Romea (SS309 north to Venice), near a local tourist information office, is the sixth-century **tomb of Barbarian King Theodoric.** Interesting is the total lack of mortar in the construction of the edifice.

Visiting hours for San Vitale, Galla Placida, and Theodoric's tomb are from 8:30 A.M. to 5 P.M. Closing time is extended to 7:30 P.M. from May to October. All three are closed January 1, May 1, August 15, and December 25.

Sant'Apollinare Nuovo and Sant'Apollinare in Classe are open 9 A.M. to noon and 2 to 5 P.M. Closing time is extended to 7 P.M. from May to October.

Monday through Saturday, the Battistero and Archbishop's Palace museum are open 9 A.M. to noon and 2:30 to 5 P.M. From May to October afternoon closing time is extended one hour. On Sunday both are open 9 A.M. to noon.

RESTAURANTS

Tre Spade, Via Rasponi 37; tel. (0544) 32382. A typical Emilia-Romagna meal will cost around Lit. 40,000. Fish specialties are in abundance. Closed Mon. and July 20–Aug. 25. All cards.

SIDETRIP

Ravenna is approximately halfway between Forli's extensive beach developments centered around Rimini, and Ferrara's Comacchio Valley marshlands that lead to the Po Delta.

North through the Po Delta to Mestre (just outside Venice) is the Via Romea, once the path for pilgrims heading to Rome. Along this 85-mile, four-lane superstrada (309) are beaches in the provinces of Ferrara and Ravenna; the **Comacchio Lagoon** that covers the Etruscan necropolis of Spina; **Comacchio,** a sand-and-water Venice noted for its three-ramp *Trepponti* (Three Bridges) and often-stagnant canals; and the sixth-century Benedictine **Pomposa Abbey,** 30 miles east of Ferrara, open in the summer only, from 7 A.M. to noon and 2 to 7 P.M.

RESTAURANTS

If traveling from Ravenna to Ferrara, stop for a meal at **Il Triga-bolo** restaurant in **Argenta**. This is an elegant dining spot on the Piazza Garibaldi (at number 4); tel. (0532) 804121. Seafood is a specialty, and everything is perfectly prepared. A dinner costs about Lit. 60,000. Closed Mon. evenings, Tues., and July 1–20. V.

Forli, Rimini, and Romagna Beach Country

The inland town of Forli is overshadowed by surrounding events (Bologna's fairs, Imola's races, San Marino's folk festivals) and highly organized provincial beach resorts. (Rimini, the heart of the Romagna beaches stretching from Cervia to Cattolica, has even become the most populated city in the province.)

Forli was a Roman outpost that became capital of Romandiola when Romagna was divided by the French. Stop here today if you want to stretch a leg, but don't go out of your way. Basically agrarian and industrial, Forli is the largest cattle market in the area.

Rimini is where the Roman Vias Emilia and Flaminia meet, and was a prosperous colony under the Romans. Having experienced a period as a mecca for foreign singles, Rimini today is evolving into a favorite beach for middle-class Italian families. Riccione is the beach resort today more likely to attract single vacationers, both locals and Northern Europeans; Cattolica absorbs some of the spillover, and there is an active nightlife throughout the area. The beaches in this region, running to the Marches border, are wide, sandy, and overcrowded, packed with umbrella and beach-chair concessions; each town is required by law to have a public beach area.

Surprisingly close to the Adriatic beach resorts are the **ski stations** of Campigna, Burraia, Monte Falco, Balze, and Verghereto. Together these tiny resorts can accommodate only about 365 people, nowhere near the capacity of the nearly 4,000 hotels along the coast, worth considering as a base.

For those interested in "taking the waters," two well-known **health spas** are at Castrocaro Terme and Bagno di Romagna. For information about these spas, contact: Azienda Autonoma di Soggiorno Turismo, Via Garibaldi 1, 47011 Castrocaro Terme; telephone (0543) 767162. Or: Azienda Autonoma di Soggiorno e Cura, Via Lungosavio 10, 47021 Bagno di Romagna (FO); telephone (0543) 911026.

❧ RESTAURANTS

In **Cattolica,** you can have a fine dinner of local specialties at the **Molo da Osvaldo** hotel, Via Mazzini 91; tel. (0541) 962438. Dinner runs Lit. 30,000–45,000. Closed Mon. and Dec. 1–27. AE, DC, V.

Between Bologna and Forli two restaurants are particularly worthwhile. About 28 miles from Bologna (26 miles from Forli) is the town of **Tossignano** and the **Locanda della Colonna,** Via Nuova 10/11; tel. (0542) 91006. A dinner of local specialties here will run about Lit. 50,000. Closed Sun., Mon., Aug., and Jan. AE, V.

Also halfway between Bologna and Forli (about 30 miles from each), in the town of **Imola** is the **San Domenico** restaurant, Via G. Sacchi 1; tel. (0542) 29000. The food here is well known, combining traditional with nouvelle. (The first chef here was the former chef to the king of Italy.) A meal here is still a royal experience—and one which you should be prepared to pay for: Lit. 75,000–90,000. Closed Mon., Jan. 1–14, July 25–Aug. 17. AE, DC, V.

Just outside of Forli in **Castrocaro Terme** is an elegant restaurant, set in the middle of a park, **La Frasca,** Via Matteotti 34; tel. (0543) 767471. Dinners cost about Lit. 40,000–60,000 without wine (La Frasca is, however, famous for its wine list). Forli itself may not be worth a special visit, but La Frasca certainly is. Closed Tues. and Aug. 1–20. AE, DC, V.

Another worthwhile gastronomical trip is to the town of **Forlim-popoli,** 5 miles from the town of Forli. The restaurant here is **Al Maneggio,** Località Selbagnone; tel. (0543) 742042. Dinner runs roughly Lit. 40,000. Closed Mon. and 15 days in July.

The Republic of San Marino

The Communist Party is the most prominent political entity in the world's smallest (38 square miles) and oldest independent republic, founded September 3, 301, as a Christian sanctuary by a Dalmatian stonecutter fleeing persecution in the Roman colony at Rimini.

Perched atop 2,400-foot Monte Titano in the Apennine foothills is the capital of San Marino, where 5,000 of the republic's total population of 19,000 reside. There are eight smaller villages scattered around the countryside below the mountain. Legend says the mountain was given to the mason Marinus by a Roman matron after he cured her paralyzed son and she embraced Christianity.

San Marino is six miles by air from the Adriatic and is connected to Rimini by a modern superstrada. Proud of its identity and independence—confirmed by the post-Napoleonic 1815 Congress of Vienna—San Marino sits atop the boundary between the Italian regions of Emilia-Romagna and Marches. Native characteristics are most similar to those of the Romagnoli.

Issuing its own stamps and coins, the republic has created a flourishing trade in them: Visit its Piazza Garibaldi **Ufficio Filatelico e Numismatico,** where collectors are habitués. A **philately museum** on Borgo Maggiore displays all stamps issued by the republic since 1877, along with collections from other Universal Postal Union member countries. Nearby are a **firearms museum** and the station for the cable-car ride up to Piazza della Libertà. The caffè-lined square, seat of the Palazzo del Governo, offers a fine view toward the Adriatic and is near the state **tourist information office,** as well as the **Basilica of San Marino,** where relics of the saint are preserved in a silver and gold case.

The **Palazzo del Governo** is open to the public from 8:30 A.M. to 12:30 P.M. and 2:30 to 6 P.M., except during official holidays and when the council is in session. Of interest are a painting of San Marino by Guercino and the chamber where the republic's 60-member council holds its sessions.

One tier below Piazza della Libertà, on the winding route through San Marino, is another square with the landmark **Rupe castle,** a short walk from the **Valloni Palace Museum-Art Gallery.** Featured are paintings by Guercino, Ribera, Strozzi, and Zampieri, Etruscan and Egyptian artifacts, and Garibaldi memorabilia. (Hours are the same as those for the Palazzo del Governo.)

Above the basilica, crowning the highest ridge of the mountaintop republic, are three fortress watchtowers (**Guaita, Cesta,** and **Montale**), which are connected by a panoramic path—the "witches' walk." The second tower—Cesta, also known as Fratta—contains an **ancient arms museum.** From the path the view sweeps across the countryside to the Adriatic resorts of Rimini, Miramare, Riccione, and Cattolica.

Sites of visitor interest in San Marino are all easy to find, with tourist markers to assist even the most confused.

Since most San Marino restaurants are generally geared to the tourist trade, plan to have your main meal elsewhere.

Ferrara

Under Ercole I, the House of Este capital at Ferrara was one of the first modern urban centers of Europe. Here the Renaissance was made to blend with the medieval.

The House of Este

The prominence of Ferrara, Modena, and Reggio nell'Emilia was determined by the rise and fall of the House of Este.

Originally from Este, near Padua, this Longobard-Guelf-aligned house represented German kings in their tenth-century Italian possessions.

Through able negotiations and manipulations the Estensi combined political and family intrigue in Verona and Padua to cover ambitious expansion south. A power base was established in Ferrara (declared a duchy by Pope Paul II), enhanced by good relations with the Viscontis of Milan and the Venetian doges.

The Estensi also courted the Vatican in extending their reign as far south as Ancona in the Marches. The house numbered three cardinals, including Ariosto's patron Ippolito II, who built the sumptuous Villa d'Este at Tivoli outside Rome.

Often merciless rulers, the Estensi were nonetheless sensitive to patronage of the arts. By the 15th century Ferrara was held in the same esteem as Florence, Venice, and Milan. By marriage, Estensi fortunes became closely integrated with those of Spanish and Austrian monarchs. Emperor Frederich II of Swabia (now southwest Germany) declared Este expansion into Modena and Reggio nell'Emilia to be another duchy for his Ferrara allies.

However, dual attempts at expansion toward Parma and Bologna were unsuccessful, even though the Estensi had the support of Spain and Florence. This mid-17th-century turning point marked the decline of the House of Este's influence.

The Marches was now directly reabsorbed into the sphere of papal states, and when Lucrezia Borgia took Este ruler Alfonso I as her third husband, Ferrara was bartered to the Vatican to assure noninterference in the Modena-Reggio nell'Emilia duchy.

Este fortunes eventually were absorbed by the Hapsburgs in Italy. These were terminated by the mid-19th-century Italian Risorgimento.

The city center is between the ornate Romanesque-Gothic 12th-century **cathedral** and 14th-century **Este Castle** (open 9:30 A.M. to 12:30 P.M., 2:30 to 5 P.M., Tuesday through Saturday, May to October; 2 to 5 P.M. October to May), facing Largo Castello from behind a moat. Both are in exceptional condition and escaped Allied bombing raids that did not pry the German army from Ferrara until April 25, 1945. A number of churches were damaged during the air raids, and the church of San Benedetto was totally destroyed.

Other artistic and historical points of interest are the 13th-century **City Hall** in front of the cathedral; the 14th-century **university** and its **library** where Ariosto (author of *Orlando Furioso*) is buried; across from the university, the 15th-century **Casa Romei** with two beautiful courtyards (open 10 A.M. to 5 P.M., Tuesday to Sunday); the **Palazzina di Marfisa d'Este,** residence of the elegant Marfisa (open 9 A.M. to 12:30 P.M. and 3 to 6 P.M. daily; behind the university); the **Schifanoia (House of Joy) Palace,** dating from the 1500s, which now contains the **city museum** and a "Salon of the Months" with one of the major 15th-century series of frescoes (it's about two blocks from the Palazzina di Marfisa); and the 16th-century Renaissance-style **Palace of Ludovico the Moor,** on Via XX Settembre, containing the **Spina Museum** with its collection of Etruscan ceramics.

The northern part of the city was built by Ercole I, with wide streets that divided the expansion from the medieval nucleus. At the junction of Corso Ercole I with Corso Porta Po and Corso Porta Mare is **Palazzo dei Diamanti,** its facade consisting of thousands of diamond-shaped blocks of marble. Inside is the **city art gallery** featuring works by leading 15th- and 16th-century artists of the Emilian and Ferrara schools. The Great Hall is adorned with 13th- and 14th-century frescoes. The art gallery is open 9 A.M. to 2 P.M. Tuesday through Saturday and 9 A.M. to 1 P.M. Sundays and holidays; closed holidays.

The local **tourist information office** is at Largo Castello 28; tel. (0532) 21267.

❧ RESTAURANTS

In Ferrara, stop at **Italia da Giovanni,** Largo Castello 32; tel. (0532) 35775. The decor and food are traditional. Dinner costs about Lit. 35,000. Closed Tues. and Aug. DC, V.

See also the **Il Trigabolo** restaurant in the Sidetrip section under Ravenna.

Modena

Between Reggio and Bologna, Modena is divided by the Via Emilia. Important points of reference are the **Este Gallery,** which is one of Italy's largest collections of foreign and Italian art, and the **Este Library,** which was transferred from Ferrara in 1598. The **Palazzo Ducale** is now the home of the Italian military academy. The **cathedral** and adjoining 290-foot **Ghirlandina bell tower** (symbol of Modena) were begun in 1099 and completed in the 14th century. Notable are sculptures by Wiligelmo and his pupils.

The **tourist information office** is at Corso Canalgrande 3; tel. (059) 237479.

🍴 RESTAURANTS

The Este Gallery is probably the sight of major importance here, and food in Modena is superb. The following restaurants offer a selection of regional specialties.

Borso d'Este, Piazza Roma 5; tel. (059) 214114. Dinner will cost about Lit. 50,000. Closed Sun. and Aug. AE, DC.

Aldo Rossi, Addition to Modena Cemetery (Competition 1971, 1976; in construction)

For a look at modern Italian architecture, visit the Modena Cemetery to see Aldo Rossi's addition. There are few who are better than Aldo Rossi at rethinking the past in order to invent a new way of building.

Though the light pink walls, sky-blue pitched roofs, simple cutout windows, and infinitely repetitive piers may appear childish, this addition to a group of existing cemeteries is based upon complex issues. When completed, the new cemetery will emulate the courtyard plans of the older cemeteries on the site. Within this *different* courtyard, Rossi will place various atypical structures, including a seven-story red cube commemorating the war dead and a 75-foot-high truncated red cone commemorating the indigent and unknown.

The architect is both playful and disturbing in his use of imagery. Rather than connecting form with function, he attaches poetic meaning to form—he is acutely aware of the transformation of a structure through time. The juxtaposition of factory, house, and prison images willfully confuse the visual and emotional associations with the work, producing an intuitive response rather than a rational reaction. Yet Rossi gives the work a tactile scale, clearly defining the individual's relationship to the building. The span of an average-sized person determines the interval between piers. The size of windows, doors, corridors, and bridges help to make passage through these spaces comfortable. The play of images invokes the idea of a city of the dead as can only be imagined for the use of the living.

—Mary Beth Betts and Charles Ayes

Fini, Piazetta S. Francesco; tel. (059) 214250. Dinners range Lit. 45,000–55,000. Closed Mon. and Tues. All cards.

Reggio nell'Emilia

Reggio nell'Emilia was the western extremity of the Estense duchy on the Via Emilia. After the demise of the Este dynasty, Reggio was a pawn in regional power plays until the population rebelled in 1848 and joined the House of Savoy in the unification of Italy.

The birthplace of Ludovico Ariosto, Reggio has several buildings and churches worth visiting, such as the 13th-century **Palace of the Captain of the People;** the 13th-century **cathedral;** the **San Prospero church,** dating from the 1500s (the facade was added in the 1600s), with its octagonal bell tower; and the early 16th-century **Parmeggiani Gallery,** featuring foreign as well as Italian artists. The **local tourist information** office is at Piazza C. Battisti 4; tel. (0522) 43370.

RESTAURANTS

La Scala, Via Blasmatorti 1; tel. (0522) 48223. Dinner at this vegetarian restaurant costs about Lit. 20,000. Specialties include herb omelets, stews, and risotto with lentils. Closed Mon. evening, Tues., and July 20–Aug. 20. No cards.

Heading west from Reggio nell'Emilia toward Parma, consider a detour to **Cavriago** and the **Picci** restaurant, Via XX Settembre; tel. (0522) 57201. Dinners of regional specialties run about Lit. 40,000. Closed Mon. evening, Tues., Dec. 26–Jan. 20, and Aug. 5–25. AE, DC, V.

Parma

On the Via Emilia and a tributary of the Po, Parma ranks second in importance only to Bologna in Emilia. With Piacenza, Parma was the duchy that Pope Paul III (Alessandro Farnese) gave to his son Pier Luigi, in 1545. While Piacenza may have been more prominent under the Farnese, Parma became the center of the Bourbon hold on the duchy from 1731 to 1801. Under Napoleon Parma came under French rule.

In 1815, after the fall of the Empire, former Empress Marie-Louise took the reigns of the duchy. Parma was as widely known then as an arts and cultural center as it is known today for its famous hams and cheese. Now the area thrives on its food-processing and curing facilities.

A number of historical palaces, monumental churches, and notable art collections are found in the city, making it worth a stop. Begin in the central **Piazza del Duomo,** where the local **tourist information office** is at number 5. Facing the square are the 12th-century **Romanesque cathedral** and its 13th-century **bell tower.** In the dome of the cathedral is Correggio's *Assumption of the Virgin,* completed in 1530. Sculptures by Antelami are in the cathedral, as well as the adjacent Baptistry, which is a splendid example of the transition from Romanesque to Gothic design that took place in the late 1100s and early 1200s. More Correggio frescoes are in the nearby **Church of San Giovanni.**

The most imposing building in Parma is just a brief stroll away toward the river. Here is the **Palazzo della Pilotta** that the Farnese began in 1583. Construction continued for several decades, but the original project was never completed. The massive structure contains the **National Museum of Antiquities,** the early 17th-century **Farnese Theater** (modeled after Palladio's Olympic Theater in Vicenza), the 350,000-volume and 40,000-print **Palatina Library,** the **National Gallery,** and the richly decorated **St. Paul's chambers** by Correggio.

Featured in the museum are artifacts uncovered at the nearby Velleia archaeological dig, including a "food table" of the Emperor Trajan, discovered in 1747 near Macinessio, which recorded taxes on farmlands to pay for food for the poor children in the Roman colony.

The art gallery features Italian painting schools from the 14th through the 18th century and is highlighted by Leonardo da Vinci's *Head of an Adolescent* and Correggio's highly acclaimed *Virgin with St. Jerome.*

The museum and gallery are open Tuesday through Saturday, 9 A.M. to 2 P.M., and Sunday 9 A.M. to 1 P.M. Both are closed major holidays.

❦ RESTAURANTS

Just outside of town is **Cocchi,** Via Gramsci 16; tel. (0521) 91990. The restaurant is simple, the specialties regional. Dinners run about Lit. 35,000. Closed Sat. and July 25–Aug. 25. AE, DC, V.

Six and a half miles southwest of Parma is the **Ceci** restaurant in **Collecchio,** Villa Maria Luigia; tel. (0521) 805489. A regional dinner costs about Lit. 40,000 here. Closed Thurs., Jan. 10–31, and Aug. 5–20. DC, V.

Piacenza

Piacenza is the northernmost of the former Roman colonies on the Via Emilia. Just across the Po from Lombardy, this agrarian-industrial center of Emilia-Romagna, once, with Parma, part of the 16th-century Farnese duchy, reflects a strong Lombard influence, making it the perfect transitional stop if traveling on to Lombardy.

Many modern buildings testify to the extensive reconstruction after Allied bombing in April 1944 devastated much of the old city near the rail terminal and the tracks crossing the Po. Two bridges were totally destroyed.

The center of town is **Piazza dei Cavalli.** The name derives from the two 17th-century **equestrian statues** featuring Alessandro and Ranuccio I of the Farnese. Around the corner is the **tourist information office** at Piazzetta dei Mercanti 10. Just off the square are the city's most fashionable stores for local shopping.

Facing Piazza dei Cavalli from behind the statues is the 13th-century Lombard Gothic **Palazzo del Comune** (City Hall), often referred to as the most beautiful public building in Italy. Featured are stately arches, mullioned windows, and rooftop battlements.

Also on the square is the 18th-century former **Governor's Palace,** adorned with statues and a sun dial that can also indicate the day of the year.

Set back just to the left of the square is the 13th-century **Church of St. Francis** with its high Lombard facade and Gothic interior. Only a five-minute walk behind St. Francis is the **Lombard Cathedral,** dating from the 12th and 13th centuries, punctuated by a rose window and other Gothic elements. Curious is the iron cage in the bell tower where sinners were put on public display stripped naked.

In the triangle between Via Roma and Via Alberoni, behind the cathedral, is the 12th-century **San Savino,** with mosaics in the church's crypt that reproduce signs of the zodiac.

Toward the center of the triangle, Via Roma intersects with Corso Cavour halfway between Piazza dei Cavalli and Piazza Cittadella. On the right of Piazza Cittadella is the unfinished, predominantly brick 16th-century **Farnese Palace** that was urged by Margherita of Austria on her husband, Ottavio Farnese, son of Pier Luigi and grandson of Pope Paul III. The duchy was a gift from pontiff father to ne'er-do-well son, a gift that was not appreciated by the local nobility held responsible for the subsequent assassination of Pier Luigi. Two other grandsons of Pope Paul III became cardinals, while the fourth, Orazio, married Diane of France (duchess of Angoulême), which added to the duchy. The political orbit of the Farnese extended from the Vatican to Spain, Austria, and France.

The **city museum** is in the Farnese Palace. Botticelli's *Madonna* heads an art collection from the 17th and 18th centuries. There is an arms collection, and the Piacenza Etruscan Liver, found by a farmer while plowing a field in nearby Settima. This engraved Etruscan bronze was allegedly used by seer-priests to read the entrails of human sacrifices.

Just a five-minute stroll to the left of Palazzo Farnese is the Latin-cross **Church of San Sisto.** Built in 874, it was reconstructed in 1499. The painting of *St. Siro with the Virgin* over the main altar is a copy of the original by Raphael, which once graced the church. The original was sold to August III in 1754 and is now in the Dresden Museum.

❦ RESTAURANTS

Antica Osteria al Teatro, Via Verdi 16; tel. (0523) 23777. Dinners range Lit. 45,000–70,000. Closed Sun., Jan. 1–6, and Aug. 1–25. AE, DC, V.

SIDETRIPS

A number of interesting sights and excursions can be found outside town and along the road to Parma.

Just outside Piacenza, the **Galleria Alberoni's** interesting art collection is open to the public on Sun. afternoons Nov.–July. (Otherwise, make arrangements with the gallery director, Via Emilia Parmense 77; tel. (0523) 63198.) The valuable collection includes works by Antonello da Messina, Bernini, Caravaggio, Correggio, Giorgione, Rubens, Signorelli, and Titian.

The village of **Bobbio** is 43 miles southwest of Piacenza via Castel San Giovanni. Its seventh-century **San Colombano monastery** was a leading cultural center in the Middle Ages. In the crypt of the 15th-century **basilica** are mosaics depicting months of the year. There is also the 11-arch undulating **San Colombano Bridge** across the Trebbia River; the bridge is referred to as the "bridge of the devil."

The village of **Bettola** lies 20 miles south of Piacenza via Grazzano Visconti, and claims in vain to be the birthplace of Christopher Columbus; in central Piazza Colombo, which hosts a characteristic market every Monday, there is a monument dedicated to the discoverer of the Americas. It has been verified that the navigator's father Domenico was from **Pradello** (3½ miles north); the family home there that he left in 1439 is now a museum.

Grazzano Visconti is a faithful reconstruction of a medieval village, surrounding the 13th-century **Visconti castle,** located just 8½ miles south of Piacenza. Wood and wrought iron handicrafts, produced in local specialized schools, are available.

About 20 miles southeast of Piacenza, Busseto and Villa Verdi are the birthplace and summer residence of composer Giuseppe Verdi. Refused admission to the Milan conservatory, Verdi returned to Busseto and directed the village band until he scored his first triumph with "Nabucco" in 1842. The home in which he was born and the villa are now museums (the latter is closed from November to April). *"Viva Verdi"* became a popular rallying cry in occupied Italy prior to the Risorgimento, not because of the composer's patriotism, but due to the coincidence that the letters of his name were also the first letters of "Vittorio Emanuele Re d'Italia."

The medieval village of **Castell'Arquato,** 25 miles west of Parma, sits on a hill overlooking the Arda valley. Facing the central Piazza Matteotti are the monumental 12th-century **Col-**

legiata and 13th-century **Pretorio Palace** and **Rocca Comunale.** This is a fine example of a Middle Ages urban center in Emilia, worth a stop on a Piacenza-to-Parma trip, especially for a picnic in the nearby Terme di Bacedasco natural park.

RESTAURANTS

For a meal in Castell'Arquato, try **Faccini,** Località Sant'Antonio; tel. (0523) 896340. Dinner will run about Lit. 30,000. Closed Wed. and July. No cards.

9

MILAN

Italy's usually sunny skies become gray and foggy; red-checkered tablecloths are replaced with neatly starched white linen; singing Don Giovannis with guitars in hand give way to efficient bankers talking lire; and the traditional three-hour lunch oozing with time, food, and wine is suddenly a hurried, on-the-way-back-to-the-office fast-food snack. This is Milan (Milano), the capital of Lombardy, the Manhattan of Italy.

As the center of finance, fashion, furniture, and publishing, this prosperous entrant into the world's competitive, cosmopolitan inner circle offers the traveler a different view of Italy. Milan is a sober town, a practical reprieve from the romantic visual overload of Florence and Venice.

The dynamic *Borsa* (Stock Exchange) and the conservatively suited Milanese prove that the city's mind is on its wallet, and it is smug about its enormously impressive success. Milan's unemployment rate of 8.4 percent is half that of Rome, and Milan continues to be the industrial baron of Italy. The city ranks next to New York and Paris as one of *the* places to be, and prides itself as a leader in style and *moda,* housing such fashion greats as Armani, Versace, Krizia, Missoni, Mila Schön, and Ferre, as well as state-of-the-art furniture and home furnishing designers. The whole aura of Milan suggests a work-in-progress . . . one big collective blueprint ready to set another unsurpassed example.

Unlike the immediate enchantment of other Italian cities, Milan works a slow spell into your heart. Its mystery, privacy, and snobbery demand patience from the traveler. The city does not have the outward beauty of Rome, Florence, and Venice, but its appeal seeps *piano piano* into the unsuspecting, not leaving you speechless at first glance, but seductively revealing its magic through random great moments.

To know Milan's charms, you must be willing to fight frustrating traffic jams, one-way streets that test even the best navigators, severe air pollution, and foggy, gray weather. But like the buildings whose stark fronts give way to concealed, flowered courtyards, every so often Milan's businesslike, metropolitan persona melts away to reveal its hidden treasures, and the Renaissance splendor created by Leonardo and Bramante suddenly surfaces to seduce even the most jaded traveler. Catch a sunlit tram inching down cobblestoned Corso Magenta and you will swear that you are visiting not a metropolis but a village, very Italian and very provincial.

Milan's Historical Mix

Milan displays an intriguing combination of Northern Europe's exacting mental nature (especially Germany's and Austria's) and Southern Europe's agricultural, more earthy feel. Milan's history reflects this mixture: The city's *padroni* have consisted of the Insubres (a Celtic tribe settling in the area around 400 B.C.); the Romans (who called the city *Mediolanum*, meaning midlands—the city lies in the middle of the Po Valley); the barbaric Longobards (hence the name Lombardy); the powerful Visconti and Sforza families (who brought to the city some of the finest minds of the day, including Leonardo and Bramante); the Spanish (who ruled for almost two hundred years); the Austrians (from the early 1700s until 1859); Napoleon; and the returning Austro-Hungarians, who ruled until Milan became a part of the Savoy Kingdom and Italy was unified in 1861. The Fascist party was founded in Milan in 1919, and the Allies bombed the city during World War II. Since then, a steady influx of Southern immigrants bringing their own agriculturally based culture has mixed with the pragmatic Northerners to create the vital Milan of today.

ORIENTING YOURSELF

Milan (population 1,700,000) is in the shape of a circle, with the Piazza Duomo as the center. The streets run from the center to the outskirts of the city, crossing three rings. The inner ring is called the Cerchia dei Navigli, and follows the walls built to protect the city in the medieval era. This ring includes the ancient *navigli* (canals) that ran throughout Milan at that time. The second ring of streets, called *Viali* or bastioni, runs along the 16th-century wall built by the Spanish. The third and outermost ring, the Circonvallazione Esterna, encircles the outskirts of Milan.

Within the center of the city, four general areas are of interest.

The Piazza Duomo/San Babila area is considered the geographical and social center of Milan. A great deal of time can be spent here exploring the sights. This area includes the Duomo itself; Palazzo Reale (Royal Palace), now used to house the Duomo Museum; the Ambrosian Library (Biblioteca Ambrosiana) and picture gallery (Pinacoteca Ambrosiana); Piazza Mercanti, dating from medieval Milan; Galleria Vittorio Emanuele II, the glass-enclosed shopping arcade dating from the 19th century; the legendary Teatro alla Scala (La Scala) and its theatrical museum; the Poldi Pezzoli Museum; and the world-renowned shopping streets Via Manzoni (named after the author of *I Promessi Sposi,* who was born and died in Milan), Via Monte Napoleone, Via della Spiga, Via Sant'Andrea, Corso Venezia, Piazza San Babila, and Corso Vittorio Emanuele.

The Brera/Stazione Centrale area is a stylish business district with galleries, shops, and sights. It starts at La Scala Theater (Teatro alla Scala) and includes the entire area extending northward to the Stazione Centrale (Central Train Station), including Via Brera, with its art galleries; the Brera Art Gallery (Pinacoteca di Brera); and the busy Via Fatebenefratelli and Piazza Cavour.

Piazza Cordusio/Corso Magenta/Parco is an area west of the Duomo, extremely rich in history. Here are found the impressive Castle of the Sforzas (Castello Sforzesco) with Sempione Park beyond it; the Arch of Peace (Arco della Pace) in Sempione Park; the church of Santa Maria delle Grazie (next door to the Cenacolo Vinciano, which houses Leonardo's *Last Supper*); the Leonardo da Vinci Museum (Museo Nazionale della Scienza e della Tecnica); the Basilica of Saint Ambrose (Sant'Ambrogio); the church of San Maurizio and its Archaeological Museum.

Porta Ticinese/Navigli is an area typical of old Milan, called the Ticinese district after the Ticino River. A tributary of the Po, the Ticino was the source of water for the active canal system that ran through the city in the 13th century. This area, quite lively in the evenings, includes the Roman ruins of San Lorenzo Maggiore; the Corso di Porta Ticinese, which connects the Roman columns of San Lorenzo and the 12th-century Porta Ticinese; the neoclassical Arco di Porta Ticinese, designed by Luigi Cagnola in the early 1800s and built along the Spanish walls; and the *navigli* (canals).

PRIORITIES

As with any city of interest, it could take a lifetime to get to know Milan. Listed here alphabetically are the sights that are most evocative of both Milan's history and present-day personality. Organize your activities by choosing what most interests you, and then seeing what's nearby.

Although many may just want to shop, first-time visitors interested in Milan's history and culture should concentrate on the Basilica of Saint Ambrose, the Duomo and the Galleria Vittorio Emanuele across the street, the Castle of the Sforzas, the Brera Art Gallery, Santa Maria delle Grazie church (with Leonardo's *Last Supper* next door), and La Scala Theater. This will give you a general idea of the many facets of Milan's persona, represented in its Romanesque, medieval, Renaissance, neoclassical, and modern architecture.

The best way to visit this suprisingly attractive city is on foot, discovering the unexpected as you go. Please be aware that Italian museums are fickle in terms of hours, and travelers must be extremely flexible. Check at the **Tourist Office** (Via Marconi 1) for a recent museum schedule and a copy of *Tutto Milano* (in English). Museum entrance fees are usually around Lit. 4,000. Although most museums are closed on Mondays, Sundays and Monday mornings are the best times to visit to avoid traffic: locals leave Milan for the weekend and stores are closed Monday morning. Take advantage of this opportunity to walk around town leisurely.

Milan is not a casual city. The Milanese are conservative in dress during the day; in the evenings, they bring out their best jewelry and furs. You can, of course, dress any way you like, but you might feel more comfortable if you observe the notion "When in Milan, do as the Milanese do" and wear business-style clothing rather than your most casual touring clothes.

Sights are keyed into neighborhoods and the color map of Milan at the back of the book; page numbers refer to the page number of the insert, map coordinates to the location of the sight.

Ambrosian Picture Gallery

PIAZZA DUOMO/SAN BABILA, P. 12, C3

This gallery in the Ambrosian Library houses works and papers by Leonardo da Vinci, Botticelli, Ghirlandaio, Caravaggio, Raphael, and Tiepolo among many others from the Tuscan, Lombard, and Venetian Renaissance. A one-hour tour of the museum is suggested. Located at Piazza Pio XI 2. Walk from Piazza Duomo or Cordusio, or take bus number 50, 54, or 60 or tram number 1, 4, 8, 12, 19, or 24. Hours are usually 9:30 A.M. to 5 P.M.

Nearby: Duomo, Piazza Cordusio.

Basilica of Saint Ambrose and Museum

PIAZZA CORDUSIO/CORSO MAGENTA/PARCO, P. 12, C3

This majestic construction honoring the patron saint of Milan, Saint Ambrose, sits on a foundation dating back to the year 386. The present structure, from the 11th and 12th centuries, is considered a prototype of Roman-Lombard churches. On view are precious relics from the history of the basilica, including jewelry, textiles, marble, mosaics, and paintings.

Plan on spending a few hours here: The Catholic university is located behind the basilica and the neighborhood is a lovely area for a *passeggiata*. The museum is open from 10 A.M. to noon and 3 to 5 P.M., and is closed Tuesday, Saturday, and Sunday mornings, and on public holidays. Located at Piazza

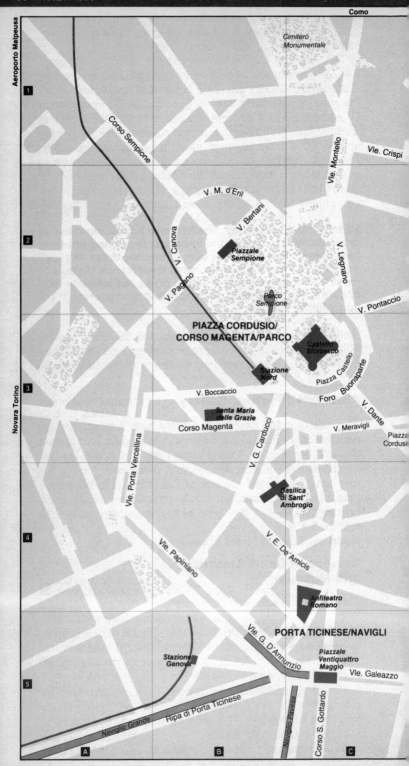

Como

Aeroporto Malpeusa

Novara Torino

Cimitero Monumentale

Corso Sempione

Vle. Montello

Vle. Crispi

V. M. d'Eril

V. Bertani

V. Canova

V. Pagano

Piazzale Sempione

V. Legnano

Parco Sempione

V. Pontaccio

**PIAZZA CORDUSIO/
CORSO MAGENTA/PARCO**

Castello Sforzesco

Piazza Castello

Foro Buonaparte

Stazione Nord

V. Dante

V. Boccaccio

Santa Maria delle Grazie

Corso Magenta

V. G. Carducci

V. Meravigli

Piazza Cordusi

Basilica di Sant' Ambrogio

Vle. Porta Vercellina

V. E. De' Amicis

Vle. Papiniano

Anfiteatro Romano

PORTA TICINESE/NAVIGLI

Vle. G. D'Annunzio

Piazzale Ventiquattro Maggio

Stazione Genova

Vle. Galeazzo

Corso S. Gottardo

Naviglio Pavese

Naviglio Grande

Ripa di Porta Ticinese

A   B   C

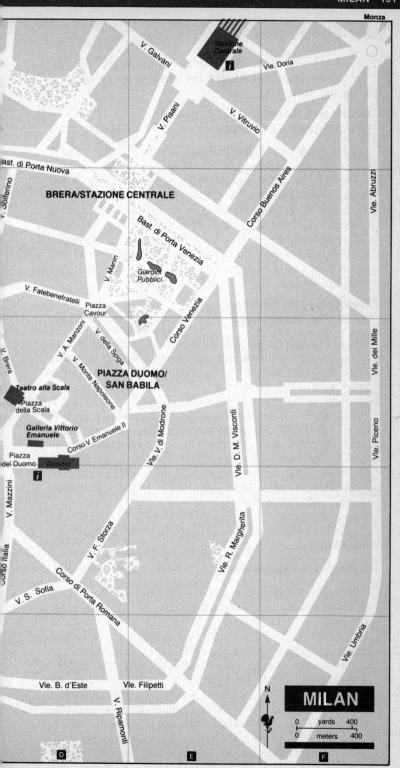

Monza

V. Galvani

Stazione
Centrale

Vle. Doria

V. Pisani

V. Vitruvio

ast. di Porta Nuova

Corso Buenos Aires

Vle. Abruzzi

BRERA/STAZIONE CENTRALE

Bast. di Porta Venezia

V. Solferino

V. Manin

Giardini
Pubblici

V. Fatebenefratelli

Piazza
Cavour

Corso Venezia

Vle. dei Mille

V. A. Manzoni

V. della Spiga

V. Brera

V. Monte Napoleone

**PIAZZA DUOMO/
SAN BABILA**

Teatro alla Scala

Piazza
della Scala

Vle. V. di Modrone

Vle. D. M. Visconti

Vle. Piceno

Galleria Vittorio
Emanuele

Corso V Emanuele II

Piazza
del Duomo

Duomo

V. Mazzini

V. F. Sforza

Vle. R. Margherita

Corso Italia

Vle. Umbria

V. S. Sofia

Corso di Porta Romana

Vle. B. d'Este

Vle. Filipetti

N

MILAN

V. Ripamonti

0   yards   400
0   meters   400

D

E

F

Sant'Ambrogio 15; take the Green Line metro to the Sant'Ambrogio stop, or buses number 50, 54, 74, 96, or 97.
Nearby: Leonardo da Vinci Museum; Santa Maria delle Grazie and the Cenacolo museum; the Castle of the Sforzas and Sempione Park.

Brera Art Gallery
(Pinacoteca di Brera)

BRERA/STAZIONE CENTRALE, P. 12, D3

This spectacular building (formerly the main Jesuit center) was built in the 17th century and houses one of the most comprehensive art collections in Italy, rich in works from the Lombard and Veneto schools (15th to 18th centuries). Plan half a day with a pleasant lunch at the bar upstairs. Located at Via Brera 28. Walk up Via Verdi from La Scala to Via Brera or take bus number 61. Hours are 9 A.M. to 2 P.M. weekdays, to 1 P.M. on Sundays and public holidays and the second and fourth Saturday of each month.
Nearby: La Scala.

Castle of the Sforzas
(Castello Sforzesco)

PIAZZA CORDUSIO/CORSO MAGENTA/PARCO, P. 12, C3

This castle, built on top of ruins in 1450 by Francesco Sforza, is the largest civil monument from the Renaissance period in Milan. Radically restored by Luca Beltrami, it is a most awesome sight in its present, square form with an expansive courtyard in the Piazza Castello. Do not miss Michelangelo's last work, *Pietà Rondanini* (*sala* 15), and Mantegna's *Madonna In Glory* (sala 20) in the museum. Plan to spend a few hours walking through the castle, and enjoy a quiet moment in Sempione Park, behind the castle. Take buses number 57, 60, 70, 96, or 97; trams number 2, 4, 8, 14, or 21. The museum hours are 9:30 A.M. to 12:15 P.M. and 2:30 to 5:15 P.M.; closed Monday. No entrance fee.
Nearby: Sempione Park; Santa Maria delle Grazie and the Cenacolo Vinciano; Basilica of Saint Ambrose; Leonardo da Vinci Museum.

Duomo and Museum

PIAZZA DUOMO/SAN BABILA, P. 12, D3

Built between 1386 and the 1800s, the Duomo is the largest cathedral and the most complex example of Gothic architecture in Italy. As the symbol of Milan, it is a center point in navigating the city. Spend some time visiting this spectacular creation, and be sure to climb up to the terrace (166 steps) or take the elevator (for a nominal fee) for a spectacular view of the city and a stroll among some of the 2,245 statutes and 135 spires that adorn this Gothic wonder. The terrace is open 9 A.M. to 4 P.M. in the winter and to 5 P.M. in the summer. There is a Treasury housing a collection of jewelry, gold, silver, and ivories; hours are 9 A.M. to noon and 3 to 5:30 P.M.

The cathedral museum is located in the Royal Palace, on the right as you face the Duomo. There are 21 rooms filled with Gothic sculpture from the Lombard and French eras, dating from the 14th and 15th centuries. The museum is open 10:30 A.M. to 12:30 P.M. and 3 to 5:30 P.M.; closed Monday. There is an entrance fee, but admission is free on Thursdays. Take the Red Line metro to the Duomo; buses number 50, 54, or 60, or trams 8, 12, 15, 19, or 24.

Nearby: Ambrosian Library and art gallery; Piazza Mercanti; Galleria Vittorio Emanuele II; La Scala and its theatrical musuem; Poldi Pezzoli Museum; and shopping streets.

Galleria Vittorio Emanuele II
PIAZZA DUOMO/
SAN BABILA, P. 12, D3

Built between 1865 and 1877, the Galleria is a beautiful glass-domed passageway between Piazza Duomo and Piazza della Scala. Its four-story arcade serves as a meeting place and elite shopping area. Enjoy a leisurely stroll here between La Scala and the Duomo.

La Scala Theater
and the Theatrical Museum
PIAZZA
DUOMO/SAN BABILA, P. 12, D3

Built in 1778 by Giuseppe Piermarini, during the reign of Maria Theresa of Austria, this unimpressive neoclassical exterior houses one of the world's most famous and acoustically perfect opera theaters, elegantly lined in red damask. The museum holds a vast collection of articles and books on opera and the history of theater (especially on Verdi). Museum hours are 9 A.M. to noon and 2 to 6 P.M.; closed Sunday. From May to October the museum is open Sundays 9:30 A.M. to noon and 2:30 to 6 P.M. The best way to experience the theater in its full glory is, of course, during a performance. Think of booking tickets before leaving home; they are difficult to get. (See "Entertainment," this chapter.) Located at Piazza della Scala. Take the Red Line metro to the Duomo stop; bus number 61; or tram number 1 or 4.

Nearby: Galleria Vittorio Emanuele; Duomo; Brera Art Gallery; Poldi Pezzoli Museum.

Leonardo da Vinci Museum
PIAZZA CORDUSIO/
CORSO MAGENTA/PARCO, P. 12, B4

Officially known as the Museo Nazionale della Scienza e della Tecnica, this museum has a fascinating collection of models representing da Vinci's technical designs. There is a saying in Lombardy that when something is well made and has a stroke of genius in it, it is (without a doubt) a da Vinci invention! Located on Via San Vittore 21; take the Red Line metro (toward Romolo) to the Sant'Ambrogio stop, or buses number 50, 54, 96, or 97. Hours are 9 A.M. to 5 P.M.; closed Mondays but open Sundays and holidays; admission free on Thursday.

Nearby: Basilica of Saint Ambrose; Santa Marie delle Grazie and the Cenacolo Vinciano; the Castle of the Sforzas and Sempione Park.

Leonardo's *Last Supper.*
See Santa Maria delle Grazie.

Navigli
PORTA TICINESE/NAVIGLI, P. 13, A/B/C5

The remaining canals of Milan are colorful, active, and characteristic of days gone by. One can easily spend an afternoon strolling along these charming waterways, and they boast some of the hot night spots in Milan. Take tram number 15 to the Columns of San Lorenzo Maggiore and stop for lunch under the Roman columns at Il Pois, nearby. From there walk down the offbeat Via Porta Ticinese to Piazza XXIV Maggio, turning right toward the canals.

Piazza Mercanti and Palazzo della Ragione
PIAZZA DUOMO/SAN BABILA, P. 12, D3

Built between 1228 and 1233, the Palazzo della Ragione was the autonomous seat when Milan won independence against the German emperors. The palace was the town hall until 1770, and was the center of the square known as Piazza Mercanti. A remnant of medieval Milan, the Piazza Mercanti was the center of daily life.

Nearby: This is a very short walk from the Duomo, heading toward the Castle of the Sforzas.

Poldi Pezzoli Museum
PIAZZA DUOMO/SAN BABILA, P. 12, D3

The collection of G.G. Poldi Pezzoli, these paintings, jewelry, and art objects from different periods deserve at least an hour's tour. Located on Via Manzoni 12; take tram number 1 or 4, or walk down Via Manzoni from La Scala Theater toward Piazza Cavour. The hours are 9:30 A.M. to 12:30 P.M. and 2:30 to 5:30 P.M. Open Thursday evenings 9 to 11 P.M. (except August); closed Monday and holidays; in the summer closed Sunday afternoons.

Nearby: La Scala Theater and its museum; the Duomo and its museum; Galleria Vittorio Emanuele II; Piazza Mercanti; the Ambrosian Library and art gallery; and shopping streets.

San Lorenzo Maggiore
PORTA TICINESE/NAVIGLI, P. 13, C4

This is Milan's most important remnant of the Roman-Christian era. Dating back to the second and third centuries, the 16 Roman columns in front of the fourth-century church are the ruins of an ancient temple.

Nearby: This is a great starting point for discovering the Porta Ticinese and Navigli areas.

Santa Maria delle Grazie
PIAZZA CORDUSIO/ CORSO MAGENTA/PARCO, P. 12, B3

This church is by far one of the most spectacular sights in Milan. The splendid apse created by Donato Bramante continues to impress visitors from all over the world. Visit the small cloister, also by Bramante. There are two forms of architecture in the church: the Gothic naves by Guiniforte Solari and the Renaissance apse of Bramante. The entrance to what was once the refectory of the Dominican convent, off the square in front of the church, contains the Cenacolo Vinciano, where Leonardo da Vinci painted his famous *Last Supper* (1495–1498) on a wall. The hours of the Cenacolo are 9 A.M. to 1:30 P.M. and 2 to 6:30 P.M. Tuesday through Saturday; Sunday 9 A.M. to 3 P.M.; closed Monday; admission is free on the first and third Tuesdays and second and fourth Sundays of every month. Located on Via Caradosso and Corso Magenta. Take the Green or Red Line metro to the Cadorno stop or tram number 19, 21, or 24.

Nearby: Leonardo da Vinci Museum; Basilica of Saint Ambrose; Castle of the Sforzas and Sempione Park; San Maurizio and the Archaeological Museum.

Via Monte Napoleone, Via della Spiga, Via Sant'Andrea, Via Manzoni, Corso Vittorio Emanuele   PIAZZA DUOMO/SAN BABILA, P. 12, D3

This is what Milan is famous for today! Visit the many designer shops along these streets, remembering that stores are usually closed from around 12:30 to 3:30 P.M. for lunch. Certain boutiques and the department store Rinascente don't close. Take the Red Line metro to San Babila, or tram number 1 or 4.

TRAVEL

Arriving in Milan

Your first and most important stop is the EPT Tourist Office, found at Linate Airport, Stazione Centrale (Central Train Station), and Via Marconi 1 in Piazza Duomo. Hours are 8:45 A.M.–12:30 P.M. and 1:30–6 P.M. weekdays; Sat. 9 A.M.–12:30 P.M. and 1–5 P.M. Closed Sun. Tel. (02)809662. Basic English is spoken here.

From Linate and Malpensa airports, there are buses going to Stazione Centrale; the fare is Lit. 3,000–5,000. There is a taxi stand at the entrance of the train station, it should cost Lit. 5,000–10,000 to reach your hotel. Taxis to or from Malpensa are very expensive because one must pay the equivalent of a round-trip fare, which is approximately Lit. 80,000. Taxis to or from Linate are approximately Lit. 15,000–20,000. Tipping is not required (it is solely up to you), but there are nighttime charges that vary according to travel time and distance.

Public Transportation

Trams and buses are generally painted orange. Buy a ticket (*biglietto*) for Lit. 700 at a *tabaccheria* (tobacco store) or bar, in the metro station, at a newsstand, or wherever there is a yellow sign saying *vendita biglietti.* There are exact-change ticket machines in the subway. Board the tram at the rear and insert the ticket in the metal box. The time will be stamped, and the ticket is good for the next 75 min. You are allowed one metro ride with a stamped ticket. All-day tickets, maps, or any and all information about getting around Milan can be obtained from the EPT (see "Arriving in Milan"). Signs mark all tram and bus stops and indicate times for the first and last bus or trolley.

The Metropolitana (**subway**) in Milan is clean and efficient. Entrances are marked with an orange-red sign with "MM" written in white. There are two lines (a third is under construction): the Red Line (MM1) and the Green Line (MM2). The two lines connect at the Cadorna stop (near the Castle of the Sforzas) and the Loreto stop (near Stazione Centrale). Signs in metro stations indicate the direction of travel and stops. Subways start running at 6:20 A.M. and stop around midnight. This can vary depending on stops. Check with the EPT for updated information.

Driving

Use public transportation (trolleys/trams, buses, the metro) rather than rent a car. Milan is a circular city, difficult to navigate, and the parking is horrendous. Save yourself a headache and rent a car only to leave the city; try one of the following agencies or at the airport. Most rental-agency employees speak English.

CAR RENTALS

Avis, tel. (02) 6981; **Hertz,** tel. (02) 20483; **Europcar,** tel. (02) 6071053. Call for the location closest to your hotel.

A word to the wise: If you must drive a car in Milan and find yourself lost, hail a cab and follow it to your destination!

Taxis

In Milan, it is better to take yellow taxis (tel. 6767, 8585, or 8388; wait at taxi stands; or just hail one). An average ride within the city should cost about Lit. 10,000. (Milanese taxi drivers are honest and friendly and will answer any question regarding the fare.)

Tours

American Express has tours every day, 9–11:30 A.M. or 2–4:30 P.M. Look for the buses marked Sightseeing in Piazza Duomo, to the right of the Duomo when facing it. Tickets are purchased on the bus for Lit. 35,000. Call American Express to confirm hours (tel. 85571). The EPT tourist office also organizes city tours, as well as boat rides on the *navigli* (canals); see "Arriving in Milan."

❧ ACCOMMODATIONS

The hotel selections here combine practicality with a sense of style, much the way Milan does. All provide the necessary comforts. Unless otherwise noted, the hotels are open year-round. Be prepared for very expensive hotel rates; Milan is considered one of the more expensive cities in Europe. In fact, the cost of living is said to be 17% higher than in New York City. Be sure to add 19% on to prices here for IVA tax.

Note: Postal codes follow the street addresses.

Rates given indicate the span between single and double rooms.

Credit cards are listed as accepted. "All cards" means that all of the following are accepted: AE—American Express; DC—Diner's Club; MC—MasterCard; V—Visa.

Hotels are keyed into neighborhoods and the color map at the back of the book; page numbers refer to the page number of the insert, map coordinates to the hotel's location.

An alternative to staying in Milan is to stay at nearby Lake Como, taking the train from the town of Como to and from the city.

LUXURY HOTELS
The hotels in this category all provide concierge service, room service, laundry service, TV, and air-conditioning, are equipped for the physically handicapped and provide excellent business facilities.

Excelsior Gallia
BRERA/STAZIONE CENTRALE, P. 12, E1

Piazza Duca d'Aosta 9, 20124; tel. (02) 6277; telex 311160. This is a favorite among business people, very near Stazione Centrale. During the thirties, the Gallia was frequented by princes and high-ranking officials. The 249 rooms just underwent a very lovely refurnishing. Rates are Lit. 340,000–450,000 with continental breakfast. Apartments run Lit. 900,000–1,400,000. All cards.

Michelangelo
BRERA/STAZIONE CENTRALE, P. 12, E1

Via Scarlatti 33, 20124; tel. (02) 6755; telex 340330. This is a favorite modern business hotel, although it is in a very chaotic part of town, close to the Stazione Centrale. Special insurance cards for theft are given to visiting business people. There are 260 rooms and a conference room for 350. The piano player in the bar is great! Rates are Lit. 260,000–340,000, breakfast included. Apartments are Lit. 420,000. All cards.

Milano Hilton
BRERA/STAZIONE CENTRALE, P. 12, D/E1

Via Galvani 12, 20124; tel. (02) 6983; telex 330433. A large hotel, with 339 rooms for those who want to feel close to home. Rates run Lit. 350,000–470,000 with continental breakfast. Apartments are Lit. 900,000–1,400,000. All cards.

Palace
BRERA/STAZIONE CENTRALE, P. 12, D2

Piazza della Repubblica 20, 20124; tel. (02) 6336; telex 311026. This hotel is similar to the prestigious Principe, but with friendlier employees. Although the feel is modern, the 187 rooms have just been redecorated in neoclassic style. Every comfort is available; there is a conference room for 140, a lovely roof garden with a terrific view, and the excellent Grill Casanova restaurant. Prices run Lit. 210,000–400,000; there are three grades of singles and doubles: low, medium, and high. All cards.

Principe di Savoia

BRERA/STAZIONE CENTRALE,
P. 12, D2

Piazza della Repubblica 17, 20124; tel. (02) 6230; telex 310052.
This 280-room hotel is a favorite of Americans. Every amenity
is available; there is a conference room for 1,000 and baby-
sitting services. The Principe is elegant in a traditional way and
caters to those who want a no-hassle, luxurious stay. Although
considered the most prestigious hotel in Milan, the service is
often less than friendly. Room prices range from Lit.
260,000–410,000; there are splendid apartments as well. All
cards.

EXPENSIVE

These hotels have the basic amenities—air-conditioning, TV,
and concierge service—and are priced somewhat more reasonably.

Carlton Hotel Senato

PIAZZA DUOMO/SAN BABILA,
P. 12, D3

Via Senato 5, 20121; tel. (02) 798583; telex 331306. A comfortable, clean 71-room hotel conveniently located near the world-
class shopping of the San Babila area. Ask for a room overlooking Via della Spiga. Rates are Lit. 155,000–195,000. Closed Aug.
All cards.

Cavour

BRERA/STAZIONE CENTRALE, P. 12, D3

Via Fatebenefratelli 21, 20121; tel. (02) 650983; telex 320498.
This is a favorite business hotel, especially for the publishing
and shopping clientele, since it is located in Piazza Cavour in
the heart of the magazine district and at the end of Via della
Spiga. The decor is more functional than pleasing. Be sure to
ask for a quiet room out of the 113 available. The restaurant is
closed on Fri. night, Sat., and Sun. lunchtime. Rates run Lit.
160,000–195,000; apartments run Lit. 210,000. All cards.

Hotel Diana Majestic

OUTSIDE CENTER

Viale Piave 42, 20129; tel. (02) 203404. Part of the Ciga chain,
this 102-room hotel is *very* in with the art and music crowd.
Newly redecorated, it is a bit off the beaten track, almost at the
entrance of the busy Corso Buenos Aires. There is a lovely garden in the back. Rates run Lit. 190,000–270,000. All cards.

Manin

BRERA/STAZIONE CENTRALE, P. 12, D2

Via Manin 7, 20121; tel. (02) 6596511; telex 320385. A very simple and homey hotel of 110 rooms that manages peace and
quiet in a busy location. There's a conference room for 100 and
a lovely garden. The restaurant is closed Sun. Rates run Lit.
155,000–200,000; apartments, Lit. 230,000–315,000. Closed
Aug. 7–23. All cards.

Grand Hotel et de Milan

PIAZZA DUOMO/SAN
BABILA, P. 12, D3

Via Manzoni 29, 20121; tel. (02) 870757; telex 334505. Located
at the end of Via Monte Napoleone on the elegant Via Manzoni,
this hotel was once Giuseppe Verdi's creative hideaway. When
he was on his deathbed, Verdi's fellow Milanese lined Via Manzoni with straw so the carriage traffic wouldn't disturb the composer. The hotel still has lovely old-world European charm

(although the lobby and various bathrooms need some refurnishing). Each of the 89 rooms has its own personality and is tastefully decorated with antiques. There is no restaurant, but there is room service and a pleasant bar in the lobby; a conference room holds 150. A favorite with the fashion crowd and serious shoppers. Prices run Lit. 220,000–325,000; apartments, Lit. 500,000–620,000. All cards.

MODERATELY PRICED
The amenities of these less expensive selections are similar to those in the higher-priced hotels, but the feel is somewhat less elegant.

Europea
PIAZZA CORDUSIO/CORSO MAGENTA/ PARCO, P. 12, C2

Via Canonica 38, 20154; tel. (02) 3314751; telex 321237. An advertising/marketing clientele frequents this 45-room hotel in the Chinese section of the city. It's very quiet, with a small garden. Rates range from Lit. 100,000–175,000. Closed Aug. All cards.

Manzoni
PIAZZA DUOMO/SAN BABILA, P. 12, D3

Via Santo Spirito 20, 20121; tel. (02) 705700. The 52 rooms are without television but in a great location in the heart of the city. Very affordable rates: Lit. 90,000–135,000. No cards; traveler's checks accepted.

Hotel Promessi Sposi
OUTSIDE CENTER, P. 12, E2

Piazza Oberdan 12, 20129; tel. (02) 203661. Take the Red Line metro to Porta Venezia. A homey, hospitable atmosphere permeates this small, 32-room hotel; fresh flowers abound. Rates are Lit. 82,000–123,000, with breakfast. No cards.

Antica Locanda Solferino
BRERA/STAZIONE CENTRALE, P. 12, D2

Via Castelfidardo 2, 20121; tel. (02) 656905. Located in the heart of Brera, this 11-room hostelry used to be a favorite with young people; models and photographers considered it charming in its simplicity. Lately, even the young think it's too simple, and the proprietors are not always the most polite. Still, be sure to reserve at least two weeks in advance. The Solferino Restaurant is attached to the hotel, and also attracts the fashion-model crowd. Prices are reasonable: Lit. 87,000 for a double. There are no singles. No cards.

Piazza Duomo/San Babila Area

The area around the Piazza Duomo is the heart of Milan and is considered the center of the city. Directions are often given "from the Duomo," and many use the steps of this masterpiece as a meeting place.

Its immense dimensions (515 feet long, 305 feet wide, and 345 feet to the tallest spire, where the gold statue of the protectress Madonnina reigns above the city) render the **Duomo** worthy of its place as Milan's proud symbol. Like all classic works, this majestic edifice seems to transcend all time. Of the largest cathedrals in the world (as well as the largest and most elaborate example of Gothic architecture in Italy), the Duomo continues to amaze.

Conceived in the 14th century, the Duomo was the project of the powerful Visconti family, who ruled the medieval city for more than one hundred years. Gian Galeazzo Visconti decreed the building of the massive church as a tribute to the Virgin, in exchange for a son. He was blessed with two, both rather eccentric and neither cut out to rule. All was not lost, however, as this architectural treasure remains.

The interior of the Duomo is divided into five naves supported by massive columns. The stained-glass windows date from the 15th century through modern times. In the south transept is the tomb of Gian Giacomo de'Medici. The remains of San Carlo Borromeo, archbishop of Milan who died in 1584, are in a crypt downstairs, where the cathedral's Treasury (Tesoro) is located. The Treasury houses a collection of gold, silver, ivories, and jewels, dating from the fourth to 17th centuries. (Open 9 A.M. to noon and 3 to 5:30 P.M.)

Duomo (1386–1806)

Started in 1386 and finished nearly five centuries later, the complexity of the Duomo's chronology and form inspires the viewer's delight and the historian's despair. Due to its large scale, the Duomo's builders consulted with Italian as well as French and German architects famed for their lofty cathedrals. The result is a building with Italian proportions and northern, Gothic details.

The form of the cathedral had been determined by the early 15th century. Soaring buttresses culminating in pinnacles separate the curved apse wall into three sections. Between the buttresses are luminous stained-glass windows interlaced with stone tracery. Italian builders balanced these Gothic aspects by introducing strong horizontal elements into the composition.

The crossing (where the transept and nave intersect), with its exterior lantern and spire, was designed in the late 15th century. Officials conferred with Leonardo da Vinci before selecting a proposal by Giovanni Amadeo. Instead of imposing classically derived Renaissance forms on the building, Amadeo designed this area using the Duomo's Gothic style. The result is a lacy octagonal cage that culminates in a 350-foot spire. Visitors can view the rooftop landscape of bristling pinnacles, statues, and the soaring spire.

Napoleon had the Duomo finished in 1805, during a period of renewed interest in Gothic forms. Despite this, the facade and north elevation completed then are considered the most uninspired parts of the Duomo.

—Mary Beth Betts and Charles Ayes

Climb or take an elevator to the roof, to admire up close the intricate carvings on the cathedral's exterior (open from 9 A.M. to 4 P.M. in winter, to 5 P.M. in summer).

To the right as you face the Duomo, the **Royal Palace** (Palazzo Reale) is a splendid example of 18th-century architecture. Once housing the Visconti and Sforza families as well as foreign diplomats, the building was eventually taken over by the city. Unfortunately, many of the neoclassical interiors were bombed during the war, and except for art exhibitions, only the **Duomo Museum** on the ground floor is open to the public. Hours for the museum are 10:30 A.M. to 12:30 P.M. and 3 to 5:30 P.M.; closed Monday; free on Thursday.

As you walk along Via Mercanti (opposite the Duomo), you will see what remains of the **Piazza Mercanti,** the center of medieval Milan. The only thing left is the **Palazzo della Ragione,** the town hall until 1770, now surrounded by banks and offices. Continuing on to Via Orefici, you will find the Ambrosian Library (Biblioteca Ambrosiana) and picture gallery (Pinacotteca Ambrosiana) at Piazza Pio XI 2, the institution founded by Cardinal Federico Borromeo in the early 1600s.

Galleria Vittorio Emanuele II (1865–1867, 1877), Giuseppe Mengoni

The Galleria Vittorio Emanuele II unites two obsessions of the 19th century, commerce and technology. The Galleria, an arcade or glass-enclosed street of stores, was made possible by the late-18th-century mastery of glass and iron construction; arcades encouraged continual shopping and strolling, regardless of time or weather.

Milan's Galleria is a cross-shaped structure with a huge central dome, designed by Giuseppe Mengoni. The long arm of the building extends from the Duomo to La Scala Theater, and thus connects two important cultural institutions. The building's triumphal arch facade was part of a scheme to aggrandize the Piazza del Duomo.

The triumphal arch also was symbolic. Constructed during the period of Italy's unification, the Galleria was named after united Italy's first king, and celebrates Italy's cultural past and Vittorio Emanuele's heritage. The arch recalls the Roman Empire, the circumference of the dome equals St. Peter's, the cross-shaped plan suggests Vittorio Emanuele's family crest, and statues in the rotunda and inside the four entrances represent a pantheon of Italian artists, scientists, and politicians.

If the decorations no longer evoke meaning for today's viewer, they enhance the Galleria's primary function as a frame for a constantly shifting display of shoppers and goods. The ornate decorations and elaborate shop windows create an almost theatrical environment.

—Mary Beth Betts and Charles Ayes

It has a vast collection of paintings and manuscripts, including works and papers by Raphael, Caravaggio, and Botticelli; a room is devoted to Leonardo da Vinci. Usually open 9:30 A.M. to 5 P.M.

Facing the Duomo once again, enter the **Galleria Vittorio Emanuele II,** on the left. There are plenty of elegant shops to visit before exiting on the opposite end at **Piazza della Scala,** facing **La Scala** (Teatro alla Scala). Completed on the site of a church in 1778, this acoustic jewel has seen and heard the best musicians in the world. Bombed during the war, it has been completely reconstructed piece by piece to its original splendor and detail. The elegant interior hall seats approximately three thousand spectators. The **Theatrical Museum** (Museo Teatrale), next to the theater, has an impressive collection of objects and literature relating to the history of opera, and especially to Verdi. You can usually see the interior of the opera house through the museum for a fee; ask the guard. Museum hours are 9 A.M. to noon and 2 to 6 P.M.; closed Sundays November through April; Sunday hours May to October are from 9:30 A.M. and from 2:30 P.M.

❦ Stop for a *panino* in any bar in the area. The **Motta** (to the left of the Duomo) is perfect for a quick lunch; the top floor of the department store **Rinascente,** across from the Duomo, offers a good selection of food. There are more expensive restaurants in the **Galleria.**

Walk down Via Manzoni toward Piazza Cavour to visit the **Poldi Pezzoli Museum** at number 12. The building was the home of Gian Giacomo Poldi Pezzoli, a member of a wealthy Milanese family, who bequeathed his house and his outstanding art collection to the city. The most important paintings hang in the Gold Saloon, and include works by Botticelli, Bernini, and Piero della Francesca. A focal point is the *Portrait of a Woman* by Antonio Pollaiuolo. The museum is well worth the visit, and reflects the elegant refinement found in Milan throughout its history. The museum is open 9:30 A.M. to 12:30 P.M. and 2:30 to 5:30 P.M.; also open Thursday evenings, 9 to 11 P.M., except in August. Closed Mondays and summer Sundays.

Continue along on Via Manzoni for preparatory window-shopping before entering into shopper's paradise: **Via Monte Napoleone** (once the headquarters for the Italian revolution against the Austrians), **Via Sant'Andrea,** and **Via della Spiga.** On these streets are the world's best-known designers and stores, whose very window displays drip with style and high prices. (See "Shopping," this chapter, for details.) Continue up Via della Spiga to Corso Venezia and turn right, heading toward **Piazza San Babila** (considered one of the wealthiest corners in Europe). Your shopping days are *not* over! **Corso Vittorio Emanuele II** is one long, tempting consumer walkway back to Piazza Duomo. Good luck!

Brera/Stazione Centrale Area

To get to the Brera district, walk up Via Verdi (to the right of La Scala when facing the theater). The street eventually turns into Via Brera, leading to the Art Academy and the **Brera Art Gallery** (Pinocoteca di Brera) at number 28. Maria Theresa of Austria turned what was at one time a grand Jesuit headquarters into this thriving cultural center. Built in the 17th century, the palace houses one of the most comprehensive art collections in Italy, rich in works from the Lombard and Veneto schools (15th to 18th centuries). Be sure to buy the catalog as the museum is enormous. Open 9 A.M. to 2 P.M. weekdays, 9 A.M. to 1 P.M. Sundays, holidays, and the second and fourth Saturday of each month.

You can also enter the Brera district by going down Via Fatebenefratelli (where the police station can be found). Pass **San Marco church** and, continuing along, Via Solferino (to the right) and Via Brera (to the left). This is an area to take map in hand and walk. There is plenty of shopping, art and antique galleries, bars, and sights (**Santa Maria del Carmine** church on Via Madonnina and the Paleo-Christian basilica of **San Simpliciano**). This used to be the bohemian section of Milan, but as all good things must come to an end, real estate prices are changing the local color.

 Stop for a coffee or salad at the **Bar Giamaica** on Via Brera, still somewhat of a hangout for locals.

Piazza Cordusio/Corso Magenta/Parco

With your back to the Duomo, you are now facing Via Dante and the **Castle of the Sforzas** (Castello Sforzesco). It was built as a fortress for Francesco Sforza in 1450 (he was the enterprising husband of the only Visconti heir, illegitimate Bianca Maria) on the ruins of the original Visconti castle. As you face this enormous structure, enter the main portals off Largo Cairoli, cross the piazza, and enter the large doorway leading into the Corte Ducale. Immediately to the right is a museum containing sculpture, paintings, and applied arts from pre-Roman times until the present. Here can be found Michelangelo's last work, *Pietà Rondanini,* Mantegna's *Madonna In Glory,* and works by Filippo Lippi, Bellini, Correggio, and Tintoretto. The museum is open 9:30 A.M. to 12:15 P.M. and 2:30 to 5:15 P.M., and is closed Mondays.

Behind the castle, covering over 110 acres, is a respite from smog and traffic—the welcoming **Sempione Park** with a Parisian-like view of the **Arch of Peace** (Arco della Pace). The arch was built by Cagnola in 1807 in honor of Napoleon, then dedicated to Francesco I of Austria in 1838, and finally, in 1859, to the independence of Italy. On the right side of the park is the **Civic Arena** (Arena Civica), constructed in the neoclassical style. On the left side of the park is the **Triennale,** where architectural and contemporary design exhibitions are often held.

Walk toward the Stazione Nord (North Train Station) in Piazzale Cadorna to Via Boccaccio. Continue on to Via Caradosso (the third street on the left). Here is the church of **Santa Maria delle Grazie,** built in the Gothic style from 1466 to 1490 by Guiniforte Solari. The High Renaissance architect, Donato Bramante, added the richly decorated apse, considered one of the purest creations of the Renaissance. From the apse, through a door on the left, pass into Bramante's exquisite cloister.

Leonardo da Vinci
Last Supper (1495–1498)

Leonardo was the most gifted inventor of the Renaissance, but sometimes his experiments failed. Not content with the standard techniques of fresco painting, he tested a new method of application on the *Last Supper* and as a result, it has been in a state of perpetual disrepair almost since the day he finished it. To make matters worse, an Allied bombing attack nearly leveled the refectory housing the painting in World War II, although somehow Leonardo's masterpiece survived. The pathos and dignity of the fresco, coupled with its fragility, have earned it the reputation as one of the world's most precious paintings.

As is the case with all of Leonardo's works, the composition is mathematically precise. The 12 disciples are arranged in four groups of three. Four panels in retreating size on each side lend perspective and lead the eye to Christ's head at the center, backed by three open panels that complete the series. The painting dramatizes the moment when Jesus reveals to his disciples that one of them will betray him. The guilty Judas, clutching his bag of silver, pushes away from Christ, his face dark with anxiety. The others protest their disbelief in a variety of expressive poses. Christ, imperturbable in his foreknowledge, gestures calmly at the center of the din. Leonardo's psychological realism is extraordinary. With the exception of Christ, he drew his figures from live models; for the face of Judas he searched through the local prison, drawing many sketches.

In the *Last Supper,* Leonardo stresses not only the betrayal of Christ, but also the symbolism of the Eucharist, the ritual sharing of bread and wine in a communal setting. Picture this refectory crowded with monks at mealtime, when the entire hall served as a living mirror for the solemn narrative on the wall.

—Michael Hinden

To the left of the entrance to the church is what was once the refectory or dining hall of the monastery, the **Cenacolo Vinciano,** where **Leonardo da Vinci's** *Last Supper* (*Cena*) can be seen. Miraculously unharmed when the building was bombed during World War II, the poor physical condition of the masterpiece has long caused controversy. Da Vinci chose to paint on dry plaster rather than moist, creating a vulnerable base for the color; the amount of time involved in its restoration has been the focus of many a sightseer as well as art historian. A copy that was made by students of da Vinci several years after the original appeared to be losing its clarity is beautifully restored and hangs in London—and, according to many, puts the original to shame. Decide for yourself. The Cenacolo is open 9 A.M. to 1:30 P.M. and 2:30 to 6:30 P.M. Tuesday to Saturday; 9 A.M. to 3 P.M. Sunday; closed Monday.

What would you think of a man who stared in ecstasy upon a desert of stumps and said: "Oh, my soul, my beating heart, what a noble forest is here!"

You would think that those men had an astonishing talent for seeing things that had already passed away. It was what I thought when I stood before "The Last Supper" and heard men apostrophizing wonders and beauties and perfections which had faded out of the picture and gone a hundred years before they were born. We can imagine the beauty that was once in an aged face; we can imagine the forest if we see the stumps; but we cannot absolutely *see* these things when they are not there. I am willing to believe that the eye of the practiced artist can rest upon "The Last Supper" and renew a luster where only a hint of it is left, supply a tint that has faded away, restore an expression that is gone; patch and color and add to the dull canvas until at last its figures shall stand before him aglow with the life, the feeling, the freshness, yea, with all the noble beauty that was theirs when first they came from the hand of the master. But *I* cannot work this miracle. Can those other uninspired visitors do it, or do they only happily imagine they do?

After reading so much about it, I am satisfied that "The Last Supper" was a very miracle of art once. But it was three hundred years ago.

—Mark Twain
The Innocents Abroad, 1869

🦐 For a quick, good lunch, try **Lo Squalo** in Piazzale Baracca. From Santa Maria delle Grazie, follow Corso Magenta in the opposite direction of the Duomo, and turn right at the piazza. The Chinese **Kota Radja** is on the other side of the square if you're looking for a change from Italian food.

From Corso Magenta, walk down Via Zenale (across from Santa Maria delle Grazie) and head toward Via San Vittore (past the 19th-century San Vittore prison). Turn left and pass the **Leonardo da Vinci Museum** (Museo della Scienza e della Tecnica), displaying a collection of da Vinci's designs. Open 9 A.M. to 5 P.M.; closed Monday; admission free Thursday. Further on is the **Basilica of Saint Ambrose** (Sant Ambrogio), honoring the saint (a lawyer by trade) who became bishop of Mediolanum (Milan) in A.D. 375 after the Roman capital had moved there. Saint Ambrose was a converted Christian who was as passionate about his church as he was about his state. It is said that he baptized Saint Augustine in the basilica.

The architecture combines work from the ninth (the apse), 12th, and 13th centuries; there was a thorough restoration in the late 19th century. Do not miss the main altar (protected by glass) with its elaborate ninth-century work in gold and jewels and engraved with images of Saint Ambrose and Christ, and the underground crypt where Saint Ambrose is buried. The **Museum** offers a step-by-step guide to the church; it's open 10 A.M. to noon and 3 to 5 P.M.; closed Tuesdays, Saturdays, Sunday mornings, and holidays.

Returning in the direction of the Castle of the Sforzas, you reach the Lombard Renaissance church of **San Maurizio,** also known as the Monastero Maggiore (usually open Wednesdays only for concerts). It contains the Archaeology Museum, open 9:30 A.M. to 12:30 P.M. and 2:30 to 5:30 P.M.; closed Tuesdays.

Porta Ticinese/Navigli

From the square in front of Saint Ambrose, you enter the Ticinese district. The name comes from the River Ticino, which used to be a vital waterway to Milan. The shops in this area are less fashionable than those on Via Monte Napoleone and Via della Spiga, but are characteristic of days gone by. The district has a refreshing avant-garde air, offbeat in a quiet way. Eventually you will reach the Corso di Porta Ticinese and the **Colonne** (Columns) of **San Lorenzo Maggiore,** the most important Roman ruins in Milan. The columns date to the second and third centuries.

Warm weather brings everyone out for lunch or a beer at night at Il Pois, under the columns.

Walk down the colorful Corso di Porta Ticinese and you will end up at the **navigli** (canals). This is where the Naviglio Pavese, Naviglio Grande, and the Darsena meet at what is the liveliest night area in town, taking over where Brera leaves off. This dynamic zone is an energetic mixture of working class and young artists, and is a nostalgic reminder of days when Milan's canals were navigable. During warm weather boats on the canals become restaurants and caffès.

A traditional dominant theme in Milan's attitude toward the rest of the world is resentment of Rome. There is nothing new about this—the Milanese have never forgiven Cavour for his insistence on making Rome the capital of his united Italy, and they still revere Napoleon for having established *his* Italian capital here—but as Milan's post-war power and influence grew, so did its traditional umbrage. The local feeling about Rome, then and now, is a compound of distrust, envy, and contempt, comparable to the reactions of Chicagoans vis-à-vis New York. Whenever anything goes wrong, the Milanese are likely to blame Rome, and "S.P.Q.R." is translated locally as *"Sono Porci Questi Romani"* ("They are pigs, these Romans"). Since Rome is, after all, the seat of government, the Milanese are inclined to believe that all governmental regulation of commerce is a heinous conspiracy to defraud them of the fruits of their genius. "Politics is a Roman industry, and the only one they have," a friend of mine said to me one day. "We make the money, and they steal it." The Milanese have long been indifferent to politics, and, consequently, are almost unrepresented in the government Ministries, where, they feel, most of the damage is done. They are likely to point with pride to all that their city is accomplishing without government help or interference—then it was the subway, two new airports, public housing, and so on—and they invariably claim that they could do much more if Rome would just leave them alone. At the time the European Common Market was being created, the city administration published a handsomely illustrated brochure in four languages touting Milan as "the Seat of European Institutions" and in which a lead article proclaimed boldly that Milan was "a capital in search of a country."

Quite apart from all the rational explanations for the Milanese grudge against Rome may lie a deeper cause. This is the gulf that separates two distinct mentalities—both Italian, but worlds apart. I once overheard a discussion between two elderly, distinguished women, one from Rome, one from Milan, on the relative merits of their hometowns. The Roman lady had been maintaining loudly that Milan was not an Italian city at all, but the moral capital of Switzerland. The Milanese matriarch's firm, final word was "I never go to Rome. Everything is so old there."

—William Murray
Italy: The Fatal Gift

SHOPPING

It's not news that Milan shares the title of "fashion capital" with Paris. It has become à la mode to go to Milan for a quick, expensive shopping spree. The city reflects the ultimate in subtle, refined style, represented by such designers as Armani. Italians have perfected the aesthetic sense, and the windows of Milan, whether displaying dresses, stockings, or lamps, subliminally influence. Shopping in Milan is sightseeing and art appreciation; by the process of osmosis, one becomes a discerning fashion expert after only a few days, squinting knowingly at every hemline and tailored jacket.

The stores listed here will satisfy every shopping and visual need. Many will ship purchases. Beware that prices are astronomical, but you will find the very best of everything—Milan and style go hand in hand, and prices reflect that. This is *not* the place to shop for bargains; if you're looking for good prices on leather goods, head for Rome or Florence.

Remember that most shops close for lunch, between about 1 and 3 P.M.; they stay open evenings until about 7 P.M.

Via Monte Napoleone to Via della Spiga

Some of the best shopping in Europe is found in this area. The streets themselves are as elegant as the fashions; some are closed to traffic, making strolling that much easier. Just a walk down Via Manzoni, Via Monte Napoleone, Via Sant'Andrea, Via Borgospesso, and Via della Spiga will introduce many of the quality designer names associated with Italian fashion—and with fashion throughout the world.

On Via Monte Napoleone, you'll find **Mila Schön,** clothing and accessories for women at number 2, for men at number 6. **Valentino Uomo** (for men) is at number 20; the entrance to **Valentino Donna** (for women) is off Monte Napoleone at Via Santo Spirito 3. You'll find **Jesurum,** for lace and lingerie, at Via Monte Napoleone number 14, and at number 21, **Pratesi** for linens.

The little streets connecting Via Monte Napoleone and Via della Spiga continue the fashion show. At Via Borgospesso 19 is **Laura Biagiotti.** Via Sant'Andrea has **Giorgio Armani** at number 9, **Ferre** (for men) at number 21, **Fendi** leather goods at number 16, and the Paris-based **Kenzo** at number 11. For a reasonably priced cashmere jacket (for men or women), try **Uomo** on Via Gesu.

Among the shops lining Via della Spiga are **Prada** (for shoes, bags, and accessories) at number 1; **Bottega Veneta** (another star in the leather goods world) at number 5; at the same address, **Maude Frizon** (also for shoes); **Fendi** at number 9; another **Ferre** shop (for women) at number 11; **Krizia** at number 23; and for daring designs, **Thierry Mugler,** at number 36.

Emporio Armani, featuring the more affordable end of the Armani collection, is on Via Durini at number 27, beyond Piazza San Babila. Near Via Monte Napoleone is **Enrico Coveri,** on Corso Matteotti 12.

A perfect place to rest your street-weary shopping feet is **Cova,** Via Monte Napoleone 8. This prestigious tearoom has been serving hungry shoppers since 1817 and continues its typically English service in high style. Or before you attack the stores on Corso Vittorio Emanuele, sip an *aperitivo* at **Gin Rosa** (Galleria San Babila 4B) at an outside table and watch your fellow shoppers pass by.

Corso Vittorio Emanuele II and Piazza del Duomo

From Piazza San Babila walk down Corso Vittorio Emanuele II toward the Piazza del Duomo, for even more serious shopping.

On Corso Vittorio Emanuele is the department store **Max Mara,** at number 7. Be sure to visit the **Max Mara annex** across from the main store; there are great bargains downstairs. There may not be a sign, so ask someone at the shop to point you in the right direction.

The oldest and largest department store in Milan is **La Rinascente,** right near the Piazza del Duomo, where many a shopper has found good selections and prices. Off Corso Vittorio Emanuele toward the Galleria are a number of shops with fashions for young people, including **Benetton** (Piazza del Duomo 22 and in the Galleria Passarella) and **Fiorucci** (two stores in the Galleria Passarella).

Along with the caffès, bars, restaurants, and people-watching in the Galleria are tobacco stores, bookstores, hatmakers, and, of course, more fashionable clothing stores.

Corso Vercelli

Corso Vercelli is an excellent shopping street at the end of Corso Magenta; its close to the fair grounds, home of the Milano Collection Fashion shows as well as industry shows of everything from computers to jewelry. Avoid the crowds in the center of town; there are branches of several shops here, including **Frette,** for the bed and bath, at Via Manzoni 11 or Via Torino 42. For lingerie, **Donini** at Via Belfiore 7 is worth a stop.

 Stop for a coffee and a mouth-watering pastry at **Biffi,** Corso Magenta 87, after you've finished your shopping.

Brera

Brera, the area north of La Scala, has a variety of less serious shopping possibilities. Most of the shops are farther north where Via Brera turns into Via Solferino. Of interest are **Drogheria Solferino** (on the corner of Via Pontaccio and Solferino); **Merù** (for jewelry) at number 3; **Guardaroba** at number 9; **Urrah,** number 3; and **La Tenda,** at Piazza San

Marco 1. Off Solferino, **Arform,** Via Moscova 22, has a tasteful range of merchandise from clothing to home accessories.

Walk down Via Fiori Chiari and Via Madonnina for a look at some beautiful antiques, jewelry, and antique clothing; **Luisa Beccaria** is at Via Madonnina 10.

On Via Brera itself is **Naj Oleari,** at numbers 5 and 8, excellent for children. Unusual decorative objects are sold at **Piero Fornasetti,** Via Brera 16. Beautiful white porcelain can be found at **La Porcellana Bianca,** Via dell'Orso 7.

Boutiques

Designer goods and other bargains can be found in the many boutiques of Milan. For offbeat, fresh design, **Komlan** on Corso Venezia II is terrific. Other great boutiques are **Biffi,** Corso Genova 6 (designers from France, Spain, Japan, and Italy); **Anni 80,** Via Fabio Filzi 14 (designs by Erreuno, Byblos, and Touche); **Cose,** Via della Spiga 8 (designs by Romeo Gigli, Norma Kamali, and jewelry from Art Wear in New York); **Bianca e Blu,** Via de Amicis 53/55, near Biffi (for a romantic, classical look); **Giusi Bresciani,** Via Morone 8, near Via Manzoni (for a stylish, traditional look; Bresciani specializes in hats of all kinds—a favorite stop before the La Scala debut!); **Zeus** is at Via Vigevano 8 (featuring crazy new styles); **Pupi Solari** is in Piazza Tommaseo, at Via Mascheroni 12 (with romantic, English-style clothing for women and children); and **Bardelli,** at Corso Magenta 13, is a favorite with Milanese gentlemen (English-style clothing for men and women—but the selection is better for men).

After you've picked out a new outfit at Bardelli, walk down Corso Magenta to **Marchesi,** Via Santa Maria alla Porta 13, for a cappuccino in one of Milan's original pastry shops.

Other men's stores include **Etro,** Via Bigli 10 (very expensive goods for the man who has everything; they sell women's clothing, too); **Boggi,** Piazza San Babila 3 (a classic men's shop); and **Tincati,** Piazza Oberdan 2 (a good selection).

Children's Stores

Fashion-conscious youngsters would appreciate grown-ups who shop at: **Pupi Solari,** Piazza Tommaseo at Via Mascheroni 12; **Emporio Armani,** Via Durini 27; **Naj Oleari,** Via Brera 5; **Luisa Beccaria,** Via Madonnina 10; **Gerry Mox,** Via dell'Orso 9; and **Calico Lion** (for newborns), Via Bigli 4.

Shoes, Leather, Accessories

To repeat, leather bargains are hard to come by in Milan. You can find good prices and quality merchandise, however, at

Serapian, Via Jommelli 35—a taxi ride from the center of the city. Other stores that have fine leather goods include **Fendi,** Via Sant'Andrea 16; **Bottega Veneta,** Via della Spiga 5; **Diego della Valle,** Via della Spiga 22; **Prada,** Via della Spiga 1 and Galleria Vittorio Emanuele; **Guido Pasquali,** Via Sant'Andrea 1; **Ferragamo,** Via Monte Napoleone 3; **Gucci,** Via Monte Napoleone 5; **Mario Valentino,** Corso Matteotti 10; **Carrano,** Via Sant'Andrea 21; and **Beltrami,** Via Monte Napoleone 16.

For jewelry try **Pellini Bijoux,** Via Morigi 9.

Furniture

The design capital of the world offers numerous goods for your home. Many Italian manufacturers have distributors abroad, so you can compare goods in Milan and buy merchandise back home.

Browse through the following: **Alchimia,** Foro Buonaparte 55 (modern Italian designs); **Arflex,** Via Borgogna 2 (designs by Marco Zanuso, Adolfo Matalini, and Cini Boeri); **High-Tech,** Corso di Porta Ticinese 77 (young, industrial style); **Cassina,** Via Durini 16/18 (classical); **Memphis,** Via Manzoni 46 (everything by the Memphis school); **Tanzi Driade,** Via Fatebenefratelli 9 (designs by Antonio Astori and Massimo Morozzi); **Zeus,** Via Vigevano 8 (avant-garde designs); and **Alias,** Via Fiori Chiari (modern and classic designs).

Lighting

Italian lighting designs are admired (and copied) throughout the world. If you're looking for the real thing, try **Arteluce,** Via Borgogna 5; and **Artemide,** Corso Monforte 19.

Food Stores

Food is an art form in Italy, and Milan takes food to its highest level. Eating takes on another meaning here; it's as much for the eyes as for the stomach!

Peck, at Via Spadari 9, is the king of the food designer group! Even if you don't buy anything, this is a delicious side trip worth taking—and it is very close to the Duomo. Be sure to visit Peck's cheese store, **Casa del Formaggio,** at Via Speronari 3, next to **Vino Vino** (a wine store not to be believed). **Il Salumaio,** at Via Monte Napoleone 12, offers a great selection of nibbles for your hotel room.

❦ RESTAURANTS

As the saying goes, "si mangia bene a Milano" (one eats well in Milan), and it is deliciously true! Among Milanese specialties are: *risotto giallo* or *alla milanese* (rice cooked in broth with saffron), *costoletta alla milanese* (breaded veal chops), *osso buco* (braised shin of veal), *polenta, lenticchie con cotechino* (sausages with lentils), *cazzoeula* (pork and cabbage casserole), and the traditional *panettone* (an egg-yellow sweet bread with currants and bits of candied orange and citron). But, being a cosmopolitan city, Milan's menus are varied and vast, and Milanese specialties are only a part of the offering.

The following restaurants are variously priced and offer a range of Italian cuisines. Higher-priced restaurants are listed first, then more moderately priced ones. These restaurants were chosen because they reflect the many sides of Milan's personality—from the unpretentious, timeless Milanese trattoria to Italy's only 3-star restaurant, nouvelle and *very* chic.

Prices given here are for a complete meal (antipasto to dessert), but do not include wine (which usually costs from Lit. 10,000 lire up) or tip (which depends on the restaurant and is usually around 10–15 percent). It is often safe to ask the waiter to choose a wine; most restaurants have their favorites and will suggest them. If you want one from a specific region, just ask.

Be sure to reserve in advance, as dining out is a favorite pastime in Milan. Dressing up is part of the fun, even when entertaining at home, so you can enjoy a fashion show with your food.

Credit cards are listed as accepted. "All cards" means that all of the following are accepted: AE—American Express; DC—Diner's Club; MC—MasterCard; V—Visa. As with hotels, restaurants are keyed into neighborhoods and the color map of the city at the back of the book.

EXPENSIVE

Bice
PIAZZO DUOMO/SAN BABILA, P. 12, D3

Via Borgospesso 12; tel. (02) 702572. Bice offers delicious classic Italian meat and fish dishes in a sophisticated atmosphere. Milan's Bice attracts a crowd—and branches in New York and Porto Cervo, Sardinia, are also known as among the very best. A dinner costs Lit. 50,000–75,000. Closed Mon., Tues. lunch, Aug., Christmas, and Easter. AE, V.

Da Aimo e Nadia
OUTSIDE CENTER, NEAR P. 13, A4

Via Montecuccoli 6; tel. (02) 416886. A creative menu from the husband-and-wife team at Da Aimo makes a cab ride to Via Montecuccoli worthwhile. Specialties include fettuccine, rabbit with mozzarella and zucchini flowers, and scampi and calamari salad with porcini mushrooms. A dinner is priced from Lit. 65,000–96,000. Closed Sat. lunch, Sun., and Aug. AE, V.

Giannino
OUTSIDE CENTER, P. 12, A4

Via Sciesa 8; tel. (02) 5452948. Traditional and elegant, Giannino features regional and Mediterranean specialties. This is one of Milan's most famous restaurants—and with good reason. The vegetable antipasto, the fresh homemade pasta, and the *risotto alla milanese* are truly excellent. A dinner will run around Lit. 65,000–85,000. Closed Sun. and Aug. All cards.

Gualtiero Marchesi
OUTSIDE CENTER, P. 12, E4

Via Bonvesin de la Riva 9; tel. (02) 741246. This is the only res-

Quick Lunches

For lunch, you may want to try fast food Italian style. Two chains are particular favorites in Milan: **Ciao** and **Italy & Italy,** with locations throughout the city. Another favorite for a quick meal is the top floor of the **Rinascente** department store, across from the Duomo. Or for another change of pace, try **Il Girasole,** Via Vincenzo Monti 32, tel. (02) 435263, a self-service health-food restaurant featuring organic dishes (even whole-meal pasta) and juices. A meal here costs about Lit. 10,000–22,000. No cards.

taurant in Italy that was awarded 3 stars from Michelin. Chef Marchesi's nouvelle Italian cuisine and ultraminimalist decoration (both in the restaurant and on the plate) puts Italian dining on a sumptuously intellectual level. Specialties include ravioli, shrimp, and lamb chops *alla milanese* with small vegetable bouquets. House wines are Breganze and Franciacorta. Worth the price of Lit. 85,000–130,000 for dinner. Closed Sun., Mon. lunch, Aug., Dec. 24–28, and holidays. All cards.

St. Andrews   PIAZZA DUOMO/SAN BABILA, P. 12, D3
Via Sant'Andrea 23; tel. (02) 793132. This is a favorite with the fashion crowd for private parties after the designer collections. The food is not always consistent (stick to more simple selections), but the service is extremely caring. The fun here is really the clientele. Dinners run Lit. 60,000–100,000. Closed Sun. and Aug. All cards.

Savini   PIAZZA DUOMO/SAN BABILA, P. 12, D3
Galleria Vittorio Emanuele II; tel. (02) 8058343. Offering a traditional bill of fare on a grand level, this restaurant is one of the oldest and most representative of 19th-century Milan. Specialties include *risotto alla milanese, filet di San Pietro alla Carlini,* and *costoletta alla milanese.* The house wines are Gavi and Magliano. Dinner will cost Lit. 65,000–110,000. Closed Sun. and Aug. All cards.

El Toulà   PIAZZA DUOMO/SAN BABILA, P. 12, D3
Piazza Paolo Ferrari 6; tel. (02) 870302. Located next to La Scala, this elegant if somewhat staid restaurant offers international cuisine by chef Alfredo Beltrame. The consistent freshness of the food (try the gnocchi with prosciutto) makes this a favorite after-theater and business locale. This is a branch of a well-respected chain that began in Treviso. Prices are high: Lit. 65,000–112,000. Closed Sun. and Aug. All cards.

MODERATELY PRICED
Alfredo-Gran San Bernardo   OUTSIDE CENTER, P. 12, B1
Via Borgese 14; tel. (02) 3319000. Some of the best Milanese cooking around, served in a simple atmosphere. Try the *risotto alla milanese* and *osso buco.* A dinner costs around Lit. 48,000–60,000. Closed Sun., Aug., and Dec. 21–Jan. 19. No cards.

Boccondivino

Via Carducci 17; tel. (02) 866040. Specializing in salami, cheese, and wine from all regions, Boccondivino offers something different from the normal restaurant fare. A meal runs Lit. 36,000–60,000. Closed for lunch, Sun., and Aug. No cards.

La Bricola

Via Solferino 25; tel. (02) 6551012. There is always a lively scene at La Bricola. The specialty is carpaccio (cooked or raw), but chicken, salads, and *risotto al sálto* (a saffron rice cake) are on the menu as well. La Bricola is usually packed, so reserve early. This is a fashion industry hangout—truly modern Milanese. Dinner costs about Lit. 40,000–50,000. Closed Sun., Mon., Aug., and Christmas. AE, DC, V.

Pizza

For some of Milan's best pizza, try these two local favorites:

Le Briciole, Via Camperio 17; tel. (02) 804114. Rustic atmosphere and a good, basic menu. No cards.

Malastrana, Corso Garibaldi 50; tel. (02) 872935. Basic pizzeria with great pizza. Seems to always be open—even in August. MC, V.

La Brisa

Via della Brisa 15; tel. (02) 872001. La Brisa has a great location, near the Roman Circus ruins behind Corso Magenta. It offers fresh salads and desserts in an open-air garden, plus an interesting architect/designer clientele. Dinners are priced Lit. 35,000–40,000. Closed Sat., Sun. lunch, 3 weeks at Christmas. No cards.

La Champagneria

Via Clerici 1; tel. (02) 800862. For something very different, try La Champagneria. Here you'll find anything and everything sexy, including oysters and clams, served with champagne. Expect to pay Lit. 60,000–70,000, not including champagne. Closed Sat. lunch, Sun., Aug. AE, DC, MC.

Al Porto

Piazzale Generale Cantore; tel. (02) 8321481. This is one of the best fish restaurants in Milan: a lively, friendly atmosphere in an old tollhouse on the canal. If it's a summer evening, stroll around the neighborhood after dinner—stopping for a drink or some jazz. Dinner runs Lit. 45,000–65,000. Closed Sun., Mon. lunch, Aug., and Dec. AE, DC.

Santa Lucia

Via S. Pietro All'Orto 3; tel. (02) 793155. Travelers love Santa Lucia for its fine food, service, and ambience. A good choice of Italian favorites are served in a formal atmosphere, especially good fish specialties. Dinner runs around Lit. 40,000–60,000. Closed Mon. No cards.

Solferino
BRERA/STAZIONE CENTRALE, P. 12, D2

Via Castelfidardo 2; tel. (02) 6599886. Known more for its good-looking model clientele and atmosphere than its food, Solferino offers such specialties as salmon and an enormous *costoletta alla milanese.* Dinners cost about Lit. 40,000–60,000. Closed Sat. lunch, Sun. and Sat. evenings May–Sept., Dec. 24–Jan. 2, and Aug. 7–17. No cards.

Il Torchietto
PORTA TICINESE/NAVIGLI, P. 13, C5

Via Ascanio Sforza 47; tel. (02) 8372910. Located on one of the *navigli* (canals), this is the perfect place for dinner before taking in some jazz at the nearby Scimmie. There's a lovely garden and specialties from Mantua (sausages, tortelli with squash, green gnocchetti, tagliatelle). A dinner costs about Lit. 36,000–45,000. Closed Mon. and Aug. V.

Trattoria al Piccolo Teatro
PIAZZA CORDUSIO/ CORSO MAGENTA/PARCO, P. 12, C3

Via Rovello 21; tel. (02) 877127. The candlelit, cozy atmosphere makes this a perfect after-theater spot. (The Piccolo Teatro is nearby.) The *costoletta alla milanese* is always good here. Dinners run Lit. 40,000–57,000. Closed Sat. lunch, Sun., and Aug. All cards.

EVENING ENTERTAINMENT

To find out what's happening in town, pick up the current *Milano Mese* and *Viva Milano* (at newstands and the EPT). The EPT should have an English copy available. Each and every event in the city is listed here. Remember that Milan is a "late night" town and dinner begins between 8 and 10 P.M.

Opera, Concerts, Theater

La Scala, of course, is a priority for opera fans, and as mentioned before, you should try to get tickets before you leave home—they are difficult to come by. Call (02) 809126 or 88791, or write: Teatro Alla Scala, Via Filodrammatici 2, Milano 20121, Italy. People in the ticket office usually speak basic English. The season begins December 7 and continues until July. If you don't have tickets, head over to La Scala Biglietteria (when facing the theater, the ticket office is to the left). The ticket office often opens at 6 P.M. and sells tickets for that evening until the performance at 8 P.M. For information, call (02) 807041; for reservations, call (02) 809126 in the morning. The concierge in major hotels may be able to help you get tickets.

Classical music is offered at the **Conservatorio** (Conservatory) on Via Conservatorio 12 (telephone (02) 701755), which presents a varied program of classical concerts throughout the year. The Conservatorio is in the San Babila area; take the Red Line metro to San Babila. During the summer, outdoor concerts are held within the walls of the Castle of the Sforzas. Check the local newspaper and the tourist agency for information.

For theater, Giorgio Strehler's **Piccolo Teatro** is numero uno. Although the performances are in Italian, Strehler is recognized internationally as one of the world's most prolific and daring directors. The theater is at Via Rovello 2 (between the Duomo and the Castle of the Sforzas on a crossroad off of Via Dante); take the Red Line metro to Cordusio or Cairoli; buses number 50, 54, 57, 60, 96, or 97; or trams number 1, 4, 8, 12, 13, 19, 21, or 24. Phone (02) 872352 for reservations and information. As it's difficult to get seats, you might think about reserving from home.

Make reservations at the nearby Trattoria al Piccolo Teatro **for an after-theater dinner. (See "Restaurants.")**

Informal Amusements

The Navigli is by far the liveliest after-hours area. You can sit on a barge with a late-night drink and talk until the rising sun reflects quietly in the still canal waters. Jazz lovers should spend an evening strolling the canals, stopping for dinner or a drink at **Scimmie,** Via Ascanio Sforza 49, telephone (02) 8391874, closed Tuesday; or **Capolinea,** Via Ludovico il Moro 119, telephone (02) 470524, closed Monday.

The **Isola Fiorita,** Ripa di Porta Ticinese 83, telephone (02) 8391060, closed Sunday and Monday, is an old trattoria transformed into a bar/restaurant with a stage for performances and readings.

Brera is another spot where something is always happening. Stop in for a drink at **L'Agora,** Via San Marco, before deciding where to go next; you can just walk around Via San Marco, Via Pontaccio, and Via Solferino to take in a bit of the night air.

For dancing the night away, try the following (all are usually closed Sunday and Monday, have an entrance fee of about Lit. 15,000–20,000, and start warming up after 11 P.M.):

Nepentha (Piazza Diaz 1 in the Duomo area) offers dinner and dancing and is quite popular with the moneyed fashion-industry crowd); **Amnesie** (Via Cellini 2) is a favorite with models; **Plastic** (Viale Umbria 120) is a stark, somewhat new wave club; **Hollywood** (Corso Como 15) is the latest favorite; and **Zeus** (Corso Garibaldi 97/99 in Brera) has a great dance floor, but not so great music.

Bars

Sip a beer, drink an *espresso,* or munch a *panino* while discussing the latest soccer scores, Italian president, or film. The following bars observe this well-thought-out bar tradition with respect.

Bar Magenta, on Via Carducci 13 in the Corso Magenta area, is a young hangout. Americans like the feeling here; there are decent sandwiches and the bar closes late. Or try **Il Pois,** Via Pioppette 3, near the Columns of San Lorenzo in the Porta Ticinese/Navigli area. In Brera, you can barhop between **El Tumbun de San Marc,** Via San Marco 20; **Moscatelli,** Corso Garibaldi 93, is a great wine-tasting bar; **Banco,** Via Pontaccio 10; and **Bar Giamaica,** Via Brera 26.

SHORT TRIPS OUT OF MILAN

Excursions outside of Milan offer the traveler a sometimes needed breath of fresh air (after time in the polluted city) and a chance to see the other, rural side of this fast-moving metropolis. Check the EPT for information on tours, but it's better to rent a car and enjoy the time as you please. Have a map handy, since the highway numbering system can be confusing. Follow signs for cities on the way to or past your destination if your desired town is not marked. See also the "Lombardy" chapter.

Unless otherwise noted, expect museums and palaces to be open Tuesday through Sunday, 9 A.M. to noon and 3 to 5:30 P.M., although hours can vary; check at the EPT.

Bergamo. Although you can fly directly into Bergamo, this town makes a splendid (and full) day trip from Milan. If driving, take autostrada 4 from Milan, or take the train. The drive should take about 35 to 40 minutes, depending on traffic.

Divided into two parts (the Lower Town and the medieval Upper Town, enclosed within a Venetian wall), Bergamo is one of the most characteristic Lombard towns. At the foot of the Pre-Alps, between the Brembana and Seriana valleys, with a dramatic setting nine hundred feet above sea level, Bergamo has been compared to a Tuscan or Umbrian village.

Since the days of the Roman Empire, this prosperous city has played an important role in Italian history. Even when under Venetian domination, it has been one of the wealthiest areas in Italy.

A funicular (cable car) connects the Lower Town (Bassa) with the Upper Town (Alta). The historical center of the Upper Town is the **Piazza Vecchia.** Here you'll find the **Palazzo della Ragione,** dating from the end of the 12th century. The palace is not generally open to the public—ask at the EPT for permission to enter. Also in the Upper Town are the elaborately decorated **Colleoni Chapel** (closed Mondays in winter) and the 12th-century Romanesque **Church of Santa Maria Maggiore,** with architectural elements from the 14th century (the north and south doorways), the 15th century (the spire on the south side), and an interior remodeled in the baroque style in the late 16th to early 17th century.

For a pleasant interlude visit the green hills of **Val Brembana** and the **San Pellegrino Terme** (Spa), about 12 miles from Bergamo, known for its fresh water and health assessments. There is bus service from Bergamo to the spa. To make reservations for a stay at the spa, contact Azienda Autonoma di Cura, Soggiorno e Turismo (Tourist Office), Via Bernardo Tasso 1, 1-24016 San Pellegrino Terme (BG); telephone (0345) 21020. For information, contact the Ente Provinciale per Il Turismo, Viale Vittorio Emanuele II 4, 24100 Bergamo; telephone (035) 242226; the Azienda Autonoma di Turismo, telephone (035) 210204; or San Pellegrino Spa, telephone (0345) 21355.

RESTAURANTS

Food specialties of the area are *polenta* (a corn-meal concoction) with game birds; *polenta taragna* (polenta made with buckwheat flour), and *casonsei* (large ravioli with butter). A good meal can be had at **Da Vittorio,** Viale Papa Giovanni XXIII; tel. (035) 218060. A regional dinner (without wine) can be enjoyed for Lit. 73,000–94,000. Closed Wed. and Aug. 8–18. AE, DC, V.

Bike Tour. For bike riders, there is many a discovery to be made by following the navigli out of Milan toward Abbiategrasso, Gaggiano, Trezzano, and Robecco. In Robecco, visit the **Villa di Ternengo,** a classic example of the 17th-century villas built by Milan's nobility.

To rent bikes in Milan, try Vittorio Comizzoli, Via Washington 60; telephone (02) 4984694. Take the Red Line metro to Wagner.

RESTAURANTS

A wonderful place to have lunch is in Cassinetta di Lugagnano (about 1½ miles north of Abbiategrasso along the Naviglio Grande), at the **Antica Osteria del Ponte,** tel. (02) 9420034. Be sure to reserve in advance. A meal costs Lit. 80,000–140,000 (without wine). Closed Sun., Mon., Aug., and Jan. 1–15. AE, DC, MC.

Chiaravalle. Visit the **abbey and bell tower,** about four miles southeast of Milan. This picturesque abbey dates from the 12th century and was one of the first Cistercian abbeys. The bell tower is from the 14th century and the church is a blend of French Gothic and Lombard Romanesque styles. The frescoes in the dome date back to the 14th-century Tuscan (especially Sienese) school.

RESTAURANTS

Try the **Antica Trattoria San Bernardo** in Chiaravalle, Via San Bernardo 36, tel. (02) 5690831. You can enjoy Milanese specialties in the middle of the Lombard countryside. A dinner without wine costs Lit. 40,000–77,000. Closed Sun. night, Mon., and Aug. No cards.

Lodi. About twenty miles southeast of Milan is Lodi, on the Adda River. The river and its terrain are said to have inspired Leonardo da Vinci's painting. Visit **Lodi Vecchio** (Old Lodi), the city center in Roman and medieval times that was destroyed in the 12th century and later revived as a small village. The **Basilica of San Bassiano,** which is the original city's only remaining structure, and **Sant'Angelo Castle** are both in Old Lodi, and the wine-producing area of **San Colombano al Lambro** is a pleasant drive.

Lodi is known for its parmesan cheese (some say there is more here than in nearby Parma) and its wine. Try a slice of cheese with some red Roverone wine or white Tonsa.

Monza A half-hour drive from Milan is Monza, at one time the summer residence of the Longobards. In A.D. 595 Queen Theodolinda built a church that was rebuilt in the Middle Ages into a spectacular **cathedral;** it houses treasures including 15th-century frescoes and pieces of gold plate. The **Villa Reale** (Royal Villa) and its surrounding park are a magnificent place to spend a lazy day.

The **Monza golf course,** on the grounds of the former estate, is considered one of Italy's best. Clubs can be rented for around Lit. 30,000. Telephone (039) 303081; closed Monday.

You might be able to catch a race at the **Monza race track,** which is on the villa grounds, or a current exhibition at the **art museum.**

RESTAURANTS

For a filling lunch in a 17th-century villa, try the **Saint Georges Premier,** tel. (039) 320600. Enter the park at the Porta Vedano entrance. Be sure to reserve a table in advance. The restaurant's garden is part of the park, and you can eat peacefully while listening to the birds. A meal without wine costs about Lit. 37,000–62,000. Closed Tues. and Aug. AE.

Pavia. To visit one of Lombardy's most famous monasteries, take state highway 35 from Milan (or take the A7 to Binasco and continue on 35) to Pavia and its **Certosa** (Carthusian Monastery). As the capital of the Longobard kingdom in the seventh and eighth centuries and a major center during the Visconti rule, Pavia has retained her regal air. The imposing **Visconti Castle** is today the site of the **Municipal Museum** (Museo Civico) and a **Museum of Archaeology and Sculpture.** (The Civic Museum is closed Monday and afternoons in January, May, July, August, and December.)

In the 15th century, the castle of Pavia expanded its property boundaries to include a park, on one side of which stood the monastery, which became a mark for the property boundary. Built under the order of Gian Galeazzo Visconti in 1386 (the same year the Duomo in Milan was begun), the Certosa was a monastery as well as a church for the Visconti family. The building is a mixture of styles (the facade dating from the 15th and 16th centuries and the guest house, designed by Francesco Maria Ricchino, from 1625) and houses a collection of artwork from various periods. Though the Certosa is still inhabited, the monastery is open to visitors from 9:30 A.M. to 12:30 P.M.; closed Monday.

Also in Pavia, the **Basilica of San Michele** is a 12th-century church built on a Longobard foundation. The exterior is an elaborate mix of sculpted animal and human figures. **San Pietro in Ciel d'Oro** is another example of Lombard-Romanesque architecture. Consecrated in 1132, it holds the **tomb** of St. Augustine. Pavia's **Duomo** was begun in 1488, with both Bramante and da Vinci contributing to the design. The cathedral's dome is the third largest in Italy.

Take a break from visiting churches to see the **covered bridge** on the Ticino River. The bridge is a replica of a 14th-century one that was destroyed during the war.

RESTAURANTS

Enjoy a pleasant lunch in the garden at the **Vecchio Mulino,** Via al Monumento 5; tel. (0382) 925894. Try the local wine. A meal without wine will run Lit. 40,000–60,000. Closed Sun. and Mon. AE, DC, V.

Varese. Spend a lovely day in the lake country at **Lake Varese, Lake Lugano** (part of which is in Lombardy, part in Switzerland) and the city of **Lugano,** Switzerland, and the Lombardy (eastern) side of **Lake Maggiore.** The province of Varese is about forty minutes by car from Milan (take autostrada 8).

The capital city Varese, often called the city of gardens and villas, is a vital town that has one of the highest incomes per capita in Lombardy. It is nestled among green hills and surrounded by Lake Varese, Lake Comabbio, Lake Monate, and Lake Maggiore.

The best spots to visit on the eastern side of Lake Maggiore (fed by the Ticino River) are Angera, Ispra, Laveno, Mombello (the most scenic from the Lombard side of the lake), and the town of Luino, where an extensive open market is held every Wednesday. Be sure to visit the **Santa Caterina del Sasso Church,** carved out of rock, between Leggiuno and Laveno. The graceful northern part of the lake is well worth a trip; or you can take a car ferry from Laveno to Intra, on the Piedmonte side of the lake.

Vigevano. Follow the signs for Abbiategrasso and Vigevano, and in about half an hour you will arrive in the shoe capital of Italy, and a part of the Lomellina region, known for its prolific rice production. From Vigevano, follow the signs for the **Piazza Ducale** and have a seat in one of the outdoor caffès around this impressive piazza for some fresh air, ice cream (a must!) and people-watching. Considered a superb example of Italian Renaissance style, the piazza, said to have been designed by Bramante, has served as a meeting place since the 15th century. Unfortunately the castle adjacent to the square, once residence of the Sforzas, is being renovated, and is closed to sightseeing.

Try not to travel on Sunday, as the traffic is fierce—and the shoe stores are closed!

CITY LISTINGS

Neighborhood keys refer to the color map of Milan at the back of the book: the page number of the insert and map coordinates at which sight/establishment is located. Page numbers within the listings refer to the text page(s) on which sight/establishment is discussed.

Churches

Basilica of Saint Ambrose   **PIAZZA CORDUSIO/CORSO MAGENTA/PARCO, P. 12, C3**

Piazza Sant'Ambrogio 15; 10 A.M.–noon, 3–5; closed Tues., Sat., and Sun. morning; pp. 188, 189, 206

Duomo   **PIAZZA DUOMO/SAN BABILA, P. 12, D3**

Piazza Duomo; terrace: winter 9 A.M.–4 P.M., summer 9 A.M.–5 P.M.; Treasury: 9 A.M.–noon, 3–5:30 P.M.; pp. 187, 192, 199–200

San Maurizio (Monastero Maggiore)   **PIAZZA CORDUSIO/ CORSO MAGENTA/PARCO, P. 12, C3**

Corso Magenta 15; only Wed. P.M. for concerts; pp. 188, 206

Santa Maria delle Grazie   **PIAZZA CORDUSIO/CORSO MAGENTA/PARCO, P. 12, B3**

Corso Magenta at Via Caradosso; pp. 188, 194–195, 204

Historic Sites

Arco della Pace   **PIAZZA CORDUSIO/CORSO MAGENTA/PARCO, P. 12, B2**

Sempione Park; pp. 188, 203–204

Colonne (Columns) of San Lorenzo Maggiore   **PORTA TICINESE/NAVIGLI, P. 13, C4**

Corso di Porta Ticinese; pp. 188, 206

Galleria Vittorio Emanuele II   **PIAZZA DUOMO/SAN BABILA, P. 12, D3**

Piazza Duomo to Piazza della Scala; pp. 187, 193, 201–202

Navigli   **PORTA TICINESE/NAVIGLI, P. 13, A/B/C5**
pp. 194, 206–207

Piazza Mercanti   **PIAZZA DUOMO/SAN BABILA, P. 12, D3**
pp. 187, 194, 201

La Scala Theater   **PIAZZA DUOMO/SAN BABILA, P. 12, D3**
Piazza della Scala; pp. 188, 193, 202

Museums

Ambrosian Picture Gallery (Pinacoteca Ambrosiana)

PIAZZA DUOMO/SAN BABILA, P. 12, C3

Piazza Pio XI 2; 9:30 A.M.–5 P.M.; pp. 187, 189

Brera Art Gallery (Pinacoteca di Brera)   BRERA/STAZIONE
CENTRALE, P. 12, D3
Via Brera 28; Mon.–Fri. 9 A.M.–2 P.M., Sun., holidays, and 2nd and 4th Sat.
each month 9 A.M.–1 P.M.; pp. 188, 192, 203

Castle of the Sforzas   PIAZZA CORDUSIO/CORSO
MAGENTA/PARCO, P. 12, C3
Piazza Castello; 9:30 A.M.–12:15 P.M., 2:30–5:15 P.M.; closed Mon.; pp. 188,
192, 203

Cenacolo Vinciano (*Last Supper*)   PIAZZA CORDUSIO/
CORSO MAGENTA/PARCO, P. 12, B3
Corso Magenta (next to Santa Maria delle Grazie); open 9 A.M.–1:30 P.M.,
2–6:30 P.M.; Sun. 9 A.M.–3 P.M.; closed Mon.; pp. 188, 195, 204–205

Duomo Museum   PIAZZA DUOMO/SAN BABILA, P. 12, D3
Ground floor of Royal Palace (Palazzo Reale), Piazza Duomo; open 10:30
A.M.–12:30 P.M., 3–5:30 P.M.; closed Mon.; pp. 187, 192–193, 201

**Leonardo da Vinci Museum (Museo Nazionale della Scienza e
della Tecnica)**   PIAZZA CORDUSIO/CORSO MAGENTA/PARCO,
P. 12, B4
Via San Vittore 21; 9 A.M.–5 P.M.; closed Mon.; pp. 188, 193, 206

Poldi Pezzoli Museum   PIAZZA DUOMO/SAN BABILA,
P. 12, D3
Via Manzoni 12; 9:30 A.M.–12:30 P.M., 2:30–5:30 P.M., Thurs. 9–11 P.M. ex-
cept Aug.; closed Mon., in summer Sun. P.M.; pp. 188, 194, 202

Theatrical Museum   PIAZZA DUOMO/SAN BABILA, P. 12, D3
Piazza della Scala; 9 A.M.–noon, 2–6 P.M., closed Sun. Nov.–April; May–Oct.,
Sun. 9:30 A.M.–noon, 2:30–6 P.M.; pp. 193, 202

Parks and Gardens
Sempione Park (Parco Sempione)   PIAZZA CORDUSIO/
CORSO MAGENTA/PARCO, P. 12, B2/3
Behind the Castle of the Sforzas; pp. 188, 203–204

Shops
Alchimia   PIAZZA CORDUSIO/CORSO MAGENTA/PARCO,
P. 12, C3
Foro Buonaparte 55; p. 211

Alias   BRERA/STAZIONE CENTRALE, P. 12, C/D3
Via Fiori Chiari; p. 211

Anni 80   BRERA/STAZIONE CENTRALE, P. 12, E1
Fabio Filzi 14; p. 210

Arflex   PIAZZA DUOMO/SAN BABILA, P. 12, D3
Via Borgogna 2; p. 211

Arform   BRERA/STAZIONE CENTRALE, P. 12, C/D2
Via Moscova 22; p. 210

Arteluce   PIAZZA DUOMO/SAN BABILA, P. 12, D3
Via Borgogna 5; p. 211

Artemide   PIAZZA DUOMO/SAN BABILA, P. 12, E3
Corso Monforte 19; p. 211

Bardelli   PIAZZA CORDUSIO/CORSO MAGENTA/PARCO,
P. 12, C3
Corso Magenta 13; p. 210

Beccaria   BRERA/STAZIONE CENTRALE, P. 12, C3
Via Madonnina 10; p. 210

Beltrami   PIAZZA DUOMO/SAN BABILA, P. 12, D3
Via Monte Napoleone 16; p. 211

Benetton   PIAZZA DUOMO/SAN BABILA, P. 12, D3
Piazza del Duomo 22 and Galleria Passarella; p. 209

Bianca e Blu   PORTA TICINESE/NAVIGLI, P. 13, C4
Via de Amicis 53/55; p. 210

Biffi   PORTA TICINESE/NAVIGLI, P. 13, C4
Corso Genova 6; p. 210

Boggi   PIAZZA DUOMO/SAN BABILA, P. 12, D3
Piazza San Babila 3; p. 210

Bottega Veneta   PIAZZA DUOMO/SAN BABILA, P. 12, D3
Via della Spiga 5; pp. 208, 211

Calico Lion   PIAZZA DUOMO/SAN BABILA, P. 12, D3
Via Bigli 4; p. 210

Carrano   PIAZZA DUOMO/SAN BABILA, P. 12, D3
Via Sant'Andrea 21; p. 211

Casa del Formaggio   PIAZZA DUOMO/SAN BABILA, P. 12, D4
Via Speronari 3; p. 211

Cassina   PIAZZA DUOMO/SAN BABILA, P. 12, D3
Via Durini 16/18; p. 211

Cose   PIAZZA DUOMO/SAN BABILA, P. 12, D3
Via della Spiga 8; p. 210

De Padova   PIAZZA DUOMO/SAN BABILA, P. 12, D3
Corso Venezia 18; p. 211

Diego della Valle   PIAZZA DUOMO/SAN BABILA, P. 12, D3
Via della Spiga 22; p. 211

Donini   PIAZZA CORDUSIO/CORSO MAGENTA/PARCO, P. 12,
                                                                A3
Via Belfiore 7; p. 209

Drogheria Solferino   BRERA/STAZIONE CENTRALE, P. 12,
                                                              C/D3
Via Pontaccio at Via Solferino; p. 209

Emporio Armani   PIAZZA DUOMO/SAN BABILA, P. 12, D3
Via Durini 27; pp. 208, 210

Enrico Coveri   PIAZZA DUOMO/SAN BABILA, P. 12, D3
Corso Matteotti 12; p. 208

Etro   PIAZZA DUOMO/SAN BABILA, P. 12, D3
Via Bigli 10; p. 210

Fendi   PIAZZA DUOMO/SAN BABILA AREA, P. 12, D3
Via della Spiga 9 and Via Sant'Andrea 16; pp. 208, 211

Ferragamo   PIAZZA DUOMO/SAN BABILA, P. 12, D3
Via Monte Napoleone 3; p. 211

Fiorucci   PIAZZA DUOMO/SAN BABILA, P. 12, D3
Galleria Passarella; p. 209

Frette   PIAZZA DUOMO/SAN BABILA, P. 12, C/D3
Via Manzoni 11 and Via Torino 42; p. 209

Gerry Mox   BRERA/STAZIONE CENTRALE, P. 12, D3
Via dell'Orso 9; p. 210

Gianfranco Ferre PIAZZA DUOMO/SAN BABILA, P. 12, D3
Via Sant'Andrea 21 (men); Via della Spiga 11 (women); p. 208

Giorgio Armani PIAZZA DUOMO/SAN BABILA, P. 12, D3
Via Sant'Andrea 9; p. 208

Giusi Bresciani PIAZZA DUOMO/SAN BABILA, P. 12, D3
Via Morone 8; p. 210

Guardaroba BRERA/STAZIONE CENTRALE, P. 12, D2
Via Solferino 9; p. 209

Gucci PIAZZA DUOMO/SAN BABILA, P. 12, D3
Via Monte Napoleone 5; p. 211

Guido Pasquali PIAZZA DUOMO/SAN BABILA, P. 12, D3
Via Sant'Andrea 1; p. 211

High-Tech PORTA TICINESE/NAVIGLI, P. 13, C4; P. 12
Corso di Porta Ticinese 77; p. 211

Jesurum PIAZZA DUOMO/SAN BABILA, P. 12, D3
Via Monte Napoleone 14; p. 208

Kenzo PIAZZA DUOMO/SAN BABILA, P. 12, D3
Via Sant'Andrea 11; p. 208

Komlan PIAZZA DUOMO/SAN BABILA, P. 12, D3
Corso Venezia 11; p. 210

Krizia PIAZZA DUOMO/SAN BABILA, P. 12, D3
Via della Spiga 23; p. 208

Laura Biagiotti PIAZZA DUOMO/SAN BABILA, P. 12, D3
Via Borgospesso 19; p. 208

Luisa Beccaria BRERA/STAZIONE CENTRALE, P. 12, C3
Via Madonnina 10; p. 210

Mario Valentino PIAZZA DUOMO/SAN BABILA, P. 12, D3
Corso Matteotti 10; p. 211

Maud Frizon PIAZZA DUOMO/SAN BABILA, P. 12, D3
Via della Spiga 5; p. 208

Max Mara PIAZZA DUOMO/SAN BABILA, P. 12, D3
Corso Vittorio Emanuele 7; p. 209

Memphis PIAZZA DUOMO/SAN BABILA, P. 12, D3
Via Manzoni 46; p. 211

Merù BRERA/STAZIONE CENTRALE, P. 12, D2
Via Solferino 3; p. 209

Mila Schön PIAZZA DUOMO/SAN BABILA, P. 12, D3
Via Monte Napoleone 2 and 6; p. 208

Naj Oleari BRERA/STAZIONE CENTRALE, P. 12, D3
Via Brera 5 and 8; p. 210

Peck PIAZZA DUOMO/SAN BABILA, P. 12, D4
Via Spadari 9; p. 211

Pellini Bijoux PIAZZA CORDUSIO/CORSO MAGENTA/PARCO,
P. 12, C4
Via Morigi 9; p. 211

Piero Fornasetti BRERA/STAZIONE CENTRALE, P. 12, D3
Via Brera 16; p. 210

La Porcellana Bianca   BRERA/STAZIONE CENTRALE, P. 12, C/D3
Via dell'Orso 7; p. 210

Prada   PIAZZA DUOMO/SAN BABILA, P. 12, D3
Via della Spiga 1 and Galleria Vittorio Emanuele; pp. 208, 211

Pratesi   PIAZZA DUOMO/SAN BABILA, P. 12, D3
Via Monte Napoleone 21; p. 208

Pupi Solari   PIAZZA CORDUSIO/CORSO MAGENTA/PARCO, P. 12, B3
Piazza Tommaseo at Via Mascheroni 12; p. 210

La Rinascente   PIAZZA DUOMO/SAN BABILA, P. 12, D3
Piazza del Duomo; p. 209

Il Salumaio   PIAZZA DUOMO/SAN BABILA, P. 12, D3
Via Monte Napoleone 12; p. 211

Serapian   OUTSIDE CENTER, P. 12, F1
Via Jommelli 35; pp. 210–211

Tanzi Driade   BRERA/STAZIONE CENTRALE, P. 12, D3
Via Fatebenefratelli 9; p. 211

La Tenda   BRERA/STAZIONE CENTRALE, P. 12, D2/3
Piazza San Marco 1; p. 209

Thierry Mugler   PIAZZA DUOMO/SAN BABILA, P. 12, D3
Via della Spiga 36; p. 208

Tincati   PIAZZA DUOMO/SAN BABILA, P. 12, E2
Piazza Oberdan 2; p. 210

Uomo   PIAZZA DUOMO/SAN BABILA, P. 12, D3
Via Gesù; p. 208

Urrah   BRERA/STAZIONE CENTRALE, P. 12, D2
Via Solferino 3; p. 209

Valentino Donna   PIAZZA DUOMO/SAN BABILA, P. 12, D3
Via Santo Spirito 3; p. 208

Valentino Uomo   PIAZZA DUOMO/SAN BABILA, P. 12, D3
Via Monte Napoleone 20; p. 208

Vino Vino   PIAZZA DUOMO/SAN BABILA, P. 12, D4
Via Speronari; p. 211

Zeus   PORTA TICINESE/NAVIGLI, P. 13, C5
Via Vigevano 8; pp. 210, 211

10

LOMBARDY

A trip through Lombardy (Lombardia) is a time-travel that will take you from the prehistoric (the carvings at Val Camonica), through Roman opulence (the villas on Lake Garda), the medieval age (the Broletto Palace in Brescia), the glittering Renaissance (Mantua's Palazzo Ducale with Mantegna's famous frescoes in the Camera degli Sposi), and the splendid remnants of Napoleon's 19th-century Repubblica Cisalpina (Cisalpina Republic), to the present day's *dolce vita* (from the shores of Lake Como to the slopes of Livigno).

You will be entering into the beloved worlds of Virgil, Catullus, Leonardo da Vinci, Bramante, D'Annunzio, Donizetti, Stradivari, Verdi, and Manzoni (to name a select few). It is a region known for Italy's largest lake (Lake Garda) and spas famed for their excellent water and fresh climate; for its incomparable wines, cheeses, and other hearty Lombard specialties; for a consistent belief in the work ethic (Lombardy has one of the highest incomes per capita in Italy); for a unique architectural style that has inspired more than one book (in the 12th century especially, the masons of Lombardy built great vaulted churches, with elaborate facades, carvings, and bell towers); for a faithful and respectful allegiance to Mother Earth; and for art treasures and historical surprises.

Lombardy is bordered by Switzerland on the north, Emilia-Romagna on the south, Veneto and Trentino-Alto-Adige on the east, and Piedmont on the west. It is the fourth largest region in Italy (following Sicily, Piedmont, and Sardinia) and can be viewed as three major areas: the Po Valley (which borders the Apennines in the south and includes the towns of Pavia, Cremona, and Mantua); the Lake Country (with Bergamo, Brescia, Como, and Varese); and the Northern Alpine Range.

Lombardy is composed of nine provinces (Milan, Pavia, Cremona, Mantua, Brescia, Sondrio, Bergamo, Como, and Varese) and is an area rich in water, with about twenty substantial lakes and innumerable small mountain lakes. The winters are cold and foggy and the summers hot and muggy for the most part, except around the large lakes such as Como, Maggiore, Garda, and Iseo, where one can find a typically pleasant Mediterranean climate.

Unjustly, Milan, Pavia, Brescia, and Varese seem to be the culprits of Lombardy's image as an industrial wasteland. It is true that there is a strong concentration of twentieth-century industrial production (mostly steel, iron, machinery, and chemicals) in and around these cities, yet they comprise only a very small part of the Lombardy region. Just a short drive outside of these so-called industrial centers will reveal very green pastures indeed.

Traveling south toward the Po Valley region of Cremona and Mantua is a solid agricultural community that earns its bread from that from which bread is made. The entire area is covered in wheat, rice, and maize, as well as cattle, swine, and dairy products; a drive through Virgil's homeland will fill the traveler's nose with the aroma of freshly tilled fertile earth—one of the most lush, satisfying terrains in Italy for the nature lover.

Lombard History

Historically, the Lombardy region is a gold mine. The Gauls (in the fifth century B.C.) and a small number of Etruscans were the first visitors. In the third century A.D., the Romans moved their capital north to Mediolanum (today's Milan). They stayed on for the next one hundred years and were followed by the Longobards (whose capital was Pavia and who also had a summer retreat in Monza) and the Franks (in the eighth century), who set up a feudal system. The rise of the feudal city-state eventually led to the formation of the Lombard League, which beat Frederick Barbarossa at Legnano in 1176. The Viscontis ruled during the 13th and 14th centuries. In the 15th century the Sforzas succeeded in uniting the region (with the exclusion of Mantua, which was under the rule of the Gonzaga family). The Duchy of Milan fell in 1499 and Lombardy was divided between Piedmont, Venice, Switzerland, France, and Sardinia. Then came the Spanish, who remained in power until 1705, when the Austrians took over. In 1796, Napoleon created the Repubblica Cisalpina, crowning himself king of Italy in 1805. Napoleon's reign ended in 1814, and the Austrian kingdom of Lombardo-Veneto was created in the 19th century. Lombardy was finally unified with the rest of Italy in 1861.

TRAVEL

Traveling is quite easy in Lombardy, as the roads are excellent and the bus (the SGEA line) and train services are efficient. The most delightful way to see the area is in a car or camper: There are approximately two-hundred camping sites (mostly in the lake region), hundreds of hotels, and much to enjoy along the way.

If driving, you can easily enter Lombardy from Switzerland at the border crossing of Chiasso, or to avoid traffic, at Ponte Tresa, Porto Ceresio, the Splügen Pass, Villa di Chiavenna, or Tirano.

Fly into the region to Milan (Linate and Malpensa airports) or Bergamo (Orio al Serio Airport). Check the EPT office of each province to find out about sightseeing tours in the area. (See "Vital Information" at the end of this book, and the Lombardy town sections later in this chapter.)

Distances from Milan to Lombardy Towns	
To Brescia	40 miles
To Como	25 miles
To Cremona	40 miles
To Mantua	75 miles
To Sondrio	60 miles
To Varese	25 miles

CAR RENTALS
Bergamo: Airport—Avis, tel. (035) 214192; Hertz, tel. (035) 221258.

Brescia: is Avis, Via XX Settembre 2, tel. (030) 295474; Hertz, Via XXV Aprile 12, tel. (030) 45132

Como: Avis, Via Manzoni 16, tel. (031) 266174; Europcar, Via M. Monti 30, tel. (031) 269108; Hertz, Via Masia 77, tel. (031) 551307

See the Milan chapter for information about car rentals at the airports there.

ACCOMMODATIONS

Each province in Lombardy has a vast selection of hotels to choose from; herein are some of those best situated for travelers who want to explore Lombardy's diversity. Credit cards are listed as accepted. "All cards" means that all of the following are accepted: AE—American Express; DC—Diner's Club; MC—MasterCard; V—Visa. Price ranges given indicate the span between the costs of single and double rooms.

The Po Valley
In the Po Valley, use Mantua (Mantova) as a base for accommodations. Next to Pavia (which can be explored as an excursion from Milan—see the Milan chapter), Mantua is the largest city, and Cremona, Sabbioneta, and the other Po Valley towns are easily accessible. You can combine an exploration of the valley with a lake holiday, staying along Lake Garda, discussed later in this chapter. The following hotels have air-conditioning unless otherwise noted; none have hotel restaurants, but are located near several of Mantua's suggested restaurants and *trattorias*.

MANTUA

Mantegna, Via Fabio Filzi 10b, 46100; tel. (0376) 350315. Accommodations are clean, simple, and pleasant in this 37-room hotel. It's a 10-min. walk from Mantua's sights. Closed Dec. 24–Jan. 5. Rates run Lit. 45,000–75,000. All cards.

San Lorenzo, Piazza Concordia 14, 46100; tel. (0376) 220500. Close to the Ducal Palace, this hotel has 43 comfortable rooms—no two are alike—and an elegant lobby furnished with antiques. The building is old but the comforts are modern. Rates are a bit high, running Lit. 80,000–125,000. Apartments are Lit. 200,000. Open year-round. AE, DC.

The Lake Country

Almost all of the hotels recommended here have air-conditioning, but inquire first at the least expensive ones.

LAKE COMO

Recommended bases for an overnight stay on Lake Como (Lago di Como) start with the city of **Como** (the closest to Milan) and move north along both sides of the lake. Stay in Como if you want to be in the center of activity. You may want to consider using Como as your base for seeing Milan, as well; it's a short train ride away.

Barchetta Excelsior, Piazza Cavour 1, 22100 Como; tel. (031) 266531; telex 380435. Right in the center of town, on a lakefront piazza, the Barchetta makes it easy to visit the town's monuments as well as enjoy the splendors of the lake by boat. The 54 attractive rooms are relatively expensive: Lit. 105,000–150,000; apartments are Lit. 250,000. There's a good restaurant as well. All cards.

Plinius, Via Garibaldi 33, 22100 Como; tel. (031) 273067. With rooms rates at Lit. 57,000–85,000, this hotel is a reasonably priced option, although there is no restaurant or beach. Most rooms have baths, and the hotel is convenient to the rail station. Open Mar.–Nov. All cards.

For those who want to enjoy a more peaceful, rural atmosphere, stay outside of Como itself. On the road between Como and Cernobbio, on the west side of the lake, is the **Villa Flori,** Strade per Cernobbio 12, 22100 Como; tel. (031) 557642. The hotel is right on the lake and has a lovely garden and terrace, with views of the water, mountains, and city. Room rates: Lit. 87,000–115,000. Closed Dec. 14–Jan. 16. All cards.

In **Cernobbio,** the most elegant lake resort town, is the Famous **Grand Hotel Villa d'Este,** 22100 Cernobbio (CO); tel. (031) 511471; telex 380025. The majestic villa, with 160 18th-century rooms and a lush park on the banks of the lake, is a world renown V.I.P. hideaway. For those who want a more adventurous holiday, this is not the best choice; the hotel caters to an older, established clientele. However, there are tennis courts, a swimming pool, a nightclub, and nearby golf course. Both the hotel dining room and the more relaxed grill are worth a visit for lunch or dinner even if you're not staying here. Room rates reflect the hotel's luxury: Lit. 315,000–520,000. AE, DC, V.

Brunate, on the west side of the lake, is a good choice if you want to be convenient to Como, yet outside. Reasonably priced rooms are offered at **Miramonti,** 22034 Brunate (CO); tel. (031) 220260. There are only 11 rooms and no restaurant, but you'll have a spectacular view of the lake and the mountains from the terrace. The rooms are very simple and very quiet. Rates: Lit. 42,000–73,000. Open May 20–Oct. 10. No cards.

Torno is north of Brunate, on a little spit of land. You'll find great value here at **Vapore,** 22020 Torno (CO); tel. (031) 419311. This ten-room hotel offers pleasant service, reasonable prices, and a lovely terraced restaurant. Rooms run Lit. 25,000–32,000; Lit. 40,000 for meals. Open Mar.–Oct. No cards.

In the center of Lake Como's two branches, in the picturesque town of **Bellagio,** is a splendid villa-turned-hotel called the **Grand Hotel Villa Serbelloni,** 22021 Bellagio (CO); tel. (031) 950216; telex 380330. The grounds are exceptional, with a beach, tennis courts, and view; the villa itself is a sight to see. Rates run Lit. 200,000–300,000; apartments are Lit. 380,000–570,000. AE, DC, V.

LAKE GARDA
For a well-rounded holiday, Lake Garda (Lago di Garda) is the spot to choose for an extended stay. From here, one can visit the entire lake area, the inland Po Valley region between Sirmione and Mantua, and the rich, historical area around Brescia and Lake Iseo. Lake Garda offers an array of fish specialties, and there are several lovely places to stay along the Lombardy side of the lake.

The small, characteristic town of **Sirmione,** on a peninsula, is a major resort area. There are pleasant hotels on the lake as well as the Sirmione Spa, and the area around Brescia is easily accessible. (Note that high season is usually July–Aug.)

Brunella, Via Catullo 29, 25019 (BS); tel. (030) 916115. Situated in the hills, this 22-room, 3-star hotel has a pleasant, terraced restaurant. Rates in high season run Lit. 60,000–75,000; in low season, Lit. 60,000–65,000 meals included, and Lit. 47,000–70,000 without meals. Open Apr. 10–Oct.

Du Lac, Via 25 Aprile 60, 25019 (BS); tel. (030) 916026. A simple 34-room hotel with a small beach on the lake. There is also a restaurant. Rates: Lit. 52,000–75,000. Open Apr.–Oct. 25. V.

Grand Hotel Terme, Viale Marconi 1, 25019 (BS); tel. (030) 916261. This is a pleasant resort with a garden on the lake. Room rates run Lit. 160,000–178,000 in high season and Lit. 150,000–165,000 in low season, with meals; Lit. 120,000–190,000 without meals. Open Apr. 10–Oct. 26. All cards.

Ideal, Via Catullo 23, 25019 (BS); tel. (030) 916020. A small, 25-room, relaxing hideaway on the lake. Rooms are Lit. 75,000–85,000 in high season and Lit. 65,000–75,000 in low season, with meals; Lit. 50,000–75,000 without meals. Open Apr.–Oct. 25. V.

Olivi, Via San Pietro 5, 25019 (BS); tel. (030) 916110. A well-run hotel 170 feet from the lake; it also has a swimming pool. Air-conditioning is a Lit. 7,000 charge. Rates are Lit. 84,000–108,000 in high season, and Lit. 73,000–89,000 in low season, with meals; Lit. 67,000–98,000 without meals. Closed Jan. AE.

Villa Cortine, Via Grotte 12, 25019 (BS); tel. (030) 916021; telex 300171. With a sloping park that borders the lake and tennis courts, this very relaxing resort offers rooms for Lit. 245,000–275,000 in high season and Lit. 225,000–255,000 in low season, with meals; Lit. 205,000–290,000 without meals. (There are many excellent restaurants in the area, so you may not want to eat in all the time.) Open Mar. 25–Oct. 25. All cards.

Continuing north up Lake Garda are even quieter getaways, typical Mediterranean landscaping, and inviting *riviere* (coastal areas). The width of the lake at certain points gives the illusion of the sea.

There is a large concentration of efficient **camping sites** north along the lake. Be sure to drive along the coast instead of along Route 572; exit at **Moniga del Garda** to find several campsites to choose from, near Manerba del Garda.

Less than 2 miles from Sirmione is **Sirmionciono,** tel. (030) 919045; 3 miles away is **Lugana Marina,** tel. (030) 919173. These campsites require advance bookings in summer. The **Tourist Office** in Brescia (ENIT), Corso Zanardelli 38, 25100 Brescia; tel. (030) 43418, and in Sirmione (ENIT), Via Marconi 2, 25019 (BS); tel. (030) 916114, will have more information.

Two of the most scenic spots on Lake Garda are farther north: Gardone Riviera and Fasano del Garda (1 mile apart).

In **Gardone Riviera** is the **Grand Hotel,** 25083 Gardone Riviera (BS); tel. (0365) 20261; telex 300254. This large hotel (108 rooms) has a garden terrace on the lake and a heated pool. Rates run Lit. 105,000–150,000 in high season, and Lit. 89,000–124,000 in low season, with meals; Lit. 116,000–215,000 without meals. Open Apr. 15–Oct. 3. AE, DC, MC.

Also here is the **Parkhotel Villa Ella,** 25083 Gardone Riviera (BS); tel. (0365) 21030. This hotel is much smaller (48 rooms) and much quieter than the Grand Hotel, but lacks air-conditioning. A view of the lake and a shadowed park with swimming pool makes for a peaceful stay. Rates: Lit. 69,000–74,000 in high season and Lit. 55,000–61,000 in low season, with meals; Lit. 58,000–100,000 without. Open Apr.–Sept. All cards.

Villa Fiordaliso, 25083 Gardone Riviera, (BS); tel. (0365) 20158. Located on the lake, this charming historical villa is primarily a restaurant, but has seven rooms. The meals are served outside and are very good. (The restaurant is closed Sun. night and Mon.) Rates: Lit. 125,000 without meals, and Lit. 182,000 with meals. (Meals taken separately cost Lit. 30,000–74,000, plus 10 percent service charge.) Closed Jan.–Feb. and Nov. AE, DC, V.

In **Fasano del Garda** is the **Grand Hotel Fasano,** 25080 Fasano del Garda (BS); tel. (0365) 21051. This is a true resort, with heated pool, tennis, beach, and gardened terrace. Rooms in high season run Lit. 89,000–117,000 with half-*pensione,* i.e., breakfast plus lunch or dinner, and Lit. 76,000–98,000 in low season; Lit. 98,000–173,000 for all meals. Open May–Sept. No cards.

Villa del Sogno, 25080 Fasano del Garda (BS); tel. (0365) 20228. This spectacular villa has a dramatic view of the lake and a well-kept park and terrace with a swimming pool—a true find. Be sure to ask for a room with a terrace overlooking the lake. Rates: Lit. 115,000–144,000 in high season, and Lit. 94,000–116,000 in low season, with meals; Lit. 88,000–160,000 without meals. Open Apr.–Oct. 15. All cards.

The Northern Alpine Range

The province of Sondrio is a haven for winter and summer sports. Consider staying in Bormio—internationally famous for its skiing—or Livigno—called the Tibet of Italy for its altitude, and loved by many for its duty-free status. Santa Caterina is only 8 miles from Bormio and promises snow and sun; Passo dello Stelvio's summer glacier skiing is a mere 12 miles from here.

Alu, 23032 Bormio, (Sondrio); tel. (0342) 904504. Thirty cozy and comfortable rooms surrounded by wildflowers in the spring. Rates: Lit. 60,000–84,000 with meals; Lit. 47,000–77,000 without meals. Open Dec. 4–Apr. 20 and June 30–Sept. 15. V.

Pare, 23030 Livigno, (Sondrio); tel. (0342) 996331. Forty peaceful rooms. Rates: Lit. 65,000 with meals; Lit. 37,000–65,000 without meals. Open Dec.–Apr. 16 and June 27–Sept. 15. V.

Restaurants

Credit cards are listed as accepted in our suggested restaurants, below. "All cards" means that all of the following are accepted: AE—American Express; DC—Diner's Club; MC—MasterCard; V—Visa. Prices given are for a complete meal (antipasto to dessert) for one person.

The Po Valley

Pavia is a city rich in history. If you don't take a day-trip from Milan (see "Short Trips Out of Milan" in Milan chapter) to see it, do visit—especially the Certosa di Pavia (Carthusian Monastery)—a priority when exploring the Po Valley.

For an adventurous drive to Cremona, follow the signs marked Varzi and Penice when leaving Pavia. (Varzi is famous for its salami and wine.) Take Route 461 toward Bobbio; from there, follow the signs for Passo di Penice (Penice Pass). This spectacular pre-Alp drive is as pretty as some of those farther north.

On the *statale* (state highway) from Pavia to Cremona, stop for an unforgettable lunch in the small village of **Maleo**, at **Sole**, tel. (0377) 58142. A meal will run Lit. 40,000–57,000. Be sure to reserve as the locals know a good thing when they taste it! Closed Sun. night, Mon., Jan., and Aug. AE.

Cremona

Cremona is the city famous for giving birth to the violin makers Stradivari, Amati, and Guarneri and the composers Claudio Monteverdi and Amilcare Ponchielli. Off the beaten track, the town has an agricultural air that emphasizes the fact that most of its inhabitants work with the land. Be sure to visit the **Piazza del Comune,** one of the finest piazzas in Italy, with the **Duomo** (built between the 12th and 14th centuries; note the frescoes decorating the central nave and chancel); the **Torrazzo bell tower** (the tallest campanile in Italy, built at the end of the 13th century); and the **Palazzo Comunale** (Town Hall), where some of the instruments made by the legendary Cremonese are on display.

For those who long to hear the legendary sounds of an authentic Stradivarius violin, call the Ufficio di Gabinetto del Sindaco at (0372) 26201, and ask for an appointment with Maestro Andrea Mosconi. He will quietly play for about ten minutes. From there, visit the **Stradivari Museum** on Via Palestro and, at Corso Garibaldi 95, the **school and violin workshop** of Hungarian Istvan Konya. It may not be easy to see this maestro, however, as he is busy filling requests for his handmade string instruments.

Unless otherwise noted, expect museums in Lombardy to be open Tuesday to Saturday, 9 A.M. to noon and 3 to 5 P.M. If you really have your heart set on exploring some place in particular, check with the local tourist offices.

Besides being one of the best places to buy a violin or guitar, Cremona is known for its delicious *torrone* (nougat) candy, *mostarda* (a kind of fruit pickle), garlic salami, and *mascarpone* (similar to soft cream cheese).

There are **boat trips** along the Po, Adda, and Oglio rivers from Cremona. At press time the *Stradivari* is offering trips all the way to Venice. Cruises leave Cremona at 10 A.M. on

Saturday and arrive in Ferrara at 4 P.M., departing Sunday at 8:30 A.M. and arriving in St. Mark's Square in Venice at 5 P.M. The trip includes hotel and breakfast in Ferrara. To make arrangements, contact: Società Navigazione Interna, Via Rubolotti 7, 26100 Cremona; tel. (0372) 31928 or 25546. The Tourist Office can also provide information; the address is **Ente Provinciale per il Turismo** (Cremona Tourist Office), Piazza Duomo 8, 26100 Cremona; tel. (0372) 23233.

❦ RESTAURANTS

Ceresole, Via Ceresole 4; tel. (0372) 23322. Excellent specialties include fresh fish and onion soup. Ask for Franciacorta and Sassella wine. Dinner without wine will run Lit. 44,000–47,000. Be sure to reserve. Closed Sun. night, Mon., Jan. 2–9, and Aug. 4–25. All cards.

Mantua (Mantova)

The ancient words of the Latin poet Virgil, written fifty years before Christ, paint the landscape of the province of Mantua.

> If life enough is left me,
> I'll be the first to bring the Muse of song to my
> birthplace
> From Greece, and wear the poet's palm for
> Mantua:
> and there in the green meadows I'll build a
> shrine
> of marble
> Close to the waterside, where the river
> Mincius wanders
> With lazy loops and fringes the banks with
> delicate reed.

This dignified, timeless city was settled by the Etruscans and made famous by Virgil (born near Mantua, in Andes); Giulio Romano, the powerful architect who left his imprint on the city; the Renaissance masters, Pisanello and Mantegna; and the powerful Gonzaga family, who ruled for four centuries from 1328. Mantua is a splendor that bears witness to the richness of the Italian Renaissance. Because masters such as Tintoretto, Rubens, and Raphael were a few of the artists commissioned during the Gonzaga reign, this was one of the richest art centers during the Renaissance.

Surrounded by three lakes formed by the River Mincio, the city feels much like a peninsula, with a very humid climate that makes the winters cold and the summers muggy. Because of all the water, the province of Mantua is a fertile area that owes its keep to its well-harvested land.

The first stop should be the **Ducal Palace** (Palazzo Ducale), seat of the Gonzaga family, in **Piazza Sordello.** There are approximately five-hundred rooms, gardens, courtyards, and squares. Built between the 13th and 18th centuries, the grandiose facade of the palace was a symbol of the city. Andrea Mantegna's masterpiece, the *Camera degli Sposi* (the frescoed Spouses' Room), completed in 1474, is in the **Castello San Giogio,** connected to the Palazzo Ducale.

Continuing on toward the Palazzo Te, visit the **Basilica di Sant'Andrea** (built by Leon-Battista Alberti); the impressive interior has a single vaulted nave and is Mantegna's funeral chapel. From there, walk to **Andrea Mantegna's house** (next to the **Church of San Sebastiano**), standing in its original cubelike form. The house is open to tourists.

Arriving at **Palazzo Te,** the country villa of the Gonzaga family, you'll find one of the most important monuments of the city. Built by Giulio Romano, the structure exhibits the creative expression unleashed by this young architect.

Check with the **Mantuan Tourist Agency** in Piazza Mantegna 5, tel. (0376) 350681, for information regarding monuments and museums (hours and prices). Guides may be reserved from this agency.

❦ RESTAURANTS

As far as food is concerned, Mantua is more influenced by its southern neighbor, Emilia-Romagna, than by Milan. Mantuans boast of their special sausage, the *salame dell'Oltrepo,* similar in flavor to sausages from Emilia-Romagna. One of the most famous agricultural fairs in the Po Valley (the Fiera Millenaria, begun in 1580) is held here during the second week in Sept., and has special days devoted to bread and wine.
Recommended restaurants in Mantua are:

Aquila Nigra, Vicolo Bonacolsi 4; tel. (0376) 350651. Excellent dining is to be had here at around Lit. 30,000–41,000 for a dinner without wine. Ask for Custoza or Franciacorta red wine. Closed Sun. night and Mon. AE, DC.

Cento Rampini, Piazza delle Erbe 11; tel. (0376) 366349. Ask for the evening's specialties—you won't go wrong. A dinner here costs around Lit. 24,000–36,000 without wine. Closed Sun. night, Mon., and Aug. 1–15. AE.

Il Cigno, Piazza d'Arco 1; tel. (0376) 327101. Considered by many to be the valley's best restaurant, Le Cigno offers typical Mantuan specialties in a 15th-century palace. Ask for Tocai or Rubino wine. A dinner without wine costs around Lit. 46,000–64,000. Closed Mon., Tues. night, and Aug. 1–15. All cards.

Sabbioneta

On the Lombardy border between Mantua and Parma is Sabbioneta, known as Little Athens. Built as a utopian city by Vespasiano Gonzaga between 1560 and 1591, it stands as an advanced urban achievement of the high years of the Renaissance. Many Jewish families were attracted to the idea of the city, and their **Synagogue** remains in the center of town (although closed to the public). Be sure to visit the **Teatro Olimpico,** a beautiful 16th-century theater unrelated to the Greek games. Entry to most buildings is by guided tour only; to schedule a tour call (0375) 52039 or go to the tourist office on Via Gonzaga.

The Lake Country

Lake Como

The closest lake to Milan, Como is perfect for those who want to combine the city and the countryside. The reflection from Lake Como has mesmerized many an innocent traveler for many a century, casting a romantic spell from its "mirror."

As the birthplace of Pliny the Elder and Pliny the Younger, the town of **Como** was an important center during Roman times. There are many monuments to appreciate (the **City Hall,** built in 1215; the Romanesque **Sant'Abbondio church,** built in the 11th century; the Lombard-Gothic-Renaissance **Duomo,** built between the 14th and 17th centuries), but you can just enjoy the natural wonder of the lake itself by driving along the banks or skimming across its waters to Tremezzo, Bellagio, Lecco, and Colico by **boat;** telephone (031) 272278 for boat information. (Sadly, due to pollution, there is no swimming in Lake Como.) There is a **cable car** (a seven-minute ride) from the shores of Lake Como to Brunate for a lovely view of the city and lake. The **Ente Provinciale per il Turismo** (Tourist Office), Piazza Cavour 17, telephone (031) 262091, or Piazza Cavour 33, telephone (031) 272518, can give all the information you need.

While staying on Lake Como, be sure to visit the **Villa Carlotta** in Tremezzo (closed November 10 to February 26), the **Villa Serbelloni** and **Villa Melzi** in Bellagio, and the **Villa d'Este** in Cernobbio (see "Accommodations," above).

Try the restaurants in the hotels discussed in "Accommodations." They are all very good, and **Villa d'Este** and **Villa Serbelloni** are fun simply to see.

For something a bit different, the Azienda di Soggiorno in Lecco organizes a **bus service with guide** every Saturday and Sunday at 3 P.M. from May to September. It visits the places mentioned in Manzoni's classic *I Promessi Sposi.* The bus leaves from the pier, and the tour lasts about three hours. The cost of the ticket is minimal. Contact the Azienda di Soggiorno, Via Nazario Sauro 6; telephone (0341) 369390, for further information.

I Promessi Sposi

Set in the chaos of early 17th-century Italy, Alessandro Manzoni's *I Promessi Sposi* (The Betrothed) has been hailed as a national institution. The love story of Renzo and Lucia, during Spanish reign and the Venetian Republic, the book glowingly paints 17th-century northern Italy, with a focus on Lombardy.

For a pleasant Sunday drive, the green, rolling hills of Brianza (between Monza, Lecco, and Como) offer fresh air and green pastures. Southeast of Como is **Bergamo,** discussed in "Short Trips Out of Milan" in the Milan chapter.

Brescia

With a population of 225,000, Brescia is the second-ranking business center (after Milan) in Lombardy. There are several Roman monuments (the **forum** and **Capitoline Temple** built by the Emperor Vespasian in A.D. 73); the **Piazza della Loggia** and **clock tower** (built during the Venetian era); the **Torre del Popolo** (built in the 12th century), which dominates the **Broletto,** a medieval communal palace; and the **Castle** (built in the 16th century), with a magnificent view of Brescia and the surrounding area, well worth seeing.

To reach Brescia, take A4 from Milan, or continue on the *statale* from Mantua, following signs for Brescia.

After exploring the city (perhaps in a morning), visit the lovely terrain outside, which includes the **Franciacorta Vineyards** (Brescia is known for its good-quality wine), Lake Garda, Lake Iseo, Lake Idro, and the Val (valley) Camonica. Check with the **Ente Provinciale per il Turismo,** Corso Zanardelli 35; telephone (030) 45052, for information on the entire province of Brescia as well as Lake Garda. Ask for a detailed map of the valleys and lakes.

Lake Iseo

Located between Val Camonica and the Franciacorta vineyards, the rocky coast of Lake Iseo provides a dramatic view, with several picturesque towns. The largest island in all the Italian lakes is found here, called **Monte Isola.** Its height reaches about 2,000 feet, and the island is full of chestnut trees. To reach Monte Isola, there are **boats** (no cars allowed on the island) from Sulzano and Sale Marasino.

 There is a delightful restaurant on the island in Peschiera Maraglio, called **Due Sorelle Archetti.** For fresh fish, cheap prices (Lit. 15,000–20,000 for dinner without wine), and a characteristic atmosphere, this is worth a stop.

Val Camonica

The northern tip of Lake Iseo, Pisogne, is a good starting point for the Val Camonica. One of the most characteristic, beautiful valleys in the Alps, covering fifty miles from Pisogne to the Tonale Pass, its scenery changes from orchards and wheat fields to steep rock walls and thick forests. The name Camonica comes from an ancient tribe of 4,000 years ago, known as the Camuni, who left engravings on large slabs of rock. Most of these are found in the **national park** at Capo di Ponte; others are the towns of Darfo, Paspardo, and Sonico. Known for its water and clean air, the famous **Boario Spa** (Boario Terme) is found in the Val Camonica; telephone (0364) 531609 or 532280 for information. Farther north is the summer/winter resort of **Ponte di Legno,** which offers downhill and cross-country skiing in the winter, and swimming and hiking in the summer. It's near **Tonale Pass,** where skiing is available throughout the summer.

Lake Garda

Called Benacus by the Romans, Lake Garda has been a refuge for water-lovers for centuries. The western shore belongs to Lombardy and the eastern shore to Trentino and Veneto. Lush Mediterranean vegetation (olive trees, lemon trees, and oleander) created by the mild climate is an elixir for the weary. Cleaner than Como, Garda is the best lake for water sports.

Sirmione, located on a peninsula, is one of the most popular resorts on Lake Garda. The **Sirmione Spa** is well-known for its treatment of deafness; telephone (030) 916114. Be sure to visit the impressive Roman villa **Le Grotte di Catullo,** and the medieval **Scaliger Castle** in Sirmione, as well as the **Vittoriale,** residence and tomb of Gabriele D'Annunzio, and the **Hruska Botanical Garden,** both in **Gardone Riviera.**

To travel north on Lake Garda, contact the **Azienda Autonoma di Soggiorno** (travel bureau) Viale Marconi 2, 25019 Sirmione; telephone (030) 916994, for information about **boat trips** (some with orchestras). These leave from various ports including Sirmione, Desenzano, Gardone Riviera, Riva del Garda, and Limone sul Garda. There is fabulous **sailing** (especially between Manerba and Campione del Garda) and **windsurfing** (between Campione del Garda and Limone sul Garda), and boats can be rented to visit **Isola di Garda,** which is only thirty minutes from Manerba. To rent a boat in Sirmione, tel. Bertoldi, (030) 916105, or Bisoli, (030) 916088; to rent a windsurfer telephone Grummelli, (030) 919130. Boats can be rented in most small towns; ask at your hotel or call the Sirmione travel bureau.

Suggested visits along the lake's Lombard coast are: **Lido di Manerba, Maderno** (Churchill's old stomping ground), **Salò, Serniga** (inland between Salò and Gardone Riviera), and the stretch of **coast between Gargnano and Limone sul Garda** (surrounded by citrus and olive groves and considered a *"piccolo Portofino"* by the many German tourists who visit Lake Garda yearly). If you're a golfer, try the **golf course** in Bogliaco, south of Gargnano; it's closed Tuesdays. Telephone (030) 643006.

SIDETRIP

There is a very compelling route from Gargnano up to **Lake Idro.** Once at the lake, continue northward through the charming village of **Bagolino,** where there is a unique **Carnevale** celebration every year. From here you can continue to the **Val Camonica** and the **Boario Spa** (see above).

❧ RESTAURANTS

Lake Garda is known for its fresh fish, excellent wines, and olive oil. Listed here are recommended restaurants for a number of towns on Lake Garda, starting with Sirmione and generally moving north.

In **Sirmione** is **Grifone da Luciano,** Via delle Bisse 5; tel. (030) 926097. The restaurant has a beautiful open-air terrace bordering the lake. Dinner will run Lit. 24,000–35,000 (without wine) plus 15% service charge. Open Mar.–Oct.; closed Wed. AE, DC, V.

Three miles from Sirmione, in **Lugana,** is **Vecchia Lugana;** tel. (030) 919012. Fabulous fresh grilled fish from the lake is served on a lakefront terrace. Dinner will run Lit. 36,000–60,000 (without wine). Closed Mon. night and Tues. AE, DC, V.

In **Gardone Riviera** have dinner at **La Stalla,** Strada per Il Vittoriale; tel. (0365) 21038. Dinner (without wine), runs Lit. 30,000–50,000. Closed Tues. except July–Sept. AE, DC, V.

Well worth the approximately 12-mile trip northwest of Gardone Riviera to **Barghe** is **Da Girelli Benedetto;** tel. (0365) 84140. There's good food here served in pleasant surroundings. Ask for the *funghi* (mushroom) specialty if it's in season. Dinner without wine will run Lit. 52,000–58,000. No cards.

In **Gargnano,** on the banks of Lake Garda, is **La Tortuga,** via XXIV Maggio 5; tel. (0365) 71251. Ask for the house specialties (fish mousse, soufflé of lettuce and spinach) and Lugana or Chiaretto del Garda wine—delicious! Dinner: Lit. 42,000–58,000 (without wine) plus 10% service charge. Closed Mon. night except June–Sept., Tues., Jan.–Feb. AE, V.

The Northern Alpine Range

Sondrio

The province of Sondrio (directly north of the province of Brescia) is in the large Valtellina (Tellina Valley) and is known for its wine (Sassella, Inferno, Francia, Grumello), considered the best in Lombardy, and specialties such as *bresaola* (raw beef fillet cured, smoked, and salted like ham), homemade sausage, and *polenta taragna* and *pizzo cher* (made with buckwheat flour, potatoes, and leeks). Sample these dishes at hotel restaurants mentioned under "Accommodations."

In addition to the good food there is fresh mountain air and relaxation at **mountain resorts** such as Aprica, Bormio, Chiesa, Val Malenco, Livigno, Madesimo/Val di Lei, and Santa Caterina Valfurva. Stay in **Livigno** (known for its duty-free shopping and its high altitude) or **Bormio,** internationally famous for skiing and its health spa. These are the largest ski areas in this region, with slopes ranging from intermediate to advanced. Lessons are available, though they are primarily in Italian. From both locations, you can enjoy the massive **Stelvio National Park,** which offers glacier summer skiing, hiking, and horseback riding. The drive over the Stelvio Pass is memorable.

The **tourist office** in Sondrio, on Via C. Battisti 12; telephone (0342) 212269, or in Brescia or Milan, can give you more information.

11

VENICE

Going, going, but far from gone, Venice enriches, embraces, refutes, fleeces, exhalts, and depresses in waves—much like the Adriatic she once dominated, but now sweeps through St. Mark's Square every winter.

This once-noble city, built on marshy islands by refugees from fifth-century barbarian invasions of the upper Adriatic, is dying a slow death. Not only is Venice sinking, but it is depopulating, as full-time inhabitants flee to the mainland at an alarming rate. Venetian doges once built villas on the mainland; today, affluent northerners who can afford high renovation costs are buying weekend homes here, as Venice becomes more and more a holiday city. Visitors continue to be awestruck by the unique atmosphere and beauty; locals, on the other hand, find Venice overpriced (true) and overcrowded with tourists (also true). But Venice remains Venice—unlike any other city in the world.

A Quick History

Venice began collecting Mediterranean possessions with the fourth Crusade, and by the 15th century was Italy's most powerful maritime republic—the spirit of which is revived every September with a colorful folk regatta. This domination of the Adriatic created continued clashes with the Ottoman Empire, but the Turks never dislodged the doges from Venice.

However, the maritime republic was no match for the Napoleonic forces that conquered the Veneto at the advent of the 19th century. With the treaty of Campo Formio, Venice passed under Austrian domination. In 1866 Venice became part of united Italy under the House of Savoy, although the island city was not physically connected to the mainland until 1846, when a rail link was constructed. A parallel highway was not completed until 1933.

The melodious Venetian cadence is one of the most easily distinguishable accents in Italy; Venice's urban structure and terminology are the most diverse.

A new urban vocabulary is needed for Venice. Besides the all-purpose gondola, which is to Venetian canals what the bicycle, auto, and truck are to mainland pavements, transportation is in the form of *vaporetti* (covered passenger boats) and *motoscafi* (speedboats), which function as buses and taxis.

Here a waterfront street is a *fondamenta* or *riva,* an inner street a *calle* or *salizzada,* a square is a *campo,* and a canal is called a *rio.* On the Lido, which is open to private motor vehicles, normal Italian terminology prevails: via, piazza, etc.

Over the past decade the Venice Carnival has catapulted from a local Mardi Gras festival to an international attraction. Jet-set parties have multiplied and hundreds of elaborately costumed celebrators turn the Piazza San Marco and surrounding calles into a giant party. Hotel reservations should be made well in advance—and bring your own costume.

ORIENTING YOURSELF

The main city of Venice is divided into *sestieri* (sixths):

Cannaregio is the northern part of Venice, including the rail terminal at Santa Lucia. Less on the tourist trails than other areas of the city, Cannaregio's attractions include the Ca'd'Oro, the "House of Gold," on the Grand Canal (Canal Grande), once opulent even by Venetian standards, the Franchetti art collection, and Venice's Jewish Ghetto.

Castello is the area beyond San Marco to and including the Arsenal. Hotels and caffès line the Riva degli Schiavoni, on the Canale di San Marco; it's perfect for strolling, taking the sun, and getting some fresh air, away from the tiny streets that make up most of Venice. Behind the Riva are San Zaccaria church, famous for its Bellini altarpiece, and the Naval Museum.

Dorsoduro is the Accademia area on the point opposite the San Marco area on the Grand Canal. Major sights include the Academy of Fine Arts (Gallerie dell'Accademia), the Peggy Guggenheim art collection, and Santa Maria della Salute church. There are a number of charming pensiones in the area as well.

Santa Croce extends from Piazzale Roma parking area; it borders the Grand Canal in front of the train station.

San Marco is the area most tourists know—central Venice, including St. Mark's Basilica, the Doges' Palace (Palazzo Ducale), and all the famous sights of the Piazza San Marco (St. Mark's Square)—"Europe's finest drawing room," to paraphrase Napoleon.

San Polo is the area of canals and streets that comprise the heart of Venice, connected to San Marco by the famous

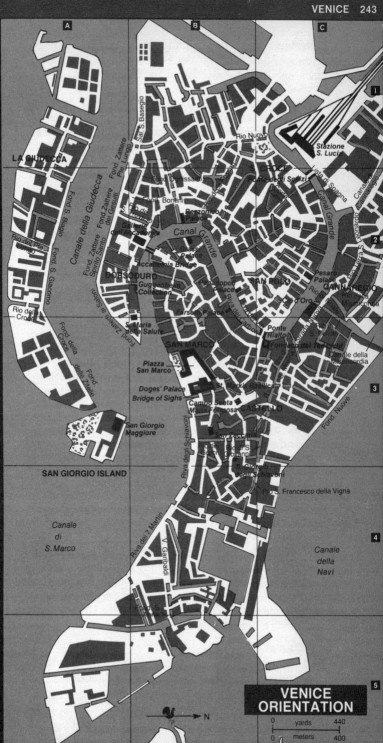

VENICE ORIENTATION

Rialto Bridge. Among the sights here are the Church of St. Mary (Santa Maria Gloriosa dei Frari), with its magnificent paintings, and the art collection of the Scuola di San Rocco.

The six teeth on the ornamental comb on the bow of gondolas represent the six *sestieri*. Some have a seventh tooth on the back of the comb, representing **Giudecca,** the large island in the lagoon between Dorsoduro and the Lido (a long coastal island that separates Venice's lagoon from the Adriatic). Off the point of Giudecca facing San Marco is the island of **San Giorgio.** Other islands of note are **Burano, Murano, Torcello,** and the **Island of the Armenians.** Even Venice's cemetery is an island, San Michele, opposite Fondamenta Nuove, the point of origin for boat service from Venice to most of these islands.

PRIORITIES

The only absolute priority in Venice is to sit in a caffè in Piazza San Marco and to wander the streets—to just experience this remarkable city. The art, the churches, the shops are all secondary. Venice is a good place to recuperate from touring Italy's endless museums and churches. Relax, enjoy; don't make lists of things to see and do. Being here is everything.

However, consider the following (keyed to page of color map insert and map coordinates at which sight is located):

Academy of Fine Arts (Gallerie dell'Accademia)   DORSODURO, P. 31, B4
Here you can see a wide range of Venetian paintings, with works dating from the 14th to 18th centuries. The vaporetto stops here; the Peggy Guggenheim Collection is nearby. Closed Monday.

Gondola Ride
Go ahead. Sure, it's overpriced. Sure, it's touristy. But this is Venice. When else are you going to get to ride in a gondola? Wait for early evening, confirm the price in advance (there are official rates—Lit. 60,000 for fifty minutes, about Lit. 25,000 for the next half-hour, but you might bargain), tell him you want to ride the small canals as well as the Grand Canal, sit back, and let Venice embrace you.

Grand Canal
The best way to see the Grand Canal is to take the vaporetto line 1 at Santa Lucia. (See "The Grand Canal," below.)

Peggy Guggenheim Collection   DORSODURO, P. 31, B4
If you've seen enough Titians and Veroneses to last you for a while, consider a visit to this eclectic collection of modern art, housed in what was Peggy Guggenheim's Palazzo home,

on the Grand Canal. Open April to October, noon–6 P.M.; to 9 P.M. on Saturday; closed Tuesday. The Accademia is nearby.

Piazza San Marco
SAN MARCO, P. 31, C4

You can just sit in this splendid, pigeon-filled square, or visit the major sights: the **Basilica** and its famous bronze horses (hours for the Treasury and Pala d'Oro are 9:30 A.M. to 4:30 P.M., to 5:30 P.M. in summer, 2 to 4:30 P.M. Sunday; hours for the Galleria and Marciano Museum are 10 A.M. to 5:30 P.M., to 4:45 P.M. in winter, 2 to 4:30 P.M. Sundays and holidays), the **Doges' Palace** (Palazzo Ducale; 8:30 A.M.–7 P.M., to 1 P.M. Sundays and holidays, to 4 P.M. in winter), the **Campanile** (bell tower; 10 A.M. to 11 P.M., to 4 P.M. in winter), the **Clock Tower** (Torre dell'Orologio; 9 A.M. to noon, 3 to 5 P.M., to 6 P.M. in summer, closed Sun. and holiday afternoons and Monday) and **Law Courts,** the **Libreria Vecchia**

And there is no use pretending that the tourist Venice is not the real Venice, which is possible with other cities—Rome or Florence or Naples. The tourist Venice *is* Venice: the gondolas, the sunsets, the changing light, Florian's, Quadri's, Torcello, Harry's Bar, Murano, Burano, the pigeons, the glass beads, the vaporetto. Venice is a folding picture-post-card of itself. And though it is true (as is sometimes said, sententiously) that nearly two hundred thousand people live their ordinary working lives in Venice, they too exist in it as tourists or guides. Nearly every Venetian is an art-appreciator, a connoisseur of Venice, ready to talk of Tintoretto or to show you, at his own suggestion, the spiral staircase (said to challenge the void), to demonstrate the Venetian dialect or identify the sound of the Marangona, the bell of the Campanile, when it rings out at midnight. . . .

When the Venetians stroll out in the evening, they do not avoid the Piazza San Marco, where the tourists are, as the Romans do with Doney's on the Via Veneto. The Venetians go to look at the tourists, and the tourists look back at them. It is all for the ear and eye, this city, but primarily for the eye. Built on water, it is an endless succession of reflections and echoes, a mirroring. Contrary to popular belief, there are no back canals where a tourist will not meet himself, with a camera, in the person of the other tourist crossing the little bridge. And no word can be spoken in this city that is not an echo of something said before. *"Mais c'est aussi cher que Paris!"* exclaims a Frenchman in a restaurant, unaware that he repeats Montaigne. The complaint against foreigners, voiced by a foreigner, chimes querulously through the ages, in unison with the medieval monk who found St Mark's Square filled with 'Turks, Libyans, Parthians, and other monsters of the sea.' Today it is the Germans we complain of, and no doubt they complain of the Americans, in the same words.

—Mary McCarthy
Venice Observed, 1956

(**Old Library**). The famous **Bridge of Sighs** is behind the Doges' Palace.

TRAVEL

Travel in Venice is highly unusual. Since there are no cars, you'll be dealing with public transportation consisting only of boats, but let's face it, this is half the fun. There are rush hours, however, with workers crowding the vaporetti toward San Marco from Piazzale Roma in the morning and heading in the other direction in the evening.

Getting lost on the city's tiny, canal-lined streets is also a part of a trip to Venice; try to pay careful attention to the turns in your explorations. Street numbers meander, and street names may be duplicated in different *sestieri.* Don't panic: just travel with a map and keep asking directions; it may take several attempts before you actually reach your destination.

Arriving in Venice

Venice is served by Marco Polo Airport, with both domestic and international flights.

Alitalia; ATI; Aliblu, tel. (041) 5216333; Alisarda; and Avianova, tel. (041) 958030, operate domestic flights. Besides Alitalia, international carriers operating out of Marco Polo are Air France, tel. (041) 5415148; Austrian Airlines, tel. (041) 988666; British Air, tel. (041) 5415629; and Lufthansa, tel. (041) 5415347.

Direct daily domestic flights connect Milan (45 min.), Naples (70 min.), Olbia (70 min.), Palermo (3 hours), and Rome (65 min.).

Daily international flights are available to Düsseldorf, Frankfurt, London, Munich, and Paris. Weekend flights are available for Amsterdam, Brussels, Cologne, and Vienna.

The airport is 8 miles from the city, and airport buses coordinate with flight times to take travelers to the Piazzale Roma (where you can pick up a vaporetto). For airport information, tel. (041) 661111. You can also take a motorboat (*motoscafo*) to Piazza San Marco for under Lit. 20,000; private water taxis also are available, but are very costly; the ride could cost well over Lit. 50,000.

Trains (including the legendary Venice-Simplon Orient Express from Paris) come into the Santa Lucia train station right on the Grand Canal; (tel. 041 715555 for information. The Venice–Rome trip takes 5 hours, 27 min. via Padua, Bologna, and Florence; Venice–Trieste, 1 hour, 37 min.; Venice–Milan, 2 hours, 45 min. The vaporetto stops outside the train station. Water taxis are available, but are quite expensive.

Buses connect Venice with towns throughout the Veneto, as well as Trieste. (See "Travel" in the Veneto chapter.)

Buses arrive at Piazzale Roma; the vaporetto number 2 line stops here. Bus lines: ATVO, tel. (041) 5205530; Brusetti, tel. (041) 9299333; and Societa Autotrasporto Padova, tel. (041) 5222099.

It is wise to call your hotel for directions from your point of arrival.

Public Transportation
TAKING THE VAPORETTO

The Venice ACTV transit company operates 21 vaporetto lines, eight of which function only in the summer, during the peak tourist season. Ticket booths are at the stops. Information on special tourist passes can be obtained at the ACTV Venice office, tel. (041) 780310, and Mestre office, tel. (041) 92073.

The number 1 line is a half-hour local run down the Grand Canal. Starting at the island of Tronchetto (also the ferry departure point behind the main maritime station), the vaporetto makes every stop (Piazzale Roma, the Santa Lucia train station—Ferrovia, S. Stae, Ca' d'Oro, Rialto, S. Silvestro, S. Angelo, S. Tomà, Ca'Rezzonico, Accademia, S. Marco, S. Zaccaria, Arsenale, Giardini, S. Elena) before arriving at the Lido.

Making the run in half the time from Piazzale Roma to San Marco are the number 2 and the summer-only number 4 lines. The number 17 from Tronchetto is the ferry line for the Lido, and passes between Giudecca and Dorsoduro on the Giudecca Canal. For Giudecca, take the number 5 from Riva Schiavoni.

The ferry to the Lido and a ride on the number 1 line provide a comprehensive water view of most of Venice. Complemented by a walk from the train station through San Polo, across the Rialto Bridge and through San Marco to Piazza San Marco, you can see as much of Venice as humanly possible in the shortest time available.

TAKING THE BUS

ACTV bus service is available on the Lido, as well as to (and in) Mestre and Marghera.

Taxis and Water Taxis

Lido taxi stands are at the vaporetto landing point at Piazzale Santa Maria Elisabetta, tel. (041) 765974; and in front of the Casinò, tel. (041) 5261064. For Mestre taxis, tel. (041) 936222, 929499, or 5057942.

Motoscafi (motorboat) stands are: Piazzale Santa Maria Elisabetta on the Lido, tel. (041) 5260059; Piazzetta San Marco, tel. (041) 5229750; Ponte della Paglia, tel. (041) 5228539; Rialto, Riva Carbon, tel. (041) 5230575; San Marco (Giardinetti), tel. (041) 5222303; and Airport, Tessera, tel. (041) 5415084. There are fixed prices for common routes.

Private water taxis are also available, but these are very expensive—the ride from San Marco to the train station will run around Lit. 50,000.

A gondola is less a method of transportation than it is a tourist experience (see Priorities). Gondola stations are located throughout Venice—you'll find plenty available in tourist haunts such as San Marco and Rialto. Official rates run around Lit. 60,000 for fifty minutes; Lit. 25,000 for an additional half hour. Be sure to confirm the price in advance—and don't be afraid to try to bargain the price down.

For a cheap thrill use the gondola ferries that cross the Grand Canal. They're strategically placed all along the canal and cost only a couple hundred lire.

CAR RENTALS

To tour outside the city, you can rent cars at the airport or at Piazzale Roma.

Airport: Avis, tel. (041) 5415030; Europcar, tel. (041) 5415654, telex 223451; Hertz, tel. (041) 5415060; Maggiore, tel. (041) 5415040.

Piazzale Roma: Avis, Piazzale Roma 496/4, tel. (041) 5237377; Europcar, Piazzale Roma 540/1/2, tel. (041) 5238616, telex 410639; Hertz, Piazzale Roma 496e, tel. (041) 522300, telex 410092.

❧ ACCOMMODATIONS

Accommodations in Venice are the most expensive in Italy. Visitors must be prepared to make do, or pay dearly. Outlying areas offer alternative accommodations that are far more in line with services received. Mestre often absorbs the overflow, but it is a drab town offering nothing more than a place to sleep.

Other towns—like Treviso, Padua, or Vicenza—are far more suitable for seeing the Veneto region, as well as for saving money, and are an easy commute into Venice.

Following are suggested lodgings in Venice. To combine a beach vacation with Venetian sightseeing, consider staying on the Lido; these hotels are listed separately.

Rates given below indicate the span between single and double rooms.

Credit cards are listed as accepted. "All cards" means that all of the following are accepted: AE—American Express; DC—Diner's Club; MC—MasterCard; V—Visa.

Note: If writing these hotels, use the appropriate neighborhood designation, as shown below. Hotels are keyed to neighborhoods, page numbers of colored map section at the back of the book, and map coordinates at which hotel is located.

Accademia Villa Maravegie

DORSODURO, P. 31, B4

Dorsoduro, Fondamenta Bollani 1058, 30123; tel. (041) 5210188. This well-managed, 3-star, 27-room hotel is always booked well in advance, so plan accordingly. A 17th-century villa, the Accademia's rooms make visitors feel as if they've stepped into a private home in another century. A relaxing garden is in the inner courtyard. Air-conditioning costs an additional Lit. 7,000. Room rates, Lit. 71,000–120,000. All cards.

La Calcina

DORSODURO, P. 31, B4

Dorsoduro, Zattere 780, 30123; tel. (041) 5206466. Many of the 37 rooms in this 2-star inn do not have private baths, but the ambience is well cured and comfortable. Said to be Venice's oldest pensione (John Ruskin stayed here), today it is a favorite for modern writers, as well as models. Meals may be required in peak summer months. Room rates with private bath, Lit. 45,000–75,000. All cards.

The place is bathed in mauve and gold and the first star is quite clearly *there* to the east of the bell tower, and the shred of a new moon is rising just *there* above the palace roof. I remember in my adolescence being patiently taught *stella* and *luna* as I stretched suntanned limbs slouched in a caffè chair. As I mimicked those words, I thought: "Nothing will ever be more beautiful than it is at this moment," and away I floated on the magic carpet of the Piazza.

Having led you this far, Venice stops. Venice, as it happens, frowns on sex.

"But this is VENice," you say to the concierge as you pass the front desk with the girl you have discovered in all that mooning and June-ing of the Piazza. *"Un momento, prego,"* he is saying. The word Venice dies on your lips. Venice, as though it was some privileged place; Venice, as in venery, venereal, venerable. You hear him tell you that it is forbidden for men to have ladies in their rooms, for ladies to have gentlemen, for any other combination to assemble, even if they register, even if you offer to pay for the other half of the room, your lonely room with only one pathetic bed out of its superfluous two meticulously turned down for the solitary night's sleep ahead.

"What," you might ask, with mounting incredulity, "what if it happened that we were both actually staying at the hotel?"

"Then under those circumstances," he replies, commerce for the moment winning out over morality in the finest Venetian tradition, "it would be your affair." He snorts, the way they did in films of the thirties and goes over to the next client requiring his attention.

—Richard de Combray
Venice, Frail Barrier, 1975

Casa Frollo

GIUDECCA, P. 31, C5

Giudecca, Fondamenta Zitelle 50, 30123; tel. (041) 5222723. Some of the 26 rooms in this 2-star inn, a 17th-century palazzo, have private baths, but these are in high demand, especially by locals in need of space for visiting relatives or friends. Off the beaten track, the Casa Frollo can be reached by vaporetto in a few minutes from San Marco. Rooms with private bath run Lit. 45,000–75,000. No cards.

Cipriani

GIUDECCA, P. 31, C5

Giudecca 10, 30123; tel. (041) 5207744; telex 410162 CIPRVE. This luxury 5-star, 98-room air-conditioned hotel is away from the crowds. Near the point of Giudecca island, on the banks of the Canale della Grazia, in front of San Giorgio Maggiore island, this is the ultimate in Venetian living. Considered by cognoscenti to be the best hotel in Venice, the Cipriani is in fact one of the finest in the world. A free motorboat ferries guests between Giudecca and San Marco. Amenities include a good restaurant (opened over 20 years ago by Giuseppe Cipriani, of the original Harry's Bar), along with a heated pool and tennis courts. Closed in winter. Rooms are a whopping Lit. 500,000–750,000. All cards.

Danieli
CASTELLO, P. 31, D4

Castello, Riva degli Schiavoni 4196, 30122; tel. (041) 5226480; telex 410077 DANIVE. This luxury 5-star, 238-room air-conditioned Ciga hotel is very popular. Behind San Marco and the cathedral, it has a good restaurant that can seat up to 100. The old section of the hotel, a 14th-century palace, has accommodated the famous, from D'Annunzio to George Sand. There's a modern addition, too—but if you're spending this kind of money, stay in the old, more atmospheric part. Room rates, Lit. 410,000–550,000. All cards.

Flora
SAN MARCO, P. 31, C4

San Marco, Calle larga 22 Marzo 2283A, 30124; tel. (041) 5205844; telex 410401 FLORA. This fine 3-star, 44-room hotel is just 10 min. from Piazza San Marco. On a tiny street, the Flora has a small, peaceful garden, but no restaurant. Air-conditioning is an additional Lit. 10,000. Rates for rooms with bath run Lit. 95,000–140,000. All cards.

Gritti Palace
SAN MARCO, P. 31, C4

San Marco, Santa Maria del Giglio 2467, 30124; tel. (041) 794611; telex 410125 GRITTI. Another Ciga 5-star luxury hotel; the chain began here. All 98 rooms are air-conditioned. At the mouth of the Grand Canal just minutes from San Marco, this is another hotel that has seen its share of famous names, Ernest Hemingway and Churchill among them. The service is as close to perfect as service can get; the hotel has a good restaurant that seats 50. Room rates run Lit. 480,000–620,000. All cards.

Montin
DORSODURO, P. 31, A4

Dorsoduro, Fondamenta di Borgo 1147, 30123; tel. (041) 5227151. Just 1 star for this little locanda and its seven rooms, all without bath. But an excellent restaurant and economy-minded clientele keep the clean rooms full, so plan ahead. Reasonable rates explain its popularity: Lit. 27,000–42,000. No cards.

La Residenza
CASTELLO

Castello, Campo Bandiera e Moro 3608, 30122; tel. (041) 5285315. Most of the 17 rooms have private bath in this clean, comfortable 2-star inn in a 14th-century building just off Rio della Pietà, 10 min. behind San Marco. There's an antique-filled common room, and a mix of older and newer guest rooms. Rates for rooms with bath are Lit. 45,000–75,000. Air-conditioning is an added Lit. 10,000. Closed Jan. 8–Feb. 15, Nov. 16–Dec. 12. All cards.

San Fantin
SAN MARCO, P. 31, C4

San Marco, Campiello Fenice 1930A, 30124; tel. (041) 5231401. Accommodations are simple but comfortable, and the location is perfect. All singles in this 2-star, 14-room inn are without bath, for Lit. 33,000. A double with bath costs Lit. 75,000. No cards.

San Stefano

San Marco, Campo San Stefano 2957, 30124; tel. (041) 5200166. All 12 rooms in this pleasant little 2-star hotel have private showers, and are in high demand. Just across from the Accademia landing stage, the San Stefano is convenient to everything. Reservations must be made well in advance. Rates are Lit. 45,000–75,000. Air-conditioning is an added Lit. 7,500. No cards.

Saturnia & International

San Marco, Via 22 Marzo 2398, 30124; tel. (041) 5208377. A 15th-century building houses this 100-room hotel. Rooms can be small, but furnishings are lovely: elaborate glass light fixtures, carved wooden headboards. Amenities are the most modern; black-and-white tile bathrooms even come equipped with hair dryers. The staff is courteous and charming: At check-out time they'll look truly disappointed you're leaving them. La Caravella and Il Cortile restaurants are downstairs. Rates, including breakfast, run Lit. 130,000. All cards.

Seguso

Dorsoduro, Zattere 779, 30123; tel. (041) 5222340. Classified 2-star, this well-kept 36-room inn faces the Canale della Giudecca. Comfortably furnished with antiques, it has a homey feel; only six rooms are without private bath. There is a restaurant, and meals may be required in peak summer months. Rates for rooms with bath are Lit. 45,000–75,000. No cards.

Lido

Biasutti Adria Urania/Nora and Villa Ada, Via E. Dandolo 29, 30017; tel. (041) 5260120; telex 410666 BIAHOT. These two 3-star hotels have a total of 89 rooms, between the casinò and the vaporetto port at Santa Maria Elisabetta. This draws strongly from the film festival crowd. Meals may be required during peak season; air-conditioning is an added Lit. 10,000. Room rates are Lit. 95,000–140,000. Closed Nov. 1–Easter. All cards.

Excelsior, Lungomare 41, 30017; tel. (041) 5260201; telex 410023 EXCEVE. This Ciga 5-star luxury, 230-room air-conditioned hotel on the sea is across the street from the Cinema Palace, site of Venice's annual film festival, and just a 10-min. seaside stroll to the summer casinò. It has a pool, private beach, tennis courts, 18-hole golf course, and a fine restaurant. Rooms cost Lit. 435,000–570,000. All cards.

Some of the restaurants on the islands in the lagoon also have rooms to let. See listings in the "Restaurant" section.

Piazzale Roma and the nearby Santa Lucia train station are the arrival points in Venice, and are at the beginning of the Grand Canal. This is an ideal starting point for touring the city.

The Grand Canal

Board the number 1 vaporetto at Santa Lucia and hustle for a vantage point for viewing both banks of the canal. The ride begins by passing under the **Ponte degli Scalzi** (translated as the "bridge of the bare-footed," in reference to the Carmelite monastery near the train station). This is the first of only three bridges that span the Grand Canal.

On the right before the first bend is the 13th-century **Fondaco dei Turchi.** Once the residence of Turkish merchants in Venice—entrance was prohibited to women and young men—it is now the Natural History Museum (open 9 A.M. to 1:30 P.M.; 9 A.M.–noon Sunday and holidays; closed Monday).

Across the canal is the 16th-century **Vendramin Calergi Palace,** where German composer Richard Wagner died on Feb. 13, 1883. Back on the right bank, halfway into the straight stretch at the S. Stae stop, are:

Pesaro Palace, an 18th-century building that is now the Modern Art Gallery and Oriental Museum. Both are currently closed for restoration.

On the opposite bank at the Ca' d'Oro stop is the Gothic 15th-century **Ca' d'Oro.** Once entirely gilded, the palace is the most elegant in Venice. Donated to the state in 1916, the adjoining Palazzetto Giusto contains the 15th- to 17th-century **Franchetti collection** of art, sculpture, and tapestries that were donated with the palace. (Calle Ca' d'Oro; open 9 A.M. to 2 P.M., to 1 P.M. Sunday and holidays; closed Monday.) On display are works by Carpaccio, Mantegna, Titian, Fra Filippo Lippi—the list goes on.

On the right bank, before the bend at Rialto Bridge, are: the 16th-century **Fabbriche Nuove,** now the Assize Court; and beside it, **Fabbriche Vecchie,** built ten years earlier. Once the meeting place for Venetian magistrates, it is now the city's main fruit and vegetable market. Just before the bridge is **Camerlenghi Palace:** Built in 1525, it was once the debtor's prison.

Before the Rialto, on the left bank, is **Fondaco dei Tedeschi.** The original 13th-century building was destroyed by fire in 1505. Rebuilt immediately, it was used by German merchants; the facade once had frescoes by Giorgione and Titian, which time and weather have now erased. The building today is the main post office.

The Rialto Bridge was once the only bridge across the Grand Canal. The original wooden Bridge of Coins (so-called because it was near the republic's mint) was built in 1264. It collapsed and was rebuilt repeatedly. The present 158-foot marble span, 73 feet wide, was inaugurated in 1592. Each base of the bridge is supported by 6,000 larch piles. (Larch is a wood that becomes as strong as steel under water; once removed and placed in the sun, it crumbles easily.)

Just beyond the Riva del Carbon on the left bank is **Farsetti Palace.** Once a hotel, the 13th-century building is now city hall. A few buildings beyond (also on the left bank) is **Grimani Palace,** built by Michele Sanmicheli in 1556 for the father of Doge Marino Grimani. Pope Clement VIII was so impressed by the building that he presented Sanmicheli with a gold rose. The palace is now the Appeals Court.

Back on the right bank are the 16th-century Renaissance **Papadopoli Palace,** which houses works by Tiepolo and Longhi, and the 1442 Gothic **Bernardo Palace** (note that its two main floors are not at all aligned). You cannot visit the palace, itself, but you can view the gardens.

Facing the latter, after the S. Benedetto vaporetto stop, is the **Benzon Palace.** A rejected suitor immortalized in song ("La Biondina in Gondoletta"—"The Blonde in Gondola") the amorous adventures of the house's 18th-century owner, Countess Benzon, with Foscolo, Byron, and Canova.

Neighboring **Corner-Spinelli Palace** is considered the Renaissance masterpiece of Venice. Built at the turn of the 15th century, it was the home of the duke of Bari, known for his household of at least three hundred servants.

At the vaporetto stop is the 17th-century **Rezzonico Palace,** which belonged to the family of Pope Clement XIII. Legend has it that Robert Browning caught a fatal cold here in 1889. With frescoes by Tiepolo, the palace houses the Museum of 18th-Century Venice (open 10 A.M. to 4 P.M.; Sunday and holidays 9:30 A.M. to 12:30 P.M.; closed Friday). The museum features period tapestries, furniture, porcelain, majolica, and so forth.

The **Accademia Bridge** is a temporary structure dating from 1930, when it was installed to replace a British-made bridge from 1854. The bridge was built to provide easy access to the Academy of Fine Arts, the **Galleria dell'Accademia** (Campo della Carità 1050; open 9 A.M. to 2 P.M.; to 1 P.M. Sunday and holidays; closed Monday). The gallery is divided between Santa Maria della Carità and the Lateran Cannon's Convent, and provides a complete panorama of 14th- to 18th-century painting.

Next to the bridge, on the left bank, is the 15th-century **Cavalli Franchetti Palace,** restored by the same Franchetti who gave the city his art collection. Across the canal is the 19th-century **Barbarigo** that is now a glassworks. The mosaics on the facade depict visits by Charles V to the studio of Titian and by Henry III of France to a glassworks.

Also on the left bank are the imposing 16th-century Corner Palace or **Ca' Granda,** by Sansovino (work was interrupted while the family decided whose inheritance would be used to pay him), and the 15th-century Pisano **Gritti Palace.** Partly restructured in 1742, the latter is now the Gritti Palace.

Giorgione, *Tempest*, Accademia (c. 1505)

Little is known about Giorgione, except that he died young and was immensely popular during his day. Only three surviving paintings can be definitely attributed to him. *Tempest* is his most intriguing work. For years scholars have quarreled over its interpretation. Is it a narrative? If so, no one has identified its source. Is it an allegory? Claims have been advanced, but no one really knows. An early catalog referred to the painting as a landscape with a tempest, gypsy, and soldier, but that seems more of a description than an answer, and a dubious one, at that. Why is a half-nude woman nursing a baby out of doors during a thunderstorm? Is she aware of the well-dressed gentleman who gazes at her? What ruins are these, and in the distance, what town?

The brooding atmosphere is alluring; perhaps nature itself is the focus. The vegetation is lush, and the human figures are posed to set off the sultry landscape. The lightning crackling in the sky is the first to be accurately recorded in Western art. The white bird perched on the slanting roof makes no sign of departure, nor do the man and woman in the foreground.

The composition is beautifully organized, leading the eye into receding space by the subtlest of techniques. Vertical forms (trees, columns) frame the river that winds into the distance. A serpentine path follows its line, stabilized by a horizontal bridge. Beyond it, the dreamy town awaits the storm. Visually, everything about the painting satisfies. Giorgione's luxurious colors and rich texture are typical of the Venetian style.

But what is the subject? Vasari, who offered the earliest appraisal of Giorgione's work, admired his fancy, but when it came to a final interpretation, shrugged: "Heaven knows what it all means." That was in 1568, and art historians are still shrugging.

—Michael Hinden

On the right bank, before arriving at San Marco, is **Santa Maria della Salute.** The 17th-century church was fulfillment of a vow by the governors of Venice for relief from a plague that was afflicting the city. The church sits on a platform supported by 1,156,000 larch piles. Longhena's masterpiece, it contains paintings by Tintoretto and Titian in the sacristy. (Open 9 A.M. to noon and 3 to 6 P.M., to 5 P.M. in winter.)

Nearly at the point where Dorsoduro ends is the **Dogana di Mare** customs station, dating to 1414. The present 17th-century building is highlighted by a golden globe and the revolving statue of Fortune weather vane.

San Marco

At the vaporetto dock at San Marco, the entrance to the piazzetta is marked by two granite columns, that were brought
from Constantinople. One is topped by a winged lion, symbol
of St. Mark, and the other by the city's original patron saint,
Theodore. The piazzetta leads to the piazza, St. Mark's
Square, the pride of Venice. Nearly the size of two football
fields back-to-back, one look explains why this is one of the
world's major tourist attractions.

> One may doubtless be very happy in Venice without reading at
> all—without criticising or analysing or thinking a strenuous
> thought. . . . Almost all the pleasures of the place are simple; this
> may be maintained even under the imputation of ingenious para-
> dox. There is no simpler pleasure than looking at a fine Titian,
> unless it be looking at a fine Tintoret or strolling into St. Mark's—
> abominable the way one falls into the habit—and resting one's
> light-wearied eyes upon the windowless gloom; or than floating
> in a gondola or than hanging over a balcony or than taking one's
> coffee at Florian's. It is of such superficial pastimes that a Vene-
> tian day is composed, and the pleasure of the matter is in the emo-
> tions to which they minister. These are fortunately of the finest—
> otherwise Venice would be insufferably dull. Reading Ruskin is
> good; reading the old records is perhaps better; but the best thing
> of all is simply staying on. The only way to care for Venice as
> she deserves it is to give her a chance to touch you often—to
> linger and remain and return.
>
> —Henry James
> *Italian Hours,* 1909

Visitors and pigeons vie for supremacy, supplanted only by
the periodic flooding. Don't wear a silk suit; the pigeons strike
back. You can escape, enter the basilica for an afternoon of
art appreciation, and walk out to find planks stretched across
a submerged piazza.

The nature of a coffee break must be given serious consideration. Head inside to a bar in one of the many caffès if you
just want refreshment. But, the view, sun, and outdoor music
are part of the square's magic, so consider an outside table—
but be prepared for a tab ten to twenty times the norm. Too
many cry scam when presented with the bill. The musicians
are, after all, not volunteers. The city also charges the caffès
exorbitant fees for each square meter of space. So don't think
you alone are paying for the caffè owner's next trip around
the world. Having paid a good grand to get here, a Lit. 20,000
table tab will buy you a unique spectacle—and you can stay
all day, if you fall into a trance. **Florian's** is the most famous
caffè; it has been a meeting place for Venetians for centuries.

Quadri across the piazza, with its rival orchestra, was favored in 18th-century Venice by supporters of the occupying Austrians. (For a tour of Venice's and northern Italy's piazzas, see "Touring" in the "Travel Arrangements" chapter.)

The view of **St. Mark's Basilica** and the **Doges' Palace** (Palazzo Ducale) proves the historical importance and wealth of the Venetian Republic. St. Mark's began as a small church to house the remains of the evangelist saint, which Venetian mercenaries "removed" from Alexandria around 824. According to local legend, the remains were hidden under a cargo of pork to avoid inspection by Islamic customs police.

The present basilica was constructed as the royal Chapel of the Doges from the 11th to 15th centuries and reflects in its Greek cross form distinctive Romanesque, Byzantine, and Gothic styling. On the loggia of the central most of five arches that dominate the facade are copies of four Hellenistic **bronze horses** that were 1204 booty from Constantinople. (The originals are on display inside the church.) Mosaics in the other arches recount the journey of the remains of Venice's patron saint and their reception in Venice. The inside of the church is covered with mosaics.

The Quadriga

So, big deal, four horses. Once you see these for the first time—a gleaming, spirited combination of weathered bronze and gold—you'll know what the big deal is. These are the only quadriga (four horses yoked together) to survive from classical times. It's believed they were cast in the fourth century, and removed from the Hippodrome in Constantinople by Venetian Crusaders in 1204. Napoleon brought them to Paris in 1797 and had them placed in the Arc du Carousel; they were returned to Venice after his reign ended in 1815.

The high **altar** over the saint's tomb supports a green marble ciborium (canopy) with six 13th-century statues. Behind the altar is the **Pala d'Oro** (open 9:30 A.M. to 4:30 P.M., to 5:30 P.M. in summer; 2 to 4:30 P.M. Sunday and holidays), an astounding gold altarpiece encrusted with silver, enamel, and jewels, a masterful display of Byzantine and Venetian gold work. The **Treasury** (same hours as the Pala d'Oro), houses precious Byzantine art that, along with the horses, was booty from the sack of Constantinople in 1204.

Entrance to the **Galleria** (gallery) and **Marciano Museum** (open 10 A.M. to 5:30 P.M., to 4:45 P.M. in the winter; 2 to 4:30 P.M. Sunday and holidays) is from the atrium. In addition to the original bronze horses, the museum contains 16th-century tapestries, Persian carpets, and paintings. The Galleria offers both a beautiful overview of the piazza as well as a closer look at the cathedral's ceiling mosaics.

Among the most majestic **mosaics** are scenes in the Emanuele dome (believed restored after a mid-12th-century fire) depicting the prophets announcing the coming of Christ. They are cornered by a human figure (Matthew), a lion (Mark), a bull (Luke), and an eagle (John). In the baptistery is the 1342–54 adoration of the Magi. The Epiphany mosaic is based on an original design by Tintoretto. The 1220 olive orchard oration depicts scenes from the life of Christ, including his preaching to sleeping disciples.

The **Doges' Palace** (Palazzo Ducale) was residence of Venice's rulers and leading magistrates. The pink-and-white marble palace was the symbol of the splendor and power of the Venetian Republic. The Porta della Carta ("door of paper," where official decrees were once posted) is the main entrance. The Renaissance **courtyard** was where Doge Faliero was beheaded in 1355 after being convicted of conspiracy.

The doges' **apartments** and chambers (open 8:30 A.M. to 7 P.M., to 1 P.M. Sunday and holidays; to 4 P.M. in winter) are reached by Sansovino's 1558 **Golden Stairway.** A lavish series of frescoes and paintings by Titian, Tintoretto, Tiepolo, Paolo Veronese, and others is found throughout the palace. Especially memorable is Tintoretto's *Paradise*—the largest oil painting in the world, in the palace's largest room—the Grand Council Chamber, where the 1,000-member Great Council met to ratify laws. Tintoretto's daughter is painted at the feet of St. Christopher.

Across the Piazzetta from the palace is Sansovino's graceful 1553 **Libreria Vecchia** (Old Library), which closes the south side of Piazza San Marco. At number 12 is the **Marciana Library,** which may be visited by guided tour only, at 10, 11, or noon. At number 17 is the **Archaeological Museum** (9 A.M. to 2 P.M.; to 1 P.M. Sunday and holidays; closed Monday).

The solitary 324-foot **Campanile** (bell tower) has an elevator to the top that offers a complete panorama of Venice (open 10 A.M. to 11 P.M. in summer and to 4 P.M. in winter). The 10th-century original collapsed in 1902 and was rebuilt. Sansovino's 16th-century **loggetta** at its base was damaged when the tower collapsed, but has been restored to its original form.

The square on the north is flanked by the **Torre dell'Orologio** (Clock Tower) and the 16th-century **Old Law Courts** (Procuratie Vecchie). The facade of the 15th-century clock tower has a zodiac dial; giant bronze Moors on the top of the tower strike the hour with heavy mallets. Be careful when emerging onto the platform if the Moors are moving; the mallets are hard and heavy (open 9 A.M. to noon and 3 to 5 P.M., to 6 P.M. in summer; closed Sunday and holiday afternoons and Mondays).

The **Ala Napoleonica** is a wing built in 1810 by Napoleon's orders to close the west end of the square. Known as the **New Law Courts** (Procuratie Nuove) they also house (at number 52) the **Correr Museum** of the city of Venice (10 A.M. to 4 P.M.; 9:30 A.M. to 12:30 P.M. Sunday; closed Tuesday). The museum's picture gallery features Giovanni and Gentile Bellini, Carpaccio and Antonello da Messina. Another section is dedicated to the Italian Risorgimento, and the history of Venice.

A Walking Tour

Like most of the rest of Venice, the area around St. Mark's is a good place for a brief walking tour. Pass through the piazzetta toward the vaporetto stop. Across the canal is **San Giorgio Island,** with the 16th-century **San Giorgio Maggiore** church, begun by Palladio but finished after his death by Scamozzi. In the church are the *Last Supper* and other paintings by Tintoretto, and Carpaccio's *St. George and the Dragon.* Vaporetto service is on the number 5 line from nearby Riva degli Schiavoni.

Walking down the waterfront, as you cross the first bridge look up behind the Doges' Palace and you'll see the **Bridge of Sighs** connecting the republic's courts with the prison. (Tours of the Doges' Palace will allow you to walk in the footsteps of condemned prisoners whose lamentations gave the bridge its name.) After crossing the third bridge (Ponte della Pietà) turn left onto Calle Pietà and keep bearing left until reaching **San Giorgio degli Schiavoni** and the **Hellenic Institute Museum** (Ponte dei Greci, Castello 3412, open 9 A.M. to 12:30, P.M. and 3:30 to 6 P.M.; Sunday and holidays 9 A.M. to noon; closed Tuesday), with a collection of Byzantine art.

Across Rio dei Greci onto Fondamenta dell' Osmarin, then right across Rio di S. Provolo, head straight to **Campo Santa Maria Formosa,** where the church of the same name (10 A.M. to 2:45 P.M., to 3:45 P.M. in summer; closed Monday) holds an interesting collection of works by Venetian artists from the 14th to 18th centuries.

At this point, the distance to both San Marco and the Rialto Bridge is about the same. Choose your destination and wander through a bit of inner Venice; every angle of the city offers another surprise. Residents claim it's the same for them: a walk down even a familiar street will turn up a carving, a window, a detail of striking beauty they've never noticed before. Practically every church, museum, and gallery has its own masterpiece; put your guidebook aside and see Venice for yourself.

OTHER CHURCHES

Church of Saints John and Paul (SS. Giovanni e Paolo). In the campo of the same name in the Castello area. The Gothic church was founded by the Dominicans in 1246, though not consecrated until 1430. Besides the tombs of many illustrious Venetians, the church, called **San Zanipolo** in the Venetian dialect, also houses Giovanni Bellini's polyptych of *St. Vincent Ferrer* and Piazzetta's *Glory of St. Dominic.*

Church of St. Mary (Santa Maria Gloriosa dei Frari). A Gothic church in Campo dei Frari in San Polo, finished in 1443, St. Mary's contains sepulchers of famous Venetians and a Gothic-Renaissance choir loft, in addition to works by Titian, Bellini, and Rizzo.

St. Zachary (San Zaccaria). In Campo San Zaccaria, Castello, this 1465 Gothic church has altarpieces by Giovanni Bellini and Vivarini and frescoes by del Castagno.

MUSEUMS AND GALLERIES

Glassworks Museum (Museo dell'Arte Vetraria). On the island of Murano, in the Palazzo Gustiniani. (Open 10 to 4 P.M.; Sunday and holidays 9:30 A.M. to 12:30 P.M., closed Wednesday.) Glass exhibits cover ancient to modern times, from the days of Rome through the 20th century, with glass for sale.

Jewish Community Museum (Museo della Comunità Israelitica). Campo del Ghetto Nuovo, Cannaregio. (Open 10:15 A.M. to 12:30 P.M. and 3 to 6 P.M.; closed afternoons in winter.) Sacred vestments and relics from various Hebrew schools are housed in this modest little museum.

Naval Museum (Museo Storico Navale). Riva degli Schiavoni, Castello. (Open 9 A.M. to 1 P.M., to noon on Saturday; closed Sunday and holidays.) The museum contains a collection of models of ships of the Venetian Republic and various maritime documents.

Peggy Guggenheim Collection. Palazzo Venier dei Leoni, Dorsoduro. (Open April to October noon to 6 P.M., Saturday to 9 P.M.; closed Tuesday.) This collection is dedicated to the most representative modern artists, with works by Picasso, Klee, Pollock, and De Kooning, among other major names. The palazzo was the home of the late Peggy Guggenheim, who personally knew most of the artists represented in her collection.

School of San Rocco (Scuola Grande di San Rocco). Campo San Rocco, San Polo. (Open April to October 9 A.M. to 1 P.M. and 3:30 to 6:30 P.M.; November to March 10 A.M. to 1 P.M.; closed Sunday and holidays.) *Scuole* were Venetian clubs, sort of fraternal guilds, that often promoted charitable works. San Rocco was one of six major scuole that existed during the days of the republic. Its quarters were begun in 1515 and completed by Scarpignano in 1549. Besides paintings by Giorgione, Titian, and Tiepolo, it houses a series of 56 works by Tintoretto painted over a period of 18 years.

SHOPPING

Venice is one of those rare cities where you can buy things that are truly unlike anything you'll find back home. Take Carnival **masks,** for instance: There are several types of masks, each representing a certain character in the centuries-old masquerade story. The most traditional is the *larva*—a black or white mask recognizable by the very prominent chin, commonly worn at February's Carnival with a black tricorner hat. Masks are all over town: cheap masks by the hundreds, expensive masks, mask makers. But don't get the idea that these are commonplace souvenirs. They are uniquely Venetian, and will recall Venice to you in a way that few souvenirs can. It's not often that you can have a memory of a trip that looks back at you.

Stores are all over the city, on tiny back streets as well as the major tourist thoroughfares of the Rialto and San Marco. Look for shops that are owned by the mask maker himself; you may well save money. Ask the story of the Carnival characters, and your mask will gain in meaning. Specifically you may want to try Mezá, Calle del Cappeller (Dorsoduro), telephone 5236832; or Balocoloc, Calle del Scaleter 2235 (San Polo); telephone 5240551.

Don't fall prey in Venice to the desire to compare prices and then "come back" for something. If you fall in love with it, buy it. The unending twists and turns of the streets often mean that you may never find a particular shop again!

Murano glass remains Venice's number one product and a favorite souvenir. Some of it is truly hideous—but don't ignore all of it; there are beautiful pieces as well. Prices at the glass factory on Murano and in Venetian stores are on a par. You may find better prices in shops that carry glass from various manufacturers, rather than those that are just showrooms for Murano. One of the more respected shops is Salviati, at San Marco 78 and 10, which sells replicas of antique glass and offers glassblowing exhibitions and showrooms on the Grand Canal (the entrance is at San Gregorio 195). Pauly is another old firm; it has several stores on the Piazza San Marco, at number 72 and 316, and an elaborate showroom at Calle Larga, Ponte Consorzi; telephone 5209899.

Like its glass, Venice's **lacemaking** industry is famous throughout the world. (Legend has it that it was born when a young woman attempted to copy the pattern of a leaf from an aquatic plant.) The most famous name in lace is Jesurum, at Ponte della Canonica 4310, just behind the Basilica; there is also a smaller shop right on St. Mark's Square.

Remember when shopping in Venice that, as elsewhere in Italy, stores are closed for two or three hours in the mid-afternoon.

You'll also find the name **fashion designers** in Venice, mostly in the San Marco area: Mila Shön, on Calle Goldoni; Gianni Versace, Frezzeria 1722; Gucci, San Marco 258; Gianfranco Ferre, Calle larga San Marco 287; Laura Biagiotti, via 22 Marzo 2400/A; and the list goes on.

Antique and modern **prints** abound; or maybe you'd be interested in an **oar lock** like those used on gondolas? You can save all your souvenir shopping in Italy for Venice, then wander the streets (probably the most fun thing to do in Venice), fall in love with the city, and find unusual gifts, all at the same time.

❧ RESTAURANTS

Dining costs are excessive in Venice, so the following restaurants have been chosen with an eye to good value for your money. Don't expect bargains—as with most things in Venice, you pay for the privilege of just being in this city. Restaurants on the lagoon islands are listed separately.

Credit cards are listed as accepted. "All cards" means that all of the following are accepted: AE—American Express; DC—Diner's Club; MC—MasterCard; V—Visa.

Prices given are for a complete meal (antipasto to dessert) for one person.

Restaurants are keyed into page of color map insert and map coordinates at which they are located.

Antica Besetta   SANTA CROCE, P. 30, B2
Calle Salvio 1395; tel. (041) 721687. Behind their picturesque entrance Nereo and Mira Volpe do it their way. Call before making a visit, because if they are not satisfied with the day's marketing, they won't open. Specialities can range from soft-shell crabs to tagliatelle with vegetables; trust their advice when ordering. Meals run Lit. 35,000–40,000, including fruit, wine, and *grappa*. Closed Tues., Wed., July 20–Aug. 20. No cards.

Antico Martini   SAN MARCO, P. 31, C4
Campo San Fantin 1983; tel. (041) 5224121. The elegant, air-conditioned inner areas and a relaxing summer garden are matched by excellent service; the atmosphere alone is worth the experience. Seafood and entrails specialties divide the tourist from the Venetian. There is an excellent wine list. Dinner is a hefty Lit. 100,000. Closed Tues., Wed. noon, Dec., Feb. All cards.

Antico Pizzo
SAN POLO, P. 30, B3

San Polo 814; tel. (041) 5231575. A Venetian's trattoria 2 min. from the Rialto. Vittorio is one of the last of a rare breed catering exclusively to Venetian seafood tastes, with fresh fish and shellfish from the Adriatic. With house wine the tab will average about Lit. 30,000–35,000. Closed Sun. P.M., Mon., Aug. No cards.

La Caravella
SAN MARCO, P. 31, C4

Calle larga 22 Marzo 2397; tel. (041) 5208901. A tribute to the glorious seafaring days of the maritime republic, La Caravella offers a voluminous menu elaborately presenting Italian and international cuisine to satisfy every possible whim. It's one of the few places in the city where you can order seafood risotto for one. An elegant experience at Lit. 90,000. Closed Wed. from Nov.–Apr. All cards.

Alla Colomba
SAN MARCO, P. 31, C3

Frezzeria 1665; tel. (041) 5223817. This refined, elegant, air-conditioned restaurant is just behind La Fenice theater, and offers for late-evening diners a classic Veneto menu. Specialties include fish pasticcio, spaghetti with clams, cuddlefish cooked in its own ink. With wine, meals run Lit. 60,000–70,000. Closed Wed. Dec.–Mar. All cards.

Do Forni
SAN MARCO, P. 31, C3

Calle Specchieri 470; tel. (041) 5237729. This modern, air-conditioned restaurant is the most recent favorite with local politicians. The menu includes wonderful seafood, fried vegetables, chicken, and rabbit. Added popularity has pushed the average tab, with wine, to Lit. 40,000–50,000. Closed Thurs. Nov.–Apr. All cards.

La Furatola
DORSODURO, P. 31, A4

Calle San Barnaba 2870; tel. (041) 5208594. If the right fish is at the market, the trattoria is open; otherwise. . . . Fish in every possible form. With a house wine, dinner runs Lit. 30,000. Closed Wed. evening, Thurs., July, Aug. No cards.

Graspo de Ua
SAN MARCO, P. 30, C3

Calle dei Bombaseri 5094; tel. (041) 5223647. For many years this has been one of the best seafood restaurants in Venice. Mounds of fresh seafood greet arrivals at this picturesque, air-conditioned spot on a little street near the Rialto. With moderation the tab can be held to Lit. 40,000. But eyes often overcome frugality, and with a good regional DOC wine the tab can reach Lit. 80,000. Closed Mon., Tues., Dec. 20–Jan. 1. All cards.

Harry's Bar
SAN MARCO, P. 31, C4

Calle Vallaresso 1323; tel. (041) 5236797. Yes, here it is, the best known name on the international tourist scene. If you can wend your way between the crowded tables and long narrow bar there may be room for another foreigner. A seafood dinner tab runs Lit. 70,000–90,000. Closed Sun. evening, Mon. Oct.–Mar., Jan. 4–Feb. 15. All cards.

Toscana
Fondamenta Cannaregio 5719; tel. (041) 5285281. This air-conditioned restaurant caters both to fish lovers and devotees of other regional recipes. Without fish and a house wine, the tab runs Lit. 25,000–35,000, depending on the second course. Closed Tues. All cards.

Lunch

Lunch can be an ordeal for the rookie traveler, a problem that is equally shared by permanent residents. They usually fall back on little *osterie* locally referred to as *bacari*. These are generally off the beaten path and offer a variety of snacks before the lunch and dinner hours. You can have a salad or a selection of tempting tarts and a glass of house wine for as little as Lit. 10,000. Ask a local for a recommendation and to point you in the right direction; the snacks disappear when the lunch hour begins.

BASIC BARGAINS
Chat Qui Rit
Frezzeria 1131; tel. (041) 5229086. Snacks, pizza, and modest meals served in the expensive San Marco area. Here hunger will generate the size of the tab. Lit. 4,000–22,000. Closed Sat., Nov.–Apr. No cards.

Al Mondo Nuovo
San Lio 5409; tel. (041) 5200698. This self-service restaurant offers a tourist menu for Lit. 16,000 with beverage. *Alla carta,* the tab runs from Lit. 5,000 for spaghetti only to Lit. 20,000 with a fish dish. Closed Tues. in winter. AE.

Rialto
Calle San Marco 4173; tel. (041) 5237909. This air-conditioned cafeteria offers a Lit. 12,000 tourist menu including beverage. *Alla carta* can run from Lit. 3,000 for a plate of spaghetti to Lit. 20,000 for something a bit more elaborate. Closed Sun. No cards.

Vino Vino
Campo San Fantin 1983. This is not self-service, but is perfect for those times you don't want an enormous dinner. A wine bar, Vino Vino also serves small pasta dishes, simple main courses, vegetables, and salads. It stays open very late and attracts tourists and residents alike. Dinner with wine will run Lit. 15,000.

Burano
Al Gatto Nero, Via Giudecca 88; tel. (041) 730120. One of the most characteristic islands in the Venetian lagoon, Burano is a 30-min. vaporetto ride from the Fondamenta Nuove. This rustic seafood restaurant offers outdoor tables in the summer, where you can enjoy a fish pasticcio with a chilled Prosecco. A full meal runs Lit. 30,000–40,000. Closed Mon. Oct.–May. All cards.

Giudecca

Altanella, Rio del Ponte Lungo 268; tel. (041) 522780. Once popular with Italian painters and writers, Gianni and Paola Stradella's trattoria provides good Venetian seafood that reclaims past glory. With the house Pinot, meals run Lit. 25,000–30,000. Closed Mon. evening, Tues., Aug 20–31. No cards.

Murano

Al Soffia d'Oro, Viale Garibaldi 11; tel. (041) 739430. Murano and its glassworks are one of the most visited points of interest in the lagoon; you could make Murano a base for visiting Venice. This recently renovated old fisherman's house by the sea not only offers a good menu of lagoon recipes, but also has five rooms with bath that look out over the Adriatic. (Room rates are Lit. 35,000–50,000; Lit. 65,000 for a triple; breakfast is Lit. 6,000.) Lunch or dinner in the trattoria, with a house wine, runs Lit. 20,000–25,000. Closed Sun. Oct.–May.

Torcello

Locanda Cipriani, tel. (041) 730757. A 45-min. vaporetto ride from the Fondamenta Nuove takes you to Torcello. Locanda Cipriani has summer garden dining for an elegant atmosphere, good seafood, a Veneto menu, and a fine selection of DOC wines. The locanda's three double and two single rooms, all with bath, have a 3-star rating; with air-conditioning, rates are Lit. 90,000–135,000. Meals run Lit. 70,000–100,000. Closed mid-Nov.–mid-Mar. All cards.

EVENING ENTERTAINMENT

The most popular evening entertainment in Venice is simply to sit in the Piazza San Marco and drink it all in: the outdoor orchestras, the people, the vistas.

You might consider taking in an **opera** at **La Fenice,** the theater in Campo San Fantin. For programs and tickets, write to Biglietteria, Teatro La Fenice, Campo San Fantin, 30124 Venice; or call (041) 5203544. The ticket office closes at midday. It's recommended that you make ticket requests in writing from home, well in advance. Occasionally, an English speaker may be found in the ticket office, but if you're trying for last-minute seats, ask your hotel to call for you.

There is one **nightclub** in Venice, truly open until the wee hours: Martini, also in Campo San Fantin, near La Fenice. There is usually some kind of mediocre entertainment (a chanteuse, perhaps); drinks are very expensive. Martini is right behind the wine bar Vino Vino, so you can linger over food and wine until closing time, then continue the evening around the corner.

The Lido **casinò** is open in the summer and fall; then business returns to the main casinò on the Grand Canal.

Consider a gondola ride, or just walk around the city. Venice at night is haunting. Some shops seem to have unusual windows eerily lit, adding to the mystery. Venice is safe at night, too.

SHORT TRIPS OUT OF VENICE

You can stay in one of these Veneto towns, or make a day trip from Venice. Cars may be rented in Venice's Piazzale Roma (see "Travel").

Padua. A 20-minute train ride or an equally easy bus trip takes you into the university town of Padua. The major sight is **St. Anthony's Basilica,** in Piazza del Santo, near the southern perimeter of the old city. The **Scrovegni Chapel** is decorated with famous Giotto frescoes and houses sculptures by Pisano. (See "Padua" in the Veneto chapter.)

Treviso. Commuter train service, running almost every hour for the 20-minute ride to Treviso, makes this an especially accessible day trip into the Veneto hinterland. The wonderful **Piazza dei Signori** is perfect for sitting and sipping an *espresso*. In the **Civic Museum** most major Venetian artists are represented. (See the Veneto chapter.)

Vicenza. Another easy train ride away is this center of Palladian architecture. The town is filled with buildings designed by the famous High Renaissance architect Palladio and his students. (See the Veneto chapter.)

❦ RESTAURANTS

If you rent a car to explore the mainland area around Venice, then visit the exceptional **Da Nalin** restaurant in **Mira,** 12 miles outside of Venice; Via Nuovissimo 29; tel. (041) 420083. (See "Outskirts of Venice" in the Veneto chapter.)

Just a few minutes by train to **Mestre** brings you to the restaurant **Dall'Amelia,** Via Miranese 113; tel. (041) 913951. This elegant, refined, air-conditioned restaurant on the mainland link to Venice steals some thunder from Venice's seafood restaurants. Lobster and shellfish *al Prosecco* along with an excellent house wine can push the tab to Lit. 70,000–90,000. Closed Wed. All cards.

CITY LISTINGS

Page numbers in neighborhood keys refer to the page of the color map insert; map coordinates refer to location of sight/establishment. Page numbers in the listings refer to the text pages in which sight/establishment is discussed.

Churches
St. Mark's Basilica (Basilica of San Marco)   SAN MARCO,
                                                           P. 31, C3

Piazza San Marco; Treasury and Pala d'Oro (altarpiece): 9:30 A.M.–4:30 P.M., to 5:30 P.M. in summer; 2–4:30 P.M. Sun. Galleria and Marciano Museum: 10 A.M.–5:30 P.M., to 4:45 P.M. in winter; 2–4:30 P.M., Sun. and holidays; pp. 242, 245, 256–258

Church of Saints John and Paul
(SS. Giovanni e Paolo)   CASTELLO, P. 30, D3
  Campo SS. Giovanni e Paolo; p. 259

Church of St. Mary
(Santa Maria Gloriosa dei Frari)   SAN POLO, P. 30, B3
  Campo dei Frari; pp. 244, 259

St. Zachary (San Zaccaria)   CASTELLO, P. 31, D3
  Campo San Zaccaria; pp. 242, 259

San Giorgio Maggiore   ISLAND OF SAN GIORGIO, P. 31, D4
  On island of San Giorgio, across canal from Piazza San Marco; p. 258

Santa Maria della Salute   DORSODURO, P. 31, C4
  On Grand Canal, across from Piazza San Marco; 9 A.M.–noon, 3–6 P.M.; 3–5 P.M. in winter; pp. 242, 254

Santa Maria Formosa   CASTELLO, P. 31, D3
  Campo Santa Maria Formosa; 10 A.M.–2:45 P.M., to 3:45 P.M. in summer; closed Mon.; p. 258

Historic Sites
Accademia Bridge   DORSODURO/SAN MARCO, P. 31, B4
  Across Grand Canal; p. 253

Bridge of Sighs   SAN MARCO/CASTELLO, P. 31, C4
  Behind Doges' Palace; pp. 246, 258

Ca d'Oro   CANNAREGIO, P. 30, C2
  Calle della Ca d'Oro; p. 252

Campanile   SAN MARCO, P. 31, C4
  Piazza San Marco; 10 A.M.–11 P.M. in summer, to 4 P.M. in winter; pp. 245, 257

Law Courts   SAN MARCO, P. 31, C4
  Piazza San Marco; pp. 245, 257–258

Libreria Vecchia   SAN MARCO, P. 31, C4
  Piazza San Marco; see Marciana Library, below, and Archaeological Museum, above; pp. 245, 257

Marciana Library   SAN MARCO, P. 31, C4
  Piazza San Marco 12; tours at 10 A.M., 11 A.M., and noon; p. 257

Papadopoli Palace   SAN POLO, P. 30, B3
  On Grand Canal; when coming from Santa Lucia train station it's on the right, just past the Rialto Bridge and Fondamento del Vin; p. 253

Rialto Bridge   SAN POLO/SAN MARCO, P. 30, C3
  Across the Grand Canal; pp. 244, 252–253

Teatro La Fenice   SAN MARCO, P. 31, C4
  Campo San Fantin (041) 5203544; p. 264

Torre dell'Orologio   SAN MARCO, P. 31, C4
  Piazza San Marco; Mon.–Sat. 9 A.M.–noon, 3–5 P.M., to 6 P.M. in summer; closed Sun. and holiday afternoons and Mon.; pp. 245, 257

Museums
Archaeological Museum   SAN MARCO, P. 31, C4
  Piazza San Marco 17; 9 A.M.–2 P.M. Tues.–Sat., to 1 P.M. Sun. and holidays; closed Mon.; p. 257

Correr Museum SAN MARCO, P. 31, C4
Piazza San Marco 52; 10 A.M.–4 P.M.; 9:30 A.M.–12:30 P.M. Sun. and holidays; closed Tues.; p. 258

Doges' Palace (Palazzo Ducale) SAN MARCO, P. 31, C4
Piazzetta San Marco; daily 8:30 A.M.–7 P.M.; to 1 P.M. Sundays and holidays; to 4 P.M. in winter; pp. 245, 256–257

Dogana di Mare customs station DORSODURO, P. 31, C4
At the point of Dorsoduro; p. 254

Hellenic Institute Museum CASTELLO
Ponte dei Greci, Castello 3412; 9 A.M.–12:30 P.M.; 3:30–6 P.M.; Sun. and holidays 9 A.M.–noon; closed Tues.; p. 258

Fondaco dei Turchi (Natural History Museum) SANTA
CROCE, P. 30, B2
On the Grand Canal; when coming from the Santa Lucia train station, it's on the right, before the first bend; 9 A.M.–1:30 P.M. Tues.–Sat.; 9 A.M.–12 P.M. Sun., holidays; closed Mon.; p. 252

Franchetti Collection CANNAREGIO, P. 30, C2
In Palazzetto Giusto; 9 A.M.–2 P.M., to 1 P.M. Sun. and holidays; closed Mon.; pp. 242, 252

Galleria dell'Accademia DORSODURO, P. 31, B4
Campo della Carità 1050; tel. 5222247; 9 A.M.–2 P.M. Tues.–Sat., to 1 P.M. Sun and holidays; closed Mon.; pp. 242, 244, 253

Glassworks Museum
(Museo dell' Arte Vetraria) MURANO ISLAND
Fondamenta Giustiniani, Palazzo Gustiniani; 10 A.M.–4 P.M., Sun. and holidays 9:30 A.M.–12:30 P.M.; closed Wed.; p. 259

Jewish Community Museum
(Museo della Comunità Israelitica) CANNAREGIO, P. 30, B1
Campo del Ghetto Nuovo; 10:15 A.M.–12:30 P.M., summer also 3–6 P.M.; p. 259

Marciano Museum SAN MARCO, P. 31, C3
See St. Mark's Basilica.

Naval Museum (Museo Storico Navale) CASTELLO
Riva degli Schiavoni; 9 A.M.–1 P.M., Sat. to noon; closed Sun. and holidays; pp. 242, 259

Peggy Guggenheim Collection DORSODURO, P. 31, B4
Palazzo Venier dei Leoni; April–Oct. 12–6 P.M., Sat. to 9 P.M.; closed Tues.; pp. 242, 244–245, 259

Rezzonico Palace
(Museum of 18th-Century Venice) DORSODURO, P. 31, B3
On Grand Canal, Fondamento Rezzonico; 10 A.M.–4 P.M.; Sun. and holidays, 9:30 A.M.–12:30 P.M.; closed Fri.; p. 253

School of San Rocco (Scuola Grande di San Rocco) SAN
POLO, P. 30, B3
Campo San Rocco; April–Oct. 9 A.M.–1 P.M., 3:30–6:30 P.M.; Nov.–Mar. 10 A.M.–1 P.M.; closed Sun. and holidays; pp. 244, 259–260

Shops
Balocoloc SAN POLO, P. 30, C3
Calle de Scaleter 2235; p. 260

Gianfranco Ferre SAN MARCO, P. 31, C3
Calle larga San Marco 287; p. 261

Gianni Versace   SAN MARCO, P. 30, C4
  Frezzaria 1722; p. 261

Gucci   SAN MARCO, P. 31, C3
  San Marco 258; p. 261

Jesurum   SAN MARCO, P. 31, C3
  Ponte della Canonica 4310; p. 261

Laura Biagiotti   SAN MARCO, P. 31, C4
  Via 22 Marzo 2400/A; p. 261

Mezá   DORSODURO, P. 31, B4
  Calle del Cappeller, Dorsoduro 3215; p. 260

Mila Shön   SAN MARCO, P. 30, C3
  Calle Goldoni; p. 261

Pauly   SAN MARCO, P. 31, C4
  Calle Larga, Ponte Consorzi, and Piazza San Marco 72 and 316; p. 260

Salviati   SAN MARCO, P. 31, C4
  San Marco 78 and 10; showroom and exhibits at San Gregorio 195; p. 260

12

THE VENETO

The Veneto is God's country. No other region of Italy has been more consistently faithful to the Christian Democratic party. And no other geographic area can offer a wider panorama of natural and artistic beauty complemented by prominent points of historical interest.

Between the majestic Dolomite setting of Cortina d'Ampezzo and the marshy Po delta's natural wildlife reserve are rolling hills, fertile valleys, sweeping rivers, the wide sandy beaches of Jesolo, and the country's largest freshwater lake, Garda, which also borders on Lombardy and Trentino.

The winged Venetian lion is still prominent throughout the empire city's former outlying domain. Roman ruins are also in abundance, reminders of a yet more ancient glory, and Verona's Roman Arena, one of the largest built, provides an unforgettable setting for summer opera performances.

While Venice has its ornate Grand Canal palaces, the mainland has the surviving genius of Andrea Palladio. The 16th-century Paduan-born architect was internationally famed for his *ville Venete* (Venetian villas). Colleagues added to this patrimony, and their skill beautifies the villas, palaces, and churches of all seven of the region's provinces. These artists included such masters of the Venetian school as Bellini, Giorgione, Titian, Veronese, Tintoretto, and Tiepolo.

The most eminent literary figure to emerge from the Veneto was Carlo Goldoni, often referred to as the Italian Molière. The contagious mysticism of the region drew Shakespeare to set plays in Venice, Verona, and Padua, though there is reason to doubt that he even visited the area. Visitors who immortalized their firsthand impressions were Byron, Keats, Goethe, Chauteaubriand, Musset, George Sand, Barrès, John Ruskin, Ben Jonson, Jules Romains, and Thomas Mann.

Folk and cultural spectacles include the biannual art show, controversial film festival, *palio,* and regatta at Venice. Besides opera, Verona offers summer theater in its Roman amphitheater on the banks of the Adige River. And there is an annual chess match, played with human chessmen in the square at Marostica, usually held the first half of September.

The region's religious shrines, sanctuaries, and outstanding cathedrals range from regal St. Mark's in Venice and St. Anthony's in Padua to cliffside Madonna della Corona sanctuary at Spiazzi di Monte Baldo, in the province of Verona.

The Ville Venete

The palatial villas throughout the Veneto are one of the most neglected highlights of the area, due to their abandonment by private owners and state officials for decades.

Classified national monuments, the villas often need restoration, but strict criteria imposed by the Fine Arts Commission made the necessary expenditures prohibitive for individual owners.

With the recent intervention of reason and state financing, one of the Veneto's proudest patrimonies is now being restored to palatial splendor. These Gothic and Renaissance 16th- to 19th-century villas are vivid testimony to the wealth accumulated during the prime of the Venetian Maritime Republic.

Most of the homes and their splendid parks were summer retreats for the lords and leading merchants of Venice. Forty villas have been officially cataloged by the Fine Arts Commission. Some are concentrated northwest of Verona, but many are found in and around Vicenza, the home of prominent architect Andrea Palladio. Thomas Jefferson was so impressed by Paladio's La Rotonda, outside Vicenza, that he used it as a model for his Monticello home at Charlottesville, Virginia.

Most of the villas are private property or belong to public administrations that use them for special events only. But a country drive, boat trip, or stroll along the Brenta Canal, between Padua and Venice, is a rewarding experience for its display of Venetian homes.

Information and itineraries may be obtained from the Regional Tourist Information Office in Venice, tel. (041) 792111, or the Provincial Tourist Information Offices at Belluno, tel. (0437) 22043; Padua, tel. (049) 8750655; Rovigo, tel. (0425) 3340; Treviso, tel. (0422) 540600; Verona, tel. (045) 30086, and Vicenza, tel. (0444) 28944.

In spite of this heritage and the everyday reminders of a long and glorious past, there is no sense of the complacency evident in other Italian regions. At one time the outlying provinces were purely agrarian. They formed a labor pool for Fascist redevelopment projects and for wealthy matrons from Rome and Milan seeking live-in domestic help. With few other avenues to explore, native sons sought escape and fortune in bicycle racing. Little space was left for other livelihoods, and the Veneto became derided as the land of bicycle racers and household servants.

But the solid, industrious character of the Veneto sired a regional revolution that can claim a good portion of the credit for Italy's modern emergence as a leading world industrial nation. Once hardly more than family companies, Benetton and Nordica have acquired international acclaim. But these are exceptions. The real base of the area's new economy is the hundreds of small processors, manufacturers, and refineries that defied the odds and have transformed the region into one of the most prosperous in the country.

The newfound prosperity was virgin territory for southern organized crime suspects exiled by national police policy and awaiting trial. Drugs certainly were not an unknown entity before, but drug traffic soon soared to a new plateau. Verona became known as the Bangkok of Europe.

Though sympathizing with the U.S. general kidnapped by the Red Brigades, Veronese welcomed the massive police intervention that had the collateral effect of momentarily stymieing the massive drug market movement.

Prices of goods in the area surprise many visitors. The Veneto is not a bargain basement. Though the region is enjoying its newfound wealth, frugal instincts of the past, traits embedded during the Austrian occupation of the region, remain.

Once obliged to emigrate to obtain any sort of work, Veneto's children can still be found in the four corners of the world, but with briefcases and professional skills. That melodious cadence so pronounced in their Italian also tinges their English. And profit has replaced survival as their major motive.

WINING AND DINING

Demanding doges and frugal farmers formulated a regional cuisine that still features centuries-old recipes. Local produce is exploited to the maximum. The Austrian occupation imported goulash, but the Veneto has remained faithful to grandmother's recipes: *risotti,* vegetable broths, and minestrone as well as rib-sticking *polenta* distinguish regional menus; specialties are *bigoli con sardelle* (wheat noodles with sardines), *baccalà alla Vicentina* (dried cod with milk and onions), *fegato alla Veneziana* (calf's liver simmered with onions), and *la pastissada* (chopped horse meat—it's true—simmered with onions and red wine).

Risotti can be as varied here as pasta dishes are in the south. Sausage, mushrooms, shellfish, and peas (*risi e bisi*) are favorites, each risotto is simmered in an open skillet to produce a distinctive broth. Choose these over pasta; pasta in the Veneto has a tendency to be overcooked.

Seafood is a favorite throughout the region, and fresh fish is at a premium. Major restaurants reportedly offer trawler captains a bonus for the privilege of making selections before the catch is passed on to the local market. The diner absorbs this expense. Better seafood restaurants demand top dollar and are not geared to the tourist market. Some of these restaurants are included here, but the emphasis is on the reasonably priced little *trattorie* out of town and tucked away in the side streets of old towns, with tasty regional cuisine and such local wines as Tocai, Soave, Valpolicella, Recioto, Amarone, and Bardolino.

Two interesting local wines that should legally no longer exist due to Common Market minimum levels of alcoholic content are fragolino and clinton. Some farmers still supply their own tables, and at times a stray bottle winds up in circulation. *Grappa* is a favorite after-dinner digestive aid in the winter. Priceless is a smoked version that is aged in cedar kegs.

Credit cards are listed as accepted in our restaurant recommendations. "All cards" means that all of the following are accepted: AE—American Express; DC—Diner's Club; MC—MasterCard; V—Visa.

Prices given are for a complete meal (antipasto to dessert) for one person.

TRAVEL

Travel in the Veneto is not complicated. Four of the seven provincial seats are connected by practically straight east-west rail routes and turnpikes from Verona, through Vicenza and Padua, to Venice. North of this line are Belluno and Treviso, while Rovigo lies south of Padua.

Flying

Two international commercial airports are in the Veneto: Marco Polo at Venice (see the Venice chapter) and Catullo at Villafranca, just outside Verona.

Catullo is 7½ miles from Verona's central Piazza Cittadella. The number 39 bus from the Porta Nuova rail station makes the 20-min. trip to the airport. For airport information, tel. (045) 513039.

Domestic flights are provided by Alitalia; ATI; Aliblu, tel. (045) 594222; Alisarda; and Avianova, tel. (041) 958222. Daily flights connect with Naples (1 hour, 45 min.) and Rome (1 hour). Three times weekly flights connect with Cagliari (1 hour, 20 min.) and Olbia (1 hour, 10 min.). Direct flights Tues., Thurs., Sat., and Sun. are available to Paris (1 hour, 45 min.).

Taking the Train

Verona is the crossroads of main north-south rail lines from Munich to Rome, and the west-east line from Turin to Trieste that also services Vicenza, Padua, and Venice.

The Milan–Venice *rapido* train takes two hours, 45 mins., or one hour, 20 min. Verona–Venice; Verona–Vicenza is 28 min.; Vicenza–Padua 19 min.; Padua–Mestre 19 min.; Mestre–Venice, 9 min.; and Venice–Trieste 1 hour, 37 min. Verona–Rome takes 4 hours, 58 min. via Bologna and Florence.

There is an average of one train every 9 min. connecting Mestre and Venice during the peak summer season. From Venice to Treviso there is a 20-min. commuter run practically every hour. The frequency of trains and the proximity of provincial seats offer many possibilities for avoiding the often exorbitant hotel rates in Venice while enjoying other areas of the Veneto.

Trains depart from both Padua and Venice for Belluno and Calalzo–Pieve di Cadore (the closest rail depot to Cortina d'Ampezzo). Padua–Calalzo is 3 hours, Padua–Belluno, 2 hours, 11 min. Venice–Calalzo is 2 hours, 26 min.; Venice–Belluno is 1 hour, 50 min.

Rail information can be obtained 7 A.M.–10 P.M. by calling: Belluno, tel. (0437) 25438; Padua, tel. (049) 8751800; Rovigo, tel. (0425) 33396; Treviso, tel. (0422) 541352; Venice (Santa Lucia and Mestre), tel. (041) 715555; Verona, tel. (045) 590688; and Vicenza, tel. (0444) 239427.

Taking the Bus and Taxis

An extensive network of provincial buses serve the Veneto. The locations of bus depots and connections between major towns in the region (and phone numbers of local taxi services) are:

Belluno: Piazzale Stazione 21; Dolomiti Bus, tel. (0437) 25112. Connects with provincial seats Bolzano, Treviso, and Venezia, many outlying villages in provincial Belluno, and the ski stations at Cortina d'Ampezzo, Moena, Passo di San Pellegrino, and Selva. Belluno taxis: tel. (0437) 32532, 27733, 940336, or 213312. Cortina d'Ampezzo taxis: tel. (0436) 2839, 4619, or 2667.

Padua: Viale Trieste; tel. (049) 8206811. Four bus lines make extensive runs throughout the provinces of Padua, Treviso, Udine (in Friuli-Venezia Giulia), Venice, and Verona, as well as to the cities of Cremona, Genoa, Mantua, Milan, Trieste, and Vicenza. Local taxi: Piazzale Stazione; tel. (049) 651333.

Treviso: Lungosile Mattei bus depot; tel. (049) 546268. SIAMIC is the point of reference for most of the 15 companies based here. Other companies are COMIN, tel. (0422) 545863; and CTT, tel. (0422) 57746. Connections to the provincial seats of Belluno, Brescia, Bolzano, Milan, Padua, Pordenone, Trento, Trieste, and Venice, and smaller towns throughout provincial Treviso; service to Canazei, Cortina, Corvara, Fiera di Primiero, Jesolo, Merano, Mestre, and San Martino di Castrozza.

Venice: Piazzale Roma; ACTV, tel. (041) 780111; ATVO, tel. (041) 5205530; Brusetti, tel. (041) 929333; and Società Autotrasporto Padova, tel. (041) 5222099. Routes to the provincial seats of Belluno, Treviso, Trieste, and Vicenza, most of provincial Venice, and Asolo, Asiago, Canazei, Cortina d'Ampezzo, Feltre, Fiera di Primiero, Jesolo Lido, and Moena. (See the Venice chapter for taxi information.)

Verona: Porta Nuova FS Station; APT, tel. (045) 8004129. Buses depart from a depot at the train station, for Brescia, Mantua, Lake Garda, and throughout provincial Verona. Local taxi: tel. (045) 532666.

Vicenza: Viale Milano 103; FTV, tel. (0444) 232950. Service is almost exclusively limited to provincial Vicenza. One exception is summer service to the beach resort at Jesolo Lido. Local taxis: tel. (0444) 235738, 544470, or 514213 during the day; tel. (0444) 235794 at night.

Driving

Verona is the hub of regional traffic, connecting Veneto with the rest of Italy as well as northern Europe.

On the A4 from Turin to Trieste, Verona offers a connection with the A22 from the Brenner Pass to Modena, which is on the Milan–Rome A1. At Padua is a connection with the A13 to Bologna, which ties into the A1 and the A14 (which swings over to Rimini and down the Adriatic coast).

At Mestre, on the A4, is a connection with the Via Romea superstrada that covers the upper Adriatic coast down to the A14.

Off the A4 at Vicenza Est (East) is a connection with the A31 Vicenza–Piovene Rocchette (22 miles). At the Thiene exit are clearly indicated provincial roads for Marostica (11 miles), Bassano del Grappa (15½ miles), Recoaro Terme (25 miles), and Monte Grappa (34 miles).

Off the A4 at Mestre is the 36-mile A27 to Vittorio Veneto, which passes 7 miles from Treviso (exit at Treviso Sud). This is also the best exit for Asolo.

At Vittorio Veneto is a 34-mile superstrada (51) for Cortina d'Ampezzo. Belluno is 5 miles from the Ponte nelle Alpi exit onto highway 50. Take the Tai di Cadore exit onto the SS51bis to reach Pieve di Cadore.

CAR RENTALS

For information on car rentals in Venice or its airport, see the Venice chapter.

The following are rental agencies throughout the Veneto:

Bardolino: Avis, Via Mirabella 9; tel. (045) 7210390.

Calalzo di Cadore (closest rail depot to Cortina): Avis, Località Noui 41; tel. (0435) 72663.

Mestre: Avis, Viale Stazione 18E; tel. (041) 935866. Hertz, c/o Hotel Plaza, Piazzale Favaretti; tel. 7000000. Maggiore, Train Station; tel. (041) 935300.

Padua: Avis, Piazzale Stazione 1; tel. (049) 664198. Europcar, c/o Garage Stazione, Piazzale Stazione 6/VII; tel. (049) 36094. Maggiore, Piazzale Stazione 15bis; tel. (049) 30031.

Verona: (Airport) All city agencies can provide service at the airport with advance notice.

(City) Avis, Porta Nuova Train Station; tel. (045) 26636. Europcar, Porta Nuova Train Station; tel. (045) 592759; telex 480845. Hertz, Porta Nuova Train Station; tel. (045) 8000832. Maggiore, Porta Nuova Train Station; tel. (045) 34808.

Vicenza: Avis, Viale Milano 88; tel. (0444) 221622. Maggiore, Train Station, tel. (0444) 545962.

❦ ACCOMMODATIONS

Growing tourism and the development of local industry often tax the capabilities of regional hotels to adequately accommodate all visitors. The problem is never so acute as in Venice during July and Aug. (see the chapter on Venice). Consider using Treviso, Padua, or Vicenza as a base for exploring the Veneto as well as Venice. In addition to its summer opera and theater programs, Verona has an active calendar of fairs and conventions; consider spending a night or two there if traveling between Venice and Milan. Belluno is a stopover on the way into the Dolomites. The skiing at Cortina d'Ampezzo attracts crowds in winter, while summer visitors come for the mountain air. If you'd like to "take the waters," then head for Abano Terme.

You must make reservations as far ahead as possible. Local tourist information boards are helpful and well organized, but beware: They strictly follow local office hours.

For accommodations in Venice see the chapter on that city.

Rates given below show the span between prices for single and double rooms.

Credit cards are listed as accepted. "All cards" means that all of the following are accepted: AE—American Express; DC—Diner's Club; MC—MasterCard; V—Visa.

Abano Terme

Grand Hotel Orologio, Viale delle Terme 66, 85031 (PD); tel. (049) 669111; telex 430254. Luxury 5-star, 65-room, air-conditioned hotel in a shady park, with in-house thermal cures, a restaurant, bar, heated outdoor and indoor pools, tennis court, parking, and facilities for the handicapped. The treatment is a real treat. The Lit. 235,000 *pensione* plan is a good idea, especially for those who want to keep a low profile while undergoing mud baths. Room rates are Lit. 195,000–295,000. All cards.

Ritz, Via Monteortone 19, 85031 (PD); tel. (049) 669990; telex 430222. In-house thermal cures in this 3-star, 149-room air-conditioned hotel with heated outdoor and indoor pools, a tennis court, shady park, and parking. Room rates run Lit. 55,000–90,000. The *pensione* plan is Lit. 120,000. All cards.

Belluno

Delle Alpi, Via J. Tasso, 37020; tel. (0437) 20545. This 3-star, 40-room hotel is the newest and highest rated in town. A block off the central park, it's 10 min. from the train station. Rates run Lit. 52,000–82,000. Cards pending.

Cortina D'Ampezzo

Cristallo, Via R. Menardi 42, 32043 (BN); tel. (0436) 4281; telex 440090 CRICOR. This 5-star, 98-room Ciga hotel in Alpine style has a good restaurant, bar, pool, tennis court, and garage. *Pensione* plan only, Lit. 300,000. Open June 1–Sept. 9 and Dec. 20–Mar. 23. All cards.

Panda, Via Roma 64, 32043 (BN); tel. (0436) 60344. This small 2-star, 19-room hotel without restaurant is just across the Bigontina stream from central Cortina. No meal obligations leave more time for the slopes. The rates are reasonable, too: Lit. 45,000–75,000. Closed May, Nov. All cards.

Lake Garda

Half of the shores of Lake Garda are in the province of Verona. This has long been a favorite German holiday spot—it can feel like you're not even in Italy. Hundreds of hotels and campgrounds are available. For any extended stay contact the Ente Provinciale per il Turismo–Verona, Via Scalzi 20, 37100 Verona; tel. (045) 26997.

Padua

Donatello, Via del Santo 102, 35123; tel. (049) 36515. Across the square from the St. Anthony Basilica, this 3-star, 42-room hotel has a roof-garden restaurant and parking facilities. Room rates are Lit. 55,000–80,000. Air-conditioning is an added Lit. 5,000. Closed Dec. 15–Jan. 15. All cards.

Monaco, Piazzale Stazione 3, 35131; tel. (049) 664344. Facing the train station just beyond the old city walls, this 3-star, 57-room hotel can accommodate the handicapped. Rooms are Lit. 52,000–73,000, plus Lit. 4,000 for air-conditioning. All cards.

Treviso

Carlton, Largo di Porta Altinia 15, 31100; tel. (0422) 55221; telex 410041. This modern, 3-star, 96-room air-conditioned hotel is 150 yards from the train station inside the old town walls. Frequented by businesspeople as well as visiting artists. Rooms are priced Lit. 70,000–110,000; air-conditioning is an extra Lit. 5,000. All cards.

NOTE: See restaurant section for further accommodations in and around Treviso.

Verona

Colombo d'Oro, Via Cattaneo 10, 37121; tel. (045) 595300; telex 480872. With 51 air-conditioned rooms, this 4-star hotel is less than a 2-min. walk from the central Piazza Bra and the Arena. There is no restaurant, but the small bar has seen local nobility pass many an interesting evening. Room rates are Lit. 95,000–130,000. All cards.

Due Torri, Piazza Sant'Anastasia 4, 37121; tel. (045) 595044; telex 480524. This luxurious, 5-star, air-conditioned hotel has 100 rooms furnished with authentic 18th- and 19th-century furniture. The illustrious guest list has included Goethe and Mozart. There is a comfortable restaurant and a tavern, and bar service throughout the spacious lobby. Less than a 10-min. walk from Piazza Dante and Piazza Erbe, the Due Torri is in the heart of old town. But you'll pay: Rooms run Lit. 200,000–305,000. All cards.

Italia, Via G. Mameli 64, 37126; tel. (045) 918088; telex 431064. Every year sees an improvement in this 3-star, 53-room hotel on the old road to Trento, a 15-min. walk to the heart of the old town's pedestrian area. Double windows eliminate noise; air-conditioning is being installed. Telephone, color TV, and minibar in each room; there is a garage. Yet the rates are reasonable: Lit. 52,000–77,000. All cards.

Rossi, Via delle Coste 2, 37138; tel. (045) 569022. Just 200 yards from the Porta Nuova train station and airport bus stop, this 3-star, 39-room air-conditioned hotel has a restaurant, bar, and parking facilities. Rooms are Lit. 59,000–86,000. All cards.

Vicenza

Alfa Hotel, Via dell'Oreficeria 52, 36100; tel. (0444) 565455; telex 434550 ALFHOT. This modern 4-star, 87-room hotel is near the industrial fairgrounds. There's a good restaurant (L'Incontro), and the Alfa can accommodate the handicapped. Rates are Lit. 77,000–100,000. Closed Dec. 20–30. All cards.

Outskirts of Venice

The principal towns in this area–Padua, Treviso, and Vicenza—can all be easily visited as day trips from Venice. However, to best experience the Veneto, consider staying in one of these towns.

Padua (Padova)

St. Anthony's Basilica is one of the most visited shrines in the Catholic world. Built to house the remains of the Lisbon-born Franciscan priest who died here at the age of 36 in 1231, the basilica is visited annually by an incalculable number of pilgrims seeking miraculous assistance.

In **The Palazzo Bo** at Via VIII Febbraio is the **University of Padua,** one of the oldest in Europe, founded in 1222; only Bologna's university is older in Italy. Galileo was once a professor here; in modern time so was Toni Negri, who used his position to recruit for left-wing terrorist cells during Italy's "years of lead." The university's renowned medical college was a sanctuary for hundreds of American students seeking to avoid induction in the armed forces during the Vietnam War.

Minutes from the university is the central **Piazza Cavour** and the **Caffè Pedrocchi,** a point of reference for local intellectuals and artists. Its neoclassical design dates from 1831. Recent rumors that it was headed for a fast-food fate sparked outrage in the nation's press; according to local tourist board officials, the reports were no more than "malicious."

Padua's major artistic attraction is the **Scrovegni Chapel,** a short stroll north of Piazza Cavour to Corso Garibaldi. The 14th-century chapel is adorned with magnificent frescoes by Giotto and sculptures by Pisano. (Open March 16 to October 15 9 A.M. to 12:30 P.M. and 2:20 to 5:30 P.M.; in winter, 9:30 A.M. to 12:30 P.M. and 1:30 to 4:30 P.M.; closed Sunday and holiday afternoons.)

The **basilica** is located in Piazza del Santo, near the southern perimeter of the old city walls. The 15th-century **equestrian statue** in the piazza is by Donatello, of Venetian commander Erasmo da Narni. Architectural styles compete in the multidomed and spired red brick structure, begun in 1232, a year after the saint's death, and completed in 1307. Fused into the structure are the Gothic, Romanesque, Venetian, and Byzantine.

The imposing three interior naves open onto lateral side

Giotto, *Frescoes* of the Arena Chapel (Capella degli Scrovegni) (1305-1306)

Chronologically, Giotto belongs to the late Middle Ages, but artistically, he opened the door to the Renaissance. His empathy, sense of drama, genius for emotion, and expressive line lend his figures a degree of naturalism never before achieved in painting. Dante was a friend from whom he may have learned the skill of story-telling, but his hero was Saint Francis, whose appealing creed of compassion and simplicity inspired his artistic style. Unlike Francis, however, Giotto was no aspirant to poverty; his commissions made him rich.

In 1305, Giotto undertook this impressive cycle of 38 frescoes illustrating the history of the Virgin and Christ. The blue barrel-vaulted ceiling of the chapel and Giotto's use of harmonious color throughout create a unified impression, although the schematization is complex. The panels "read" horizontally, left to right. Three tiers of frescoes line the side walls, one devoted to the life of Mary (the top row of panels on both walls), another to the life of Christ (the middle rows), and a third to the events leading up to and following the Crucifixion (the lower panels). The entrance wall is given to *The Last Judgment,* which may be compared with Michelangelo's treatment of the same subject two centuries later. As you follow the sequence, notice the wonderful variety of facial expressions—Giotto's specialty.

Pause on your way out at *The Lamentation,* three panels from *The Last Judgment* on the lower band to your right. Here Giotto's skill is shown to great advantage. Each mourner is individualized, yet the sense of collective grief is palpable. The diagonal rocky ledge, emphasized by the outstretched arms of one disciple, draws our attention to Christ's face in the lower corner where Mary cradles his head. Two mourners seen from the rear frame the tableau. In anguish, angles twist in the sky.

—Michael Hinden

chapels. Main points in the richly decorated basilica are the principal **altar** and the **saint's chapel,** from the 16th century and containing nine marble sculptures depicting miracles attributed to the saint. Decorating the main altar is a bas-relief in bronze by Donatello.

❦ RESTAURANTS

Il Burchiello, Via Venezia 42, Oriago; tel. (041) 429415. On the Brenta near some of the more famous Venetian villas, this air-conditioned restaurant affords the opportunity for a pleasant stroll along the canal to admire the villas and observe the barge traffic; it all puts the area into another dimension. Fish is the main fare; there is a house wine and a good selection of local DOC brands. Meals run Lit. 70,000–90,000. Closed Thurs. evening and Mon. No cards.

Cavalca, Via Manin 8; tel. (049) 39244. In the heart of Padua's old town near the cathedral, this air-conditioned restaurant has a local menu featuring *gnocchi* and *pasta e fagioli.* With a good house wine the tab will be Lit. 25,000–30,000. Closed Tues. evening, Wed., Jan., and July 1–10. All cards.

Alle Magnolie, Via Nazareth 39; tel. (049) 756155. This modern, air-conditioned restaurant featuring Veneto meat and fish recipes is just beyond the old city walls off Via Iacopo Facciolati. An open inner court is available for dining. Well managed, the Magnolie has a wide selection of local DOC wines and its own house wine. Dinners run Lit. 25,000–40,000. Closed Mon., Aug. 1–15. AE.

Da Nalin, Via Nuovissimo 29, Mira; tel. (041) 420083. The Nalin's seafood dining experience is well known through northern Italy. *Alla carta* dining is possible for Lit. 40,000–50,000. But that's not the only reason to visit this air-conditioned restaurant 12 miles from Venice and 13 from Padua. Smile and let the house's parade begin—the feast will continue until you say stop. The whole experience, including an excellent house wine, will run Lit. 70,000–90,000. Closed Sun. evening, Mon., and Aug. All cards.

Alla Posta, Via Ca'Tron 91, Dolo; tel. (041) 410740. This characteristic restaurant 13 miles from Venice and 10½ from Padua is a converted Italian mail way station along the Brenta River. Dine in a picturesque converted stable that is modern enough to be air-conditioned. Fresh seafood is the house specialty, with a good house wine and DOC selection. A full meal with wine runs Lit. 50,000–70,000. Closed Tues. No cards.

Treviso

The old town of Treviso is surrounded by 15th-century ramparts and a moat. This delightful hinterland surprise is only twenty to thirty minutes north of Venice. Navigation was once possible from Venice to Treviso on inland canals; the town and its province were summer holiday retreats for Venetian nobility.

Spas and Springs

Besides the country's most professional and efficient hospital and preventive-medicine systems, the Veneto can claim one of Europe's most extensive thermal cure and rehabilitation centers.

Roman ruins date the origin of the spas at **Abano** and **Montegrotto Terme,** which have expanded with additional treatment centers at **Battaglia** and **Galzignano.** Only 15 minutes south of Padua, the area seems more luxurious than would be expected of a refuge for the relief of rheumatic and arthritic disturbances.

More than 150 hotels from luxury to modest, able to accommodate 16,000, provide a holiday retreat atmosphere with 151 indoor and outdoor pools, tennis courts, golf courses, and organized galas that have been known to include early-morning spa treatments.

Less mundane is the mineral-water spa at **Recoaro Terme.** Eight different springs have brought fame over the last three hundred years to this area northwest of Vicenza in the upper Agno valley, tucked between the Little Dolomites.

Information may be obtained from Laura Graziano, Dipartimento per il Turismo–Regione Veneto, Palazzo Sceriman, Cannaregio 168, 30100 Venezia; tel. (041) 792646.

The city's pedestrian inner center, around **Piazza dei Signori,** is the gathering point for an *aperitif,* espresso, or just pure gossip. The narrow, porticoed aisles weaving past shops, caffès, and inner-city canals are a lesson in relaxation, welcome breaks from the tourist trail. This is the beauty of the former agrarian center that is now the home of the clothing firm Benetton.

Main points of interest include the **Luigi Bailo Civic Museum,** Borgo Cavour 22 (open 9 A.M. to noon and 2 to 5 P.M.; closed Monday, Sunday afternoon, and holidays). On exhibit are Roman relics and a picture gallery with paintings and sculptures by prominent Veneto artists: Titian, Lorenzo Lotto, Cima da Conegliano, and Jacopo Bassano, among others. Of medieval origin, the **Cathedral,** on Piazza del Duomo, was rebuilt in the 15th, 16th, and 18th centuries. In a chapel is Titian's *Annunciation,* along with works by Paris Bordone and Girolamo da Treviso il Vecchio.

Treviso's countryside is dotted with a number of Venetian villas, the most impressive being **Villa Barbaro (Volpi),** thirty miles northwest of Treviso at Maser, just beyond Asolo (hometown of Eleonora Duse, Italy's famous tragic actress). The villa was constructed by Palladio in the mid-16th century. Containing frescoes by Paolo Veronese and statues and stuccoes by Alessandro Vittoria, the villa has limited hours: Tuesday, Saturday, Sunday, and national holidays from 3 to 6 P.M. June through September; 2 to 5 P.M. October through March.

Closed Easter, August 15, November 1, December 8, and December 24 to January 7.

❧ RESTAURANTS

Le Beccherie, Piazza Ancillotto 10; tel. (0422) 540871. The air-conditioned restaurant also offers outdoor dining in the heart of old Treviso. Try the *baccalà* and *polenta* with the local house white wine. The restaurant is part of a 28-room, 2-star hotel; 16 of its rooms have private bath, and rates are Lit. 32,000–57,000. In the restaurant, a meal with house wine is Lit. 30,000–35,000. A *pensione* plan is available. Closed Thurs. evening, Fri., July. All cards.

Ciarnie, Via Chiesa 2, Località Pagnano, Asolo; tel. (0423) 52237. If you're visiting the Villa Barbaro, stop at this hillside restaurant, with outdoor summer dining and an assortment of roast and boiled meats and fowl from the serving cart. Dinners run Lit. 20,000–25,000 with house wine. Closed Mon. evening, Tues. No cards.

Due Mori, Piazza Duse 229; tel. (0423) 52256. This atmospheric *locanda* even has three rooms to let (Lit. 22,000–37,000 without bath) if the meal is too filling. *Pasta e fagioli* and grilled chicken are house specialties in this well-known glimpse into yesteryear. Dinner runs Lit. 30,000–35,000 with wine. Closed Wed. All cards.

La Piola, Via Filodrammatici 9; tel. (0422) 540287. Just 50 yards from the Piazza dei Signori heart of Treviso, this elegant air-conditioned restaurant is a favorite with local "young lions" and visiting theater troupes. *Gnocchi* heads the list of local specialties, along with (deliberately) room-temperature soups, appealing in any season. There are two dining areas inside and one on the balcony. Dinners range Lit. 20,000–35,000 with a regional wine. Closed Mon. All cards.

Righetto al Cacciatore, Via Ciardi 2; tel. (0422) 370804. In Quinto di Treviso, 4 miles from Treviso, this is typical of the *trattoria-albergo* found in the Veneto's rural areas. Freshwater fish leads a regional menu that also includes a rabbit cacciatore. A full meal with house wine runs Lit. 30,000. The 2-star hotel has nine rooms with shower for Lit. 26,000–42,000. Closed Mon., Jan. All cards.

Toni del Spin, Via Inferiore 7; tel. (0422) 543829. This rustic, family-style, air-conditioned trattoria in the heart of Treviso is a step into the past. The home cooking includes *risotto con luganega* (soft sausage found only in the Veneto), a good meal starter. A full meal with house wine runs about Lit. 25,000. Closed Sun., Mon. morning, and Aug. No cards.

Vicenza

This is the heart of Palladio country. Appropriately, the main street in Vicenza is **Corso Andrea Palladio,** and climaxes at his most famous work, the **Teatro Olimpico** (Olympic Theater) in Piazza Matteotti. Severely damaged by Allied bombing raids, this outstanding architectural legacy has been lovingly restored. A walking tour of Vicenza should start in **Piazzale De Gaspari** at the beginning of Corso Palladio east to Piazza Matteotti, with a detour to the central **Piazza dei Signori** off Via Cavour.

Palladio's magic touch has been described as the perfect architectural union of the grandeur of Rome with the brightness of the Venetian painting traditions. This Venetian-Roman unity of Palladio and his leading pupil Scamozzi can be compared with the pure Renaissance early 16th-century structures of the **Angaran** and **Negri palaces,** both in Vicenza on Contra Zanella.

Palladio's most famous projects in Vicenza are the white marble 16th-century **basilica** in Piazza dei Signori (the symbol of Vicenza; the name is used in the Roman sense of a hall of justice), and the **Chiericati Palace,** now the Civic Museum, at Piazza Matteotti 39 (near the Teatro Olimpico). Another outstanding work is **La Rotunda** or **Villa Capra,** which Scamozzi completed. Only the park is open to the public (9 A.M. to noon and 3 to 6 P.M.; closed November 16 to March 14; to reach the villa, leave Vicenza by Route 4 and take the

Andrea Palladio, Villa Capra (La Rotonda), (1569)

This is a house where the enlightened Renaissance Man could retire to an antique dream of a beautifully ordered natural life. Palladio laid out his principles of architecture in his still influential book, the *Quattro Libri* (1570). The villa was designed for the papal prelate Paolo Almerico and is currently owned by the Valmarana family.

La Rotunda commands the top of a gentle hill a few minutes outside of Vicenza, where it takes advantage of pastoral views. Seeking to evoke associations with the splendors of Imperial Rome, Palladio joined four classical temple fronts with the solid cubic form of the main block. A central cupola over the rotunda, (which gives the villa its nickname) crowns the composition. Impressive runs of stairs join the temple facades to the ground. One front is used as the main entry (not the one originally intended), with a landscaped drive and court. Sculptures for the grounds and building were completed around 1600, based on Palladio's published intentions in *Quattro Libri.*

The interior, not open to the public, is featured in Joseph Losey's film *Don Giovanni.* The traditional Mediterranean atrium house is successfully blended with the monumentality of the central church. Rooms, vestibules, and stairs are arranged around the domed rotunda, which originally had an oculus (a circular opening) at the top. Mannerist frescoes by various artists decorate the walls.

—Mary Beth Betts and Charles Ayes

second road to the right). Also on Piazza dei Signori are the Palladio-designed **Loggia del Capitanito,** formerly the home of the Venetian governor, and the 12th-century **Torre di Piazza** or **Bissara.**

Arriving in **Piazza Matteotti,** the **Civic Museum** (open 9:30 A.M. to noon and 2:30 to 5 P.M.) exhibits 14th- to 18th-century Veneto artists, projects by Palladio, archaeological exhibits from the province, coins, and stamps. Also on Piazza Matteotti is Palladio's **Teatro Olimpico,** completed by Scamozzi in 1583 after his master's death (open 9:30 A.M. to 12:30 P.M. and 3 to 5:30 P.M., 2 to 4:30 P.M. in winter; closed Sunday afternoons, holidays, and during theatrical productions). Sophocles's *Oedipus Tyrranus* was the first play performed here, in 1585.

Slightly over a mile south of Vicenza, on **Monte Berico,** is a 17th-century **basilica** reputedly originally erected in the 15th-century in just three months as a sign of devotion during a plague that was devastating Vicenza; the basilica completed, the pestilence subsided in 1428. The cry of miracle attracted pilgrims from throughout the Veneto, and the church was expanded in the late 17th century. From Monte Berico there is a fine view of the area. Finer feasts for the eyes are Bartolommeo Montagna's *Madonna with Christ* to the right of the main altar and his *Pietà* in the vestry. In the adjacent refectory is the 1572 *Feast of Saint Gregory The Great* by Paolo Veronese, measuring over 15 by 30 feet.

For those with a serious interest in Palladio, all information can be obtained from: Centro Internazionale di Studi di Architettetora Andrea Palladio, Basilica Palladiano, Piazza dei Signori, 36100 Vicenza; telephone (0444) 23224.

❦ RESTAURANTS

Al Cappello, Via Fogazzano 82; tel. (0445) 368066. In one of the province's most industrialized towns, Thiene, 12 miles north of Vicenza off A31, this air-conditioned restaurant specializes (reservations only) in wine tastings accompanied by samples of local food. Here mushrooms are in expert hands. Special Veneto recipes will be made on advance request. The cellar includes a wide variety of wines from other regions. The noontime sampling runs Lit. 30,000–40,000 (depending on the wine and food sampled). Closed Sun., Aug. 10–20. No cards.

Cinzia e Valerio, Piazzetta Porta Padova 65/67; tel. (0444) 512796. Part of this air-conditioned restaurant is in (and under) the old walls of the city. Fresh flowers and friendly service complement good seafood and Vicentine recipes; there is outdoor dining in the summer. Dinner can run Lit. 50,000, if you're not tempted by the prestigious wines on offer. Closed Mon., Aug. All cards.

Scudo di Francia, Contrà Piancoli 4; tel. (0444) 228655. This air-conditioned restaurant offers a comfortable step into the 1700s a block from the old town's Piazza delle Erbe. *Risotti* and roasts top a gourmet Veneto menu. Dinners range Lit. 50,000–60,000. Closed Sun. evening, Mon. All cards.

Da Pippo, Via Rendola 53; tel. (0424) 462722. Located in Asiago, 32 miles north of Vicenza in the Sette Comuni highlands, which are a local cool-air summer retreat. The area is known for Asiago cheese, one of the best found in the Veneto. Pippo specializes in seasonal local offerings in his regional recipes. Dinner in the air-conditioned restaurant runs Lit. 35,000–45,000. Closed Tues. evening and Wed. in the off-season. All cards.

Alla Scacchiera, Piazza Castello 49; tel. (0424) 72346. In Marostica, 15 miles north of Vicenza, a town that stages an annual chess match with living chessmen. The characteristic restaurant features *bigoli all'anatra* (pasta with duck), *baccalà alla Vicentina* and *scaloppe* (veal) with mushrooms. Dinners run Lit. 30,000. Closed Sun. evening, Mon. No cards.

Verona

The hub of the Veneto's national and northern European rail and highway traffic, Verona has become the most important mainland center in the region. Its Roman past is vividly evident throughout the city. The Adige flows through Verona in much the same way as the Tiber weaves through Rome, and the city of the Scaligeri is second only to Rome in the importance of its ancient monuments. Verona is a good example of competent management and civic pride.

Immortalized by William Shakespeare's *Romeo and Juliet* and *The Two Gentlemen of Verona,* the city was already an important Roman municipality on the Via Augusta in 49 B.C. In later centuries Verona was the center of the rule of the Scaligeri family, who dominated most of the Veneto and parts of Lombardy and Emilia in the 13th and 14th centuries. The city spent nearly four hundred years under the doges of Venice, until Napoleonic forces arrived. Ceded to Austria in 1814, Verona became part of a united Italy in 1866.

After the fall of Fascism in the final stages of the World War II campaign in Italy, the German high command established its headquarters in Verona and backed former dictator Benito Mussolini's puppet regime at Salò on the western coast of Lake Garda. The city suffered heavy damage in Allied bombing raids. Verona was also site of the Republic of Salò's mock trial and execution of former members of the Fascist hierarchy. Mussolini refused to intervene, despite his daughter Edda's pleas for the life of her husband, former Italian foreign minister Count Galeazzo Ciano. The German troops abandoned Verona before the arrival of Allied forces, but destroyed all bridges across the Adige before departing.

Dominating Verona is the spacious **Piazza Bra,** with its promenade and caffès and restaurants that flow onto the sidewalks during the warmer months. At opposite extremes of the promenade, facing one another across the Bra gardens, are the first-century **Roman Arena** and the early 17th-century **Gran Guardia,** which hosts most of the major exhibits and cultural events in the city. The nearly perfect acoustics in the Arena make it an ideal (and impressive) outdoor setting for the city's annual summer opera spectaculars.

Tickets for the Verona Opera must be ordered in advance. Contact: Ente Lirico Arena di Verona, Piazza Bra, 37100 Verona; (045) 8003520.

The two **14th-century arches** opening onto Corso Porto Nuova, which leads to the major rail terminal, are a reminder of the brief rule of the Viscontis.

Off the Piazza Bra is the **Via Mazzini** promenade past the city's most fashionable shops, leading to **Piazza Erbe** and its open-air fruit and vegetable market. To the right, before entering the market, is the 13th-century **Capuleti home** at Via Cappello 23, with **Juliet's** famous **balcony** within the small courtyard.

Piazza delle Erbe is on the site of the forum of the old Roman city where chariot races were once run. At the north end of the square is one of the city's few baroque monuments, the 17th-century **Palazzo Maffei,** crowned with statues of Hercules, Jupiter, Venus, Mercury, Apollo, and Minerva. In front of the building is a Venetian marble **column** topped by the winged lion. In the center of the square is the 14th-century **Madonna of Verona fountain,** in the shadow of the over 270-foot-high **Lamberti clock tower.** Its hourly gongs are not conducive to sleep in nearby hotels. To climb the tower for a fine view over old town, enter through the arch to the right of the Bar Trieste. This **Arco della Costa** (so-called for the rib bone of a whale that hangs from its center) leads into the Romanesque-Gothic **Old Market courtyard** with its ornate **Stairs of Reason.**

Continue on through the arch into **Piazza dei Signori** (known locally as Piazza Dante because of the statue of the author in the center; Dante's first refuge after exile from Florence was in Verona). To the right, before reaching the Scaligeri tombs, are recently uncovered **archaeological ruins** from Roman times.

The **Tombs of the Scaligeri** family are surrounded by wrought iron grills featuring the Scaligeri crest, in places linked but not fixed, testifying to the master workmanship of local craftsmen. Overlooking the tombs and closing most of the east end of the square is the late 13th-century **Scaligeri residence,** which became the **Governor's Palace** under the rule of the Venetians. The lower building to the north is the 15th-century **Loggia del Consiglio,** Verona's most graceful Renaissance remnant. Off the square on Via Arche Scaligere is the **Casa Montecchi,** Romeo's home.

The best time to walk through the heart of old Verona is in the morning, when the colorful Erbe market is in full swing under its picturesque umbrellas.

Unless otherwise noted, historic sites are open 9 A.M. to 12:30 P.M. and 2:30 to 5:30 P.M., to 6 in summer. Closed Monday.

Other sightseeing suggestions include **Castelvecchio,** five minutes from Piazza Bra on Via Roma or a straight 15-minute walk from Piazza Erbe beginning on Corso Porta Borsari. This will take you through the first-century Roman **Arco dei Gavi** and **Porta Borsari,** once a gate to the Roman city. The 14th-century castle, built by a Scaligeri, has undergone extensive renovation, especially after World War II. The **Bridge of the Scaligeri** behind the castle and across the Adige was totally destroyed by retreating German troops, but was reconstructed. The castle houses the city art museum, with works by Pisanello, Mantegna, Gentile and Giovanni Bellini, Liberale da Verona, Veronese, Brusasorci, Tintoretto, and so forth. (Open 9 A.M. to 12:30 P.M. and 2:30 to 5:30 P.M., to 6 P.M. in summer; closed Monday and holidays.)

The **Church of San Zeno Major** and its cloisters, in Piazza San Zeno, were founded in the fifth century over the tomb of the first bishop and patron saint of Verona. Destroyed by the Lombards, San Zeno was rebuilt in the 12th century. The basilica is an Italian Romanesque masterpiece; its 12th-century bronze sheathing has just been restored and stolen portions replaced. Highlight of the splendid interior is Mantegna's triptych altarpiece, once removed by Napoleon. Enter the graceful cloisters through the left aisle of the basilica; they were once part of a Benedictine monastery.

The **Duomo,** in Piazza del Duomo, is a 12th-century cathedral built on the site of an earlier church and enlarged between 1444 and the end of the 16th century. Inside is Titian's *Assumption.* The cathedral complex includes two smaller churches, a cloister, library, and bishop's residence.

The exact age of the Roman **Ponte della Pietra** across the Adige is unknown. Faithfully reconstructed after it was destroyed in World War II, the bridge connects the Castel San Pietro and the Roman Theater area with a rebuilt old town that has become one of the most exclusive areas of Verona.

Straight up from the Ponte della Pietra is the **Castel San Pietro,** begun by the Venetians on a Visconti plan and completed by the Austrians at the end of the 19th century. Legend says this was the site of the castle of Ostrogoth King Theodoric; the Romans built fortifications here. The patio offers the most splendid view of Verona along the Adige.

The best-preserved **Roman Theater** in the Veneto, from the first century B.C., is built into the hillside below Castel San Pietro. It is the site of Verona's summer theater festival. On its site is the 10th-century **Santa Libera Church** and the former **San Girolamo monastery.** An elevator is available for the hillside archaeological museum. (Open 9 A.M. to noon and 2:30 to 5:30 P.M., to 6 P.M. in summer; closed Monday and holidays.)

For tickets and information about the summer theater program, contact Estate Teatrale Veronese, Teatro Romano, Rig. Redentore, 37100 Verona; inquiries can be made in English—or telephone in Italian (045) 8000360.

The **Giusti Gardens,** on Via Giusti, are a ten-minute walk from the amphitheater. This terraced labyrinth of well-manicured hedgerows and flowerbeds framed by cypress trees is a fine example of 17th- and 18th-century Italian gardens. Hidden behind walls on a narrow street, the gardens offer more fine views of Verona across the Adige.

In **Juliet's Tomb** and the **Fresco Museum** on Via del Pontiere, legend reigns over fact, dramatized in Shakespeare's play and Zeffirelli's film of Verona's feuding Guelph and Ghibelline clans. A former custodian at the Tomb, whose fertile imagination fielded thousands of questions about one of the most celebrated love stories of all times, passed his retirement days traveling through the generosity of honeymooners and the lovelorn who made pilgrimages to Verona.

RESTAURANTS

Arche, Via Arche Scaligere 6; tel. (045) 8007415. A fine example of local ingenuity is Giancarlo Gioco's cuttlefish and eggplant soup. For pasta lovers, the shellfish ravioli comes highly recommended. A well-supplied *cantina* can make the tab soar. Reservations are suggested. With a house wine dinner runs Lit. 60,000. Closed Sun., Mon. noon, and June 20–July 18. AE.

Al Cristo, Piazzetta Pescheria; tel. (045) 30550. In the heart of old Verona is this characteristic 18th-century trattoria offering outdoor summer dining. *Pasta e fagioli* or *lesso con pearà* (boiled meat or chicken with a local gravy) are a must. Dinners run Lit. 15,000–20,000. Closed Sat. evening, Sun., and July. No cards.

Il Desco, Via dietro San Sebastiano 7; tel. (045) 595358. Seafood reigns in the kitchen of two youngsters (Elia and Natale) who can claim one of the best restaurants in the Veneto. Shellfish *antipasti,* tagliatelle with crabmeat sauce, and a wide range of tempting second courses plus a good Veneto DOC wine can cost around Lit. 65,000. Closed Sun. All cards.

Osteria La Fontanina, Portichetti Fontanelle 3; tel. (045) 973305. In the oldest section of Verona (San Stefano) 100 yards from the historic Ponte della Pietra is this den featuring home-style Veronese fare such as *gnocchi* and *pastissada.* Dinner runs Lit. 18,000–20,000 with house wine. Closed Sun. and Aug.

All'Oste Scuro, Vicolo San Silvestro 10; tel. (045) 592650. This warm, friendly osteria is off the central Via Roma connecting Castelvecchio and the Piazza Bra. Specialties include *pastissada* and *pasta e fagioli* prepared in the best Veronese fashion. With a house wine dinner runs Lit. 20,000–30,000. Closed Sun., Aug. No cards.

Re Teodorico, Piazzale Castel San Pietro; tel. (045) 49990. The terrace over the old Roman theater offers an unforgettable view of the Adige and the old town of Verona. Regional fare with a seafood accent is accompanied by a good Veneto wine selection. Dinner runs Lit. 40,000–60,000. Closed Wed., Nov. All cards.

Lake Garda

Lake Garda (Lago di Garda) is the largest freshwater body in Italy. It is bordered by Lombardy's Brescia on the south and west, Trentino on the north, and Veneto's Verona province on the east and south.

Just 17 miles from Piazza Bra in the center of Verona is **Peschiera del Garda,** the first major town on the nearly 50 miles of Veronese shoreline along SS249 north to Trentino's Riva del Garda.

Spring and fall are the best months to enjoy the natural beauty of this "Riviera of Olives," overrun by elbow-to-elbow German and Dutch mobs in the peak summer months.

After a brief bout with pollution, the lake once again has crystal-clear waters yielding delicious fish dinners. The cypress-lined, craggy coast is interrupted by the private park and gardens of **Villa Guarienti** on Punta di San Vigilio, between the towns of Garda and Torri del Benaco. The 16th-century villa and grounds are private, but they can be opened to the public on special request; Prince Charles was a recent houseguest on a visit to northern Italy.

Local fishermen can be hired from Garda and Torri del Benaco for cruises to admire the lake and the beauty of the coast, villa, and park, with Monte Baldo as a backdrop.

On the short drive from Verona, three miles from the lake at Castelnuovo del Garda, is **Gardaland,** one of Europe's largest amusement parks, with rides and intents to re-create the fantasy of Disneyland. Planned expansion was underway for the 1989 summer season.

The Dolomite Alps

Rising from the Bardolino wine country on the eastern shore of Lake Garda (Lago di Garda), Monte Baldo and the Lessini foothills of the **Dolomite Alps** extend to the Sette Comuni highlands of northern Vicenza and soar to the Alpine peaks of northern Belluno.

Here legend and history are easily apparent, from the Montecchio castle ruins west of Vicenza, north to the "petrified lagoon" of Bolca where archaeologists are still uncovering fossils of saltwater fish believed to be millions of years old, to today's "paths of peace" for hikers, following World War I front lines.

Tens of thousands of Italians and Austro-Hungarians died during the war years in this Alpine area. A Monte Grappa **war memorial** and two cemeteries contain nearly 25,000 war dead, while another 10,000 are buried near Pocol, along the scenic SS48 Grand Highway of the Dolomites, which links Cortina d'Ampezzo with its winter wonderland counterparts in Trentino-Alto Adige (see the Northeast Italy chapter).

Belluno

This provincial seat north of Treviso is overshadowed by its surrounding winter and summer resorts in the Dolomites.

On the Piave River, with a population of just over 36,000, Belluno's past can be seen through porticoed old-town streets and Gothic and Renaissance buildings. On Piazza del Duomo are the 16th-century **baptistery** and **cathedral,** with some intriguing paintings from the Venetian school, and an 18th-century bell tower by Filippo Juvara.

RESTAURANTS

Alle Schiette, SS51 at Ponte nelle Alpi, Località Ponte delle Schiette, near Lago Santa Croce; tel. (0437) 900203. Located on the highway for Cortina d'Ampezzo between Vittorio Veneto and Belluno, this rustic hillside trattoria offers open-air dining in the summer and a blazing fireplace in the winter to accompany its assortment of regional wines and fare. Dinners range Lit. 25,000–30,000. Closed Mon., July 4–Sept. 3. AE, V.

Taverna, Via Cipro 7; tel. (0437) 25192. Near the cathedral in the center of Belluno, local game is featured along with regional wines. With a good house wine dinner can run Lit. 20,000–30,000. Closed Sun., Aug. AE.

Tre Gai, Via Villapaiera 45, Feltre; tel. (0439) 80260. The name is not deceiving. A good local menu with mushrooms prepared in a variety of recipes has made the restaurant a favorite with locals and visiting businessmen. Feltre is southwest of Belluno, off SS50. Even with wine the tab rarely goes over Lit. 25,000. Closed Wed. AE.

Cortina d'Ampezzo

Site of the 1956 Winter Olympics, Cortina is the most complete **winter sports center** in the Dolomites. Miles of downhill runs and cross-country courses are serviced by lifts and cable cars. The cable ride from the pinewood **Ice Stadium** to the 10,673-foot summit of Tofane di mezzo unveils the pure beauty of the vista from the central Alps to the Po plain.

For better or worse, Cortina emerged as a winter resort when such pastimes were considered a monopoly of the more affluent. While Cortina still maintains this poshness, other more affordable areas are developing close to neighboring Trentino ski stations.

The **Agordino Dolomites** offer more than 140 hotels that can accommodate 5,000, while six campgrounds can host 2,000-plus, and private homes and apartments can accommodate nearly 12,000. The area offers 166-plus miles of ski runs and nearly one hundred miles of cross-country courses serviced by cable cars and chair lifts.

The area is tied into the **Dolomiti Superski circuit** and the run around the Sella and the Tre Valli ski area to San Pellegrino and Moena (see the "Northeast Italy" chapter).

The summer season offers hikers a complex web of safe trails in the Pale Mountains, between the provinces of Belluno and Trento, well marked at altitudes of over 2,700 feet and lined with bivouac areas, refuges, and refreshment points.

Information can be obtained from the Azienda di Promozione "Dolomite Agordine," Palazzo del Municipio, 32020 Falcade (BL); tel. (0437) 59241; telex 440821 AAST FC I.

❦ RESTAURANTS

Baita Fraina, Località Fraina 1; tel. (0436) 3634. The Menardi family's rustic little restaurant a mile from the center of Cortina d'Ampezzo also offers several modest, comfortable rooms. Try the *zuppa d'orzo* and grilled meats; in winter go local with *polenta,* melted cheese, and sausage. With a local wine, a meal runs Lit. 40,000. Closed Mon., Oct. 1–Nov. 30. No cards.

Il Meloncino, Località Gillardon 17; tel. (0436) 861043. On SS48 south of Cortina d'Ampezzo toward Pocol, the Melòn family has acquired a strong following for one of the best local restaurants. Since settings are limited to just 25, reservations are a must. An added venture is **Il Meloncino al Lago,** tel. (0436) 60376, almost 2 miles away overlooking Ghedina's lake; it's managed by the same five-member clan. Dinner at either, without wine, runs Lit. 40,000. Closed Tues., June, and Nov. No cards.

13

NORTHEASTERN ITALY

Northeastern Italy offers one of Europe's most complete vacation experiences. Considering the multitude of alternatives—world-class skiing, hiking, houseboating on the Adriatic, relaxing beside mountain lakes—the biggest dilemma facing the visitor is what, when, and where.

Northeastern Italy consists of the autonomous provinces of Trento (also called Trient or Trentino) and Bolzano (or Bozen, Alto Adige, or the Südtirol), which together form the Trentino-Alto Adige region; as well as the Friuli-Venezia Giulia region along the Adriatic, which became Italian in 1919 when the Treaty of Versailles eviscerated the Austro-Hungarian Empire following World War I. (In doing so, the territorial limits of the Augustan era of the Roman Empire were restored.)

Volcanic eruptions and Ice Age glaciers created towering Alpine peaks and graceful valleys along the area's northern borders with Switzerland, Austria, and Yugoslavia. The south is contained by the Adriatic and the eastern extreme of the Venetian lagoon.

German-speaking Bolzano and the ethnic Italian territory of Trentino provide two international experiences. In Bolzano's Alta Badia Valley the Ladin dialect provides a lexical link between northern and southern European civilizations.

Supreme in the area's Alpine system are the Dolomites, named after French geologist Déodat de Dolomieu, who discovered in these mountains the magnesium-calcium rock that also bears his name. Minerals in the range form a rocky rainbow with blue-black streaks, yellow spots, and brilliant reds that leap to life at sunset.

Flanking the Dolomites are the Brenta and Adria Alps, which also warrant stops on the ski circuit. Four-time World Cup winner Gustav Thöni is from Trafoi, in western Bolzano.

Modern chalet-style hotels and lodgings in medieval castles are both available, especially around the towns of Merano and Bolzano. This Tyrolean area traces its origin to the Counts of Tyrol, who reigned in Merano until the 14th century. It is certainly one of the most picturesque areas in the entire territory.

In the summer the mountain resorts are perfect for escaping the heat and urban chaos. There's a bit of a *paesano* in every Italian, and the return to small-town living—though some areas can be crowded in summer—is a call from the past, when simple, friendly human contact was the norm. The towns and hillsides are full of strollers—you don't need to hike or climb to fully enjoy the area, though this is serious hiking country: paths are marked, and hikers can get detailed information from local tourist offices.

When the winter mantle of snow melts into streams and rivers nature's beauty flowers here. The tri-regional (Lombardy, Trentino, and Veneto) Lake Garda comes to life, along with the summer Gulf of Trieste resorts at Grado and Lignano, where houseboats are available to tour the lagoon.

But nature has not always smiled on northeastern Italy. Scars are still evident from the 1976 earthquakes that devastated the area west of Udine, and the 1963 dam disaster at Vajont in that sliver of the Veneto province of Belluno that finds its way into the Dolomites.

TRAVEL

Flying

The only commercial airport in the Bolzano-Trentino and Friuli-Venezia Giulia regions is Ronchi dei Legionari, 21½ miles northwest of Trieste. The airport is 14 miles from Gorizia, 26½ miles from Udine, and 47 miles from Pordenone. Alitalia airport bus service is available to these Friuli-Venezia Giulia provincial capitals; details are given below.

Trento and Bolzano must rely on the Villafranca airport at Verona. The two provincial capitals are 66 and 98 miles north of Verona, respectively. Villafranca is only 7½ miles from Verona's main rail terminal and just a 5-min. drive to the Brenner–Moden Autostrada 22.

Daily flights connect Ronchi dei Legionari with Linate airport in Milan (a 50-min. trip) and Leonardo da Vinci in Rome (70 min.). There are Wed., Thurs., and Sun. flights to Forlì (1 hour), 38 miles southeast of Bologna. For airport information on Alitalia, Ati, and Aliblu flights tel. (0481) 7731.

Bus service from Trieste to the airport is available at the main rail terminal, Piazza della Libertà. Additional information is provided by the Cosulich Agency, Piazza Sant'Antonio 1; tel. (040) 68017, 630143, or 65108.

Taking The Train

The Brenner–Bolzano–Trento–Verona rail line is an intricate component of the international Trans-European Express (TEE) route to Innsbruck, Munich, and large portions of northern Europe. The Venice–Udine line is on the most direct route to Vienna and other central European destinations.

Cortina d'Ampezzo is the most notable exception to the identical rail-and-road-access rule. Rail travel to this town is through Venice to Calalzo di Cadore, while the most convenient automobile access is by the SS241 from Bolzano that connects with SS48, the scenic Dolomite Drive.

Taking the Bus

Provincial bus service is available, but since it is the only public transportation between valley villages and larger towns it can be a time-consuming milk run.

Driving

Terrain and weather dictate travel throughout most of northeastern Italy. Though snow can close Alpine passes to Switzerland and Austria from Nov. to May, removal efforts are always at a maximum to ensure that the Brenner Pass to Innsbruck remains open, as well as routes connecting valley villages to mainstream mountain road and rail traffic.

The Alps have obliged major highway and rail routes to follow the same "L" pattern from Brenner, Bolzano, and Trento to Verona, then eastward to Vicenza, Padua, Venice-Mestre, and around the northern shores of the Adriatic to Trieste.

The principal north–south highway is the A22, which joins the Milan–Rome A1 at Modena, while east-to-west is the A4 Trieste–Turin highway. The A22 and A4 cross at Verona near the airport.

CAR RENTALS

In proportion to the geographic size of the region, auto rental service is limited. Here is what is available:

Bolzano: Avis, Piazza Verdi 18; tel. (0471) 971467. Hertz, Via Alto Adige 30; tel. (0471) 977155. Maggiore, Via Garibaldi 32; tel. (0471) 971531.

Calalzo di Cadore (18½ miles southeast of Cortina): Avis, Localita Noai 47; tel. (0435) 72663.

Riva del Garda: Avis, Viale Rovereto 76; tel. (0464) 552282.

Trieste (Airport): Avis, tel. (0481) 777085. Europcar, tel. (0481) 778920; telex 461173. Hertz, tel. (0481) 777600.

    (City): Avis, Via S. Nicolò 12; tel. (040) 68243. Hertz, Via Mazzini 1; tel. (040) 60650; telex 410092. Maggiore, Viale Miramare 2; tel. (040) 42323.

Note: Verona information is listed in the Veneto "Travel" section.

✿ ACCOMMODATIONS

Area accommodations offer a number of pleasant surprises, as the local classification system tends to underrate. Most local tourist information offices are highly efficient.

Credit cards are listed as accepted. "All cards" means that all of the following are accepted: AE—American Express; DC—Diner's Club; MC—MasterCard; V—Visa. Price ranges given indicate the span between single and double rooms, unless otherwise indicated.

Two exceptional regional experiences are staying in castle hotels in the Südtirol and traveling by houseboat to Adriatic coasts and lagoons.

Houseboats

The houseboat is an unforgettable experience. Solo and caravan excursions can be arranged (with the Trident company coordinating mooring) from Trieste to Venice, where only the Grand Canal is off limits. Shorter runs are possible to Grado, just across the local lagoon.

For the more sun-and-fun-inclined, anchoring offshore avoids crowded beaches and the murky water along the immediate shore. The top of the cabin is a perfect sun deck, as well as a diving platform. Underfoot are food and drink, easily stocked from a local store, as well as shade for a siesta. At the end of the day you just chug back to a mooring slot and dine in a nearby restaurant or trattoria to sample the local food and wine.

The houseboats are based behind Lignano's three lidos—Riviera, Pineta, and Sabbiadoro—12 miles south of the A4, halfway between Venice and Trieste, less than 50 miles to either.

Each trailer-style cabin usually is equipped with three sets of bunk beds, a kitchenette, shower, and toilet. Usually 10½ feet by 25 feet, the boats are powered by 20-horsepower diesel engines. No special nautical license is required to operate one. The July–Aug. weekly rate is Lit. 1,500,000. The May–June–Sept. weekly rate is Lit. 1,120,000. During the rest of the year the rate is only Lit. 770,000. Arrangements are coordinated with Ezio Conti, Trident Sail, Darsena Aprilia Marittima, 33050 Pertegada (UD); tel. (0431) 53301 or 53345; telex 461059 APRIMA I. No permanent staff member is fluent in English, so if you don't speak Italian, write or wire; replies will be in English.

Bolzano (Südtirol)

Any of these accommodations make good bases from which to explore the mountains and colorful Tyrolean towns of the Bolzano area (also called the Südtirol). Merano is typical of these towns, and is a known health center for its pleasant climate and spa waters. It's only 17 miles from the town of Bolzano, and is perfect for exploring the castles of the area. The wine town Appiano and nearby Missiano and San Michele are right outside Bolzano.

A good base for exploring the slopes of the Val Gardena is Corvara in Badia, which also can act as a base for skiers wanting the Alta Badia and Canazei slopes. Also listed are a few recommendations for Stelvio National Park—in both summer and winter.

Don't expect air-conditioning in the Bolzano area, although you probably won't need it. Nor should you count on castles and inns accepting credit cards.

Skiers should also see the "Skiing" section for accommodations and transportation information.

SÜDTIROL CASTLES

The castles in the province of Bolzano are not a state-run chain like Spain's *paradores* or the *posadas* in Portugal. But Bolzano's efficient Provincial Tourist office can furnish complete information, including prices. Write to Bozen Tourist Office, Attn: Frau Frass, Pfarrplatz 11/12, 39100 Bolzano; tel. (0471) 993808; telex 400158.

The castle experience, in which you can live the past today, is concentrated between Merano and the town of Bolzano.

To visit the famous wine town of **Appiano sulla Strada del Vino** (Eppan an der Weinstrasse), stay in **Missiano** or **San Michele:**

Aichberg, Bergstrasse 31, 39057 San Michele (BZ); tel. (0471) 52247. Three stars, 12 rooms, pool, bar, no restaurant, in nearby San Michele. Room with breakfast for two, Lit. 74,000. Open Easter–Nov.

Ansitz Wendelstein, St. Annaweg 9, 39057 San Michele (BZ); tel. (0471) 52122. Three stars, all 19 rooms with bath, diet meals. Room and breakfast for two, Lit. 84,000. Open Easter–Nov.

Matschatsch, Mendelstrasse 32, 39057 San Michele (BZ); tel. (0471) 52035. Two stars, 10 rooms with bath, restaurant, bar, tennis courts. Room and breakfast for two, Lit. 56,000. Open Easter–Nov.

Schloss Kobb C.M./HH, Hocheppanerweg 5, 39057 Missiano (BZ); tel. (0471) 633222. A 4-star, 30-room hotel. Indoor and outdoor pools and tennis courts, restaurant, and bar. Room with breakfast for two costs Lit. 134,000. Open Easter–Nov.

In **Merano:**

Castel Freiberg, 39012 Freiberg (BZ); tel. (0473) 44196. Superior 4 stars, 36 rooms with bath, restaurant, bar, indoor and outdoor pools, tennis courts. Outside Merano. Room and breakfast for two, Lit. 280,000. Open Easter–Nov.

Kur-Hotel Schloss Rundegg, Schenna Strasse 2, 39012 (BZ); tel. (0473) 34364; telex 400840. Superior 4 stars, 30 rooms with bath, restaurant, diet meals, bar, indoor pool. Room and breakfast for two, Lit. 212,000. Open year-round.

SÜDTIROL INNS

From castle to chalet: At **Corvara in Badia,** in the Alta Badia east of the town of Bolzano, it's amazing that **Pensione Christian,** Peskosta 96, 39033 (BZ); tel. (0471) 836201, has just a

2-star rating. This immaculate, four-story *pensione* run by the Pezzei family has 15 rooms with bath and a characteristic Alpine dining room and bar. Bed and breakfast for two is Lit. 70,000; full board in this Ladin inn is only Lit. 65,000 each. Open June–Sept. and Christmas–Easter.

When the Christian is full, the Pezzeis will make arrangements with relatives across the street at the **Piz da l'Ander,** Peskosta 157, 39033 (BZ); tel. (0471) 836185. Seven of the 11 rooms in the Dejacos' newer but less elaborate inn have baths. Here room and breakfast for two is Lit. 52,000.

Nestled amid the trees in **Stelvio National Park** are two fine choices in **Campo Tures** (Sand in Taufers). Both 2-star inns are open all year. The **Berger,** Rein in Taufers 1, 39032 (BZ); tel. (0474) 62507, has a restaurant, bar, indoor pool, and sauna. Room and breakfast for two, Lit. 40,000. Full board is Lit. 41,000 per person. And at the **Moosmair,** Ahornach 44, 39032, (BZ); tel. (0474) 68046, all 15 rooms have bath. Room and breakfast for two, Lit. 38,000. Full board per person, Lit. 37,000.

Trentino and Lignano

In the seasonal Trentino valley mountain hotels and Lignano beach hotels and *pensioni,* minimum stays of three to seven days may be required. The capricious and undecided cannot expect a refund if they move on earlier than planned. These Trentino towns are wonderful for two-season holidays. Enjoy the cool mountain in summer; ski in the winter.

Cavalese (southeast of the town of Bolzano, northeast of Trento) can be a skier's base for Moena, Val di Fiemme, and San Martino ski stations. (See "Skiing," this chapter.) Madonna di Campiglio is a perfect base for—obviously—the skiing at Madonna di Campiglio. Levico Terme is on Lake Caldona. Don't expect air-conditioning at these hotels, or depend on the acceptance of credit cards.

A few suggestions in Trentino are:

CAVALESE
Hotel Cavalese, 38033 (TN); tel. (0462) 30306. Most of Renzo Bonelli's 25 rooms with bath are booked in high season on a year-to-year basis by a faithful clientele, but it's worth a try. Room rates in the 3-star hotel are Lit. 32,000–58,000. Open all year.

LEVICO TERME
Bellavista, Via Vittorio Emanuele 7, 38056 (TN); tel. (0461) 706136 or 706474. The Galvans have renovated an attractive villa into a 3-star, 78-room hotel complete with conference facilities, restaurant, bar, and outdoor pool. Room rates, Lit. 45,000–75,000. In May–June and Sept.–Oct. special weekend rates with full board are offered.

Florida, Viale Segantini 20, 38056 (TN); tel. (0461) 706400 or 707194. A new, 3-star hotel, 43 rooms with bath under the watchful eye of Sergio Arnoldo. Only 30 yards from the lake, the hotel has separate breakfast and dining areas, and a bar and terrace for refreshments in the summer. Room rates, Lit. 47,000–65,000.

Al Sorriso, Viale Segantini, 38056 (TN); tel. (0461) 707029. All the Bommassar family gets in the act to run this 3-star hotel, 42 rooms with bath, just off the lake. Winter evenings are especially enjoyable around the sitting-room fireplace. For warmer weather an outdoor pool and two tennis courts are next to the chalet-style hotel. Room rates, Lit. 47,000–65,000.

MADONNA DI CAMPIGLIO

Cristallo, 38080 Madonna di Campiglio (TN); tel. (0465) 41132. Three stars, 41 rooms with bath, as well as suites. There's a fine view of the Brenta range from the sun terrace. The restaurant is all'italiana. Rooms run Lit. 75,000–118,000.

Crozzon, 38080 Madonna di Campiglio (TN); tel. (0465) 42217. Family-run and centrally located, this is a 3-star hotel with restaurant. All 16 rooms have bath. Doubles are Lit. 90,000. No singles available.

Palù, 38080 Madonna di Campiglio (TN); tel. (0465) 41280. A suggestive mountain-style chalet at the beginning of the road to Vallesinella. Three stars, all 17 rooms with bath (no singles). Doubles are Lit. 105,000.

Outside Madonna di Campiglio, try:

Costa Rotian, Località Costa Rotian, 38020 Almazzago (TN); tel. (0463) 94307. A modern, 3-star hotel 10 miles before Madonna di Campiglio on the road from Trento. Indoor pool, mini-ice rink, and tennis court, plus beautiful views of the surrounding mountains. Rooms average Lit. 41,000–67,000.

In Lignano, contact the courteous and highly efficient local **tourist board,** Azienda Autonoma di Soggiorno e Turismo, Via Latisana 42, 33054 (UD); tel. (0431) 71821; telex 450193 LIGN I; telefax 70449. You'll be submerged with brochures, price lists, maps, etc., and it is always abreast of what hotels have accommodations available, and can make bookings.

Trieste

Colombia, Via della Geppa 18, 34100; tel. (040) 69434. This 40-room hotel is just two blocks from the central rail terminal. No dining facilities. Rooms run Lit. 58,000–91,000. All cards.

Duchi d'Aosta, Piazza dell'Unità d'Italia 2, 34100; tel. (040) 62081; telex 460358. This first-class CIGA hotel is a Trieste landmark. Its ornate facade blends harmoniously with the city's piazza next to the sea. Heavily geared for conferences and banquets, the hotel has 48 rooms and two suites, averaging Lit. 135,000–350,000.

The hotel's **Harry's Grill** is a local institution (enter at Via dell'Orologio 2; tel. 62081) and reflects the city's *mitteleuropa* character. In addition to regional specialties, diet and kosher food can be prepared with advanced notice. A full meal with wine begins at Lit. 70,000. All cards.

SKIING

The northeastern half of Italy's winter wonderland has a heavy accent on skiing, though other sports are well represented: ice skating, curling, and tobogganing, as well as indoor swimming and tennis.

For diehards, there is summer skiing in both Bolzano (the Südtirol) and Trentino. Fledgling Friuli-Venezia Giulia most take a back seat to the highly organized Tyrol-Trento facilities. Some Friuli-Venezia Giulia areas are now beginning to attract world-class competition, such as at Piancavallo, but generally speaking, Trentino-Alto Adige holds sway.

Note: The Belluno spur into the Dolomites is covered in the "Veneto" chapter.

Computerized ski-pass systems are found throughout the Südtirol, Trentino, and Veneto. The most comprehensive is the **Dolomiti Superski pass,** valid on 457 lifts to 651 miles of runs in 11 specific areas: Cortina d'Ampezzo, Plan de Corones, Alta Badia, Gardena/Alpe di Siusi, Fassa and Carezza, Arabba, Upper Pusteria, Fiemme/Obereggen (San Floriano), San Martino di Castrozza/Rolle Pass, Isarco, and Tre Valli. And there are a series of local passes often coordinated with neighboring ski stations.

Lifts will vary, from cable cars to chair lifts to tow ropes. Ski schools and rentals are found in all the areas mentioned. A wide assortment of caffès, bars, restaurants, discos, and movie theaters will easily satisfy after-ski enthusiasts. Provincial bus service is available to all areas from either Bolzano or Trento.

Bolzano (Südtirol)

Alta Badia. This Sella group of four Ladin valleys extends from central Corvara. There are 142 hotels and *pensioni* in this Dolomiti Superski area, with 100 miles of runs serviced by 53 lifts, to a maximum of 9,200 feet near Stern. Winter camping is available. For information, contact Silvestro Kostner, Agenzia Autonoma di Soggiorno e Turismo, Casa de Comun 198, 39033 Corvara in Badia (BZ); tel. (0471) 83176; telex 401555 CORVAS I.

Grödner-Seiser Alm (Val Gardena). The 1970 world ski championships, international hockey tournaments at Ortisei (St. Ulrich), and an annual December World Cup visit have guaranteed this area's prominence. On Seiser Alm alone 25 lifts reach Dolomiti Superski runs scattered over 30 square miles. Bus service connects Castelrotto (Kastelruth), Siusi (Seis), and Alpe di Siusi (Seiser Alm) to Bolzano (Bozen), Chiusa (Klausen), and Bressanone (Brixen). At Ortesei there are 117 hotels, with another 108 divided between Siusi, San Valentino, and Castelrotto. For information, contact Uwe Von Exeli, Agenzia Autonoma di

Soggiorno e Turismo, Via Rezia 1 (Palazzo dei Congressi), 39046 Ortisei-St. Ulrich (BZ); tel. (0471) 76328; telex 40035 TURIST.

Ortles Group. One of the most reliable northeast winter sports areas, rising to 12,800 feet, the Ortles (Ortler) group has its own Ortles Skiarena pass for 11 different areas serviced by four cable cars and 59 lifts. Ski runs total 110 miles. Summer skiing is possible at the over 11,000-foot Stelvio Pass (Stilfser Joch). Fifty-one hotels are available between Solda (Sulden) and Trafoi. There is no local tourist information office, but information for all ski resorts in the province of Bolzano (or Alto Adige/Südtirol) can be obtained from: Landesverkehrsamt für Südtirol, Pfarrplatz 11/12, 39100 Bolzano-Bozen; tel. (0471) 993808; telex 400158.

Trentino

Canazei. One of the leading ski stations in Trentino, this Dolomiti Superski circuit is also tied into the Fassa-Carezza pass system and runs in neighboring Bolzano and Belluno provinces. Artificial snow machinery is a guarantee for vacationers. In the immediate area 25 lifts service 27 runs ranging from 360 to 4,050 yards. Summer skiing on the Marmolada is available. The area's 167 hotels can accommodate 5,925 persons; rooms and apartments are available. There is a public indoor pool and a sauna at Canazei, and an ice rink at neighboring Alba. For specific information, contact Azienda Autonoma di Soggiorno, Via Roma 34, 38032 Canazei (TN); tel. (0462) 61113; telex 40012 TURISM I.

Madonna di Campiglio. Long a national favorite, Campiglio is becoming a top international draw. Sixty-one hotels can accommodate 4,185 persons, and there also are rooms and apartments to let. The Skirama Dolomiti di Brenta pass covers 31 lifts and also ties into the Folgarida and Marilleva runs in the Sole Valley. Campiglio's 20 runs vary from 250 to 3,690 yards. Added attractions are a public indoor pool, Olympic skating circuit, and cross-country ski centers. For specific information contact the Azienda Autonoma di Soggiorno, 38084 Madonna di Campiglio (TN); tel. (0465) 42000; telex 40082 CARUPI I.

Moena. Part of the Dolomiti Superski circuit, Moena is also in the Skiarea Tre Valli pass plan. Included in this downhill ski triangle are Luisa, San Pellegrino Pass, and Valles Pass. Besides two downhill and one cross-country school, the Italian Border Police ski school is in Moena. Twenty-four lifts service 18 runs ranging from 350 to 4,000 yards. Sixty-nine hotels can accommodate 3,046 persons; rooms and apartments are also available. For information contact the Azienda Autonoma di Soggiorno, 38035 Moena (TN); tel. (0462) 53122; telex 400677 MOENA I.

San Martino di Castrozza and Fiera di Primiero. In both the Dolomiti Superski and Skipass di Valle systems, the area also offers cross-country centers, a toboggan run, a ski jump, and two public indoor pools. Twenty-nine lifts service 33 runs ranging from 400 to 2,650 yards. Ninety-three hotels can accommodate 4,217 persons; private rooms and apartments are available, and there are three winter campsites. For information, contact the Azienda Autonoma di Soggiorno e Turismo di San Martino di Castrozza, 38058 San Martino di Castrozza (TN); tel. (0439) 68101; telex 401543 ASMART I. Or: Azienda Autonoma di Soggiorno e Turismo del Primiero e Vanoi, 38054 Fiera di Primiero (TN); tel. (0439) 62407.

Val di Fiemme. The most extended ski area in Trentino includes the towns of Cavalese and Predazzo. In the Dolomiti Superski system, the area also offers the Fiemme and Obereggen network of 60 lifts, for 90 miles of downhill runs. Accommodations for 5,346 persons are available in 127 hotels. Private rooms and apartment rentals also are available, as are two cross-country centers, a toboggan run, an ice rink, and indoor pool and tennis courts. Information can be obtained from the Azienda Autonoma di Soggiorno, Centro Fiemme, 38033 Cavalese (TN); tel. (0462) 30298; telex 400096 TUROF I. Or: Azienda Autonoma di Soggiorno Alta Val di Fiemme, 38037 Predazzo (TN); tel. (0462) 51237; telex 401329 FIEMME I.

General information for the entire Trentino area can be obtained from the Azienda per la Promozione Turistica, Provincia Autonoma di Trento, Corso 3 Novembre 132, 38100 Trento; tel. (0461) 980000; telex 401382 PTNTUR I.

Restaurants

The cuisine of the northeast is very varied—details are discussed below.

Credit cards are listed as accepted in our restaurant suggestions. "All cards" means that all of the following are accepted: AE—American Express; DC—Diner's Club; MC—MasterCard; V—Visa. Prices given are for a complete meal (appetizer to dessert) for one person, unless otherwise specified.

Bolzano

Whether you call the region Bolzano, Bozen, Südtirol, or Alto Adige, this area possesses the most colorful Austro-Germanic flavor in the Alps. A fierce pride and intensive desire to perpetuate its distinctive cultural heritage gives the Italian territory even more of a Tyrolean atmosphere than its northern neighbor across the Austrian border.

Brenner Pass Towns

Historically, the Brenner Pass has been northern Europe's corridor to the Mediterranean. Three of the Italian Tyrol's five most prominent towns are along this route: Bolzano, (Bozen), Bressanone (Brixen), and Vipiteno (Sterzing).

All three are along the 53-mile tract of A22 and SS12, running parallel to the Isarco (Risack) River, which converges with the Adige south of Bolzano.

Of the other two major towns, Merano (Meran) is 17 miles northeast of Bolzano on the SS38 to Stelvio National Park, while Brunico (Bruneck) is 21 miles east of Bressanone on SS49, which continues through the Austrian Dolomites to Lienz.

A stop in one of these towns is a must: Arcades, battlements, elaborate wooden ornaments, wrought iron signs colorfully announcing hotels, and beer halls, all are within a picturesque floral frame.

Most characteristic are the **Via dei Portici** in **Bolzano** and in **Merano,** and **Via Città Nuova** in **Vipiteno.** These old-town promenades pass between inviting bakeries, caffès, stores, and handicraft shops featuring local wood sculptures.

A number of fascinating castles and monasteries turn back the pages of time. Two Bolzano castles of particular interest are **Mareccio** (Maretsch), sometimes used as a venue for art shows and conventions, and **Roncolo** (Runkelstein), about one mile north of town. Both have been restored and are maintained by local administrations.

Begun in the 12th century, Mareccio assumed its present size and shape with walls and four circular towers built in the 15th century. Roncolo (open 10 A.M. to noon and 3 to 7 P.M., closed Sunday, Monday, December, and January) is noted for its medieval frescoes.

🐾 Both have characteristic restaurants to complete the atmosphere.

Merano's reputation as a health center is due to its moderate climate and spa waters. The 13th- and 14th-century **Gothic cathedral** and 15th-century **Principesco Castle** (visitors welcome) are in the center of the old town. Nearby is the 12th-century **Tyrol Castle** (three miles north on SS44; open 9 A.M. to noon, 2 to 5 P.M.; closed Monday and Sunday, and holiday afternoons). It was once seat of the Counts of Tyrol.

Unless otherwise noted, castles and other attractions are open to the public from Tuesday to Saturday mornings.

Mountain Touring

Further west are **Stelvio National Park,** the inviting slopes of the **Val Venosta** (Vinschgau) region, and the curious church steeple in the middle of **Lake Resia** (Reschen). In 1949 the village of Curon Venosta gave way to an artificial lake, and today only the steeple sees the light of day.

Stelvio National Park surrounds imposing Stelvio peak, covered with snow most of the year. There is perhaps excessive development on the outer fringes, but the park itself is a treat. There's abundant skiing, camping, and hiking; hiking trails are well marked. Information about skiing and camping can be obtained from the Bolzano tourist office, Landesverkehrsamt für Südtirol, Pfarrplatz 11/12, 39100 Bolzano-Bozen; tel. (0471) 993808.

Northeast of Bolzano is the Val Gardena and a seemingly indeterminable number of ski slopes. For those who prefer more sedentary sightseeing to hiking or skiing, this is magnificent country just to drive through.

❧ RESTAURANTS

Bolzano's government-controlled wines are Alto Adige, Casteller, Colli di Bolzano, Lago di Caldaro, Meranese in Collina, Santa Maddalena, Terlano, and Valdadige.

Distilled locally are Cabernet, Küchelberger, Merlot, red and white Pinot, Reisling, Sylvaner, and Traminer, as well as Moscato and Spumante. Grappa with fruit or berries is a Südtirol specialty.

Gastronomical treats are the local bread, butter, cheese, ravioli from the Val Venosta, *gnocchi* (knödel), *würst, speck, goulasch, craut,* and wild berries.

In **Appiano** sulla Strada del Vino, the restaurant to try is **Zur Rose,** Josef Innerhoferstrasse 2; tel. (0471) 52249. This rustic, family-style restaurant with just 60 settings provides an authentic Tyrolese menu and wine list. Smoked trout is a house specialty. Dinner will cost about Lit. 30,000 without wine. Closed Sun. and Feb. No cards.

In **Bolzano,** try **Da Abramo,** Piazza Gries 16; tel. (0471) 280141. Fish is featured, especially the hot antipasto selections. Abramo Panterri's small, 40-seat, elegant restaurant took over the Gries civic administration offices when the town became part of Bolzano. Luncheon specials can go for Lit. 25,000. The evening fare is around Lit. 50,000 without wine. Closed Sun. and June 20–July 10. AE.

Or try **Rastbichler,** Via Cadorna 1; tel. (0471) 41131. Adolfo Tauber has created a hospitable little restaurant with 60 settings in traditional Tyrolean rustic decor. He and his son prepare local fare in the kitchen while his wife acts as hostess. Dinner runs about Lit. 30,000 without wine. Closed Sun. and Jan. 10–Feb. 1. No cards.

The recommended restaurant in **Bressanone** is **Fink,** Via Portici Minori 4; tel. (0472) 23883. Helmuth Fink is a pure traditionalist with his Südtirol menu and wine list. A fruit *grappa* is a must to end the meal. Dinners range Lit. 18,000–20,000 without wine. Closed Wed. and 20 days in June. No cards.

The best choice in **Merano** is **Andrea,** Via Galileo Galilei; tel. (0473) 37400. Andreas Hellrigl established a reputation in the kitchen at the Hotel Villa Mozart, where his wife, Emmi, now runs the restaurant (open only to nonguests for parties of at least four). Once this little 26-seat restaurant was established, Andreas put it in the competent hands of chef Walter Oberrauch and opened the Palio with Tony Mei in New York. It all began here in Merano, where rigorous equilibrium of flavors and appearances is maintained to please not only the palate, but the eye as well. Dinner will run approximately Lit. 70,000 without wine. Closed Mon. and Jan. 1–Mar. 15. DC, MC.

Trentino

Trentino is the southern, ethnic Italian Dolomite stalwart. Though *all'italiana,* local culture reflects a strong Austro-Germanic influence. This is most evident in local organizational ability.

Trento

Capital of the autonomous province is Trento (Trent), whose place in history was permanently carved by the 1545–1563 Council of Trent's counterreforms to the Reformation Proclamation that Martin Luther nailed to the door of All Saints Church in Wittenberg.

An ill-fated and bloodstained contemporary reform effort emerged from the Trento University School of Sociology in the 1960s when socioeconomic debates evolved into the political platform of a phenomenon that threatened to destabilize Italian democracy—the Red Brigades.

The Council of Trent was held in the sixth-century **cathedral** that still dominates the center of the old town in **Piazza del Duomo.** The original basilica was expanded in 1145 and more solemn Gothic designs were added in the 13th century. In the **Alberti Chapel** is the same crucifix in front of which the Catholic Church's decisions to combat Protestantism were decreed in 1563. Heading north from the square is the picturesque Via Belenzani, the most attractive street in town.

Mountain Resorts

Less than 11 miles from the center of Trento is **Monte Bondone,** the urban ski station. However, the main Trentino winter sports center is west, around the Brenta group to **Madonna di Campiglio,** with the largest concentration of ski facilities in all northeastern Italy and popular with the Milanese.

Not to be ignored is **San Martino di Castrozza.** Situated in what has been called "the most superb natural amphitheater in the Dolomites," San Martino is the most eastern Trentino ski station included in the Dolomite Superski pass system. San Martino is accessible on SS50 through the Valle Travignolo east of Predazzo.

Lakes

Trentino is spotted with a number of attractive lakes—such as Lake Caldonazzo, close to Trento—but the most popular is **Lake Garda,** the largest freshwater body in the country. Its boundaries are shared with the regions of Lombardy and Veneto. Be aware, however, that beaches at Garda are small, overcrowded and rocky; mostly, it's a favored lake for water sports (see the "Lombardy" chapter). Riva del Garda on the northern peak of the lake is less than an hour's drive south of Trento on A22 to SS240 from the Rovereto Sud exit. Northern Garda's summer atmosphere is totally German. Italian visitors are foreigners at home. A gesturing sign language is more productive than English.

Castles and Monasteries

Trentino has its share of castles and monasteries. One of the most picturesque is **St. Romedio Sanctuary,** a mountain-top complex of churches dating from the 12th to 16th centuries, located seven miles east of Cles overlooking Lake Santa Giustina.

In Trento proper is **Castello del Buon Consiglio,** once residence of the prince-bishops who dominated the area. This maze of multiform constructions houses the **Trentino provincial museum** as well as a **Risorgimento Museum.**

⚜ RESTAURANTS

Trentino fare is rather simple and relies strongly on local produce season by season. The *luganeghe* sausage is a treat, especially when prepared in a *risotto.* Then there is local salami, speck, black polenta (made with Saracen wheat instead of cornmeal), mushrooms, asparagus, chestnut cakes, strudel, apples, pears, plums, and grapes.

In Trentino, government-controlled DOC wines are Rotaliano, Sorni, Trentino, Teroldego, and Valle Isarco. These are used for the best local Cabernet, Casteller, Lagrien, red and white Pinot, and Riesling.

In **Cavalese,** try **Cantuccio,** Via Unterberger 14; tel. (0462) 30140. Down-to-earth home cooking mountain-style, with a good choice of local wines and grappas. Dinner will run about Lit. 25,000. Closed Tues. and Nov. No cards.

In **Rovereto,** south of Trento, try **Al Borgo,** Via Garibaldi 13; tel. (0464) 36300. Rinaldo Dalsasso has attended to every detail in this elegant restaurant, considered one of the best in Trentino. A meal will provide a gastronomical tour of the region. Dinners run Lit. 45,000–50,000. Closed Sun. evening, Mon., and Feb. 1–10. AE, DC, V.

In **San Martino di Castrozza,** try **Malga Ces,** Località Ces; tel. (0439) 68145. The fine view of the Dolomites and surrounding woods is just a bonus. The grilled meats and game are designed for a meat-and-potato appetite. But first try the barley soup, a real Alpine specialty. The mushroom soup is also an attraction. Dinner will cost about Lit. 30,000 with house wine. Closed Apr. 15–May 31 and Oct. 1–Nov. 30. No cards.

In **Trento,** try **Accademia,** Via Colico 6; tel. (0461) 981580. It's worth arriving early for a drink at the beautiful, well-stocked bar. This sober, elegant creation of Andrea Bassetti and Antonio Grasso in the Hotel Accademia presents a menu of excellent local cuisine. Dinners cost about Lit. 28,000. Closed Mon. and Aug. 4–20. AE, DC, V.

Friuli-Venezia Giulia

Too often Friuli-Venezia Giulia is a footnote to presentations of Venice and the Veneto region. This is a mistake.

Comprised of four provinces—Gorizia, Pordenone, Trieste, and Udine—with its capital in Trieste, the region is one of five in Italy with autonomous status.

Though ethnically Italian and once under Venice, the region—Trieste in particular—under the Hapsburgs assimilated central European traits foreign to the rest of Italy. In 1382 the city even sought and obtained Hapsburg protection, though security was probably a stronger motivation than loyalty for the decision.

Whereas the northern border province of Bolzano was World War I booty, the eastern frontier with Yugoslavia was greatly redimensioned after Italy's World War II ordeal. In the waning days of the war, Yugoslav troops arrived in Trieste, but the Allies resisted territorial claims and installed a military government. Eventually the city became a United Nations free-port protectorate, but in 1954 by a popular referendum it decided on union with Italy. Trieste escaped Tito's grasp, but lost most of its province, including the Italian Capodistria.

There, as along most of the border with Italy, extensive resettlement programs were forced on the population to assure Belgrade's domination of as much of the territory as possible.

Gorizia suddenly became a border town, and is now a divided city. It certainly has not had Berlin's dramatic confrontations, but it is strange to see a street in Italy that ends against a cyclone fence. The asphalt continues to a former rail station that is now a border police office under a Yugoslav flag.

Castles

The scenic drive along the coast to Trieste belies the travails of Italy's largest Adriatic port. Two beautiful castles line the 13-mile SS14 from Monfalcone through the sliver of Italian coast between the Gulf of Trieste and Yugoslavia.

The first is cliffside **Duino Castle** (open to the public), which once offered refuge to Dante. Another famous guest was the German poet Rilke, whose *Duino Elegies* are said to have been written here during a sojourn with Maria von Turn und Taxis.

The second castle, just four miles before Trieste, is **Miramare,** which Archduke Maximilian of Austria and Princess Carlotta received as a wedding gift. It certainly wasn't a good omen; after proclaiming himself emperor of Mexico, Maximilian was executed by a firing squad of Mexican insurgents, and Carlotta went mad with grief. Miramare is also open to the public.

The beautiful gardens and a summer sound-and-light performance of Maximilian's tragedy (held in the port below Miramare) are added attractions. A refreshment caffè is on the grounds.

Trieste

The port is the most characteristic part of Trieste. To the left is the Mandracchio inlet (for small, private boats) conforming perfectly with the symmetry of surrounding Borgo Teresiano.

Along the seafront at Riva Tre Novembre 5 is **Caffè Tommaseo,** one of the most characteristic in the city. The **San Marco** at Via Battisti 18 is also a pleasant experience.

Facing the sea is the city's summer *salotto* in **Piazza dell'Unita d'Italia,** where one can relax in an outdoor caffè while the north-wind *bora* is on vacation.

The most notable spot for refreshment is the **Caffè degli Specchi.**

The chain-and-rope railings on many sidewalks are necessary when the bora is in town—this Adriatic wind reaches gale proportions.

Next to the **old fort** atop the hill of San Giusto, where the fortified village of Tregeste was founded in 1200 B.C., is **St. Justus (San Giusto) Basilica.** The 15th- and 16th-century fort's parapets and the basilica's 14th-century bell tower offer fine views over the city. Arms and furniture museums are inside the fortress.

The city's most characteristic restaurant—**La Bottega del Vino**—occupies the old stables.

The basilica was constructed in three separate periods. One wing dates to the sixth century, another to the 11th century. The central connecting nave, framing a Gothic rose window in its facade, was completed in the 1300s. Among the church's

13th-century mosaics and 11th-century frescoes is a beautiful 12th-century north apse mosaic depicting the apostles in adoration of Mary as she appears between the angels Gabriel and Michael.

Aquileia

In the Middle Ages Trieste was under the Patriarch of Aquileia. Aquileia is now little more than a dot on a detailed map, but once it was the home of Rome's Adriatic fleet and the largest city in the Empire after Rome. When Attila raided and razed Aquileia in 452, the inhabitants fled to islands in the Venetian lagoon. These refugees were the founders of Venice. **Ruins** of the town and an **archaeological** museum, with numerous artifacts from extensive excavation, are open to the public.

Grado

Six miles south of Aquileia on SS352 is Grado. This lagoon isle is one of the most characteristic in the northern Adriatic. It was a favorite vacation spot during the Hapsburg reign, and is still avidly frequented by Austrians and Germans.

Palmanova

Back to Aquileia and 9½ miles north is the star-shaped city-fortress of Palmanova. Constructed in perfect symmetry by the Republic of Venice in 1593, the town is surrounded by fortified walls that form a nine-point star. The entire town has been declared a national monument. Unfortunately, a full perspective of Palmanova can only be obtained from the air, but guides and the local museum can provide an impressive picture of this unique city-fortress.

Villa Manin (Passariano)

The region presents a number of beautiful castles and villas, but the most impressive is Villa Manin at Passariano. Visitors are welcome at the 16th-century village, which has been restored and is now used for cultural events and international meetings. This is where Napoleon signed the Campoformido Treaty relinquishing Lombardy and Veneto to the House of Savoy (in exchange for Corsica and Nice), as well as renouncing any future claims to Friuli-Venezia Giulia and Trentino.

Passariano is 1½ miles from Rivolto on SS252, 33 miles west of Udine. Farther west on SS252 after Codroipo (about four and a half miles) is a junction with SS463, which runs north parallel to the Tagliamento River. A 14-mile drive north is **San Daniele,** paradise of prosciutto lovers. The only rivals to these cured hams are those of Parma (and many consider that statement a heresy).

Adriatic Beaches

From Codroipo, following signs to San Martino, Muscletto, Varmo, Ronchis, and Latisana onto SS354, you return to the Adriatic and the extensive **Lignano beach complex** across the lagoon from Grado. The wide sandy beaches (each town has a designated public beach) are lined with wall-to-wall hotels. Like most of the Adriatic, coastal waters can be very shallow, even one hundred yards offshore. The tides constantly bring sea-bottom sand to the surface, making the water murky.

You can avoid murky beach water by hiring a houseboat. (See "Accommodations.")

Ski Areas

Since over half of the region is mountainous, local skiing necessitates mention. Pioneer resorts in the interior, which once had the highest emigration rate in northern Italy, are beginning to emerge.

Friuli's most prominent ski resort is **Piancavallo** in the eastern tip of the Dolomites. Created just twenty years ago, the center now hosts a mid-December event on the women's World Cup ski circuit. Piancavallo's four snow cannons guarantee snow throughout the season.

Other prominent skiing areas are Forni di Sopra in the eastern Dolomites, Sella Nevea and Tarvisio near the Yugoslav border, and Ravascletto and Zoncolan, northeast of Cortina in the Carnia Alps near the Monte Croce Pass to Austria. The truth is that if one is in the area in season and wants a day of skiing the Friuli-Venezia Giulia area is fine—but these cannot compare with those in Bolzano and Trentino.

❧ RESTAURANTS

The region's cuisine is simple, not sophisticated. Mountain areas rely heavily on game and *polenta,* while soups and fish are in abundance in coastal restaurants. Try checking the plate of the day and the best local wine to accompany it.

Friuli-Venezia Giulia's government-regulated DOC list includes Carso, Collio Goriziano, Colli Orientali del Friuli, Grave del Friuli, Latisana, Isonzo, and Aquileia. Featured in regional restaurants are Cabernet, Merlot, gray and white Pinot, Tocai, and Verduzzo. A local dessert wine is Picolit. Grappa is also found in abundance.

If in **Grado,** the restaurant to try is **Antica Trattoria Nico,** Via Marina 10; tel. (0431) 80470. Nico greets the fishermen at the docks, then hustles back to his kitchen to begin preparations for his guests. Hope the lobster soup is on the menu. The desserts are homemade. Lit. 40,000 is a bargain for dinner. Closed Thurs. and Jan. AE, DC, V.

In **Trieste** try:

Suban, Via Comici 2; tel. (040) 54368. The Suban family has run this restaurant since 1865, when they emigrated from France. Mario now runs this "gastronomic temple of Trieste," turning out Russian, Austrian, and Hungarian dishes with the same ease as local Friuli fare. For the diet-conscious, there is a fine view. Dinner runs about Lit. 50,000. Closed Mon., Tues., and 20 days in Aug. All cards.

Ristorante Locanda Mario, Draga Sant'Elia, Basovizza; tel. (040) 228173. The biggest obstacle is finding Mario Lupidi's characteristic restaurant just outside Trieste. Take the road for Fiume, Yugoslavia; Mario's is just a mile to the left after Basovizza. Deer, snail, and frog recipes dot the menu; the restaurant seats 100, including the summer garden facilities. The locanda has ten rooms, all with private bath. Dinner with local wine will cost about Lit. 35,000. Closed Tues. No cards.

See also **Harry's Grill,** under "Accommodations," above.

14

NORTHWESTERN ITALY

The Valle d'Aosta is Italy's northwest passage from Francophone Europe to the Piedmont capital of Turin, cradle of a united Italy under the House of Savoy. The proximity of the Mediterranean has mellowed French haughtiness; the transition to an Italian experience has combined graceful sophistication with the sober outdoors.

The labyrinth of valleys in the region of Valle d'Aosta is one of the most scenic areas in the Alps. The 15-mile tunnel through Monte Bianco (Mont Blanc), Europe's highest peak, remains a Franco-Italian engineering marvel, proudly indicating the industrial prowess that lies to the south.

Aosta, seat of the autonomous province-region's administration, is in the center of the main valley. It is a perfect base for visiting the entire valley, from Gran Paradiso National Park to the internationally acclaimed ski stations and seasonal resorts at Courmayeur and Breuil-Cervinia, as well as the spa with adjacent casinò at St.-Vincent.

Once the Po Department of Napoleonic France, the region of Piedmont has long been Italy's leading textile and clothing manufacturer. The more mundane presentations—i.e., the fashion shows—have moved to Milan.

Turin (Torino), first capital of a united Italy and center of Piedmont's regional administration, is the keystone to industrial Italy. Ironic is the address of Italy's citadel of capitalism, the Fiat autoworks: Corso Unione Sovietica. The enterprising skills and foresight of the Agnelli family have provided a solid foundation for Italy's industrial establishment.

Provincial industry is no lesser-known entity. Under the guidance of Carlo DeBenedetti, Ivrea's Olivetti computer corporation has exploded onto the world market. Here also is the most prominent wine patrimony in the country, and the creative goldsmiths in the town of Valenza.

The largest mainland region in Italy, Piedmont is comprised of the provinces of Alessandria, Asti, Cuneo, Novara, Torino, and Vercelli. Castles and ruins are abundant in both regions. Vacation meccas are as diverse as the Sestriere winter-summer resort near the western border with France and captivating Stresa and the Borromean Islands in Lake Maggiore, on the border with Switzerland.

There are a number of enchanting Piedmont valleys, such as Susa, Lanzo, Valsesia, and Val d'Ossola. The latter, scene of the most bitter combat between partisans and retreating German forces at the end of World War II, briefly was an independent republic when Italy emerged from Nazi occupation.

WINING AND DINING

Piedmont presents the most aristocratic wine list in Italy. Renowned aperitifs, sparkling spumantes, and rugged grappas can make the experience even more exciting.

Asti Spumante, Barbera, Barolo, Dolcetto, Gattinara, Grignolino, Malvasia, and Nebbiolo head the list of 39 government-regulated DOC wines produced in the region.

And in spite of its limited territory, the Valle d'Aosta can claim six DOC wines: Boca, Carema, Fara, Ghemme, Sizza, and Valle d'Aosta.

Northwestern cuisine is jealously limited almost exclusively to local produce. Hearty appetites in Alpine Aosta are appeased by recipes featuring local fontina cheese, salted meats, and Valdostan steak.

Piedmont is famous for its wide variety of *antipasti* (appetizers), *bagna cauda* (a condiment for vegetables), *polenta* and rice recipes, and *bolliti* (mixed boiled meat platters). Here French presentation and Italian substance leads the renaissance of old regional recipes to make local dining a real treat.

There is one major drawback in Turin. Since most of the more established and acclaimed restaurants cater to the industrial and financial communities, finding a place open for Sunday dining often poses a problem.

Credit cards are listed as accepted under our restaurant suggestions in this chapter. "All cards" means that all of the following are accepted: AE—American Express; DC—Diner's Club; MC—MasterCard; V—Visa. Prices given are for a complete dinner (antipasto to dessert) for one person, unless otherwise indicated.

TRAVEL

Flying

Turin's Caselle International Airport is 10 miles from the center of the regional capital. However, Milan's Malpensa and Genoa's

Cristoforo Colombo airports may be more convenient for the eastern and southern extremes of the region (see "Travel" in the Milan and Liguria chapters).

Most Alitalia international flights are shuttled through Milan. International carriers serving Turin are Air France, British Air, Lufthansa, and Sabina. Further information is available by calling the airport; tel. (011) 5778.

Direct, daily international flights are to London (Alitalia, British Air), Paris (Air France, Alitalia), and Zurich (Swissair).

Direct, Mon.–Fri. flights are available to Düsseldorf, Frankfurt, Munich, Stuttgart (Lufthansa), Liege (Sabina), and Lyon (Aliblu).

Bus service from Turin to Caselle (70 min.) is available from the intersection at Corso Inghilterra and Corso Vittorio Emanuele II.

Downtown Alitalia, Ati, Aliblu, Alisarda, and Avianova information can be obtained at Via Lagrange 35; tel. (011) 55911. World Jet Services offices are at Via Arsenale 27; tel. (011) 542566.

Direct, daily national service is to Alghero (1 hour, 35 min.), Cagliari (1 hour, 15 min.), Catania (2 hours, 55 min.), Naples (1 hour, 20 min.), Pisa (50 min.), and Rome (1 hour, 5 min.). Mon.–Fri. service is to Bologna (1 hour) and Pescara (2 hours, 40 min.). There are flights every other day to Olbia.

Taking the Train

Turin's Porta Susa and Porta Nuova rail terminals are on two principal national lines: Milan via Vercelli and Novara (1½ hours) and Genoa via Asti and Alessandria (1 hour, 50 min.) (times are for inter-city service). Cuneo is tied to the main Turin–Savona line by secondary service to both Fossano and Mondovi.

Aosta connects with the main Turin–Milan line at Chivasso via Ivrea and St.-Vincent.

Taking the Bus

Bus service should not be considered an alternative, but rather a complement, to the national rail network. Depots are in the vicinity of principal rail stations.

Driving

Turin is the hub for all travel and transport throughout northwestern Italy. Four of the six regional turnpikes originate on Turin's Tangenziale (the beltway circumventing three-quarters of the city; it does not cover the eastern flank).

The turnpikes originating at Turin are:

The **A4** east to Trieste (320 miles) via Novara, Milan, Bergamo, Brescia, Verona, Vicenza, Padua, and Venice.

The **A5** north to Aosta (62 miles) via Ivrea and St.-Vincent; to reach the Monte Bianco tunnel to France (27 miles from Aosta), proceed on E21b and then SS26.

The **A6** south, then east to Savona (78 miles).

The **A21** east to Brescia (148 miles) via Asti, Alessandria, Piacenza, and Cremona.

Two other turnpikes cut through southeastern Piedmont:

The 83-mile Milan–Genoa **A7** crosses both A21 and A26. It also connects with the A10 (Genoa–Ventimiglia on the French border) and A12 from Genoa to Livorno. For Rome connect with the SS1 to Civitavecchia, where the A12 resumes, or take the A11 Firenze–Mare for Florence, which is on the A1 Milan–Rome. (The A12 has not been completed due to bureaucratic problems in Rome.)

The 83-mile **A26** connects the Voltri exit on the A10 (Genoa–Ventimiglia) to the Santhia exit on the Turin–Trieste A4.

CAR RENTALS

Local auto rental agencies are available in many small centers. National service in Piedmont:

Stresa: Maggiore, Corso Umberto I 4; tel. (0323) 30252.
Turin (Caselle Airport): Avis, tel. (011) 4701528. Europcar, tel. (011) 4701926; telex 214553. Hertz, tel. (011) 4701103; telex 222381. Maggiore, tel. (011) 4701929.

(Porta Nuova Rail Terminal): Avis, tel. (011) 6699800. Hertz, tel. (011) 6699658. Maggiore, tel. 6503013.

(City): Avis, Corso Turati 15G; tel. (011) 501107, and Via Cibrario 18; tel. (011) 482948. Europcar, Via Madama Cristina 72; tel. (011) 6503603; telex 212269. Hertz, Corso Marconi 19; tel. (011) 6504504; telex 224544. Maggiore, Via Saorgio 67; tel. (011) 259309.

❦ ACCOMMODATIONS

A good base for viewing the Valle d'Aosta region is the town of Aosta. In the center of the main valley, it is well located for exploration, as well as for visits to the ski resorts at Monte Rosa (Ayas, Gressoney-la-Trinite, Gressoney-Saint-Jean, and Macugnaga), Valtournenche, Breuil-Cervinia, Courmayeur, La Thuile, and Sauze d'Oulx. (Serious skiers will probably want to stay at the resorts; see "Skiing," this chapter.)

Sestriere is, of course, the base for those who want to ski at Sestriere—site of Europe's largest artificial snow-making system, which guarantees skiing six months of the year. You also can stay at Sestriere and ski at Sauze d'Oulx.

For a lake vacation, consider a stay in Stresa.

Do not expect air-conditioning unless otherwise noted—but since the Northwest's mountain areas are usually cool, air-conditioning is probably unnecessary.

Credit cards are listed as accepted. "All cards" means that all of the following are accepted: AE—American Express; DC—Diner's Club; MC—MasterCard; V—Visa.

Room rates given indicate the span in prices between single and double rooms, unless otherwise specified.

Aosta

Don't try potluck in Aug. when seeking lodging. Even July may pose problems. Other times of the year are not that difficult, but advance reservations are always recommended. When in need, contact the local tourist board—one of the most efficient in

Italy—at Piazza Narbonne 3, 11100; tel. (0165) 303718. Otherwise, try:

Bus, Via Malherbes 18, 11100; tel. (0165) 43645. You guessed wrong. The name is that of former owner Adolfo Bus. This 40-room, 3-star hotel changed hands in 1983. The clean, comfortable rooms are conveniently located in the center of town. The hotel has a restaurant and limited parking, though trying to access it can be maddening; it's in a labyrinth of alleys winding around a pedestrian island. Rooms run Lit. 50,000–85,000. Open all year. All cards.

Roma, Via Torino 7, 11100; tel. (0165) 40821. Appearances can be deceiving. The entrance from Via Torino is a passage to an inner courtyard, with limited parking in front of the main entrance. Access to the parking lot is from Via Veney. This 3-star hotel has 33 rooms and is a block from the main promenade and half a minute from the Tues. open-air market. Surprisingly, no early-morning noise invades the small but comfortable rooms. No restaurant, but a warm breakfast room. Rates for rooms run Lit. 52,000–83,000. Closed mid-Jan.–mid-Feb. All cards.

Sestriere

Grand Hotel Principi di Piemonte, 10058 Sestriere (TO); tel. (0122) 7941; telex 221411 Turin Pal. Built in the 1930s when Sen. Giovanni Agnelli constructed Sestriere (the building is still part of the family fortune), the hotel recently reopened after a decade. Renovation was extensive, making this the most modern hotel in Sestriere; it's in the competent hands of Cesare Clemente, who was number 2 in the Turin Palace for four years. Nearby golf course. Rates run Lit. 140,000–220,000. Open pre-Christmas–Easter holidays. All cards.

Miramonti, 10058 Sestriere (TO); tel. (0122) 77048. Right on the finish line of the annual Cesana–Sestriere summer hill-climb rally, this 3-star, 36-room hotel with slate roof has that characteristic appearance of local mountain lodges. A restaurant and bar are on the premises. Room rates run Lit. 50,000–65,000. Open Nov. 25–Apr. 25 and July–Aug. DC, MC, V.

Stresa

La Fontana Meublé, SS del Sempione 3, 28049 (NO); tel. (0323) 32707. A small (19-rooms), 3-star hotel in a pleasant little park on the lake, the Fontana offers just bed and breakfast. Room rates are Lit. 50,000–72,000. AE, V.

Hotel des Iles Borromées, Lungolago Umberto I 67, 28049 (NO); tel. (0323) 30431; telex 200377; telefax (0323) 32405. This luxury-class, CIGA hotel has one of the most enviable locations in Europe. Right on Lake Maggiore in acres of lush parkland, it offers a wonderful view of the three Borromean Islands. The 115 rooms, nine suites, and 47 apartments in the hotel and its annex are served by two heated outdoor pools, an indoor pool, a gym (an in-house health center is manned by a permanent professional staff), sauna, Turkish bath, and Jacuzzi. **Il Borromeo** restaurant features regional and Mediterranean specialties. The hotel's convention and banquet facilities can competently accommodate up to 350 people. Room rates run Lit. 250,000–350,000. Open all year. All cards.

Royal, SS del Sempione 22, 28049 Stresa Lido (NO); tel. (0323) 32777. Frequented by Italian writers and journalists, this 3-star hotel with a relaxing garden is quiet, comfortable, and efficient in a family atmosphere. Located just 50 yards from the lake, rates for the 45 rooms are Lit. 53,000–78,000. AE, V.

BORROMEAN ISLANDS
Verbano, Isola dei Pescatori, 28049 Stresa (NO); tel. (0323) 30408. Reservations are needed well in advance for this charming 3-star hotel on the most characteristic of Lake Maggiore's three Borromean Islands, only 10 min. by boat from Stresa. There are only 12 rooms, all with bath. The good restaurant features fresh lake fish and homemade lemon cake. Room rates run Lit. 52,000–79,000. Open mid-May–Nov. 1. All cards.

Turin (Torino)
Turin's industrial expansion has created an acute hotel shortage. The demand is increasing while the supply is decreasing. A number of smaller hotels in the center have been bought out by expanding banks requiring more office facilities.

However, a disadvantage can be an advantage. Since the squeeze of business travelers is on Mon.–Thurs., space is no longer at a premium over the weekend. Some of the larger hotels even offer special weekend rates just to maintain occupancy.

In Aug., when the FIAT auto works close for the annual holidays, the city empties, as do the hotels. However, some hotels do close during this period. Check this on a year-to-year basis.

City, Via Filippo Juvarra 25, 10100; tel. (011) 540546; telex 216225. Visiting industrialists are quick to compliment the efficient staff. Many believe it is the best-run hotel in the city. The modern (1970), 4-star, 44-room hotel is just around the corner from the Porta Susa rail terminal. Secretarial services, a meeting room overlooking the courtyard garden, and airport pickups are just a few of the amenities for visiting businesspeople. There is a Cartier shop on premises. Rates run Lit. 175,000–230,000. AE, DC, V.

Jolly Hotel Ambasciatori, Corso Vittorio Emanuele II 104, 10100; tel. (011) 5752; telex 221296. Utilized by Alitalia for its flight crews, this is considered the most comfortable of the three Turin Jollys. Rates for the 197 rooms of this 4-star hotel are Lit. 160,000–200,000. The other 4-star Jollys are the **Ligure,** Piazza Carlo Felice 85, 10100; tel. (011) 55641, just renovated; and the **Principe di Piemonte,** Via P. Gobetti 15, 10100; tel. (011) 532153, in need of renovation. Rates for both are Lit. 195,000–248,000. All hotels, all cards.

Stazione e Genova, Via Sacchi 14b, 10100; tel. (011) 545323; telex 224242. A 3-star, 40-room hotel next door to the Turin Palace and across the street from the Porta Nuova rail terminal, the S e G has recently been renovated in modern decor. Rooms are soundproofed. A bar and restaurant are on the premises. Rates run Lit. 65,000–90,000. All cards.

Turin Palace, Via Sacchi 8, 10100; tel. (011) 515511; telex 221411. This is status in Turin: A 5-star, luxury 125-room establishment across from the main Porta Nuova rail terminal. The hotel, part of the Italhotel chain, has a highly acclaimed restaurant. All rooms are soundproofed and equipped with air-conditioning. Rates run Lit. 210,000–250,000. All cards.

SKIING

Valle d'Aosta and Piedmont winter sports facilities are not as inter-organized as those of their northeastern neighbors. These are more exclusive areas, on the southern slopes of Monte Bianco, Cervinia (the Matterhorn), and Monte Rosa, plus some international and local favorites.

The Valle d'Aosta

The Aosta Tourist Board is one of the most efficient and best organized in Italy. The hub of the country's smallest region's ski information center will rapidly reply to all requests: **Tourist Information Office,** Piazza Chanoux 8, 11100 Aosta; tel. (0165) 35655. Or contact Anna Carsone, Assessorato Regionale Turismo, Valle d'Aosta, Piazza Narbonne 3, 11100 Aosta; tel. (0165) 303718.

Monte Rosa. The Champoluc crest at Ayas, with neighboring slopes that include Gressoney-la-Trinité and Gressoney-St.-Jean, offers 42 lifts with cable cars to 51 downhill runs of nearly 80 miles. Nearly 40 miles of cross-country runs also available. Lessons are available, but there are no rentals. The 45 hotels can accommodate 1,529 persons; there is also winter camping. For local **tourist information,** tel. (0125) 307113, 356143, or 355185, respectively, for the three main areas.

Valtournenche. The lower valley leading to the Matterhorn has 15 lifts to 25 miles of downhill and nearly 30 miles of cross-country runs. Winter camping is available here, too. The 23 hotels can accommodate 743 persons. Lessons. Tel. (0166) 92029 for information.

In the upper valley, at the foot of the Matterhorn, is the prime ski attraction, **Breuil-Cervinia.** Here 37 cable and lift facilities access 54 downhill runs that total 63 miles. Schools. There are cross-country courses, ice skating, bowling, and a bobsled run. The 62 hotels accommodate 2,784 persons. For tourist information, tel. (0166) 949136; telex 211822.

Courmayeur. Outside of one of Italy's most exclusive winter resorts at the base of Monte Bianco (Mt. Blanc) are 32 cable and lift facilities to 23 downhill runs of 60 miles, plus 20 miles of cross-country courses. You'll find ski schools here. There are 65 hotels with room for 2,516 persons. An indoor pool is also available. A rail terminal is 3½ miles away at Pré-St.-Didier. Tourist information: tel. (0165) 842060; telex EPT CYI 215871.

La Thuile. This popular local resort, in the Little San Bernardo Valley before the climb to the French border, has 15 lifts to 45 miles of downhill and 10 miles of cross-country runs. Eleven hotels can accommodate 1,958 persons. There is an indoor pool and a ski school. For information, tel. (0165) 884179.

The Piedmont

Piedmont stations are generally divided between the Valle di Susa, Val d'Ossola, and the so-called Seven Sisters of the Monregalese.

Sestriere. Created over 50 years ago by Sen. Giovanni Agnelli, Sestriere remains the regional pacesetter. Europe's largest artificial snow system guarantees snow for six months a year. Bus service is available from the Frejus rail depot at Oulx (13 miles away), as well as from Turin and Pinerolo. There are 22 lifts to 62 miles of downhill runs; a ski school with over 100 instructors; and rentals. Here you'll also find a cross-country course, a go-cart ice track, skating, an indoor pool, discotheques, nightclubs, and cinemas. Sixteen hotels can accommodate 1,305 persons; 319 miniapartments can accommodate up to 1,199. For information, contact Sergio Pezzotti, Ufficio di Informazione e Assistenza Turistica, Piazza Giovanni Agnelli 11, 10058 Sestriere (TO); tel. (0122) 76085.

Sauze d'Oulx. Billed as the balcony of the Alps, this Upper Susa Valley area is the home of World Cup champion Piero Gros. There is a bus connection to the Frejus rail depot at Oulx (2½ miles away). Snow season is generally Dec.–April. Artificial snow guarantees major runs. There are 26 lifts servicing 60 miles of downhill runs; a ski school with 100 instructors; and rentals. Other attractions include a 3½-mile cross-country circuit, an ice rink, indoor tennis, discotheques, and cinemas. There are 35 hotels with rooms for 1,539; two apartment complexes can house 70. For information, contact Mario De Salvia, Ufficio di Informazione e Assistenza Turistica, Piazza Assietta, 10050 Sauze d'Oulx (TO); tel. (0122) 85009.

Lesser known but more economical areas are:

Bardonecchia. From Turin, 54 miles on SS24 or SS353. Snow season is generally Dec.–Apr. There are 20 lifts to 85 miles of downhill runs; 4 semicircular cross-country courses; 100 ski instructors; and rentals. The area has 30 hotels with a capacity for 1,230; two apartment complexes contain 95 flats. For information, contact Ettore Giordana, Azienda Autonoma di Soggiorno, Viale Vittoria 44, 10052 Bardonecchia (TO); tel. (0122) 99032.

Claviere and Cesana. From Turin, 53 miles on SS24. Bus service is available from Frejus rail depot at Oulx (5½ miles from Claviere, 9½ miles from Cesana). Claviere is on the French border and has connections with San Sicario and Montgenévre. Cesana is at the foot of the Monti della Luna. The area's 66 miles of downhill slopes are served by 11 lifts. There are an additional 90 miles of external runs; a school with 40 instructors; rentals; a sled run; horseback riding; an ice rink; nightclubs; and discotheques. The area's 21 hotels and pensiones can accommodate 437 persons; there are three apartment complexes with 247 flats. For information, contact Orlando Tiani, Azienda Autonoma di Soggiorno di Claviere e Cesana, Via Nazionale 30, 10050 Claviere (TO); tel. (0122) 878856.

Limone Piemonte. Less than 20 miles from Cuneo (68 from Turin) on the SS20 and on the Cuneo–Ventimiglia–Nice rail line (station at Limone). Snow season is Dec.–Apr. There are 33 lifts to 63 miles of downhill runs. Also available are cross-country circuits; a school with 70 instructors; rentals; an ice rink; a tennis court; indoor pool; nightclub; cinemas; and discotheques. The area's 25 hotels can accommodate 891; apartment rentals are available, too. For information, contact Nicola Bottero, Azienda Autonoma di Soggiorno e Turismo, Via Roma 38, 12015 Limone Piemonte (CN); tel. (0171) 92101.

Macugnaga. On the SS549 on the eastern slope of Monte Rosa, across the Alps from Zermatt, Macugnaga is 113 miles from Turin and 87 miles from Milan. It is 20 miles from the Domodossola station on the Milan–Domodossola–Sempione rail line and 17 miles from the local station at Piedimulera. Macugnaga is unique for the modern facilities that serve an area that still preserves its old mountain outpost characteristics in a rich pinewood setting. Snow is generally available Nov.–May. There are 13 cable cars and lifts to serve 22 miles of downhill runs. There are skating and hockey rinks; a cross-country course; and discotheques. The 21 small hotels can accommodate 564 persons; 25 apartments are also available. For information contact Giuseppe Burgener, Azienda Autonoma di Soggiorno, Piazza Municipio, 28030 Macugnaga (NO); tel. (0324) 65119.

The Valle d'Aosta

The call of the ski resorts of Courmayeur and Breuil-Cervinia make the Aosta Valley a winter attraction, but the best time of year to visit is between late spring and early autumn, when the cool, dry evenings provide needed relief from hot, humid urban areas.

Aosta

A town of just 40,000, Aosta traces its history to the first century B.C. All major points of interest, as well as handicraft shops (don't be duped by the many ceramics and wood carvings from the Tyrol—the "friendship cups" are authentic local products), caffès, restaurants, banks, and other commercial establishments are along or just off the half-mile promenade from the **Arch of Augustus** (25 B.C.) through Porta Pretoria, Piazza Chanoux, and down to Piazza della Repubblica.

Off the promenade, clearly marked by yellow tourist signs, are the medieval tenth-century **St. Orso church** with its fine 12th-century cloister and ruins of a **Roman theater** and **amphitheater.**

RESTAURANTS

Brasserie Valdotaine, Via Xavier de Maistre 8; tel. (0165) 32076. In the heart of Aosta, Rocco Colucci's renovated brewery is spacious and comfortable. The rustic ambience is complemented by the good local fare and national specialties. A Lit. 20,000 tourist menu is offered; dining outside during the summer. The more frugal can lunch on pasta and salad for Lit. 15,000. A full *alla carta* meal is Lit. 35,000. Closed Wed. All cards.

Cavallo Bianco, Via Aubert 15; tel. (0165) 362214. Every small town has "the" restaurant. Voila! With its garden, this hardly seems like a place where weary travelers once changed horses on trans-Alpine trips. Totally renovated six years ago, the atmosphere is elegant and intimate. "I don't know the menu until I get back from the market at 9 A.M." claims cook Paolo Vai, who runs the restaurant with brother Franco. Paolo is a firm believer of renaissance cuisine: traditional regional recipes in a more contemporary fashion. The results are excellent. A regional menu is Lit. 40,000 (without wine). A *degustazione* (samples of a wider variety of delicacies) menu is Lit. 90,000, also without wine. Closed Sun. evening, Mon., and July. AE, DC, V.

Vecchia Aosta, Porta Pretoria 4; tel. (0165) 361186. Being more picturesque would be difficult. Ennio and Maria Giovanna Brochet's beautiful restaurant is tastefully tucked into the city's old Roman walls along the promenade. An interior garden in the summer expands capacity to 150. Dining is by candlelight; a good regional meal is Lit. 30,000–35,000 with wine. Closed Wed. AE, MC, V.

Vecchio Ristoro, Via Tourneuve 4; tel. (0165) 33238. Situated in a renovated mill 300 yards from the intersection of the roads for Monte Bianco and the Gran San Bernardo tunnels. This small restaurant seats only 35–40, so it's best to reserve. Such specialties as smoked breast of goose, smoked fish, and cabbage soup are worthy contributions to the regional menu. Dinners cost Lit. 35,000–40,000 without wine. Closed Sun., Feb. 19–28, June 20–July 10, and Nov. 1–10. No cards.

Around the Valley

Traveling the valley for a day or two while based in Aosta can cover most of the region and some exceptional scenery. A casual day's drive is from Aosta to Courmayeur and through the Monte Bianco tunnel to Chamonix, continuing through the valley into Switzerland, then returning through the Gran San Bernardo tunnel to Aosta. Local caffès and picnic possibilities are everywhere.

Leave Italy through the Little San Bernardo Pass via La Thuile and Lake Verney. This and the drive to Annecy—an Alpine Venice on a beautiful scenic lake—make for a splendid side trip while en route to Geneva. There is a popular ski station here, too.

If gambling is your game, take the 17½-mile drive down A5 toward Turin. The **St. Vincent casinò**—never forget the accent (without it, the literal translation is "whore house")— could pay the hotel bill, if you're optimistic—and lucky!

Beautifully illuminated on the right, halfway to St. Vincent, is the magnificent 14th-century **medieval castle of Fenis.** Despite its fortifications, like most castles in the Valle d'Aosta it was built as a Middle Ages status symbol with the lucrative farming income provided its feudal owners. Visitors are welcome.

Two other day trips are through the Val Savarenche and the Valtournenche.

The first enters the heart of **Gran Paradiso National Park;** the Val Savarenche provides a glimpse at the best-preserved part of the vast natural reserve.

The Gran Paradiso is a beautiful area of mountains and streams. **Trout fishing** is possible in the many streams— although licenses are required. You'll also need a membership card from the Italian Fishing Federation (FIPS). You can reach the office in Rome at Viale Tiziano 70; tel. (06) 36851; or contact the **Aosta Tourist Information Office,** tel. (0165) 35655 or 303718. The tourist information office can provide information on Alpine guides if climbing is your sport. Campsites abound in the park.

Piedmont

Turin (Torino)

The most provocative baptism to Turin is a stroll under the elegant, baroque arcades along the central **Via Roma** from **Piazza Carlo Felice,** in front of the main Porta Nuova railroad station, to **Piazza Castello.**

The stores tastefully display the city's sophisticated sense of elegance, along with sweets and pastries that are unrivaled in Italy. Most of Turin's principal attractions are also in this area.

One block off Piazza San Carlo (halfway down Via Roma) is the **Egyptian Museum** at Via Accademia delle Scienze 6. Only Cairo has a larger display of Egyptian artifacts and relics.

To enter Turin then of a lovely August afternoon was to find a city of arcades, of pink and yellow stucco, of innumerable cafés, of blue-legged officers, of ladies draped in the North-Italian mantilla. An old friend of Italy coming back to her finds an easy waking for dormant memories. Every object is a reminder and every reminder a thrill. Half an hour after my arrival, as I stood at my window, which overhung the great square, I found the scene, within and without, a rough epitome of every pleasure and every impression I had formerly gathered from Italy: the balcony and the Venetian-blind, the cool floor of speckled concrete, the lavish delusions of frescoed wall and ceiling, the broad divan framed for the noonday siesta, the massive mediaeval Castello in mid-piazza, with its shabby rear and its pompous Palladian front, the brick campaniles beyond, the milder, yellower light, the range of colour, the suggestion of sound.

—Henry James
Italian Hours, 1909

Unless otherwise noted, museums and historic sights are open Tuesday through Sunday mornings (closed Mondays and holidays).

Next door is the **Sabauda Gallery,** featuring primitive to 18th-century art. The Dutch and Flemish collections are considered by many to be the finest in Italy. Across Via Bertola on the left is the **Risorgimento Museum,** with the first chamber occupied by a united Italian parliament.

At the end of Via Roma, on Piazza Castello, is the **Palazzo Madama** (open 9 A.M. to 7 P.M. Tuesday through Saturday, 10 A.M. to 6 P.M. Sunday; closed Mondays and holidays), the most representative building of Turin's history. The 18th-century baroque facade is by Filippo Juvara, the Sicilian architect responsible for most of Turin's major monuments and shrines. The building incorporates the original castle of the local lord (Marquis Guglielmo VII of Monferrato) and the two towers of Porta Decumana, built by Augustus. Juvara also built the fascinating entrance, staircase, and large upper vestibule. The palace now houses the Ancient Art Museum, featuring Antonello da Messina's 15th-century *Portrait of a Man* and admirable collections of works in gold, glass, bronze, marble reliefs, medals, and sculptures.

Across the square are the Royal Palace, home to the princes of the House of Savoy, and the Royal Chapel of the Holy Shroud. Enter the **Royal Palace** through its ornate iron gates. On the right are the Armory, with an elaborate display of armor and weapons, and the Library (Biblioteca), with da Vinci sketches, including a self-portrait. Modified at various stages over the years, the palace was created by Amadeo di Castellamonte in the 1600s. Most interesting are the richly decorated throne room, the reception chamber with Carlo Alberto's collection of Oriental vases, the European-style ballroom with a decorative inlaid wooden floor by Capello and the apartment of Queen Maria Teresa.

The House of Savoy

For almost nine centuries the House of Savoy, a dynasty descended from Umberto the Whitehanded, ruled over the Savoy region (now in southeastern France) and the Piedmont. In 1720 it gained control of Sardinia, and from 1860 to 1945 ruled over all of Italy. Turin was the first capital of the Kingdom of Italy—although unification wasn't complete until 1870, when the capital became Rome after a brief stop in Florence.

Access to the **Chapel of the Holy Shroud** is around the corner on Via XX Settembre, through St. John's Cathedral, Turin's only example of Renaissance architecture. The 17th-century chapel is by Guarino Guarini. The shroud—once believed to be the cloth in which the body of Christ was wrapped after it was removed from the cross—is preserved in an urn on the chapel's marble altar. Despite recent proof that the shroud is not old enough to have been Christ's burial cloth, it is still revered as a work of art. The shroud is on public display only under exceptional circumstances.

To the right on leaving the cathedral is **Piazza della Repubblica,** where there are a number of **open-air markets.** Don't be confused by references to the Balon, Porta Palazzo, and Porta Pila markets, all are at Piazza della Repubblica. Monday through Friday mornings and all day Saturday, the area is a food and fruit market. On Saturday, the side streets are taken over by the Balon flea market. The honky atmosphere that has invaded Rome's Porta Portese open-air market is not present, but bartering is still the order of the day.

The **Mole Antonelliana,** at Via Montebello 20 (to the right of the palace toward the Po), is a 19th-century construction by Antonelli that is the symbol of Turin. Once a synagogue, the building was severely damaged by a windstorm in 1953, and was gutted and reinforced. An elevator takes visitors to an observation platform for the best view available over the inner city.

The **Parco del Valentino** extends over one hundred acres on the left bank of the Po between Corso Dante and Corso Vittorio Emanuele II, which passes in front of the nearby Porta Nuova rail terminal. The park features the original 17th-century French Renaissance Valentino castle and botanical gardens, exhibit hall, and a re-creation of a 15th-century

Piedmont village. The park is open 9:30 A.M. to noon and 3 to 6 P.M.

The **Automobile Museum,** Corso Unità d'Italia 40, is open 9:30 A.M. to 12:30 P.M., and 3 to 7 P.M. April to October; 10 A.M. to 12:30 P.M. and 3 to 5:30 P.M. November to March; and is closed Monday, Tuesday, and two weeks at Christmas and New Year's. The low-slung modern building offers an interesting display of the evolution of automotive engineering, along with a number of vintage automobiles. Nearby is Fiat's original Lingotto plant, now site of Turin's **automobile show.** Once held every other year in the fall, the show has gained more prominence and is now held every year in the spring.

❦ RESTAURANTS

Break, Piazza Carlo Felice. Strong fast-lunch trade with employees from area business, banks, and exchanges. An inside garden is open during the summer. Nothing elaborate, but satisfactory for a quick noon meal. Lunches run Lit. 13,000–15,000. Closed Sun. and Aug. No cards.

Del Cambio, Piazza Carignano 2; tel. (011) 546690. Some claim the Risorgimento was born here. The restaurant was the favorite of regular customer Camillo Benso, Count of Cavour, who was the political mind behind the unification of Italy. The restaurant is a national monument and is the best known in Turin. A good regional menu is offered, utilizing top regional wines in a number of traditional recipes. Dinners run about Lit. 60,000–80,000 with wine. Closed Sun. and Aug. AE, DC, V.

I Due Lampioni, Via Carlo Alberto 45A; tel. (011) 546721. Reservations are a must at this elegant restaurant in the heart of Turin. Giancarlo and Pierina Bagatin are constantly improving the ambience to make the restaurant more comfortable. Be sure to try the *antipasti.* Full meals cost Lit. 50,000–60,000. Closed Sun. and Aug. V.

Gatto Nero, Corso Turati 14; tel. (011) 590414. A favorite with Turin industrialists. The regional touch prevails, from antipasto to dessert. Both of the Montecarlo red and white wines available are produced from vineyards owned by the restaurant. Dinner costs about Lit. 60,000–70,000 with wine. Closed Sun. and Aug. AE, DC.

Vecchia Lanterna,Corso Re Umberto 21, tel. (011) 537047. Armando Zanetti is a perfectionist with over 50 years' experience for the diner's benefit. This restaurant is a Turin favorite, so making reservations is a must. Specialties embrace the unusual: brains, tortelloni with squid ink sauce, rice with frog sauce, breast of frog with cranberry sauce. Dinners will cost about Lit. 80,000. Closed Sat., Sun., and mid-Aug. AE, DC, V.

Turin also has a strong caffè tradition, so try:

Baratti e Milani, Piazza Castello 29; tel. (011) 511481. This 200-year-old-plus caffè has a 19th-century atmosphere catering to 20th-century needs, such as the noon salad bar. House specialties are pastry and minichocolates. Outdoor tables are set in the adjoining gallery from May to early fall. Open 8 A.M.–8 P.M.; closed Tues. and Aug. No cards.

Caffè Torino, Piazza San Carlo 204; tel. (011) 547356. Appropriately named, this caffè is strictly Torinese, from the 19th-century decor to the bread sticks. Both snacks and hot meals are available. Open 8:30 A.M.–1 A.M. Closed Tues. and June 15–July 15. All cards.

SIDETRIPS

Two interesting excursions around Turin are to the Superga Basilica and Stupinigi royal hunting lodge. Both works by Filippo Juvara were commissioned by Victor Amadeus II.

Superga, considered Juvara's greatest work, is across the Po and six miles east. At the Chieri intersection turn left and wind to the top of the hill, where there is a fine view of Turin as well as the Alps, from the Matterhorn to Gran Paradiso.

Considered the most noble baroque building of central symmetry, the **Basilica of Superga** was built by Victor Amadeus II to fulfill a vow he made before battling the French at La Feuillade on Sept. 7, 1706. Next to the basilica is a monastery, and the courtyard leads to tombs of the Kings of the House of Savoy.

Stupinigi Palace is seven miles southwest of Turin on the SS23 for Pinerolo. To call this minipalace by Juvara a hunting lodge must be the understatement of the year. Set in a park of over 1,000 acres, it was completed in 1730. It is now open to the public as a furniture museum.

❧ RESTAURANTS

Consider a gastronomical excursion to Costigliole d'Asti, 8 miles from Asti and 42 from Turin, off A21. The restaurant is **Da Guido,** Piazza Umberto I 27; tel. (0141) 966012. Reservations are required in this small, 36-seat, elegant restaurant that is acknowledged as one of the best in Italy. Comment is superfluous—it must be experienced. Management is strictly a family affair between Guido Alciati, his wife, Lidia, and their three sons, Ugo, Piero, and Andrea. Specialties include *agnolotti* (meat-and-cabbage ravioli), mushroom soup, warm duck-liver salad, nougat ice cream with peaches, and marinated rabbit (a 15th-century recipe). Dinner with wine will cost around Lit. 80,000. Closed Sun. and Aug. 1–15. AE.

Sestriere

The sixth milestone (Petra Sixtraria) on the 22 B.C. crossing of the Alps by Hannibal's army and elephants, this annual stop on the World Cup ski circuit was created by automobile tycoon Sen. Giovanni Agnelli in the 1930s for his son Edoardo. In just three years all basics and access roads were constructed, bringing urban conveniences into the mountains and making winter sports facilities available to more than just the elite. In addition to a number of fine **ski slopes** serviced by cable cars and chair lifts, there is also an **ice rink** in the center of town. For summer mountain enthusiasts there is a **golf course;** yellow signs point the way.

Sestriere is 58 miles west of Turin via SS25 to Susa, then left on SS24 to Cesana and left again onto SS23. Superstradas 25 and 24 continue on to France.

The eight-mile road from Cesana was also used to test autos produced in the old Fiat Lingotto factory in Turin. Rising over 2,200 feet from Cesana to Sestriere (an altitude of over 6,600 feet), the road is now site of an annual summer car rally.

Other popular ski stations are Sauze D'Oulx, San Sicario, and Limone Piemonte.

Stresa

With its three Lake Maggiore islands (the Borromeans), this little town 32 miles north of Novara is the most picturesque in all of northern Italy's lake district. The ornate villas (Ducale, Pallavicino, and Taranto), though not open to the public, provide a beauty that is amplified by **Bella, Madre,** and **Pescatori islands,** in the gulf between Stresa and Pallanza.

❧ RESTAURANTS

L'Emiliano, Corso Italia 48; tel. (0323) 31396. Romano Felisi has made this Stresa restaurant a shrine to Emilian cuisine, but no one's complaining. Assisted by wife Maria and two children, he offers a new menu daily in this intimate and elegant restaurant. The likes of his Emilian regional menu, featuring homemade pasta with either Bolognese sauce or ricotta cheese, and costing Lit. 40,000, would be difficult to top even in Emilia. A special *degustazione* menu for Lit. 80,000 is also available. Closed Tues. and Nov. 20–Dec. 20. AE, DC, V.

The 18-acre Madre is the largest of the Borromean trio; Bella is the site of the splendid Borromeo Palace and a superb garden; but Pescatori, the smallest, is the most scenic. This "Fishermen's Island," with its 11th-century **San Vittore church,** is only 110 by 380 yards. Its appeal is legendary, especially to the British, from George Bernard Shaw to Anthony Eden.

The islands, obtained by the Borromeo family from the bishop of Vercelli in the 1500s, are all connected to Stresa by regular **boat service.** Contact Navigazione Lago Maggiore, telephone 30393, or in Milan, Società Navigazione Laghi, Via Ariosto 21; telephone (02) 4812086.

One of the most attractive villas in Stresa is **Villa Taranto,** on SS34 toward Pallanza. The twenty-acre park offers a beautiful variety of exotic plants and flowers as well as statues, fountains, terraces, and lawns. Nearby is the Romanesque **San Remigio church,** dating from the 1100s and adorned with 16th-century frescoes.

Stresa is 48 miles from Milan and 80 miles from Turin. On the A8 Milan–Verese, turn west after Gallarate, then take the SS33. At Comignago there is an intersection with the SS32 from Novara. SS33 continues on to Domodossola and through the Simplon pass into France. At Feriolo on the most western tip of the lake, an intersection with SS34 offers a beautiful scenic drive along the western shore of Maggiore into Switzerland.

15

LIGURIA

Liguria looks to the sea. With its back to the Apennine off-shoot from the Alps, this quarter-moon stretch of coast from Tuscany to France is the second smallest region in Italy.

Centrally located on the coastal bend is the regional capital of Genoa (Genova). The massive port complex, stretching 23 miles west toward Savona, divides the two Italian Rivieras: the Ponente (also known as the Riviera dei Fiori) to the French border, and the Levante, south to La Spezia, a natural harbor that is one of Italy's largest naval bases.

Once inhabitants of one of the Mediterranean's most powerful maritime republics, the austere Genoese were not blessed with foresight when approached by an adventurous weaver's son.

Consequently, the city lost a chance for preeminence in history, and its participation in the worldwide celebrations in 1992 to fete native-born Christopher Columbus will be mostly congratulatory. The five-hundredth anniversary of the epic voyage that changed the world will be marked by international festivities, especially in Spain. (This was one of the prime motives for awarding the 1992 Olympic Games to Barcelona, where a replica of the Genoese mariner's caravel is moored.)

The "Red Belt" anchor on the Tyrrhenian, Genoa concentrates on "quality tourism" and gladly forfeits "mass appeal to those who were still watching sheep twenty years ago," according to one Ligurian regional official.

The above allusion to Adriatic beaches is thinly veiled. But the more sedate and affluent Ligurian clientele has never been tempted by the Adriatic beaches. Ligurian prices help maintain the upper-class clientele. Daily excursions cater to the curious, anxious to sample the international charm of Portofino, on the Levantine coast. Luxury yachts under foreign flags are constantly present, as are the pretentious and the pretenders settled under caffè umbrellas at water's edge.

Still, the natives are not to be denied. Recent government statistics listed Portofino as leading the nation in average per-capita income. "Let the foreigners overrun Portofino," comments a young La Spezia attorney, "as long as they don't spoil the Cinque Terre." A localism indeed, but this enchanting stretch of Ligurian coast is a scenic wonder.

Generally, the Ligurian coast is rocky; beaches are pebbly. There is always some area of public beach, but 90 percent of the shoreline here is privately owned (by hotels and such), making public access difficult.

Kingpin on the Ponente coast is San Remo. Much of the local activity revolves around the scandal-ridden *casinò* (remember the accent). When croupiers aren't favoring generous clients, national attention focuses on the February **pop music festival** that has drawn the tops in international entertainment, from Louis Armstrong to Boy George.

Liguria has her pride as well as her price. For those who can afford it, disappointment is rare.

WINING AND DINING

"Pesto and rustic wine" is the most simple synopsis of the cuisine of Liguria, whose maritime traditions are not as evident as their consequences. Long tenures at sea meant less time to terrace the hilly terrain for vineyards; it also meant a strong desire for vegetables and other sources of vitamins on return to home port.

Only three DOC (government-controlled) wines are produced in Liguria: Rossese di Dolceacqua, Cinqueterre, and Cinqueterre Sciacchetrà. But every area has its own local wine, which is probably a more suitable accompaniment for the local cuisine—they were born together.

Pesto is that mortar-crushed mixture of basil, garlic, olive oil (Liguria's is exceptional), pine nuts, and pecorino cheese. In Liguria pesto is destined as a condiment for minestrone or to garnish *trenette* (long pasta), *trofie* (potato gnocchi), and lasagna.

A few regional specialties often subjected to local variations:

cima ripiena—whole veal bacon rolled around a stuffing of ground meat, eggs, peas, and slices of artichokes or carrots.
cappon magro—a pyramid-shaped seafood and vegetable "queen of salads."
frittelle—fried vegetable and legume fritterlike pancakes. The *ceci* (garbanzo) bean frittella is particularly popular.

A favorite pastime of Ligurians is to stroll through town searching for that aroma that will lead to a characteristic trattoria specializing in local cuisine. This is an art; the uninitiated may be guided by the suggestions that follow below.

Credit cards for our suggested restaurants are listed as accepted. "All cards" means that all of the following are accept-

ed: AE—American Express; DC—Diner's Club; MC—
MasterCard; V—Visa. Prices given estimate the cost of a
complete dinner (antipasto to dessert) per person.

TRAVEL

Flying

The only airport in the four-province region of Genoa, Imperia,
La Spezia, and Savona is Cristoforo Colombo, 4½ miles from
downtown Genoa. Bus service is available at the AMT stops on
Via Petrarca and at Piazza Acquaverde 2. Departure is recommended at least 80 min. prior to flight time; the fare is Lit. 2,500.
By cab the ride averages Lit. 10,000, and is 20 min. from downtown. For airport information tel. (010) 54930.

Daily direct national flights reach Alghero (1 hour, 20 min.),
Cagliari (1 hour, 10 min.), Milan (50 min.), Naples (1 hour, 15
min.), and Rome (1 hour). There are Tues., Thurs., and Sat.
flights to Olbia (50 min.)

For information on national flights contact Alitalia/ATI/Aliblu,
Via XII Ottobre 188 R, Genoa; tel. (010) 54931, or Alisar-
da/Avianova, Via Martin Piaggio 15R, Genoa; tel. (010)
5489317.

International service (duty-free shop available) is provided by
Alitalia, Air France, British Caledonian, Lufthansa, and Swissair.

Both Alitalia and Lufthansa, tel. (010) 580436, fly direct daily
to Frankfurt (1 hour, 25 min.). British Caledonian, tel. (010)
541411, flies direct daily to London-Gatwick (2 hours). Swissair,
tel. (010) 542841, flies direct daily to Zurich (1 hour, 20 min.).
For the 1 hour, 25 min. flight to Paris, Alitalia flies direct daily,
and Air France, tel. (010) 594710, has direct flights four times
a week—Mon., Wed., Fri., and Sun.

Keep in mind that Nice's Côte d'Azur airport is much closer
to western Imperia than is Cristoforo Colombo Airport. Approximately 40 miles from the Italian border, it may be much more
convenient, especially for reaching San Remo.

Taking the Train

All means of mass transportation are concentrated along the
region's extensive coastline.

Genoa is the hub of the rail network in Liguria. The city's main
terminal is Stazione Principe; the other is Brignole. They are only
an 8-min. rail ride from one another and both are approximately
the same distance from the city center, Piazza De Ferrari.

There is almost hourly service from Genoa (Stazione Principe)
to Ventimiglia (2½–3 hours) via Savona, Imperia, and San
Remo. Inter-city (IC) service to La Spezia (1 hour, 13 min.) does
not stop at either Rapallo or Santa Margherita Ligure, where
transportation must be arranged for Portofino. To reach either,
a local train is the answer.

Genoa is on the main west coast line south to Naples. Many
of the stops in Rome are at the Ostiense Station, and not at
Rome's Termini. IC service to Rome takes 5 hours, 15 min.

Other principal IC trains from Genoa reach Milan in 1½ hours and Turin in 1 hour, 42 min.

Local train service to the five towns (Monterosso al Mare, Vulnezia or Vernazza, Corniglia, Manarola, and Riomaggiore) on the Levante's 11½-mile Cinque Terre coast is available at both Sestri Levante and La Spezia. There is no road connecting these five villages; the hourly trains are the only means of public transportation between these villages and the rest of the region.

Driving

Though bordering the inaccessible, the hinterland of Liguria is pierced by modern turnpikes linking the region with other major cities of the so-called industrial triangle between Genoa, Turin, and Milan.

The A10 and A12 provide complete coverage for the entire length of the region. The two meet at Genoa and form an Italian highway engineering masterpiece. Before their conception, the grueling drive on the coastal SS1 was tedious and time-consuming. But for the holiday traveler, the scenary may be worth the time.

The A10 covers the nearly 100-mile tract to the French border near Ventimiglia to link with France's turnpike network; Nice is only 24 miles west, via Monte Carlo.

The A12 south to La Spezia (60 miles from Genoa) seemingly spends more time under mountains than in open air, whereas SS1 makes just two deviations from the coastal Tyrrhenian arc: around the Tigullio Peninsula (the peninsula of Portofino) between Camogli and Rapallo and around the eastern extreme of the rugged Cinque Terre, from Sestri Levante to La Spezia.

Four turnpikes tie into the A10-A12 semicircle. Off the A10, at Savona there is the A6 to Turin (70 miles), and at Voltri the A26 to Milan (96 miles) via Alessandria (26 miles).

Where the A10 and A12 meet at Genoa Ovest is the A7 for Milan (66 miles). At La Spezia the A12 meets the A15 for Parma (65 miles), which is on the Milan–Rome A1. (There is no straight turnpike route down the west coast to Rome, since the proposed Livorno–Civitavecchia tract of highway cannot be untangled from red tape in Rome.)

CAR RENTALS

Genoa

Airport	City	Principe Rail Terminal
Avis; tel. (010) 607280	Avis, Via Balbi 190R; tel. (010) 255598	Maggiore; tel. (010) 255342
Europcar; tel. (010) 604881	Europcar, Via Ramassia 106R; tel. (010) 565153; telex 285294	
Hertz; tel. (010) 607422	Hertz, Via Casacce 3; tel. (010) 564412; telex 270373	
Maggiore; tel. (010) 607467	Maggiore, Corso Sardegna 275/281; tel. (010) 892153	

Riviera di Levante

La Spezia	Santa Margherita Ligure
Avis, Via Frat. Rosselli 86/88; tel. (0187) 33345	Avis (open Apr. 1–Oct. 31), Garage Cattoni, Via Solimano 20; tel. (0185) 286833
Europcar, Viale S. Bartolomeo 371; tel. (0187) 512140	
Hertz, Viale S. Bartolomeo 665; tel. (0187) 516712; telex 282644	
Maggiore, Via XXIV Maggio 45; tel. (0187) 36168	

Riviera di Ponente

San Remo

Avis (open Apr. 1–Oct. 31),
Corso Imperatrice 96; tel.
(0184) 73897
Hertz, Garage Italia,
Via XX Settembre 17; tel.
(0184) 85618
Maggiore, Piazza Colombo 19;
tel. (0184) 85165

Taking the Ferry

Genoa is one of the principal mainland ports for ferry service to both Sardinia and Sicily. For information, see the "Travel" sections of each region. Access to the Genoa ferry port is from Strada Aldo Moro.

❦ ACCOMMODATIONS

Liguria has one of Italy's most formidable hotel traditions. On the Rivieras in particular a cult thrives to maintain the true sense of luxurious, first-class hotels, in a region where substance is more important than appearance. Appropriately, the country's most attended hotel trade show is held every Nov. at Genoa's modern and extensive industrial fairgrounds on the waterfront.

Here are a few of the more picturesque hotels along the coast and an in-town alternative or two. Try combining a night in the city with a Riviera holiday.

Expect to pay top dollar in San Remo, Portofino, and Santa Margherita Ligure. More reasonable rates are to be found elsewhere along the rivieras—and especially inland. Hotels usually are open year-round, unless indicated otherwise. Don't expect air-conditioning unless specified.

Credit cards are listed as accepted. "All cards" means that all of the following are accepted: AE—American Express; DC—Diner's Club; MC—MasterCard; V—Visa.

Rates given are for the range between single and double rooms, unless otherwise specified.

Genoa

Bristol Palace, Via XX Settembre 35, 16126; tel. (010) 592541; telex 216550 BRISTL. This 4-star hotel with 130 air-conditioned rooms is just minutes from the central Piazza de

Ferrari. No restaurant, but bar service is available. Room rates with breakfast run Lit. 143,000–220,000. All cards.

Colombia, Via Balbi 40, 16126; tel. (010) 261841; telex 270423. A luxury, 5-star hotel with 172 air-conditioned rooms. Parking is available and the hotel is near the Porta Principe rail terminal. Considered *the* address by VIPs. Room rates with breakfast, Lit. 240,000–340,000. All cards.

Riviera di Levante (East of Genoa)

LA SPEZIA
Astoria, Via Roma 139, 19100; tel. (0187) 35122. This 3-star hotel with 51 rooms is centrally located in a quiet area, but parking can be adventurous. Wall safes are in every room. Room rates: Lit. 50,000–75,000. All cards.

LERICI
Venere Azzurra, Lungomare Biaggini 29, 19032 (SP); tel. (0187) 965334. With a fine view of the Gulf of the Poets, this is a 3-star hotel with 22 rooms but no restaurant, in one of the most popular lower Levante resorts. The beach is close by. Room rates, Lit. 50,000–75,000. All cards.

PORTOFINO
Splendido, Salita Baratta 10, 16034 (GE); tel. (0185) 269551; telex 281057. This 1901 villa right on the coast was built by Marquis Baratta in a tropical garden. It has a fine view of the sea and now a luxury-class 5-star hotel with two lauded restaurants: One is on the villa's terrace, the other is next to a heated pool. Regional cuisine is featured. Rates for the 65 air-conditioned rooms, with breakfast, are Lit. 280,000–470,000. Closed Nov. 1–March 25. All cards.

SANTA MARGHERITA LIGURE
Grand Hotel Miramare, Lungomare Milite Ignote 30, (GE); tel. (0185) 287013; telex 270437. Open all year, the hotel was built in 1904 as a Costa family summer residence. The facade was returned to its original Liberty style in May 1988. On Aug. 26, 1933, Guglielmo Marconi successfully conducted his first wireless experiments (transmitting nearly 100 miles) from the hotel terrace. In 1951 Italian Prime Minister Alcide De Gasperi hosted the preliminary conference leading to the formulation of the European Coal and Steel Community. The hotel is just 50 yards from the coast in a floral park; a snack bar is on the shore. Summer dining is in the Barracuda restaurant alongside the pool; in the winter dining moves to the panoramic La Terazza. Rates for the 81 air-conditioned rooms of this first-class hotel, including breakfast, run Lit. 168,000–292,000; suites, Lit. 325,000–480,000. AE, V.

Imperial Palace, Via Pagana 19, 16038 (GE); tel. (0185) 288991; telex 271398. This 98-room, luxury hotel was once the summer residence of Italy's Queen Elena. It was purchased by the Costa family in 1889 and became a hotel in 1910; the 1922 Rapallo Treaty between Russia and Germany was finalized here. The hotel's floral park leads directly to the beach and one of two restaurants. The other is in the main villa. Rates for the air-conditioned rooms, with breakfast, are Lit. 220,000–380,000; suites, Lit. 565,000–780,000. Closed Oct. 31–Easter. All cards.

Moderately priced accommodations are available around the Cinque Terre: for example **Nido** at Fiascherino, **Miramare** at Tellaro, **Due Gemelli** at Riomaggiore, and **Marina Piccola** at Manarola. These are simple, but clean; explore locally for other options.

Riviera di Ponente (West of Genoa)

BORGIO-VEREZZI
Villa Rose, Via Sauro 1, 17022 (SV); tel. (019) 610461. This 3-star hotel with restaurant is on the coast in a small floral park. Lit. 40,000–50,000. No credit cards.

SAN REMO
Royal, Corso Imperatrice 74, 18100 (IM); tel. (0184) 79991; telex 27054. Situated in a colorful 3-acre park, this luxury-class 5-star hotel is protected by the Italian Fine Arts Commission. Miniature golf, tennis courts, and a swimming pool are available, along with conference halls with capacities for up to 300. Two restaurants are available. Rates for the 138 air-conditioned rooms, with breakfast, are Lit. 170,000–295,000. Closed Oct. 15–Dec. 20. All cards.

Genoa

Genoa is a reminder of grandmother's house. Severe facades protect privacy; warm and elaborate interiors commemorate an active and productive past.

Though Italian industrial production is rising, Genoa is in a recession. Many local industries are concentrating efforts elsewhere; the local population is declining. Genoa is the only major Italian city to have experienced such a phenomenon in the last decade.

The port is still one of the most active in the Mediterranean, with Italian seemingly a foreign language in the old-town fringe near the port, frequented by merchant seamen. After dark the area can yield unpleasant surprises as seamen who have jumped ship ply dubious trades.

But the past prominence of the once prestigious city republic, former home of wealthy merchants and financiers, warrants more than just a casual visit. Begin in the central **Piazza de Ferrari.** Via Dante runs into Piazza Dante, where there is an 18th-century reconstruction of the alleged childhood **home of Cristoforo Colombo** better known as Columbus (visitors welcome). In fact, many towns and villages in Liguria claim to be the birthplace of the great navigator; the name Colombo was once almost as common as Smith is today, which has easily led to confusion in reconstructing the past.

Behind *casa Colombo* is the 12th-century **St. Andrew cloister** and the medieval **Porta Soprana** in the old city wall. Through the gate, after a straight five-minute walk, is the Gothic black-and-white facade of **San Lorenzo Cathedral.** In the **Treasury museum** (open 9:30 to 11:45 A.M. and 3 to 5:45 P.M.; closed Sundays and holidays), in Piazza San Lorenzo, are displays of the evolution of the craftsmanship of Genoese goldsmiths and silversmiths, 13th-century Byzantine crosses, and 16th-century processional coffers.

To the right of Piazza San Lorenzo, toward Via San Luca, is the **Risorgimento Museum,** Via Lomellini 11 (open 9 A.M. to 1 P.M., and 3 to 6 P.M.; closed Sundays and Mondays), in the home where Italian patriot Giuseppe Mazzini was born. Just beyond is the **Palazzo Spinola,** Piazza Pellicceria 1, once the residence of Genoese nobility.

Within is the **Spinola Art Gallery** (open 9 A.M. to 5 P.M.; Sunday, 9 A.M. to 1 P.M.; closed Monday). The collection includes major Genoese painters and other masters such as Antonello de Messina, Joos Van Cleve, Mattia Preti, and Filippo Parodi.

Only five minutes away is **Via Garibaldi,** lined with fine palaces, two of which also contain interesting art collections.

Palazzo Bianco, Via Garibaldi 11, is open Tuesday through Saturday, 9 A.M. to 1 P.M., and 2 to 6 P.M.; Sunday, 9 A.M. to noon; closed Monday. The 18th-century palace is a reconstruction of the 16th-century Grimaldi palace and includes works by prominent Italian and Flemish artists (Gerard David, Matsys, Rubens, and Van Dyck, among others).

Palazzo Rosso, Via Garibaldi 18, has the same hours as Palazzo Bianco. Titian, Tintoretto, Guercino, and De Ferrari head a long list of Italian artists who are represented.

North on the "street of palaces" is Via Balbi and the finest palace of them all, the former House of Savoy residence in Genoa: **Palazzo Reale,** Via Balbi 10; open 9 A.M. to 1 P.M. on Sunday, Tuesday, Thursday, and Saturday. The richly decorated interior is abundant with *stucchi* and frescoes. The ornate Hall of Mirrors is a reminder of Versailles. The Throne Room and Reception Hall still contain Savoy furnishings, and there is an abundant collection of paintings and sculptures by leading Italian and Flemish artists.

Genoa has not neglected its past maritime prestige; it can be seen in the **Naval History Museum,** near Piazza Principe and the rail terminal; open Tuesday through Saturday, 9 A.M. to 1 P.M. and 2 to 5 P.M., closed Sunday and Monday. The 18 rooms of the 16th-century **Doria Palace** present a chronological study of over four centuries of naval history, up to the technical advances at the beginning of the 19th century. Many items came from the arsenal and arms collection of the maritime republic.

More detailed information on the more than 20 museums in Genoa can be obtained from **local tourist offices,** at Via Roma 11, tel. (010) 581405; Via Pittaluga 4R, tel. (010) 321504, or Via Porta d'Archi 10, tel. (010) 541504.

Before leaving Genoa, see the floral composition representing Columbus's three ships in Piazza della Vittoria. Shoppers should keep their eyes open for silver- and gold-plated filigree jewelry, blown glass, and ceramics.

RESTAURANTS

Antica Osteria del Bai, Via Quarto 12, Località Quarto dei Mille; tel. (010) 387478. This historic anti-Saracen fort is allegedly where Risorgimento warrior Giuseppe Garibaldi met with Italian patriot Nino Bixio before heading for Sicily with his Redshirts task force of 1,000 (Garibaldi's army of volunteers who set out to liberate the island). Though the restaurant will seat 100, reservations are recommended if you want to enjoy a Ligurian banquet. Lit. 60,000–65,000 with wine. Closed Mon. and July 20–Aug. 10. All cards.

Da Giacomo, Corso Italia 1R; tel. (010) 369647. When the Genoese aren't seeking a little, unknown trattoria, this elegant, comfortable "old faithful" gets the nod. Lit. 75,000–85,000 with local wine. Closed Sun. and Aug. AE, DC, V.

Zeffirino, Via XX Settembre 20; tel. (010) 591990. The five Belloni brothers and their families run this "pesto palace" that has attracted Frank Sinatra and Luciano Pavarotti. Though Pope John Paul II dined in the curia on his visit to Genoa, Zeffirino supplied the meal. Lit. 50,000–60,000 without wine. Closed Wed. All cards.

Riviera di Levante

Though Portofino is considered by many the crown jewel on this coast, east of Genoa, there are two specific areas rivaling one another in scenic beauty: Portofino's peninsula and the Gulf of La Spezia-Cinque Terre.

The former is the small peninsula jutting into the Tyrrhenian between the seaside towns of Camogli and Rapallo. No coast road traverses the entire peninsula, although there is a provincial road crossing Monte Portofino from Camogli via Ruta to Santa Margherita Ligure.

SIDETRIPS

Brief sidetrips may be taken to San Rocco and Portofino Vetta (nearly 2,000 feet above sea level; *vetta* means summit). There are beautiful views of the coast up to Genoa and, from Portofino Vetta, all of the Gulf of Tigullio.

Camogli

Camogli literally means "wives' homes," dubbed such due to the extended absences of maritime husbands. Some of the picturesque homes appear to drop straight into the sea. The town must be seen by foot; autos should be parked just outside of town. From Camogli there is a **boat service** to the village of San Fruttuoso (also accessible by boat from Portofino), which has no road links. The view of the coast from the sea is more than rewarding on the brief boat trip.

Portofino

Portofino is off-limits to automobiles, and parking can be a problem on the outskirts of the beautiful little village, situated in a natural inlet lined with renovated homes around the port. Outdoor caffès are abundant, and there are many tiny shops offering quality merchandise.

When the water is calm the **Cristo degli Abissi** (Christ of the Depths) **bronze statue** is visible in the center of the harbor. On the point of the peninsula is the 16th-century **San Giorgio castle** (open 10 A.M. to 5 P.M. everyday except Tuesday).

❧ RESTAURANTS

Il Pitosforo, Molo Umberto 1; tel. (0185) 69020. Mario Vignelli and family have one of the most picturesque positions on the Ligurian coast—right on the small port in Portofino. Clients are warmly greeted; Ligurian and international cuisine professionally served. Dinner will cost about Lit. 100,000 (yes, that's per person!). Closed Tues., Wed. noon, Jan., Feb. All cards.

Santa Margherita Ligure

The narrow coast road from Portofino to Rapallo passes through evocative Paraggi and Santa Margherita, a beautiful but highly commercialized seaside resort that is dominated by the 16th-century **Villa Centurione** (Durazzo) and its extensive **park,** now open to the public.

❧ RESTAURANTS

Cesarina, Via Mameli 2E; tel. (0185) 286059. The Bonardi brothers and Angelo Cozzi offer the best seafood specialties in Liguria. A full meal with a good Vermentino wine will cost around Lit. 65,000. Closed Wed., Mar. 5–17, and Dec. 12–27. V.

Rapallo

In Rapallo stroll along the Lungomare Vittorio Veneto coastal promenade, lined with enticing shops and caffès. At the end of the street is the small 16th-century **castle** that has become the symbol of the town. It is often used as a venue for shows and exhibits of artistic and cultural interest.

A reminder of the "tourism of the elite" that flourished in Rapallo at the beginning of the 19th century is the **Chiostro della Banda Cittadina,** something like a bandstand, where local bands played for the pleasure of holidayers.

La Spezia and the Cinque Terre

The Gulf of La Spezia and the Cinque Terre are equally pleasant and picturesque. The Cinque Terre are five villages, rising from seaside cliffs, east of La Spezia. The town of La Spezia is a military town and bears all the consequences, but it can provide a reasonable base of operations, especially for boat tours. Parking is available (on Viale Italia) between the public park and the seaside mooring of the touring boats.

The Gulf of La Spezia is known as the Gulf of Poets, as it was a favorite with two of England's most prominent romantic poets, Percy Bysshe Shelley (1792–1822) and Lord George Gordon Byron (1788–1824). Shelley drowned off the coast of Viareggio just south of La Spezia.

Two museums in La Spezia are worth a visit.

The Civic Museum, on Via Curtatone, is open 9 A.M. to 1 P.M. and 3 to 7 P.M., Tuesday through Saturday; and 9 A.M. to 1 P.M. Monday; it is closed Sunday. The most important of the three sections in the museum contains prehistorical archaeological artifacts from the nearby isle of Palmaria and stelae from the 177 B.C. Roman colony at Luni. The **excavations** and the **Luni Museum** (Via S. Pero, open 9 A.M. to noon and 4 to 7 P.M.; 2 to 6 P.M. only in the winter; closed Monday) are just off the A12 heading south (a thirty-minute drive from La Spezia).

The Naval Museum, Piazza Chioco, is open Tuesday, Thursday, and Saturday, 9 A.M. to noon and 3 to 6 P.M. This museum, next to the military arsenal, centers around relics collected in the Villafranca arsenal near Nice by Savoy regent Emanuele Filiberto in 1560. The collection has been in La Spezia since 1870. It contains relics of sea battles up to the two world wars, and an interesting hall dedicated to ships' figures.

❦ RESTAURANTS

La Locandina, Via Sapri 10; tel. (0187) 27499. Good Ligurian and fish offerings are the fare in this small, rustic, family-run restaurant. A full meal without wine runs Lit. 45,000. Closed Mon. and Aug. No cards.

Trattoria Toscana da Dino, Via Da Passano 17; tel. (0187) 21360. Tuscan cuisine has precedence, but when it's difficult to find a place open in Aug., this oasis on the park is a blessing.

Good seafood with local wine runs Lit. 40,000. Closed Sun. eve., Mon., and June 25–July 10. No cards.

From La Spezia only the first two of the Cinque Terre villages, Monterosso and Riomaggiore, can be reached by automobile. The Via Cinque Terre, up Monte Santa Croce, leads through a tunnel, and at the opposite end there is a fantastic view of the coast from a wide parking area adjacent to Lombardo's Trattoria delle Cinqueterre.

Lombardo's is nothing extravagant and is at times chaotic, but the seafood antipasto and *frittura di mare* make a stop here worthwhile.

A meal break can be particularly enjoyable after trying to reach Riomaggiore by auto, not recommended during July and August in particular. The long line of autos parked along the road often restrict travel to just one lane, which can be disastrous because the road is not one-way. The main square at Riomaggiore is about the size of an ancho-vy—picturesque but not conducive to a joy ride.

For the more fortunate, the scenic **"Lovers' Walk"** weaves along the craggy coast. At times it is interrupted by damage from the pounding surf, so the hike to the next town is not always possible; try a boat ride instead.

SIDETRIP TO LERICI AND PORTOVENERE

A particularly pleasant all-day boat trip from La Spezia with sight-seeing, shopping, and bathing possibilities takes in Lerici and Portovenere. (Boat departure times are posted at the dock.) Two of the most photographed sights on the trip are the 13th-century **castle** built by rival Pisans at the entrance of the harbor at Lerici, and the strait between Palmaria Island and the main-land past Portovenere. On the point of the peninsula is the **church of San Pietro,** built in the 13th century on the founda-tions of a temple to the goddess of love. Across the strait are the remains of a **Romanesque abbey.**

RESTAURANTS

In **Portovenere,** try a meal at **Del Corsaro,** Lungomare Doria 102; tel. (0187) 900622. Seafood is obviously the fare at this small restaurant on the sea across the strait from Palmaria Is-land. With only 60 settings, it's popular with tourists and locals alike. Lit. 45,000 without wine. Closed Thurs., May 25–June 15, and Jan. 6–31. All cards.

Riviera di Ponente

Known as the Riviera dei Fiori, or the Floral Coast, this is Italy's most extended stretch of natural beauty; picturesque towns and villages complement nature's work, making the ex-perience unforgettable. Several hinterland excursions are equally as rewarding, and are probably the best alternatives for lodging during the peak July and August months.

Noli, Varigotti, and Finale Ligure

Nearly every inch of the seventy-mile coast, between Noli and Ventimiglia in particular, offers enchanting variations. A few highlights are the old town at the base of the **Ursino castle at Noli,** the Mediterranean **rainbow of houses** at Varigotti, and the historic, **colorful parades** in Finale Ligure.

Borgio and Verezzi

Borgio and Verezzi defy being charted on most maps, but they represent a highlight on the Ligurian cultural summer calendar. A gold statue of Verezzi's symbolic **mill** is presented every summer to a leading Italian actor during a series of **theatrical presentations** staged in the square in front of the church of St. Agostino. Verezzi is just a short drive up the hill from coastal Borgio; take relaxing, scenic strolls along the Viale del Tramonto and Viale del Sole.

Loano

Loano also has a picturesque old town and promenade along the coast, but above the town is the most interesting attraction, the **Toirano caverns** (five miles inland from Borghetto Santo Spirito). The thirteen-hundred-yard-long caverns were not discovered until 1950. In addition to the spectacular natural sculptures, in the Bàsura cave there is the petrified footprint of a prehistoric man.

Alassio, Imperia, and Bussana

Alassio offers one of the area's widest selections of souvenirs, **local ceramics,** in particular. And from the little church atop Santa Croce cape there is a fine view over the town and Gallinara Island.

Imperia's history dates to the time of the Romans. The provincial capital is the result of a 1923 union of the towns of Porto Maurizio and Oneglia. City hall is halfway between the two on the connecting artery of Via Giacomo Matteotti.

This area marks the beginning of Liguria's extensive "flower industry," which stretches all the way to Bordighera; greenhouses outnumber vineyards on the terraced hillsides.

Bussana is just before San Remo. The old town, abandoned after a devastating 1887 earthquake, has now developed into an **artist's colony;** the artists may sell their work, if you make a good enough offer.

RESTAURANTS

In Imperia, stop at **Lanterna Blu,** Via Scarincio 32, Porto Maurizio; tel. (0183) 63859. Neapolitan Tonino Fiorillo's seafood is particularly enjoyable on the comfortable terrace. A full meal without wine will come to around Lit. 75,000. Closed Wed. and Nov. 5–Dec. 5. AE, DC.

San Remo

San Remo is considered the capital of the flower coast. From October to June, the **flower market** blooms between 6 and 8 A.M., as flowers are gathered to be sent all over Italy and abroad. The town consists of two distinct sections. The **old town,** *Pigna* (meaning "beak"; it has a pointed shape), is all twisting alleys and stairways. The more modern complex, centering around Corso dell'Imperatrice and Via Matteotti, is the site of the **Casinò.** Unusual is the town's onion-domed **Russian church.**

Forgetting the accent on casinò is offensive; San Remese are proud of this reminder of *la Belle Époque,* and won't appreciate it being called a "whorehouse"—the literal translation of the unaccented casino.

RESTAURANTS
Giannino, Lungomare Trento e Trieste 23; tel. (0184) 70843. Light, well-balanced Ligurian recipes are served in this elegant restaurant under the watchful eye of proprietor Giuseppe Gasparini. Wife Anna commands in the kitchen. A full meal without wine runs Lit. 60,000. Closed Sun. and Mon. noon, 15 days in July, and 15 days in Dec. DC, MC, V.

Bordighera

Bordighera is another of the major floricultural centers of the region. Since 1586 it has furnished the Vatican with the palms that are blessed and distributed in Rome on Palm Sunday.

The privilege of supplying the Vatican with palms was granted by Pope Sixtus V after the ceremony to install the obelisk in the center of St. Peter's Square. Architect Domenico Fontana was directing nearly one thousand men and 140 horses in the operation; the pope had ordered silence, with the death penalty for anyone who violated the decree. But the ropes for the operation proved too long, and as the obelisk was being erected it began to tilt out of position. "Water the ropes," screamed a laborer from Bordighera. The water caused the hemp ropes to shrink, and the obelisk was righted to its position of today. Instead of having the man from Bordighera executed, the pope complimented him on his courage, and granted the palm privilege to his hometown.

Bordighera today offers a fine view from its Lungomare Argentina along the coast. And its old town provides a pleasant stroll into the 15th-century. The **Bicknell Museum** is a major attraction, named after Englishman Clarence Bicknell, who founded it in 1888. The museum features Roman archaeological finds and plaster casts of Neolithic and Iron Age rock engravings. Located at Via Bicknell 3, the museum is open 10 A.M. to noon and 3:30 to 5 P.M., Tuesday through Saturday; it is closed Sunday and Monday.

⁂ RESTAURANTS

Carletto, Via Vittorio Emanuele 339; tel. (0184) 261725. Mamma's helping hand in the kitchen enables the Pessina brothers to provide a good selection of Ligurian specialties with a little fantasy and innovation. Meals run Lit. 50,000 without wine. Closed Wed. and Nov. 10–Dec. 20. AE, DC, V.

Ventimiglia

Ventimiglia is the last Italian town on the Ponente Riviera before the French border. Besides the town's **Roman theater** and interesting hillside **old town,** there is more testimony to transplanted Englishmen three miles west of town, at **Mortola Inferiore.**

In 1867 Sir Thomas Hanbury purchased a 16th-century villa; he transformed the villa's park into a botanical paradise, **Hanbury Gardens,** Italy's largest. Mediterranean maquis and local flora flourish alongside numerous species of rare exotic and tropical plants that Sir Thomas succeeded in acclimatizing to temperate Liguria. The gardens are open 10 A.M. to 4 P.M., Sunday 9 A.M. to 4 P.M.; they are closed Wednesday.

Off the Coast

There are a number of excursions off the coast, the most enjoyable are usually the pot-luck turns inland. A brief jaunt is the drive up the Val di Nervia from Ventimiglia. The first rural settlement, Camporosso, is one and a half miles inland, then comes **Dolceacqua,** another two and a half miles along. This quaint little village, settled alongside the Nervia torrent passed from the counts of Ventimiglia to the Dorias in the 12th century. Now in ruins, the **Doria castle** is where the local lords exercised their rights of *ius primae noctis.* (When any of their peasants married, the lords had the right to opt for the first night with the maiden.)

Continuing on the minitour inland are Isolabona, Rocchetta Nervina, and **Pigna,** which actually proclaimed itself an independent republic on September 18, 1944, in northern Italy's war of liberation against occupying German troops. Characteristic is the medieval loggia in Pigna's Piazza Vecchia.

The last stop before the 28-mile return to the coast (or the exploration of neighboring valleys) is **Castel Vittorio.** The tiny town of 520 inhabitants is typical of inner-Ligurian hilltop villages. The highest point of the hill is dominated by a church steeple that seems to watch over the valley below. The tiny cascade of houses flows down the slopes from the church.

16

NAPLES AND CAMPANIA

Campania is an aging beauty. The memories of her lustrous past linger, but require a dose of imagination to complete the picture.

The region is divided into five provinces: Avellino, Benevento, Caserta, Naples, and Salerno. Inland Avellino and Benevento are dwarfed by the historic attractions in Naples and Salerno. Caserta is almost ignored by tourists turnpike-dashing between Pompeii and Rome, yet the drab provincial seat lies next to one of Italy's architectural triumphs, La Reggia and its park, which rival the French royal palace at Versailles.

Naples, the former Bourbon capital, lies on a scenic gulf stretching from Cape Miseno to the Sorrentine Peninsula. Besides the nearby unique archaeological ruins at Pompeii, Herculaneum, and in the Phlegrean Fields, there are the intriguing gulf islands of Capri, Ischia and Procida.

The town of Salerno is anticlimactic compared to the natural beauty of its province. The drive along the Amalfi Coast from Positano to Cetara is legendary for its views. Thirty miles south of Salerno on the west coast of Campania are the ancient Greek temples at Paestum and the fine Cilento beach areas.

For the less adventurous, one, two, and three-day tours of Campania's highlights are available from Rome. At first glance all-inclusive prices may seem high, but remember that all meals, lodging, transportation, admission fees, and guide costs are included.

This chapter is geared for those seeking their own experience. Campania unfortunately has more drawbacks than most other regions. But it also has one of the most hospitable, helpful, and cheerful populaces on the Italian peninsula. And, surprisingly, even the hawkers have a heart.

WINING AND DINING

Campania cuisine is simple but satisfying fare. Seafood, tomatoes, and mozzarella assume various forms with basil seasoning. Pasta, pizza, fish soups, *pasta e fagioli*, shellfish sauce, smoked provolone, and grilled scamorza cheese are all to be tried here; don't forget that perfect summer salad, *la Caprese* (tomatoes, mozzarella, and basil). Ischia and Capri produce the best regional DOC (government-controlled) wines; notable others are Fiano di Avellino, Greco di Tufo, Solopace, and Taurasi di Vesuvio. Good local wines are Falerno, Gragnano, Ravello, and Boscotrecase's Lacrima Christi from the slopes of Vesuvius.

Credit cards are listed as accepted in our restaurant suggestions. "All cards" means that all of the following are accepted: AE—American Express; DC—Diner's Club; MC—MasterCard; V—Visa.

Prices given are for complete meals (antipasto to dessert) for one person.

CAMPANIA TRAVEL

See also "Travel in Naples," under the Naples section, below.

Flying

The only commercial airport in Campania is Capodichino, 4 miles north of the center of Naples off the Tangenziale Ovest (West) toll expressway. City ATAN bus service (the number 14 line; these buses are red) makes the 25-min. trip between the airport and Piazza Garibaldi, in front of the main rail terminal. The fare is Lit. 600. Cab fare from the airport is Lit. 18,000. Direct domestic flights (on Alitalia, Ati, Aliblu, Alisarda, and Avianova) are available to Bari (55 min.), Bologna (65 min.), Brindisi (1 hour, 10 min.), Catania (50 min.), Florence (1 hour, 45 min.), Genoa (1 hour, 15 min.), Milan (1 hour, 20 min.), Olbia (1 hour), Palermo (45 min.), Rome (50 min.), Torino (1 hour, 25 min.), Venice (1 hour, 15 min.) and Verona (1 hour, 45 min.).

Alitalia, Ati, and Aliblu information is available at Via Medina 41/42; tel. (081) 5425222. For Alisarda and Avianova information contact ALI Travel, Via Cavour 2; tel. (081) 421808.

All Alitalia international flights go through Rome or Milan. Lufthansa, Piazza Municipio 72; tel. (081) 5515440, offers daily flights to Frankfurt via Genoa (3 hours, 20 min.). British Air, tel. (081) 7803087 for Capodichino information, flies direct to London's Gatwick Airport (2 hours, 40 min.) Tues., Thurs., Sat., and Sun. Air France, Via San Carlo 32/34; tel. (081) 5520547; at Capodichino, tel. (081) 7804700, flies direct to De Gaulle Airport in Paris Tues., Wed., Sat., and Sun. (2 hours, 15 min.).

Taking the Train

Campania is served by public and private rail lines that center around Naples. The main Naples rail stations are Centrale and Piazza Garibaldi, which actually are in the same complex on different levels at Piazza Garibaldi. This is the most convenient point for arrivals transferring to the private Circumvesuviano line (EuRail passes not valid). The complex also contains a stop for the Naples Metropolitana (subway) that is basically a state railroad-run city service connecting minor depots around the gulf as far west as Pozzuoli.

Naples is on the principal north–south rail route from Milan down Italy's west coast to Reggio di Calabria and Messina. It is also the terminal for a principal east–west route through Caserta and Benevento to Foggia, in Apulia. Avellino is reached via Benevento (36 min.), on an 18-mile local route.

There are two routes between Rome and Naples. One is via Latina and Formia, the other via Frosinone and Caserta. An Inter-city (IC) train makes the 133-mile trip in 2½ hours. There is also IC service to Salerno (35 min.), requiring nearly 1½ hours on a local from Naples.

Italian state rail service is available to Pompeii via Portici–Herculaneum, Torre del Greco, and Torre Annunziata. With intricate planning one-day excursions can be made to Pompeii from Rome, but very little time will be available to visit the ruins.

There are also two private railroads operating in Naples and environs. The eastbound Circumvesuviana leaves from Corso Garibaldi 387; tel. (081) 7792111; its lines to Sorrento, Sarno, and Baiano pass through the state Gianturco station in Naples that is accessible by escalator from the lower-level Piazza Garibaldi Station.

Circumvesuviana trains also leave Naples every 20–40 min. (depending on the time of day) for the 35-min. ride to Pompeii. Sorrento service takes 65 min.

The Ferrovia Cumana private railroad operates westbound routes from its Montesanto terminal, Piazza Montesanto; tel. (081) 313328. **Do not confuse this with the state-run Montesanto station 200 yards away.** Between the two stations is the Montesanto funicular (cable car) to San Martino. Cumana operates two routes through the volcanic Phlegrean Fields west to Torregaveta, beneath Monte Procida on the Tyrrhenian coast. This is the best service to Baia and Pozzuoli.

Taking the Bus

Ten provincial bus companies connect Naples with other provincial capitals and villages throughout the region (these buses are blue):

Amalfi, Maiori, Minori, Pompeii, Praiano, Ravello, and Salerno: SITA buses depart from Via Pisanelli 3/7; tel. (081) 616080.

Avellino: Gestione Straordinaria Regionale Servizi Extraurbana Avellino buses depart from Piazza Garibaldi 38; tel. (081) 334677, at the central station. Circumvesuviana buses from Avellino, tel. (081) 779211, depart from Porta Vesuviana.

Benevento: Buses are operated by ETAC, Via Marina Nuova, tel. (0824) 24126; Gestione Commissariale Governativa Ferrovia, Piazza Garibaldi, tel. (0824) 24961; and Palombi, Via Marittima, tel. (0824) 21804. These stops are in Naples; the phone numbers for information are for offices in Benevento.

Caserta: Two bus companies offer service: Consorzio Trasporti Pubblici Napoli, Porta Capuana, tel. (081) 261333; and Gestione CGF, Piazza Garibaldi, tel. (0824) 24961.

Potenza: Liscio buses depart from Piazza Garibaldi at the main rail station, tel. (0971) 54673.

Driving

Naples and environs are the heart of Campania. Other provincial seats are Avellino, Benevento, Caserta, and Salerno. Major turnpike arteries are the Rome–Naples A2, which passes Caserta 18 miles north of Naples; and the Naples–Reggio di Calabria A3, which passes Salerno, 33 miles south of Naples.

Skirting Naples and its gulf to the north is the toll Tangenziale Ovest (West) from the Napoli Nord (North) A2 exit. This is the only advisable route through Naples traffic to Capodichino Airport, Pozzuoli, and the Phlegrean Fields.

A mile before the Napoli Nord exit is a cloverleaf onto the A16 for Bari, which bypasses Avellino (37 miles east of Naples, 22 miles north of Salerno) and continues on to the Adriatic, passing 8½ miles east of Benevento. A more direct route to Benevento from the A2 is the state road (SS7) from Caserta (34 miles).

The coastal SS18 south from Naples to Pompeii and the Sorrentine Peninsula is clogged with traffic and exhaust fumes. The A3 runs parallel, and has much less congestion, though even this should be avoided on Sundays, when beach traffic to the Sorrentine Peninsula is intense. The same is true for the Sorrentine and Amalfi drives, which on weekends overflow with day tourists from Naples and Salerno.

CAR RENTALS

Caserta: Avis, Stazione Centrale; tel. (0823) 443756. Europcar, Via Gaspari 64; tel. (0823) 351333. Hertz, c/o Hotel Reggia Palace, San Nicola La Strada; tel. (0823) 458500; telex 710037.

Ischia: Nonresidents are not allowed to bring automobiles onto the island during the high-season summer months. Local rental agencies at Port Ischia are Di Meglio, tel. (081) 991275; Mazzarella, tel. (081) 991141; and Rent-a-Car, tel. (081) 992444. At Forio is Davidauto, tel. (081) 998043.

Salerno: Avis, Corso Garibaldi 144; tel. (089) 229686. Europcar, Corso Garibaldi 29/7; tel. (089) 226257. Maggiore, Corso Garibaldi 106; tel. (089) 228879. (The Hertz office in Naples also handles bookings.)

Sorrento: Avis, Corso Italia 155; tel. (081) 8782459. Europcar, Via degli Aranci 29/E; tel. (081) 8773234. (The Hertz office in Naples also handles bookings.)

Taking the Ferry

Naples, Sorrento, the Amalfi Coast, and the gulf islands are connected by a network of ferries and hydrofoils. The Naples Port
Authority is at Molo Angioino, tel. (081) 206133. *Molo* means
pier; Angioino and Molo Beverello are in front of Castel Nuovo.
Trolley number 1 is the most direct connection between the port
and the main rail terminal; buses number 106 and 150 pass
through Piazza Municipio, a 100-yard walk from the port.

This is the main departure point for boats to Capri (about an
hour and a half trip direct), Ischia, Procida, Sorrento, Sardinia,
Sicily, Tunisia, and Libya. There are also hydrofoils to Capri, Ischia, Procida, and Sorrento.

Destinations and companies providing service:

Capri, Ischia, Procida: Caremar, Molo Beverello; tel. (081)
320763.

Capri, Castellammare di Stabia, Sorrento, Ischia: Navigazione Libera del Gulfo, Molo Beverello; tel. (081) 320763.

Corsica, Sardinia, Sicily, Malta, Tunisia, Libya: Tirrenia, Stazione Marittima; tel. (081) 312181.

A port for hydrofoils only is at Mergellina (Via Caracciolo), just
beyond the Villa Comunale park. The port is about 300 yards
from the Mergellina train station. Trains from Rome via Latina
stop here before going on to the main Naples terminal. A subway connects the main train station to Mergellina. Hydrofoil
companies operating are:

Capri, Ischia, Sorrento, Amalfi, Positano: Alilauro, Via Caracciolo 11; tel. (081) 684288.

Capri, Ischia, Sorrento: Aliscafi, SNAV, Via Caracciolo 10; tel.
(081) 660444.

From the small port at Pozzuoli there are boats to Procida and
Ischia; operators are Caremar, tel. (081) 8671335; or Lauro, tel.
(081) 8673736.

For information in Sorrento, contact Caremar, tel. (081)
8781282.

❦ ACCOMMODATIONS

Naples, Pompeii, Herculaneum, and the towns in the surrounding area are all within easy driving distance from one another.
However, be aware that the Amalfi Drive can be very slow going,
so don't put yourself in the position of having to adhere to a strict
schedule. If you're catching an early flight out of Naples, do stay
there the night before. Otherwise, the area you choose for your
base is a matter of personal priorities: If you'd like to get a good
feel for Naples, then stay there. Avellino, Benevento, and Caserta, off-the-beaten-track towns in the hills east of Naples, make
an unusual base from which to visit the city. Scenic alternatives
would be in Bácoli, on the bay west of Naples; or in towns on
the Sorrentine Peninsula (Massa Lubrense, Sant'Agnello, Sorrento, or Piano di Sorrento) and its Amalfi Coast (Amalfi, Maiori,
Positano, or Ravello). Further south is Salerno, a good stopover
if you're heading into the deep south. If island life is appealing,

stay on Capri or Ischia. (Although you can make daytrips there from Naples and Sorrento, and elsewhere along the coast.)

Credit cards are listed as accepted. "All cards" means that all of the following are accepted: AE—American Express; DC—Diner's Club; MC—MasterCard; V—Visa.

Rates given show the range of prices between single and double rooms.

Naples

LUXURY HOTELS

Most top-rated hotels in Naples are on the waterfront Via Partenope, which connects the Villa Comunale (bordering Via Francesco Caracciolo) with Via Nazara Sauro.

Excelsior, Via Partenope 48, 80121; tel. (081) 417111; telex 710043 EXCENA I. This CIGA hotel is the only 5-star luxury hotel in Naples. All amenities are available for the 138 air-conditioned rooms. The hotel's Casanova Grill is an added treat. Garage parking available. Room rates run Lit. 279,000–393,000. All cards.

Jolly Ambassador, Via Medina 70, 80133; tel. (081) 416000; telex 720335. This 4-star, 251-room hotel is Naples' skyscraper, just off central Piazza Municipio and minutes from the port for Capri, Ischia, and Procida. The hotel is popular with visiting major-league soccer teams and sports personalities. The rooftop restaurant has sweeping views of the gulf. Room rates run Lit. 156,000–203,000; air-conditioning is an added Lit. 15,000. All cards.

Mediterraneo, Via Nuova Ponte di Tappia 25, 80133; tel. (081) 5512240; telex 721615 MEDHOT I. A modern 4-star, 256-room hotel close to Piazza Municipio and the Via Roma shopping area. Rooms run Lit. 94,000–148,000; air-conditioning is an extra Lit. 12,000. All cards.

Royal, Via Partenope 38, 80121; tel. (081) 400244; telex 71067 ROYAL I. This 4-star, 300-room hotel has its own pool, bar, and restaurant. Lit. 123,000–203,000; air-conditioning is an extra Lit. 12,500. All cards.

Vesuvio, Via Partenope 45, 80121; tel. (081) 417044; telex 710127. This 4-star hotel was a favorite with Enrico Caruso and Princess Grace of Monaco. The roof garden offers a beautiful view over Borgo Marinaro and the Castel dell'Ovo. Rates for the 174 air-conditioned rooms are Lit. 173,000–247,000. All cards.

MODERATELY PRICED

Hotels in the lower price ranges in Naples can be adventuresome for a variety of reasons. But these have standards of cleanliness and conscientious management:

Belvedere, Via Tito Angelini 51, 80129; tel. (081) 364540. This small 2-star, 22-room hotel is in Vomero, practically facing the San Martino museum and 500 yards from the Montesanto funicular stop to the lower city, next to the Cumana rail depot. The hotel has a bar and restaurant. Double room rates (with and without private bath) run Lit. 38,500–66,000. AE, DC, V.

Rex, Via Palepoli 12, 80132; tel. (081) 416388. This 3-star, 40-room (35 with bath) hotel has a bar, but no restaurant. It is 5 min. from the Campania region tourism offices and is popular with touring theatrical troopers. Rates run Lit. 60,000–86,000. All cards.

Amalfi

Cappuccini Convento, Via Annunziatella 46, 84011 (SA); tel. (089) 871008; telex 770134. A converted convent in the center of Amalfi, this 4-star, 41-room hotel has a well known, atmospheric restaurant. You'll need to reserve in advance for most of July and Aug. Rates run Lit. 66,000–110,000. AE, DC.

Miramalfi, Via Quasimodo 3, 84011 (SA); tel. (089) 871588; telex 720325. This 3-star, 44-room hotel is a half-mile from the center of Amalfi on a seaside precipice (an elevator takes guests to the bathing platform with bar). The hotel has parking, a restaurant, a second bar in the hotel, and a pool. Rates run Lit. 45,000–79,000. All cards.

Avellino

Jolly, Via Tuoro Cappuccini 97a, 83100; tel. (0825) 25922; telex 722584. This 4-star hotel with 74 air-conditioned rooms is the best and most consistent refuge in town. The hotel has a restaurant, bar, and private parking. Rooms range Lit. 95,000–130,000. All cards.

Bácoli

Hotel Club Cala Moresca, Via del Faro 28, 80070 (NA); tel. (081) 8670595; telex 720161 DORASPED I. A pragmatic young management team took over this floundering 5-star hotel three years ago, axed 2 stars, lowered prices, offered special weekend rates, and began attracting more guests to its beautiful location atop the western end of the gulf of Naples. All 30 rooms overlook the sea. The hotel has a restaurant, bar, and pizzeria with wood oven. The pool and tennis courts will open in 1989. Located 15 miles from Capodichino Airport; transport can be arranged by hotel. The weekend package with meals is a bargain. Daily rates run Lit. 75,000–99,000. All cards.

Benevento

President, Via Perasso 1, 82100; tel. (0824) 21000. The only first-class hotel in the entire province. Its 76 air-conditioned rooms are across Piazza IV Novembre from the 14th-century Rocca dei Rettori. The hotel has a restaurant, bar, and private parking. Rooms run Lit. 51,000–84,000.

Capri

Quisisana e Grand Hotel, Via Camerelle 2, 80073; tel. (081) 8370788; telex 710520. If the walls could only talk; this is "the" address in Capri, with 5 stars, 143 rooms, air-conditioning, a restaurant, bar, and pool. The name recalls the structure's past as a hospital; *quisisana* means "here one's cured." Rooms run Lit. 220,000–330,000. All cards.

Hotel-Club Villa Pina, Via Tuoro 11, 80073; tel. (081) 8377517. The 2-star rating is due to plain but adequate furnishings. Most of the 45 rooms have a private bath and sun terrace. Located 10 min. form the piazzetta, the hotel overlooks the sea and has private steps down to the water; the return climb is invigorating! The hotel has a restaurant, bar, pool, and disco. Rooms run Lit. 44,000–66,000. Open June 1–Sept. 30. No cards.

Caserta

Centrale, Via Roma 170, 81100; tel. (0823) 321855. A 3-star hotel in the center of town with 41 air-conditioned rooms furnished in antique style, a restaurant, and bar. Parking is nearby. Reservations required weekdays. Rooms run Lit. 52,000–65,000; air-conditioning is Lit. 2,000 extra. AE, V.

Houston, Via Nazionale Appia, 81100; tel. (0823) 467755. A 3-star, modern, 124-room air-conditioned hotel open year-round. The hotel, at the A2 Caserta Nord exit ½ mile from La Reggia, has a restaurant, bar, pool, tennis court, and parking. Rooms run Lit. 35,000–57,000. All cards.

Ischia

Grande Albergo delle Terme, Via A. de Luca 42, 80070 (NA); tel. (081) 991744; telex 710267 JOLLIS. A 4-star Jolly hotel with 208 air-conditioned rooms facing a small park, 5 min. from a thermal center and 15 min. from the port. There is a bar and restaurant, and heated and indoor pools. The hotel is equipped to accommodate the handicapped. Rooms run Lit. 150,000–265,000. All cards.

Villa Maria, Via Osservatorio 2, 80070 (NA); tel. (081) 9922117. A simple, 2-star, 24-room (14 with private bath) hotel with restaurant, open all year. A 5-min. stroll from the port to the mainland. Rates run Lit. 21,000 for a bathless single, Lit. 40,000 for a double with bath. Meals may be required July–Aug. No cards.

Maiori

Reginna Palace. Costa d'Amalfi, 84010 (SA); tel. (089) 877183. Located in the center of Maiori across the street from a sandy beach, this 4-star, 67-room hotel is 9 miles from the A3 Vietri sul Mare exit. The hotel has a seawater pool, an illuminated tennis court, disco, restaurant, bar, and roof garden, and can accommodate the handicapped. Rooms are air-conditioned and run Lit. 67,000–125,000 in high season. Open Apr. 15–Sept. 30. All cards.

Massa Lubrense

La Certosa, Località Marina del Cantone, 80061; tel. (081) 8081029. Owner Corrado's unrivaled knack for confusion reigns, but his 1-star, 14-room renovated monastery survives. *Pensione* meals are sufficient, but an occasional sway to the *alla carta* menu is more than worth the added cost. Don't be dissuaded by screams from the kitchen—just be patient. The breakfast veranda is three steps above the pebble beach. Try for one of the top rooms with a private sun terrace. Room rates run Lit. 30,000–50,000.

Taverna del Capitano, Località Marina del Cantone, 80061; tel. (081) 8081028. This 2-star, 15-room modern hotel is located in an old fishing village on an enchanting inlet lined with Saracen towers. All rooms are doubles; rates are Lit. 54,000. When meals are required, *pensione* plan is Lit. 77,000 per person. Open Mar. 1–Oct. 31. AE, DC.

Paestum

Le Palme, Località Laura, 84063 (SA); tel. (0828) 851080; telex 721397 PALME I. A good overnighter for visiting the Greek ruins, this 3-star hotel has 50 air-conditioned rooms, a restaurant, bar, pool, tennis court, and private beach. Rooms run Lit. 45,000–56,000. Open Mar. 1–Sept. 30. All cards.

Piano di Sorrento

Klein Wien, 80063 Piano di Sorrento (NA); tel. (081) 8786746. This 1-star, 55-room (31 with bath) hotel occupies part of a postwar apartment building on a tree-lined street overlooking the Piano port and its black sandy beach. The gracious and accommodating proprietor, Comandante Donatantonio, has several fine rooms on the top floor with private sun terraces. Rooms run Lit. 33,000–55,000 when meals are not required. Open Mar. 1–Oct. 31.

Positano

Pupetto, Via Fornillo 31, 84017; tel. (089) 875087. A real bargain, so reserve well in advance. Just 1 star, but all 20 rooms have private bath. Meals may be required. Rooms run Lit. 28,000–45,000; *pensione* plan is Lit. 60,000 per person. Open Apr. 10–Sept. 30.

Le Sirenuse, Via Colombo 22, 84017 (SA); tel. (089) 875066; telex 770066. When Marquis Paolo Sersale decided in 1951 to convert his family's 18th-century home he created one of Europe's most noted 5-star luxury hotels, with 58 rooms. Le Sirenuse stands next to the majolica-domed Santa Maria Assunta church. The views from the terrace extend to Li Galli Islands. The hotel has a restaurant, bar, air-conditioned rooms, and heated pool. Double rooms run Lit. 375,000; apartments run Lit. 590,000. All cards.

Ravello

Palumbo, Via San Giovanni del Toro 28, 84010 (SA); tel. (089) 857244; telex 770101. The eight rooms in the 12th-century Confalone Palace are luxury-class, while the eight rooms in the annex have 1 less star and go for half the price. The complex has a bar and a good, well-known restaurant. Palace room rates with breakfast are Lit. 200,000–330,000; annex rooms are Lit. 138,000 (doubles only). All cards.

Parsifal, Piazza Fontana Moresca, 84010 (SA); tel. (089) 857144. An ex-convent, 16 of its 19 rooms have private bath. The 2-star hotel offers a fine view from a garden terrace. A restaurant is open Apr. 1–Oct. 10. Room rates run Lit. 35,000–55,000. All cards.

Salerno

Jolly Hotel delle Palme, Lungomare Trieste 1, 84100; tel. (089) 225222; telex 77050. A 4-star hotel with 105 air-conditioned rooms, a restaurant, bar, and private parking, this chain hotel is at the north end of Salerno near the port, and overlooks the waterfront park. Rooms run Lit. 82,000–136,000. All cards.

Sant'Agnello

Grand Hotel Cocumella 7, Sant'Agnello di Sorrento; tel. 8782933; telex 720370. In an enchanting position atop the Sorrentine coast is this 16th-century Jesuit monastery that has just been awarded a merited 5th star. The 61-room, air-conditioned hotel has undergone extensive modernization of services and renovation over the past decade. The hotel has a pool, tennis court, and an elevator to the private beach below with a beautiful tree-lined promenade overlooking the gulf and coast. Bed and breakfast rates run Lit. 117,000–194,000. All cards.

Sorrento

Excelsior Grand Hotel Vittoria, Piazza Tasso 34, 80067; tel. (081) 8781900; telex 720368. This 4-star, 125-room hotel sits atop a precipice that drops straight down to the ferry port. The elegant prewar atmosphere is complemented by modern amenities including a pool, surrounded by fruit trees. Rooms run Lit. 165,000–220,000. All cards.

Faro, Marino Piccolo 5, 80067; tel. (081) 8781390. This recently renovated 2-star, 23-room hotel with restaurant and taverna faces the ferry port for Capri and Naples. Rooms range Lit. 30,000–45,000. Open Mar. 1–Oct. 31.

Michelangelo, Corso Italia 275, 80067; tel. (081) 8781816; telex 722018. This 4-star, 100-room modern hotel with a restaurant, bar, pool, and garage is located on the main street through the center of Sorrento, near the Circumvesuviano rail terminal. Rooms run Lit. 50,000–86,000. Open Mar. 1–Dec. 31. AE, DC, V.

President, Via Nastro Verde 26, 80067; tel. (081) 8782262; telex 710687. A 4-star, 82-room modern hotel with bar, restaurant, and private pool, set in the comfortable wooded area just outside Sorrento on the road to Sant'Agata. The hotel has fine tree-framed views over the gulf. Rooms run Lit. 75,000–140,000. Open Mar. 1–Oct. 30. AE, DC, V.

Camping

The Cilento district in the southern part of the province of Salerno has undergone tourist development in the past decade. Among the campgrounds that have sprung up are:

In **Acciaroli, Camping Ondina,** off SS267, Marina di Mezzatorre km. 35.4, 84041 Acciaroli (SA); tel. (0974) 904040. Regular camping facilities are supplemented by wood and brick bungalows in this area, on one of the cleanest stretches of Tyrrhenian coast. Both rock and sandy beaches are nearby. Bungalows for four run Lit. 66,600 per night. Open Apr. 4–Sept. 30.

In **Caprioli** is **Villaggio-Camping Baia del Silenzio,** Via Valle di Marco, 84040 Caprioli (SA); tel. (0974) 976079. Situated on the coast near the Palinuro caverns, this campground offers bungalows, *tukuls* (African-style huts), and trailers. All are furnished and sleep 2–6 persons. Week-long stays are required July–Aug. Special weekend rates of Lit. 80,000 per person for full board are available the rest of the season. For reservations contact: Reservation Office, Via Tertulliano 30, 20137 Milan; tel. (02) 5483323 (in Milan). Open mid-May–Sept. 30.

In **Marina di Camerota** try **Happy Camping Village,** Località Arcorete, 84059 Marina di Camerota (SA); tel. (0974) 932326. This family-oriented center has minimum three-week stays July–Aug., but shorter sojourns are possible in mid and low seasons. *Tukuls* are available in the olive groves and on the hillside overlooking the sea and sandy beaches. Full-board weekly rates per person in a *tukul* range Lit. 350,000–740,000, depending on season and number of persons per hut.

Naples

Naples is another world. The adage "See Naples, then die" has contrasting connotations for admirers and detractors. Despite its exceptional artistic and archaeological heritage, enviable climate, and pure popular love for living, neglect prohibits prosperity. Often described as the city of sun, songs, and slums, Naples is a showcase for the worst aspects of Italian bureaucracy.

Natural calamities have also intervened. The latest was the November 1980 earthquake that damaged many buildings and forced the evacuation of hundreds into makeshift shanty-towns. Inspection teams converged on Naples. All state, para-

One of the greatest delights of Naples is the universal gaiety. The many-colored flowers and fruits in which Nature adorns herself seem to invite the people to decorate themselves and their belongings with as vivid colours as possible. All who can in any way afford it wear silk scarves, ribbons and flowers in their hats. In the poorest homes the chairs and chests are painted with bright flowers on a gilt ground; even the one-horse carriages painted a bright red, their carved woodwork gilded; and the horses decorated with artificial flowers, crimson tassels and tinsel. Some horses wear plumes on their heads, others little pennons which revolve as they trot.

We usually think of a passion for gaudy colours as barbaric or bad taste, and often with reason, but under this blue sky nothing can be too colourful, for nothing can outshine the brightness of the sun and its reflection in the sea. The most brillant colour is softened by the strong light, and the green of trees and plants, the yellow, brown and red of the soil are dominant enough to absorbe the more highly coloured flowers and dresses into the general harmony. The scarlet skirts and bodices, trimmed with gold and silver braids, which the women of Nattuno wear, the painted boats, etc., everything seems to be competing for visual attention against the splendour of sea and sky.

—J. W. Goethe
Italian Journey, 1786–88

state, city, provincial, regional and military entities each sent their own inspectors. One multistoried office building was visited and declared safe by nearly a dozen teams. Within a week the building collapsed. In hand-washing statements each team declared that the faulty foundation was beyond their respective realms of competence. Once again the total lack of bureaucratic coordination prevailed.

Most visitors to Campania come to see Naples and its environs. Founded by Greek colonists in 600 B.C., the city of the siren Parthenope succumbed to the Romans nearly three hundred years later. Emperors and aristocracy constructed sumptuous holiday villas around the entire gulf coast from Baia to Sorrento. After the fall of the Roman Empire came the Goths, Byzantines, and Lombards (or Longobards), before a period of independence under the dukes of Naples. But the reign of foreign domination was resumed in the 12th century with the arrival of the Germanic Swabians, followed by the Normans, Angevins, and Aragons. In the early 1500s Sicily and Naples became a province of the Kingdom of Spain, and Naples was ruled by a viceroy for two hundred years.

After a brief Austrian rule Naples became capital of the Bourbon kingdom, in 1734. Except for the 1789 popular upheaval that sought to create the Parthenopaean Republic and the 1806–1815 reigns of Napoleon's brother and brother-in-law, Joseph Bonaparte and Joachim Murat, the Bourbons controlled the region until it was annexed by the Kingdom of Italy in 1860.

When the Bourbons departed, a needy Naples was on its knees in the shadow of a volatile Vesuvius. More than one hundred years after the Bourbon departure, Naples and the south are still recovering from the pillaging of its wealth before its liberation by Garibaldi.

No wonder Neapolitans are so ready to embrace a miracle. Twice a year on local feast days, anxiety can evolve into delirium when patron saint San Gennaro's blood, preserved in two flasks in Naples' cathedral, does not liquefy, signaling a disaster for the town. Though the Vatican scratched San Gennaro from its roster of saints, the enthusiasm of Naples' faithful has not been dampened.

Petty crime is a problem for locals as well as tourists, and police patrol the city center. Much like in New York, the best deterrent is common sense and elementary precaution. Gold jewelry should be momentarily shelved, along with expensive watches and the like. Street urchins (the *scugnizzi* so aptly described in Morris West's *Children of the Sun*) can snatch a watch from an arm resting on an open car window in traffic and be gone before you're out of the car. A baggage-packed auto should never be left unattended on the street (common sense in almost any city). But don't think that Naples is an armed camp to be avoided. It has its share of street crime, but its attractions are unique.

Naples is a challenge. Many note that it is the least Italian of the metropolitan areas in Italy. But, what is the most Italian metropolis? Is there one Italian city that can symbolize all the diverse ethnic and cultural origins of the entire peninsula?

Naples and Neapolitans are an integral and vital force in Italy today. The noise and confusion may rival the decibel levels of a Manhattan disco, but can be just as entertaining. This is another dimension that merits its proper perspective.

Travel in Naples

ATAN provides public transportation throughout the city of Naples. All **city buses** are yellow, as are all legitimate metered taxis.

ATAN operates four funicular lines, three cable bus routes, three **trolley** lines and 138 bus routes. Principal terminals are in Piazza Garibaldi in front of the main rail station and Piazza del Plebiscito in front of the Royal Palace, on the waterfront.

Funicolari (funiculars) are cable-car-like trolleys used from the lower city to its hilltop backdrop. Three routes go to wealthy Vomero, overlooking old Naples (see "Vomero" in the Naples city section). The fourth rises from near the Mergellina port to Via Manzoni.

The Metropolitana (**subway**) is the most convenient form of transport, due to Naples' chaotic traffic conditions. A separate subway on state rail tracks connects all state-run train stations, from Bagnoli (on the northern perimeter of the Gulf of Naples) to Centrale at Piazza Garibaldi. There are eight state train stations within Naples city limits. The two main stations are Centrale and Piazza Garibaldi, both actually on different levels in the terminal at Piazza Garibaldi.

The Ferrovia Cumana private railroad operates westbound trains from the Montesanto terminal, Piazza Montesanto; tel. (081) 313328. Between this terminal and the state-run Montesanto station is the Montesanto funicular to San Martino, an area of Naples on high ground overlooking the city. See the "Campania Travel" section above for further details on train connections from Naples.

The five taxi co-ops in Naples are Autoradio Taxi Partenope, tel. 364340; Cooperativa Radio Taxi, tel. 322232; COTAR, tel. 402640; Radio Taxi, tel. 245745 and Tassisti Città di Napoli, tel. 269884.

If you need to rent a car in Naples, contact the following. At Capodichino airport: Avis, tel. (081) 7805790; Europcar, tel. (081) 7805643, telex 720698; Hertz, tel. (081) 7802971; Maggiore, tel. (081) 7803011.

In the city: Avis, Via Partenope 31–34, tel. (081) 417226 and Piazza Garibaldi, tel. (081) 284041; Europcar, c/o Hotel Royal, Via Partenope 38, tel. (081) 413307, telex 720044; Hertz (local office also handles bookings for Salerno and Sorrento), Via Partenope 29, tel. (081) 400400, telex 710037 and Piazza Garibaldi 69, tel. (081) 206228; Maggiore, Via Miguel Cervantes 92, tel. (081) 5524308 as well as in the main Centrale rail terminal, tel. (081) 287858 and Arzano, Via Rettifico al Bravo Contrada Agnolo, tel. (081) 7318781; Prestige, Via Petronio 6, tel. (081) 415157.

Naples is divided into *quartièri* (districts), the oldest being Forcella, Pignasecca, Sanità, Santa Lucia, and Spagnoli. The center of old town is Piazzetta Nilo, at the intersection of Via Benedetto Croce and Via Giovanni Paladino near the university.

Spacca Napoli

Cutting through the heart of old town is the so-called Spacca Napoli section. This is the street that begins at Santa Chiara church as Via Croce and becomes Via San Biagio di Librai at Piazza Nolana, Via Vicaria Vecchia at Via del Duomo, and Via Guidecca Vecchia just before it ends.

Lined with ornate palaces and gateways at its beginning, the street turns into an open-air bazaar in a poorer section of the Forcella district and is reputedly capable of providing anything from toothpicks to tanks. Tourists stand out immediately in Forcella, so be careful of petty theft.

The major points of interest in the Forcella section are readily accessible by public transportation or just a few minutes' walk from the Spacca Napoli:

The **Duomo San Gennaro** is on Via del Duomo between Via Tribunali and Largo Donnaregina. A neo-Gothic facade was added to the 13th-century cathedral in the 19th century. A magnificent wood ceiling highlights the elaborately decorated interior. Oriental and African granite columns support the original structure, built in the form of a Greek cross. Housed within are paintings by Luca Giordano, Stefano Pozzi, Aniello Falcone and sculptures by Domenico Fontana, Lorenzo Vaccaro, and Girolamo d'Auris. The 17th-century **Chapel of San Gennaro** holds the head and two vials of the dried blood of San Gennaro, patron of Naples. It was built to fulfill a vow made by Neapolitans during a 16th-century plague that swept the city. Though the Vatican has removed Gennaro from its roster of saints, Neapolitans still gather twice yearly, on September 19 and the first Saturday in May, for the Feast of the Miracle, when the blood is said to liquefy; if it does not, a disaster supposedly will fall on the town.

Off the left aisle of the Duomo complex is the small fourth-century **Santa Restituta church,** the oldest in Naples.

A little ways down Via del Duomo, behind the baroque facade facing Largo Donnaregina is the 14th-century Gothic **Santa Maria di Donnaregina church,** with 14th-century frescoes by Pietro Cavallini and the elaborate **tomb of Mary of Hungary.**

In the opposite direction (toward the waterfront) at Via del Duomo 288 is the **Filangieri Civic Museum** in **Palazzo Cuomo,** telephone (081) 203175 (open 10 A.M. to 4 P.M., Sunday and holidays; closed Monday). This 15th-century Florentine Renaissance-style building houses a vast collection of paintings, sculptures, porcelain, and 16th- to 18th-century weapons.

Back up Via del Duomo and left to Via Tribunali 316 is **San Lorenzo Maggiore.** This 13th- to 14th-century church is the finest example of Gothic architecture in Naples. An archaeological site is through the adjoining convent. In this church Giovanni Boccaccio first met his Fiammetta (Maria d'Aquino).

Down the Spacca Napoli at Piazza San Domenico Maggiore is the **church of San Domenico Maggiore.** St. Thomas Aquinas lived in the monastery next to the 14th-century Gothic church that houses his famous crucifix. The building has undergone various renovations.

Continue down Via Croce to **Santa Chiara church and convent,** at Piazza del Gesù Nuovo 18. Severely damaged by Allied bombing in 1943, the church has been fully restored in its original 13th-century Gothic-Provençal style. In the church are beautiful medieval tombs and memorials of the Anjou dynasty (including the tomb of King Robert the Wise) and frescoes. Stairs lead to the strange 18th-century inner-courtyard cloister of the Clarisse nuns.

Leaving the Spacca Napoli and up Via Roma (previously Via Toledo) is the most worthwhile stop in Naples: the **National Archaeological Museum,** at Piazza Museo Nazionale 35; telephone (081) 440166. Open 9 A.M. to 2 P.M., to 1 P.M. Sunday and holidays; closed Monday. Once a military barracks, then the university, the 1585 palace became a museum under the Bourbons and now houses one of the richest Greco-Roman collections anywhere, including all major finds from Pompeii, Herculaneum, and other Vesuvian excavations, as well as artworks, statues, and bronzes from the Villa Pison (or Villa dei Papyri). The museum's collection of sculptures, bronzes, ceramics, paintings, mosaics, and jewelry is priceless.

Capodimonte

In the hills north of the museum is the royal palace of Bourbon King Charles, begun in 1738, in a wooded park that was once a hunting reserve overlooking the city. Today it is the **Capodimonte Museum and National Gallery,** Via Capodimonte; telephone (081) 7410801. (Open 9 A.M. to 2 P.M., to 1 P.M. Sunday and holidays; closed Monday.) The Tangenziale passes under the park, with an exit to Via Capodimonte; on weekdays buses from Piazza Dante (red and black lines number 137, 160, and 161) pass the National Museum en route to Via Capodimonte. Well worth a visit, the gallery includes Titian, Caravaggio, Simone Martini, Correggio, Luca Giordano, Aniello Falcone, Giovanni Bellini, and Giovanni Lanfranco among the many artists represented. There is also a rich display of porcelain and majolica (Italian earthenware with an opaque glaze). In the park are the famous Capodimonte porcelain works.

RESTAURANTS
Stop for lunch at **Berganino,** Vico San Felice 16/20 (tel. 081-310369), in the old Sanità *quartiere* halfway between the National Archaeological Museum and the Capodimonte Museum, just 5 min. from the Piazza Sanità. One of the oldest restaurants in Naples, Bergantino still attracts a solid, middle-class clientele. Open at lunch time only; meals run about Lit. 30,000. Closed Sat. and Aug.

The Waterfront

The area along the waterfront *quartiere* of Santa Lucia from the Maritime Station to Castel dell'Ovo has more historical sites than the Spacca-Napoli. West of Via Roma (Via Toledo) is the Spagnoli *quartiere,* picturesque in the day, but best avoided after dark. The same holds for the Pallonetto area of Santa Lucia, on the bay in the heart of the old Greek area of Naples.

Major points of interest are:

Castel Nuovo, also called **Maschio Angioino** (open 9 A.M. to 7 P.M.), is between the Beverello port for the gulf islands and Piazza Municipio. The imposing 13th-century castle is surrounded by moats and faces Via Parco del Castello, which separates it from the Royal Palace. Built by Charles I of Anjou at the end of the 13th century and added to by Alfonso I and other Aragons, it has undergone various renovations. The notable **Triumphal Arch** commemorates the 1443 entry of Alfonso into Naples; other interesting sights are the Palatine Chapel, the Sala dei Baroni (where the Naples City Council holds its sessions), and the apartments of the viceroy. All look onto an inner courtyard.

After its original 1600 design by Domenico Fontana, the **Palazzo Reale (Royal Palace)** on Piazza Plebiscito was enlarged and restored, and eventually became the official residence of Bourbon and Savoy kings. Umberto I ordered the eight statues in the facade of famous kings who represent the dynasties that have reigned over Naples. The **royal apartments** may be visited. The National Library occupies part of the palace. (Open 9 A.M. to 2 P.M., to 1 P.M. Sunday and holidays; closed Monday.)

Adjacent to the Royal Palace is the **Teatro San Carlo** opera house, Via Vittorio Emanuele III (open 9 A.M. to noon). With perfect acoustics, the theater is second only to Milan's La Scala in national importance. The interior is richly decorated.

For ticket information for the theater, reserve in advance by contacting: Biglietteria, Teatro San Carlo, Via San Carlo, 80132 Naples; telephone (081) 416305.

Across Piazza Trento e Trieste from the San Carlo opera house is **Galleria Umberto I,** a complex of shops, caffès, and offices typical of Umbertine architecture. Built ten years after Milan's Galleria, the glass and iron building has ornate marble walks, and is a favorite meeting place among the artists and intellectuals of Naples.

Back at the waterfront in the *borgo marinaro,* hovering over the old fishing village at Santa Lucia Port is **Castel dell'Ovo,** connected by a small bridge to mainland Via Partenope. One of the more picturesque symbols of Naples, the 12th-century Norman fort was built on the ruins of a Roman villa. It is not open to visitors.

On the waterfront between Via Francesco Caracciolo and Riviera di Chiaia, a 15-minute stroll from Castel dell'Ovo, is **Villa Comunale,** the kilometer-long public park designed by Luigi Vanvitelli in 1780. Public transportation from the main train station via Piazza Plebiscito includes bus routes FT, 106, and 150 to Piazza Vittorio on the eastern flank of the park. Caffè concerts are staged at four chalets located in the villa; each caffè can seat three hundred to four hundred people and offers a variety of Neapolitan music, as well as other types of Italian and popular music.

In the park, facing Via Caracciolo, is the **Aquarium** (open 9 A.M. to 5 P.M.; closed Monday). Founded by Polish naturalist Anton Dohrn in 1872, it is the oldest aquarium in Europe, and features the sea life from the Bay of Naples.

Behind the park, off Riviera di Chiaia at Largo Principessa Pignatelli 200, is the **Villa Pignatelli** (open 9 A.M. to 2 P.M., to 1 P.M. Sunday and holidays; closed Monday). Once the cultural center of Naples, the elegant neoclassical villa was built for Ferdinando Acton in 1826. It now houses the **Principe Diego Aragona Pignatelli Cortes Museum of Art,** and a collection of 19th- and 20th-century carriages from across Europe.

Vomero

Vomero overlooks old Naples. Three of the city's four funicular lines connect Vomero with the lower city. The Chiaia line links Villa Floridiana with the Piazza Amedeo metro stop; Centrale departs from Galleria Umberto to a point halfway between Villa Floridiana and the monastery at San Martino; while the Montesanto line runs from near the Montesanto Cumana terminal to upper Castel San Elmo.

The main points of interest in Vomero are good places to head to get a little perspective on the city.

Villa Floridiana, on Via Cimarosa, is a neoclassical villa in Pompeii style surrounded by a park (open 9 A.M. to 2 P.M., to 1 P.M. Sunday and holidays; closed Monday). Views extend across the gulf to Capri. Built for Ferdinando I, the 18th-century villa contains the **Duca di Martina National Ceramics Museum** with priceless porcelain and European and Oriental ceramics.

The 14th-century **Carthusian Monastery of St. Martin** (Certosa di San Martino), originally of Gothic design, was converted into the **San Martino National Museum,** Largo San Martino 5 (open 9 A.M. to 2 P.M., to 1 P.M. Sunday and holidays; closed Monday). The museum houses historical memorabilia of the Kingdom of Naples; it is in a beautiful park that offers fine views of the lower city and gulf.

Beautiful views are also plentiful at next-door **Castel San Elmo,** Via Angelini (open 9 A.M. to 2 P.M., to 1 P.M. Sunday and holidays; closed Monday). Visitors are allowed on the bastions and into the old prison beneath the 14th-century castle.

SHOPPING

The main attractions of shopping in Naples and environs are **Capodimonte porcelain** (Bourbon kings founded the Capodimonte school in the 18th century) and **coral jewelry** and **cameos** from Torre del Greco. Prices are not necessarily the best at the source, so compare prices in reputable shops in Naples. Capodimonte is in Naples west of Capodichino Airport; Torre del Greco is on the gulf coast just below Herculaneum.

In Naples, the smartest shops are found on Via Chiaia heading west from Piazza Trento e Trieste. On the square at number 56 is Neapolitan Mario Valentino, one of Italy's leading leather fashion designers.

Across the square in the Galleria Umberto are a number of fine shops catering to Naples' smart set; small caffès offer a break from shopping.

Leather goods and **furs** can be found in the market area on Corso Malta, which connects the Tangenziale to the main rail terminal. For **old books** and **silverware** try the Spacca-Napoli quarter, the heart of old Naples.

Other good shopping areas are centered around Via Roma (called Via Toledo), Via dei Mille, Via Carlo Poerio and the Piazza dei Martiri, and Piazza Amedeo.

RESTAURANTS

The preparation of pasta with seafood sauces or simply with tomato and basil is a religious rite in Naples, cherished by even the most diet-conscious Neapolitan. The city is also the home port for pizza. And Neapolitans claim their espresso is the only real coffee. Satisfying most, if not all, of these simple requisites are the following suggested restaurants. They have been tested by time and are the most consistent.

Amici Miei, Via Monte di Dio 78; tel. (081) 405727. Next to the Politeama Theater off Via Chiaia near Piazza Plebiscito is this small, elegant restaurant catering primarily to habitués and theatergoers. The flavor of Old Naples reigns, from homemade pasta to sweets. Reservations suggested. Dinner runs Lit. 25,000–35,000. Closed Sun. evening, Mon., Aug. AE, DC, V.

La Cantinella, Via Cuma 42; tel. (081) 404884. Halfway between the Beverello port and Borgo Marinara, the swordfish and dried cod specialties are supplemented with a good selection of meat dishes. A full meal including a wide choice of sweets runs about Lit. 40,000–50,000. Closed Sun., Aug. All cards.

Ciro a Santa Brigida, Via Santa Brigida 71; tel. (081) 324072. One of the most authentic Neapolitan restaurants left in the city, Ciro occupies two floors next to Galleria Umberto I and has a late closing to accommodate theatergoers and artists alike. Dinners run Lit. 40,000. Closed Sun., Aug. No cards.

Dante e Beatrice, Piazza Dante 44; tel. (081) 349905. At the end of Via Roma between Santa Chiara and the Cumana station, this trattoria with a long list of local faithfuls is popular with the "young lions" of Naples. Dinner will run Lit. 20,000–30,000. Closed Wed., Aug. 24–31. No cards.

Harry's Bar, Via Lucilio 11; tel. (081) 407810. Behind the Excelsior hotel, the bar is open to early morning for after-dinner drinks around the piano bar; it is a favorite with theater troupes. The bar's elegant atmosphere also draws a good luncheon clientele. Meals run Lit. 25,000–40,000. Closed Sun. AE, DC.

Around Naples

Posillipo

Escape from the city and take a drive to the promontory of Cape Posillipo, separating the Bay of Naples and Pozzuoli Bay. The coast road through Mergellina climbs to become Via Posillipo; nine miles southwest of central Naples, the area is now considered part of the metropolitan urban area, although explorations of Campania's upper coast could begin here. Development of this area first began during Joachim Murat's Napoleonic reign in Naples. Today Posillipo's buildings range from luxury villas to aged fishing villages such as Marechiaro, a small port on the northern gulf spur approximately halfway between Herculaneum and Miseno. There are fine views and good restaurants to stop at.

❦ RESTAURANTS

If a trip to Cape Posillipo is on your schedule, consider stopping for a meal at **Rosiello,** Via S. Strato 10; tel. (081) 7691288, where Salvatore Varriale has revolutionized the old family restaurant; it's intimate with beautiful gulf views from its terraces. Closed Wed., Aug. 10–20. Dinners range Lit. 50,000. AE, DC, V.

Phlegrean Fields (Campi Flegrei)

This hilly, volcanic area west of Naples at one time extended all the way to Ischia. There is more breathing room here than in the Vesuvian ruins of the central gulf (from Portici to Castellammare di Stabia). Besides beautiful panoramas, the area includes Pozzuoli, port for Ischia and Procida, and the picturesque fishing village of Bacoli.

Bacoli, almost at the tip of Cape Miseno, is a fishing village 18 miles from Naples with an impressive archaeological patrimony. The **Piscina Mirabile** is an enormous underground freshwater cistern created in the Augustan era to supply water to the Roman fleet based at neighboring Miseno. Nearby are the Cento Camerelle (one hundred rooms)—cisterns begun in the first century that stored water for a Roman villa. Also in town is the tomb of Agrippina, Nero's mother.

❧ RESTAURANTS

In Bàcoli, try **Campi Elisi,** Via Miseno 41; tel. (081) 8670432. Across the street from the waterfront public park, this pine-paneled tavern specializes in seafood and wood-oven pizzas. Meals range Lit. 20,000–50,000. Closed Wed. No cards.

The oldest archaeological site in Italy, **Cumae,** on the Campania coast, traces its origin to eighth-century B.C. Greek colonists. The fifth-century B.C. **acropolis** walls contain the **temples of Apollo and Jupiter,** the **Sibyl's cavern** cited in Virgil's *Aeneid,* a **Roman crypt,** remains of thermal **baths,** and an **amphitheater.**

Vesuvius, Pompeii, and Herculaneum

Just 14 miles south of Naples, along the coast, are some of the most famous archaeological sites in the Western world.

Vesuvius

Mainland Europe's last active volcano has been behaving since March 1944, when it showered soot on Naples and environs for 13 days. The dramatic ruins of Pompeii and Herculaneum are evidence of more destructive times. Today the rich, fertile slopes of the mountain are encircled by a series of villages that have gained dubious fame in *camorra* gang wars. (Often cited in crime reports is inland Ottaviano, home of reputed underworld lord Raffaello Cutolo, now serving a life sentence.)

The best routes to visit Vesuvius' crater are from Herculaneum, Torre del Greco, and Boscotrecase, just north of Pompeii. A chair lift (closed November 5–30) is available almost to the lip of the crater, whose cone disappeared during the eruptions of March 18–31, 1944.

Coastal road SS18 to Vesuvius is choked with traffic and should be avoided. The A3 is better, but avoid even this on a Sunday, when Neapolitans travel to the Sorrentine Peninsula.

Pompeii

Shortly after noon on August 24, A.D. 79, the fury of Vesuvius buried Herculaneum under nearly twenty feet of mud and lava. Neighbor Pompeii had a more agonizing death. Sulfuric gasses emitted by the volcano choked its more than 20,000 inhabitants; then an incessant three-day flow of lava and ash buried both Pompeii and the nearby town of Stabiae.

A Roman colony since 80 B.C., Pompeii, founded in the eighth century B.C., was a commercial center that had also belonged to the Samnites and Greeks. After the eruption, Pompeii (the Italian spelling has one *i*) was a forgotten city for over fifteen hundred years, until architect Domenico Fontana accidentally uncovered its amphitheater in the late 1600s while supervising construction of a canal.

The first archaeological digs did not begin until 1748, at the order of Bourbon King Charles. These were not serious excavations, but a basic attempt to recover relics and art objects. The first serious excavations began during the Napoleonic reign; between 1815 and 1832 the forum, basilica (the largest building in Pompeii), House of the Faun, House of the Tragic Poet, the Casa di Pansa, and smaller baths were uncovered.

In 1860, under the Kingdom of Italy, Giuseppe Fiorelli was placed in charge of excavations that today have uncovered most of the town. Fiorelli devised the system that produced plaster casts from cavities made by bodies of victims in the hardened mud. These casts of agonized, contorted humans and animals are on display in the baths at Pompeii and in the Archaeological Museum in Naples.

The houses of Pompeii are notable for their atriums and wall paintings. But few artifacts remain—after theft, vandalism, and the 1980 earthquake it was decided to move all relics from both Pompeii and Herculaneum (except for a few casts) to the National Archaeological Museum.

Visiting hours vary; ruins usually are open 9 A.M. to 2 P.M., to 7:30 P.M. in June, July, and August. Information may be obtained from the Pompeii tourist office, telephone (081) 8610913. English-speaking guides are available at the Porta Marina entrance, but to make advance arrangements call the guides' co-op, telephone (081) 8615628.

Entrance fee is Lit. 5,000, which also includes admission to the Villa dei Misteri (with paintings depicting the introduction of young brides into the cult of Dionysius), about five hundred yards from the Porta Marina entrance outside the walls of Pompeii. Porta Marina is close to the train station and private parking lots. The Circumvesuviana Pompeii Scavi train depot is in front of the Porta di Nola entrance on the opposite side of Pompeii.

Among the highlights of Pompeii is the first building discovered, the **amphitheater,** the oldest such structure in existence, dating from 80 B.C. In the southeast corner of the site, near the Porta di Nola entrance, it could seat 12,000. The **Palestra** (gymnasium) is opposite.

The **Stabian Baths** (Terme Stabiane) were for both men and women. They had both cold baths and hot baths, swimming pools, and a gym. The men's baths have well-preserved dressing rooms. The baths are on Via dell'Abbondanza (from the Amphitheater area, walk to Via dell'Abbondanza and turn left; the baths are at Via Stabiana).

At **Lupanare African et Victoris** the pornographic paintings on the ground floor seem to be over bed stalls—which indicates that this was indeed a brothel (*lupanare*). If the area is open to the public, follow Via dell'Abbondanza to Vico del Lupanare and turn right; the building is on the left, just before Via degli Augustali.

The **House of Loreius Tiburtinus** (or Octavius Quartio), a residence, is known for its Roman garden, featuring trellises and formal paintings. It's next to the Palestra, as you head away from the entrance toward Via dell'Abbondanza.

The **Forum** (Foro), an immense square that served as town hall, was planned so that Vesuvius dominates the central axis. Surrounding the square are the larger buildings: the Basilica, temples, and a large covered market. The Forum is at the end of Via dell'Abbondanza, near Porta Marina.

The **House of the Vettii** belonged to two brothers, wealthy merchants. The most completely restored house in Pompeii, it is known for its well-preserved paintings and the skill of the reconstruction. Head away from the Forum, past the Temple of Jupiter, turn right on Via di Nola, then left on Vicolo dei Vettii.

🐾 RESTAURANTS

Several restaurants line the parking area near the Porta Marina entrance to the ruins. All offer tourist menus that are basically the same with slight price variations. Stick to the basic offering without trying to substitute, or you'll pay. About half a mile away in Pompeii proper, on Via Roma, is a good local favorite—**Zi Caterina,** tel. (081) 8631263. Closed Tues.

Herculaneum (Ercolano)

While Pompeians were given no warning of death, Herculaneans had time to flee their city when Vesuvius struck. But death caught up with them in the seaside caves where they took refuge. Herculaneum itself was buried under boiling mud, rather than the burning cinders that buried Pompeii. Consequently, wooden house frames and furnishings, including artworks, were encased in a shell of hardened mud, and what has been laboriously uncovered is more complete and better preserved than in Pompeii. But ancient Herculaneum may never fully see light; the lower town has been uncovered, but the upper town lies under modern-day Ercolano and wealthy 18th-century villas designed by Luigi Vanvitelli, the architect of La Reggia.

Herculaneum, by legend founded by Hercules, was rediscovered in 1709 by the prince of Elbeuf, who was having a well dug. Though the excavated site at Herculaneum is smaller than at Pompeii, it is more intimate, and gives a much fuller picture of Roman life of the first century.

The hours at Herculaneum are the same as Pompeii's; guides are available at the entrance to the site.

Among Herculaneum's highlights is the

House with the Mosaic Atrium (Casa dell'Atrio a Mosaico), with, indeed, an atrium beyond the entrance paved with mosaics; there is also a garden and a terrace overlooking the sea. The entrance to the house is on Cardo IV.

Baths (Terme). Continue up Cardo IV and cross Decumanus Inferior to reach these well preserved public baths, dating from the time of Augustus.

The **House of Neptune and Amphitrite** (Casa di Nettuno and Anfitrite) is so-called because there's a mosaic of Neptune and Amphitrite in the inner court. Some furniture remains in the upper floor of this building; downstairs is a well-preserved shop, with all its goods containers as they once stood ready for sale. Also on Cardo IV, the house is across from the Baths.

The House of the Stags (Casa dei Cervi) is from the time of Nero. Red and black frescoes decorate this home, whose name comes from the stag sculptures beyond the atrius. To reach the house, continue up Cardo IV to Decumanus Maximus, then right on Cardo V to the end of the street.

The Sorrentine Peninsula

The Sorrentine Peninsula is one of the most captivating corners of Europe. Rugged natural beauty combines with colorful dwellings and sumptuous and discreet villas and hotels to create an unforgettable experience. Particularly beautiful is the drive along the lower Amalfi Coast.

Extending into the Tyrrhenian, this finger of land pointing at Capri divides the gulfs of Naples and Salerno. Its territory is divided between the provinces of Naples and Salerno.

Sorrento

Sorrento, largest town on the peninsula, was once a quaint holiday resort favored by Northern European senior citizens. A tremendous postwar hotel boom has brought a new festive air. Due to the proximity to Capri, Amalfi, and even Pompeii, the town's hotels now attract the tourist coach trade that once frequented Naples. Impossible traffic conditions in Naples help to popularize the detour to Sorrento. Although the town's quiet charms may be gone forever, off-season visitors, particularly, may appreciate the activity here, when other towns along the coast may just seem a little *too* quiet.

The drive to Sorrento on SS145 from the A3 turnpike exit at Castellammare di Stabia has been modified extensively over the past decade to accommodate the ever-increasing influx of tourists. The drive is fascinating, but is second to the more picturesque Amalfi Drive (SS163) on the underside of the peninsula.

Both of these roads should be avoided on Sundays, when both Naples and Salerno empty out. Traffic nearly always manages to keep moving to and from Sorrento, but one poorly parked auto near Positano can paralyze the entire Amalfi Drive.
    To fully appreciate the peninsula's scenery, head westward toward Sorrento and eastward toward Salerno, to get the view from the outside lanes instead of the rock-confined inner lanes.

❧ RESTAURANTS
O'Parrucchiano, Corso Italia 71; tel. (081) 8781321. Any VIP who has ever passed through Sorrento has made an appearance here. What came first, the garden or the restaurant? This is more than just a meal, it's a full evening out. Dinners run Lit. 30,000–40,000. Closed Wed. Nov.–May. AE, V.

The Lower Peninsula
Off the beaten path and just off the point of the peninsula are several places to satisfy the more adventurous: Sant'Agata sui Due Golfi, Massa Lubrense, and best of all, Marina del Cantone. The cooler evening air at **Sant'Agata** is a treat, but in August crowds can be heavy.

Massa Lubrense's port is crammed with yachts and boats of all dimensions then, too, and crowds also fill **Marina del Cantone,** a natural inlet under the watchful eye of Saracen towers. In the summer local fishermen find that hiring their boats for trips to Capri and Positano is more lucrative than their usual trade. Above the inlet beyond the settlement of Nerano, practically on the point of the peninsula, there is a peaceful chapel. From this point Capri appears at arm's length, and there is an unforgettable panorama down the length of the peninsula, and across the Gulfs of Naples and Salerno, and down the Calabrian coast to where the Appennines begin rolling into the Tyrrhenian.

❧ RESTAURANTS
In Sant'Agata, stop for a meal at **Don Alfonso,** Piazza Sant'Agata; tel. (081) 8780026. Alfonso Iaccarino is the don with elegance, in one of Campania's leading restaurants. Three gourmet possibilities are the Lit. 45,000 "traditional meal," the Lit. 65,000 *degustazione* special, and the *alla carta* dinners that average about Lit. 70,000. Specialties include lobster and shellfish pâté, linquine with shellfish, mozzarella flambé with a basil cream sauce. All prices are without wine. Reservations suggested June–Aug. Closed Sun. evening, Mon. except summer, Jan. 7–Feb. 25. All cards.

The Amalfi Drive

The Amalfi Drive (SS163) affords picturesque glimpses of rainbow-tinted tiers of houses clinging to hills that drop into the sea and slope to scenic inlets with sandy or pebble beaches. With some of Italy's best scenery, it runs along the underside of the Sorrentine Peninsula, through several charming towns.

POSITANO

Above Positano, the most beautiful of the drive's coastal towns, there is a small parking area beside a statue of the Madonna, who appears to offer her protection to the town below. This spot offers an exceptional view of the coast and offshore Galli islands, once the property of an exiled Russian ballet dancer, Leonid Massine.

A narrow winding road leads off SS163 and down into the upper half of Positano. If no parking is available in the limited areas before the pedestrian-only lower half, continue on the one-way street back to the state highway; this loop is serviced by municipal shuttle minibuses.

The pergola-shaded walk through the lower half of Positano is lined with shops offering tempting sweets and ices and boutiques displaying blouses, skirts, shirts, and other items from the flourishing local cottage industries. Occasionally sidewalk cobblers offer handmade, loose-fitting moccasins ideal for sockless relaxation. One visit is enough to understand why globe-trotting director Franco Zeffirelli built his home in Positano.

❦ RESTAURANTS

Costantino, Via Corvo 95; tel. (089) 875738. With a theater career that has covered the local Sirenuse as well as stages in Paris and London, Costantino Buonocore now has his own rustic restaurant just outside Positano. Patio dining offers superb views to complete an enjoyable evening. Try the homemade tagliatelle with eggplant or spaghetti with clam sauce. Fish is prepared almost every way imaginable. Call to reserve and make arrangements for minibus transportation. Dinner will come to about Lit. 30,000. Closed Wed., Nov. 1–Dec. 31. No cards.

CONCA DEI MARINI

East of Positano, on the water's edge below Conca dei Marini is the **Grotta di Smeraldo** (Emerald Cave). Both an elevator and steep stairs lead to the ticket booth in front of the opening to the cavern. The light filtering underwater creates a magical bright emerald green around the stalagmites and stalactites. (Open March through May 9 A.M. to noon, June through September 8:30 A.M. to 6 P.M., October through February 10 A.M. to 4 P.M.)

AMALFI

Once a prosperous maritime republic, Amalfi rivaled Genoa and Venice between the ninth and 11th centuries. Most of the town was destroyed by a tidal wave in 1343. Just off the coast road, facing Amalfi's main square from atop a wide 55-step ramp, is the 11th-century **cathedral of St. Andrew.** The saint's relics are in the crypt; the black and white facade was reconstructed in the 19th century. At the far left of the baroque atrium is the entrance to the **Chiostro del Paradiso** (Paradise Cloister), a 13th-century cemetery for nobility with Arabesque arches supported by a series of twin columns. (Open 9 A.M. to 6 P.M., to 7 P.M. in summer.)

In the local **Museo Civico,** Piazza del Municipio (open 9 A.M. to 2 P.M., to 1 P.M. Sunday; closed Monday), are the 11th-century **Tavole Amalfitane** (Amalfi Tablets), the world's oldest maritime code. According to local legend Amalfi's Flavio Gioia invented the mariner's compass in the 11th century. Two sections of the original 12th-century maritime republic's **arsenal,** on Via M. Camera near Piazza Flavio Gioia, are of interest; this is where galleys with 112 to 116 oars were constructed.

Costume parades and a regatta are held every year between Italy's four former maritime republics—Amalfi, Genoa, Pisa, and Venice—with the site rotating among the four.

☞ RESTAURANTS

La Caravella, Via Nazionale 36; tel. (089) 871029. Angelo and Franco have put their wives in the kitchen and entertain diners with jovial Campania hospitality. The *spaghetti alla Caravella* can be a meal in itself for weight-watchers and rookies. Full meals run around Lit. 35,000. Closed Tues., Nov. 10–30. No cards.

RAVELLO

Overlooking the coast and most of the Gulf of Salerno is this jewel, three and a half miles up a winding road from Atrani (at an altitude of about 1,200 feet). Refreshing sea breezes make a stop even more delightful when darkness sweeps away the rays of a torrid summer sun. Local attractions include the **Villa Cimbrone** (open 9 A.M. to sunset), a neo-Gothic building with a park and terrace, which symbolically condenses the entire fascination of the Amalfi Drive—natural beauty accentuated by the artistic and creative imagination of man.

The **Villa Rufolo,** at Piazza Vescovada (open 9:30 A.M. to 1 P.M. and 3 to 6:30 P.M.), is an 11th-century Arab-Sicilian complex, begun by the Rufoli family. The cloister, court, and gardens are ideal for appreciating another fine view over the sea. Giovanni Boccaccio was so charmed that he set one of the tales from his *Decameron* here. Another enchanted visitor was composer Richard Wagner.

The 11th-century **cathedral** (restructured in the 1700s) is flanked by a 13th-century bell tower. Beyond a 12th-century bronze door by Barisano da Trani in the baroque nave is a pulpit commissioned by Nicola Rufolo in 1272. The mosaic-decorated pulpit is supported by six columns resting atop marble lions, and is a classic example of southern Romanesque sculpture. In the church is a cracked vessel reputed to contain the blood of Ravello's patron San Pantaleone, which supposedly liquefies each July 27.

✤ RESTAURANTS

Cumpà Cosimo, Via Roma; tel. (089) 857156. This is what happens when the local butcher is a relative next door. Nella and Luca Bottone offer good fresh meat along with traditional varieties of fish. The summer pizza menu satisfies everyone. Dinners run Lit. 20,000–30,000. Closed Mon. Oct.–May. AE, DC, V.

The Gulf Islands

Of the three Tyrrhenian islands looking into the Gulf of Naples, Capri is probably the most celebrated. It is three miles off the tip of the Sorrentine Peninsula. The two other islands, Ischia and Procida, are just off the northern end of the gulf near Pozzuoli.

Capri

The eden of Naples, fairy-tale Capri is accessible by boat or hydrofoil from Naples, Ischia, Sorrento, and Positano. The name Capri is derived from the Greek *kapros* (boar), for the wild boar that once roamed the isle. Two small mountains— 1,100-foot Tiberio to the east and 1,940-foot Solaro in the southwest—give the lovely island the appearance of a saddle.

The major port to the mainland is **Marina Grande,** with the local tourist information office. On the opposite side of the island is the smaller **Marina Piccola,** at the foot of Solaro, with beautiful beaches. Open-air taxis and shuttle buses connect the two main villages on the island, **Capri** and **Anacapri.** Besides public buses and taxis, there is a cable car every 15 minutes from Marina Grande to Capri village from April through September. Anacapri is connected to the top of Monte Solaro by a 12-minute chair-lift ride.

The island has startling blue waters and a rich variety of Mediterranean flora and fauna. Beaches are few, pebbly and, unfortunately, usually overcrowded. But the two natural phenomena highlighting any visit are the Blue Grotto (Grotta Azzurra) and the Faraglioni rock formations.

The **Blue Grotto,** the most famous of Capri's sea caves, is on the northwest coast, near Anacapri. It is accessible only by flat-bottom boat, through a small opening obliging visitors practically to lie down. If the sea is even slightly agitated, the entrance is closed. Inside, the filtered light colors everything a heavenly blue. Boat excursions from Marina Grande transfer in open water to smaller boats to enter the Blue Grotto.

The **Faraglioni** are a symbol of Capri, twin rock formations off Punta di Tragara on the southeastern coast below Capri village. The water-carved rocks appear to be guarding the access to Marina Piccola from the mainland.

There are archaeological remains on the island, such as the sixth- to fifth-century B.C. **Greek acropolis,** the **Baths of Tiberius,** and the **Villa Jovis,** the palace of the Emperor Tiberius, who spent the last ten years of his life on Capri. **Villa San Michele** was built by Swedish physician-naturalist Axel Munthe on the remains of one of Tiberius's villas, near Anacapri. Its enchanting position offers a sweeping panorama from the island of Ponza (off the southern coast of Lazio) across the entire Gulf of Naples, with Vesuvius in the background, down to the Apennines in Calabria. (You can walk to the sights; follow signs.)

RESTAURANTS

La Capannina, Via le Botteghe 14; tel. (081) 8370732. In the village of Capri, 100 yards from the central piazzetta, Antonio De Angelis has the only restaurant on the island that does not have a view to entice diners: His smooth accommodating manner, excellent wine cellar, and good food—especially seafood—are the selling points. This air-conditioned restaurant is not just a tourist eatery. Dinner runs about Lit. 40,000. Closed Nov.–Easter. AE, V.

Da Luigi, Strada dei Faraglioni; tel. (081) 8370591. Open for lunch only. A good, open-air restaurant with a private beach 200 yards from Marina Piccola. If a view is essential, what could be better? The restaurant offers boat service to the beach; otherwise it's an adventurous walk on a steep downhill trail. Shellfish and a Capri DOC wine can be had for as little as Lit. 30,000. Closed Nov.–Easter. No cards.

Ischia

The largest island in the gulf, about 18 miles from Naples, Ischia was once part of the mainland Phlegrean Fields. Divided into six municipalities, the island is noted for its mild climate and thermal spas, and a beautiful coastline with inviting pebbly beaches punctuated by picturesque cliffs and bays.

Ischia has long been a favorite therapeutic and holiday spot with Germans; during the high season beaches will usually be quite crowded.

RESTAURANTS

Giardini Eden, Via Nuova Cartaromana, Ischia Ponte; tel. (081) 993909. Open for lunch only. Peace and quiet can have their price. So do the lobsters and fish from Ugo's personal preserves, not to mention his homemade wine. Swimming on the Ischia Ponte islet is available to guests, so a meal can be an all-day affair. Meals run Lit. 60,000. Closed Oct.–Mar. AE, V.

Procida

The smallest of the three gulf islands, Procida is 15 miles from Naples and lies halfway between Ischia and the mainland point of Monte di Procida. Probably the most characteristic of the three, it still preserves a quaint fishing village atmosphere around its port, and has fewer crowds. Camping is available.

RESTAURANTS
La Medusa, Via Roma 112 , near the port; tel. (081) 8967481. On an island that relies on fishing for its livelihood it's difficult to go wrong choosing seafood. Medusa is slightly above average for pasta as well as fish. Dinners range Lit. 25,000–40,000. Closed Tues., Jan.–Feb. AE, DC.

Salerno

The seat of the southernmost province in Campania, Salerno for a brief period was once capital of the Kingdom of Naples. It was also the site of Allied headquarters in World War II after the September 5, 1943 landing of the U.S. Army just south of the port. The anteroom to the Amalfi Coast, the city straddles the rolling hills along the Gulf of Salerno. The attractive park-lined **Lungomare Trieste** runs along Salerno's waterfront, a good spot for a summer evening stroll.

Parallel to the coast, just beyond Lungomare Trieste and Via Roma, is **Via dei Mercanti,** the most characteristic street in Salerno, which runs through the city's old town. Here are signs of the city's medieval, Renaissance, baroque, and Greco-Roman past.

Main points of interest are the **cathedral** and its **museum** between Via del Duomo and Via Guiscardo. The 11th-century cathedral dedicated to patron San Matteo was ordered by Norman leader Robert Guiscard and consecrated by Pope Gregory VII, who was entombed there after he died in Salerno in exile in 1085. The cathedral's 11th-century **bronze doors** open onto two naves that are believed to have been at one time part of the Salerno **School of Medicine,** the oldest in the Western world, which in the 11th century became famous throughout the Mediterranean and Europe. The 12th-century mosaic-decorated pulpits are supported by 12 columns with elaborately sculptured capitals.

Besides paintings by Giordano, Stanzione, and Ribera, the cathedral museum (the **sala degli avori** or "hall of ivories") houses the 12th-century Salerno ivories, which depict 54 scenes from the Old and New Testaments.

❧ RESTAURANTS

Rugantino, Lungomare Trieste 180; tel. (089) 229768. On the most picturesque street in Salerno, the scent of the sea prevails. Linguine with lobster sauce is an ideal first course; go with the house wine. Dinner runs about Lit. 30,000. Closed Sun. No cards.

Paestum

Along the coast 31 miles southeast of Salerno, Paestum was the ancient Greek colony of Poseidonia, founded in the sixth century B.C.

The ruins of the **ancient city** and the **museum** are open from 8 A.M. to 2 P.M. only, so start your day early if you're not staying nearby. Highlights in the old city include the so-called **Basilica,** actually a **temple** dedicated **to Juno** (Hera); the remains of the altar of sacrifice are visible at the entrance. The massive **Temple of Neptune** (Poseidon) is one of the best-preserved temples in Europe. The **Temple of Ceres** is surrounded by 34 columns. The **museum** (closed Mondays) includes fifth-century B.C. frescoes found in nearby tombs and 34 *metopes,* bas-reliefs which decorated the base of the Temple of Juno near the Sele River.

Rural Campania

An inland loop from Naples traverses the rolling hills of Campania, passing three towns of interest—Avellino, Benevento, and Caserta.

Avellino

The agricultural center Avellino, 37 miles northeast of Naples, is a provincial seat and the largest urban settlement in the area known as Irpinia. This is the backyard of Christian Democratic leader and Italian prime minister Ciriaco DeMita. Hilly and wooded, the town and province of Avellino were hard-hit by the November 23, 1980, earthquake that took a heavy toll throughout Campania and western Basilicata.

Most of the old town around the 12th-century **cathedral** was damaged by the quake. Under the cathedral is the modified Romanesque crypt now known as **Santa Maria dei Sette Dolori.** Of particular interest is the **Irpino Museum** (open 9 A.M. to 2 P.M., to 1 P.M. Sunday, closed Monday), at the far corner of the Villa Comunale off Corso Europa. Besides a collection of 18th- and 19th-century ceramics and paintings, there is a rather complete documentation of Irpinia's history from prehistoric times.

❦ RESTAURANTS

La Caveja, Via Tuoro Cappuccini 48; tel. (0825) 38277. The best restaurant in town is a popular local spot for receptions—which means it's often closed to the passerby. But if things are calm, Alba Galasso's touch of Romagna added to traditional Campania recipes is enjoyable. The restaurant is air-conditioned. Dinners will cost Lit. 30,000–40,000. Closed Mon., Aug. 5–20. AE, V.

Benevento

North of Avellino, the hilltop provincial seat of Benevento is halfway between Campobasso and Naples. Conquered by the Romans in the third century B.C., and an important agricultural center on the ancient Appian Way, it became a cultural center during medieval Lombard domination.

Before joining the House of Savoy's united Italy in 1860, Benevento was a papal principality for nearly two hundred years. The 12th-century **cathedral** was practically destroyed by World War II bombing raids, but has been reconstructed. The 13th-century **bell tower** is adorned with many sculptures. Also of interest in town are **Trajan's Arch** (from A.D. 114), remains of the second-century **Roman theater** (one of the largest in existence), and the seventh-century **Santa Sofia church** and its 12th-century **Lombard cloisters.** Inside is the **Samnium Museum** (open 9 A.M. to 2 P.M., to 1 P.M. Sunday; closed Monday), **Library,** and **Historical Archives.** Housed in the museum are Egyptian sculptures from a temple to Isis in Benevento, Greek and Byzantine coins and objects, and medieval and even modern art. Ten minutes away on Piazza IV Novembre are two 14th-century buildings known as **Rocca dei Rettori** that contain relics from the history of Benevento.

Benevento is known for **Strega** liqueur and **nougat.**

❦ RESTAURANTS

Antica Taverna, Via Annunziata 41; tel. (0824) 21212. This rustic trattoria is the best in town. Homemade pasta is done in the best country tradition. Consider finishing off your meal with a glass of Strega. Meals costs around Lit. 25,000. Closed Sun. AE.

Caserta

Once known as Villa Reale, Caserta, west of Benevento, has all the appearances of a military town. A national police academy and air force NCO school have encroached on one of Italy's architectural gems—the royal palace and park of **La Reggia.**

Half a mile from the Caserta Nord (North) A2 exit (18 miles from Naples, 109 from Rome), La Reggia was Bourbon King Charles III's answer to Versailles. The five-floor, 1,200-room

Palazzo Reale and extensive park were created by architect Luigi Vanvitelli between 1752 and 1774. (La Reggia's apartments are open 9 A.M. to 1:30 P.M., to 12:30 P.M. Sunday; the park is open to 2:30 P.M., to 4:30 P.M. in March, and to 6 P.M. from April to September.)

The Royal Apartments are entered through an ornate vestibule and the "stairs of honor," an imposing marble ramp that divides into two parallel stairs up to the first floor.

The lavishly decorated and furnished Royal Apartments occupy the front of the palace, and are complemented by interior chambers such as the Palatine Chapel, with its paintings and marble walls.

Before the rooms of the Bourbon kings are the Hall of Alessandro and the Hall of the Guards, which are dedicated to the Farnese family. The Hall of Alessandro overlooks Piazza Carlo III, embraced by Bernini-style wings, in front of La Reggia.

To the right of the hall two waiting rooms, Salone di Marte and Sala di Astrea, richly decorated with gold ornaments and chandeliers, precede the Throne Room of the King of Naples, with its arched ceiling and elaborate gold stuccoes. The gold and wood throne is carved with likenesses of former kings and crests of provinces in the kingdom.

The king's chambers include the bedroom of Francesco II, his bath with sculpted lions' heads on a granite tub, and the Council Chamber, featuring an elaborately styled table given to Francesco I as a wedding gift from the City of Naples.

Also on this side of the Hall of Alessandro are the study and bedroom occupied by Joachim Murat when he governed the Kingdom of Naples during the Napoleonic domination of Italy.

To the left of the Hall of Alessandro are the older royal apartment and four frescoed rooms dedicated to the four seasons of the year. Occupying an inner wing is the U-shaped Court Theater, with five tiers of boxes decorated with paintings of mythological subjects.

The **park** extends over 150 endless acres behind La Reggia. There is bus service from the rear of the Royal Palace along the canal to Diana Falls, at the opposite end of the park. These falls feed the canal and fountains in the park. The water is channeled under five mountains from the Taburno spring nearly 25 miles away.

The winding and relaxing **English Garden** is to the right of the cascade, with its Bath of Venus pool and Lake of the Swans.

17

THE DEEP SOUTH

A sun-drenched corridor to elsewhere, the Deep South is Italy's problem child.

The Basilicata wedge and its Apulia (Puglia) and Calabria peninsulas form the over 26,500-square-mile, boot-shaped extremity of mainland Italy, isolated from the north for millenia by the curve of the Apennines from the Adriatic to the Tyrrhenian toe.

The extensive coastline of the three regions has been pierced by more foreign forces than any other area in Italy. Striking contrasts in cultural origin are visible on the streets in more populated areas.

When the three regions joined the Piedmont's unification of Italy, with Rome as the capital, Rome itself was as distant as the foreign powers that had alternated domination to assure control of the middle Mediterranean. For many succeeding generations of southerners "the capital" remained Naples, in the region of Campania, where the Bourbons had reigned over the Deep South and Sicily. The magnetism of Neapolitan grandeur attracted ambitious southern mothers convinced that "born in Bari" would handicap their children's future. (Mothers made arrangements with Neapolitan maternity clinics, and when the time was ripe, they went to Naples to give birth, returning home with their child afterwards.) The phenomenon long threw a curve to demographic experts.

The degeneration of Naples and evolution of Adriatic Bari has muted such emigration today. With the political patronage of academic-statesman Aldo Moro, the capital city of the Apulia region has become the most important in the Deep South. Its annual Levant Fair is a Mediterranean showcase for Italian industry and products. Apulia has also escaped the plague of organized crime that heavily weighs in most of the south: the Mafia in Sicily, the *camorra* in Campania, and the *'ndraghetta* in Calabria.

Its neighbor Basilicata is the poorest region in the entire country. And the southern unemployment rate has soared. For many youngsters the only recourse is emigration, the military, or the national police corps.

The *Mezzogiorno* (Italy's south—literally translated as "midday" as well as "South") always is a priority on the political platforms of incoming governments.

Yet some economists have estimated that squandered funds alone would have been more than sufficient to completely vitalize the entire *Mezzogiorno*. Too many projects were literally "castles in the sand," concerned more with creating jobs than economic feasibility. The Taranto steelworks have been scaled down, and the Gioia Tauro port and industrial complex has been abandoned.

Only within the past twenty years have two modern turnpikes been completed on both the eastern and western coasts of the South, to finally link most of the area directly to Rome and Europe. The roads are godsends for Southerners obliged to seek work away from home in Lombardy, Piedmont, and abroad.

With the tourist influx to the recent rampant coastal developments, a trip through Italy's Deep South can be an overwhelming experience. As elsewhere in Italy, August is the problem month for tourism, since northern industrial complexes close in toto for vacation.

Though various locales throughout the three regions are discussed, of prime concern will be those points of interest along the east coast route to Brindisi (for the ferry to Greece) and the west coast road to the ferry for Sicily.

WINING AND DINING

The texture and taste of the Deep South's food and wines appear exaggerated compared to the offerings elsewhere in Italy, but until recently it typified Italian cuisine to the rest of the world due to mass emigration from the underdeveloped South.

Basilicata produces just two government-controlled DOC wines: Aglianico del Taburno and Aglianico del Vulture. These also serve as the base for local muscatels (*moscati*). Regional cuisine follows basic, simple recipes using local produce, especially vegetables, lamb, entrails, and eel. There is an overlap in cooking styles from neighboring Puglia and Calabria.

Apulia (Puglia) is the largest wine-producing region in the European Economic Community. Local wines are often used to blend with northern Italian and French wines, due to their hearty texture and high alcohol content. Twenty-three DOC wines are recognized; among those beginning to emerge on their own merit are Aleatico di Puglia, Castel del Monte, Locorontondo, Martina Franca, Matino, Ostuni, and San Severo.

Apulia is also the home of *orecchiette,* an ear-shaped, hard-grain pasta served with a tart tomato sauce. The extensive coast provides a good fishing base to satisfy tastes for fish stew, squid, and octopus casserole. Lamb is also a local favorite; in addition to local flocks, there are sheep from Abruzzi which migrate to the Tavoliere plain for winter grazing.

A broad-bean puree is one of many legume-based recipes popular in Apulia. Local cheeses are provolone, *cacioricotta, burrata, caciocavallo,* and pecorino.

Calabria definitely offers the strongest wines and spiciest menus. Local DOC wines are Cirò, Donnici Sanuto, Greco di Bianco, Lamezia, Melissa, Polinno, and Sant'Anna di Isola Capo Rizzuto.

Highlighting local menus are such regional pasta variations as *pizzicotti, ricchielle,* and *ricci di donna,* and vegetable soups spiced with strong pecorino cheese. Red peppers are used in abundance in many local *insaccati,* as well as some pecorino. *Butirri* is a curious local cheese with a butter heart.

Unfortunately, many southern restaurants may be a bit rustic by North American standards. Cleanliness was a prime consideration in selecting the establishments listed here.

Credit cards for recommended restaurants are listed as accepted. "All cards" means that all of the following are accepted: AE—American Express; DC—Diner's Club; MC—MasterCard; V—Visa. Prices given are for a complete dinner (from antipasto to dessert) for one person, unless otherwise noted.

TRAVEL

Flying

Air service is available to the cities of Bari, Brindisi, Foggia, Lamezia Terme (for both Cosenza and Catanzaro), and Reggio di Calabria.

Taking the Train

Major state rail routes cover both coasts and make two trans-Apennine crossings. Along the west coast is the 359 line originating in Rome, and stopping in all major coastal towns and cities down to Reggio di Calabria. It connects with ferry service for Sicily and elsewhere at both Reggio and Villa San Giovanni.

The major east coast route 286 begins in Bologna and continues, via Ancona, Pescara, and Termoli, through to Foggia (with a connection to Manfredonia) and Bari and on to Brindisi.

The two mountain routes (west to east) are 361 from Caserta (just north of Naples) to Foggia, and 364 from Battipaglia (south of Naples) via Potenza to Metaponto. A major coastal route along the Ionian Sea is the 365 from Reggio Calabria northeast via Catanzaro Lido-Crotone-Sibari-Metaponto to Taranto. Minor links are the 358 Taranto-Brindisi and the 285 Brindisi-Lecce.

FLIGHT DETAILS

Town	Airport	Connections	Airport Bus Transport	Flight Information
Bari	Palese Airport (7½ miles)	Bologna (1½ hrs.) Cagliari (3½ hrs.) Florence (1 ¾ hrs.) Foggia (30 min.) Milan (1½ hrs.) Naples (50 min.) Olbia (4 hrs. 40 min.) Palermo (1 hr.) Pescara (1 hr.) Rome (1 hr.)	From/to Morfini Agenzia, Via Calefati 37; tel. (080) 216609	Alitalia/ATI/Aliblu, tel. (080) 369288; Alisarda/Avianova, tel. (080) 235860; airport, tel. (080) 374654
Brindisi	Casale Airport (4 miles)	Catania (1½ hrs.) Milan (1½ hrs.) Naples (65 min.) Rome (1 hr.)	From/to Daversa bus line stop, in front of main rail station. Also connections with Lecce (Piazza Mazzini, 45 min.) and Taranto (Piazza Umberto, 51, 90 min.)	Alitalia/ATI/Aliblu, tel. (0831) 29091; airport, tel. (0831) 418805
Catanzaro	Sant'Eufemia Airport (in Lamezia Terme)	Milan (1½ hrs.) Rome (65 min.)	From/to Piazza Matteotti	Airport, tel. (0968) 51766
Cosenza	Sant'Eufemia Airport (in Lamezia Terme)	Milan (1½ hrs.) Rome (65 min.)	From/to Platform 1, Stazione Centrale (unavailable Sun.)	Airport, tel. (0968) 51766
Foggia	Gino Lisa Airport (2 miles)	Milan (Mon–Fri, 2 hrs.) Rome (Mon–Fri, 70 min.) San Domino–Tremiti Islands (by helicopter), depart 8 A.M. 6 P.M. (20 min.); return 9:10 A.M. 6:40 P.M.	None—taxi required	Aliblu, tel. (0881) 24798
Lamezia Terme	Sant'Eufemia Airport	Milan (1½ hrs.) Rome (65 min.)		Airport, tel. (0968) 51766
Reggio di Calabria	Tito Minniti Airport (3 miles)	Milan (1 hr., 40 min.) Rome (70 min.)	From/to Port, AMA line 125	Alitalia/ATI/Aliblu, tel. (0965) 320095

The private Calabro–Lucano railroad, complemented by rural bus service, links all Deep South provincial capitals with provincial urban areas. EuRailpasses are not valid on these lines. As a general rule C–L depots either share or are in the immediate vicinity of FS (Italian state railroad) stations in provincial seats. C–L bus connections are generally in the immediate vicinity of the company's rail depots.

Driving

Road connections continue to improve in the Deep South, but too often means of mass transportation—especially in the hinterland—remain, at the most, primitive.

Three major turnpikes serving the area are:

A3 (Naples–Reggio di Calabria, 306 miles). Traversing northwestern areas, the A3 ties into both A1 and A2 (Naples–Florence–Bologna–Milan) as well as the SS94 to Potenza and SS407 to Metaponto, in the middle of the Basilicata coast on the Ionian Sea. There is no toll between Salerno and Reggio di Calabria.

A14 (Bologna–Taranto, 461 miles). Running along the east coast, the A14 ties into the A1 between Milan and Rome and the Rome superstrada along the Adriatic coast to Venice.

A16 (Naples–Canosa, 107 miles). Running east-west, this trans-Apennine highway connects with the A14 30 miles south of Foggia and 44 miles north of Bari.

CAR RENTALS

The following auto rental facilities are available in the Deep South:

Bari: (Palese Airport) Avis, tel. (080) 373390; Europcar, tel. (080) 371092; Hertz, tel. (080) 373666; Maggiore, tel. (080) 374647.

(City) Avis, Via L. Zuppetta 5A; tel. (080) 540266. Europcar, Piazza Aldo Moro 58; tel. (080) 213936; telex 810851. Hertz, Piazza Aldo Moro 47; tel. (080) 225616; telex 810192. Maggiore, Via Carulli 12/22; tel. (080) 544300.

Brindisi: (Casale Airport) Avis, (0831) 418826; Europcar, (0831) 412061; Hertz, (0831) 412109; Maggiore, (0831) 418155.

(City) Avis, Via del Mare 50; tel. (0831) 26407. Europcar, Via Sacramento 16; tel. (0831) 29104; telex 813363. Hertz, Via San Francesco 13; tel. (0831) 26515. Maggiore, Piazza Francesco Crispi 13; tel. (0831) 25838.

Cosenza: Maggiore, Viale degli Alimena 31H; tel. (0984) 71249.

Foggia: Avis, Stazione Centrale; tel. (0881) 78912. Europcar, c/o Hotel Palace Sarti, Viale XXIV Maggio 48; tel. (0881) 76495. Maggiore, Viale XXIV Maggio 76/78; tel. (0881) 73173.

Lamezia Terme: (Sant Eufemia airport) Avis, tel. (0968) 51508; Europcar, tel. (0968) 51541, telex 912594; Hertz, tel. (0968) 51533, telex 890034; Maggiore, tel. (0968) 51331.

Lecce: Maggiore, Via Daurio 76; tel. (0832) 20184.

Potenza: Avis, Via Tecnica 18; tel. (0971) 54722.

Reggio Calabria: (Tito Minniti airport) Avis, tel. (0965) 320023; Europcar, tel. (0965) 320431, telex 912578; Hertz, tel. (0965) 320093, telex 890034; Maggiore, tel. (0965) 320148.

(City) Hertz, Via V. Florio 19 (port); tel. (0965) 332223; telex 890034. Maggiore, Corso Garibaldi 320; tel. (0965) 94980.

Taranto: Avis, Corso Umberto 61; tel. (099) 26071. Europcar, Via Nitti 16; tel. (099) 23592. Hertz, Via Pupino 19; tel. (099) 91943. Maggiore, Via T. d'Aquino 52; tel. (099) 24881.

Vibo Valentia: Maggiore, Viale Kennedy 13/23; tel. (0963) 42165.

Taking the Ferry

International ferry service is available at Bari for Greece and Yugoslavia, at Brindisi for Greece, and at Reggio di Calabria for Malta. For service from Calabria (Reggio and Villa San Giovanni) to Sicily, see "Travel" in the Sicily chapter.

There is sea service around the Gargano Massif to the Tremiti Islands. Hydrofoil service to the Tremiti is available from Rodi Garganico, Peschici, Termoli, and Vasto. Information numbers of the Compagnia Adriatica are: Manfredonia, tel. (0884) 22888; Peschici, tel. (0884) 94074; Rodi Garganico, tel. (0884) 95031; Vieste, tel. (0884) 78501; Tremiti, tel. (0882) 663008; Termoli, tel. (0875) 2429; and Vasto, tel. (0873) 516180.

❧ ACCOMMODATIONS

In Italy's Deep South accommodations have evolved from the days when a northern industrialist had to create the Jolly hotel chain to assure himself clean, comfortable lodgings when he was obliged to visit the area. (Today, the Jolly chain has altered its scope, now more concerned with 4- and 5-star hotels.)

This points to a missing link in southern hospitality—the medium-range vacation hotel (though, as a rule, the tab at leading southern hotels is much less than at northern counterparts).

The recent tourist boom has seen the rise of a number of fine seasonal establishments. Unfortunately, organization can at times be a severe shortcoming—even a beautiful facility surely needs more than to simply open its doors. Concepts of cleanliness on the part of cleaning personnel is another handicap—but one that experience seems to be resolving. The transition from plow to mop has its consequences.

There are a number of camps with bungalows, often on private beaches, as well as well-equipped tourist villages, which attract northern Italians. These usually require minimal stays of seven days, with arrangements made with the tourist villages; shorter stops may be arranged on a walk-in basis if space is available.

Hotels are listed on a regional basis, along with tourist villages that are equipped with pools, private beach facilities, and so forth.

Credit cards are listed as accepted. "All cards" means that all of the following are accepted: AE—American Express; DC—Diner's Club; MC—MasterCard; V—Visa. Range of rates given are for single to double rooms.

Basilicata

Described loosely, Basilicata is shaped like a strap across Italy's instep. Three types of terrain predominate: sandy beaches on the Gulf of Taranto; craggy coastline on the Gulf of Policastro; and rugged interior.

To base yourself on the Gulf of Taranto, stay at the coastal town of Metaponto, from which you can also visit the Greek ruins at Metapontum.

On the Gulf of Policastro, Maratea would be a good base for accommodations.

Inland, the artistic center of Matera makes a good base, as does Potenza, about 2½ miles away. Only an hour's drive from the Gulf of Policastro, Potenza has cool Alpine air and is well located as a base for drives through western Basilicata.

MARATEA

Santavenere, Località Fiumicello, Punta Santavenere, 85046; tel. (0973) 876910; telex 760087. This luxury hotel in a 22-acre private park faces the sea and its own private beach. With 44 air-conditioned rooms, the hotel also offers a beachfront restaurant and bar, piano bar, pool, and tennis courts. Just a mile from the Maratea tourist port, rooms run Lit. 124,000–212,000, to Lit. 500,000 in Aug. Open June 1–Sept. 30. AE, DC, V.

Villa del Mare, SS18, Località Acquafredda, 85046; tel. (0973) 878007; telex 812390. This 4-star, air-conditioned, 75-room hotel is 1½ miles from the Maratea tourist port and 6 miles from the San Pietro caverns. The hotel has a restaurant, bar, pool, park, and private beach, which is served by a private elevator. Half-board rates run: Lit. 90,000–140,000 (singles); Lit. 70,000–120,000 per person for double occupancy. Open Easter–Oct. 31. V pending.

MATERA

Park Hotel, SS99; 75100; tel. (0835) 263625. This 3-star hotel is less than 2 miles from the center of Matera on the state highway for Altamura. In open country, the hotel has 56 double rooms at Lit. 59,000. It is equipped with ceiling fans, but no air-conditioning. No cards.

METAPONTO LIDO

Turismo, Via delle Ninfe 5, 75010; tel. (0835) 741918. Only 50 yards from the sea, this 3-star, 62-room hotel has an air-conditioned restaurant and bar. Rates run Lit. 35,000–55,000; with meals Lit. 72,000. Open April 1–Oct. 10. No cards.

POTENZA

Park Hotel, SS Basentana, 85100; tel. (0971) 69031; telex 812471. Part of this 100-room, 3-star hotel was totally remodeled last year. Located 2½ miles from the center of Potenza, it is the best in the area, with a bar and air-conditioned restaurant (no air-conditioning in the rooms, however). Rooms will run Lit. 55,000–100,000; apartments Lit. 140,000. All cards.

Calabria

Calabria is the toe of the Italian boot. You'll find major beach development along the Tyrrhenian coast, from Lamezia Terme to Reggio di Calabria—but despite the development, this area of rocky shore broken by sandy stretches is one of Italy's loveliest areas. The beach towns best as bases are: Lamezia Terme (about 2 miles from the sea; there is also an airport); Soverato; and Tropea. Reggio di Calabria is the gateway to Sicily (one of the major ferry ports for the island), with historical interest in its own right.

Cosenza is recommended for exploring the mountainous La Sila area. You can ski 15 miles from Cosenza at Camigliatello, and 34 miles from Cosenza at Lorica.

Because Catanzaro is a major city in the region, lodgings are listed, but the city is not of major tourist importance.

CATANZARO

Guglielmo, Via Azaria Tedeschi 1, 88100 tel. (0961) 26532; telex 880025. This remodeled former Jolly hotel now has 4 stars and 50 air-conditioned rooms in the heart of Catanzaro. The hotel has a bar and restaurant. Rates are Lit. 80,000–120,000. All cards.

COSENZA

Centrale, Via Macallé trav., Corso Mazzini (once Via dei Tigrai 3), 87100; tel. (0984) 73681; telex 912599. This centerally located 3-star, 48-room, air-conditioned hotel can also claim a good restaurant and bar. It is about a mile from the main rail terminal. Rates run Lit. 65,000–95,000. AE, MC, V.

San Francesco, Via Ungheretti, contrada Commenda, Rende (CS), 87100; tel. (0984) 861721; telex 800048. On the SS19 north, 2½ miles from the center of Cosenza, this 4-star hotel with 144 air-conditioned rooms is just beyond the city limits and 20 miles from the fabulous Sila mountains. Built in 1980, the hotel offers the largest conference facilities (for 500) in Calabria, and has a restaurant, bar, and pool. Rooms will run Lit. 70,000–119,000. All cards.

LAMEZIA TERME

Grand Hotel Lamezia, Località Sant'Eufemia, 88046 (CZ); tel. (0968) 53021. Less than 2 miles from the sea and only a half-mile from the airport serving both Cosenza and Catanzaro, this 3-star hotel built in 1971 has 104 air-conditioned rooms. Rates run Lit. 42,000–58,000. All cards.

REGGIO DI CALABRIA

Grand Hotel Excelsior, Via Vittorio Veneto 66, 89100; tel. (0965) 25801. This 4-star, 92-room hotel is conveniently situated between the port for ferries to Sicily and the National Museum. The supplement for air-conditioning was not fixed at press time. Room rates Lit. 95,000–100,000. All cards.

Primavera, Via Nazionale 177, 89100; tel. (0965) 47081. Just 300 yards from the A3 north, this 3-star, 60-room hotel has both a restaurant and bar. Rooms will run Lit. 60,000–90,000. All cards.

SOVERATO

San Domenico, Via della Galleria, 88068 (CZ); tel. (0967) 23121. This 3-star hotel sits right on the beach and 49 of its 80 air-conditioned rooms look out on the Ionian Sea. A well-traveled northern Italian businessman claims to have gone "100 kilometers (60 miles) out of my way to stay" here. Open all year, the San Domenico has one of the best hotel restaurants in Calabria. Just 15 miles from Catanzaro Lido, 18 miles from Catanzaro, and 34 from the Lamezia airport. For Lit. 70,000 the hotel will arrange for a taxi pickup at the airport. Single room rates run Lit. 45,000–58,000, doubles Lit. 65,000–85,000, depending on the season. DC, MC.

TROPEA

La Pineta, Via Marina 150, 88038 (CZ); tel. (0963) 617000. This 3-star, 59-room air-conditioned hotel with restaurant and bar is just 100 yards from a beautiful sandy beach. Tennis court and pool table are available for guests. Double room rates range Lit. 52,000–96,000; in low season doubles are let for single occupancy at Lit. 39,000. Open April 1–Oct. 10.

Apulia (Puglia)

Simply put, Apulia (Puglia) is the heel of the boot.

The Gargano Peninsula is a magnificent area of woods, beaches, and rocky coast; the best bathing in Puglia is found here. Foggia is an inland town, gateway to the Gargano. Vieste del Gargano is right on the coast.

A beach alternative to the Gargano is the coastal area south of Brindisi: from San Cataldo south around the cape and up the western coast of the peninsula's "heel," to the promontory of Gallipoli. Stay either at Gallipoli, on the rocky Ionian shore; Alimini, near sandy Adriatic beaches and inland lakes, or at Lecce, which is inland, but convenient for exploring the entire area. Martina Franca is another inland option, also convenient for exploring the region.

Another seaside option is Taranto, a barrier island between the bay and Ionian Sea. And Bari has much to offer visitors, including ferry service to Greece. About 20 miles away is the coastal town of Polignano a Mare, on the sandy Adriatic shore; farther south is coastal Ostuni Marina.

BARI

L'Approdo, Via del Mare 50, 70122; tel. (0831) 29667. Not all of the 24 rooms in this 3-star hotel have baths, but the location 10 min. from ferry service to Greece is convenient. Rooms run Lit. 42,000–65,000. All cards.

Palace, Via Lombardi 13, 70122; tel. (080) 216551; telex 81011. Bari's prestige address on the edge of old town near the new port is a 4-star, 204-room air-conditioned hotel with restaurant, bar, and parking facilities. Rooms run Lit. 163,000–260,000. All cards.

7 Mari, Via Verdi 60, 70122; tel. (080) 441500. This 3-star hotel with 56 rooms is just 300 yards from the *Levante* fairgrounds and stadium. Air-conditioning is available at a supplement of Lit. 6,000. Room rates run Lit. 66,000–85,000. All cards.

BRINDISI
L'Approdo, Via del Mare 50, 72100; tel. (0831) 29668. Most convenient for ferry transport to Greece, this 24-room, 3-star hotel is just 200 yards from the port. There's a restaurant and bar. Rooms with baths run Lit. 42,000–65,000. AE, DC, V.

FOGGIA
President, Via degli Aviatori 80, 71100; tel. (0881) 79648. Just 10 min. from the rail terminal, this 3-star, 130-room hotel will have a pool ready by 1989. There is a restaurant and bar on the premises. Air-conditioning costs an extra Lit. 5,000. Room rates run Lit. 50,000–78,000. All cards.

GALLIPOLI
Le Sirenuse, Litorale per S. Maria di Leuca, 73014 (LE); tel. (0833) 22536. Less than 2 miles from the center of characteristic Gallipoli is this modern, 3-star hotel between the coast road and an inviting sandy beach. The 120 air-conditioned rooms are served by a restaurant and bar. Open all year, the hotel has a private pool and tennis court. Rooms will cost Lit. 57,000–89,000. No cards.

LECCE
Risorgimento, Via Augusto Imperatore 19, 73100; tel. (0832) 42125; telex 860144. In the heart of old town, just 800 yards from the rail terminal, this 3-star hotel has a strong business clientele. Rates for the 57 air-conditioned rooms run Lit. 51,000–95,000. All cards.

MARTINA FRANCA
Dell'Erba, Viale dei Cedri 1, 74015 (TA); tel. (080) 901055. Both the hotel and its restaurant are strong favorites with business people traveling in Apulia. The 3-star, 49-room hotel has a private pool. Rooms run Lit. 45,000–85,000. All cards.

POLIGNANO A MARE
Hotel Grotta Palazzese, Via Narciso 59, 70044 (BA); tel. (080) 740261. The 14 rooms of this 4-star hotel and its four-room annex sit atop a rocky coast that drops straight into the sea. Under the hotel, in a natural cavern facing the sea, is a restaurant that seats 250 in the summer. Just a mile off the main Bari–Brindisi coastal road, the Grotta Palazzese is 20 miles south of Bari. The rooms are air-conditioned. Rates run Lit. 48,000–92,000. All cards.

TARANTO
Delfino, Viale Virgilio 66, 74100; tel. (099) 3205; telex 860113. A 4-star, 198-room, air-conditioned hotel on the Mare Grande coast, with a bar, restaurant, and private pool, the Delfino offers a fine view over the Gulf of Taranto. The hotel has a strong business clientele. Rooms will run Lit. 86,000–128,000. All cards.

TREMITI ISLANDS

Gabbiano, 71040 San Nicole di Tremiti (FG); tel. (0882) 663044. This 35-room hotel, just off the coast in a pine wood, has a good restaurant. Board is generally required in high season. Room rates run Lit. 36,000–65,000. AE.

VIESTE DEL GARGANO

Hotel degli Aranci, Piazza Santa Maria delle Grazie 10, 71019 (FE); tel. (0884) 78557. This 3-star, 86-room hotel provides shuttle service to the beach, 100 yards off; there is also a private pool. The management coordinates bookings for three nearby camps with bungalows. English replies to correspondence are guaranteed. Room rates run Lit. 61,000–88,000. Closed Jan. and Feb. AE, MC, V.

Basilicata

Basilicata is Italy's time machine. In most of the country, progress has canceled nostalgic concepts; "today," comments an observer, "traces of pre-1950 Italian lifestyle can only be found in Toronto (Canada) or Basilicata."

The smallest Deep South region, Basilicata is also Italy's poorest. A strap-shaped wedge between the Apulian heel and Calabrian toe of the Italian boot, over 90 percent of the area separating Apulia and Calabria is mountainous or pre-Appennine foothills. The lowlands are the Ionian plains stretching south of Matera to the sea. Here wide sandy beaches contrast sharply with Basilicata's craggy Tyrrhenian coast separating Calabria from Campania.

A chronicle of his political exile for anti-Fascist sentiments, Carlo Levi's *Christ Stopped at Eboli* captures the desolation haunting most of the region in its title alone.

In Basilicata, nature reigns and man has had to adapt. An earthquake in 1980 devastated large portions of the region. Some towns have been abandoned in heaps of rubble, forcing survivors to relocate.

Refuge has always been a key to Basilicatan settlements. Apart from the regional capital of Potenza and the provincial seat at Matera (with a combined population of nearly 100,000 out of the region's total population of slightly over 600,000), rural towns all are hilltop or mountainside sites chosen as defensible against foreign invaders, bandits, and even rampant malaria, which once ravaged the lower valleys, which were subject to flooding.

Consequently, most hinterland roads are one time-consuming series of curves after another through the Apennines. Public transportation is a combination of rail lines through the valleys and bus service to highland villages. Both are private concessions, and do not honor EuRail passes valid on the nationwide state rail network (see "Travel," this chapter).

This is a prime example of the region's abandonment to its own limited means. But Rome appears to be making overtures; public works projects such as the superstrada from the A3 south of Salerno, through the heart of the region to Metaponto, on the Ionian coast, are beginning to emerge.

The name Basilicata is believed to be derived from that of Byzantine Emperor Basil II. The Romans referred to the area as Lucania; this name was revived by the Fascists in 1932. But under the new republic that emerged following WWII, the region again became Basilicata.

The time machine may not be the easiest of experiences, but it can be rewarding for the curious as well as the nostalgic.

Potenza

The regional capital, Potenza still shows scars from the 1980 earthquake, the latest in a series (in 1273, 1694, 1806, and 1930) that has ravaged Potenza. Though the medieval old town, divided by the Via Pretoria promenade, is not a major tourist attraction, cool Alpine air less than an hour's drive from the heart of the sun-baked Mediterranean is an attractive calling card for the highest regional capital in Italy (at an altitude of over 2,700 feet).

Like most of Basilicata, Potenza is not for first-timers to Italy. It is one of those quaint little pockets of hinterland that merit consideration on a leisurely return to the peninsula. The **Provincial Archaeological Museum,** Via Lazio, Santa Maria (open 9 A.M. to 2 P.M. Tuesday through Saturday, 9 A.M. to 1 P.M. Sunday; closed Monday) has the richest collection of regional artifacts, including a sixth-century B.C. warrior's helmet, fourth-century B.C. soldier's armor, and Greek and Roman statues.

There is also the 12th-century **San Gerardo cathedral** (rebuilt in the 1700s), and several **12th- and 13th-century churches** reflecting the various architectural styles that have influenced the region.

Unless otherwise mentioned, sights (including museums) are usually open Tuesday through Sunday mornings.

🍴 RESTAURANTS
Fuori le Mura, Via IV Novembre 34; tel. (0971) 25409. The reception may be brusque, but the soups and local pasta sauces merit being patient. Dinner will run about Lit. 28,000. Closed Mon. No cards.

SIDETRIPS
Potenza is a good base for panoramic drives throughout western Basilicata. The *tufo* (tufa) caves at **Pietragalla** are still used for producing and storing wine; **Melfi** (north of Potenza off route 93) has the **Hohenstaufen castle museum,** a **12th-century Norman cathedral,** rebuilt with a baroque facade after the 1694

quake; and the Roman archaeological site at **Grumentum** is on picturesque **Lake Pietra del Petrusillo,** southeast of Potenza.

Maratea

This picturesque three-village complex south of Potenza lies in the center of the Basilicata Tyrrhenian coast, on the Gulf of Policastro. The upper and lower old towns (Maratea Superiore and Maratea Inferiore) look over the small holiday port of Marina di Maratea. Atop nearby Monte San Biagio is a 70-foot-high **statue of Christ the Redeemer** and the **17th-century San Biagio Sanctuary chapel.** Just three miles south is the **Maratea cavern,** rich in stalagmites and stalactites.

❦ RESTAURANTS

If you're in Maratea in the summer, be sure to stop at **Taverna Rovita,** Via Rovita 13; tel. (0973) 876588. A characteristic little place with just 34 settings in the heart of old town; reservations are recommended. Dinner costs about Lit. 40,000. Open June 1–Sept. 30 and weekends for special parties year-round. AE, DC, V.

South and inland from Maratea is Calabria's best restaurant, in the town of **Castrovillari: Alia,** Via Jetticelle 71; tel. (0981) 46370. *Degustazione* menu runs Lit. 50,000; there is also a more moderately priced daily special for Lit. 30,000. Closed Sun. and Aug. 10–25. All cards.

Matera

In the center of an Apulian-penetrating territory, the provincial capital of Matera is divided into two worlds by a single ridgetop drive. Atop the ridge is the modern new town of this agricultural center. Appearing to flow down the side of the hill are the Arabesque old-town *sassi,* homes built into the rocky cliffs. **Sasso Caveoso** and **Sasso Barisano**—the two sections of old-town Matera—are eroding *tufo* houses and cave dwellings that once sheltered farmers and animals alike. The chaotic composition has often served as the backdrop for biblical films.

Local efforts are intent on preserving the depopulating old town as an artistic, cultural, and handicraft center. The two *sassi* and surrounding farmlands also conserve some 120 **rock churches.** These crypts, carved into the porous *tufo* by monks fleeing persecution from foreign invaders, span the 6th to 18th centuries. Many can be visited, while others are private property; some even serve now as stables. Information and tour itineraries can be obtained from the local **tourist information office** at Via de Viti de Marco 9; tel. (0835) 212488.

❦ RESTAURANTS

Cucina Casalinga, Via Lucana 48; tel. (0835) 216779. A small, rustic trattoria that lives up to its name, which means "home cooking." Featured is the best produce available that day in the local market. Dinner runs about Lit. 20,000. Closed Sun. No cards.

SIDETRIPS

There are points of historical and cultural interest elsewhere in the province, such as the 11th-century **Sanctuary of Santa Maria d'Anglona,** six miles from **Tursi,** between the Agri and Sinni rivers—42 miles southwest of Potenza. This was the cathedral of the town of Anglona, which no longer exists; part of the structure dates from the 8th century. Drives that take in the **lunar landscapes** of **Aliano** (where Carlo Levi was in exile) and the **white-tiered houses** at **Pisticci** can be a photographer's delight.

Metaponto

Metaponto is in the center of Basilicata's Ionian coast. The Lido and its wide sandy beaches are a marked contrast to the rugged and often isolated interior. Nearby are the **ruins** of the once flourishing seventh-century B.C. Magna Graecia center of Metapontum.

Calabria

This 9,300-square-mile toe of the Italian peninsula provides a topographical slice of the entire nation, from its craggy, Tyrrhenian coast across often snowcapped mountains to the sandy, Ionian beaches. The region is divided into the three provinces of Catanzaro, Cosenza, and Reggio di Calabria.

Political infighting and gerrymandering established the regional seat at Catanzaro, which divides administrative offices with Reggio di Calabria, nearly one hundred miles southwest. Cosenza is the most northern provincial seat, nearly sixty miles from Catanzaro and about 118 miles from Reggio di Calabria.

Calabria has experienced a national summer beach boom, but the most beautiful area remains the Sila pine forests in the forty-thousand-acre Calabria National Park, near Cosenza, in the heart of the region.

Like most of Italy's Deep South, Calabria has a long history of foreign domination. Unique was the urge by each new intruder to rename the area. Once, the tip of Calabria was even considered part of Sicily.

The tremendous contrasts of the terrain have equal rivals in local characteristics, which can range from gracious hospitality to vindictive blood feuds. In spite of the exaggerated contradictions and history of abandonment, Calabria is certainly a land of pleasant surprises.

Cosenza

In the Crati Valley, at the merger of the Busento and Crati rivers, the agricultural-commercial city of Cosenza was once an important link in Rome's trade with Sicily. A 16th-century cultural center, it is now site of the University of Calabria. For tourists, Cosenza is important as a gateway to La Sila.

🌿 RESTAURANTS

La Calvarisella, Via Gerolamo de Rada 11a; tel. (0984) 28012. Noted for consistently offering a fine panorama of Calabrian cooking. Air-conditioned. Dinner runs Lit. 28,000. Closed Sat. night and Sun. AE, V.

La Sila

Improved roads over the past decade have opened the beautiful area of La Sila to tourism. Tourism has gained—the fragrant scent of pines is everywhere; picturesque mountain lakes augment the natural splendor of one of the most beautiful regions of Italy.

The pine- and oak-covered granite massif called La Sila is divided into three sectors: the northern Sila Greca, central Sila Grande, and southern Sila Piccola. The **Cosenza Tourist Information Office,** Via Tagliamento 15; tel. (0984) 27821, can provide information on the ever-increasing number of hotels, pensiones, and tourist villages being developed in the park.

Catanzaro

The regional capital of Calabria, the city of Catanzaro was founded by the Byzantines in the ninth century. Its position between the southern Sila and the Ionian coast creates a climate that is temperate year-round. The commercial and agricultural center for the province of Catanzaro, the city has gained importance with the installation of major regional administrative offices. Catanzaro is not of primary tourist importance; World War II bombing totally destroyed the 16th-century **cathedral,** though it has been completely rebuilt.

🌿 RESTAURANTS

Uno più uno, Galleria Mancuso; tel. (0961) 23180. This is an ice cream parlor plus restaurant that is strongly favored by local inhabitants. A meal runs Lit. 29,000. Closed Sun. night, Mon., and Aug. 10–20. DC, V.

The Tyrrhenian Coast

Beach development has boomed along the Tyrrhenian coast, which is accessible from the major A3 turnpike (Naples–Reggio di Calabria). (The nearly 160 miles of more isolated Ionian coast should be left for a more extensive exploration of the region.)

Most of the A3 is inland, except for the southern stretch, from Lamezia Terme to Reggio di Calabria. Calabria's Tyrrhenian coastal drive is the longest stretch of natural beauty in Italy. Even questionable development in some areas has been unable to detract from the scenery. Isolated stretches of sandy shore can still be found where the craggy Apennines roll into the sea.

Take swimsuits as well as picnic baskets on a Tyrrhenian drive. At the least expected moment a stretch of isolated sandy shore will appear from nowhere.

The Capo Vaticano promontory immediately west of Vibo Valentia cannot compete with the natural beauty of Apulia's Gargano spur, but the picturesque village of **Tropea** warrants a detour off coastal SS18, which does not cover the spur. Just south of Pizzo, SS522 turns right to swing around to Nicotera via Tropea.

Unfortunately there are a few Environmental League red flags warning of unsafe water along the coast around Tropea, but the 12th century **cathedral** and offshore, reeftop **Santa Maria dell' Isola church** are worth the detour. At the southern extreme of the cape is another picturesque village, **Nicotera,** four miles inland. There is a splendid view of the gulf from the square in front of the baroque **cathedral;** also of interest is the Archaeological Museum in the castle on Via Umberto I.

Before reaching the ferry crossings for Sicily at either Villa San Giovanni or Reggio di Calabria, stop at **Bagnara Calabra** and **Scilla.** Both are directly on the coast and have fine views over the Messina Strait to Sicily. Both are fishing villages that capitalize on the swordfish spawning run in July, when Bagnara features a local *sagra* (festival), and swordfish steaks are in abundance.

Reggio di Calabria

Rebuilt after the 1908 earthquake that also leveled Messina, Reggio is the largest city in Calabria. Of historical interest are the fourth-century B.C. **Greek walls** and **Roman baths** at the end of the coastal promenade, **Lungomare Giacomo Matteotti,** which extends toward the main rail terminal. The promenade looks out over the Strait of Messina, between Sicily and the peninsula. In nearby Piazza Castello is the 15th-century **Aragon castle,** and around the corner, off Via Ciminio in Piazza Duomo, is the **cathedral,** totally rebuilt after the destructive 1908 quake.

The city's main attraction, however, is in the **National Museum,** Piazza de Nava (open 9 A.M. to 1 P.M. and 3 to 6 P.M. Tuesday through Saturday, 9 A.M. to 1 P.M. Sunday, closed Monday; in winter, Tuesday, Thursday, and Saturday only, 9 A.M. to 2 P.M.). In a special display off the courtyard are the fifth-century B.C. bronzes. These two Greek warriors, magnificent testimony to the art of ancient Greece, were discovered off the Calabrian coast near the village of Riace in 1972. A complete documentation of the restoration of the ancient statues is also on display.

🦅 RESTAURANTS

Baylik, Via Leone 1; tel. (0965) 48624. Good fish and home-made sweets as well as a fine view over the Strait of Messina. Dinner runs Lit. 35,000. Closed Thurs. and Aug. 10–20. AE, DC, V.

Collina dello Scoiattolo, Località Gallina, Via Provinciale 34; tel. (0965) 682255. Just a short drive out of town, this is a pleasant change of pace from the confusion in Calabria's largest city. A good selection of regional recipes makes the trip worth the effort. Dinner will cost about Lit. 38,000. Closed Wed. No cards.

Apulia

Apulia, Puglia, or Le Puglie, it's the heel of the boot between the Adriatic and Ionian seas. The nearly 12,000-square-mile territory begins with the Tavoliere and Murge plains that undulate south along the Apennine perimeter with Molise and Basilicata.

The region's name derives from prehistoric inhabitants known as the Apulians. From that time, no other Italian region has had such an unenviable history of foreign invasion and domination.

Prehistoric monuments and relics remain preserved. Villages trace their origin to Greek colonization. This is the end of the Via Appia (Appian Way) from the center of the Roman Empire.

After the Romans came the Goths, Byzantines, Longobards, Saracens, Normans, Angiones, Aragons, and Bourbons, before the unification of the modern state of Italy.

The tables momentarily turned in the early 1940s when Apulia became Fascism's base of operations for its war on Greece. Then, in 1943, an armistice was signed with the Allies, in Cassibile, Sicily. With the Allied move into the Deep South came a new provisional government. The provisionals established a mainland base behind Allied lines in Brindisi, while the Germans sought to resurrect Fascism and placed Mussolini at the helm of the puppet Republic of Salò. A full-fledged civil war erupted while World War II still raged.

Except for Foggia, most of Apulia escaped relatively unscathed from the ensuing horrors, while northern regions became trapped in the vengeful vise of German ground forces who considered the inhabitants traitors.

Today Bari is the regional administrative capital. Because of its strategic location at the center of Apulia's Adriatic Coast, Bari's development was promoted by Napoleon's Gen. Joachim Murat, who became king of Naples. Expansion of Bari was resumed during Fascism, and it became the second most important southern city after Naples, due to the hometown efforts of former Christian Democratic leader Aldo Moro, before his assassination in Rome by the Red Brigades.

A modern turnpike system today extends across the region, abbreviating distances. This has enabled Apulia to draw heavily from the national holiday pool over the past decade. The woods, beaches, and rocky shores of the Gargano promontory in the province of Foggia have become particular favorites.

Over five hundred miles of coastline, two-thousand-year-old olive orchards, the Castellana Caverns, Alberobello's curious cone-shaped *trulli* dwellings, the imposing octagonal Castel del Monte, the Tremiti Islands, Salento's botanical splendor, and the recently uncovered mosaics at Otranto are all reasons to consider a trip through Apulia as more than a dash to the ferry to Greece.

Foggia and the Gargano Peninsula

Situated in the center of the Tavoliere plain, the agro-industrial city of Foggia is the capital of the northernmost province in Apulia. Of local interest is the 12th-century **cathedral** that was largely rebuilt in the 1700s. But with its modern turnpike connections, Foggia's main interest is as the gateway to Gargano. Twenty-four miles east via modern superstrada is Manfredonia, at the beginning of SS89, which takes in the peninsula's entire coastal loop and links with the A14 north near Poggio Imperiale.

Near Manfredonia are two of Apulia's most important religious shrines at **San Giovanni Rotondo** and **Monte Sant'Angelo,** visited annually by thousands. The coast road is the most characteristic and beautiful drive in Apulia: rocky coasts, sand and pebble beaches, caves, quaint little villages, modern yet scenic tourist complexes, and ancient settlements such as Vieste and Peschici. Inland, off the point of the promontory, is the **Umbra Forest National Park,** rising to 2,600 feet in the center of the spur.

For an offshore coastal view there is **boat service** from Manfredonia via Vieste to Rodi Garganico. This line continues to the **Tremiti Islands,** where there are connections to Termoli (in Molise) and Marina di Vasto and Ortona, in Abruzzi.

The Tremiti are thirteen and a half miles north of the mainland. The total surface area of the four main islands is less than two square miles of natural beauty. Between the islands of San Domino, the largest; San Nicola, the most populated (with approximately three hundred year-round residents); Ca-prara; and Il Cretaccio are reef formations that frame crystal-line waters for bathing, diving, and fishing. Although not well known by foreigners, the islands become extremely crowded in the summer with Italians.

✦ RESTAURANTS

Cicolella means the finest in Foggia. Alberto and Antonio Cico-lella have spread their talents to three corners of the city:

Cicolella in Fierra, at Via Fortore and Via Bari; tel. (0881) 32166. Delicious dinners run Lit. 45,000. Closed Mon., Tues. AE, DC, V.

Hotel Cicolella, Viale XXIV Maggio 60; tel. (0881) 3890. Din-ners in the hotel restaurant run Lit. 40,000. Closed weekends. AE, DC, V.

Self-Service Cicolella, AGIP Station, Via Bari; tel. (0881) 84136. Very reasonable meals at Lit. 15,000. Closed Mon., Dec. 26–Jan. 1. AE, DC.

Bari

The regional capital of Bari is two cities in one: the medieval-Byzantine old town centered around the Basilica of San Ni-cola, and the 19th-century symmetrical urban center initiated by Napoleonic General Murat in 1813.

Under the Normans, Bari was a major port of embarkation for the Crusades. Now, in terms of population and economic importance, Bari is second only to Naples in southern Italy.

Old Town is the spur between the old fishing port and the new industrial harbor that offers ferry service to Greece and Yugoslavia. Just beyond the western extremity of the modern harbor is the site of the **Levante industrial fair.** There are permanent exhibits, but the main fair each September is the largest of its kind in southern Italy. This is the showcase for Italian economic penetration throughout the Mediterranean.

East of the old town is the picturesque coastal promenade, **Lungomare Imperatore Augusto,** which wraps around the old port and joins **Lungomare Nazario Sauro** to flank the new city.

Flanked by Corso Vittorio Veneto and Piazza Federico II, between the old town and the new port, is the **Byzantine-Norman castle-fortress** expanded by Emperor Frederick II of Hohenstaufen in 1233. (Open 9 A.M. to 1 P.M. and 4 to 7 P.M. Tuesday through Saturday, 9 A.M. to 1 P.M. Sunday; closed Monday.) The castle hosts the **Festival castello**—a celebration of theater, cinema, and music held in July and the first half of August. A museum is on the first floor, off the courtyard. Nearby **Petruzzelli Theater,** an opera house, hosts a popular music festival at the end of August.

To the right of the castle, just a few minutes by foot into old town, is the **11th-century cathedral, San Sabino,** that was rebuilt at the end of the 12th century. The Romanesque facade is ornamented with a rose window and three baroque portals. The remains of San Sabino are under the main altar.

A short walk brings you to the **Basilica of San Nicola** (St. Nicholas). Built between 1087 and 1197 to house the remains of the saint who would become Santa Claus, the church is just behind the cathedral, on the site of the former palace of Byzantine governors in the center of old Bari. The simple, solid facade is considered a prototype of Romanesque architecture in Apulia. In front of the church is the reconstructed **pilgrim's gate.** On the left is the **local history museum** (open 9 A.M. to 1 P.M. and 4:30 to 7 P.M.; closed Friday).

San Nicola

San Nicola was the bishop of Myra, in Asia Minor. He was renowned (understandably) for having resurrected three children who had been cut up and placed in brine by a local butcher. His remains were returned to Bari in 1807 by local sailors who stole them from Myra; the Basilica of San Nicola was built to hold them. The saint's day is May 8, when those who worship him come by boat to pray before his statue in Bari. There is also a procession through town on the eve of the feast day.

The **Provincial Art Gallery** (Lungomare Nazario Sauro, open 9 A.M. to 1 P.M. and 5 to 7 P.M., Sunday 9 A.M. to 1 P.M., closed Monday) features Apulian and Neapolitan artists. In Sala VI are paintings by Tintoretto and Veronese that originally were in the cathedral. **Walking tours of the old town** are organized here every Thursday morning in July and August.

To see the most complete collection of artifacts (particularly ceramics and bronzes) uncovered in Apulia, visit the **Archaeological Museum** (University Palace, first floor, Piazza Umberto I; open 9 A.M. to 2 P.M., holidays to 1 P.M.; closed Sunday). Some items date from the seventh to third centuries B.C.

The main shopping district of Bari is along Via Sparano, which runs the entire length of new Bari, from Piazza Aldo Moro in front of the rail terminal to the Corso Vittorio Emanuele promenade lined with shops and caffès. Prices in Bari tend to be high. Locals often come to Rome to shop and claim that the better prices more than make up for transportation costs.

RESTAURANTS
Ai 2 Ghiottoni, Via Putignani 11; tel. (080) 232240. Fresh fish and roast meats, all prepared with a fine local touch. You'll

also find a good choice of regional wines. Dinner will cost Lit. 40,000. Closed Sun. and Aug. 1–21. All cards.

La Formica Rossa, Via G. Bozzi 53; tel. (080) 235617. In the evening this is also a piano bar, with over 50 varieties of beer. Good light meals go for as little as Lit. 20,000. Closed Mon. and Aug. DC.

La Pignata, Via Melo 9; tel. (080) 232481. Located near the Palace Hotel, this restaurant offers a good *degustazione* menu (for a minimum of 2) for Lit. 55,000. Closed Wed. and Aug. 2–28. All cards.

Vecchia Bari, Via Dante 47; tel. (080) 216496. Near the rail station, off Piazza Aldo Moro, this place has a strong regional atmosphere in every respect; ambience, menu, and wine. Dinners cost about Lit. 40,000. Closed Fri. and Aug. 5–20. AE, DC, V.

The Adriatic Coast

One of the most interesting sections of Adriatic coast in Apulia, combining beaches with points of historic interest, is the nearly twenty-mile strip north of SS16 between Bari and Barletta.

In the center of **Barletta,** at the intersection of Corso Garibaldi and Corso Vittorio Emanuele, is a **16-and-a-half-foot bronze Colossus** dating from the fourth century B.C. that the Venetians abandoned on the beach during a sea storm in the thirteenth century, having removed it from Constantinople (Istanbul). It is believed to be the likeness of a Byzantine emperor, perhaps Valentinian I. The statue is in front of the **San Sepolcro** (Holy Sepulcher) **church,** a Gothic structure dating from the 13th century, which has just been restored. Down Corso Garibaldi toward the port are the 12th-century **Romanesque cathedral** and the 13th-century Hohenstaufen **castle-fortress** that was re-enforced by the Spaniards in the 16th century.

Just 18 miles inland on SS170d via Andria is one of Apulia's major historic monuments, the medieval octagonal **Castel del Monte,** built for Frederick II between 1240 and 1250. On each angle of the castle is an octagonal tower. The complex is on a small plateau overlooking the Murge plain, and offers views as far north as the Tavoliere Plain. In summer the castle is open 9 A.M. to 1 P.M. and 3:30 to 6 P.M., in winter 9 A.M. to 2 P.M.; Sundays and holidays 9 A.M. to 1 P.M.; closed Monday.

Worth a swing south (where you can pick up 96 for the coast) is Altamura, the bread capital of Apulia. Along with Emilia Romagna's Ferrara, it undoubtedly makes the best bread in Italy. A swing into a local deli to have a few sand-

wiches made for a countryside picnic more than repays the effort.

Back on the coast road are **Trani** and the picturesque towns of **Bisceglie, Molfetta,** and **Giovinazzo.** Trani's **waterfront** and its 12th- and 13th-century **cathedral** (with its bronze door and steeple, one of the more beautiful religious structures in Apulia), are sights of interest. In Trani's **Antonacci Palace** are forty perfectly preserved 19th-century carriages.

The coastal route south of Bari becomes a superstrada at Polignano, and parallels a series of Adriatic beach resorts all the way to the port of Brindisi.

Trulli

Trulli are domed structures whose design dates from prehistoric Saracen and Christian civilizations. Two to three hundred years old, they usually stand in groups of three or four, and are whitewashed—except for the roofs, which often are covered in tiles and decorated with crosses and what are thought to be symbols from the spiritual Rosicrucian society that spread through Europe in the 17th and 18th centuries. *Trulli* are also found between Monopoli, Castellana Grotte, and Martina Franca.

SIDETRIPS INLAND
A rewarding inland detour will take in the beautiful caverns at **Castellana Grotte,** the unusual **trulli village** of **Alberobello,** the **white-tiered houses** at **Locorotondo,** and the **17th-century Ducal Palace,** now city hall, at **Martina Franca,** the only building designed by Bernini in southern Italy.

RESTAURANTS
In Alberobello, try a meal at **Trullo D'Oro,** Via Cavallotti 29; tel. (080) 721820. Simple, down-to-earth regional cuisine and wines. Dinner costs around Lit. 30,000. Closed Mon. AE, DC, V.

Brindisi
The history of Brindisi, situated on a promontory within a natural harbor protected by strips of the Adriatic coast, reads like a scorecard of foreign invasions. Before the onslaught of Goths, Byzantines, Longobards, and so on, Brindisi was the port of embarkation for Roman legions heading for Macedonia, Greece, and Asia Minor. A column with a richly decorated *capitello* bearing the heads of Roman gods marks the end of the ancient **Appian Way** near the port (Via Taranto and Viale Regina Margherita). The base of a second column that was destroyed in 1528 also remains.

Just five minutes away in Piazza del Duomo is the **Francesco Ribezzo Provincial Archaeological Muse-**

um (open Monday through Friday, 9 A.M. to 1:30 P.M., Saturday 9 A.M. to noon; closed Sunday), the **14th-century Balsamo loggia,** the two Gothic arches of the **Cavalieri Templari** (Knights Templar) **Gate** and the reconstructed 18th-century **Romanesque cathedral** with its 12th-century mosaic pavements.

Other interesting churches of Romanesque origin are the 11th-century **San Giovanni al Sepolcro,** the 11th-century **San Benedetto,** and the 12th-century **Santa Lucia,** which has undergone much alteration. On the inlet, opposite the main port for ferry service to Greece and the tourist information office, is the 13th-century **Swabian castle** constructed by Emperor Frederick II and expanded in successive eras by Ferdinand II of Aragon and Charles V.

RESTAURANTS

Trattoria Acropolis, Via San Francesco 1; tel. (0831) 29173. Facing the port near the fish market, the seafood here is a real treat. Dinners cost Lit. 40,000. Closed Wed., Sun. dinner, and Aug. 10–Sept. 10. V.

Lecce and Its Environs

Just a half-hour south of Brindisi on the 613 superstrada is the provincial capital of Lecce, in the heart of the Salento. This area extends to the southern extremity of Apulia at Cape Santa Maria di Leuca, which divides the region's sandy Adriatic beaches and its rocky Ionian shores. Except for the Gargano, the area from San Cataldo, six miles east of Lecce on SS543 and extending all the way around the cape and up the western coast to Gallipoli, is the best bathing area in Apulia.

The salt-water **Alimini lakes,** surrounded by pine groves and favored by fishermen, just north of the enticing walled old town of **Otranto; Gallipoli,** with it's medieval old town on an island connected to the mainland by a 16th-century bridge, on a coastal spur pointing toward Sant'Andrea island; and the **village-fortress** at **Nardó** are all strong regional attractions. These are the environs of Lecce, where a bland complacency seems to surround the art center of the region.

Defined the "baroque Florence," the city has not been invaded by rampant urban development—although auto traffic can border on the ridiculous. A "viale loop" contains the **old town,** which must be seen on foot. Every alley seems to hide a baroque surprise with peculiar interpretations. The center of town is Piazza Sant'Oronzo, also site of the **tourist information office.** On the square are the ruins of a **Roman amphitheater;** the alleged reconstruction of the **second Roman column** that once marked the end of the Appian Way in Brindisi; the **Government Palace,** once a Celestine convent; the **Basilica of Santa Croce**—the most expressive example of Leccese baroque architecture, and the **Provincial**

Museum, containing artifacts from the Rudiae archaeological site (one and a half miles from Lecce).

Ten minutes down Via Vittorio Emanuele is another major attraction, **Piazza del Duomo,** with its perimeter of baroque facades featuring the early 18th-century **Seminario,** 17th-century **Vescovile** (Bishop's) **Palace,** and late 17th-century **cathedral.**

RESTAURANTS
Gino e Gianni, Via 4 Finite 2; tel. (0832) 45888. About 1½ miles from the center of Lecce on the Via Adriatica per Torre Chianca, this restaurant offers a good regional menu, but try to avoid it on weekends and when it hosts wedding receptions. Dinners run Lit. 35,000. Closed Wed. and Aug. 5–20. No cards.

Taranto
At the peak of the Ionian Gulf of Taranto, the old-town island of Magna Graecia prominence is a barrier between the bay (Mare Piccolo) and open sea (Mare Grande). Both ends of the island are bridged to the mainland.

A distinct picturesque facade for Italy's largest southern naval base is provided by palm-lined seaside drives. The creation of the Italsider steel mill brought about radical changes in the city that had once been mostly a naval town.

Old town is definitely the most interesting attraction with its **San Cataldo cathedral** dating to the 11th century. The baroque facade was added in the 1700s. Under the church is a crypt that dates to the dawn of Christianity.

On the most eastern extremity of old town is the 10th-century **Sant'Angelo castle** that was further fortified by Aragon King Ferdinand II in 1492.

In the new town, two blocks from the canal separating the new from the old, and between Via Pitagora and Corso Umberto I, is the **National Museum** (open 9 A.M. to 2 P.M. Tuesday through Saturday, 9 A.M. to 1 P.M. Sunday and holidays; closed Monday). This is one of Italy's most intriguing museums; most of the artifacts are from the Taranto area and cover prehistoric as well as the Bronze and Iron ages. Jewelry, terra-cotta, statues, art, and mosaics are many of the relics on display from Roman and Greek colonies.

RESTAURANTS
Il Caffè, Via d'Aquino 8; tel. (099) 25097. This small 60-seat restaurant near the coast has a fine view of the Aragon castle and offers a good *degustazione* menu for Lit. 40,000–50,000. Closed Sun. night, Mon. noon, and Aug. 10–20. AE, DC, V.

18

SICILY

Since erupting out of the Mediterranean over two hundred million years ago into a strategic position between two worlds, Sicily's fate has remained on course. The Mediterranean's largest island has had an unenviable history of natural calamities and regional conflicts since Syracusae rivaled Athenae for Magna Graecia supremacy in the eighth century B.C. (Sicily's Lampedusa Island was even the target for an abortive missile attack by Libya after the 1986 U.S. bombing raid on Tripoli.)

There is yet a third historical source of death and destruction. A multitentacled phenomenon has unjustly made the island synonymous with the Mafia. Once romanticized in song and verse, this folk facade has been permanently obliterated by the list of murdered and vanished, written in blood from Palermo to Catania.

An immensely proud, temperamental, and volatile people are obliged to pay a tremendous price. "Go, Etna, we're with you" insults were bannered in northern Italy when the volcano regurgitated destructive lava—and drug-war massacres erupted on the island.

The island's organized crime is no longer confined to Palermo and western Sicily. Almost simultaneously with the completion of a modern turnpike through the island's rugged interior, the bloody beast appeared at the doors of Catania. It is one of the few common denominators found in the contrasting cultures of Sicily's two major cities.

Sicily's principal city since it was proclaimed the capital by invading Arab forces, Arabic-Castilian Palermo has always been an administrative center; today it is capital of the largest Italian region's autonomous government. Greek-Catalan Catania has always been the commercial and industrial center of the island, which made it such an appetizing prey to invaders.

With its beaches and historic sites, Sicily's possibilities as a European vacation mecca are unlimited. But preconceptions

A Glance at Sicilian History

8 c. B.C.		Sicily is part of Magna Graecia; Syracusae is the main city
3 c. B.C.		Romans drive out Greeks
9–10 c. A.D.		Saracens take over; Sicily becomes a Muslim outpost, second only to Spain in importance
11–12 c. A.D.		Normans dislodge the Arabs; Sicily becomes seat of the Norman court
12 c. A.D.		Descendants of Holy Roman Emperor Frederick Barbarossa come into power; poetry, science, music flourish under Frederick II
13 c. A.D.		Charles of Anjou, King of Naples, rules
1282	A.D.	Sicilian Vespers massacre; House of Aragon rules, followed by Castilian princes
15 c. A.D.		Sicily is joint Spanish possession
1720	A.D.	At the end of the War of the Spanish Succession, Sicily given to Savoy, then to Austria
1734	A.D.	Sicily taken over by Charles III of Bourbon
1860	A.D.	Garibaldi's troops land and Sicily unified with the rest of Italy under Vittorio Emanuele
1943	A.D.	Allied landings between Licata and Syracuse force Germans to abandon the island
1948	A.D.	Sicily achieves autonomy as a region within the Italian Republic

persistently plague the island's present, though Sicilian hospitality is exceptional. Here continues the ancient belief, "the guest is sacred." Another characteristic inconsistency: July and August find the coasts and smaller islands crowded to the extent of taxing health standards and limited water supplies, yet in the spring and fall the dust has settled, the beaches are clear, and there are no more crowds in the Valley of Temples where the Magna Graecia ruins are second only to the Parthenon in Athens.

Two Sicilian jewels that are musts for any visit to the island are the former Greek and Sicilian town of Erice, just outside Trapani, and the seaside town of Taormina, between Messina and Catania.

WINING AND DINING

Food-loving Sicilians claim they were eating pasta before Marco Polo even left for China. With the island's extensive coastline, there is a heavy accent on seafood in most menus. Though the sweets can be too sweet, local ice cream, and ices in particular, have few rivals; homegrown oranges and lemons provide a genuine source of flavor.

Oregano is a favorite herb, and finds its way into about every tomato sauce. Though used elsewhere in Italy, it is a particularly Sicilian ingredient. Though rice is primarily a northern commodity, it is used in a favorite local snack, *arancine.* These fried rice balls can have either a mozzarella or ground-meat heart. Rice also is used as a substitute staple for a Trapani favorite, fish *couscous*.

Sicily can claim ten government-controlled (DOC) wines: Alcamo, Cerasuolo di Vittoria, Etna, Faro, Malvasiz delle Lipari, Marsala, Moscato, Moscato Passito di Pantelleria, Moscato di Noto, and Moscato di Siracusa. Most are sweet, syrupy dessert wines. But a chilled local Corvo is a fine example of local table wines, and is a perfect companion for *pasta con le sarde* and a wide variety of swordfish and tuna recipes.

Credit cards for suggested restaurants are listed as accepted. "All cards" means that all of the following are accepted: AE—American Express; DC—Diner's Club; MC—MasterCard; V—Visa. Prices given are for complete dinner (antipasto to dessert) for one person.

TRAVEL

The most populated areas of this 16,000-square-mile triangular island are well served by public transportation and turnpikes.

Flying

The island's two main airports are at Catania (on the east coast) and Palermo (northwest). Messina (on the northeastern tip) relies on the airport at mainland Reggio di Calabria (accessible by ferry and bus). Smaller air terminals are at Trapani (just west of Palermo and a ferry port to other islands), and the islands of Lampedusa and Pantelleria. Complete information is listed here.

Taking the Train

Sicily's main rail routes are Palermo–Messina (3 hours) on the northern Tyrrhenian coast and Messina–Taormina–Catania–Syracuse (3 hours, 10 min.) along the eastern Ionian shore. By train, the ferry port of Trapani is 2 hours west of Palermo. Inland, Caltanissetta and Enna are connected to both the Palermo–Messina and Syracuse–Messina lines. A secondary Trapani–Marsala–Agrigento–Ragusa–Syracuse tract provides rail service to the more isolated western coast. Any other rail and bus travel can be adventurous.

Driving

The western coast of Sicily is the least served by the island's turnpike network, though a proposed Catania–Syracuse–Gela turnpike would cover the southwestern tip.

Four turnpikes have been completed over the past twenty years. The major artery is the 138-mile Messina–Palermo A20. Twenty-eight miles east of Palermo, at Buonfornello, the 124-mile A19 turns inland and south for Enna (where there is a 7½-mile connection to Caltanissetta) and on to coastal Catania. The A18 Messina–Catania covers 47 miles.

The 72-mile A29 Palermo–Mazara del Vallo has turnpike connections to Trapani and Birgi (18½ and 27 miles, respectively) from the exit just south of Alcamo.

Flight Information

Airport	Connections	Airport Bus Transport	Flight Information
Catania and Syracuse	Fontanarossa Airport (4¼ miles from Catania; 33 miles from Syracuse)	Bologna (1½ hrs.) Brindisi (1½ hrs.) Milan (1¾ hrs.) Naples (55 min.) Rome (1 hr., 20 min.)	Catania: To/from Piazza della Repubblica, bus no. 24; Syracuse: tel. (0931) 66710	Catania: Alitalia, tel. (095) 252111, 349837, or 346966 Syracuse: SAIS, tel. (0931) 66710
Lampedusa	Lampedusa Airport (½ mile)	Palermo (45 min.)		ATI, tel. (0922) 970229
Messina	Tito Minniti Airport (in Reggio di Calabria, 4½ miles)	Milan (1 hr., 40 min.) Rome (1 hr., 10 min.)		Alitalia, call Meo Travel Agency, Via del Vespro; tel. (0965) 719192
Palermo	Punta Raisi Airport (20 miles)	Bari (1½ hrs.) Bologna (1½ hrs.) Lampedusa (45 min.) Milan (1 hr., 50 min.) Naples (45 min.) Pantelleria (35 min.) Pisa (1½ hrs.) Rome (1 hr., 10 min.) Turin (2¾ hrs.) Venice (2¾ hrs.)		Alitalia/ATI, tel. (091) 591692; Alibiu, tel. 591275.
Pantelleria Island	Pantelleria Airport (3½ miles)	Trapani (30 min.) Palermo (35 min.)	To/from La Cossira Agency, Via Borgo; tel. (0965) 719192	
Trapani	Sen. V. Floris Airport (at Birgi, 10½ miles)	Pantelleria (30 min.) Rome (1 hr., 40 min.)	To/from Corso Italia 52/56, tel. (0923) 23819	Alitalia/ATI, tel. (0923) 27480

*Note: All international flights connect in either Rome or Milan; see flight information in Rome and Milan chapters.

CAR RENTALS

Catania: (Fontanarossa airport) Avis, tel. (095) 340500; Europcar, tel. (095) 348125, telex 911403; Hertz, tel. (095) 341596; Maggiore, tel. (095) 340594.

(City) Avis, Via S. Giuseppe Larena 87; tel. (095) 347116. Or: Via Federico de Roberto 10; tel. (095) 374905. Europcar, Via L. Sturzo; tel. (095) 531329. Hertz, Via Toselli 45; tel. (095) 322560; telex 970092. Maggiore, Piazza G. Verga 48; tel. (095) 310002. Or: Piazza Gioeni 6; tel. (095) 338306.

Gela: Maggiore, Circolvallazione G. Verga 100; tel. (0933) 91009.

Messina: Avis, Via V. Emanuele 35; tel. (090) 58404. Europcar, Via Pozzo Leone 9; tel. (090) 45079. Hertz, Via V. Emanuele II 113; tel. (090) 363740. Maggiore, Via T. Cannizzaro 46; tel. (090) 675476.

Palermo: (Punta Raisi airport) Avis, tel. (091) 591684; Europcar, tel. (091) 591688; Hertz, tel. (091) 591682, telex 910449; Maggiore, tel. (091) 591681.

(City) Avis, Via Principe Scordia 12/14; tel. (091) 586940. Europcar, Via C.B. Cavour 77A; tel. (091) 321949; telex 911009. Or: Main rail terminal; tel. (091) 6165050. Hertz, Via Messina 7E; tel. (091) 331668; telex 910094. Maggiore, Via Agrigento 27/33; tel. (091) 6257848.

Syracuse: Avis, Piazza della Repubblica 11; tel. (0931) 69635. Maggiore, Via Tevere 14; tel. (0931) 66548.

Taormina: Avis, Via S. Pancrazio 6; tel. (0942) 23041. Europcar, Via Iannuzzo 14 (Giardini Naxos); tel. (0942) 54027. Hertz, through Catania office. Maggiore, Giardini rail terminal; tel. (0942) 51511.

Trapani: Hertz, from Birgi airport; through Palermo's airport office.

Taking the Ferry

Principal ferry service to the mainland ("the continent") is from Messina to Villa San Giovanni and Reggio di Calabria. If you want to avoid traveling the entire length of the Italian peninsula, service is also available from Genoa, Livorno, and Naples. Complete information is listed here.

Ferry Service from Sicily to the Peninsula

	Connections	Information
Catania	Reggio di Calabria (3 hrs.) Mon., Wed., Sun.	Tirrenia: Catania, tel. (095) 316394, telex 960326; Reggio di Calabria, tel. (0965) 94003; telex 890082
	Naples (15 hrs.) Wed.	Tirrenia: Catania, tel. (095) 316394; Naples, tel. (081) 5512181, telex 710030
Messina	Villa San Giovanni (30 min.)	F.S.: Messina, tel. (090) 775234; Villa San Giovanni, tel. (0965) 775582

From Sicily to Peninsula (cont.)

	Connections	Information
Messina (cont.)		Private Service via Caronte: Messina, tel. (090) 44982; Villa San Giovanni, tel. (0965) 751413
	Reggio di Calabria (45 min.)	F.S.: Messina, tel. (090) 775234; Reggio di Calabria, tel. (0963) 97957
	By hydrofoil (15 min.)	SNAV: Messina, tel. (090) 364044; Reggio di Calabria, tel. (0963) 29568
Palermo	Genoa (22 hrs.) Mon., Tues., Fri., Sun.	Tirrenia: Palermo, tel. (091) 333300, telex 910020; Genoa, tel. (010) 258041, telex 270186
	Tues., Fri.	Grandi Traghetti: Palermo, tel. (091) 587832, telex 910098; Genoa, tel. (010) 589331, telex 271132
	Livorno (18 hrs.) Mon., Wed., Fri.	Grandi Traghetti: Palermo, tel. (091) 587832, telex 910098; Livorno, tel. (0586) 28314, telex 500044
	Naples (11 hrs.)	Tirrenia: Palermo, tel. (091) 333300, telex 910020; Naples, tel. (081) 5512181, telex 710030
Syracuse	Reggio di Calabria (6½ hrs.) Mon., Tues., Sat.	Tirrenia: Syracuse, tel. (0931) 66956, telex 970283; Reggio di Calabria, tel. (0965) 94003, telex 890082
	Naples (18 hrs.) Wed.	Tirrenia: Syracuse, tel. (0931) 66956, telex 970283; Naples, tel. (081) 5512181, telex 710030

Ferry Service from Sicily to Other Islands

	Connections	Information
Milazzo	Lipari Islands (Lipari) By ferry (1¼ hrs.) By hydrofoil (40 min., weather permitting*)	Siremar: Milazzo, tel. (090) 9283242, telex 980090; Lipari, tel. (090) 9811312, telex 980120
Palermo	Ustica By ferry (2½ hrs.) By hydrofoil (1¼ hrs.)	Siremar: Ustica, tel. (091) 8449002, telex 910586; Palermo, tel. (091) 582403
	Cagliari (Sardinia) (12 hrs.)	Tirrenia: Cagliari, tel. (070) 666065, telex 790013; Palermo, tel. (091) 333300, telex 910020
Trapani	Egadi Islands (Favignana) By ferry (1 hr.) By hydrofoil (20 min.)	Siremar: Favignana, tel. (0923) 91368; Trapani, tel. (0923) 40515, telex 910132

*Turbulent seas can prolong a 40-min. ride to as long as 6 hours; a 40-min. hydrofoil ride can take 2½ hours.

From Sicily to Other Islands (cont.)

	Connections	Information
Trapani (cont.)	Pantelleria (4½ hrs.)	Siremar: Pantelleria, tel. (0923) 911104, telex 910109; Trapani, tel. (0923) 40515, telex 910132
	Cagliari (Sardinia) (10 hrs.)	Tirrenia: Cagliari, tel. (070) 666065, telex 790013; Trapani, tel. (0923) 27480, telex 910132

✣ ACCOMMODATIONS

Attending a medical conference in Palermo, a Rome doctor complained to the management of his first-class hotel that his room was not sufficiently heated. "Look at that sun, doctor. It's December, and feel the warmth of that sun," he was told. "That's out there, and I'm inside where it's cold," he replied. The room remained cold. And the daily tab for a single was a discounted Lit. 100,000 a day.

Air-conditioning is not a problem in Sicily in the summer, when it is a must. But should you consider cutting corners on the selection of a hotel, give it a thought. And remember, as elsewhere in Italy's Deep South, local concepts of cleanliness on the part of cleaning personnel can sometimes leave something to be desired by North American standards.

The major base for northern and western Sicily is Palermo. From here, you can visit the beach towns of Mondello, Cefalù, and—farther away—Sciacca, Erice, Marsala, and Agrigento. However, consider a night or two in Palermo and then a more relaxing night or two out of the city, in Mondello (Palermo's beach town); cool, scenic Erice; Sciacca (a convenient beach base for the Agrigento ruins); or Agrigento itself, gateway to the majestic ruins of the Valley of Temples.

Catania is the major city in the east. There is much to see here, and the area includes the ruins in Syracuse, a charming town itself and worth a stay. North of Catania, Taormina is a perfect beach base, and allows day trips to Catania. Beautiful Taormina is also close to the ferry port of Messina. Messina is not as centrally located as Catania, but is a major entry point to Sicily and offers much for travelers in its own right.

Credit cards are listed as accepted. "All cards" means that all of the following are accepted: AE—American Express; DC—Diner's Club; MC—MasterCard; V—Visa. Room rates given cover the range in prices from singles to doubles.

Agrigento

Villa Athena, Via Passeggiata Archeologiche 33, 92100; tel. (0922) 56288; telex 910617. This 4-star hotel with 40 air-conditioned rooms has a pool, bar, and good restaurant. Room rates run Lit. 69,000–106,000. All cards.

Catania

Centrale Palace, Via Etnea 218, 95131; tel. (095) 325334; telex 911383 Palace. This centrally located, 4-star hotel is in the middle of the main shopping district and near the Villa Bellini park. There are 99 air-conditioned rooms plus one of the best restaurants in town. Rooms run Lit. 74,000–108,000. All cards.

Poggio Ducale, Via Gaifami 5, 95126; tel. (095) 330016. With just 25 rooms, this 3-star hotel is air-conditioned and maintains a bar and good restaurant. Rooms run Lit. 50,000–70,000. All cards.

Erice

Moderno, Via Vittorio Emanuele 63, 91016; tel. (0923) 869300. Located on the highest point in western Sicily, this 3-star hotel offers a welcome respite for vacationers seeking relief from the torrid summer heat. Advance reservations are recommended June–Aug. The hotel has a restaurant and bar. Rates in high season for the 40 rooms are Lit. 46,000–72,000. All cards.

Messina

Royal Palace, Via T. Cannizzaro Isolato 224, 98100; tel. (090) 21161; telex 912413. Around the corner from the main rail station and 10 min. from the ferry to the mainland, this 3-star, air-conditioned hotel is also equipped to accommodate the handicapped. Fixed rate for the 83 double rooms is Lit. 88,000. All cards.

Palermo

Motel AGIP, Viale Regione Siciliana 2620, 90145; tel. (091) 552030; telex 911196 MOTE PA. Outlets of this national chain are usually a safe selection in Italy's South and in Sicily. On the loop around the city center, this one provides easy access to both the A19 for Messina and the Palermo airport. The 3-star hotel has a restaurant and 105 air-conditioned rooms. Rates run Lit. 48,000–88,000. All cards.

Politeama Palace, Piazza Ruggiero VII 15, 90141, tel. (091) 322777; Telex POLHOT. This 4-star hotel is a popular choice for visiting businessmen, with its 102 air-conditioned rooms, restaurant, and bar. Rooms run Lit. 81,000–105,000. DC, V.

Grand Hotel Villa Igea, Salita Belmonte 43, 90142; tel. (091) 543744; telex 910092 IGIEAH. This luxury hotel, on the coast in the shadow of Monte Pellegrino, has become Palermo's prestige address. The hotel has 92 air-conditioned rooms, a restaurant, bar, pool, tennis courts, and bus service to the city center. Rates run Lit. 190,000–330,000. All cards.

Palermo—Mondello

Palermo's lido is 5½ miles from the city center. Local bus service is good, making lodgings here a good alternative for avoiding the traffic chaos of Palermo proper. Both selections here are attractively situated in private gardens facing the sea, and offer pools and private beach facilities. Both have bars and restaurants.

Mondello Palace, Viale Principe di Scalea, 90151; tel. (091) 45001. A 4-star hotel with 83 air-conditioned rooms. Rooms run Lit. 105,000–143,000. All cards.

Splendid—La Torre, Piano Gallo 11, 90151; tel. (091) 450222; telex 910183 LATORREH. A 3-star hotel with 177 air-conditioned rooms. Rates run Lit. 52,000–83,000. All cards.

Sciacca

Torre Macauda, SS115, 92019; tel. (0925) 26800; telex 910108 TORMAC. On the beach 5 miles from the thermal baths, this ultramodern 3-star complex has 249 air-conditioned rooms, indoor and outdoor pools, a private beach, and tennis courts. Coach service is provided to the spa. Room rates run Lit. 60,000–95,000. Open Feb. 1–Oct. 31. AE.

Syracuse

Motel AGIP, Viale Trento 30, 96100; tel. (0931) 66944; telex 912480 MOTESI. Ten min. from both the local information office and the Greek theater, this 3-star hotel offers 83 air-conditioned rooms, a restaurant, and bar. Rooms will cost Lit. 58,000–70,000. All cards.

Taormina

San Domenico Palace, Piazza San Domenico 5, 98039; tel. (0942) 23701; telex 980013 DOMHOT. This luxury hotel has been classified a national monument by the state Fine Arts Committee. Situated in a truly panoramic position, with a fine view of the coast and Mount Etna from the private garden. The hotel has a heated pool and provides private coach service down to a private beach area at Giardini. Rooms run Lit. 230,000–385,000. All cards.

Villa San Michele, Via Damiano Rossi 11bis, 98039; tel. (0942) 24327; telex 980062 ASOTEL I. Reserve well in advance as this 3-star hotel has only 23 air-conditioned rooms. The view sweeps along the Ionian coast down to Naxos bay. Room rates run Lit. 45,000–79,000. All cards.

Tourist Villages

Worthy of consideration for extended stays in Sicily are the tourist villages operated by national and international organizations. Those listed here are all on the coast and serve as excellent bases for sightseeing; all operate May–Sept. Advance bookings for minimum stops of seven days are required. The **Club Mèditerranèe** offers a village at Cefalù (just east of Palermo):

Club Med Cefalù, Località Santa Lucia, 90015 Cefalù; tel. (0921) 23977.

Club Vacanze operates a village on the west coast of Favignana Island, in the Egadi archipelago just off the western coast of Sicily near Trapani. For information, contact the organization's Milan office: Vacanze S.r.l., Via Rastrelli 2, 20122 Milan; tel. (02) 85391; telex 312372 VCZMIL I.

Valtur operates tourist villages at Brucoli, 18 miles from Syracuse, and Pollina, just outside Cefalù:

Hotel-Villaggio Valtur, 96010 Brucoli (SR); tel. (0931) 991333; telex 970172.

Hotel-Villaggio Valtur, 90010 Finale di Pollina (PA); tel. (0921) 26243; telex 910129.

Sacked, shaken, and eroding, Sicily's monuments struggle to exist. Invading armies, earthquakes, and volcanic eruptions have all taken their toll. And the sandstone *tufo* blocks used in so many constructions have certainly not been as resistant as the marble and stone more readily accessible on the mainland.

Long reeflike stretches of coast occasionally pause around stretches of sandy beach. Many coastal villages appear parched and forgotten, in a context more Arab than European. Ornate urban architecture is often exaggerated. Seemingly impossible combinations of styling, such as Arab and Norman, are incorporated into one structure.

Miles of green interior pastures contrast with the black lava remains of past eruptions. Crystal-clear Mediterranean waters tease empty torrent beds that often are occupied by heavy equipment extracting gravel. The contrasts continue, until the island assumes an exotic fascination unparalled in mainland Italy.

Northern Sicily

Palermo

This natural harbor (called Panormus—all harbor—by the Romans when they took it from the Carthaginians in 254), at the foot of Monte Pellegrino in the Conca d'Oro valley, has seen four distinct cultural periods: Arabic-Norman, Renaissance, baroque, and the indiscriminate post-World War II expansion plagued by the collusion of city officials and unconscionable speculators, perhaps best dubbed the "modern Mafia" period. The city today is chaotic, overcrowded, stifling in the summer.

In the **old town,** buildings are exuberant, with often exaggerated exterior decorations of sculptured figures and cornices, and lavish interiors adorned with stuccoes and frescoes.

Here the influence of Rome on apprenticing architects is easily identifiable at the **Quattro Canti** (note the similarities to Rome's **Quattro Fontane**) intersection on Via Maqueda—the center of old town—and the city hall at **Piazza Pretoria** (similar to Rome's **Piazza del Campidoglio,** designed by Michelangelo). In Piazza Pretoria is Francesco Camilliani's 16th-century fountain that was originally built for a Florentine villa, but was purchased by the city in 1573.

Le Martorana church stands at Piazza Bellini, adjacent to Piazza Pretoria. A prime example of Norman art, the church has been restored to its original form. Norman King Roger II's Admiral George of Antioch commissioned the church in 1143. In 1433 it was given by King Alphonse to a monastery founded by Elvisa Martorana, after whom it was named. This was where the nobles elected Peter of Aragon ruler, after the Sicilian Vespers.

At Piazza del Cattedrale, a few blocks west of the Quattro Canti, is **Assumption Cathedral.** Built by Arab architects under the Normans in 1185, the fortress-cathedral reflects the changes in the course of Palermo's history and moods: The Normans built the cathedral on the foundation of a mosque; an elaborate Catalan-Gothic entrance was added in the 15th century, and at the end of the 18th century, the interior was rebuilt and the dome added. In different chapels are tombs of Norman and Hohenstaufen royalty.

The Sicilian Vespers

Charles of Anjou was not a popular ruler in 13th-century Sicily. Consequently, the French were the subject of local ridicule—called *tartaglioni,* meaning "stammerers," because of their poor Italian. In 1282, on Easter Monday, as church bells were ringing for vespers, some Frenchmen insulted a young Sicilian woman. A revolt broke out; all Frenchmen who could not correctly pronounce the word *cicero* (chick pea) were killed.

Access is limited to the **Palace of the Normans,** on Piazza della Vittoria at the end of Via Vittorio Emanule; the building is now seat of Sicily's Regional Assembly, and is open Monday, Friday, and Saturday only, 9 A.M. to noon. Originally a ninth-century Arab fortress, the palace was expanded by the Normans, using Arab and Byzantine artists for elaborate decorative mosaics, in particular in the Palatine Chapel and King Roger's Hall. Many of the treasures in the palace did not resurface until extensive restoration in 1921.

Another fine example of Norman art, **St. John of the Hermits,** at Via dei Benedettini 18, off Corso Ruggero, to the left of the Norman Palace, was converted from a mosque by Roger II in 1132. The interior is comprised of one simple nave. A colorful garden is next to the pink-domed church and is framed by a 13th-century twin-columned cloister.

The **Capuchin Convent,** in Piazza Cappuccini behind the Palace of the Normans, is famous for its catacombs. Visitors must be accompanied: The catacombs under the 17th-century convent and 16th-century church contain the macabre skeletons and mummified remains of more than 8,000 of the richer and more notable Palermitans of the 17th to 19th centuries. Open daily 9:30 A.M. to 12:30 P.M. and 3:30 to 5:30 P.M.; closed Sunday afternoons.

The **Chiaramonte Palace** (Piazza Marina 60) is a severe three-story Gothic building that served as a model for the ornate, patrician baroque villas in and around Palermo in the 17th and 18th centuries.

Also of interest is the **Zisa Palace,** in Piazza Zisa, commissioned by King William I in 1154. The Arab flavor of this Norman palace is evident in the interior fountain and mosaics depicting animals, plants, and hunters.

If your interest is museums, there are several in Palermo worth seeing. **The National Archaeological Museum,** on Piazza Olivella, features practically all the relics and artifacts uncovered from the ancient Greek settlement of Selinunte (12 miles south of the A29 Castelvetrano exit before Mazara del Vallo). Besides other Greek and Roman relics, the three-story museum has a fine Etruscan collection from Tuscan necropolises in the Chiusi area.

The National Gallery of Sicily, in the Palazzo Abatellis, Via Alloro 4, is a 15th-century Gothic-Catalan building with Renaissance tones. Featured is an art and sculpture collection covering the Middle Ages to the 18th-century, including Francesco Laurana's bust of Eleonora of Aragon, Antonello da Messina's *Annunciation* and images of three saints, a series of works by Flemish artists, and the 15th-century fresco *Triumph of Death,* by an unknown artist.

Sicilian *Pupi*

Sicily's *pupi* (puppets) date back to the Middle Ages. The marionettes, about four feet tall with painted faces, almost always represent the same characters, acting out various chapters in the same story: Orlando and the paladins, with the help of Charlemagne, are fighting the Saracens, usually avenging an insult to their honor. The performance always ends before the resolution, but don't worry—the paladins always win. Many of the puppets wear real metal armor and swords (the swords clang around a lot during the performance). The original story was brought to Sicily by the Normans, and the Sicilians adopted it as their own.

Sicily's famous puppets *(pupi)* are legendary. Not only have the large, ornate puppets entertained children over the centuries, but during foreign domination their shows were the most effective means of local communication. Opened in 1975, the **International Puppet Museum** (Palazzo Fatta, Piazza Marina 19; telephone (091) 328060) displays Sicilian puppets, complemented by displays from other countries. Elsewhere, you may want to attend a puppet show; or consider buying one as a souvenir (they're expensive, however).

Unless otherwise noted, museums are usually open Tuesday through Sunday mornings.

With all that Palermo offers it's difficult to leave town, but there are a number of pleasant surprises in the immediate environs.

The prime excursion attraction is the 12th-century **cathedral at Monreale,** two and a half miles southwest of Palermo on SS186. Ordered by William II in 1174, the cathedral dominates the Conca d'Oro valley, and with its magnificent cloisters is considered one of the most beautiful religious complexes in Italy. The cathedral alone warrants a trip to Palermo.

A number of **bathing areas** are available both east and west of Palermo, but the most favored is **Mondello,** six and a half miles to the west along coastal A29, in the natural cove between Monte Pellegrino and the smaller Monte Gallo. Several popular restaurants relocate here during the summer.

On Monte Pellegrino is the **Sanctuary of Santa Rosalia,** the patron of Palermo. Nearly one hundred feet beneath the 1625 convent is a grotto where the saint (supposedly the niece of Norman King William II) used to meditate; the grotto has been converted into a chapel with a 17th-century marble statue of the saint by Gregorio Tedeschi. The statue is cloaked in a silver-gilt mantle donated by Bourbon King Charles III.

RESTAURANTS

Charleston, Piazzale Ungheria 30; tel. (091) 321366. Angelo Ingrao and Antonio Glorioso don't really take the entire summer off; they just move their exhalting regional cuisine to the beach at Mondello (**Charleston le Terrazze,** Viale Regina Elena; tel. (091) 450171). Both are considered temples of Sicilian dining pleasure. Dinner runs Lit. 60,000. Closed Sun. and June 15–Sept. 25. All cards.

Gourmand's, Via della Libertà 37a; tel. (091) 323431. Rosario Guddo divides his time in summer between Gourmand's and his Mondello restaurant on Via Torre Mondello. Guddo's smoked swordfish is a must. Dinner will cost Lit. 60,000. Closed Sun. and Aug. 10–20. All cards.

La 'ngrasciata, Via Tiro a Segno 12 (Sant'Eurasmo); tel. (090) 230947. Where the two halves meet: The atmosphere is pure decadence, but Palermo's upper crust refuses to abandon the

good fish dinners. Dinners run Lit. 30,000–40,000. Closed Sun.
No cards.

Renato L'Approdo, Via Messina Marina 28; tel. (091) 470103.
Francesca and Gianrodolfo Botto have created one of the best
restaurants on the island. Subdued lighting and antique furniture
provide an elegant atmosphere for the best of Sicilian cuisine.
The wine list offers a number of very particular (and costly) attractions. Dinner will cost about Lit. 60,000 without wine. Closed
Wed. AE.

Cefalù

About 37 miles east of Palermo, now little more than a fishing
village and bathing resort, Cefalù boasts an interesting 12th-
century **Norman cathedral** that was once center of a separate diocese. It was ordered in 1133 by Norman King Roger
II, who vowed to build a church if he survived turbulent seas.
Various phases of construction continued for nearly a century.
Worthy of a visit are the cloister and the mosaics (especially
the 1148 *Christ Pantocrator*) covering the apse, presbytery
walls, and ribbed vault of the cathedral.

Walk down Via Mandralisca in front of the cathedral to the
Mandralisca Museum, housing Baron Enrico Piraino's collection of prehistoric tools, Greek vases, coins from the Cefalù mint and other towns of ancient Sicily, and an art gallery
featuring Antonello da Messina's *Portrait of an Unknown
Man.*

✎ RESTAURANTS
Da Nino al Lungomare, Via Lungomare, tel. (0921) 22582.
The Moceo brothers can provide pleasant surprises, from *antipasti* to pasta or *risotti marinari,* plus fish in any fashion. Dinner
will cost about Lit. 30,000–35,000. AE, DC.

Western Sicily

Erice and Trapani

The former Greek and Phoenician colony of Eryx, Erice is
nine miles northeast of the port town of Trapani, atop the
nearly 2,500-foot-tall Monte Erice, the highest point in western Sicily. Some of the triangular-shaped **town walls** date
from the Punic era. The cool evening air is a welcome relief
from the torrid heat on the beaches below, around Trapani,
62 miles west of Palermo. Once the eternal flame in Erice's
Temple of Venus was a beacon for sailors in the Mediterranean world; a **Norman castle** now stands on the site.

Erice draws an international spotlight every summer when
it hosts seminars condemning nuclear warfare, which have
drawn prominent physicists from the political superpowers
and their respective allies.

Trapani is the port town for ferries to the Egadi Islands, Pantelleria Island, and Sardinia. There is not much of interest here, other than ferry connections—stay in Erice.

❧ RESTAURANTS

A pleasant surprise in the bleak coastal city of Trapani is **P e G,** Via Spalti 1; tel. (0923) 47701. The air-conditioning is a must. The imaginations of Paolo Gallo and Giacinto Spano thrive on Sicilian adaptations of such recipes as North African couscous. Dinner will cost about Lit. 25,000–40,000. Closed Sun. and Aug. AE, DC.

SIDETRIPS

The islands of the Egadi archipelago center around the largest island of Favignana. Fishing is still the major activity for islanders; the season peaks during the May–June tuna run.

The island of Pantelleria is seventy miles southwest of Trapani. Arab-style dwellings (called *dammuso*) line the coast around 2,800-foot high Montagna Grande and its 24 ancient volcanic craters. You can stay in a *dammuso* house; contact Dammuso, Contrado San Vito, 91017 Pantelleria; tel. (0923) 911827. For ferry information to these islands, see "Travel" in this chapter.

Marsala

The name of this prominent wine and liqueur region on the west coast is traced to the Carthaginian domination, when it was known as Marsá Alí (harbor of Alí). On May 11, 1860, Giuseppe Garibaldi and his thousand-man army landed at Marsala and paved the way for Sicily to join a united Italy. Recent archaeological excavations have uncovered ruins of the old Roman town. The area was also the site of Carthaginian and Phoenician settlements.

Sciacca

Between Mazara del Vallo (just south of Marsala and center of Sicily's largest fishing fleet) and Agrigento (on the western coast), the sandy bathing center and popular spa of Sciacca is 28 miles east on the SS115 from the Castelvetrano A29 exit. Development in recent years has increased the area's prominence as a holiday resort. Of historic interest are the 15th-century Sicilian-Catalan **Steripinto Palace** on Via Pietro Gerardi, the 12th-century **cathedral** (rebuilt in the 1700's) with its three original apses and 16th-century statues by Antonio and Gian Domenico Gagini, and the 14th- to 15th-century **St. Margaret's Church** on the northern outskirts of town, with its Gothic-Renaissance portal by Laurana.

Agrigento

Agrigento is the gateway to the **Valley of Temples** 75 miles south of Palermo, said to be finer than many ruins in Greece. It is also the birthplace of Sicily's most prominent literary figure, Luigi Pirandello, the Nobel laureate, considered by many to be the inventor of modern drama. Most of the artifacts and relics discovered in the valley, from the Greek colony of Akragas settled by Rhodians from Gela in 581 B.C., are preserved in the **National Archaeological Museum,** Contrada San Nicola.

Unless otherwise noted, museums are open Tuesday through Sunday mornings.

The **Temple of Juno** dominates the valley from the hilltop where it was constructed in 460–440 B.C. (It is often erroneously referred to as the Temple of Hera; the real Temple of Hera is at Crotone.) Of the 34 original pillars, 25 are still standing. Akragas was razed by invading Carthaginians in 406 B.C., and scars from the fire can still be distinguished.

The **Temple of Concord** was built in the middle of the fifth century B.C. This hilltop temple is one of the best preserved in the world. The deity to which it was dedicated remains unknown; the name is derived from a Latin inscription discovered in the vicinity.

Believed to be the oldest of the temples, the **Temple of Hercules** was constructed in the sixth century B.C. Only eight of the original 38 columns are still standing. Archaeologists believe it was adorned with statues and paintings.

Though of Greek origin, from about the fifth century B.C., the remains of the **Temple of Castor and Pollux (Dioscuri)** reflect restoration in the area above the four columns still standing. This temple is believed to have been built after the Carthaginian invasion.

Archaeologists did not uncover the **Temple of Esculapios** until 1926. Just south of the main valley on the banks of the Akragas river, it once contained the statue of Apollo. There is a fine view of the old walls and the Temple of Concord.

Three other temples collapsed in December 1401; their remains, along with those of four telamones (figure-pillars) uncovered in the 1926 excavations, complete most of the Greek ruins in the area. The **Ekklesiastirion** was a third-century B.C. Roman amphitheater dug into the rocky terrain; it is believed to be the only civic complex in the valley. The **Oratory of Phalaris** is believed to have been a first-century B.C. tomb of a Roman matron. This small rectangular temple was transformed into a chapel in the Middle Ages.

🍴 RESTAURANTS

Besides a good restaurant at Villa Athena (see "Accommodations"), outside Agrigento is **Taverna Mosè,** Contrada Mosè; tel. (0922) 26778. Located between the Valley of Temples and San Leone Lido, on the road from Porto Empedocle to inland Caltanissetta. The choice is pork or sole, with Pino Catalano's distinct local flare. Dinner will cost about Lit. 30,000. Closed Mon. No credit cards.

SIDETRIP

The **Pelagie Islands**—Linosa, Lampedusa, and Lampione—are actually nearer to North Africa than Sicily and their administrative capital of Agrigento. A wild beauty and long stretches of black lava make the islands unusually appealing. A U.S. satellite tracking station on Lampedusa was the alleged target of an unsuccessful Libyan missile attack in 1986. Ferry service to the islands is available from Porto Empedocle, Agrigento's port town (see "Travel").

Eastern Sicily

Catania

The most prominent town on the eastern coast is Catania, halfway between Messina and Syracuse at the foot of Mount Etna. It is the only major Sicilian city that was not occupied by Arab invaders. The birthplace of Vincenzo Bellini (1801–35; composer of "Norma"), the town is a monument to Palermo-born, Roman-trained architect Giovan Battista Vaccarini.

A 1669 eruption of Mount Etna destroyed the western side of Catania and filled in part of the harbor (now nearly five hundred yards from the coast, the Ursino Castle was once at sea's edge). A 1693 earthquake that destroyed 25 nearby towns claimed 16,000 of the city's population of forty thousand. Vaccarini was entrusted with rebuilding Catania in the 18th century, and academics call it one of the most beautiful cities of that era in Italy. Vaccarini was responsible for the facade (1730) of the **cathedral, City Hall** (1732), **Sant'Agata Church** (1735), and the **Cutelli College** (1754).

Modern structures appeared as the city emerged from the debris of World War II Allied bombing raids prior to the Allied landing in Sicily. There are many similarities with Rome in Catania's urban reconstruction. The principal street, **Via Etnea,** a two-mile stretch of elegant shops, banks, and commercial centers, is reminiscent of Rome's Via del Corso; **Piazza del Duomo** reminiscent of Piazza del Popolo.

Via Garibaldi, through the old city to the black and white (lava and stone) 17th-century **Porta Uzeda,** lost its prominence as the city regrouped and expanded north. Both streets begin at the base of the **Elephant Fountain** facing the cathedral in Piazza del Duomo.

The city has amply commemorated Bellini with a monument, the **Bellini Gardens** just off Via Etnea, and a richly decorated **opera house,** built in the 1800s by Andrea Scala and Carlo Sada—just off Piazza Bellini.

The **Ursino Castle** was ordered built by Frederick II in 1239. It has been a residence of the Aragons, a military barracks, a prison, and now (after complete restoration in 1932) the **Civic Museum.** Prominent works are *St. Christopher* by Pietro Novelli, considered Sicily's most outstanding 17th-century painter; an 11th-century statue of Venus, and Antonello Saliba's *Madonna with Child.*

If you understand Italian, visit the **Museo di Vulcanologia** at the University of Catania before making the 53-mile trip up the slopes to visit the nearly 11,000-foot-tall **Mount Etna.** From the more than two hundred groups of craters, approximately one hundred and forty eruptions have been recorded in local annals. The peak averages seven months of snow a year and is Sicily's **ski station.**

Driving to Etna from Catania via Nicolosi or turning west from Giarre presents the widest variety of landscapes, from squat little villages to fruit groves, from wooded areas where makeshift stands offer wood carvings to the eerie, black lunar scenario of solidified lava surrounding the Rifugio Sapienza cable car base.

Guides are required when renting four-wheel-drive vehicles from **la Montagnola** to visit the still-active craters. (The guides are right there, you pay on the spot.) The cable car is recommended only if it's a clear day: then, from la Montagnola, the panorama will extend from the northern coast of Tunis to the western coast of Calabria.

❧ RESTAURANTS

Besides good restaurants at the Central Palace and Poggio Ducale hotels (see "Accommodations"), try **La Siciliana,** Viale Marco Polo 52A; tel. (095) 376400. Vito, Salvo, and Ettore La Rosa seem to be on a mission to establish local cuisine and Sicilian wines. It's all to the diner's advantage. The summer garden dining area is an added treat. Dinners cost Lit. 35,000–40,000. Closed Sun. evening and Mon. All cards.

Syracuse (Siracusa)

Originally founded in 734 B.C., the sun-baked Sicilian city of Syracuse dominated Sicily and the southern areas of both the Adriatic and Tyrrhenian seas before being conquered by the Romans in 212 B.C. It was successively ruled by the Normans, Swabians, Angevins, Aragons, Spaniards, and Bourbons. The picturesque **old town** is on an insular tip of the Ortigia peninsula that is connected to the main island by New Bridge.

Favorite son Archimedes (287–212 B.C.) is commemorated by a statue depicting the absentminded mathematician at work with his "burning-glass," a magnifying glass with which he supposedly set fire to invading enemy ships and staved off invasions. (The conquering Romans attacked from the land.)

Maniace Castle (a military zone off-limits to visitors) covers most of the southern extreme of the old town. **The Cathedral,** in Piazza Duomo, was completed between 1728 and 1754. The original construction, built on the foundation of the fifth-century B.C. Temple of Minerva, underwent restructuring in the 1600s. Inside are two 16th-century statues by Antonello Gagini.

Bellomo Palace, Via Capodieci 14, has a rich collection of sculptures from the Byzantine era to the Renaissance, and an art gallery covering the 15th to 18th centuries.

The **Paolo Orsi Regional Archaeological Museum,** in Villa Landolina, at Viale Teocrito 66, is a modern brick and glass complex exhibiting a wonderful variety of artifacts uncovered in Sicilian excavations, as well as plastic models presenting monuments in their ancient splendor.

Neapoli Archaeological Park, at Largo Anfiteatro, is an extensive area enclosing the third-century Roman amphitheater, the third-century B.C. Altar of Hiero II (used for public sacrifices), the fifth-century B.C. Greek theater (in front of the entrance to the park, it is the best preserved in Italy; almost the entire theater was carved out of the rocky hillside), and the Paradise Quarry (with the Ear of Dionisio grotto and Cordmakers' Cavern). (In summer, the park is open daily until 7 P.M.)

Unless otherwise noted, museums are open Tuesday through Sunday mornings.

An interesting shop in Syracuse is the **Centro Papiro,** Via San Metodio 1/3; tel. (0931) 32916. Paper is produced here, from papyrus found along the banks of the nearby Ciane river. Visitors are allowed to follow the production process as well as the artistic decoration of the final product. Naturally, items are for sale.

❧ RESTAURANTS

Darsena da Januzzo, Riva Garibaldi 6; tel. (0931) 66104. A typical Sicilian trattoria on the waterfront. The air-conditioned restaurant specializes in fresh fish and shellfish. Dinner will cost about Lit. 30,000–35,000. Closed Wed. and Oct. No cards.

Jonico'a Rutta 'e Ciauli, Riviera Dionisio 194; tel. (0931) 65540. The four Giudici brothers have accumulated an extravagant range of objects to decorate the inside, but nature gets the upper hand on the refreshing seaside patio. Good regional fare is Lit. 40,000 for a full meal without wine. Closed Wed. AE, DC, MC.

Taormina

About halfway between Messina and Catania is Taormina, one of the most beautiful spots in Italy. Some 675 feet above sea level, the town offers one fine view after another, from Mount Etna to the Calabrian coast. An ill-fated attempt to open a casinò saw Rome draw the line on the autonomy of the Sicilian regional government.

The center of tourist interest now is the third-century B.C. **Greek Theater** that was extensively remodeled by the Romans in the second century. A summer film festival is held here (the Italian Cannes), where the Davids of Donatello (the Italian version of the Academy Awards' Oscar) are presented annually.

At the foot of Taormina is the seaside town of **Giardini,** which extends to a fine **sandy beach**—Sicily's finest—and four miles south is Cape Schisò, where there are the remains of the 735 B.C. **Greek colony of Naxos.**

Messina

The Greek humanistic center of Messina gained importance under the Byzantines and Normans. The tide turned under the Catalans; a serious earthquake ravaged the city in 1638, and then in 1674 a rebellion against the Spanish government resulted in a massacre. Another earthquake in 1783 and an 1854 cholera epidemic took turns at trying to erase the city. Finally, on December 18, 1908, a devastating combination of earth and sea quakes succeeded, turning practically the entire town into a mass of rubble.

By comparison, World War II's fire and fury seems inconsequential. First, British bombers attacked from nearby Malta; then joint Allied raids in 1943 softened Sicily's underbelly for the Allied invasion from North Africa.

Astonishingly, a few precious pearls of the past have survived, though massive rebuilding has often been required. Foremost is the **cathedral** built by Norman King Roger II in the late 12th century. Modified in the 14th and 16th centuries, the cathedral, with three Gothic portals, is symbolic of the city's ability to reemerge. Next to the cathedral is a two-hundred-foot **bell tower** gabled to house gilded statuettes that move every 15 minutes. At noon, the entire tower and its astronomical and calendar clocks come to life, and its various figures and animals act out an ancient legend.

In front of the cathedral in **Piazza Duomo** is Giovanni Angelo Montorsoli's **Orion Fountain** (1547–1550). Montorsoli was one of the more prominent disciples of Michelangelo.

Near the cathedral on Via Garibaldi is the 12th-century Norman church **Our Lady of the Annunciation.** At the base of the statue of John of Austria in front of the church is a **reproduction of the original complex,** which included a castle with six towers, the royal residence of Roger II. To the right is the church of **St. Julian** and its roof adorned with a number of small domes.

All of the city's relics and artifacts that were salvaged after the 1908 quake are now displayed in the 16 halls of the two-story **National Archaeological Museum,** Viale della Libertà 465 (open Tuesday through Saturday mornings). Highlights of the museum are the signed and dated *Polyptych of St. Gregory* (1473) by Antonello da Messina and the *Resurrection of Lazarus* and *Adoration of the Shepherds* by Caravaggio, painted during his refuge in Sicily at the outset of the 1600s. Other interesting pieces are Flemish artist Colin van Coter's 15th-century *Descent from the Cross,* Montorsoli's 15th-century sculptures of Scylla and Neptune, Laurana's gilded and colored marble 15th-century statue of *Madonna with Child,* Gagini's 16th-century *St. Catherine,* and a wooden crucifix by an unknown Sicilian artist.

❦ RESTAURANTS

Alberto, Via Ghibellina 95; tel. (090) 710711. The air-conditioned restaurant has a wide variety of *antipasti* that can detract from Alberto Sardella's noted swordfish and stockfish specialties for the uninitiated. Patience and pace is of primary importance to enjoy a full meal, which will run Lit. 35,000–50,000. Closed Sun. and Aug. 5–Sept. 5. AE, DC.

Central Sicily

Piazza Armerina and Enna

The town of Piazza Armerina is 25 miles south of the provincial capital of Enna, west of Catania on SS117bis from the A19. This is the most central part of the island, and the green, rolling hills are a stark contrast to the sunbaked coasts. The most interesting attraction is the third-century **Roman Villa Casale,** three and a half miles south of Piazza Armerina on SS117bis. Since 1960 an exceptional series of mosaics have come to light. They cover most of the over 23,000 square feet of the villa and feature colorful, natural scenes.

An interesting folk festival is the **Norman Palio** (festival), celebrated every August 15 to commemorate the arrival of Count (soon to be King) Roger. Horsemen in costumes represent the various quarters of the town in jousting events.

Isolated Enna, over three thousand feet above sea level, is a favorite retreat for foreign kings in the summer. It has a richly sculptured 13th-century **cathedral,** rebuilt in the baroque style.

❦ RESTAURANTS

When in **Piazza Armerina,** try **Al Ritrovo,** SS117bis; tel. (0935) 80648. Avoiding the tour-bus temptation, Nunzio Palermo works his grill overtime to satisfy locals as well as discriminating travelers. Don't expect to be overpowered by the service, but for Lit. 20,000. . . . Closed Mon. No cards.

19

SARDINIA

Sardinia is Italy's island in the sun. The crystal-clear water bathing the rectangular isle's 1,054-mile coastline is Italy's best, according to national ecological reports. Lured by Aga Khan's northeastern Costa Smeralda development, luxury yachts are a marked contrast to the rigors of pastoral life still prevalent in the hinterland.

The **Nuraghe su Nuraxi** village-fortress near Barumini north of Cagliari proves Sardian settlement on the island nearly 1,500 years before Christ. In the nearly 3,500 years that have followed, the island has been invaded by Phoenicians, Carthaginians, Vandals, Saracens, Romans, Byzantines, Aragonese, Spaniards, Piedmontese, and the Maritime Republics of Pisa and Genoa. Today the U.S. nuclear submarine station on the northern Maddalena archipelago between Sardinia and Corsica dissuades attack.

Nuraghi

Nuraghi are odd, conical structures, believed to date from 1,200 to 1,500 years before Christ. They are thought to have been fortress–houses, used to protect the ancient Sardes from invaders. The *nuraghi* are made of stones piled one on top of another without mortar; they are unique to Sardinia. Artifacts found in the *nuraghi* can be viewed at the National Museum in Cagliari.

However, new barbarians have islanders in alarm. Backpackers who improvise camping on island beaches are under attack; "Nature is our patrimony," proclaims a regional tourism official, concerned that Sardinia may become another Rimini (that is, a cheap beach resort). "If we don't take steps to preserve this patrimony now, tomorrow may be too late."

A proposed remedy to the destruction of Sardinia's patrimony is to require all prospective visitors to provide proof of hotel or camping reservations before being allowed to embark by air or sea for Sardinia. Officials acknowledge that such drastic measures would be difficult to enforce, but stress their determination to eliminate the new barbarians.

Crafts

Despite the Sardinian resistance to some forms of tourism, local craftsmen offer a variety of goods, including filigree jewelry in gold and silver, ornamental throw rugs and tapestries, handmade doilies, coral jewelry, dolls in native costume, ceramic plates and vases, and rustic wood, leather, and palm pieces.

After all, nature is Sardinia's appeal. Most of the ruins and monuments are of secondary importance; the coast and its northern and southern islets are the strong attraction. Typical are rocky, reeflike formations extending into the sea, and steep cliffs, making diving the favored sport here; windsurfing and waterskiing are also possible, but there is a lack of equipment rentals.

Sardinia's interior remains underdeveloped, and there is little appeal to the rugged, lunarlike Barbagia mountains. Rising to nearly three thousand feet in the center of the island and extending to the eastern coast, the Barbagia were long a cove for bandits during the rash of kidnappings twenty years ago that forced landowners to relinquish coastal property at rock-bottom prices for ransom cash.

The interior reflects centuries of Sardinian isolation. Central and southern speech is not a dialect, but a recognized Romance language. In the north the dialect is more Catalan than Italian. And Sardinians in many respects have more in common with their northern island neighbors in Corsica than with mainland Italians.

Corsica was ceded to France along with Nice by the House of Savoy in 1859 in exchange for support in the revolt against Austro-Hungarian domination in northern Italy, during the phase of the Risorgimento that led to the unification of the entire peninsula. Napoleon III also renounced all claims to Lombardy and the Veneto, which then became permanent Italian possessions. (Victor Amadeus II of the Savoy monarchy was forced to relinquish Sicily to Austria in exchange for Sardinia. But the Savoys were absentee regents who preferred Turin, the first capital of united Italy.)

Multimillionare Aga Khan's heavy investments began the break from an isolationist past—coastal development fever has rapidly circumvented the island. The national and international favor thus scored has provided a tremendous economic boom for Sardinia.

WINING AND DINING

Sardinia complements a wide variety of seafood recipes with a fine assortment of local wines. Maybe the lobsters that enter the wicker basket traps fishermen use subconsciously consider the *vermentino* or *vernaccia* on the table of a holiday diner.

The island's government-regulated DOC wines are: Cannonau di Sardegna, Campidano di Terralba, Carignano del Succis, Giro de Cagliari, Malvasia di Bosia, Malvasia di Cagliari, Mandrousai, Monica di Cagliari, Monica di Sardegna, Moscato di Cagliari, Moscato di Sardegna, Moscato di Sorso Sennori, Nasco di Cagliari, Nuragus di Cagliari, Vermentino di Gallura, and Vernaccia di Oristano.

Sardinia is surely where the craving for lobster, shrimp, and other shellfish can be satisfied. Preparing shellfish is a cult, and local prices for lobster are more attractive than those on the mainland. On the other hand, since large quantities of produce are imported by boat, fruit and vegetable prices can appear a bit high.

Lamb, wild boar, and roasted suckling pig are other local favorites, but are more suitable to fall and winter dining. Be sure to try Sardinia's *pecorino* cheese. Another must is a dessert recipe combining ricotta cheese and local honey. To finish the evening (and how!), try a local double whammy called *fil'e ferru* (iron wire). This white lightning will put anyone into high gear.

Credit cards are listed as accepted. "All cards" means that all of the following are accepted: AE—American Express; DC—Diner's Club; MC—MasterCard; V—Visa. Prices given in our recommended restaurants are for a complete dinner (antipasto to dessert) for one person.

TRAVEL

European and especially Italian vacation schedules create a July–Aug. crush that makes sea and air passage practically impossible for the spontaneous. Local rates are tailored accordingly. June, May, Sept., and even Oct. visits can be equally rewarding at almost half high-season rates.

Since the island measures only about 91 by 168 miles, and north–south highway connections are excellent, you can tour the whole island easily regardless of your port of entry.

Flying

Sardinia is less than an hour by air from Rome. Various air connections are listed here; entry is at Alghero-Sassari, Olbia, and Cagliari.

Flying

	Airport	Connections	Airlines	Airport Bus	Flight Information
Alghero (northwest coast)	Fertilia (8 miles)	Bologna; Cagliari; Genoa; Milan; Pisa; Rome; Turin.	Alitalia; ATI; Air Sardinia	Agenzia Oliva, Corso V. Emanuele II; tel. (079) 979395	Alitalia, ATI; tel. (070) 60108; Air Sardinia, tel. (079) 975017
Cagliari (southern coast)	Elmas (4½ miles)	Alghero; Bari; Bologna; Genoa; Milan; Naples; Palermo; Rome; Turin; Pisa; Verona; Olbia	Alitalia; ATI; Aliblu; Alisarda; Avianova; Air Sardinia	Piazza Matteotti at Via Sassari; tel. (070) 651381	Alitalia, ATI, Aliblu, tel. (070) 60108; Alisarda, Avianova, tel. (070) 669161/2/3; Air Sardinia, tel. (070) 240458
Olbia (northeast coast)	Costa Smeralda (2½ miles)	Bergamo; Bologna; Cagliari; Genoa; Milan; Naples; Pisa; Rome; Turin; Venice; Verona; Frankfurt	Alisarda; Avianova; Air Sardinia; Lufthansa	City bus No. 2, Piazza Margherita; tel. (0789) 52600	Alisarda, Avianova, tel. (0789) 69300; Air Sardinia, tel. (0789) 69191; Lufthansa, tel. (0789) 69517
Sassari (northwest coast)	Fertilia (19 miles)	See Alghero	See Alghero	Sardaviaggi, Via Cagliari 30; tel. (079) 234784	See Alghero
Tortoli (east coast)	Arbatax (2 miles)	Olbia (3 times weekly); Cagliari (daily)	Air Sardinia	Taxi only	Air Sardinia, tel. (0782) 623123

Driving

If traveling by rented car, to eliminate round-trip ferry expenses turn in your car on the mainland and arrange for a new rental in Sardinia. The savings practically pay for the difference between a one-hour flight and a seven- to 12-hour boat ride. Major international rental agencies are represented in all major ports of entry; there are also a number of local organizations listed here.

There are no toll roads in Sardinia. The main north–south artery is the 145-mile superstrada 131 from Porto Torres to Cagliari via Sassari and Oristano, near the west coast. All major routes to the east spring from the SS131.

Another route north from Cagliari, administrative capital of the the autonomous region, is the SS125, covering most of the eastern coast to Olbia and connecting with a provincial route to reach Golfo Aranci. This highly scenic route passes through Tortoli, only three miles from the central eastern port of Arbatax. This often winding road has to contend with the Barbagia mountains, and service areas are few and far between, so be sure to have a full tank of petrol when starting off.

A minute isthmus connects the isle of Sant'Antioco to the main island, making it reachable by automobile in about one hour from Cagliari. The most scenic route is the provincial road along the southern coast, which passes points of historical interest.

CAR RENTALS

Alghero: (Airport) Avis-Demontis, tel. (079) 935064; Europcar, tel. (079) 935032; Hertz, tel. (079) 935054; Italia, tel. (079) 977879; Maggiore, tel. (079) 935045.

   (City) Demontis, Piazza Sulis 7; tel. (079) 976435. Maggiore, Piazza Sulis 1; tel. (079) 979375.

Baia Sardinia (near Costa Smeralda): Avis, Via Tre Monti; tel. (0789) 99138. If your car cannot be delivered to your hotel, take a taxi to the agency.

Cagliari: (Airport) Avis-Demontis, tel. (070) 240081; Europcar, tel. (070) 240126; Hertz, tel. (070) 240037; Maggiore, tel. (070) 240069.

   (City) Avis-Demontis, Via Sonnino 87/89; tel. (070) 668128. Hertz, Piazza Matteotti 8 (near airport bus); tel. (070) 668105. Italia, Via Sonnino 95; tel. (070) 664940. Maggiore, Via XX Settembre 1A; tel. (070) 650919. Rental agencies are all near the ferry.

Olbia: (Airport) Avis-Demontis, tel. (0789) 69540; Europcar, tel. (0789) 69548; Hertz, tel. (0789) 69389; Italia, tel. (0789) 69501; Maggiore, tel. (0789) 69457.

   (City) Avis-Demontis, Via Genova 67; tel. (0789) 22420. Hertz, Via Regina Elena 34; tel. (0789) 21274. Maggiore, Via Mameli 2; tel. (0789) 22131. Rental agencies are near the ferry and the bus.

Porto Cervo (near Costa Smeralda): Avis, Piazza Clipper; tel. (0789) 91244. Hertz, Localita Sottovento; tel. (0789) 94132. Costa Smeralda hotels can arrange for airport and ferry pickups, and then you can get your rental car near the hotel.

Porto Torres: Maggiore, Via Losto 18; tel. (079) 514652. The rental office is near the ferry.

Porto Vesme: Hertz, Via G. Cesare; tel. (0781) 509531.

Santa Teresa Gallura: Europcar, Via Lu Pultali; tel. (0789) 754381. Hertz, Via M. Teresa 29; tel. (0789) 754247. Rental agencies are near the ferry.

Sassari: Demontis, Via Mazzini 1/2; tel. (079) 235547. Italia, Viale M. Coppino 2; tel. (079) 238079. Maggiore, Viale Italia 3; tel. (079) 235507.

Taking the Ferry

Sardinia is well connected by ferry to the mainland. However, any Aug. travel should be booked months in advance. The Tirrenia Line has the most complete service. Other private carriers are Navarma, Grandi Traghetti, and Sardinia Ferries. On round-trip tickets, Navarma offers a 50% reduction on the return fare for both cars and motorcycles. The most competitive prices are those on the Italian State Railroad (FS) tie between Golfo Aranci and Civitavecchia. This is the *only* FS run. Crossing times vary depending on ports of call, with trips to Cagliari generally taking the longest; for example, Civitavecchia–Golfo Aranci takes 8 hours; Naples–Cagliari, 15 hours; Genoa–Cagliari, 19 hours. Most connections are daily, but longer voyages can be limited to once or twice a week.

Bookings **must** be verified well in advance. Foreign travelers seeking bookings are advised to deal directly with the shipping line in major cities once in Italy. It will help to have someone who speaks Italian handle this; ask for Riparto Nautico (sea service) and be very specific with your questions.

In the past there has been an unfortunate history of strikes during peak Aug. travel that has created extreme inconveniences.

FERRY SERVICE

	Connections	Information
Arbatax (east coast)	Cagliari; Civitavecchia; Genoa; Olbia	Tirrenia, tel. (0782) 667067
Cagliari (southern coast)	Arbatax; Civitavecchia; Livorno; Naples; Palermo; Trapani; Tunis (Tunisia)	Tirrenia, tel. (070) 666065
Golfo Aranci (northeast coast)	Civitavecchia; Genoa; Livorno.	FS:tel. (0789) 46910, 46956; Sardinia Ferries, tel. (0789) 25200; Tirrenia, tel. (0789) 24691
Olbia (Costa Smeralda)	Arbatax; Civitavecchia; Genoa; Livorno	Navarma, tel. (0789) 22086; Sardinia Ferries, tel. (0789) 25200; Tirrenia, tel. (0789) tel. 24691
Porto Torres (northwest coast)	Genoa; Toulon (France)	Grandi Traghetti, tel. (079) 514477; Navarma, tel. (079) 516151; Tirrenia, tel. (079) 514107
Porto Vesme (southwest coast)	Carloforte (San Pietro); Calasetta, via Carloforte (Sant'Antioco)	Tirrenia, tel. (0781) 854005

	Connections	Information
Santa Teresa Gallura (north coast)	Bonifacio (Corsica); La Maddalena, via Palau	Navarma: tel. (0789) 755260; Tirrenia, tel. (0789) 754156

✣ ACCOMMODATIONS

In Sardinia, hotels are an imported commodity. Even today, there is no 4-star (first-class) hotel in the capital city of Cagliari. National and international businessmen have to rethink habits and preferences.

Development of the Costa Smeralda has introduced the island to luxury (5-star) and first-class hotels. The best base for accommodations is along the northern coast between Alghero and Olbia (including Porto Cervo on the Costa Smeralda and the island of Santo Stefano) or the southern shores east and west of centrally situated Cagliari (including Carloforte on San Pietro Island and Santa Margherita di Pula). Both areas offer hotels and residences as well as tourist villages and an abundance of campings—more than campsites, these are often tourist village complexes complete with bungalows, restaurants, pools, and tennis courts. A number of scenic drives and historical sites can easily be reached during a day's excursion from both of the above areas.

There are several tourist villages and campings along the coasts that are worthy of consideration (see Arbatax, Castiadas, and Villaputzu). The campings mentioned offer mini-bungalows.

Keep in mind, however, that since the peak July–Aug. season has a high demand, minimum stays are often imposed. Potlucking it for a shorter stay may result in fruitless knocking on doors.

The best advice is to try the island in late May, June, or early Sept. when the price is right, it's not too hot, and all the advantages are still available in a less crowded and more relaxed atmosphere.

Credit cards are listed as accepted. "All cards" means that all of the following are accepted: AE—American Express; DC—Diner's Club; MC—MasterCard; V—Visa. Rates given are for the span of prices between single and double rooms.

Alghero

Villa las Tronas, Lungomare Valencia 1, 07041; tel. (079) 975390. This 3-star, 30-room (plus seven more in adjoining annex) hotel, open all year, has a beautiful location a mile south of the port between the coastal road and the sea. The entire coastal spur is hotel property, with a private beach as well as a pool. Air-conditioning has just been installed. Rates run Lit. 75,000–130,000. Annex rates are Lit. 55,000–70,000. AE, DC.

Arbatax

Three miles from Tortoli and a half-mile from the port of Arbatax is **Cala Moresca,** tel. (0782) 667366; telex 790085 VCZTEL I, a reconstruction of a typical Sardinian hillside village. It can accommodate up to 600 persons, with more space in a newly opened 17-room hotel. Both are modernly equipped. Air-conditioning is available. The village has a pool and offers a wide selection of activities, from squash to skeet shooting. Weekly rates per person with full board range Lit. 605,000–1,305,000, plus Lit. 40,000 application fee.

A half-mile away is **Telis,** tel. 667126; telex 790085 VCZTEL I. This village consists of cottages and bungalows that can accommodate up to 600, and extends over 50 acres along a sandy and rocky coast. There is a pool, activities for children as well as adults, and four restaurants to choose from in the evening, with wine and iced tea included in full board. Fees range seasonally, from Lit. 440,000–990,000, plus application fee of Lit. 40,000.

Both villages are open from the end of May–Sept. Catalogs can be obtained by writing Vacanze S.r.1. of Milan, Via Rastrelli 2, 20122; tel. (02) 85391; telex 312372 VCZMIL I.

Cagliari

Motel AGIP, Circonvallazione Pirri; tel. (070) 561645; telex 792104. This link in a nationwide chain carries a 3-star rating with its 57 air-conditioned rooms. The motel has a restaurant and bar, and is equipped to accommodate the handicapped. Room rates run Lit. 45,000–69,000. AE, MC, V.

Al Solemar, Viale Armando Diaz 146, 09100; tel. (070) 301360. Though not the most central hotel in town (it's near the industrial fair grounds), this 3-star, 42-room hotel is a favorite with touring theater companies. Air-conditioned, but no restaurant. Room rates are Lit. 45,000–77,000. AE, DC.

Carloforte (Isola di San Pietro)

Riviera, Carloforte (Isola San Pietro) 09014 (CA); tel. (0781) 854004. Without a restaurant, this 3-star hotel with 27 rooms is for those not wanting a compulsory meal plan. The hotel is on the sea, although the nearest beach is 2½ miles away. There is a bar on the premises. Room rates run Lit. 45,000–70,000. Air-conditioning is an added fee of Lit. 1,000 per day. Closed Jan.–Feb. No cards at press time.

Castiadas

Camping Cala Sinzias, Strada Panoramica Villasimius-Costa Rei, 09040 (CA); tel. (070) 995037; winter information, tel. (070) 891069. Located on a long sandy beach on the southeastern tip of the island, the site offers tents to sleep four with refrigerators and gas burners for cooking. Furnished trailers are also available. No linens, blankets, or kitchen utensils provided. The site is a favorite with Germans and Austrians, and comes recommended by their respective automobile clubs. Daily tent fee for four is Lit. 36,700–47,000. Daily trailer fee for four is Lit. 44,000–58,000. Both rates vary according to season. Open April–first week in Oct.

Olbia

Hotel Royal, SS 125N Olbia-Palau, 07026 (SS); tel. (0789) 50253. Romolo Saba's 3-star, 65-room hotel with pool is less than two miles from the airport, a mile from the port, and only a half-mile from the rail depot. Pickups can be arranged, but public bus service from the port to Palau stops right in front of this clean, comfortable, fully air-conditioned hotel, which is open all year. Rates are Lit. 60,000–93,000. All cards.

At the opposite end of the port, Saba has just opened a seaside residence, the **Royal Beach** at Porto Istana, offering fully furnished mini-apartments that will be available on a weekly basis in May, June, Sept., and Oct. Monthly rentals are required in the peak summer months of July–Aug. The residence was being completed at press time, and rates were not available.

A prominent local building contractor, Saba, through his Hotel Royal, also leases **apartments** at Arbatax and Santa Maria Navarrese, and **villas** at Capo Ferro.

Porto Cervo (Costa Smeralda)

Three 5-star, luxury hotels that need no introduction to those familiar with the Costa Smeralda are listed here. All three are seasonal, but reservation offices function all year. No brief description could adequately justify room rates ranging from Lit. 480,000 for a single to Lit. 950,000 for a double (per night!). These are obviously not walk-in accommodations; brochures should be ordered directly from the hotels and bookings made well in advance.

Cala di Volpe, Costa Smeralda, Arzachena (SS); tel. (0789) 96083; telex 790274 CAVOP. On a cove in Cala di Volpe, this hotel has 125 air-conditioned rooms, a bar, restaurant, pool, tennis courts, and discotheque. Open May 1–Sept. 30.

Pitrizza, Costa Smeralda, Arzachena (SS); tel. (0789) 91500; telex 792079 PITRIZ. Air-conditioned accommodations for 56, on the coast 12 miles from Porto Cervo. Considered by some to be Italy's most discreet beach resort. Open May 15–Sept. 30.

Romazzino, Costa Smeralda, Arzachena (SS); tel. (0789) 96020; telex 790059 HTLMZ. This hotel has 93 air-conditioned rooms on a splendid bay in Romazzino. Open May 15–Sept. 30.

Santa Margherita Di Pula

Forte Village, 09010 (CA); tel. (070) 921520; telex 790117 FHVILL. This is another link in the worldwide British Trusthouse Forte chain under the guidance of Italian-born (in Campobasso) Sir Charles Forte. The village, 25 miles west of Cagliari, consists of 564 bungalows and the 144-room **Hotel Castello.** It is serviced by three restaurants and four snack bars as well as a bar with facilities for a maximum of 1,500. Cagliari air and port pickup service is offered for a fee of Lit. 75,000. The village is on a long stretch of sandy beach and offers a number of activities including 12 illuminated tennis courts, two squash courts, four for mini-tennis, volleyball and basketball courts, a gym, bicycles, horseback riding, shops, and congress halls. Normal policy is a minimum sojourn of three days; walk-in possibilities for a briefer period exist. The village's reservation office is open all year, but information and accommodations can be arranged with Trusthouse Forte offices worldwide. U.S. representatives are in New York, Los Angeles, Chicago, and Atlanta. Room rates, from low season to mandatory half-board rates in high season, are Lit. 75,000–175,000 per person for bungalows, Lit. 88,000–222,000 in the Hotel Castello. Open Mar. 24–mid-Nov. All cards.

Santo Stefano Island

Hotel Villaggio Valtur, 07024 La Maddalena (SS); tel. (0789) 737061; telex 792094. This 222-room complex offers a vast assortment of activities, from underwater diving to tennis (six illuminated courts) to bridge tournaments. The village wraps around an inlet on the island in the La Maddalena archipelago. There is no commercial boat service to the island, so all transportation to La Maddalena is organized by Valtur. Pickups can be coordinated from the port at Olbia as well as the airport. Minimum stay is one week; arrangements and information can be obtained from Valtur's Milan offices, Corso Venezia 5; tel. (02) 791733; their Rome location, Piazza di Spagna 85; tel. (06) 6784588; or their Turin office, Via Alfieri 22; tel. (011) 516016. Foreign correspondent for Valtur is Club Méditerranée. Full-board rates per person range Lit. 520,000–950,000 for one week. Open June 2–Sept. 22.

Villaputzu

Porto Corallo, Coop. Coosviturs, 09040 (CA); tel. (070) 997017. This camping has furnished bungalows and huts *(tukuls)* that can sleep four persons each. For these accommodations at least half-board is required in July and Aug.; the season runs May–Sept. The rocky shore (4 miles from Villaputzu on the east coast) alternates with wide stretches of sandy beach on one of the most scenic coastal drives in Sardinia, 42 miles from Cagliari. Per person rates with full board range Lit. 35,000–45,000.

The North Coast

Costa Smeralda

Sardinia's Costa Smeralda consists of what are probably Europe's most famous and most expensive **beachfront** properties. Along the shore, clear, emerald-tinted water slides between reeflike islets and craggy points to tease an occasional stretch of sandy beach. The emerald hue of the waters easily explains the origins of the name Costa Smeralda. The natural beauty is the main attraction at this summer playground, which does offer well-manicured 18-hole **golf courses** and moorings for forty-foot yachts. The rich and ultrarich have given new significance to such barely distinguishable geographic distinctions as Porto Cervo and Cala di Volpe.

It seems the least likely locale for a nuclear submarine base, but just across the strait dividing the main island from the La Maddalena archipelago is a U.S. nuclear complex that has drawn sharp criticism from Italian ecologists, and startled more than one sunbather with the sudden appearance of an offshore periscope.

Unfortunately, prices at this paradise have discouraged many common mortals from exploring. To safeguard vacationers and their property, the area maintains private police and fire departments, with a chain of watchtowers and a fleet of helicopters in constant surveillance. Despite the holiday atmosphere, it can be a bit unsettling.

While on the Costa Smeralda, take a **scenic drive** from Porto Cervo on the provincial road to Baia Sardinia, and continue around the Golfo di Arzachena to Capo d'Orso, where the wind and sea have molded the cliffs into the strangest of shapes. West of Porto Cervo and Capo d'Orso is Palau, the junction for ferry service between the Maddalena archipelago and Santa Teresa Gallura.

❧ RESTAURANTS

In the Baia Sardinia town of Arzachena, try **Casablanca,** Club Hotel; tel. (0789) 99006. After elevating his La Frasca restaurant at Castrocaro Terme to the upper echelon of Italian gastronomy, Gianfranco Bolognesi has moved to the Costa Smeralda to team with Renzo Bongiovanni in the restaurant of a 4-star, 85-room hotel. Soft music accompanies dining on the small terrace overlooking the bay. Dinner with wine costs about Lit. 80,000. All cards.

In **Palau,** try **Da Franco,** Via Capo d'Orso 1; tel. (0789) 709558. The antipasto spread is incredible in this elegant place run by Salvatore Malu and father-in-law Franco Aversano: lobster, shrimp, squid, and oysters. Pace is the name of the game, or you'll be stuffed halfway through the first course. A full meal runs Lit. 40,000–50,000 with local wine. Closed Mon. (except in summer) and Dec. All cards.

Santo Stefano, La Maddalena, Caprera, and Santa Maria Islands

Less than a mile from Palau, to the east of the ferry route to the island of La Maddalena, is the smaller island of **Santo Stefano,** considered of strategic importance even by the Romans. Many galley remains have been found submerged in the turquoise waters off the island's pink granite coasts. Now the island hosts the U.S. Navy and a Valtur **tourist village** (an Italian version of Club Med), but relics testify to the former presences from Spain, Liguria, and Africa.

While travelers must make their own boat arrangements to Santo Stefano, Valtur provides boat service for its guests from **La Maddalena,** the island center of the archipelago and a giant campground. Rocky shores and sandy beaches alternate around the town of La Maddalena.

A small road crosses the strip of land leading from La Maddalena to **Caprera,** where the "hero of two worlds," Giuseppe Garibaldi, died and was buried on June 2, 1882. The home where the leader of the Italian Risorgimento passed his final years is a **national monument** full of memorabilia. The house is open 9 A.M. to 1 P.M. and 3 to 6 P.M.; closed Sunday afternoon, Monday, May 1, June 3, the first Sunday in June, and August 15.

Northwest of La Maddalena in the Bonifacio Strait is the isle of **Santa Maria,** a remnant of the fracture of the earth's surface that separated Corsica from Sardinia. A convent dating to 1198 is on the one-and-a-half-square-mile island. There is no commercial boat service to Santa Maria, but you can strike a deal with a local fisherman.

If you don't speak Italian, write "Santa Maria" on a piece of paper and hand it to a fisherman. Point at him, then at his boat, then to your group. Extend your right hand, rubbing your thumb and first finger together to request a price. Hand him the pen. If he's willing to take you, he'll write the fee on the piece of paper.

Olbia

Southeast of Palau (62 miles east of Sassari and 166 miles north of Cagliari on SS125) is Olbia, sea and airport for the Costa Smeralda. Its 11th-century **Santo Simplicio** is one of the oldest churches on the island.

❧ RESTAURANTS

Gallura, Córso Umberto 145; tel. (0789) 24648. Appearances can be deceiving. Rita Denza must have a magic wand in the kitchen of this restaurant, located in a simple 21-room, 2-star hotel. Here it's the food (certainly not the decor) that counts, and if the multipage menu fails to offer anything that strikes your fancy, all hope is lost. Dinners range Lit. 30,000–45,000 with wine. Closed Fri. and Dec. 20–Jan. 7. AE.

Tavolara Island

A natural sea-breaker for Olbia's port is Tavolara Island, a nearly four-square-mile sea mountain that was once the world's smallest kingdom. The highest point on the island, locally known as *Gruviera* (Swiss cheese) because of the numerous caves offering refuge to submarines, is nearly 1,900 feet above sea level.

Savoy regent Carlo Alberto enjoyed hunting on the island. A companion on these forays was Paolo Bertoleoni, who reportedly maintained homes on both Tavolara and Santa Maria—each with a different wife. After one successful hunt,

Carlo Alberto proclaimed Bertoleoni king of Tavolara. Once the "king" was reportedly visited by England's Queen Victoria.

Part of the Tavolara today is a military district. On the free, accessible side are a pair of seasonal restaurants and a dock for fishermen who bring the curious from Olbia. There is no organized transportation; find a fisherman at the dock in Olbia and strike a deal with him (see the tip offered above for getting to Santa Maria).

Castelsardo

Castelsardo is a picturesque **beach** town on the sea, 21 miles east of the ferry port Porto Torres. The provincial road from the northernmost ferry port of Santa Teresa Gallura is only a 45-mile drive, and skirts the Nur Tuttusoni *nuraghi* on Costa Paradiso. The 12th-century town of Castelsardo sits atop a small coastal knoll surrounded by **fortified walls.** Once called Castel Genovese as well as Castel Aragonese, foreign invasion is well recorded in its history.

Sassari

Sassari, the island's second largest city, lies 11 miles inland and southeast of Porto Torres on SS131. The central **Rosello Fountain** (1605–06) is the emblem of this medieval nucleus. The **San Nicola of Bari cathedral** dates from around 1400. The **Civic Theater** (Teatro Civico), modeled after Turin's Carignano in 1830, is one of the most attractive in the country and hosts a popular fall opera program.

A celebrated folk festival is the **Cavalcata Sarda,** held the third Sunday in May, and featuring a parade of decorative native costumes from all over Sardinia.

Alghero

Alghero, air and sea center for Sassari and northwestern Sardinia, is on the Riviera del Corallo, twenty miles west of Sassari on SS291. Of Catalan origin and surrounded by Spanish **fortress walls,** Alghero was actually the first Sardinian city to crack the national tourist market. The city's **15th-century cathedral** is of Gothic-Catalan design.

❧ RESTAURANTS

La Lepanto, Via Carlo Alberto 135; tel. (079) 979116. Moreno Cecchini is the lobster lord here on the Riviera del Corallo. He also offers a good variety of Catalan and local recipes featuring shrimp, squid, fish soup, and *risotti.* All can be enjoyed on the terrace overlooking the sea or in the air-conditioned interior. Dinner will run about Lit. 35,000 with local wine. Closed Mon. except in July and Aug. All cards.

Central Sardinia

Off the coasts, most of central Sardinia is desolate and mountainous. It basically consists of Nuoro, its province, and most of the province of Oristano.

Probably the most photographed church on Sardinia is the 12th-century Romanesque-Pisan, black-and-white Holy Trinity Church, in open country near Saccargia, about ten miles southwest of Sassari off SS131 and to the left of SS597 (toward Olbia).

Nuoro

Nuoro is 22 miles west on SS129 from Marina di Orosei, which is on the east coast, and 108 miles north of Cagliari. At the northernmost extreme of the Barbagia mountains, Nuoro is the provincial seat that has been least affected by the island's tourist boom. Home of Sardinia's best-known poet, S. Satta, as well as 1926 Nobel laureate Grazia Deledda, Nuoro's roots are in the 12th century. The city's **Sardinian Museum of Life and Popular Traditions** provides a good insight into island folklore. The museum is open June through September from 9 A.M. to 1 P.M. and 4 to 8 P.M., October through May from 9 A.M. to 1 P.M. and 3 to 6 P.M.; closed Monday.

Grotta del Bue Marino

On the Golfo di Orosei is one of the most spectacular views on the eastern coast. From Nuoro, go twenty miles east on SS129, then take the provincial road to the right, to Dorgali. After a twisting five-mile drive to Cala Gonone on the coast, a turn right onto another provincial road begins a five-mile drive that dead-ends at the Grotta del Bue Marino. At the opposite end of the **cavern** is a straight drop to the sea; from this point is one of the most extensive **views** of all the eastern coast. The area around this uninhabited cliff-side coast is even more spectacular when visited from the sea.

Arbatax

Slightly less than forty miles south of Dorgali on SS125 is Tortoli and the port of Arbatax. All the coast north from Arbatax to Capo di Monte Santu is a **marine national park.** The coves and caves now can only be visited by sailboat. For information, contact EPT in Nuoro, Piazza Italia 9, tel. (784) 30083. Off the port of Arbatax, three miles east of Tortoli, is a red reef resembling a cathedral rising from the sea.

SIDETRIP

Inland on SS198 13½ miles from Tortoli is Lanusei, nearly 2,000 feet above sea level. Only 86 miles north of Cagliari, this town provides one of the best views of Barbagia's lunar landscape.

> This is very different from Italian landscape. Italy is almost always dramatic, and perhaps invariably romantic. There is drama in the plains of Lombardy and romance in the Venetian lagoons, and sheer scenic excitement in nearly all the hilly parts of the peninsula. Perhaps it is the natural floridity of limestone formations. But Italian landscape is really eighteenth-century landscape, to be represented in that romantic-classic manner which makes everything rather marvellous and very topical: aqueducts, and ruins upon sugar-loaf mountains, and craggy ravines and Wilhelm Meister water-falls: all up and down.
>
> Sardinia is another thing. Much wider, much more ordinary, not up-and-down at all, but running away into the distance. Unremarkable ridges of moor-like hills running away, perhaps to a bunch of dramatic peaks on the south-west. This gives a sense of space, which is so lacking in Italy. Lovely space about one, and travelling distances—nothing finished, nothing final. It is like liberty itself, after the peaky confinement of Sicily. Room—give me room—give me room for my spirit: and you can have all the toppling crags of romance.
>
> —D. H. Lawrence
> *Sea and Sardinia,* 1921

Oristano

On the west coast of central Sardinia is Oristano, one and a half miles off SS131 and 55 miles north of Cagliari. Seat of the most recently created Italian province (in 1974), Oristano is the largest urban center on the west coast. The city's **L'Annunziata Cathedral** features 14th-century wood statues by Nino Pisano. The area is the center of one of Sardinia's best-known wines, Vernaccia.

✤ RESTAURANTS

Il Faro, Via Bellini 25; tel. (0783) 70002. The husband-and-wife team of sommelier Giovanni and cook Giovannina Brai have one of the best restaurants on the west coast of the island. In an elegant atmosphere they serve the best of Sardinia, with the freshest produce available in the market. A full meal costs Lit. 45,000–50,000 with wine. Closed Sun. AE.

The Sinis Peninsula

Extending into the sea west of Oristano is the Sinis peninsula. From northern Capo Mannu to the sliver of land known as Capo San Marco is one of the last extensions of sea-level terrain resisting development. The fragile rock formations have been less fortunate with the weather and sea.

At the southern end of the peninsula in Capo San Marco are the remains of the sixth-century B.C. development of

Tharros, which introduced one of the first systems of urban development to the island.

SIDETRIP

Twenty miles north of Oristano and west of SS131 are the *nuraghi* of Nur Atzara and Nur Losa, reportedly connected by a 5-mile underground tunnel. A little farther north, at Abbasanta, there is a provincial road leading to Santu Lussurgiu, 8 miles west. Turn right before Santu and head north for about 5 miles to the **Church of San Leonardo de Siete Fuentes.** This 12th–13th-century Romanesque church is isolated in a wood, where the silence is interrupted only by the murmur of nearby streams. This is an ideal picnic spot on any north–south drive.

Southern Sardinia

Cagliari

Southern Sardinia literally centers around Cagliari and its natural harbor. Capital of the region as well as the province of the same name, Cagliari is of Phoenician origin. Other visitors over succeeding centuries were the Romans, Byzantines, Pisans, and Aragonese. The **National Archaeological Museum** is the custodian of a collection of Roman as well as prenuraghic artifacts. Located at Piazza Indipendenza, it is open Tuesday through Sunday from 8:30 A.M. to 1:30 P.M., and closed Monday.

The city's **Roman amphitheater** is largely carved out of rock. The **San Saturnino** church, off Via Dante, is an exceptional example of early Christian architecture; the central portion dates to the fifth century. On the Piazza Palazzo, Pisan Maestro Guglielmo's pulpits and stone lions can be found inside the **13th-century cathedral.**

RESTAURANTS

Dal Corsaro, Viale Regina Margherita 28; tel. (070) 664318. Near the port, Giancarlo and Gianluigi Deidda own what many consider the best restaurant on the island, serving seafood fare. During the summer they offer an open-air restaurant, with a terrace and piano bar. The open-air version is just outside Cagliari at Marina Piccolo, tel. (070) 370295; it's open from the end of May–Sept. 15. The main restaurant is air-conditioned. At both, dinner with wine runs Lit. 45,000–50,000. Closed Tues. and Aug. 1–15. All cards.

Saint Rèmy, Via Torino 16; tel. (070) 657377. Atmosphere is abundant in this renovated 17th-century pharmacy once used by monks to prepare medicinal herbs. Now the fare ranges from fresh fish (stored in an old stone well inside the air-conditioned restaurant) to T-bone steaks. Dinner runs about Lit. 50,000 with wine. Closed Sat. noon, Sun., Aug. 1–15, and Dec. 1–15. AE.

SIDETRIPS

The drive eastward on a provincial road from Quartu Sant'Elena (east of Catania) provides a series of beautiful **views** all the way to Villasimius (29 miles) and then up the Costa Rei to Capo Ferrato, where the road ends. For most of the trip shade is an unknown entity.

Near the Variglioni islands, just off the Isle of Cavoli (3½ miles south of Villasimius), the remains of a Spanish galleon were recently discovered. For information on the site, try Luisa Mereu, tel. (070) 371643; she is an expert on local lore and a perfect source of help.

Those with more time might plan a trip westward from Cagliari. A superstrada is being built toward Capo Spartivento, on the Costa del Sud, but in the meantime SS195 is more than sufficient. Just before the cape are the **Phoenician tower** at Chia and then the **necropolis of Bithia** (3rd century B.C.), which was not discovered until 1935, when it was uncovered by a sea storm.

Three scenic islands off the coast near the cape are **Su Cardulinu,** linked to the main isle by a narrow sandy beach that emerges at low tide; **Tuaredda;** and **Su Gideu.** A literal translation of the last is "The Jew," attesting to early settlement by Jewish families; it lies in the center of the bay between Capes Spartivento and Mallafano.

Sant'Antioco Island

Continuing westward on SS195, a junction with SS126 leads to **Sant'Antioco** island, Italy's largest small isle, after Elba (which belongs to Tuscany). This summer resort was the site of Carthaginian human sacrifices, and is linked by a man-made isthmus to the main isle, built by Phoenicians and Romans. This 38-square-mile island 54 miles from Cagliari was one of the first Phoenician bases in Sardinia, founded in the eighth century B.C. In 258 B.C. Rome's fleet defeated the Phoenicians in a naval battle and gained control of the island. The two principal centers on the island are **Sant'Antioco** and **Calasetta,** just five miles apart. Today, visitors to Sant'Antioco can watch the **tuna run,** the blood from which stains the water a deep red, or visit the **site of the human sacrifices,** complete with an urn allegedly containing ashes of youths sacrificed to the gods.

San Pietro Island

At Calasetta there is ferry service for Carloforte, on the island of **San Pietro.** This is one of four islands named San Pietro in Italy that allegedly hosted the saint during his pilgrimage to Rome. Home of the Italian Merchant Marine Academy, San Pietro is known for its **tuna cannery,** which works around the clock in May as fishermen swarm to the waters off Carloforte during the annual tuna run. Migrating with aquatic currents, schools of tuna are temporarily at the mercy of harpooning fishermen while seeking to escape from the waters between San Pietro, Sant'Antioco, and the main island.

❧ RESTAURANTS

In Carloforte, try **Tonno di Corsa,** Via Marconi 47; tel. (0781) 855106. Appropriately named after the tuna run, this seafood restaurant practically overlooks the tuna fishing spectacle just off the island's coast. Relatively small but very Sardinian, the restaurant provides a full meal with local wine for Lit. 30,000. Closed Mon. and Tues. (except during the tourist season), and Oct. 1–Dec. 15. No cards.

Inland from Cagliari

A worthwhile inland visit from Cagliari is the 42-mile drive to see the ancient fortress-houses called *nuraghi,* found nowhere in the world except Sardinia. Head north on SS131, then turn right at Villasanta on the provincial road to Barumini. Less than a mile to the left, on the provincial road to Tuili, is the **Nuraghi su Nuraxi.** Construction of this outstanding Sardinian village-fortress supposedly began around 1500 B.C. This 12-tower complex with inner court, outer village, and perimeter walls was discovered by chance in 1949, when it was uncovered by a torrential rainfall. If not for the bar-restaurant and souvenir stand, the open-country setting could easily transplant you into the distant past.

Just to the north of the fortress is the Giara di Gesturi plain amid the Marmilla mountains. This area, overlapping the provinces of Cagliari and Oristano, is where the famous **Sardinian ponies** can be found running wild.

20

TRAVEL
ARRANGEMENTS

For Information

Tourist Offices

With more than 50 offices worldwide, the **Italian Government Tourist Office (ENIT)** is the official source of information and advice on planning a trip to Italy. They are happy to provide information, maps, and literature. These are just a few of their locations:

UNITED STATES

New York: 630 Fifth Ave., Suite 1565, New York, NY 10111; tel. (212) 245-4961

Chicago: 500 N. Michigan Ave., Suite 1046, Chicago, IL 60611; tel. (312) 644-0990

San Francisco: 360 Post St., Suite 801, San Francisco, CA 94108; tel. (415) 392-5266

Dallas: c/o Alitalia, 8350 Central Expressway, Dallas, TX 75206; tel. (214) 692-8761

Atlanta: c/o Alitalia, 223 Perimeter Center Parkway, Suite 530, Atlanta, GA 30346; tel. (404) 223-9770

CANADA

Montreal: 3 Place Ville Marie, Suite 2414, Montreal, PQ H3B 3M9; tel. (514) 866-7667

Toronto: c/o Alitalia, 120 Adelaide St. West, Suite 1202, Toronto, Ontario; tel. (416) 363-1348

GREAT BRITAIN

London: 1 Princes St., London W1R 8AY, England; tel. (01) 408-1254

AUSTRALIA

Sydney: c/o Alitalia, 124 Philip St., Sydney, 2000, New South Wales; tel. (02) 221-3620

Melbourne: c/o Alitalia, Pearl Assurance Bldg., 143 Queen St., Melbourne 3000, Victoria; tel. (03) 601171

Communications

Letters

Full addresses are given herein for hotels and agencies in Italy. Writing to a hotel or other establishment for information can take time and be frustrating. Always be sure to send your letters air mail (*via aerea*). Street numbers in Italian addresses *follow* the name of the street. Postal codes (akin to U.S. zip codes) *precede* the name of the city. The names of smaller towns or common town names sometimes are followed by an abbreviated provincial code (given herein in parentheses). A full street address would run like this:

American Embassy, Via Vittorio Veneto 121, 00187 Rome.

When addressing an envelope, set it up like this:

> American Embassy
> Via Vittorio Veneto 121
> 00187
> Rome (Provincial code here for smaller towns; these are in parentheses in our hotel listings when necessary.)
> ITALIA

Telephones

From a phone booth in Italy you can call just about anywhere in the world. The telephones take a token called *gettone,* which is valued at Lit. 200 and can be purchased at bars, telephone offices, and vending machines often found at airports and railway stations. Otherwise you can pay with Lit. 100 or 200 coins or magnetic phone cards.

There are SIP (Italian State Owned Telephone Company) offices in every city where you can purchase the magnetic telephone cards for external use (in the streets) or internal use (in SIP offices); denominations range from Lit. 1,000 to 10,000. They're a handy tool if you plan to use the telephone often or for long distance calling. SIP offices have phone books for every town, province, and city in Italy, and most can place operator-assisted calls for you.

OVERSEAS CALLING

If you find you must call home, here's the cheapest ways of doing it.

(1) Charge it to an international telephone credit card, which you can apply for before you leave home.

(2) Go to a SIP office and have the operator place the call for you (you will have to pay in cash, but there is no premium placed on the call).

(3) Buy a stack of Lit. 10,000 magnetic telephone cards, dial direct, and keep feeding them into the phone.

(4) Call collect but be sure that the operator understands that the charges are to be reversed. When in doubt, just say, "a carico del destinario" and any baffled operator will be sure to get it right.

> NEVER call direct from your hotel because by the time they finish sticking on the surcharge you will have shelled out an exorbitant sum of money that is sometimes more than double the usual rate. We cannot stress this enough; your call home can be higher than your hotel bill.

To telephone outside of Italy, the international access codes are 001 for calls to the U.S., 0044 to the U.K., 001 to Canada, and 0061 to Australia. When making long distance calls within Italy, dial the city code including the zero and follow with the telephone number. When calling Italy from abroad, you won't need the zero in the city code; the county code is 39.

Mail/Telegrams

Within Italy you can purchase stamps at tobacconists or at any one of the 14,000 Post and Telegraph (P&T) offices whose services also include telegrams and telexes. Hours of operation vary, but for the most part, offices in the main cities stay open from 8:30 A.M. to 7:30 or 8 P.M., while their counterparts in the smaller villages close at 2 P.M. The offices at international airports remain open 24 hours to send telegrams and registered letters.

If you are on the receiving end of a package or letter, have the mail addressed to you in care of *Fermo Posta,* along with the town or city name. To claim it, present your passport and a small fee to the *poste restante* desk at the city's central station.

Anything that is urgent or timely should be shipped by special delivery or courier. Federal Express offices are found in the major cities and you can expect delivery in 2–3 days.

Language

In all of the tourist towns, English is widely spoken. Only when you venture out of the mainstream may you encounter some difficulty. Don't be shy. Harbor your inhibitions and take a stab at speaking the language. Italians are genuine, fun-loving people and will be honored at the attempt.

PRONUNCIATION GUIDE

Vowels	Sound in English	Example in Italian
a	(ah) as in f**a**ther	casa (kAH-sah)—house
e	(eh) as in b**e**t	prendere (prEHn-deh-reh)—to take
i	(ee) as in t**ee**th	libri (lEE-bree)—books
o	(oh) as in b**o**rder	loro (lOH-roh)—they
u	(oo) as in b**oo**t	uno (OO-noh)—one
Consonants		
c	before i, (ch) as in **ch**urch	cibo (cHEE-boh)—food
c	before e, (ch) as in **ch**urch	cena (chEH-nah)—dinner
c	before a, (k) as in s**k**y	caro (kAH-roh)—dear
c	before o, (k) as in s**k**y	come (kOH-meh)—how
c	before u, (k) as in s**k**y	cura (kOO-rah)—care
c	before he, (k) as in s**k**y	perchè (pehr-kEH)—why or because
g	before e, (j) as in **j**elly	gente (jEHn-teh)—people
g	before i, (j) as in **j**elly	girare (jee-rAH-reh)—to turn
g	before a, (g) as in **g**oal	gatto (gAHt-toh)—cat
g	before o, (g) as in **g**oal	gola (gOH-lah)—throat
g	before u, (g) as in **g**oal	guidare (gooEE-dah-reh)—to drive
g	before he, (g) as in **g**oal	spaghetti (spah-gEHt-tee)—spaghetti
g	before hi, (g) as in **g**oal	funghi (fOOn-ghee)—mushrooms
gn	(ny) as in ca**ny**on	signore (see-nyOH-reh)—Mr. or Sir

Consonants	Sound in English	Example in Italian
q	(koo) as in quick	quando (kooAHn-doh)— when
s	between two vowels, (z) as in as	isola (ee-zOH-lah)—island
s	at the beginning of a word, (s) as in sea	sera (sEH-rah)—evening
ss	between vowels, (s) as in sea	rosso (rOHs-soh)—red
sce	(sh) as in ship	scendere (shEHn-deh-reh)—to go down
sci	(sh) as in ship	piscina (pee-shEE-nah)—swimming pool

GENERAL USEFUL WORDS AND EXPRESSIONS

Yes	Sì (see)
No	No (noh)
Please	Per favore (pEhr fah-vOH-reh)
Thank you	Grazie (grAH-tsee-eh)
You are welcome	Prego (prEH-goh)
Excuse me	Scusi (skOO-zee)
I am sorry	Mi dispiace (mEE dees-peeAH-cheh)
It's all right	Va bene (vAH bEH-neh)
It's not all right	Non va bene (nOHn vAH bEH-neh)
It doesn't matter	Non importa (nOhn eem-pOhr-tah)
Just a second	Un momento (OOn moh-mEHn-toh)
I don't understand	Non capisco (nOhn kah-pEEs-ko)
Please speak more slowly	Per favore parli più piano (pEhr fah-vOH-reh pAHr-lee peeOO pee-AH-noh)
Please repeat	Per favore ripeta (pEhr fah-vOH-reh ree-pEH-tah)
Sir, Mr.	Signore, signor (see-nyOh-reh, see-nyOhr)
Madam, Mrs.	Signora (see-nyOH-rah)
Miss	Signorina (see-nyOH-ree-nah)
Good morning	Buon giorno (boo-OHn-jeeOhr-noh)
Good evening	Buona sera (boo-OH-nah sEH-rah)
Good night	Buona notte (boo-OH-nah nOHt-teh)
Good-bye	Arrivederci (ahr-ree-veh-dEHr-chee)
Bye-bye	Ciao (chee-AH-oh)
See you later	A più tardi (AH pee-OO tAHr-dee)
See you tomorrow	A domani (AH doh-mAh-nee)

INTRODUCING YOURSELF AND BASIC CONVERSATION

What is your name?	Come si chiama? (kOH-meh sEE kee-AH-mah)
My name is John Miller.	Mi chiamo John Miller. (mEE kee-Ah-moh J.M.)
Nice to meet you!	Piacere! (pee-ah-chEH-reh)
Where are you from?	Di dov'è? (dEE dOH-v'EH)

I am an American from New York.	Io sono Americano/a (for women) di N.Y. (EEoh sOH-noh ah-meh-ree-kah-noh/nah dEE N.Y.)
Do you speak English?	Parla Inglese? (pAhr-lah een-glEH-zeh)
Yes I speak English, and you?	Si parlo Inglese, e Lei? (sEE pAHr-loh een-glEH-zeh, EH lEH-ee)
No, I don't speak Italian.	No, io non parlo Italiano. (nOH, EEoh nOHn pAHr-loh ee-tah-leeAH-noh)

USEFUL QUESTIONS

How do you say in Italian . . .	Come si dice in Italiano . . . (kOH-meh sEE dEE-cheh EEn ee-tah-lee AH-noh)
What does it mean?	Che cosa vuol dire? (kEH kOH-zah vooOHl dEE-reh)
Do you understand?	Capisce? (kah-pEE-sheh)
Is it far?	È lontano? (EH lohn-tAH-noh)
Can I go there walking?	Posso andarci a piedi? (pOHs-soh ahn-dAHr-chee AH peeEH-dee)
Where is the bus stop?	Dov'è la fermata dell'autobus? (dOHv-EH lAH fehr-mAH-tah dEHll'AHoo-toh-boos)
Where is the train station?	Dov'è la stazione ferroviaria? (dOHv'EH lAH stah-zeeOH-neh fehr-roh-veeAH-reeah)
. . . bank?	. . .la banca? (bAHn-kah)
. . . pharmacy?	. . . la farmacia? (fahr-mah-chEE-ah)
. . . rest room	. . . il bagno? (EEl bAH-nyoh)
. . . ticket office?	. . . la biglietteria? (bee-lleeEHt-tehr-EEah)
. . . police station?	. . . l'ufficio di polizia? (l'oof-fEE-choh dEE poh-lee-zEE-ah)

AT THE TRAIN STATION

I want a one way ticket for Rome.	Vorrei un biglietto di andata per Roma. (Vohr-rEH-ee OOn bee-llEHt-toh dEE ahn-dAH-tah pEHr rOH-mah)
I want a round trip ticket for . . .	Vorrei un biglietto di andata e ritorno per . . . (vohr-rEH-ee OOn bee-llEHt-toh dEE ahn-dAH-tah EH ree-tOHr-noh pEHr . . .)
From which track does the train leave?	Da quale binario parte il treno? (dAH kooAH-leh bee-nAH-ree-oh pAHr-teh EEl trEH-noh)

AT THE AIRPORT

Flight	Volo (vOH-loh)

Gate

Sala 'dimbarco (sAH-lah d'eem-bAHr-koh)

Smoking, nonsmoking

Fumatori, non fumatori (foo-mah-tOH-ree, nOHn foo-mah-tOH-ree)

The flight number 104 is boarding now.

Il volo numero 104 è in partenza ora. (EEl vOH-loh nOO-meh-roh 104 EH in pahr-tEhn-zah Oh-rah)

AT THE HOTEL

I would like a single room.

Vorrei una camera singola. (vohr-rEH-ee OO-nah kAH-meh-rah sEEn-goh-lah)

. . . double room.

. . . matrimoniale (. . . mah tree-moh-neeAH-leh)

. . . a room with two beds.

. . . una camera a due letti. (. . . OOnah kAH-meh-rah AH dOO-eh lEHt-tee)

. . . a room with a bathroom.

. . . una camera con il bagno. (OOran kAH-meh-rah kOHn EEl bAH-nyo)

. . . a room for one night.

. . . una camera per una notte. (OO-nah kAH-meh-rah pEHr OO-nah nOOt-teh)

. . . a room for three or four days.

. . . una camera per tre o quattro giorni. (. . . OOnah kAH-meh-rah pEHr trEH OH koo-AHt-troh jeeOHr-nee)

Do you have a reservation?

Ha la prenotazione? (AH lAH preh-noh-tah-zee-OH-neh)

I'm sorry there is no vacancy.

Mi dispiace è tutto esaurito, completo. (mEE dees-pee-AH-cheh EH tOOt-toh eh-zah-oo-rEE-toh)

Can you direct me to another hotel?

Mi puo indicare un altro albergo? (mEE poo-OH een-dee-kAH-reh OOn AHl-troh ahl-bEHr-goh)

AT THE RESTAURANT

I would like a table for two.

Vorrei un tavolo per due. (vohr-rEH-ee OOn tAH-voh-loh pEHr dOO-eh)

What would you like as an appetizer?

Che cosa desidera per antipasto? (kEH cOH-zah deh-zEE-deh-rah pEHr ahn-tee-pAHs-toh)

. . . as a first dish?

. . . per primo piatto? (. . . pEHr prEE-moh pee-AHt-toh)

. . . as an entree?

. . . per secondo piatto? (. . . pEHr seh-cOHn-doh pee-AHt-toh)

. . . as a side dish?	. . . per contorno? (. . . pEHr kohn-tOHr-noh)
. . . for dessert?	. . . per dolce? (. . . pEHr dOHl-cheh)
I would like some fruit.	Vorrei della frutta. (vohr-rEH-ee dEHl-lah FrOOt-tah)
A bottle of red (white) wine.	Una bottiglia di vino rosso (bianco). (OO-nah boht-tEE-llah dEE vEE-noh rOHs-soh [bee-AHn-koh])
A glass of wine.	Un bicchiere di vino. (OOn beek-kee-EH-reh dEE vEE-noh)
Mineral water.	Acqua minerale. (AHk-koo-ah mee-neh-rAH-leh)
Sparkling water.	Acqua minerale gassata. (AHk-koo-ah mee-neh-rAH-leh gahs-sAH-tah)
Plain water.	Acqua naturale. (Ahk-koo-ah nah-too-rAH-leh)
Waiter!	Cameriere! (kah-meh-ree-EH-reh)
The check please.	Il conto per favore. (EEl kOHn-toh pEHr fah-vOH-reh)
I did not order this.	Io non ho ordinato questo. (EE-oh nOHn OH ohr-dee-nAH-toh koo-EHstoh)

The Seasons in Italy

Seasonal Temperatures

While Italian weather is mild-mannered on the whole, temperatures vary regionally and seasonally.

In summer, to escape the heat, humidity, and stillness of the cities head for the cool mountain air of the mountains or gentle coastal breezes by the sea. In winter, bitter cold, rain, and snow can plague parts of the north; this can be a nuisance in Venice but welcome to ski enthusiasts in the Dolomite Alps. The Po Valley and Central Apennines are prone to fog in these months; sun-drenched Sicily is a heartwarming alternative. Almost anywhere in Italy, spring and fall can't be beat.

Monthly Average Temperatures in Fahrenheit											
	Jan.	Feb.	March	April	May	June	July	Aug.	Sept.	Oct.	Nov.	Dec.
BOLZANO	22	28	46	55	60	68	72	70	65	53	42	29
CORTINA	29	36	41	49	58	64	72	70	64	55	47	40
FLORENCE	45	47	50	60	67	75	77	70	64	63	55	46
GENOA	48	50	55	61	68	73	78	75	70	62	54	45
MILAN	36	40	50	58	66	72	75	74	67	56	45	39
NAPLES	50	54	58	63	70	75	83	79	74	66	60	52
ROME	49	52	57	62	70	77	82	78	73	65	56	47
TAORMINA	56	60	64	70	75	80	86	83	80	73	65	57
TURIN	31	38	48	55	61	70	74	72	66	56	45	35
VENICE	43	48	53	60	67	72	77	74	68	60	54	44

Time Zones

Italy lies in the Central European time zone, which is six hours ahead of New York and Montreal, one hour ahead of the U.K. and Ireland, and eight hours behind Sydney. Italians have daylight savings time, but they "spring ahead" a few weeks earlier, on March 28, and "fall back" a month earlier, at the end of September.

Timing Your Trip

If you can choose when you travel, avoid Italy in Aug., when most of the country is on hiatus. Businesses virtually shut down, and the cities are empty of Italians, who are replaced by hordes of students and tourists. July is the next least preferable month; not only have the tourists begun to arrive for summer break, but Italians are still around, and the crowds can be unbearable. Easter is another time to avoid; Italians hide away in the country, and foreigners fill up the cities.

May, June, Sept., and Oct. are the golden months when the weather is the sweetest and the Italian-to-tourist ratio is at its lowest. Some resort areas are seasonal, so it's best to visit no earlier than April and no later than Nov. The ski season is at its peak in Feb. and March, when the Dolomites become a playground for the chic and daring. Christmas week usually finds SRO crowds. Or you may wish to plan your trip to coincide with yearly events such as Venice's historical regatta or open-air summer opera in Verona's Roman Arena.

Annual Events

Check the Italian Tourist Office for a detailed list of annual events. Among some of the offerings are:

FEBRUARY

Carnevale, pre-Lenten festivities; the best are in Venice and Viareggio

Baccanale del Gnocco, crowning of the *gnocchi* king, last Friday of *carnevale;* Verona

MARCH

Scoppio del Carro, a float is exploded in Piazza del Duomo to celebrate Easter; Florence

Mid-Lent Festivities; nationwide

APRIL

Fiera Internazionale di Milano (Milan Trade Fair); Milan

Holy Week Processions, Holy Thursday and Good Friday; nationwide

Urbi et Orbi, papal blessing "to the city and the world," at St. Peter's, Easter; Rome

MAY

Maggio Musicale Fiorentino (May Musical Festival), through June; Florence

Cavalcata Sarda, Sardinian costume parade; Sassari (Sardinia)

Corsa dei Ceri (Race of the Candles); an uphill race in ancient dress on May 15; Gubbio

Miracle of San Gennaro, when the saint's blood allegedly liquifies, on the first Sun. in May and Sept. 19; Naples

Palio della Balestra, an archery contest between the towns of Gubbio and Sansepolcro, last Sunday (held in Sansepolcro in September); Gubbio

JUNE
Festival of Two Worlds, a panorama of performing arts, mid-June to mid-July; Spoleto

Shakespearean Festival and Drama Festival, through Sept.; Verona

JULY
Verona Opera Festival, through Aug.; Verona

Il Palio, horse race and procession on July 2 and Aug. 16; Siena

Baths of Caracalla Opera Season, through Aug.; Rome

AUGUST
Rossini Opera Festival, through mid-Sept.; Pesaro

Festa dei Candelieri (Feast of the Candles); Aug. 14; Sassari

International Film Festival at the Biennale, late Aug. to early Sept.; on the Lido; Venice

Il Palio, horse race and procession, on Aug. 16 and July 2; Siena

SEPTEMBER
Regata Storica (Historical Regatta), on the Grand Canal, the first Sun.; Venice

Miracle of San Gennaro, when the saint's blood allegedly liquefies, on Sept. 19 and the first Sun. in May; Naples

Palio della Balestra, an archery contest between the towns of Gubbio and Sansepolcro (held in Gubbio in May); Sansepolcro

Formula One Grand Prix, Monza

OCTOBER
Musical Autumn, two-month-long music festival; Como

DECEMBER
Christmas and **New Year's Festivities,** mostly in the tradition of the Roman Catholic Church; throughout Italy

Opening Night at La Scala, season runs through June; Milan

Opening Hours

Opening hours of museums and churches can be whimsical. If you're anxious to see a particular museum or church, check with the ENIT Tourist Office for up-to-date information on hours and holiday closings. Generally, hours begin and end early. Most stores, many churches, and some museums close for a prolonged lunch hour, a tradition in Italy. Most museums are closed Mon. If you're sightseeing and not attending mass, Sun. morning is not a good time to visit churches. In general, it's best to start your day early, especially when heading for major attractions such as the Uffizi Gallery or Vatican City.

Admission fees are common, but usually moderate: Lit. 3,000–7,000. Some attractions have free admission on certain days.

SIESTA

From around 1 to 3 or 4 P.M. every day, shops, pharmacies, some churches and museums, banks, and most businesses close their doors. Generally speaking, the further north you go, the less drawn-out the lunch break tends to be. This can be disconcerting to the tourist in mid-swing, who'd rather sightsee or shop than eat lunch. Learn to live with it (there's not much else you can do); start your day early, and tour the streets (or take a nap!) if you don't want a protracted lunch.

The flip side to the siesta is that many restaurants close between lunch and dinner. Just as you may have trouble finding an open store in the early afternoon, so you may have difficulty finding food between 3 and 5 P.M.

Packing

Other than an adapter plug or electrical converter for your hairdryer or electric shaver (a shaver will only need an adapter plug), there are no real prerequisites for packing for a trip to Italy. Use common sense and forget about loading your luggage with all but the kitchen sink—if you think it is better to be safe than sorry, you are bound to be sorry when lugging your overloaded bag around.

The life expectancy of high heels on cobblestone streets is less than zero; bring some good walking shoes. Remember that shorts, bare backs and arms, and miniskirts aren't allowed at the Vatican and in many churches and cathedrals. You'll find that in cities, Italians often dress elegantly, so you may want even your most comfortable touring clothes to have some sense of style. Consider packing nicer trousers along with jeans; a basic dress; or a well-tailored jacket.

Binoculars come in handy for a close-up look at frescoes and mosaics on church ceilings. If you're packing a camera, don't worry—major film brands are available throughout Italy.

ELECTRICITY

The current that flows through Italy is 220 volts, 50 cycles. Any appliances that run on 110 volts will need a converter and all equipment must be fitted with a two-pin, round-shaped plug. Come prepared.

Formalities at the Border

Passports

To enter Italy, all you'll need is a valid passport. Citizens of EEC countries, such as France, need only a national identity card. Children under 16 who are traveling with an adult of the same nationality can be entered in the adult's passport. Minors over 16 need special documents. Unless you are planning to stay longer than three months or to work abroad, a visa is not necessary.

Customs

You can bring in as many items for personal use as you like, as long as they are not intended for trade, given as gifts, or sold. Besides clothing and related accessories, personal items include books, household and camping equipment, one sporting gun and 200 cartridges, one pair of skis, two tennis rackets, a portable typewriter, record player, baby carriage, two cameras with ten rolls of film, binoculars, personal jewelry, 400 cigarettes, and no more than 500 grams of tobacco for cigars or pipes. If you are in doubt about other items, check with the Italian Tourist Office.

You may enter or leave Italy with a maximum of Lit. 500,000. To reconvert your lire at the airport, you'll need the original exchange slip from the bank to prove original lire conversion. There is no limit on how much foreign currency you may bring in (which comes as no surprise), but to leave the country with more than the equivalent of two million lire in foreign currency, avoid any hassles by filling out *on arrival* a V2 customs form declaring how much you are bringing in, to serve as proof of import when you exit.

Money Matters

The Italian unit of currency is the *lira,* or *lire* in the plural; the common abbreviation in Italy (and used herein) is *Lit.* Thus, 1,000 lire would be Lit. 1,000. There are a few more zeros in Italian denominations than you probably are used to, so it's wise to sort that out before you start to spend. There has been some talk in Italy of re-valuing the currency and dropping three of the zeros, but so far it's just talk. Bank notes come in denominations of Lit. 1,000, 2,000, 5,000, 10,000, 50,000, and 100,000. Coins come in denominations of Lit. 10, 20, 50, 100, 200, and the two-toned Lit. 500 piece. With the fluctuation of foreign currency, it's impossible to predict rates of exchange. In fall 1988, the U.S. dollar was valued at Lit. 1280, the Canadian dollar at Lit. 1042.35, the British pound at Lit. 2346.25, and the Australian dollar at Lit. 1100. Call any international bank or check the financial section of your local newspaper for current conversion rates.

Credit Cards

American Express once (abbreviated here as AE) was *the* credit card used by all and accepted by everyone. Those times have changed; look for window stickers in shops, restaurants, and hotels indicating acceptance of *Diner's Club* (DC), *Visa* (V), *MasterCard* (MC), and the new *Si* card.

Traveler's Checks

Since traveler's checks are accepted just about everywhere, they are preferable to carrying large sums of cash around. You can cash them as you need them, and if they're lost or stolen, you're insured as long as you report it right away. Buy a popular brand of checks, such as American Express or Visa Barclay checks, to avoid potential hassles.

Changing Money

A daily official exchange rate is posted in Italy, but this is just a guideline, and *cambio* (exchange) rates vary, so shop around. Many exchange offices charge a fee per transaction, so you may want to change several days' pocket money at one time.

Banks usually give the best rate of exchange. Banking hours are from 8:30 A.M. to 1:30 P.M. and from 3 to 4 P.M.; banks are closed on weekends and national holidays. All banks are affiliated with a major credit card company and can advance you cash on your card. Currency may also be exchanged at *cambio* offices at airports, main train stations, and border crossings, as well as some hotels, but use hotels only as a last resort; they usually will cost the most.

Tipping

Italians partake in tipping wholeheartedly and seriously; many of their livelihoods depend on it. But don't feel obligated or intimidated about tipping, unless it is a pleasurable payoff.

Hotels tack on a service charge somewhere between 15 and 18% to your bill. In restaurants, read the menu carefully: A supplement of 15% is usually added for service (*servizio*), but some restaurants also list a *coperto* (cover charge). It is expected of foreigners to leave a 5 to 10% tip in addition to the *servizio,* or to tip 15% if no service charge is listed.

Other considerations are: rewarding the chambermaid Lit. 1,000 for each day of your stay; giving a bellhop or porter Lit. 1,500 for each piece of baggage carried; tipping a room-service waiter Lit. 1,000 or up, depending on the delivery; and slipping the doorman Lit. 1,000 for hailing your cab. Your resident concierge is at your beck and call; expect to reward him an additional 15% over the cost of the service rendered. In top-class luxury hotels it is not uncommon to tip the concierge a few thousand lire per day to guarantee service with a smile and some sincerity. Taxi drivers are tipped 10 to 15%; (you can usually just round your fare off to the next highest thousand) helpful theater and opera ushers merit a minimum of Lit. 1,000, and tour guides, about Lit. 3,000.

Transportation

Flying

TO ITALY

Since air fares can vary so widely, check with a good travel agent and stay abreast of promotional fares advertised in the newspaper or on the radio before buying.

Once ticketing is taken care of, getting there is a cinch. Italy's two international airports are Rome's **Fiumicino** and Milan's **Malapensa,** which handle all incoming flights from the United States, Canada, Australia, and the U.K. During peak travel periods, flights from the U.K. may be routed into the smaller international airports, in Turin, Venice, Palermo, Naples, Genoa, Cagliari, Bologna, Costa Smeralda, Genoa, Rome's **Ciampino,** and Milan's **Linate.**

WITHIN ITALY

Given Italy's rather small size and its extensive network of domestic air service, traveling by plane takes less than an hour's flying time for most connections within Italy. That's just about as much time as it takes to reach Rome's center from Fiumicino airport in the afternoon rush hour. The drawback lies in the time it takes to get to and from the airport. Chances are you will spend more time in a taxi, car, or bus getting to the airport than on the plane; it may not be worth the bother or the price. Taking a train or driving often proves to be much more practical.

Alitalia and its domestic subsidiary ATI serve 25 cities within Italy, from Rome and Milan. Internal flights are fairly expensive unless you can make use of one of the special fare discounts available:

Nastro Verde fares call for a 30% reduction on specific domestic routes, and must be paid for when the booking is made.

Fine Settimana provides a 30% discount on Saturday and Sunday travel, with a maximum stay of four weeks; tickets must be paid for when booking the flight.

Plan Famiglia is available to families of three or more. One adult must pay full economy fare; the other receives a 50% reduction, as does a child aged 12 to 22. Children under 12 are entitled to a 75% discount; those under two pay only 10% of the economy fare.

By Train

A lot can be said about train travel within Italy, both pro and con. The Italian State Railway (*Ferrovie dello Stato* or FS) has improved significantly in recent years, adding new, air-conditioned InterCity (IC) express trains providing comfortable and efficient service (when operating on time). Main train stations usually are situated in the heart of the city, so you don't waste time en route to congested airports. More popular routes are serviced frequently enough to allow you to maintain a flexible schedule. And most of all, with the high cost of car rental, gas, and air travel, you just can't beat the price.

On the flip side, schedules are not always adhered to, and strikes can be a frequent occurrence—although they rarely last more than one day. Few railway personnel speak English, which may make the less seasoned and timid traveler slightly uneasy. During rush hours and the busy tourist season, trains are extremely crowded, and traveling in second class often means standing.

To make your travels go a lot smoother, be sure to make a reservation whenever possible, take the *rapido* or *espresso* trains rather than the *diretto* or *locale* (which make many more stops), and for long hauls, go first class (and assure yourself a seat).

As a foreigner traveling within Italy, you are eligible for certain discounted tickets, which can be bought either in Italy or before you leave home.

The **BTLC (Italian Tourist Ticket)** train pass can be purchased for 8, 15, 21, or 30 days of unlimited, unrestricted first- or second-class travel on all types of trains, and is good for a period of six months. Children under 12 pay half fare; children under four travel for free.

The **Italian Kilometric Ticket** is good on regular trains for a period of two months, for a total of twenty trips or 1,875 miles in first or second class. It is sometimes possible to upgrade to an InterCity train by paying a surcharge. As many as five people can use one ticket at the same time; the mileage or trip total is multiplied by the number of people traveling.

The Italian State Railroad is now working on a time-pass to accompany its current offerings. The time-pass will not calculate the days spent in any one tourist attraction, but only actual time spent in transit. This is still on the drawing board, though railroad officials in Rome seem determined to capture a larger share of the tourist transportation market. (Let's hope as much effort will be devoted to resolving the strikes that can play havoc with a limited time schedule.) Stay atop your travel agent to see the outcome of this interesting proposal.

A **EuRailpass** could be a good buy if you plan to travel extensively in any of the other 16 participating countries in continental Europe. The pass enables you to unlimited first-class travel for periods of 15 or 21 days, or one, two, or three months. Those under 26 are eligible for a EuRail Youthpass, good for one or two months but for second-class travel only. EuRailpass tickets must be purchased before arriving in Europe, from any of the member national railroads; from CIT Tours, currently the official representative of the Italian State Railways; or apply through your travel agent or contact EuRailpass, c/o WBA, 51 Ridgefield Ave., Staten Island, NY 10304.

If most of your traveling is to be done in Italy, it is better to buy an Italian train pass rather than a EuRail pass, as Italy's train fares are generally much lower than Northern Europe's. Within Italy, train tickets may be purchased at train stations or, to avoid long lines, through authorized travel agents (recognized by the *FS* logo). Italian train passes can also be bought through CIT Tours.

Driving in Italy

Traveling by car in Italy can put your vacation on a new plane. You can explore every nook and cranny, travel when you want to, and avoid the hordes of fellow tourists. That's not to say you won't be stuck in a traffic jam now and then, or that every experience will be action-packed. Nor is gasoline cheap, nor tolls on the *autostrade*. But you may never match the experience gained off the beaten path.

Getting around is usually a cinch. Maps generally are clearly marked for all routes, and highway, city, and road signs are efficient and explicit. If you're heading for a small town, though, you'll need to follow signs for the nearest provincial seat or urban area. White signs give urban directions.

Sprawling over 6,000 kilometers, the *autostrade* (highways or expressways) are an extensive network of toll roads stretching across the country, marked by green road signs. Tolls are according to the distance traveled and the size of your vehicle. Highways have plenty of pit stops for fuel, food, rest rooms, and telephones. But if you prefer a scenic route to a fast and direct one, opt for the state roads (with blue color-coded signs, and indicated by SS and a number.), provincial roads, or even narrow and winding (but very lovely) local roads. Yellow signs indicate points of tourist interest.

Traveling north–south, you can generally follow turnpikes up and down the coasts. Still to be completed is the west coast Pisa–Civitavecchia turnpike. The main route here remains the SS7 (Via Appia). Be careful north of Grosseto where there is a high accident rate. The Venice (Mestre)–Ravenna gap on the Adriatic is covered by SS309 (Strada Romea).

Coast to coast routes over the rugged Apennines south of Bologna are the Naples–Bari (A17) and Rome–Pescara (A24) turnpikes. A branch of the latter extends from L'Aquila under Gran Sasso d'Italia, the highest Apennine peak, to the Adriatic coast near San Benedetto del Tronto. There is also a toll-free superstrada (SS3bis) from the Orte A1 exit to Perugia. The remaining 120 miles north to Ravenna on the Adriatic are over a well-surfaced but slow two-lane scenic route.

Turnpike connections in Sardinia and Sicily are limited. The former has a good north–south run from Sassari to Cagliari. Sicily's northern and eastern coasts are well connected, including a heartland Catania–Enna–Palermo link. The western coast of the triangular shaped island is serviced by the state highway system.

A few rules of the road in Italy: Be sure to buckle up. Seat belts are compulsory for the driver and front-seat passenger. Drive in the right lane; where multiple lanes exist use the left lane for passing. Always signal when changing lanes, passing, or entering the highway. At crossroads, give the right-of-way to cars on the right, and always give streetcars and trains the right-of-way. Blowing horns is considered impolite, although it seems to be an art form in Rome. Speed limits vary with the size of the car and the road traveled, so pay attention to signs and check with the car rental firm. A *zona pedale* is a street open to pedestrians only and closed to cars during the posted hours. If an approaching vehicle blinks its lights at you, even in broad daylight, it probably means that a little distance down the road is the friendly neighborhood *polizia* or *carabinieri*, so slow down. Be prepared to pay for gasoline in cash; while some stations accept credit cards and travelers' checks, the majority do not.

Parking is a perennial problem within cities. Pay careful attention to signs in the city, and always park on the right side of the road when on the outskirts of town. Italians abide by road signs, but may park facing into traffic, or with one or two tires up on the curb. They have even been known to park on sidewalks in narrow city centers.

If you see a sign that has a picture of an auto in midair, it marks a tow-away zone. Don't think for a second that because you are a foreigner or that the car is a rental that you won't get towed—it's quite the opposite. You'll get slapped with two tickets and have to unearth the car. Retrieving it will run you at least Lit. 60,000, payable in cold cash.

RENTING A CAR

You often can save up to 50% of a rental cost by reserving a rental car before you leave home. The best deals are on weekly rentals, which include unlimited mileage and usually require a one- or two-day advance booking. If you're not sure you need a car, you can reserve one and cancel later if need be.

Stick with major companies like Avis, Hertz, Europcar (National in the U.S.), Budget (Italy by Car), and Maggiore, all of which have many locations, in cities, train stations, and airports.

There are substantial price breaks for rentals of more than 21 days, one month, two months, and more. Shop around; prices can vary, and not all companies offer discounts on long-term rentals.

If you're planning to drive in more than one country, check rental offices at borders for cars with foreign license plates that must be returned to their country of origin. You may be able to trade cars and save the dropoff charge, which can start at 200,000 lire. Airlines may offer fly/drive packages with your airfare similar to ones available within the U.S.

If you are driving an auto bearing foreign plates in Italy, you qualify for fuel coupons for discounts averaging 15%. Also available are discounts for toll roads. They can be bought from ENIT or the Italian Automobile Club (ACI). For this reason you may seriously want to consider picking up a rental in Nice or Zurich, near Italy's northern border.

To rent a car you will need a valid driver's license and a major credit card, with enough credit available to cover the cost of the rental plus some. You have the option to settle your account in cash upon return.

Taking Ferries

Ferry service connects the Italian peninsula with its islands: Sardinia, Sicily, Capri, Ischia, Procida, Elba, and lesser-known islands such as the Aeolian Islands, the Egadi Islands, Ustica Islan, Pantelleria Island, Pelagie Islands, Pontine Islands, the Tremiti Islands.

You can also enter or leave Italy via ferries that connect the country with Corsica; Toulon, France; Greece (and via Greece to Egypt); Malta, Tunisia, and Yugoslavia.

Summer travelers especially should book ferries months in advance.

There are numerous ports throughout the country. Contact ENIT for complete information.

Bus Service

There is no coordinated national bus service in Italy; systems vary greatly from province to province. Accurate, published schedules are virtually an unknown commodity and English-speaking assistance is nearly impossible to come by. We have given bus information for areas that have adequate service—although, on the whole, trains are far preferable.

Taking Taxis

The novice may not take kindly to the lightning speed and feisty finesse of many an Italian cabbie. In big cities, traffic is inescapable by day, but if there is an alternate route, your driver will find it.

Taxi rides are not cheap. At the drop of the meter's flag you're out anywhere from Lit. 2,500 to Lit. 4,000, and the meter adds Lit. 500 every 300 meters or 60 seconds. Miscellaneous surcharges include a Lit. 2,500 charge between the hours of 10 P.M. and 7 A.M. Weekend and holiday travel cost an extra Lit. 1,000, and airport runs can shoot up the fare by Lit. 15,000, plus a possible Lit. 500 to Lit. 1,000 for each piece of baggage. Tip around 10 to 15%, which can usually mean just rounding up to the next Lit. 1,000.

To hail a taxi, look for the light on the cab's roof that indicates it's available. Taxis may be hard to find outside the center of a city; you may find one at a taxi stand, or call for one. Any hotel or restaurant will telephone for you. Be aware that the meter of a radio taxi will be running on the way to pick you up.

Touring

Package Deals

If you are uneasy about traveling alone and want the security and comfort of a prearranged plan, by all means shop for a package tour. Or you can travel with a tour group to take advantage of reduced airfares and hotel prices, but explore and eat on your own. The package alternatives are endless, and range

Driving Distances

Mileage is based on the most direct route between cities.

	BARI	BOLOGNA	BOLZANO	FLORENCE	GENOA	MILAN	NAPLES	PALERMO	ROME	TURIN	VENICE
AOSTA	670	242	280	326	159	113	629	1,132	485	78	289
BARI	—	422	589	486	599	557	200	455	299	632	500
BOLOGNA	422	—	180	66	177	135	397	877	253	210	99
BOLZANO	589	180	—	246	247	171	577	1,044	433	253	140
COMO	587	165	175	231	126	30	562	1,042	418	106	182
FERRARA	430	29	159	95	199	152	426	885	282	236	69
FLORENCE	486	66	246	—	166	201	331	834	187	274	164
GENOA	599	177	247	166	—	97	470	973	326	108	240
MILAN	557	135	171	201	97	—	532	1,012	388	86	495
NAPLES	200	397	577	331	470	532	—	503	144	578	955
PALERMO	455	877	1,044	834	973	1,012	503	—	647	1,081	352
RAVENNA	384	48	205	84	224	183	344	839	233	257	115
ROME	299	253	428	187	326	388	144	647	—	434	826
SIENA	443	109	290	43	184	244	288	791	144	29	115
TAORMINA	326	748	915	705	844	884	374	165	518	952	826
TURIN	632	210	253	274	108	86	578	1,081	435	—	257
VENICE	500	99	140	164	240	177	557	955	352	257	—
VERONA	496	87	93	153	175	102	484	951	340	183	74

from budget to sky-high super deluxe, from independent to near-claustrophobic, from student to the over-60 set, and so on.

All of the major airlines serving Italy have their own tour packages. And there are countless tour operators who have been guiding vacationers around Italy for many years now. Travel agents, tourist offices, and the tour operators themselves can provide more detailed information, but here is just a sampling of agencies:

CIT Travel Service, 666 Fifth Ave., New York, NY 10103; tel. (212) 397-2666 or (800) 223-7987 (forty offices in the U.S., eighty worldwide)

Perillo Tours, 577 Chestnut Ridge Rd., Woodcliff Lake, NJ 07675; tel. (800) 431-1515

Italiatour, 666 Fifth Ave., New York, NY 10103; tel. (212) 262-0650 or (800) 237-0517

Donna Franca Tours, 470 Commonwealth Ave., Boston, MA 02215; tel. (617) 227-3111 or (800) 225-6290

Italia Adagio, 55 N. Ocean Ave., Freeport, NY 11520; tel. (516) 868-7825 or (516) 546-5239

Maiellano Tours, 441 Lexington Ave., New York, NY 10017; tel. (212) 687-7725 or (800) 223-1616

Central Holiday Tours, 206 Central Ave., Jersey City, NJ; tel. (800) 742-2838

Pan Am, Alitalia, TWA, British Airways, and Qantas package their own tours to Italy.

Accommodations

Regulated by each provincial tourist board, hotels are classified by price and provisions, with a rating system of stars, ranging down from the top-of-the-line 5-star (luxury) to 4-star (first class), 3-star (second class; 3 stars and above always offer private baths), 2-star (third class), and 1-star hotel, which will provide only the barest of essentials and is probably best to avoid. Centrally located hotels are always rated with more stars. Within each category a minimum and maximum rate is allowed by law that fluctuates according to season; if there is a *fiera* (trade fair) in town, expect rates to skyrocket. Very often rates include *piccola colazione* (the equivalent of a continental breakfast), which is not obligatory and in many hotels not worth the price you pay (although you may prefer having coffee without having to leave your hotel in the morning).

Leading the luxury lineup are CIGA Hotels' superdeluxe (and super-expensive) establishments, whose penchant for style, elegance, and impeccable service have made them favorite with the international jet set. Other luxury chains are the Italian consortium Italhotels' impressive 5- and 4-star properties, Leading Hotels of the World/Italy's top-notch lodgings, and the more intimate, highly celebrated Relais et Chateaux select hotels and resorts.

Other reputable chains or hotel groups throughout the country are Jolly Hotels, Starhotels, Space Hotels, City Hotels, Eurotel, and Best Western, as well as the token high-rise Hiltons and Sheratons found only in major cities.

Scrimping and saving does not have to mean settling for or sacrificing. Thanks to a host of small family-run hotels and quaint *pensioni* on back streets and in hillside villages, Italy has many budget offerings redolent with character. And if you care to sidestep tradition altogether, a few offbeat and out-of-the-ordinary alternatives are worth consideration.

Religious institutions such as convents and monasteries offer a glimpse of a very different way of life at rock-bottom rates. Be forewarned that accommodations will be the most basic, and you will be expected to respect any rules and curfews that are generally practiced. Information and arrangements can be made by contacting the archdiocese of the city you are planning to visit.

A 17th-century **farmhouse,** isolated **cottage,** or even an elegant **country home** are just a few examples of what you can expect on a **farm holi-**

day. Details of country living on more than 5,000 farms across the country are available from Agriturist, Corso Vittorio Emanuele 101, 00186 Rome; tel. (06) 6512342.

Camping out may mean roughing it a bit, but it's a good way to discover the natural beauty and serenity of Italy's countryside. The Italian Federation of Camping and Caravanning (Federcampeggio) can provide information on more than 1,700 official campsites; contact them at Casella Postale 23, 50041 Calenzano (Florence), or ask for the book *Guida Camping d'Italia* at the Italian tourist office nearest you. Some campsites are more elaborate than others, with bungalows, shopping centers, even hotels.

Renting a **private villa** or **apartment** can be exciting; just how much you are prepared to spend will determine whether you end up in a stunning *palazzo* or a more modest and affordable villa or apartment. The tourist board can supply the names of companies that will arrange villa rentals for a week or longer.

Throughout this book, the rates we've given for rooms show the range between single and double accommodations.

Health Concerns

Italy is a Westernized country, and you don't need special vaccinations to visit. It offers all the amenities of home: pharmacies are plentiful, and there is an Italian equivalent for just about everything (and indeed, your favorite products may *be* Italian)—aspirin, cough syrup, toothpaste and shampoo, makeup, tampax, contraceptives, and so on. Pharmacy hours are generally 8:30 A.M. to 1 P.M. and 4 P.M. to 7:30 or 8 P.M. Some skip the lunchtime closing, and one pharmacy in the vicinity always stays open overnight. This works on a rotation system, so if you need a pharmacy at an odd hour, check their windows for a sign indicating which one is on duty.

The water is safe to drink (except perhaps from rural pumps), but as in any unfamiliar place, your body may take some time to get used to it. To be safe, drink bottled water.

If the food and water are having an adverse effect on your plumbing system, try squeezing a lemon into a glass of water.

Avis car rental has a service that began in Britain a while back offering renters in Italy access to a 24-hour hotline, *On Call Europe.* For the cost of a toll call, you can talk to an English-speaking doctor or dentist about whatever ails you. Ask about details when you rent your car.

Safety

You'll probably hear a hundred stories about Italian street scenes before you go. Everyone knows someone who heard about someone else whom something happened to. The stories never end, and the question of safety will always remain a question. Italy's south doesn't have a monopoly on crime; it can happen anywhere.

The best advice is to be wise and be cautious. Always ask when in doubt. If you're in unfamiliar surroundings, ask the hotel if it's safe to take a stroll at night. When you drive a long distance after dark, take the main highways rather than the smaller byways. Keep a close watch on your purse and never leave your bags unattended. Keep your money, traveler's checks, and credit cards in different places and keep some identification in your wallet in case it is lost or stolen. Don't leave anything in a car—and that means the trunk and the glove compartment, too. Never keep valuables in your hotel room while you are out. If anything should be lost or stolen, report it immediately to the police and your embassy. (See Vital Information.)

Business Brief

Italy has been one of post-war Europe's great success stories. Currently, the country is undergoing a major economic boom; doing business in Italy can hold many profitable rewards.

The following are tips on the business protocols of Italy that will assist you in the successful conduct of business with the Italians:

- Northern Italians consider their sophisticated lifestyle to be in direct contrast to the more relaxed southern Italian way of life. Incomes in the North are almost twice those in the South. You will quickly learn that to confuse the two could add both insult and injury to your business relationship.
- Be prepared to use a translator during negotiations, unless you are certain that the person you are conducting business with is fluent in English. Have important documents and agreements translated to avoid any misunderstandings. This could also help to speed up the negotiation process.
- Money is not the only motivation in business. Italians value good relationships with the people they are dealing with.
- Learn to speak a little Italian. This will show the respect you have for the Italian people both as friends and business associates.
- The business day generally begins at 8:30 A.M. and ends around 6 or 7 P.M., usually with a two-hour lunch beginning around 12:30 P.M. Be punctual about your appointments.
- In the past, the head of an Italian firm had the power to make the final decisions. However, today this top-down management style is being replaced by a more democratic group consensus.
- The Italians are known to be tough, shrewd negotiators. Agendas set for meetings should be flexible and good-faith negotiations are expected. However, it is advised to involve an attorney in final agreements so that terms can be clearly defined and not left in the abstract.

Metric Conversions

Weight			
1 ounce	28.3 grams	1 inch	2.54 centimeters
1 pound	454 grams	1 foot	.3 metre
2.2 pounds	1 kilo	1 yard	.91 metre
1 quart	.94 litre	1.09 yards	1 metre
1 gallon	3.78 litres	1 mile	1.61 kilometers
		.62 mile	1 kilometer
		1 acre	.40 hectare
		2.47 acres	1 hectare

Distance (header for third and fourth columns)

Temperature: To change Fahrenheit into centigrade, subtract 32 and divide by 1.8. For the reverse calculation, multiply by 1.8 and add 32.

CULTURAL TIMELINE

Ancient Rome

70	Titus destroys the Temple in Jerusalem
79	Eruption of Vesuvius; **Pompeii** and **Herculaneum** buried
81	Completion of the **Colosseum, Arch of Titus, Rome**
96–180	Height of the Roman Empire
107–117	**Trajan's Column, Arch of Trajan, Rome**
c. 126	Completion of the **Pantheon, Rome**
138–192	Antonine Emperors (Marcus Aurelius and others)
120–127	**Villa of Hadrian at Tivoli**
c. 161	***Equestrian Statue of Marcus Aurelius,* Piazza del Campidoglio, Rome**
164–180	Plague ravages the Roman Empire
193	**Temple of Vesta, Rome**
211	Caracalla becomes emperor; builds the luxurious **Baths of Caracalla**
284–305	Reign of Diocletian; Christian persecutions
306–337	Reign of Constantine; Christianity established as the state religion; **Arch of Constantine, Rome**

The Early Christian Era

c. 324	**Old St. Peter's Basilica**
330	Constantinople (formerly Byzantium) becomes the new capital of the Roman Empire
354–430	St. Augustine
402–476	Barbarians attack Rome; Ravenna becomes the capital of the Western Roman Empire
c. 432–40	***Mosaics,* Santa Maria Maggiore, Rome**
476–540	Ravenna under the Ostrogoths ruled by Theodoric (474–526)
c. 527	**Church of San Vitale, Ravenna,** begun
c. 533	Justinian codifies Roman law and reconquers Italy through his general, Belisarius
542–594	Plague in Europe
c. 547	***Mosaics* of San Vitale, Ravenna**
590–604	Pope Gregory the Great; Gregorian chants
730–843	Iconoclasm; ban on religious imagery and destruction of art
800	Charlemagne crowned emperor by Pope Leo III; after his death, the empire fragments
811	Founding of Venice by refugees fleeing the Franks; building of the **Doge's Palace,** begun c. 825; rebuilt 1345–48.
962	Otto founds the Holy Roman Empire
998	**Monastery of Sacra di San Michele** (near Turin)

The Middle Ages

| 1000–1150 | Romanesque art and architecture at its height in Europe |

1063	**Cathedral of Pisa**
1066	Norman invasion of England; Normans also enter Italy
1077	Emperor Henry IV bows to Pope Gregory VII at Canossa
1094	**St. Mark's, Venice,** completed
1096–1291	Period of the Crusades
1140	Guelph and Ghibelline wars begin
1147	Second Crusade
1155	Frederick Barbarossa emperor; struggle between the empire and the papacy
1154–90	Growth of the Italian city-states
1174	**Leaning Tower of Pisa** begun (completed 1350); **Cathedral of Monreale, Sicily**
1209	St. Francis founds the Franciscan Order at Assisi
1228–1253	**Basilica of St. Francis at Assisi;** *frescoes* on the life of St. Francis (1296–1300)
1260	**Pulpit by Nicolò Pisano, Baptistery, Pisa**
1271	Travel by Marco Polo
1280	**Façade, Cathedral of Siena**
c. 1285	**Cimabue,** *Madonna Enthroned,* **Ufizzi, Florence**
1296–1436	**Florence Cathedral**
1299–1314	**Palazzo Vecchio, Florence**
1305–1306	**Giotto,** *frescoes* **in the Arena Chapel,** Padua
1308	**Duccio,** *Maestà altarpiece,* **Siena Cathedral**
1308–1321	Dante, *Divine Comedy;* founding of Rome University
1309–1377	Pope Clement V (French) moves the papal seat to Avignon
1310	**Giotto,** *Madonna Enthroned,* **Uffizi, Florence; façade of Orvieto Cathedral**
1337–1339	**Ambrogio Lorenzetti,** *Allegory of Good and Bad Government,* **Palazzo Pubblico, Siena**
1347–1351	Black Death takes 75 million lives in Europe
1377	The papacy returns to Rome
1378–1418	The Great Schism in the Western Church; two popes, one at Rome, the other at Avignon
1386	**Milan Cathedral** begun

The Renaissance (Rinascimento)

1417–1420	Brunelleschi designs the **dome** for the **Florence Cathedral** (completed 1436)
1423	**Fabriano,** *Adoration of the Magi,* **Uffizi, Florence**
1427	**Masaccio,** *The Tribute Money,* **Brancacci Chapel, Church of Santa Maria del Carmine, Florence**
c. 1430	**Donatello,** *David,* **Bargello Museum, Florence**

1434–1494	The Medici dominate Florence (Lorenzo the Magnificent rules from 1469–92); Florence the center of Renaissance humanism
1445–1450	**Fra Angelico, *frescoes,* Convent of San Marco, Florence**
c. 1452	**Ghiberti completes *The Gates of Paradise,* Baptistery Doors, Florence**
1453	Fall of Constantinople to the Turks
	Piero della Francesca, *Legend of the Holy Cross,* Church of St. Francis, Arezzo
c. 1466	**Mantegna, *Dead Christ,* Pinacoteca di Brera, Milan**
1471–1484	Pope Sixtus IV
1473–1474	**Mantegna, *Ceiling Fresco,* Camera degli Sposi, Palazzo Ducale, Mantua**
c. 1480	**Botticelli, *Birth of Venus, La Primavera,* Uffizi, Florence**
1482	Plato's *Dialogues* printed in Italy
1484–1492	Pope Innocent VIII
1492–1503	Pope Alexander VI
1492	Columbus discovers the New World; Lorenzo the Magnificent dies
1494	Medici in exile; Savonarola rules Florence; Charles VIII of France invades Italy; many artists flee Florence for Rome
1495–1497	**Leonardo da Vinci, *Last Supper,* Santa Maria delle Grazie, Milan**
1498–1499	**Michelangelo, *Pietà,* St. Peter's Basilica, The Vatican, Rome**
1501–1504	**Michelangelo, *David,* Accademia, Florence**
1503–1513	Pope Julius II
1505	Michelangelo summoned to Rome to work on Pope Julius's tomb; **Giorgione, *The Tempest,* Accademia, Venice**
1506	Unearthing of the **Laocoön** sculpture group, with Michelangelo in attendance; Bramante begins **New Basilica of St. Peter's**
1508–1512	**Michelangelo, *Sistine ceiling frescoes,* The Vatican, Rome; Raphael, *The School at Athens,* The Vatican, Rome**
1512	Copernicus argues that the Earth and planets revolve around the sun
1513–1521	Pope Leo X (a Medici); **Raphael, *Pope Leo X,* Uffizi, Florence; Michelangelo, *Moses,* San Pietro in Vincoli, Rome**
1517	Luther's 95 Theses; Protestant Revolution
1523	**Michelangelo, The Medici Tombs, Florence**
1527	Luther's Reformation in Germany; German and Spanish mercenaries under Emperor Charles V sack Rome; Sistine Chapel used as a stable; the end of the High Renaissance

The Baroque Age

1534	Beginnings of the Counter-Reformation; **Parmigianino, *Madonna with the Long Neck,* Uffizi, Florence**
1535–1541	**Michelangelo, *The Last Judgment,* Sistine Chapel, Rome**
1538	**Titian, *Venus of Urbino,* Uffizi, Florence**
1540	Founding of the Jesuit Order by Ignatius of Loyola
1542	Pope Paul III establishes the Inquisition in Rome
1545–1563	The Council of Trent
1547	Michelangelo becomes architect of St. Peter's
1550	**Villa d'Este, Tivoli;** Vasari, *Lives of the Artists*
c. 1560	Development of opera in Florence
1565	St. Teresa of Avila, *Autobiography*
1573	**Paolo Veronese, *Feast in the House of Levi,* Accademia, Venice;** Veronese questioned by the Inquisition
1588–1592	Construction of Rialto Bridge
1594	**Tintoretto, *Last Supper,* San Giorgio Maggiore, Venice**
1595–1600	**Annibale Carracci, *Ceiling Frescoes,* Palazzo Farnese, Rome**
1601	**Caravaggio, *Conversion of St. Paul,* Cerasi Chapel, Church of Santa Maria del Popolo, Rome;** Jesuit missionaries sent to China; in England, Shakespeare writes *Hamlet*
1607–1614	**Carlo Maderno, façade for St. Peter's, Rome**
1616	Galileo forbidden by Pope Paul V to teach the Copernican theory
c. 1618	**Gentileschi, *Judith and Holofernes,* Uffizi, Florence**
1622–1623	**Bernini, *Apollo and Daphne, The Rape of Proserpina, David,* Galleria Borghese, Rome**
1638–1641	**Borromini, San Carlo alle Quattro Fontane, Rome**
1645–1652	**Bernini, *St. Teresa in Ecstasy,* Cornaro Chapel, Church of Santa Maria della Vittoria, Rome; *Fountain of Four Rivers,* Piazza Navona, Rome**
1656	Academy of Painting founded in Rome
1656–1667	**Bernini designs St. Peter's Square and Colonnades**
1687	Isaac Newton, *Principia Mathematica*
c. 1715	The rococo style emerges
1716	First Italian newspaper published, *Diaria di Roma*

1721	**Spanish Steps, Rome** completed
1725	Vivaldi, *The Four Seasons*
1738–1748	Excavations at **Herculaneum and Pompeii**
1752–1774	**Luigi Vanvitelli, *The Great Cascade,* royal palace, La Reggia, Caserta**
1762	**The Trevi Fountain, Rome, designed by Salvi (1732)**
1776	The American Revolution
1796	Napoleon's campaign in Lombardy
1798	Roman Republic proclaimed; Death of Casanova

After 1800

1804	Napoleon crowned emperor of France
1808	**Antonio Canova, *Pauline Bonaparte Borghese as Venus Victorious,* Borghese Gallery, Rome**
1809–1814	Napoleon takes Pope Pius VII prisoner
1815	Defeat of Napoleon at Waterloo
	Congress of Vienna; Austria dominates Italian affairs
c. 1820	Rise of the Romantic movement throughout Europe in art, music, and literature
1821	Napoleon dies
1831	Mazzini founds the Young Italy movement; stirrings to unite a fragmented Italy
1848	Uprising against Austria; Marx and Engels, *The Communist Manifesto*
1853	Verdi, *La Traviata*
1859	Darwin, *On the Origin of Species*
1860	Garibaldi unifies the South
1861–1878	Victor Emmanuel II, King of Italy
1870	Italian unity achieved; Rome becomes capital
1872	Impressionism in France
1884	**Sacconi, Memorial to King Victor Emmanuel II, Rome**
1887	Verdi, *Otello*
1899	Freud, *The Interpretation of Dreams*
1900–1904	Puccini, *Tosca, Madame Butterfly*
1905	Einstein's theory of relativity
1906–1925	Cubism developed in Paris by Picasso
1915	Italy joins the Allies in World War I
1922–1926	Rise of Fascism; Mussolini becomes *Duce*
1940	Italy enters World War II on the side of Nazi Germany
1943	Italy surrenders unconditionally to the Allies
c. 1945	International art scene shifts to New York; notable Italian artists: Frank Stella (1877–1946), Umberto Boccioni (1882–1916), Gino Severini (1883–1966), Amedeo Modigliani (1884–1920), Giorgio

	de Chirico (1888–1978), Alberto Giacometti (1901–1966)
1957–1960	**Pier Luigi Nervi, Palazzo dello Sport, Rome**
1964	**Giacomo Manzù, door panels of St. Peter's, Rome**
1978	Election of Pope John Paul II

VITAL INFORMATION

Emergencies

For emergencies, dial 113.

Lost Credit Cards

If you lose your American Express Card, call the local American Express office:
Rome: (06) 72280204
Milan: (02) 85571
Florence: (055) 278751

If you lose your Visa card in Italy, dial the U.S., (415) 574-7700.

If you lose your Diner's Club card, call collect to the U.S., (303) 790-8632.

For a lost MasterCard, call the U.S. collect: (605) 335-2222.

Embassies and Consulates

Should you find yourself passportless, penniless or posed with any sort of problem, contact your embassy or consulate.

ROME

United States, Via Vittorio Veneto 119A; tel. (06) 46741

Canada, Via G.B. de Rossi 27; tel. (06) 855341

Britain, Via XX Settembre 80A; tel. (06) 4155441

Australia, Via Alessandria 215; tel. (06) 841241

New Zealand, Via Zara 28; tel. (06) 851225

FLORENCE

United States, Lungarno Amerigo Vespucci; tel. (055) 298276

Britain, Lungarno Corsini 2; tel. (055) 212594

GENOA

United States, Banca d'America e Italia Bldg., Piazza Portello 6; tel. (010) 282741

MILAN

United States, Piazza della Repubblica 32; tel. (02) 652841

Canada, Via Vittor Pisani 19; tel. (02) 6697451

Britain, Via San Paolo 7; tel. (02) 8693442

Australia, Via Turati 40; tel. (02) 8598727

NAPLES

United States, Piazza della Repubblica; tel. (081) 660966

Britain, Via Francesco Crispi 122; tel. (081) 663511

PALERMO

United States, Via Vaccarini 1; tel. (091) 291532

TRIESTE
United States, Via Rome 9; tel.
(040) 68728

Tourist Information

Regional Tourist Boards
Abruzzi, Viale G. Bovio, 65100 Pescara; tel. (085) 75094 or 73895
Apulia, Via Capruzzi 212, 70124 Bari; tel. (080) 291111
Basilicata, Via Crispi, Palazzo ex Gil, 85100 Potenza; tel. (0971) 3590
Bolzano (Alto Adige), Via Raiffeis 2, 39100 Bolzano; tel. (0471) 993666
Calabria, Vico III Raffaelli, 88100 Catanzaro; tel. (0961) 44319 or 45196
Campania, Via Santa Lucia 81, 80132 Naples; tel. (081) 400044
Emilia-Romagna, Viale Silvani 6, 40122 Bologna; tel. (051) 559111
Friuli-Venezia Giulia, Via S. Francesco d'Assisi 37, 34133 Trieste; tel.
   (040) 7355
   Azienda Regionale per la Promozione Turistica, Via Rossini 6, 34133 Tri-
   este; tel. (040) 60336
Lazio, Via F. Raimondi Garibaldi 7, 00145 Rome; tel. (06) 54571 or 517991
Liguria, Via Fieschi 15, 16121 Genoa; tel. (010) 54851
Lombardy, Via Fabio Filzi 22, 20124 Milano; tel. (02) 62621
Marches, Via Gentile de Fabriano, 60100 Ancona; tel. (071) 8061
Molise, Via Mazzini 94, 86100 Campobasso; tel. (0874) 65841/2/3
Piedmont, Via Magenta 12, 10128 Turin; tel. (011) 57173230
Sardinia, Viale Trento 69, 09100 Cagliari; tel. (070) 650971
Sicily, Via Emanuele Notarbartolo 9, 90141 Palermo; tel. (091) 251266
Tuscany, Via di Novoli 26, 50127 Florence; tel. (055) 439311
Trentino, Corso 3 Novembre 132, 38100 Trento; tel. (0461) 895111
Umbria, Corso Vannucci 30, 06100 Perugia; tel. (075) 6961
Valle d'Aosta, Piazza Narbonne, 11100 Aosta; tel. (0165) 35653
Veneto, Palazzo Balbi Dorsoduro 3901, 30123 Venice; tel. (041) 707700
   Dipartimento per il Turismo, 30100 Venice
   Palazzo Sceriman-Cannaregio 168; tel. (041) 717922

Local Tourist Boards
Agrigento, Viale della Vittori 255, 92100 Agrigento (Sicily); tel. (0922)
   26926
Ancona, Via Marcello Marini 14, 60100 Ancona (Marches); tel. (071) 201980
Aosta, Piazza Narbonne, 11100 Aosta (Valle d'Aosta); tel. (0165) 35654
Arezzo, Piazza Risorgimento 116, 52100 Arezzo (Tuscany); tel. (0575)
   23952
Ascoli Piceno, Corso Mazzini 229, 63100 Ascoli Piceno (Marches); tel.
   (0736) 51115
Asti, Piazza Alfieri 34, 14100 Asti (Piedmont); tel. (0141) 50357
Avellino, Via due Principati 5, 83100 Avellino (Campania); tel. (0825) 35169
   or 22626
Bari, Piazza Aldo Moro, 70122 Bari (Apulia); tel. (0800) 369228
Benevento, Via Nicola Sala, 82100 Benevento (Campania); tel. (0824) 21-
   960/21947
Bergamo, Viale Vittorio Emanuelle II 4, 24100 Bergamo (Lombardy); tel.
   (035) 242226
Bologna, Via Marconi 45, 40122 Bologna (Emilia-Romagna); tel. (051) 237-
   414
Bolzano, Piazza Walther 22, 39100 Bolzano (Alto Adige); tel. (0471) 26991
Brescia, Corso Zanardelli 38, 25100 Brescia (Lombardy); tel. (030) 45052
Brindisi, Via Cristoforo Colombo 88, 72100 Brindisi (Apulia); tel. (0831)
   222126 or 222813

Cagliari, Piazza Deffenu 9, 09100 Cagliari (Sardinia); tel. (070) 654-811/663-207

Campobasso, Piazza della Vittoria 14, 86100 Campobasso (Molise); tel. (0874) 95662

Caserta, Palazzo Reale, 81100 Caserta (Campania); tel. (0823) 322233 or 322170

Catania, Largo Paisiello 5, 95124 Catania (Sicily); tel. (095) 317720

Catanzaro, Via F. Spasari-Piazza Stocco 5, 88100 Catanzaro (Calabria); tel. (0961) 29823

Chieti, Via B. Spaventa 29, 66100 Chieti (Abruzzi); tel. (0871) 65231

Como, Piazza Cavour 17, 22100 Como (Lombardy); tel. (031) 262091

Cosenza, Via Tagliamento 15, 87100 Cosenza (Calabria); tel. (0984) 27821

Cremona, Galleria del Corso 3, 26100 Cremona (Lombardy); tel. (0372) 21722

Cuneo, Corso Nizza 17, 12100 Cuneo (Piedmont); tel. (0171) 68015

Ferrara, Largo Castello 28, 44100 Ferrara (Emilia-Romagna); tel. (0532) 21267

Florence, Via Manzoni 16, 50121 Florence (Tuscany); tel. (055) 2478141/2/3/4/5

Foggia, Via Senatore Emilio Perrone 17, 71100 Foggia (Apulia); tel. (0881) 23650 or 23141

Forli, (Emilia-Romagna) Corso della Repubblica 23, 47100 Forli (Emilia-Romagna); tel. (0543) 25532 or 25545

Genoa, Via Roma 11, 16121 Genoa (Liguria); tel. (010) 581407

Grosseto, Via Monterosa 206/A, 58100 Grosseto (Tuscany); tel. (0564) 22534

Imperia, Via Matteotti 54bis, 18100 Imperia (Liguria); tel. (0183) 24947

Isernia, Via Farinacci, 86170 Isernia (Molise); tel. (0865) 3992 or 59590

L'Aquila, Piazza Santa Maria di Paganica 5, 67100 L'Aquila (Abruzzi); tel. (0862) 25149

La Spezia, Viale Mazzini 47, 19100 La Spezia (Liguria); tel. (0187) 36000

Lecce, Via Monte San Michele 20, 73100 Lecce (Apulia); tel. (0832) 54117

Livorno, Piazza Cavour 6, 57100 Livorno (Tuscany); tel. (0586) 33111

Lucca, Piazza Guidiccioni 2, 55100 Lucca (Tuscany); tel. (0583) 41205

Macerata, Via Garibaldi 87, 62100 Macerata (Marches); tel. (0733) 46320

Mantua, Piazza Andrea Mantegna 6, 46100 Mantua (Lombardy); tel. (0376) 321601

Massa-Carrara, Piazza 2 Giugno 14, 54033 Massa-Carrara (Tuscany); tel. (0585) 70668

Matera, Via De Viti De Marco 9, 75100 Matera (Basilicata); tel. (0835) 221758

Messina, Via Calabria, Isolato 301bis, 98100 Messina (Sicily); tel. (090) 775356

Milan, Via Marconi 1, 20123 Milan (Lombardy); tel. (02) 870016

Modena, Corso Canalgrande 3, 41100 Modena (Emilia-Romagna); tel. (059) 237479

Naples, Via Partenope 10-A, 80121 Naples (Campania); tel. (081) 418988

Nuoro, Piazza Italia 9, 08100 Nuoro (Sardinia); tel. (0784) 30083

Oristano, Via Cagliari (Palazzo SAIA), 09170 Oristano (Sardinia); tel. (0783) 74191

Padua, Riviera Mugnai 8, 35100 Padua (Veneto); tel. (049) 25024

Palermo, Piazza Castelnuovo 35, 90141 Palermo (Sicily); tel. (091) 586122

Parma, Piazza Duomo 5, 43100 Parma (Emilia-Romagna); tel. (0521) 33959

Pavia, Corso Garibaldi 1, 27100 Pavia (Lombardy); tel. (0382) 27238

Perugia, (Umbria) Corso Vannucci 30, 06100 Perugia (Umbria); tel. (075) 6961

Pesaro and Urbino, Via Mazzolari 4, 61100 Pesaro (Marches); tel. (0721) 31433 or 30258

Pescara, Via Nicola Fabrizi 171, 65100 Pescara (Abruzzi); tel. (085) 22707

Piacenza, Via S. Siro, 29100 Piacenza (Emilia-Romagna); tel. (0523) 34347

Pisa, Lungarno Mediceo 42, 56100 Pisa (Tuscany); tel. (050) 20351 or 47290

Pistoia, Corso Gramsci 110, 51100 Pistoia (Tuscany); tel. (0573) 34326

Potenza, Via Ciccotti 12, 85100 Potenza (Basilicata); tel. (0971) 21839

Ravenna, Piazza San Francisco 7, 48100 Ravenna (Emilia-Romagna); tel. (0544) 36129

Reggio di Calabria, Via Demetrio Tripepi 72, 89100 Reggio di Calabria (Calabria); tel. (0965) 9849

Reggio nell'Emilia, Piazza C. Battisti 4, 42100 Reggio nell'Emilia (Emilia-Romagna); tel. (0522) 43370

Rieti, Via Cintia 87, 02100 Rieti (Lazio); tel. (0746) 41146

Rome, Via Parigi 11, 00185 Rome (Lazio); tel. (06) 461851

Rovigo, Via J.H. Dunant 10, 45100 Rovigo (Veneto); tel. (0425) 3611481

Salerno, Via Vella 15, 84100 Salerno (Campania); tel. (089) 224322

Sassari, Piazza Italia, Palazzo Giordano 19, 07100 Sassari (Sardinia); tel. (079) 230129

Siena, Via di Citta 5, 53100 Siena (Tuscany); tel. (0577) 47051

Syracuse, Via S. Sebastiano 43, 96100 Syracuse (Sicily); tel. (0931) 67607

Sondrio, Via Cesare Battisti 12, 23100 Sondrio (Lombardy); tel. (0342) 212269

Taranto, Corso Umberto 121, 74100 Taranto (Apulia); tel. (099) 24457

Teramo, Via del Castello 10, 64100 Teramo (Abruzzi); tel. (0861) 51222

Turin, Via Roma 222, 10121 Turin (Piedmont); tel. (011) 535181

Trento, Corso 3 Novembre 132, 38100 Trento (Trentino); tel. (0461) 895111

Treviso, Via Toniolo 41, Palazzo Scotti, 31100 Treviso (Veneto); tel. (0422) 40600

Trieste, Via Rossini 6, 34132 Trieste (Friuli-Venezia Giulia); tel. (040) 62812 or 60336

Udine, Piazza Venerio 4, 33100 Udine (Friuli-Venezia Giulia); tel. (0432) 204205 or 23707

Varese, Piazza Monte Grappa 5, 21100 Varese (Lombardy); tel. (0332) 283604

Venice, Castello, Calle del Remedio 4421, 30122 Venice (Veneto); tel. (041) 22373

Verona, Via Scalzi 20, 37122 Verona (Veneto); tel. (045) 25065

Vicenza, Piazza Duomo 5, 36100 Vicenza (Veneto); tel. (0444) 44805

Index

For index reference, "hotels" is used for *all* types of accommodations. Camp. = Campania; Em.-Rom. = Emilia-Romagna; Flor. = Florence; Lig. = Liguria; Lomb. = Lombardy; Mil. = Milan; Mar. = Marches, Abruzzi, Molise; NE = Northeast Italy; NW = Northwest Italy; Sard. = Sardinia; Sic. = Sicily; Tusc. = Tuscany; Umb. = Umbria